CIVILIZATION IN THE WEST

FOURTH EDITION

CIVILIZATION IN THE WEST

Part 2 1600 to the Present

CRANE BRINTON

JOHN B. CHRISTOPHER
Professor of History Emeritus,
University of Rochester

ROBERT LEE WOLFF
Archibald Cary Coolidge, Professor of History
Harvard University

Prentice-Hall, Inc., Englewood Cliffs, New Jersey 07632

Library of Congress Cataloging in Publication Data
Brinton, Clarence Crane, 1898–1968.
    Civilization in the West.

    Includes bibliographies and index.
    CONTENTS: pt. 1. Prehistory to 1715.—pt. 2. 1600
to the present.
    1. Civilization, Occidental.   I. Christopher,
John B., joint author.   II. Wolff, Robert Lee, joint
author.   III. Title.
CB245.B72 1981   909'.09821   80–28369
ISBN 0–13–134924–4 (v. 1)
ISBN 0–13–134932–5 (v. 2)

CIVILIZATION IN THE WEST, fourth edition
Part 2: 1600 to the present
Brinton/Christopher/Wolff

© 1981, 1973, 1969, 1964
by Prentice-Hall, Inc.,
Englewood Cliffs, N.J. 07632

Editorial/Production Supervision by Cathie Mick Mahar
Interior Design by Lee Cohen
Cover Design by Lee Cohen
Acquisition Editor: John Busch and Stephen Dalphin
Manufacturing Buyer: Edmund W. Leone
Cover Art: Einstein bust by Jacob Epstein
                Bettman Archive photograph

Printed in the United States of America

10 9 8 7 6 5 4 3 2 1

PRENTICE-HALL INTERNATIONAL, INC., *London*
PRENTICE-HALL OF AUSTRALIA PTY. LIMITED, *Sydney*
PRENTICE-HALL OF CANADA, LTD., *Toronto*
PRENTICE-HALL OF INDIA PRIVATE LIMITED, *New Delhi*
PRENTICE-HALL OF JAPAN, INC., *Tokyo*
PRENTICE-HALL OF SOUTHEAST ASIA PTE. LTD., *Singapore*
WHITEHALL BOOKS LIMITED, *Wellington, New Zealand*

Contents

Preface

This fourth edition of *Civilization in the West* is more than a mere revision of preceding volumes; it is in many respects a whole new book. Many chapters from older editions have been rewritten in the light of recent scholarship and have also been restructured in order to make the narrative more coherent and the chapters more nearly uniform in length. Sentences and paragraphs have been shortened and the vocabulary simplified to fit the reading skills of a new generation of students. The particular interests of this generation are reflected in additional material on social history and on new advances in science. Some traditions of historical writing are maintained, such as the use of "man" for human beings of both sexes in sections of the text. This is merely a convenient form of shorthand.

This new edition is available in a two-paperback format. The first volume, with ten chapters, extends from the earliest civilizations through the seventeenth century. A full chapter (the second) is devoted to the Greek world. The Roman world, previously coupled with the Greek, is now treated in Chapter 3, along with the Christian revolution which emerged in part from the shortcomings of the Roman Empire. Chapter 4 is a survey of the feudal and Byzantine successors of the Roman Empire through the eleventh century, together with the rapidly advancing Islamic rival of Christianity.

Developments in the later Middle Ages are analyzed in Chapter 5 (Western Europe) and Chapter 6 (Eastern Europe). The latter extends from the Crusades to the establishment of the Ottoman and Russian successors of Byzantium and their history down to the seventeenth century. Chapters 7 through 9 cover the transition in the West from the declining medieval world through the Renaissance and the upheavals resulting from the Protestant revolt, the growth of ambitious dynastic states, the expansion of European power abroad, and the growing unrest in the mother countries.

Chapter 10 replaces two short chapters in the third edition. It links the two volumes of the fourth edition by evaluating the contribution of both the seventeenth and eighteenth centuries to the Great Modern Revolution. This transformation of science and economic life also had important side effects on literature and the arts; it stimulated the program of the Enlightenment for political and social reform. The results were evident in the enlightened despotism of the eighteenth century (Chapter 11) and the French Revolution (Chapter 12).

The overloaded chapter in the preceding edition narrating the renewal of revolution from 1815 to 1870 has been divided in two. The new Chapter 13, Industry and Democracy, is centered on the Atlantic world, mainly Britain, France, and the United States. Chapter 14, also new, focuses on nationalism and reform in southern, central, and eastern Europe. Chapter 15 discusses the principal developments in ideas and culture during the nineteenth century.

Four chapters cover social, economic, and political events from 1870 to 1970. Chapter 16—Prelude, Theme, Coda (the terms are borrowed from music)—takes the story from the birth of the Second German Empire to the peace settlement after World War I. Chapter 17, Interlude and Repetition, steps back to the Russian Revolution of 1917, then discusses the Nazi dictatorship and other totalitarian regimes, and describes the Second World War which they precipitated. Chapter 18, the Cold War and Great Power Domestic Politics, notes the breakdown of the wartime alliance between the Soviet Union and the western democracies together with subsequent developments in the major states. Chapter 19, Great Power Foreign Policy and the Emerging Nations, records the strains between the democracies and the communist bloc from the Berlin blockade and Korean War to the Vietnam problem; it also assesses the growing importance of the newly independent states in Asia, the Middle East, and Africa.

Chapter 20 (The World Since 1970) breaks new ground as an impressionistic survey of an important and disturbing decade. And the final chapter, 21, Science and Culture in the Twentieth Century, reviews the chief advances in the sciences and arts and concludes that, though sometimes improving the quality of life, they often left countless millions of people still struggling to survive.

We thank the following people who were asked to review part or all of the book: Anthony M. Brescia, Nassau Community College; Elizabeth Carney, Clemson University; Charles W. Connell, West Virginia University; Glen H. Coston, Pensacola Junior College; Robert Feldman, California State University at Fullerton; Thomas Hachey, Marquette University; C. Douglas McCullough, DeKalb Community College; James Muldoon, Rutgers University; Cedric Ward, Andrews University; Robert Welborn, Clayton Junior College.

* * * * * * * * * * * * * *

This preface ends on a somber note as it records the death in November, 1980, of Robert Lee Wolff, who assumed responsibility for preparing fourteen of the twenty-one chapters in the fourth edition. All of us involved in this project are grateful that he had completed his assignments. He would join in expressing the authors' gratitude to members of the staff at Prentice-Hall for their patience and expert assistance in preparing these new volumes. All of us mourn the loss of this lively, many-faceted scholar who was an important contributor to all the editions of *Civilization in the West* and its parent volumes, *A History of Civilization*, during the past quarter of a century.

Maps

Illustrations

The Seventeenth Century:

War, Politics, And Empire

In this chapter we deal with the 1600s and the first few years of the 1700s. Modern complexity has set in. Within each state domestic issues are closely related to foreign issues. Political issues and religious issues are so intertwined that matters which at first seem political prove to have important religious implications, and the other way around. Economic and social values become tangled up with politics and religion.

We have already seen, for example, that the French nobles who turned to Calvinism did so in part to defend their traditional privileges against the encroachments of the king. Queen Elizabeth helped the Dutch against the Spaniards partly because the Dutch were fellow Protestants but more because of Philip II's threat to herself. The Catholic Reformation failed to win back some areas of Europe because Hapsburgs headed the Catholic cause, and many powerful Catholics who otherwise would have helped Rome did not want to help the Hapsburgs. The papacy itself was determined to avoid Hapsburg domination.

The Peace of Augsburg of 1555, the triumph of Henry IV in France, and the execution of Mary

Queen of Scots all contributed to the containment of Hapsburg power. But in 1598, when the Hapsburg Philip II died in his colossal monastic palace of the Escorial in the bleak hills near Madrid with an open coffin standing at his order beside his bed, and a skull grinning at him beneath a golden crown, all these related problems remained unsettled.

We turn first to the continental political and religious struggle known as the Thirty Years' War (1618–1648). It had an earlier background in the Low Countries, Spain, and Germany. It convulsed the German lands and ended in the Peace of Westphalia (1648).

England's part in the Thirty Years' War was small, because the Stuart monarchy, new in 1603, created so tense a situation at home that it led to the Civil War, which lasted from 1642 to 1649. The king was executed and a republic established for eleven years. Even after the Stuarts were restored in 1660, the mingled religious and political issues remained unsettled until a new overturn in 1688. To this revolution and its aftermath we devote the second part of this chapter. It was of the utmost importance for future American attitudes toward government.

In the third section we examine the political, religious, and economic developments in France throughout the century. After the 1640s, King Louis XIV personifies the country. Crown and governmental machinery, economic policy, religious issues, and especially Louis's efforts to dominate Europe all pass in review.

And in the final portion we turn to the imperial developments of the century—the growth of English and French overseas empires in America, Asia, and Africa, and their involvement in the affairs of the mother countries. Here and from now on our view must be not merely continental but global.

THE THIRTY YEARS' WAR

The Dutch and Spanish Background

After the Dutch had won the truce of 1609 with Spain and so achieved independence, they took a leading part in European affairs. Each of the seven "United Provinces" of the Dutch Republic preserved its local traditions of government and sent delegates (the *Hooge Moogende,* High Mightinesses) to the Estates-General, which was more like a diplomatic congress than a central

legislature. Each province elected its own chief executive, the *Stadholder,* but often several of them elected the same man. After the truce of 1609, Maurice, prince of Orange, son of William the Silent, was chosen Stadholder by five of the seven.

Religious differences also divided the Dutch nation. There was a large Catholic minority. The Protestant majority was split between orthodox Calvinists and moderates called Arminians (after Arminius, a Dutch theologian). Arminians believed that people's behavior in this life might change God's original intentions about their salvation hereafter. So for them, predestination was not unchangeable.

The Dutch were the world's best businessmen. By the early seventeenth century they controlled most of the coastwise shipping of Europe. They went into the wine business in France and into the fishing grounds of the Arctic. In 1602 they organized the Dutch East India Company and soon launched other ventures overseas.

The Bank of Amsterdam (1609) minted its own florins, which became standard in Europe. Its services to its depositors were so much in demand that Amsterdam became the financial capital of Europe. The Dutch invented life insurance and made it a big business. Diamond-cutting, shipbuilding, gin-distilling, and tulip-growing all made the Dutch provinces rich and famous. Their opulent middle-class way of life is mirrored in the domestic scenes and lifelike portraits of Hals, Vermeer, and Rembrandt.

No wonder Philip II's Hapsburg successors in Spain dreamed of reconquering the United Provinces. Although, as we have seen (Chapter 8), Spanish strength was declining by the seventeenth century, Spain still had the wealth of the Americas, the military manpower of north Italy, and the loyalty of the Catholic Belgian provinces.

After the Dutch revolt, the Spaniards wanted to stabilize a line of communications between their Italian and Belgian lands, so that they could move men and money over the Alps and down the Rhine. This route crossed the lands of some rulers who were friendly to the Hapsburgs and others who were hostile. The Dutch worked hard to deny this communication line to the Spaniards. So did the French, who were still working to break Hapsburg encirclement of France.

The German Background

Geographically, of course, Germany was the key. By the early seventeenth century, it had be-

The emperor Rudolf II, king of Bohemia 1575–1611, shown with the electors on a Bohemian enameled glass beaker.

come a truly fantastic conglomeration of states. Some of the German principalities had been divided and subdivided until an "independent" princeling might rule over only a village or a few hundred acres of forest. Free cities acknowledged no authority but the emperor. Some of them held vast lands outside their walls, others not. The Church governed certain cities and regions which also varied greatly in size. There were more than two thousand governing authorities. Since many of the smaller ones combined or reached understandings locally, this number can be reduced to perhaps three hundred.

Particularly influential were the seven electors, who chose each new emperor. One elector, the king of Bohemia, was in practice always a Hapsburg, so that the imperial family always had at least one vote at election time. Three electors were Catholic—the archbishops of Mainz, Trier, and Cologne. The electors of Saxony and Brandenburg were Lutheran. The elector of the Palatinate, with his capital at Heidelberg, was a Calvinist. His lands, in a rich vineyard area along the Rhine, blocked the Hapsburg communication line to the Low Countries. Some princes who were not electors were very powerful anyhow, especially the Catholic duke of Bavaria.

All this naturally weakened the central institutions of the empire. The imperial diet, consisting in theory of all the independent German rulers, always quarreled when it met. Some princes refused to accept its decisions. The emperor had to try to rule by decree and pressure.

So Germany had no machinery to deal with

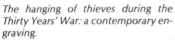

The hanging of thieves during the Thirty Years' War: a contemporary engraving.

Israel ex. Cum Privil. Reg.

the religious difficulties arising from the Peace of Augsburg of 1555 (see p. 259). This peace had not even recognized Calvinism. But after 1555 Calvinism spread rapidly both in Lutheran and in Catholic areas. Where a prince was suddenly converted, all his subjects either had to follow his lead or be persecuted. This led to riots and disorder. In 1600 the Calvinist princes formed the Calvinist Protestant Union, in 1609 the Catholics the Catholic League under Maximilian of Bavaria.

War broke out in Germany in 1618. It lasted for thirty years, drew in all the important states of western Europe, and devastated and depopulated Germany. Its grim progress is best understood if one divides the thirty long years into a Bohemian period (1618–1625), a Danish period (1625–1629), a Swedish period (1629–1635), and a Swedish and French period (1635–1648).

Count Wallenstein: a portrait by Van Dyck.

The Bohemian Period, 1618–1625

Among the seven electorates the kingdom of Bohemia, as the only one held by a Catholic layman, assumed special importance. Since the other three Catholic electorates were always held by archbishops, Bohemia offered the only hope for the Protestants ever to get a majority of four of the seven electoral votes. So, Frederick of the Palatinate, head of the Protestant League in 1618, had his eye on Bohemia. Moreover, in German-dominated Bohemia, the native Czechs expressed their national antagonism to Germans by following the religious teachings of John Hus (p. 207), which included the practice of giving both wine and bread to the laity in communion *(utraquism)*.

With the emperor Matthias (reigned 1612–1619) both old and childless, and Ferdinand of Hapsburg, a strong Catholic, slated to become king of Bohemia and emperor, Protestants took alarm, despite Ferdinand's promise that they would have freedom of worship. In 1618, the arrest of some Protestants touched off a revolt in Prague. Two Catholic imperial governors were thrown out of a window into a courtyard seventy feet below, and were saved only by landing in a pile of dung.

The Czechs offered the kingship of Bohemia to Frederick of the Palatinate, who went to Prague. But he left his Rhineland holdings, so coveted by Spain, without adequate defenses, and the Spaniards occupied them. Everywhere in the empire, Catholics rallied against the rebellion. Ferdinand of Hapsburg was duly chosen emperor (1619), and Maximilian of Bavaria, head of the

Catholic League, defeated the Czechs (1620). Maximilian got Frederick's electoral post for Bavaria. In Bohemia, Ferdinand took a fierce revenge against utraquists and Calvinists, sparing Lutherans because of obligations to the Lutheran princes. Frederick of the Palatinate fled Bohemia.

But the continued Spanish occupation of the Palatinate frightened the Protestant Dutch and Danes, as well as the Catholic French, who faced a new Hapsburg encirclement. Cardinal Richelieu, emerging as chief minister of King Louis XIII (reigned 1610–1643), was ready to join the Protestant rulers of Europe, including the English, against the growth of Hapsburg power. Even the pope looked understandingly on the growth of this French-Protestant coalition, fearing unchecked Hapsburg preponderance. New Catholic victories over Frederick of the Palatinate (1625), and Ferdinand's transfer of Frederick's lands to Maximilian of Bavaria gave still more urgency to the anti-Hapsburg cause.

The Danish Period, 1625–1629

For the next four years, however, only Christian IV of Denmark (1588–1648) bore the burden of the Protestant struggle. It proved too much for him, since he was opposed not only by Maximilian's Catholic League, but by the private Catholic armies of Count Wallenstein. A convert to Catholicism, Wallenstein bought up a quarter of the lands of Bohemia after Ferdinand had defeated the Czechs, and was now dreaming of converting Germany into a new-model monarchy. The Catholic forces defeated the Danes and moved into Denmark. Christian IV promised in the Treaty of Lübeck (1629) never again to interfere in Germany.

The victorious emperor Ferdinand celebrated his triumph by the Edict of Restitution (1629). It reaffirmed the Peace of Augsburg of 1555, still making no provision for Calvinists. And it turned back to Catholics all Church property that had passed to the Lutherans since 1551. Throughout northern and western Germany many Lutherans were dispossessed, and boundaries were changed. By his behavior Ferdinand showed that the Hapsburgs were ruthless to defeated enemies and that the Protestants had nothing to hope for. From then on it became the chief Protestant goal to overthrow the Edict of Restitution.

The victory still further enriched Wallenstein, who planned to open the Baltic to the Spaniards and let them attack the Dutch from the rear. Wallenstein's ambitions and independence led Ferdinand to dismiss him. But the Catholic armies now had to face Swedish armed intervention.

The Swedish Period, 1630–1635

King Gustavus Adolphus of Sweden (reigned 1611–1632), a first-rate administrator and general, had checked his own nobility at home and defeated the Russians and Poles abroad. He was a devout Lutheran himself and tolerant to Calvinists. With an efficient army, subsidized by Richelieu, Gustavus now joined the German Protestant forces of the electors of Saxony and Brandenburg. The terrible sack of Magdeburg by the Catholics in 1631, followed by a massacre of 20,000 Protestants, galvanized the Protestant resistance.

The Protestant counteroffensive of 1631 and 1632 not only recovered northern Germany but captured much of the southern Catholic territory as well. Prague fell to the Saxons, fighting for Frederick of the Palatinate. Gustavus Adolphus took Mainz and Frankfort. At Lützen he defeated Wallenstein, who had returned to Ferdinand's service, but Gustavus Adolphus himself was killed in the battle (1632). He had planned to become emperor and to reorganize Germany, uniting Lutheran and Calvinist churches.

Famine and plague ravaged the war-stricken lands of Germany. But fighting continued, as Gustavus Adolphus' chancellor, Oxenstierna, became chief of the Protestant cause. Wallenstein's power was diminishing, as Ferdinand suspected him of treachery, and in 1634 he was murdered by an assassin, whom Ferdinand rewarded. In the same year, Ferdinand won a victory at Nordlingen. This meant that Swedish influence lessened and French increased. Richelieu wanted the war to continue in order to further France's territorial ambitions in the Rhineland.

The Swedish and French Period, 1635–1648

In the final phase of the Thirty Years' War, the Protestant cause was dependent upon a French Catholic cardinal. Protestant commanders had to promise that after the war Catholics would not be persecuted in Germany. The religious character of the conflict became less important and the dynastic character more important. In both Hapsburg and Bourbon armies, mercenaries from every nation in Europe took service, switching sides when they thought it advantageous, taking their women and children with them everywhere.

By abandoning the Edict of Restitution at last in 1635, Emperor Ferdinand was able to make a separate peace with most of the Lutheran princes. Richelieu himself had to declare war on Spain to keep the war going. French, Swedes, and a few Calvinist princes struggled on in Germany against the Hapsburgs. The four years between 1639 and 1643 saw the destruction of Spanish hopes. The Dutch defeated the Spanish fleet at sea. Portugal, annexed by Philip II in 1580, revolted in 1640. The French won the battle of Rocroy (1643), and the ambitions of Charles V and Philip II were ended forever.

French policies continued unaltered after the deaths of Richelieu (1642) and King Louis XIII (1643). Negotiations for peace began in 1643 and took five years to complete, as fighting continued sporadically. The issues were many and complex. The Dutch made a separate peace with Spain. And finally on October 24, 1648, the Peace of Westphalia, the first major international settlement of modern times, brought the wretched war to an end at last.

The Peace of Westphalia: Impact of the War

The peace extended the principles of the Peace of Augsburg to Calvinists as well as Lutherans and Catholics. For the status of Church prop-

Europe in 1648

- Brandenburg-Prussia
- Austrian Hapsburg lands
- Spanish Hapsburg lands
- Swedish possessions
- Venetian possessions
- Ottoman Empire

····· Boundary of the Holy Roman Empire

■ Battle sites

Approximate division line between Puritans and Cavaliers in England, May 1643

NORWAY
Oslo

S W E D E N
Stockholm

DENMARK
Copenhagen

Baltic Sea

North Sea

SCOTLAND
Edinburgh
Dunbar
Berwick

ULSTER
Drogheda

IRELAND
Dublin
Wexford

Preston
Marston Moor

ENGLAND
Cavaliers
Worcester
Nottingham
Naseby
London
Puritans

see inset
Texel

UNITED NETHERLANDS

SPANISH NETHERLANDS
Osnabrück
Bremen
Münster
WEST-PHALIA

Lübeck
Hamburg
Elbe R.

POMERANIA
Danzig
BRANDENBURG
Berlin
Frankfort
Magdeburg
Breitenfeld
Lützen
SAXONY

Oder R.
SILESIA

THE
Rhine R.
Mainz
PALATINATE
Heidelberg
EMPIRE
BOHEMIA
Prague

MORAVIA

AUSTRIA
Vienna

STYRIA

Atlantic Ocean

Rocroy
Paris
Verdun
Metz
Toul
Strasbourg
ALSACE
Nördlingen
BAVARIA
Danube R.

Seine R.

Nantes

Orléans

Loire R.

F R A N C E

FRANCHE-COMTÉ

SWITZERLAND
Geneva
VALTELLINE
CARINTHIA
CARNIOLA

HUN

Bordeaux

SAVOY
PIEDMONT
MILAN
TYROL
Venice

Rhône R.

Avignon (to the papacy)
Marseilles
Genoa
Po R.

VENETIAN REPUBLIC
Ragusa

PORTUGAL
Lisbon

Burgos
Madrid
Tagus R.
Ebro R.

S P A I N

Barcelona

Valencia

Florence
PAPAL STATES
Rome

NAPLES
Naples

CORSICA
(to Genoa)

Guadalquivir R.
Seville
Granada

BALEARIC IS.

SARDINIA

M e d i t e r r a n e a n   S e a

Palermo
SICILY

ALGIERS
(Tributary to Ottoman Empire)

TUNIS

MALTA

FINLAND

L. Onega

L. Ladoga

Gulf of Finland

INGRIA

ESTONIA

Novgorod

LIVONIA

Pskov

COURLAND

W. Dvina R.

Volga R.

Moscow

Vilna

Smolensk

LITHUANIA

Oka R.

Königsberg

PRUSSIA

Warsaw

R U S S I A

POLAND

Ural R.

Kiev

Vistula R.

Dnieper R.

Dniester R.

Volga R.

55

45

Don R.

MOLDAVIA

TRANSYLVANIA

C R I M E A

Caspian Sea

uda

40

GARY

Belgrade

WALLACHIA

Moraca R.

Danube R.

50

Black Sea

MONTE-NEGRO

O T T O M A N

Vardar R.

Constantinople

Salonika

Tigris R.

E M P I R E

Aegean Sea

IONIAN IS.
(to Venice)

Athens

Euphrates R.

RHODES

(to Venice)

CYPRUS

CRETE

20   25   30   35   40   45

North Sea

UNITED NETHERLANDS

Zaandam

Haarlem

Leiden

Amsterdam

Schiedam

Rotterdam

Calais

Bruges

Antwerp

Scheldt R.

Meuse R.

SPANISH NETHERLANDS

Cambrai

Rhine R.

F R A N C E

erty, the year 1624 was chosen as the normal year, far better for the Protestants than the Edict of Restitution. States forcibly converted to Catholicism during the war won the right to revert to Protestantism. But there was still no toleration for Protestants in the Hapsburg lands.

Territorially, France secured Alsace and three important frontier fortress towns. Sweden received most of the Baltic shore of Germany, a large cash indemnity with which to pay the huge armies still mobilized, and three votes in the German Diet.

The family of Maximilian of Bavaria kept the electorate of the Palatinate and a part of its territory. The rest was returned to the son of Frederick, who was restored as an elector, thus raising the total number of electors to eight. The many individual German states secured the right to conduct their own foreign affairs, making treaties among themselves and with foreign powers if these were not directed against the emperor. The Dutch and Swiss republics were recognized as independent.

Despite the peace, the danger was great that fighting would resume. Sweden had 100,000 soldiers in Germany, mostly mercenaries whose whole life was war. A similar problem of demobilization and resettlement faced the imperial authorities. Many soldiers hired themselves out to any ruler who would pay them. Some simply became brigands. Moreover, since the treaty did not provide a means for enforcing the new religious property settlement, any attempt to recover lost property might provoke a new fight. The huge amount of money to be paid the Swedes gave rise to such bitterness that this too endangered the peace.

For more than two centuries after 1648, the Thirty Years' War was blamed for everything that later went wrong in Germany. We now know that the figures given in contemporary sources are inflated and unreliable. Sometimes the number of villages allegedly destroyed in a given district was larger than the whole number of villages that had ever existed there. Economic decline in Germany was not wholly due to the war, but had begun well before the war opened in 1618.

Nonetheless, contemporaries everywhere in Germany felt the catastrophe to have been overwhelming. The population fell from about 21 million in 1618 to less than 13½ million in 1648. Individuals suffered terribly. The war was partly responsible for the long delay in achieving German national unity, for the German yearning for authority and eagerness to obey, and even for a kind of national inferiority complex. But how much these later developments can be blamed on the Thirty Years' War remains debatable.

After it was over, the nobility often succeeded in forcing the peasants back onto the soil by denying them the right to leave their villages or to engage in home industry. Politically the main change was probably the shrinking of the power of the empire. The recognition that individual German states could, in effect, conduct their own foreign policies limited direct Hapsburg power to Hapsburg lands. Bavaria, Saxony, and especially Brandenburg-Prussia would now be able to emerge as powers in Germany.

Non-Austrian Germans always afterwards hated the Hapsburgs for having fought a terrible war chiefly to protect family interests. German particularism received yet another long lease on life.

All these issues remained to cause more European wars. Nobody liked the Peace of Westphalia. The pope denounced it. Many Protestants felt betrayed by its provisions. Its only merit was that it ended the fighting in a war that had become intolerable.

II REVOLUTION AND SETTLEMENT IN ENGLAND

Background: The First Stuarts

During the Thirty Years' War, the English went through a major domestic crisis of their own, which continued almost to the end of the seventeenth century. Trouble began under James I, son of Mary Stuart, Queen of Scots, and continued under his son Charles I in a prolonged civil war. In 1649 Charles was beheaded. Thereafter, for eleven years, England was a republic until 1660, when Charles's son, Charles II, was restored. The Stuart family got a second chance and threw it away.

James I was a Scot, a foreigner with none of Elizabeth's enormous popularity. He believed that he ruled by divine right. Kings, he said, were God's "vice-gerents*" on earth, and so adorned and furnished with some sparkles of the Divinitie." James went on repeating his opinions insistently and boringly. His son, Charles I, was personally far more attractive, but neither Stuart

* The word is "gerents" meaning "managers," not "regents."

understood the kind of compromises the Tudor monarchs had made in order to keep their Parliaments contented.

Like other contemporary European monarchs, James and Charles worked to make the royal administration strong. But unlike the continental rulers, they found themselves infringing on what the gentry in Parliament and in the countryside felt to be their established rights. The kings also tried to force submission to the Church of England, alienating those Protestants who could not accept the Church. So political and religious questions were knit together.

Worse still for the monarchy: both the king's political and his religious policies angered the same group of important people. Since the English king was obliged to ask Parliament for funds, quarrels over money proved critical. Also, Charles lacked a bureaucracy of the kind that ruled France. The unpaid English justices of the peace rendered justice in the parishes, administered poor relief, and indeed managed the administration in the countryside. The knights of the shires and burgesses who made up the House of Commons came from the same class of gentry. Many of them were "Puritans," English Calvinists. Finally Parliament grew suspicious that the king was pro-Spanish and pro-Catholic, and no longer trusted him on issues of foreign policy.

Both parties to the quarrel were trying to make revolutionary changes in the traditional system. The crown was trying to make England more like a continental divine-right monarchy, in which the king was the earthly representative of God. The idea, as old as the Roman Empire, was strongly revived in the sixteenth and seventeenth centuries. It was completely different from the Tudor compromise in which a strong monarch worked with and through his Parliament and satisfied the goals of the gentry and commercial classes.

On the other hand, the parliamentarians who revolted against the Stuarts were trying to secure for Parliament final authority in the execution of policy as well as in the making of law. This was something equally new, not only for England but for the Western world as a whole.

The Reign of James I

All the issues began to ripen during the reign of James I (1603–1625). James once said about the House of Commons, "I am surprised that my ancestors should ever have permitted such an institution to come into existence. I am

Portrait of James I by Daniel Mytens, 1621.

a stranger, and found it here when I arrived, so that I am obliged to put up with what I cannot get rid of."

When the Commons objected to James's insistence on certain legal but out-of-date royal rights, he acted as though they were personally insulting him. He tried to develop sources of income outside parliamentary control. Parliament insisted on the principle that it had to approve any new methods of raising revenue. When Parliament did not pass a law he wanted, he would try to get the courts to declare the measure legal.

One case, seemingly on a small point, illustrates the question of principle: John Bate, a merchant, refused to pay duty on imported currants. The judges ruled that there was no parliamentary authority for James to levy these customs duties, but that nonetheless he had the right to levy them. In a matter concerning the common good, they ruled, the king had absolute power, and all foreign affairs, including foreign trade, fell within this category.

So James's officials joyfully began to levy sales taxes without parliamentary authority, and when Parliament showed alarm at the possibility that James might make himself financially independent, he tried to forbid discussion of the question. Finally, James dissolved his first Parliament, which had sat from 1604 to 1611. Another met briefly in 1614, but thereafter none was elected until 1621. To raise money in these years, the king relied partly on "benevolences," supposedly free gifts granted by the subject to the monarch when he asked for them, but often in fact extracted under pressure.

James also behaved as if Parliament had no legitimate concern in foreign affairs. For years, in the face of the popular hatred for Spain, he tried to arrange a Spanish royal marriage for his son Charles. In 1621 when Parliament petitioned James to go to war with Spain instead and marry Charles to a Protestant, he threatened to punish the "insolent behavior" of anybody who continued to discuss the question. The members admitted that the king alone had the right to make war and peace and to arrange for the marriage of his son, but said that they wished to call his attention to the European situation as they saw it. James answered that this was merely a way of concealing their real intention to usurp royal prerogative.

The House of Commons then presented the Great Protestation (1621), which denied the king's right to imprison its members at will, and asserted their right to discuss and resolve any question concerning the state. James dismissed Parliament and imprisoned three of its leaders. In fact, James was right in alleging that the Commons were making a new claim, but the unpopularity of his Spanish policy made their protest a popular one. And James himself threw his case away in 1624, when—the Spanish match having fallen through—he summoned Parliament, gave it a complete report on foreign affairs, and asked its advice on the very same questions he had been ready to punish them for discussing.

In religion James was determined to enforce conformity to the Church of England. He rejected a moderate appeal presented by Puritans inside the Church: to relax or make optional certain requirements of the ritual. This probably reflected the majority sentiment in the House of Commons, but James told the Puritan leaders (1604) that he would make them conform or harry them out of the land.

James summed up his view as "no bishop, no king," stressing his belief that each depended on the other. The bishops did depend on the king for their continued support against the Puritans and he did depend on them to preach his views of divine right and to urge obedience to the royal will. One great service was rendered the English-speaking world by James's love of uniformity: between 1604 and 1611 a commission of forty-seven scholars prepared the King James version of the Bible, a major influence in the shaping of literary English.

Charles I and Parliament

Charles I (1625–1649) shared his father's theories of monarchy. He wrote less about it but acted on it even more vigorously. His first Parliament voted him only a fraction of what he asked for and needed for wars against Spain and France. Charles raised money by forced loans, always unpopular, and arrested some who refused to contribute. The courts upheld the legality of both loans and arrests.

In 1628 both houses of Parliament produced the Petition of Right. This document listed Charles's infringements of ancient statutes. It demanded no royal taxes without the consent of Parliament, no billeting of troops in private houses, no imprisonment without a charge or legal protection. The king assented. But by his assent, he later said, he had meant only to affirm previously existing rights, not to grant any new ones. Nor was his assent to the petition a law. Indeed, after Parliament had voted the subsidies he asked for, he went right on collecting customs duties that Parliament had not voted. Parliament protested.

Sir John Eliot, leader of the House of Commons, attacked Charles's religious policies. Eliot denounced the bishops as unfit to interpret the Thirty-nine Articles (see p. 244). So Eliot was in effect claiming for Parliament the right to determine the religion of England. Amid protests, Charles dissolved Parliament in 1629 and had Eliot and others arrested; Eliot died in prison, the first martyr in the parliamentary cause.

For the next eleven years (1629–1640) Charles governed without a Parliament. He totally failed to sense the rising popular support for the views of Eliot and the Puritans. To him any subject who did not adhere to the Church of England was disloyal. The whole duty of a loyal subject consisted in obeying king and bishop. Like James, he referred questions of legality to the courts, but if the judges did not say what he wanted to hear, they were dismissed and replaced by judges who would.

To save money and postpone indefinitely the recall of Parliament, Charles made peace with France and Spain. He revived obsolete medieval (but perfectly legal) ways to collect money. He forced all those who owned land worth forty

Van Dyck's portrait of Charles I hunting, ca. 1635.

pounds a year and who had not been knighted to pay large fines. He said that large areas now in private hands were in fact royal forest, and collected fines from their owners. He enforced feudal wardships.

All this aroused the wealthy against him. He also regularly collected from all of England a tax called ship money, which had been traditionally levied only on coastal towns to pay for defensive ships. John Hampden, a rich gentleman from Buckinghamshire, an inland county, refused to pay it and lost his case (1637). But the case dramatized the issue, since the judges who found for the king echoed the divine-right theory. They said that the king was *lex loquens,* the law itself speaking.

Charles's unpopularity grew as his archbishop of Canterbury, William Laud, drove the Puritans from their pulpits and censored all but approved books on religious subjects. The Puritans denounced the established ritual as "popish" and contrary to the Bible, and gave their resistance the color of martyrdom.

In Scotland, by reannexing in 1625 all the Church and crown land that had fallen into private hands since 1542, Charles enraged all Scotch nobles who had acquired the land in the interim. English and Scots often disliked each other, the English thinking of the Scots as barbarous and greedy, the Scots of the English as too rich for their own good and inclined to "popery." Unable as usual to judge public opinion, Charles decided in 1637 to impose a Book of Common Prayer on the Scots. They rose in their wrath, as if "the Mass in Latin had been presented."

In March 1638, the Presbyterians of Scotland banded together in a Solemn League and Covenant (its members were called Covenanters) to defend their faith. In November, a general assembly—despite royal objections—abolished bishops and prescribed a definitive ritual for the Scottish Kirk (church).

The Covenant united almost all Scots, who insisted all along that they were undertaking nothing against Charles as their king. But it was impossible to do away with bishops and still uphold Charles as king. Charles went to war in Scotland (1639). Immediately the question arose: how could he pay for the war? In 1640 Charles summoned Parliament once more.

Reforms of the Long Parliament

The Short Parliament of 1640 would vote no money until the piled-up grievances of almost forty years were settled. Charles refused all compromise and dissolved it. But a defeat in Scotland forced him to promise to buy off the Scots, and since he could not find the money, he had to summon another Parliament. This was the Long Parliament, which sat for twenty years, 1640–1660.

It began by arresting the most powerful royal favorite, Thomas Wentworth, earl of Strafford. Strafford was tried for high treason without a verdict being reached. But Charles eventually sacrificed him to the passions of the public and let him be executed. Archbishop Laud also was imprisoned and later executed.

Parliament now passed the Triennial Act, providing machinery for summoning Parliament if the king did not summon it himself within three years after a dissolution. It also passed a revolutionary act making it illegal for Charles to dissolve the present Parliament without its own consent. It abolished the Court of Star Chamber (see p. 212), reversed the judgment against Hampden in the ship money case, abolished ship money, reverted to the forest boundaries of 1623, and declared it illegal to require anybody to become a knight. Charles assented to all of these antiroyal measures, gritting his teeth. Many suspected that he was only waiting for a favorable moment to repeal them.

The Long Parliament, however, could not agree on Church affairs. The House of Lords would not accept a bill excluding bishops from their house, largely because they resented the Commons' interference. A "root and branch" bill abolishing bishops altogether had passionate defenders and a good many lukewarm opponents. The Commons favored, but the Lords did not, various regulations of ritual and Sabbath observance. The extreme radicalism of some of the Puritans began to produce a reaction among the milder ones.

The king's position was improving, when it was damaged by an Irish Catholic revolt that began in October 1641 with the massacre of some thirty thousand Protestants who had been settled in Ulster by James I. Parliament suspected that Charles had encouraged the Irish rebels. It refused to entrust to royal command an army to put down the revolt, and threatened to take the appointment of officers into its own hands. Finally, Parliament produced a monster list of grievances, the Grand Remonstrance, and so advertised its anger to the public. It began to discuss the appointment of a "lord general" who would have power to raise and pay troops. It talked of impeaching the queen (the French princess Henrietta Maria) on suspicion of instigating the Irish rebellion.

Charles unwisely tried to arrest five leading members of the Commons for treason and for complicity with the Scots. He took the unprecedented step of entering Parliament with a group of armed men, but found that the five had fled. They returned to Parliament in triumph (January 1642). Charles consented to a bill removing bishops from any temporal position and depriving them of any private law court. But he refused Parliament's "Nineteen Propositions" (June 1642), demanding the right to veto appointments to the great offices of state, to approve the education and marriages of the royal children, to consent to all appointments of new peers, and to dictate further reform of the Church.

England was now dividing into two camps and heading into civil war. Leadership of the Commons passed to the Independents, who were Brownists, or extreme Calvinists (see p. 245). Around Charles there gathered a party loyal to the Church and to him, including members of both houses. When Parliament announced that the cost of its own military operations would be borne by its opponents, many who had been neutral joined the king. For Charles money continued to be the problem: he depended on gifts from rich individuals. The north and west of England were largely royalist, the richer and more populous south and east, including London, largely parliamentarian.

In recent years, English historians have argued heatedly over the economic motives of the parliamentary side. Much of the writing has tended to reflect the individual author's political position on twentieth-century questions in England. Those who favor the present-day Labour party have argued that the Puritans of the Civil War included the most enterprising, advanced, and successful members of the gentry. Present-day Tories have answered that the gentry who backed the Puritans were actually those on the way down in the economic competition and unable to face inflation, the enclosure of lands for sheepraising and other economic threats. Neutral scholars enjoy the argument, but accuse both sides of oversimplification. Economic motives alone, they argue, did not determine allegiance in the English Civil War any more than they have in any other complex political and social and religious struggle.

Civil War, 1642–1649

In the Civil War the early advantage lay with the king. But he could not win a quick decisive victory, and this cost him the war in the end. He made peace with the Irish rebels in 1643, intending to use Irish Catholic forces in England. This increased the fear of "popery" that all along had driven neutrals toward Parliament, which now reached a "Solemn League and Covenant" with the anti-Catholic Scots.

This brought Scottish forces into England against Charles, in exchange for a promise to make English and Irish religion as nearly like Scottish Presbyterianism as possible. Parliament won the battle of Marston Moor (1644) largely owing to specially trained cavalry led by Oliver Cromwell, one of the radical Puritan gentry. Soon afterwards, Cromwell reorganized the parliamentary forces into the "New Model" army. At Naseby (1645) his Roundheads (so termed from their close-cropped hair) decisively defeated the Cavaliers (royalists).

In 1646 Charles surrendered to the Scots and stalled for time by launching prolonged negotiations with them and with Parliament. Dissension now developed among his opponents. The army, representing the radical, Independent (Congregationalist) wing of Puritanism, quarreled with the moderate Presbyterian leadership of Parliament that had begun the Civil War. The Independent members (about sixty) and the speakers of both houses fled London and joined the army, which marched on London and forcibly restored them to their places. Even more radical than Cromwell and the Independents was one faction in the army called Levellers. They advocated a universal franchise and relief from social and economic grievances.

In December 1647, the king secretly agreed with the Scots to establish Presbyterianism in England for three years and to suppress the Independents. Parliament thereupon renounced its allegiance to the king, and a "second" Civil War began. The Presbyterians, who had formerly supported Parliament, now joined the royalists and the Scots against the army. Most Englishmen, however, seem to have remained neutral.

In August 1648, Cromwell thoroughly defeated the Scots at Preston Pans and ended the second Civil War. The army seized Charles. Colonel Pride, acting for the army, excluded 140 Presbyterian members from Parliament in "Pride's Purge," leaving only about 60 Independents as members. The "Rump" as this much reduced body was called, created a special court to try the king. In January 1649, Charles was tried, condemned, and executed. The killers of the king believed that they were acting as agents of God. But the execution aroused genuine horror in England and abroad.

The Commonwealth and Protectorate

The Rump now abolished the monarchy and the House of Lords. England became a republic, called the Commonwealth (1649–1653), ruled by a Commons comprising only about one tenth the original membership of the Long Parliament. This minority regime depended for support on the radical army of Cromwell, who was the dominant personality of the republican experiment.

Cromwell himself with the utmost ruthlessness began the reconquest of rebellious Ireland (1649–1650). Next he turned to the Scots, who supported Charles I's son, Charles II. Cromwell defeated them, and Charles fled to France in disguise.

The Navigation Act of 1651 forbade the importation of goods into England or the colonies except in English ships or in ships of the country producing the goods. The Dutch carrying trade was so damaged that they went to war. Cromwell won.

But England itself remained Cromwell's greatest problem. Government by Rump and army aroused much bitter opposition. To grant

The House of Commons as shown on the Great Seal of England used by the Commonwealth, 1651.

an amnesty to the royalists and to enact conciliatory reforms seemed impossible in the face of parliamentary opposition. Under pressure the Rump did fix a date for new elections, but its members voted to keep their own seats in the new Parliament and to accept or reject all other representatives.

Discarding the last pretensions to be acting legally, Cromwell and his musketeers dissolved the Rump (1653), thus earning the eternal hatred of the extreme republicans. Then the army itself elected a Parliament of members nominated by Congregational ministers in each county.

After a few months, the members of this new Parliament resigned their powers to Cromwell, who became Lord Protector of England, thus inaugurating the second phase of the republican experiment—the Protectorate (1653–1660). It had a written constitution, the Instrument of Government, drawn up by some of the army officers. The Instrument restricted voting to those with an estate worth two hundred pounds, so the new Parliament proved to be an upper-class body. It proved so uncooperative that Cromwell—who believed that only a military dictatorship could govern England properly—dissolved it in 1654.

After a royalist uprising in 1653, Cromwell ordered Catholic priests exiled, forbade Anglicans to preach, and divided England into eleven military districts. In each, the major-general in command collected the taxes, policed his district, and served as censor of public morals. Many popular sports were prohibited. Alehouses, gambling dens, and brothels were closed or regulated severely. The theater was forbidden.

The English hated this Puritan regime and its attempts to impose Calvinist morality by force. The revulsion of opinion was evident in the parliamentary election of 1656. Even when the army had purged members of whom it did not approve, those who were left still produced the "Humble Petition and Advice," revising the Instrument of Government in the direction of traditional English monarchy. It asked Cromwell to become king (he refused), gave the House of Commons the right to exclude any elected member, and created a second house to be nominated by Cromwell. Though Cromwell accepted some of the amendments, he dissolved this Parliament too (1657).

Cromwell died September 3, 1658, and was succeeded as lord protector by his son, Richard, who proved unable to reorganize the army and weed out the most fanatical extremists. The army forced Richard to recall the Rump and resign (May 1659). As tension grew between the army

officers and the Rump, royalist activity increased. In October, General Lambert expelled the Rump and set up a Committee of Safety to govern England.

But a popular reaction soon set in against the assumption of such a major political role by the military. General George Monck (or Monk), a leading Cromwellian officer who had always upheld the principles of military obedience to properly constituted civil authority, emerged as the decisive figure in ending the political turbulence. In December 1659, the army gave in and restored the Rump for the third time. Monck allowed the surviving members excluded by Pride's Purge to take their old places.

The partially reconstituted Long Parliament prepared to restore the monarchy as the only barrier to chaos. At Monck's suggestion, the exiled Charles II issued the Declaration of Breda, promising a free pardon, confirmation of all land sales during the Civil Wars, payment of the soldiers' back pay, and liberty of conscience. Charles added, however, that on each point he would be bound by what Parliament wanted. A new Parliament, chosen in free election, summoned the king home in a burst of enthusiasm. On May 29, 1660, Charles II (reigned 1660–1685) arrived in London.

The English Revolution in Review

Revolutionary changes had occurred in England since 1642. Divine-right monarchy had been challenged, and a constitutional and representative government set up, based on a legislature backed by politically active private citizens. Though the Stuarts were restored, no English king ever again could hope to rule without a Parliament or to reinstate the Court of Star Chamber or to take ship money, benevolences, and other controversial taxes. Parliament thenceforward retained its critical weapon: ultimate control of the public purse by periodic grants of taxes.

Moreover, minority groups had gone much further toward political and social democracy. The Levellers put forward a program (later carried by emigrants to the American colonies) that favored universal suffrage, progressive taxation, separation of church and state, and protection of the individual against arbitrary arrest. A more extreme group called the Diggers actually dug up public lands near London and began planting vegetables in a kind of communistic enterprise. They were driven off, but not before they had got their ideas into circulation. The Fifth Monarchy men, the Millenarians, and a dozen other radical sects preached the Second Coming of Christ and the achievement of some kind of utopia on earth.

During the English struggles the Puritans urged freedom of speech and of the press, although when they came to power they often failed to practice what they had preached. Another basic liberal idea to emerge from the Civil War was religious toleration. Some of the Puritans believed that compulsion should not be exercised to secure conformity, and at least one sect held that religious toleration was a positive good.

The Quakers—more properly, the Religious Society of Friends—led by George Fox (1624–1691), were Puritans of the Puritans. They rejected all worldly show: for example, they regarded the polite form "you" as hypocritical, and so addressed everyone as "thou" or "thee." They took so seriously the basic Protestant doctrine of the priesthood of all believers that they had no ordained ministry and encouraged any worshiper to speak out in meeting if he felt the spirit move him. The Friends were—and still are today—pacifists, who opposed all use of force and would have no part in war.

The Restoration

Although many of the ideas advanced during the civil wars were much too revolutionary to win easy acceptance, the Restoration settlement showed a high degree of political tolerance. Except for a few revolutionaries, including the surviving judges who had condemned Charles I to death, Parliament pardoned all those who had been involved in the Civil War or the republican regimes. It made every effort to injure as few people as possible in settling the claims of royalists and churchmen to their former lands.

Political forbearance was not matched in religious matters. Though personally rather disposed to toleration, Charles II governed a country where very few people were yet ready to accept it. Parliament enacted many acts aimed at the Puritans but hitting at Catholics also. Bishops were restored. The Corporation Act (1661) required all magistrates to take the sacraments according to the Church of England. The Act of Uniformity (1662) required clergymen and teachers to subscribe to the Book of Common Prayer; those who refused were known as Nonconformists or Dissenters. The Conventicle Act (1664) limited to five the number of persons allowed to attend a Nonconformist meeting in a private household. The Five Mile Act (1665) forbade those who had not accepted the Act of Uniformity to come within five miles of any town unless they swore a special oath.

Much of this was impossible to enforce. It placed the Dissenters under disabilities but did not cause them great suffering. The Test Act (1673) required that all officeholders take communion in the Church of England and renounce transubstantiation (the Catholic doctrine of the Eucharist). One way around this was "occasional conformity," whereby a Dissenter whose conscience was not too strict might worship as a Presbyterian or Congregationalist most of the time, but take Anglican communion occasionally. Another way, common after 1689, was to allow Dissenters to hold office, and each year pass a special bill legalizing their acts.

The revulsion against Puritanism carried over into all aspects of the Restoration period. The Commonwealth and Protectorate had forbidden all theatrical performances. Restoration England thoroughly enjoyed them, the more indecent the better. Charles II himself and his court led cheerfully immoral lives.

Everywhere in Europe there was a trend back toward Catholicism. In Sweden, for instance, Gustavus Adolphus' own daughter, Christina, abdicated and became a Catholic (1654). Charles II sympathized with Catholicism and in 1672 tried but failed to free both Catholics and Dissenters from restrictions.

Charles greatly admired the flourishing monarchy of Louis XIV across the Channel. Without the knowledge of Parliament, he made a secret treaty with Louis (1670) and promised, in exchange for an annual subsidy, to support the French in their wars and to become a Catholic as soon as he could. His brother James, duke of York and heir to the throne, openly practiced Catholicism.

English popular suspicion of the Roman Church, however, was still strong. In the late 1670s a series of disclosures about alleged "popish" plots to murder the king and restore Catholicism aroused great popular excitement. One faction in Parliament wanted to exclude the Catholic and pro-French James from the succession.

These were called *Whigs,* a Scotch variant of "wigs." They included many well-to-do urban merchants and certain very powerful peers, who hoped to enhance their own political influence if the monarchy should be weakened. Supporting Charles and the succession of James were the landed gentry, lesser lords and country gentlemen who had been pro-Stuart all along and who suspected the newly rich townsmen. They were called *Tories,* a Gaelic term for "robber."

James II and the Glorious Revolution

James II (reigned 1685–1688) alienated even the Tories. He put down an ineffectual effort of a bastard son of Charles II, the duke of Monmouth, to invade England (1685), and sent a brutal judge to try and punish those suspected of sympathizing with Monmouth. Disregarding the laws, James appointed Catholics to high office. His Declaration of Liberty of Conscience (1687), extending religious toleration, was issued without parliamentary approval or support.

When a son was born to James (June 1688) and the prospect of a Catholic dynasty loomed, seven Whig and Tory leaders offered the throne jointly to James's daughter Mary, a Protestant, and to her husband, William of Orange. Stadholder since 1673 of six of the seven Dutch provinces, William was a vigorous enemy of Louis XIV. When William landed in England (November 1688), James fled to France. Elections were held. The throne was formally offered to William and Mary. They ruled as William III (1689–1702) and Mary II (1689–1694).

The invitation to them was accompanied by the Declaration of Rights, summing up what had been won in the long struggle with the Stuarts. Parliament alone makes or suspends laws.

Seventeenth-century Dutch engraving: fireworks in London celebrating the coronation of King William III and Queen Mary II.

The king cannot tax without Parliament. Freedom of election, freedom of debate, freedom of petition, frequent elections, no trial without jury, no excessive bail: all these William and Mary accepted as the rights of Englishmen. Parliament made them into laws as the Bill of Rights (1689), adding that in the future no Catholic could become king of England. A Toleration Act (1689) allowed Dissenters to practice their religion freely but excluded them from public office.

The sum total of the almost bloodless events of 1688–1689 is called the Glorious Revolution. In 1690 at the battle of the Boyne in Ireland, William secured it by defeating James II with his army of Irish Catholic rebels and French troops.

After the Glorious Revolution three major steps still lay ahead before England could become a full parliamentary democracy. First: the cabinet system, whereby a committee of the majority party would manage affairs of state would take shape in the eighteenth and early nineteenth centuries. Second: universal suffrage and payment of salaries to members of the Commons was gradually achieved during the nineteenth and early twentieth centuries. Third: curbs on the power of the Lords to veto legislation did not begin before our own twentieth century.

William and Mary were childless, and Mary's sister Anne, who succeeded as queen from 1702 to 1714, had no living children. Parliament, fearing that James II's son, the Catholic "James III," would try to seize the throne, settled the succession upon the descendants of Sophia, granddaughter of James I, twelfth child of Frederick of the Palatinate (see p. 268), wife of the elector of Hanover. When Anne died in 1714, Sophia's son George, elector of Hanover, became king of England as George I, and his descendants have sat on the throne ever since. By excluding the elder Catholic line of succession, Parliament had shown who really made the kings of England.

There remained the danger that the Scots might prefer a Stuart monarch to a Hanoverian. But under Anne, in 1707, the old problem of Anglo-Scottish union was worked out. Scotland accepted the Protestant succession, would send its own members to both houses of Parliament, and would join its cross of Saint Andrew with the English cross of Saint George on one flag, the Union Jack—symbol of Great Britain. Despite two efforts (1715 and 1745) of the Catholic Stuarts to rouse the old Scotch loyalties, Protestantism was too strong. And despite Scottish nationalism, revived in our own day, the Union of 1707 still holds.

The lot of the Irish was far harsher. After his victories in the Boyne and at Aughrim (1691), William III agreed to the generous Treaty of Limerick, but Parliament never ratified it. Penal laws imposed galling disabilities on the Catholics. Irish trade was stifled by mercantilist regulation. Irish misery was so acute that the Anglican Jonathan Swift made with bitter irony his famous "modest proposal" that they solve their economic problems by selling their babies to be eaten.

III DIVINE-RIGHT MONARCHY IN FRANCE

Henry IV, Richelieu, and Mazarin

The real danger that a Hapsburg combination—Spanish and Austrian—would upset the balance of power was dead after Rocroy (1643; see p. 269). But by repeatedly leading the other powers in checking any Hapsburg threat, France prepared to make its own bid for European supremacy. At home, France recovered quickly from the wounds of the sixteenth-century religious wars (see Chapter 8). Henry IV (reigned 1589–1610), dashing and popular, took a real interest in the popular welfare. His economic experts reclaimed marshes for farmland, encouraged the luxury crafts of Paris, and planted thousands of mulberry trees to feed silkworms and nurture a silk industry. They built the canals, roads, and bridges that made the French communications system the best in Europe.

Faced with a deficit, Henry IV found an efficient finance minister in Sully (1560–1641), who gradually brought income up and expenditure down until they balanced. Monarch and minister even toyed with an advanced idea for a general European international Christian republic that would include everybody but the Hapsburgs. This "grand design" obviously was conceived in the interest of France, but it also was an ancestor of future leagues of nations.

Assassinated in 1610 by a madman, Henry IV was succeeded by his nine-year-old son, Louis XIII (reigned 1610–1643). His mother Marie de' Medici became regent and her favorites almost undid what Henry IV had accomplished. But in 1624 Richelieu became the king's chief minister. We have already seen him allying France with the Protestants during the Thirty Years' War. Ev-

Triple portrait of Richelieu by Philippe de Champaigne.

erywhere the interests of the state *(raison d'état)* governed his policy.

Richelieu subsidized Lutherans and Calvinists in Germany. But in France he felt that the Edict of Nantes (see p. 260) had given too many privileges to the Huguenots. The hundred-odd fortified towns in Huguenot hands seemed potential centers of disorder and a threat to his program of increased royal centralization. Foreseeing punitive measures against them, the Huguenots rebelled. Richelieu's forces had trouble taking their key port of La Rochelle (1628), largely because he had no navy.

Over the next decade, Richelieu built French Atlantic and Mediterranean fleets. He tried to curb the French nobility by ordering some of their chateaux destroyed and by forbidding their favorite pastime of dueling. But he by no means succeeded in taming them completely. He did successfully transfer responsibility for local administration from the nobles to royal officials, the *intendants,* who obtained greatly increased power to assess and collect taxes.

Without Richelieu, later French greatness under Louis XIV would have been unthinkable. He left little place for government by discussion. Except for a few highly trained professional bureaucrats, the middle classes took little part in government. He handpicked and trained his immediate successor, the Italian-born Cardinal Mazarin, who inherited an efficient centralized administration.

Succeeding to power in 1642, Mazarin soon faced the crisis caused by the death of Louis XIII (1643), whose heir, Louis XIV (1643–1715), was only five years old. Mazarin's foreign birth, his failure to pay the interest on government debts, and his amassing of a huge personal fortune antagonized the French nobility.

The nobility consisted not only of the descendants of the feudal aristocracy—the nobility of the sword *(noblesse d' épée)*—but also of those who had been given titles because of their services as judges or administrators—the nobility of the robe *(noblesse de robe).* The old nobility of the sword hated Mazarin partly for snobbish reasons, partly for keeping them out of power; the newer nobility of the robe worried about his fast-and-loose ways with money.

This discontent and the ambitions of rival cliques of nobles led to the complex disturbances known as the Fronde, 1648–1653 (the name refers to a slingshot used by Parisian children to throw mud at passersby). In the end, Mazarin defeated both old and new nobles. He maintained himself in power until he died in 1661. By then Louis XIV was twenty-three and ready for personal rule in the fullest sense of divine-right absolutism.

Louis XIV: Le Grand Monarque

It is not James I—despite all his theorizing on the subject—nor even Philip II of Spain whom we think of as *the* divine-right monarch, but Louis XIV. Of course, he is supposed to have summed it all up by saying, "L'état, c'est moi" (I am the State). God had from the beginning destined this descendant of Hugh Capet for the throne of France. To challenge his right to it was to challenge the structure of God's universe.

Louis was able to act as a divine-right monarch partly because of the revival of the concept from Roman law that God directs the affairs of states through his chosen agents. Moreover, the French monarchy had for centuries combatted the old deep provincial loyalty—to Normandy, Brittany, Burgundy—and emphasized instead a loyalty to France.

Louis XIV.

The subjects of the French crown spoke several different languages or, at least, dialects. They had no common educational system, or press, or political life. What they had in common was the king, a symbol of common "Frenchness," who collected taxes and raised armies. Frenchmen had to feel that he had a right to do these things, and was doing it *for* them, not just *to* them.

Of course, Louis lacked the physical means for controlling all the actions of all his subjects. Indeed no ruler was ever absolute in this sense until the days of the twentieth-century dictatorships, with all their totalitarian techniques of propaganda, surveillance, and terror. Medieval local survivals in language, law, customs, weights and measures all stood in the way of real uniformity in France. Louis could not ride roughshod over city corporations that appealed to their ancient charters granting them immuni-

ties, or over guilds that could show a privileged status that they had "always" possessed. He could not force nobles and clergy to conform completely.

He did, however, deprive the nobles of their political function, and left them only their social and economic privileges and their military careers. Louis XI had begun to tame them in the fifteenth century. Henry IV's victory in the religious wars was a defeat for them. So was Richelieu's increased use of nonnobles as intendants, judges, and local officials. Louis XIV finished the job.

The French Church, too, had gradually come under the control of the crown. Under Louis XIV it was "Gallican"—that is to say, national, though of course Catholic. His bishops supported the monarchy. But the French clergy were not subject to royal taxation. Of their own free will

The noblesse de robe:
Municipal councillors of Toulouse.

in their own assembly they voted gifts of money to the king.

Louis abolished the religious toleration that Richelieu had left the Huguenots after taking away their fortresses and political privileges. In 1685 he revoked the Edict of Nantes. Fifty thousand Protestant families fled abroad. In Prussia, some of the exiles found a place in the military services, and their descendants fought against the French in the wars of the nineteenth and twentieth centuries. In Holland, England, North America, and South Africa the talents and skills of these refugees greatly strengthened the lands that received them. Some Huguenots remained in France, where they had to worship secretly.

Within the Catholic Church itself, Louis had to deal with enthusiastic mystics (Madame Guyon and the Quietists) and with puritanical Jansenists, named after Cornelius Jansen, bishop of Ypres in the early seventeenth century. The Jansenists, who virtually agreed with Calvin on predestination, questioned the authority of both pope and king, since both were mere men. Their most distinguished spokesman was the scientist and philosopher Pascal (see Chapter 10). Though Louis contained the threat that they posed to uniformity, he did not succeed in suppressing them.

Intent on his own glory, Louis worked hard and in his youth played hard. In middle age, after his Spanish queen's death, he contracted a morganatic marriage with Mme. de Maintenon, former governess of his illegitimate children. She was a devout Catholic, and it seems certain that she influenced Louis's decision to revoke the Edict of Nantes.

Louis installed the French court at Versailles, where he built a splendid palace on the site of a former hunting lodge. Almost half a mile long, the main buildings at Versailles housed a court of ten thousand tame nobles and their families, followers, and servants.

So completely did Louis make Versailles the center of French social life that everything else in Europe seemed provincial. The proper standard

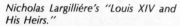

Nicholas Largilliére's "Louis XIV and His Heirs."

of sophisticated behavior for all Europe was set here: how to dress, how to speak French, what to read, what sort of story to tell, how far to go in gossip, what games to play, what food to eat at what times of day, what music to listen to, and what dances to dance. At every European court and in every nobleman's private house, the master and mistress would ask what Versailles did and imitate it.

Here Louis met with his ministers, the heads of departments like those in any modern state: war, finance, foreign policy, interior. They were directly responsible to him and not to any legislative body. Indeed, the Estates-General never met at all during Louis's entire reign of seventy-two years. From the top, the chain of command went down through the intendants, in charge of the *généralités,* or large province-sized administrative units, to smaller regional units, and then to the towns and villages. Even Louis could exercise only a general supervision.

His subjects had to fill out all sorts of official forms. Many thousands of them remain today duly filed in the French local archives. As members of the noblesse de robe, the intendants transmitted their titles and rank to their heirs and so formed a new kind of privileged corporation. They got more power than the theory of royal absolutism ideally would have allowed and so asserted provincial initiative against the monarchy.

The judges of the high courts of appeal, too, could not be removed by the king and therefore exercised considerable independence. These courts were the *parlements,* of which the Parlement of Paris enjoyed the widest jurisdiction and the most prestige. The parlements had to register each royal edict. But they claimed the right to refuse if they thought an edict violated the law of the land. Louis intimidated the Parlement of Paris by summoning the judges before him in a formal session *(lit de justice,* "bed of justice") and commanding them to register a royal edict. The claim that the parlements might throw out a royal edict, however, remained to plague his successors.

Mercantilism and Colbert: Economic Policy under Louis XIV

The economic policies of Louis XIV's government reflected mercantilist theories and practices. Mercantilists believed that hard money, gold and silver, was the basic wealth. Therefore, the state should try to get as much of it as possible and to arrange that more should come in than

go out. It should maintain this "favorable balance of trade" by encouraging exports (which bring in cash from abroad) perhaps by bounties, and discouraging imports (which cause cash to flow out) perhaps by tariffs. Carried to its extreme, this would be absurd, since gold and silver were of no use to the state except as media of exchange.

But the mercantilists were not absurd. They were trying to make their own state as self-sustaining as they could. National production, they argued, should provide the necessities of life for the population and the sinews of war for the armed forces. They favored rigorous planning and control, sweeping away the traditional ways of manor and guild and the medieval notion of the just price. Instead, mercantilists favored directing the economy by subsidies, grants of monopolies, government participation in industry, encouragement of research, and imposition of tariffs.

As we have seen in the case of Spain, they viewed the overseas colonies of the mother country as a source of necessary raw materials. Possession of these made it unnecessary to import from rival states and encouraged manufacturing at home. Therefore, the colonies must be strongly governed and their economies directed as the mother country saw fit.

Louis XIV's finance minister, Jean Baptiste Colbert (1619–1683), was a thorough-going mercantilist. He exercised more influence over the king than any other royal servant. Colbert supported new inventions, improvements in ship building, technological education, the settlement of foreign experts in France, and the founding of new industries. This was the first major experiment in a modern controlled economy, and the result was prosperity.

In Colbert's time nobody had yet put forward the rival theory of free trade *(laissez-faire),* which would leave businessmen alone, arguing that the mere removal of regulations enables the individual entrepreneur and therefore the whole economy to enrich itself still further. So we cannot say whether France would have been richer under laissez-faire.

Colbert's system gave France the economic leadership of Europe. During the eighteenth century, France would lose this lead. England would adopt new methods of power machinery and large-scale production of inexpensive goods, while the French would cling to small-scale production of a large variety of products, chiefly luxuries and consumer goods. England also had more easily exploitable resources, like coal, iron, and water power, and so would get a head start in modern industrialization. Very important too were the expensive wars of Louis XIV. They built up a burden of debt that depressed the economy in the latter part of his reign and even after his death.

The Wars of Louis XIV

As the real victor in the Thirty Years' War, France had defeated the Hapsburgs and got new territory cheaply. Louis XIV set out to expand still farther. France took the Hapsburgs' place as the threat to the European balance of power. Louis wanted to push French boundaries east to the Rhine, annexing the Spanish Netherlands (Belgium) and the Franche Comté (Free County of Burgundy). As time went on, he hoped also to secure Spain and the Spanish Empire. He also wanted to assert the predominance of France in every part of the globe and in every area of human life.

Louis had agents in India, in Canada, in Holland, and on the Rhine. He regarded it as natural and proper that French culture, French taste in the arts, French social ways should influence all of Europe. To an astonishing degree they did. But when other European rulers felt France was too threatening, they united against Louis XIV.

A legal quibble gave Louis the excuse for his first war, the War of Devolution (1667–1668). When he had married the daughter of Philip IV of Spain, his wife had renounced her right to inherit her father's lands. But her dowry had not been paid, and Louis claimed that this voided her renunciation. After the death of Philip IV (1665), Louis claimed that his queen ought to inherit the Spanish Low Countries by virtue of an old Flemish law of "devolution."

The threat to Belgium aroused the Dutch, who made an alliance with England and Sweden against France, thus joining their old enemies, the Spaniards, in supporting the balance of power. Louis made peace at Aix-la-Chapelle in 1668, collecting twelve fortified Flemish towns.

Furious at the Dutch, Louis bought off Charles II by a secret treaty in 1670 (see p. 279) and also made a treaty with the Swedes. Then he began his second war, the Dutch War (1672–1678), quickly occupying large areas of southern Holland. Six of the seven Dutch provinces elected William of Orange stadholder and decided that the office should be hereditary in his family. William allied himself with both Spanish and Austrian Hapsburgs and prevented a decisive French victory. At the Peace of Nijmegen (1678–1679), the Dutch lost no territory but had to promise future neutrality. Spain gave Louis the Franche Comté and some towns in the Spanish Netherlands.

The superb French armed forces now dominated Europe. On the eastern frontiers, special French courts ("chambers of reunion") decreed annexations of still other areas that could be shown to have belonged at any time to any of the territories newly acquired by France. Louis's armies would then proceed to take over these too. In this way France "reunited" Strasbourg (1681) and Luxembourg, all of Lorraine (1683), and the Rhineland bishopric of Trier (1684). These French aggressions in time of peace met with no resistance. Europe was busy with the Ottoman siege of Vienna (1683) and its aftermath (see Chapter 7).

Louis now put in a farfetched claim to the lands of the Palatinate and insisted on pushing his own candidate for the archbishopric of Cologne (1688). The revocation of the Edict of Nantes (1685) had distressed the Protestants of Europe. Sweden, the Palatinate, Saxony, Bavaria, the Austrian and Spanish Hapsburgs, together with William of Orange, who was soon to be king of England, formed the League of Augsburg against Louis XIV. In the War of the League of Augsburg (1688–1697), Louis was defeated, and by the Treaty of Ryswick (1697) had to give up much of the land "reunited" since Nijmegen, including Lorraine.

The War of the Spanish Succession

But within four years Louis embarked on his last and most adventurous war. When Louis's brother-in-law, the Hapsburg king of Spain, Charles II (1665–1700), died childless, his will left all the vast Spanish possessions in Europe and overseas to his great-nephew, the grandson of Louis XIV, Philip of Anjou. Louis could not resist the temptation. He proclaimed his grandson King Philip V of Spain. At once, England, Holland, the Empire, and the German states, which had been trying to avert this overwhelming addition to Bourbon strength, formed a new grand alliance against the French.

The War of the Spanish Succession (1701–1713) was fought in Italy and overseas, and especially in the Low Countries. The allies gradually wore down the French. Queen Anne's great general, John Churchill, duke of Marlborough and ancestor of Winston Churchill, won battles at Blenheim (1704), Ramillies (1706), Oudenarde (1708), and Malplaquet (1709). Malplaquet alone cost the victorious allies twenty thousand casualties, which in those days seemed "butchery" to the people of England.

In 1711 the threat arose that the new Hapsburg emperor might inherit all the Spanish possessions. This would have recreated the old empire of Charles V. Once more, the balance of power would be upset by the Hapsburgs. The English feared this as much as a French victory. Negotiations for peace began, culminating in the Treaty of Utrecht (1713), a major event in the diplomatic and territorial history of Europe.

Philip V was accepted as king of Spain, but Louis XIV promised that the crowns of France and Spain would never be united. He recognized the Protestant succession in England. In America, France gave up Newfoundland, Acadia (Nova Scotia), and the Hudson's Bay territory to England, but retained Quebec and Louisiana. From Spain the English obtained Gibraltar, which they still hold. Because the Austrian Hapsburgs lost their claim to the Spanish throne, they received the former Spanish Netherlands (Belgium). The duke of Savoy, a great general, eventually got Sardinia in 1720. As kings of Sardinia, the dukes of Savoy would later unite the rest of Italy into a kingdom. The elector of Brandenburg was recognized as "king in Prussia."

Utrecht was on the whole a moderate and sensible peace. Yet it did not end overseas rivalry between the French and English. It did not really protect the Dutch, satisfy the Hapsburgs, or settle the tangled affairs of Italy. French aggression was halted, but only temporarily, for it would be resumed at the end of the century under the impulse of the great Revolution (see Chapter 12).

The wars of Louis XIV, however, despite their great cost in human life and in treasure, and despite the popular hatred aroused by the French in their drive into Dutch and German territories, were less savage than the Thirty Years' War or the wars of nationalism and revolution that would follow after 1789. Religion played a minor role. Although Louis regarded himself as a Catholic champion, and William of Orange was hailed as a Protestant one, hundreds of thousands of Catholics were lined up against Louis on the "Protestant" side. Louis's aggressions were not religious or political crusades. His wars were more measured and "classical," as befitted le Grand Monarque.

IV EUROPE OVERSEAS

At Utrecht, we saw, Nova Scotia and Newfoundland changed hands as well as Gibraltar. Indeed, the last war of Louis XIV was almost a world war, fought not only to maintain the balance of power in Europe but to gain advantages and resources overseas. The increased concern with the world beyond Europe resulted from the faster pace of colonialism in the seventeenth century, when the English, French, and Dutch all joined the ranks of empire builders.

The Thirteen Colonies

The English got their first two permanent footholds in North America at Jamestown in Virginia (1607) and at Plymouth in Massachusetts (1620). At first similar to Spanish or Portuguese trading posts, these were established by English trading companies which vainly hoped to find gold and silver as the Spaniards had. Both settlements barely managed to survive the early years of hardship. Then the sparse Indian population was gradually replaced by immigrants of English stock.

Tobacco and the resourcefulness of Captain John Smith saved Virginia. Furs, codfish, and Calvinist toughness saved Massachusetts. Both gradually built up an agricultural economy and traded with the mother country. Neither received more than a few tens of thousands of immigrants from abroad, but the population grew steadily.

In 1664 the English defeated the Dutch in a round of the warfare for economic advantage. They took over New Amsterdam, founded in 1626, which became New York. Its important Dutch families—Stuyvesant, Schuyler, Roosevelt—would supply some leading participants in American development. In 1655 the Dutch had already eliminated the Swedish settlement at Fort Christina on the Delaware, and here, too, the English now ousted the Dutch. Pennsylvania, chartered in 1681 to the wealthy English Quaker William Penn, filled the vacuum left by the expulsion of the Swedes and the Dutch from the Delaware.

By the early eighteenth century, the English settlements formed a continuous string of thirteen colonies from Maine to Georgia. The new settlers came from all strata of English life except the very top. New England was for the most part

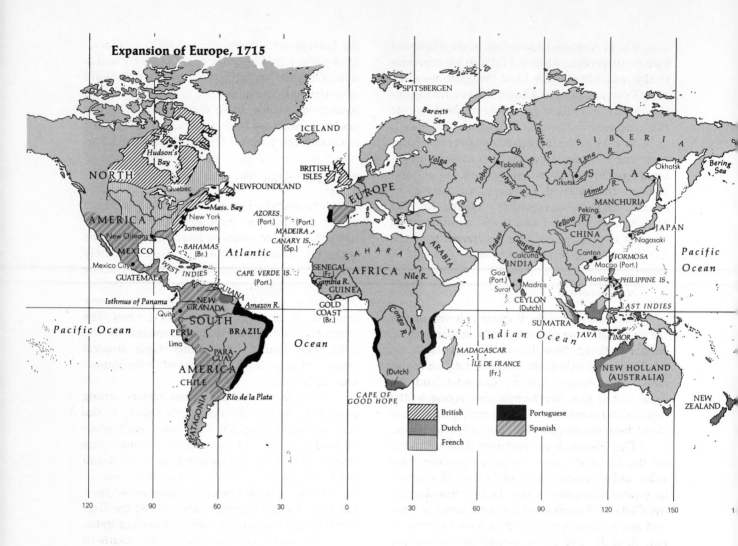

Expansion of Europe, 1715

settled by Calvinist Independents (Congregationalists), who believed in local self-government, and who set up their own Puritan state church, like Calvin's in Geneva or Cromwell's in England. Yet "heresy" appeared from the start, as Baptists, Quakers, and even Anglicans came to New England.

The southern colonies, especially tidewater Virginia, were settled for the most part by Anglicans, comfortable with the social distinctions and the large landholdings of rural England. The Church of England became the established church in Virginia. Yet in the Piedmont section of Virginia and the Carolinas, there were small farmers—"Scotch-Irish" Presbyterians and Germans from Pennsylvania. Geography and climate played their part, making the South the land of one-crop plantations producing tobacco, rice, or indigo, while New England and the Middle Colonies went in for small farming, fishing, and small-scale industry and commerce.

Maryland was founded partly to give refuge to Catholics. Rhode Island was founded by Roger Williams and others unwilling to conform to the orthodoxy of Massachusetts. Pennsylvania was founded by Quakers who believed in the separation of church and state. Such variety lay at the base of the religious freedom later prescribed in the Constitution of the United States. During the eighteenth century, it came to be recognized that people should be free to belong to any church or even to no church at all.

The colonists, as men of the seventeenth century, accepted class distinctions as a matter of course. Yet the seeds of democracy were present. There was no titled colonial nobility. The egalitarianism of the frontier and the career open to talent in the town balanced the privileged gentry in the coastal cities and in the Hudson Valley. Each colony had some sort of legislative body. Government by discussion was firmly planted from the beginning.

The crown was represented in most colonies by a royal governor. But the English government, in the instability of the Civil War, Cromwellian rule, Restoration, and Glorious Revolution, exerted no continuing bureaucratic or absolute rule over the colonies, as the Spaniards and French did over theirs. The English royal governors bickered with the colonial assemblies and often lost. Local government—in village and town and county—fostered wide popular participation. The English common law, which provided for trial by jury and lacked bureaucratic administrative regulation, perpetuated a very different tradition from that of the Spanish or French.

New France

To the north of the thirteen colonies, in the region around the Bay of Fundy and in the St. Lawrence Basin, New France for a century and a half posed a serious threat to the English North American colonies. The St. Lawrence and the Great Lakes gave the French easy access to the heart of the continent, whereas the Appalachians stood between the English and the Mississippi.

The French were also impelled westward by the fur trade. Furs are goods of very great value and comparatively little bulk, easily carried in canoes and small boats. Led by the Jesuits, the Catholic French were far more eager to convert the American Indians than were the Protestant English. The priest as well as the trapper led the push westward. In North America, the French were also moved to advance by the conscious imperial policy of the Bourbon monarchs.

The result was that the French, not the English, explored the interior of the continent. The names and accomplishments of the French explorers, missionaries, and traders—Marquette, Joliet, La Salle, Frontenac, Cadillac, Iberville—are a part of our American heritage. By the early eighteenth century, the French had built up a line of isolated trading posts—with miles of empty space between, thinly populated by Indians—which encircled the English colonies on the Atlantic coast.

From Quebec, one line of outposts led westward. From Mobile and New Orleans, in a colony founded at the beginning of the eighteenth century and named Louisiana after Louis XIV, other lines led northward up the Mississippi to join with those from Canada and Illinois.

But there were too few Frenchmen to contain the English. The French loss of Newfoundland, Acadia, and Hudson's Bay to England in the Utrecht settlement reflected their weakness. Theirs was a trading empire with military ambitions. Only in Quebec did it become a true colony of settlement. The Huguenot French, who might have come to settle as did the Puritans, were deliberately excluded by a royal policy determined to uphold the Catholic faith in New France.

The Indies, West and East; Africa

The French, Dutch, and English intruded upon the pioneer Spanish and Portuguese throughout the overseas empires. They broke the Spanish hold over the Caribbean and ultimately made that sea of many islands a kaleidoscope of colonial jurisdictions and a center of continuing naval wars and piracy. The West Indies were then one of the great prizes of imperialism. The cheap black slave labor that had replaced the exterminated Indians raised the staple tropical crops—tobacco, fruits, coffee, and, most important, cane sugar.

In India, the Mogul Empire proved strong enough to confine the Europeans chiefly to the coastal fringes. Gradually the French and English nibbled away at the Portuguese holdings. The English defeated a Portuguese fleet in 1612 and got trading rights at Surat on the west coast of India. The Mogul emperor, Aurangzeb, tried vainly to exclude them in 1685. In 1690 the English founded Calcutta in Bengal in eastern India.

The French got footholds on the southern coast near Madras at Pondichéry and soon had established other stations. Early in the eighteenth century, the stage was set in India as in North America for a decisive struggle between France and Britain. Both countries operated in India, as they had initially in North America, by means of chartered trading companies, the English East India Company and the French Compagnie des Indes Orientales. The home governments backed the companies when it came to annexing bits of land around the trading posts. Gradually both England and France became involved in Indian politics and wars. But neither country made an effort to found a New England or a New France in the East.

The Dutch, who operated the most profitable of all the East India companies, bypassed India but drove the Portuguese from the nearby island of Ceylon. In the East Indies proper, they built Batavia (from the Latin name for Holland) on the island of Java and founded an empire in Indonesia which they held until after World War II.

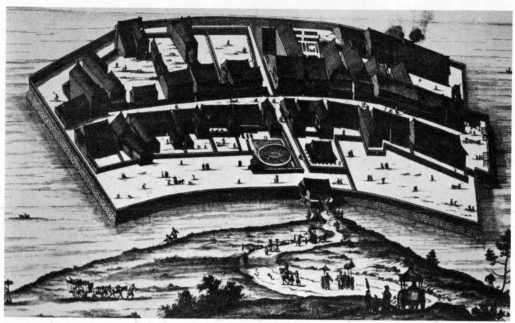

The island in Nagasaki harbor to which the Dutch were confined, 1699.

When the Dutch reached Japan in 1609, the Japanese rulers were already suspicious of Christian penetration and irritated at the bickerings between Portuguese Jesuits and Spanish Franciscans. Gradually the Japanese expelled all Christians. In 1641 only the Dutch alone were left, confined to an island in Nagasaki harbor. Japan remained sealed off from the West until the American Commodore Perry arrived in 1853, more than two centuries later.

In Africa, the Dutch took over the Cape of Good Hope from the Portuguese in 1652 and settled there—the ancestors of today's Afrikaners in South Africa. The French, too, were moving into Africa, first into Senegal on the west coast (1626). In the Indian Ocean, Louis XIV annexed the large island of Madagascar in 1686, and in 1715 the French took the island of Mauritius from the Dutch, rechristening it the Île de France.

The British broke into the competition by securing a foothold at the mouth of the Gambia River in West Africa (1662) and later added other acquisitions at French and Dutch expense. Thus a map of Africa and adjacent waters in the eighteenth century shows a series of coastal stations controlled by European states. Until the nineteenth century the interior remained untouched, except by slavers and native traders.

The Balance Sheet of Imperialism

Seen in terms of economics, the expansion of Europe in early modern times was by no means pure "exploitation" and "plundering." There was robbery, just as there was murder and enslavement. In dealing with the American Indians, the Europeans often gave far too little in exchange for land and goods of great value. The Indians sold the island of Manhattan to the Dutch for $24.00 worth of trinkets.

And the almost universally applied mercantilist policy kept money and manufacturing in the hands of the home country. It limited the colonies to the production of raw materials, a role that tended to keep even colonies of settlement economically dependent. Yet the expansion of Europe did add to the goods available to non-Europeans. Although few Europeans settled in India or Africa, their wares, and especially their weapons, gradually began the process of Europeanizing the rest of the world. By the eighteenth century this process was only beginning. The improvements in public health that Europeans would later discover and bring to the East were still unknown. But in America especially there were signs of the westernization to come.

The West in its turn was greatly affected

by the world overseas. The long list of items from the colonies included foodstuffs, utensils, and gadgets like pipes for smoking, hammocks and pajamas, and style of architecture and painting like bungalows and Japanese prints. Some novelties caught on more quickly than others. Tobacco, brought into Spain in the mid-sixteenth century as a soothing drug, had established itself by the seventeenth century as essential to the peace of mind of many European males. Potatoes, on the other hand, though highly nourishing and cheaper to grow than the staple breadstuffs, did not immediately catch on in Europe.

Among Westerners, knowledge of non-European beliefs and institutions eventually penetrated to the level of popular culture, where it is marked by a host of words—*powwow, kowtow, tabu, totem.* At the highest level of cultural interchange, that of religion and ethical ideas, however, the West imported little. The first impression of Westerners, not only when they met the relatively primitive cultures of the Americas, but even when they met the ancient cultures of the East, was that they had nothing to learn from them.

In time the West would learn to respect the other worldliness of Hinduism and the dignity and simplicity of primitive peoples. But for the most part what struck the first generations of Europeans—when they bothered to think about anything but money-making and empire-building—was the poverty, dirt, and superstition they found in India and China, the low material standards of primitive peoples, the heathenness of the heathens.

But even then exposure to these very different cultures acted as a stimulus in the West. It increased the fund of the marvelous, the incredible. The early accounts of the New World are full of giants and pygmies, El Dorados with gold-paved streets, fountains of eternal youth, fantastic plants and animals. The literary and artistic imagination revelled in all this, from the island of Shakespeare's *Tempest* to the Xanadu of Coleridge's *Kubla Khan,* two hundred years later.

Science, too, was stimulated. A dip into any of the early collections of voyages gives an impression of the realistic sense and careful observations of European travelers rather than of their credulity and exaggerations. Here is the modern science of geography already well on the way to maturity, and here too are contributions to the modern social sciences of anthropology, comparative government, and economics.

The effects of expansion were harsh and unsettling as well as stimulating. The great new supplies of gold and silver from the Americas pushed European prices up. This inflation accompanied, perhaps indeed "caused" or at least helped, general economic expansion. In this process, the merchants and financiers gained. People on fixed incomes suffered. The income of wage earners and peasants increased but usually not as fast as prices.

The Beginnings of One World

By the early eighteenth century the interior of Africa and our Pacific Northwest were still blank spots on the map. Yet it was already clear that only one system of international politics existed in the world. From now on, all general European wars tended to be world wars, fought on all the seas and all the continents. By the eighteenth century the world was already one world.

Of course, no common authority of any kind could reach all men. There were pockets of isolated peoples. And the masses of the world, even in Europe, remained ignorant of, and uninterested in, what went on in the heads and hearts of people elsewhere. But already Western goods had penetrated almost everywhere. Already an educated minority was growing up: professional geographers, journalists, diplomatists, men of business, specialists who had to deal with the problems of remote places and even of the world as a whole.

READING SUGGESTIONS on The Seventeenth Century: War, Politics, and Empire
(Asterisks indicate paperback.)

General Treatments

C. J. Friedrich, *The Age of the Baroque, 1610–1660;* F. L. Nussbaum, *The Triumph of Science and Reason, 1660–1685;* and J. B. Wolf, *The Emergence of the Great Powers, 1685–1715* (*all Harper Torchbooks). Three consecutive volumes in the Harper Rise of Modern Europe series, with good bibliographies. The first is particularly original in its treatment.

G. N. Clark, *The Seventeenth Century* (*Galaxy); and D. Ogg, *Europe in the Seventeenth Century* (*Collier). Two briefer treatments.

R. S. Dunn, *The Age of Religious Wars, 1559–1689* (*Norton). A valuable survey.

M. Ashley, *The Golden Century* (1969). The entire century in perspective.

A. Vagts, *A History of Militarism* (*Free Press); and E. M. Earle, *Makers of Modern Strategy* (*Athenaeum). Both include good treatments of seventeenth-century warfare.

E. F. Heckscher, *Mercantilism*, 2 vols. (1955). Standard advanced work by a distinguished Swedish economist. Controversial and not for beginners.

T. Aston, ed., *Crisis in Europe, 1560–1660*. The essays examine the upheaval of the century and include some very distinguished historical writing.

The Thirty Years' War and Germany

C. V. Wedgwood, *The Thirty Years' War* (*Anchor). Good full-length treatment, perhaps underemphasizing the destructiveness of the conflict.

S. H. Steinberg, *The "Thirty Years' War" and the Conflict for European Hegemony* (*Norton). Shorter than Miss Wedgwood's masterly book.

G. Pagès, *The Thirty Years' War* (*Harper Torchbooks). Heavily diplomatic in its emphasis, not so recent as the two books listed above.

T. K. Rabb, ed., *The Thirty Years' War* (*Heath). Collected modern essays on the war's motives and impact.

M. Roberts, *Gustavus Adolphus*, 2 vols. (1953, 1958). A solid, detailed biography.

H. Holborn, *History of Modern Germany*, 2 vols. (1959, 1963). Volume I includes the Thirty Years' War.

Revolution and Settlement in England

M. Ashley, *England in the Seventeenth Century* (*Penguin); and C. Hill, *The Century of Revolution, 1603–1714* (*Norton). Two surveys by well-known scholars, the latter a Marxist.

G. Davies, *The Early Stuarts, 1603–1660* (1949); and G. N. Clark, *The Later Stuarts, 1660–1714* (1949). Two good but more detailed volumes in The Oxford History of England.

W. Notestein, *The English People on the Eve of Colonization, 1603–1660* (*Harper Torchbooks). A fine brief account of the earlier period from the social historian's point of view.

D. H. Wilson, *King James Sixth and First* (*Galaxy). Good study of the first Stuart.

C. V. Wedgwood, *The King's Peace 1637–1641* (1955); *The King's War, 1641–1647* (1959); and *A Coffin for King Charles* (1964). *The* detailed study of the entire English Civil War.

L. Stone, *The Causes of the English Revolution, 1529–1642* (*Harper Torchbooks). Modern interpretations of the key event.

C. Hibbert, *Charles I* (1968). Useful biography.

C. V. Wedgwood, *Oliver Cromwell*, (1973). By the same specialist we have cited so often above.

C. Hill, *God's Englishman* (*Harper Torchbooks). Authoritative study, strongly pro-Cromwellian in tone. M. R. Ashley, *Oliver Cromwell and the Puritan Revolution* (*Collier). A more conventional but reliable brief work.

S. R. Gardiner, *The First Two Stuarts and the Puritan Revolution* (*Apollo). A textbook first published just over a century ago. Gives a good example of the work of the learned author of a multivolume history of seventeenth-century England.

J. H. Hexter, *Reappraisals in History* (*Harper Torchbooks). The controversy over the role of the gentry, masterfully summarized.

L. Stone, *The Crisis of the Aristocracy, 1558–1641* (*Oxford), and *Social Change and Revolution in England, 1540–1640* (*Barnes and Noble). Two fundamental, more detailed studies of the same subject.

C. Hill, *The World Turned Upside Down* (*Compass). The "far-out" radicals of the English Revolution and their ideas.

M. Walzer, *The Revolution of the Saints* (*Athenaeum). Another sympathetic account of the extreme radicals.

W. Haller, *The Rise of Puritanism* (*Harper Torchbooks). By a leading authority on the religion and politics of the Puritans.

G. Davies, *The Restoration of Charles II, 1658–1689* (1955). Good detailed study.

F. C. Turner, *James II* (1948). Makes the best possible case for James.

G. M. Trevelyan, *The English Revolution, 1688–1689* (*Galaxy). The Glorious Revolution as seen by a master historian.

G. M. Straka, ed., *The Revolution of 1688* (*Heath). A collection of modern studies on the subject.

S. B. Baxter, *William III and the Defense of European Liberty* (1966). A sympathetic account.

J. T. Tanner, *English Constitutional Conflicts of the Seventeenth Century* (*Cambridge). Extremely useful and comprehensive work.

Divine-Right Monarchy in France

G. R. R. Treasure, *Seventeenth-Century France* (1966). Clearly written and detailed survey.

J. D. Lough, *An Introduction to Seventeenth-Century France* (*McKay). Primarily designed for the student of literature, but useful for anybody interested in the subject.

A. Guérard, *France in the Classical Age: Life and Death of an Ideal* (*Harper Torchbooks). An original interpretation of the period.

C. V. Wedgwood, *Richelieu and the French Monarchy* (*Collier); and M. Ashley, *Louis XIV and the Greatness of France* (*Free Press). Good brief introductions.

J. B. Wolf, *Louis XIV* (*Norton). A detailed political biography.

P. Goubert, *Louis XIV and Twenty Million Frenchmen* (*Vintage). The king and his subjects.

W. H. Lewis, *The Splendid Century* (*Morrow). Social France under Louis XIV.

W. F. Church, ed., *The Greatness of Louis XIV* (*Heath), a collection of modern scholarly studies; and *The Impact of Absolutism in France* (*Wiley), source materials and commentaries on the Age of Richelieu and Louis XIV.

C. W. Cole, *Colbert and a Century of French Mercantilism*, 2 vols. (1939). A standard work.

Europe Overseas

J. B. Brebner, *The Explorers of North America, 1492–1806* (*Meridian). Good brief survey.

D. J. Boorstin, *Americans: The Colonial Experience* (*Vintage). A short introduction.

C. M. Andrews, *The Colonial Period of American History*, 3 vols. (*Yale). A detailed treatment.

L. B. Wright, *Cultural Life of the American Colonies, 1607–1783* (*Harper Torchbooks). An excellent study.

J. H. Elliott, *The Old World and the New, 1492–1650* (*Cambridge). The impact of the New World on the Old.

G. M. Wrong, *The Rise and Fall of New France*, 2 vols. (1928). Solid study by a Canadian scholar.

S. E. Morison, ed., *The Parkman Reader* (1955). Selections from Parkman's many volume classic history, *France and England in North America*.

C. R. Boxer, *The Dutch Seaborne Empire, 1600–1800* (1965). By a leading authority.

B. H. M. Vlekke, *Nusantara: A History of Indonesia* (1959). Where the Dutch founded their most important colony.

CHAPTER TEN

The Great Modern Revolution Begins

Twice in human history a chain of developments has enabled civilization to make a great leap forward. About 10,000 years ago people began to grow the food they consumed rather than to depend upon hunting and wild crops. Then, hundreds or even thousands could settle in one community and begin to trade with other settlements. These advances led to the formation of governments and to the evolution of the written languages needed by merchants and officials in their expanding activities. Together, these achievements constituted the Neolithic Revolution.

No advances of comparable significance were made until the beginning of the scientific revolution less than five hundred years ago. The rapid progress in astronomy, physics, and mathematics during the sixteenth and seventeenth centuries awakened new interest in the forces of nature. Thinkers turned away from traditional religious teachings to explore nature on their own. Their studies led many intellectuals to champion the new ideas for the improvement of humanity known as the Enlightenment. The Enlightenment, in turn, set the stage for the dramatic innovations that would begin to transform the economy and politics of the West during the last quarter of the eighteenth century.

I. THE SCIENTIFIC REVOLUTION

The scientific trailblazers of the 1600s relied both on their own insights and on the development of new instruments and techniques. The new approach was defended most forcefully by the English politician and intellectual Francis Bacon (1561–1626), who insisted on the systematic accumulation of data. The empirical method—the careful observation of experience—would enable the human mind to understand nature. Bacon asserted that valid conclusions about natural events could be reached only through the process of *induction,* proceeding from the evidence of details to a general conclusion. Bacon's faith in empiricism and induction departed sharply from the widespread acceptance of *deduction,* which proceeded from the general to the particular. Bacon deplored the continued reliance upon views of the universe many centuries old, particularly those of Aristotle (4th century B.C.) and Ptolemy (2nd century A.D.). Bacon's great Italian contemporary, Galileo, ridiculed the blind acceptance of ancient authority and thereby came into conflict with the teachings of the Catholic Church.

Galileo (1564–1642) and other scientists devised new instruments that made possible more exact measurements of the natural world. These in turn promoted the inductive approach to science. By putting two lenses together, an experiment probably originated by Dutch glassmakers, scientists obtained greater magnification of the natural phenomena they were studying. Galileo applied the new technique to devise a telescope that revealed new details about heavenly bodies. The Dutchman Van Leeuwenhoek (1632–1723), using the same method, made a microscope that enabled him to discover tiny organisms hitherto unknown—red blood cells, bacteria, protozoa, and spermatozoa. Working from the experiments of Galileo, other technicians developed the thermometer and the barometer. Employing the barometer a Frenchman, Blaise Pascal (1623–1662), proved that what we term "air pressure" diminished as altitude increased, and he went on to explode the old adage, "Nature abhors a vacuum," by showing that a vacuum is possible.

King Charles II of England roared with laughter on being told that members of his Royal Society were weighing the air. Nevertheless, the Royal Society for Improving Natural Knowledge, founded in 1662, and the French Academy of Sciences, founded in 1666, were important promoters of scientific investigation. In characteristic English fashion, the Royal Society was a private undertaking, though with a royal charter. Its French counterpart, sponsored by Colbert for the greater glory of Louis XIV, was a government institution whose fellows received salaries along with instructions to avoid discussion of religion and politics. Meantime, two important societies had already appeared in Italy: in Florence an academy to promote experimentation, and in Rome the Academy of the Lynx-Eyed (the lynx is a wildcat with acute eyesight).

Through the formal correspondence of their secretaries and informal letters between members, these institutions fostered the growth of an international scientific community. They admitted as members both professional men and inquisitive aristocrats. Among the aristocrats was Robert Boyle (1627–1691), the son of an Irish earl, who discovered the law of physics that bears his name. Boyle's Law states that under compression the volume of a gas is inversely proportional to the amount of pressure.

Although many scientific works were published in Latin, they were often translated into the vernacular to reach a wider public. The basic language for scientific computation, however, was mathematics. This branch of knowledge was benefiting from a series of innovations that made it possible to perform traditional calculations more quickly and to make new ones never before possible. In 1585 Simon Stevin, who came from the Low Countries, published a book with a wonderfully explicit title: *The Decimal, Teaching with Unheard-of Ease How to Perform All Calculations . . . by Whole Numbers without Fractions.* In 1614 John Napier of Scotland devised another mathematical shortcut with his *Marvelous Rule of Logarithms,* which simplified the processes of multiplying, dividing, and finding square roots. The French mathematician and philosopher, René Descartes (1596–1650), invented analytical geometry, which brought geometry and algebra together. His "Cartesian coordinates" made it possible to solve an algebraic equation by plotting it on a graph.

The most brilliant mathematical achievement of the century was the devising of ways to deal with such uncertain quantities as variables and probabilities. Pascal contributed his studies of games of chance, and Dutch insurance brokers drew up the first actuarial tables predicting the life expectancy of their clients. Then Isaac Newton (1642–1727) and the German philosopher Leibniz (1646–1716), apparently quite independently of each other, invented the calculus. This new mathematical tool, together with Cartesian geometry, enabled Newton to make the calculations supporting his revolutionary hypotheses in astronomy and physics.

Astronomy and Physics

In astronomy the heliocentric theory of Copernicus (see Chapter 7) had raised many difficulties. Subsequent observations had failed to confirm his belief that the planets revolved about the sun in circular paths. The German astronomer, Kepler (1571–1630), opened the way to a resolution by proving mathematically that planetary orbits were elliptical. Then Galileo's telescope revealed spots on the sun, rings around Saturn, and moonlike satellites around Jupiter. This evidence of "corruption in high places" led Galileo to publish a book in 1632 defending the heliocentric concept and ridiculing supporters of the geocentric theory. Traditionalists in the Church thereupon brought Galileo before the Inquisition, which placed his book on the *Index* of prohibited works. He was subjected to a kind of house arrest and forced to make a public recantation of his unorthodox views. However, Galileo is reported to have had the last word: "and yet it does move"—the Earth is not stationary, as the Church insists, but behaves as the other planets do.

An even more celebrated story recounts how Galileo dropped balls of different weights from the Leaning Tower of Pisa to test Aristotle's theory that objects fall with velocities proportional to their weight. Although the story may be untrue, Galileo did in fact prove Aristotle wrong. His studies of the motion of projectiles, of pendulums, and of falling and rolling bodies helped to establish the concepts of acceleration and inertia, which were later refined by Newton.

Isaac Newton (1642–1727) made many of his most exciting discoveries when he was still a student at Cambridge University. When a severe outbreak of plague forced the university to close in 1665, he returned home; there, according to the well-known tale, he observed an apple falling to the ground in his family's orchard.

Wondering why the apple fell as it did, he found the answer in the force of gravity, which attracted the apple to the vastly larger earth. Later he drew up laws of motion, arguing that the force of gravity operated throughout the universe in a more complex fashion. He concluded that it was mutual attraction that caused the planets to move in orbit around the sun, and satellites, such as the earth's moon, to move in orbit around the planets. In mathematical terms Newton stated the force of gravity as directly proportional to the masses of two bodies attracted one to the other, and inversely proportional to the squares of the distance between them. Put very simply, his laws of motion argued that bodies were not in effect "self-starters" but moved in response to forces imposed upon them.

Newton waited until 1687 to publish his theories in *The Mathematical Principles of Natural Philosophy*, better known by its Latin title, *Principia Mathematica*. Newton also contributed to the development of optics by using a prism to separate the rays of sunlight into the colors of the spectrum. He demonstrated that objects themselves have no intrinsic color; rather, the color of an object depends on what light it absorbs and reflects. In contrast to Galileo, Newton gained full recognition for his achievements from the "establishment" of his own day. He was awarded a professorship at Cambridge University, the presidency of the Royal Society, a knighthood with the title of "Sir Isaac," and the well-paid post of Master of the Mint. But even Newton was not quite the model scientist, for he put consider-

Newton.

able energy into the pseudoscience of alchemy and unscientific efforts to determine the precise dates of events related in the Bible.

During the eighteenth century, physicists and astronomers consolidated the great advances made in the seventeenth. The versatile Benjamin Franklin (1706–1790) helped found the American Philosophical Society in Philadelphia, which still exists today. He demonstrated the identical nature of lightning and electricity by obtaining an electrical charge from a key attached to the string of a kite he sent aloft during a thunderstorm. The experiment aroused much interest in Europe and was repeated at Versailles for the instruction of the French royal family. The "Newton of France," the Marquis de Laplace (1749–1827), rounded out Sir Isaac's investigation of celestial mechanics, as Newton's theories were termed, and described the movements of the solar system in mathematical formulas and theorems.

Geology, Physiology, Biology, and Chemistry

The mechanistic views of the physicists and astronomers spread to other fields of science. In geology the English physician William Gilbert (1540–1603) published in 1600 a study of magnetism suggesting that the earth itself was a giant magnet. In physiology another Englishman, William Harvey (1578–1657), physician to King Charles I, argued that the human heart was a pump that drove the blood through a single circulatory system. He thus challenged the idea handed down from Galen in the second century A.D. that the arteries and the veins were two entirely separate systems. Harvey's challenge was confirmed when a microscope revealed that tiny blood vessels called capillaries linked the arteries to the veins. In biology proper, progress advanced with the careful collection of specimens and the classification of plants and animals according to genus and species. This classification, still employed today, was perfected by the Swedish botanist Carolus Linnaeus (1707–1778), who followed the old custom of Latinizing his Swedish name (Carl von Linné).

Modern chemical analysis came of age when the Scottish professor, Joseph Black (1728–1799), exploded the theory that the air was composed of a single element by proving that it contained several different gases. Continuing the study of gases, the Frenchman Antoine Lavoisier (1743–1794) demonstrated that water was formed by a union of hydrogen and oxygen, the familiar H_2O. Lavoisier also contended that all substances were made up of certain basic chemical elements, of which he identified twenty-three.

World Machine and Rationalism

These scientific advances had a revolutionary effect beyond the realm of science proper. They exalted rationalism (reliance on reason) and innovation at the expense of religious belief and old established authority. The new mechanistic interpretation of the universe transformed the concept of God from an incomprehensible creator and judge to the chief architect of a world machine. Humans could grasp the operations of that machine if they applied their reasoning faculty, as Newton had demonstrated. The new view of humanity stressed the mechanical aspects of the human body—the heart was seen to be a sort of pump, the arm a lever.

A century earlier the materialism and rationalism promoted by the scientific revolution had found a most articulate spokesman in the Frenchman René Descartes. When he was a young man, as his *Discourse on Method* (1637) relates, he resolved to mistrust all authorities, theological and intellectual. His skepticism swept everything aside until he concluded that there was just one thing he could *not* doubt: his own existence. The self engaged in the processes of thinking and doubting must be real—"I think, therefore I am" (in Latin, *Cogito ergo sum*). Descartes then reconstructed the world until he arrived at God, whom he viewed not as a patriarch but as a master of geometry whose mathematical order-

Descartes: portrait by Frans Hals.

liness foreshadowed the great engineer of the Newtonian world machine. But where Newton would proceed inductively by drawing on the data compiled by the observations and experiments of earlier scientists, Descartes proceeded deductively, deriving both the universe and God from himself in the act of thinking.

The world that Descartes reconstructed proved to be two separate worlds—one composed of mind and soul, the other of body and matter. Descartes himself claimed competence only in dealing with the material world, yet the way in which he dealt with it suggested that only the world of science and reason counted. He even boasted that if given matter and space, he could construct the universe itself.

Not all the contributors to the new age of science abandoned traditional religious concerns. Pascal, the great mathematician and experimenter, was also an eloquent spokesman for the Jansenists, a puritanical sect of French Catholics who accepted the belief in predestination taught by Cornelius Jansen, a Dutch theologian (see Chapter 9). Repelled by the idea that God was merely a master engineer, Pascal sought the Lord of Abraham and the Old Testament prophets. And one night in November 1654 he had a mystical experience during which he felt with absolute certainty the presence of God and Christ.

Baruch Spinoza (1632–1677), a Dutch Jew, tried to reconcile the God of science and the God of Scripture. He constructed a system of ethical axioms as logical as a series of mathematical propositions. He also attempted to reunite the two separate worlds of Descartes by linking matter with mind and body with soul. Spinoza concluded that God was present everywhere and in everything—an acceptance of pantheism that horrified many of his contemporaries. His fellow Jews ostracized him, Christians shunned him as an atheist, and intellectuals deplored his rejection of rationalism and materialism.

‖ THE ECONOMIC REVOLUTIONS

Matching the scientific revolution in importance were the advances in commerce, agriculture, and industry that together constitute the great modern economic revolutions. They began earlier, in the late Middle Ages, but proceeded more slowly with many ups and downs. There were no dramatic breakthroughs comparable to those of Galileo and Newton until the industrial revolution "took off" in late eighteenth-century Britain. By then commerce and agriculture had already made many significant advances.

Commerce

The oldest component of the economic revolution was commerce, which included many of the activities Americans call "business." Banking, accounting, and insurance had all become prominent factors in urban Europe during the fourteenth and fifteenth centuries. The sixteenth added the institution of the regulated trading company, which pooled the resources of individual merchants to make long and risky voyages. It became a more tightly organized association with the development of the joint-stock company, in which many individuals bought shares but left management in the hands of a few specialists.

Earlier chapters have noted how some governments brought commerce under strict controls in order to advance national self-interest—the policy known as mercantilism. The most prominent examples were the Spain of Philip II and his successors, and the France of Louis XIV and Colbert. The do's and dont's of mercantilism, however, seldom solved the complex economic problems that confronted Europe in the seventeenth century. The huge imports of gold and silver from the New World caused prices to rise rapidly, which in turn increased the difficulties stemming from inflation. Then, during the 1600s, the population of European states either ceased to grow or actually declined as the result of a series of unfavorable factors—prolonged warfare, crop failures, famine, very high death rates among the young, and epidemics of bubonic plague. In 1665 an outbreak of plague in England is estimated to have killed 100,000 in London and its environs—twenty percent of the area's population. The calamities of the seventeenth century rivaled those of the fourteenth.

Despite a prolonged depression and other woes, the 1600s scored important advances in commerce. The newly independent Dutch republic became "the schoolmaster of Europe," thanks to the leadership of Dutch merchant vessels in seaborne trade, of Dutch brokers in life insurance, and of the Bank of Amsterdam in international finance. But the republic, which was a very small state, became exhausted by its wars against the

France of Louis XIV. By the early eighteenth century, economic leadership passed to Britain and France.

At the same time, the long depression of the seventeenth century ended. Renewed growth in population caused a rising demand for food and goods, which in turn stimulated maritime trade. Many ports enjoyed great prosperity—London, Bristol, and Liverpool in England; Nantes, Bordeaux, and Marseilles in France; Hamburg in Germany; and in Italy Leghorn, the admirably managed free port of the Grand Duchy of Tuscany. As the growth of trade increased the demand for insurance of ships and cargoes, insurance brokers in early eighteenth century London gathered at Edward Lloyd's coffee house in Lombard Street to discuss business, news, and politics. Thus was born Lloyd's of London, the firm that developed the standard policy for marine insurance and published *Lloyd's List*, the first detailed shipping newspaper.

Improved charts and a greater number of lighthouses and buoys made navigation safer. And so did two new instruments: the sextant, an elaboration of the telescope that showed the altitude of the sun at noon, and the chronometer, a timepiece unaffected by the motion of a ship. The sextant determined the ship's latitude, its position measured by degrees north or south of the equator. Longitude was determined by the difference between local time aboard ship calculated by the sextant, and Greenwich Mean Time, the hours and minutes on the zero meridian at Greenwich near London registered by the chronometer. East of Greenwich local time was faster, and to the west it was slower.

Advances in land transport came more slowly. Except in France, which continued Henry IV's example of building good highways, "roads" were often mere paths or trails. The shipment of goods was slow, costly, and unsafe until the construction of turnpikes and new canals gradually improved the situation after 1750. Business was also handicapped by the restrictive practices of guilds and by the enormous variety of coins, weights and measures, and local tolls. Baden, one of the smaller German states, had 112 separate measures for length, 65 for dry goods, 123 for liquids, and 163 for cereals, and 80 different pound weights! A merchant who shipped 60 planks down the Elbe River from Dresden to Hamburg had to pay so many tolls to the towns and principalities along the way that only 6 of the 60 would reach Hamburg.

The vigorous survival of local vested interests revealed the limitations of mercantilism, which in theory required the regulation of trade at the national level. But no eighteenth-century government had the number of officials needed for effective regulation. Austria, Prussia, and some other German states tried to assimilate mercantilism into the more systematic policy of *cameralism* (from the Latin *camera*, chamber, in this instance a council dealing with expenditures and income). The cameralists devoted their main effort to the management of state budgets and the increase of revenues. Other European states relied heavily on private companies and individuals to execute national policies. The English and Dutch East India Companies exercised not only a trading monopoly in their colonial preserves but also virtual sovereign powers, including the right to maintain soldiers and conduct diplomacy. On the whole, private initiative did more than sluggish governments to advance the commercial revolution.

The Mississippi and South Sea Bubbles

In the years after 1715, when almost every state in Europe staggered under the debts piled up during the recent wars, France and Britain both turned to the private sector. To meet the large annual interest on bonds and other obligations, they transferred the management of state debts to joint-stock companies. They awarded trading concessions to the companies which, it was hoped, would prove so lucrative that the companies' profits would easily cover the interest due on government bonds.

In France the Duke of Orléans, regent for the boy king Louis XV, allowed his crony John Law (1671–1729) to try out his "system." The system of this Scottish adventurer and mathematical wizard was mercantilist but with a difference. Where orthodox mercantilism measured the worth of a state by the amount of silver and gold it possessed, Law claimed that the limited supply of precious metals made it difficult to increase the coins in circulation and therefore difficult to promote business. Law's solution was to issue paper money, backed by the nation's wealth in land and in trade. The amount of paper in circulation would be increased or decreased according to the needs of the business community. A new central bank established by Law, following the practice of the Bank of Amsterdam, issued paper notes of stable value. Business activity at once increased.

Law then set up the Mississippi Company,

which monopolized commerce with the Louisiana colony and soon absorbed the other French colonial trading companies. Law's system reached to almost every corner of the French economy, as the Mississippi Company took over the government's debt. When it agreed to accept government bonds in partial payment for shares of its stock, the bondholders responded with enthusiasm, for their bonds had fallen to 20 percent of their face value. To obtain working capital, however, the company had to sell additional shares of stock, and Law painted the company's prospects in vivid colors to attract cash purchasers. Investors, large and small, caught the fever of speculation, and by the close of 1719 Mississippi stock was selling for forty times its par value. Cautious investors began to sell their shares, receiving payment in banknotes, which they took to Law's bank for redemption into specie. The Mississippi Bubble burst when the bank used up its reserves of gold and silver and suspended specie payments in February 1720. Law, whose talents might have revitalized the French economy

had he used them more discreetly, fled from France.

In England, meanwhile, the South Sea Company had paid the government an exorbitant sum for the privilege of managing the debt. The company's resources consisted mainly of the right to furnish slaves to Spain's American colonies under the Asiento agreement of 1713 between Britain and Spain. The South Sea Company, like the Mississippi, invited government creditors to exchange their bonds for stock. To make the stock more attractive, the directors of the company bought and sold shares in secret and permitted new investors to obtain stock with a down payment of only 10 percent in cash. They also circulated reports of forthcoming and immensely profitable voyages by the company's ships. Like Law, the South Sea directors created a speculative boom, in which South Sea shares, with a par value of £100, sold for £129 in January of 1720, and for £1,050 in June. The bubble then burst, and by September the company's shares had fallen to £150. Parliament ordered an investigation and

London during the South Sea Bubble: a Hogarth engraving. The sign above the door at the upper left reads "Raffleing for Husbands with Lottery Fortunes—in Here."

seized properties of the directors to protect the company's creditors. Many reputations were ruined or tarnished, and the future development of stock companies was impeded by the new requirement that they buy costly charters.

The Mississippi and South Sea Bubbles were acute examples of the economic growing pains affecting the states of Europe as they groped for solutions to baffling financial problems. The end results were not always unfortunate. Voltaire, who was a very successful and not very scrupulous speculator, observed that Law's "imaginary system gave birth to a real commerce," and released French business from the torpor created by the defeats of Louis XIV. The Mississippi Company, reorganized after 1720, consistently made a handsome profit. In England, the political overturn after the South Sea Bubble brought to power the Whig leader Robert Walpole with a program of honoring the debt as a *national* debt. This was a novel concept and a great advance in fiscal morality, for most states still treated their debts as the personal obligations of the monarch, to be repaid or repudiated as he saw fit.

The Agricultural Revolution

The second force modernizing the economy, the revolution in agriculture, centered on improvements that enabled fewer farmers to produce more crops. The Dutch Republic and its southern neighbor, the Spanish Netherlands (Austrian after 1713), pioneered in the culture of new crops—the potato, the turnip, and clover. Turnips furnished feed for livestock over the winter, thus eliminating the traditional slaughter of stock in the autumn. Clover, by fixing nitrogen in the soil, increased the fertility of the land and eliminated the need to let fields lie fallow every second or third year.

In England the new crops were introduced during the seventeenth century and vigorously publicized by "improving landlords" in the eighteenth. Charles Townsend (1674–1738), nicknamed "Turnip," promoted a four-year crop rotation, planting a field to turnips, then barley, then clover, then wheat. Jethro Tull (1674–1741) was impressed by the high yields obtained in small French vineyards and truck gardens where seeds were planted individually and each plant cultivated by a hoe. In *The Horse Hoeing Husbandry* he informed his countrymen how he adapted French methods to larger English fields. Instead of the wasteful practice of scattering seed broadcast, he planted it deep in regular rows by using a horse-drawn "drill," and he cultivated crops with a horse-drawn hoe.

For such improvements to be efficient, large farms were required on land that was not subdivided into long narrow plots or used in common with neighboring farmers. Improving landlords therefore sought to fence off common lands as their private property; thus enclosures, which in Tudor times had served to enlarge sheep pastures, now increased the amount of crop land. The enclosure movement reached a peak in the last decades of the eighteenth century and the first of the nineteenth, as Parliament passed hundreds of separate acts that affected several million acres. Rural England began to assume its modern aspect of large fields fenced by hedgerows, and an important transition had occurred from the nearly self-sufficient manor of the Middle Ages to the capitalist farm that produced a specialized crop.

Enclosures enabled England to feed a growing population, but they also caused widespread social misery. In eighteenth-century England, as in ancient Greece and Rome, the development of capitalistic estates ruined many yeomen. These small farmers could not get along without rights to use common land, nor could they afford to buy tools, install fences, and become improving farmers themselves. Many of them reluctantly became hired hands on big farms or sought work in the rapidly growing towns.

The Industrial Revolution Begins

By increasing productivity and releasing workers for jobs off the farm, the agricultural revolution assisted the industrial revolution. But industry also required capital to finance buildings and equipment, raw materials, and markets for its manufactures. The colonies helped to provide the last two items, and merchants who traded overseas supplied part of the capital. Thus the commercial revolution assisted industrial growth.

In textiles, the making of yarn and cloth had long been under the "domestic system." Spinners and weavers worked at home on simple wheels and looms, often as laborers for a middleman who furnished materials and sold the finished yarn and cloth. In some industries which also depended on hand processes, many laborers were assembled in a single large workshop. The industrial revolution made the domestic system obsolete and converted the large workshop into a factory. Machines replaced the spinning wheel, the loom, and other simple hand tools; and water or steam replaced human and animal muscle as the source of power. Because power-driven machines were often cumbersome and complicated, sizable factories were needed to house them.

By 1789, these revolutionary changes had affected only a few industries—mining, metallurgy, and textiles. Coal-mining was already a big business, mainly because of the demand for coke by iron smelters. Smelters had formerly used charcoal to convert ore into iron, but as more and more English forests were cut down charcoal became so scarce and expensive that it constituted 80 percent of the cost of producing iron. Raw coal could not serve as smelter fuel because the chemicals it contained would make the iron brittle. Then in the eighteenth century the Darby family of Shropshire discovered how to remove the chemical impurities by an oven process that converted coal into coke.

The revolution in textiles centered on the cheaper production of cotton cloth. The flying shuttle, a device first applied to the hand loom in England (1733), enabled a single weaver to do work that had previously required the services of two. Looms equipped with the flying shuttle used up the supply of hand-spun thread so fast that the London Society for the Encouragement of Arts, Manufactures, and Commerce offered a prize for improving the spinning process. It was won in 1764 by James Hargreaves for his "spinning jenny," a series of spinning wheels geared together to make eight threads simultaneously. Soon the jenny was adapted to water power and its output grew to a hundred or more threads at once. The eventual release of industry from dependence on unreliable water power was foreshadowed in the 1760s when the Scotsman James Watt introduced the steam engine.

But large-scale production of Watt's engine was delayed for a generation by the difficulties of making the precisely fitting parts it required. And, although Britain had nearly 150 cotton mills by 1789, woolens and dozens of other basic commodities continued to be made by hand. Full industrial development depended on skilled labor forces using precision technology and also on the extension of canals and the building of railroads to make possible the cheap shipment of heavy freight. While the eighteenth century took many of the initial steps in the industrial revolution, it remained for the next century to apply them on a truly revolutionary scale.

The *Encyclopédie* and the *Philosophes*

The new industrial machines and the details of their operation were illustrated in elaborate plates that filled eleven of the thirty-three volumes comprising the French *Encyclopédie.* This ambitious publishing venture, which began in 1751 took three decades to complete. It was committed to ending the superstition, intolerance, and inequality in existing society, and to instructing its readers in the wonders of science and the virtues of nature. Its editor, Denis Diderot (1713–1784), was a prominent spokesman for the Enlightenment who devoted many years of fourteen-hour working days to a crusade on behalf of reason and progress.

Among the 160 contributors to the *Encyclopédie* were many leading figures of the Enlightenment—Voltaire, Montesquieu, Rousseau, Condorcet, Quesnay, and Turgot. They were called *philosophes* (French for "philosophers"), although few of them were philosophers in the scholarly sense. They were critics, publicists, economists, political scientists, and champions of projects for the improvement of mankind. What linked many of them together was the conviction that human reason could cure people of past ills and enable them to discover the natural laws regulating human existence, thereby assuring humanity's

Smelting copper: an engraving from Diderot's "Encyclopédie."

progress toward perpetual peace and a utopian society.

Not all the philosophes were so optimistic, however. Voltaire devoted his most famous tale, *Candide,* to ridiculing the idea that all was for the best in the best of all possible worlds. Nevertheless, the mainstream of the Enlightenment was optimistic. A famous example is the American Declaration of Independence, which listed the pursuit of happiness as a fundamental human right along with life and liberty. The idea that a human being could pursue and perhaps achieve happiness was indeed a revolutionary departure from the traditional Christian belief that happiness could be found only in heaven. Still more optimistic was Condorcet's *Progress of the Human Mind,* written, ironically, when the author was in hiding from the French Revolution's Reign of Terror. "Nature has placed no bounds on the perfecting of the human faculties," Condorcet concluded, "and the progress of this perfectibility is limited only by the duration of the globe on which nature has placed us."*

The philosophes' belief in human potential derived in part from Descartes, who had deduced a whole philosophy from the fact that he reasoned at all. And it derived still more from John Locke (1632–1704), who eloquently defended England's Glorious Revolution in two works published in 1690. *The Second Treatise of Government* argued that a government must respect human life, liberty, and property. When it fails to do so, as it did under James II, then the overthrow of the monarch is justified. The *Essay Concerning Human Understanding* strengthened Locke's case against the defenders of absolute monarchy. The *Essay* ridiculed their argument that the inclination to submit to authority was present in human beings from birth. Locke denied the existence of innate ideas and compared the mind of the newborn to a blank slate, which would later acquire knowledge from experience. Locke's reliance on empiricism and his common sense place him among the rationalists. Although he acknowledged that human reason cannot account for everything in the universe, "the candle that is set up in us shines bright enough for all our purposes."

The philosophes also hailed Newton's discoveries as revelations of ultimate truth. By claiming that the forces of gravitation held the universe together, for instance, Newton made the universe make sense. The philosophes then dramatically asserted that laws of comparable importance could be discovered to govern all phases of human activity. They claimed to be the Newtons of statecraft, justice, and economics.

The Physiocrats and Adam Smith

Foremost among these "Newtons of the social sciences" were the French *Physiocrats* (believers in the rule of nature) and Adam Smith. The leading Physiocrat was the versatile François Quesnay (1694–1774), biologist, surgeon, and personal physician to King Louis XV and his mistress, Madame de Pompadour, herself a patroness of the philosophes. In articles Quesnay wrote for the *Encyclopédie,* he claimed that the natural laws of economics prove that "land is the only source of wealth, and that agriculture increases wealth.* The mercantilists, therefore, were mistaken in attaching so much importance to the accumulation of money. They tried to regulate commerce, when they should have freed it from controls; they made goods more expensive by levying tariffs and other indirect taxes, when they should have collected only a single direct tax on the net income from land. "Laissez faire, laissez passer" (let do, let pass), the Physiocrats urged, let nature take its course.

Adam Smith.

* Condorcet, *Esquisse d'un tableau historique des progrès de l'esprit humain* (Paris, n.d.), p. 5. Our translation.

* From E. Daire, ed., *Physiocrates* (Paris, 1846), I:82. Our translation.

The most famous statement of laissez-faire economic doctrine was made by the Scottish professor Adam Smith in *The Wealth of Nations* (1776). Smith, too, attacked mercantilist attempts to protect industries by high tariffs:

> It is the maxim of every prudent master of a family never to attempt to make at home what it will cost him more to make than to buy. The tailor does not attempt to make his own shoes, but buys them of the shoemaker. The shoemaker does not attempt to make his own clothes, but employs a tailor. . . . What is prudence in the conduct of every private family, can scarce be folly in that of a great kingdom. If a foreign country can supply us with a commodity cheaper than we ourselves can make it, better buy it of them. . . .*

Like the Physiocrats, Adam Smith attributed the wealth of nations to the production of goods, but, unlike them, he argued that production depended upon the labor of farmers, craftsmen, and millhands. Again like the Physiocrats, he minimized the role of the state, claiming that men freely competing to seek their own wealth would enrich the whole of society. It was as if they were being guided by "an invisible hand"—that is, by nature. Smith advised governments to limit their role to providing defense, a police force, and little else.

The mercantilists had placed the state above the individual and expected ceaseless trade warfare among nations. Adam Smith and the Physiocrats proclaimed that both the economic liberty of the individual and free trade among nations were natural laws. Their program of laissez-faire marked a revolutionary change in economic thought. But economic practice was slow to change, and the great powers continued to follow mercantilist policies. In the 1770s Turgot, the chief minister of the French government, tried in vain to free farming and business from the restrictions of mercantilism by applying physiocratic teachings. The Physiocrats overlooked what many other philosophes also neglected: the difficulty of adjusting the simple and reasonable dictates of natural law to the complications of politics and to the irrational side of human nature.

Justice and Education

Letting nature take its course was also the Enlightenment's prescription for improving law

and justice. The philosophes were horrified by the unjust and antiquated laws, the cumbersome legal procedures, and the frequent recourse to torture and capital punishment. New lawgivers were needed to simplify legal codes, and a new science was needed to make punishments both humane and effective.

The new science, which laid the foundations for modern sociology, was projected by the Italian philosophe, Cesare Beccaria (1738–1794). His *Essay on Crimes and Punishments* (1764) formulated three basic laws of justice, which are good examples of the Enlightenment's effort to express nature's truths. First, punishments should aim to "prevent the criminal from doing further injury, and to prevent others from committing the like offense. Such punishments ought to be chosen, as will make the most lasting impressions on the minds of others, with the least torment to the body of the criminal." Second, justice should act swiftly, "because the smaller the time between the punishment and the crime, the stronger and more lasting will be the association of the ideas of *Crime* and *Punishment.*" Third: "Crimes are more effectively prevented by the *certainty* than by the *severity* of the punishment. The certainty of a small punishment will make a stronger impression than the fear of one more severe."*

In education, as in justice, the philosophes found that existing institutions failed the tests of reason and natural law. They deplored the control of education by the churches and the stress placed on theology, ancient history, and the Greek and Latin languages. They demanded greater emphasis on science, modern history, and modern languages.

In primary education the most sweeping revisions were advanced by Jean-Jacques Rousseau (1712–1778). Rousseau rebelled against the strict traditions of Calvinist Geneva, his birthplace, and against the intensely bookish studies forced upon him as a boy. The result was *Émile* (1762), half treatise and half novel, with two heroes—Émile the pupil, and Rousseau himself the teacher. The training he prescribed was a total departure from eighteenth-century practice: "Life is the trade I would teach him. When he leaves me, he will be neither a magistrate, a soldier, nor a priest; he will be a man."* He did not discipline Émile or force him to read at an early age. Émile observed the world of nature at first hand, not from books; he learned farming by working in the

* *The Wealth of Nations*, Book IV, Ch. 2.

* From *Essay on Crimes and Punishments*, Chs. 12, 19, 27.
* *Émile* (New York: Everyman's Library, 1911), p. 9.

fields and geography by finding his way in the woods. And when, in his teens, he was finally taught to read, his first assignment was Defoe's *Robinson Crusoe* (1719), in Rousseau's view, "the best treatise on an education according to nature."

Deism and Atheism

Defenders of the Enlightenment campaigned against the role of the clergy in education, particularly the Jesuits, the symbol of militant Catholicism. A campaign for the dissolution of the Society of Jesus won the backing of Catholic monarchs who were angry over Jesuit interference in politics. In the 1760s the Jesuits were expelled from Portugal, France, and even Spain, the homeland of Loyola. The pope dissolved the order in 1773; it would be revived forty years later in a different political and intellectual climate.

On the positive side, the religious program of the Enlightenment was marked by the cultivation of "deism," which had emerged in the seventeenth-century England of Civil War and Newtonian science. Deists like John Locke sought to settle religious strife by reason rather than by resort to arms. All men, they argued, can agree on a few broad religious principles and tolerate any remaining differences. The deists accepted God as the creator of the universe, but they doubted that he was concerned with the daily activities of people or would respond to prayer or bestow grace. Deists attacked as irrational the doctrines associated with the Trinity, the Virgin Birth, and the Eucharist.

The leading exponent of deism in France was Voltaire (1694–1778), who published a stream of letters, plays, tales, epics, histories, and essays. Clear, witty, and sometimes satirical, his writings were enormously popular, especially when they were printed under an assumed name or outside France to evade censorship. Voltaire's histories stressed economics and culture in addition to the conventional concern with war and politics. He also made his French readers aware of the contributions of Locke, Newton, Shakespeare, and other Englishmen. As a young man he had spent three years of exile in England after he had criticized the French government and offended a member of the privileged nobility. Voltaire was enormously impressed by British tolerance:

> If there were just one religion in England, despotism would threaten; if there were two, they would cut each other's throats; but there are thirty religions, and they live together peacefully and happily.*

Jean Antoine Houdon's bust of Voltaire, 1781.

Voltaire carried on a lifelong crusade for tolerance. His most famous "case" was that of Jean Calas, a Protestant merchant of Toulouse, executed for allegedly murdering his son to prevent his conversion to Catholicism. Voltaire discovered that the case against Calas was based on rumor and that the court condemning him had acted out of anti-Protestant hysteria. And so Voltaire campaigned for three years until the original verdict was reversed and the name of Calas cleared.

The existence of evil, of an injustice like that suffered by Calas, confronted the Enlightenment with a major problem. Few of the philosophes accepted the Christian teaching that evil arose from the original sin of Adam and Eve. If God is purely benevolent, they asked, why then does evil so often prevail in the world he created? They rejected the pessimistic answer provided a century earlier by Thomas Hobbes in *Leviathan,*

* *Lettres Philosophiques,* No. 6. Our translation.

published in 1651 and much influenced by England's Civil War. Unless men accept an all-powerful authority, Hobbes argued, the state of nature will become a state of war; men will prey on their fellows and human life will become "solitary, poor, nasty, brutish, short." At the other extreme, many philosophes could not accept the jaunty assertion of Alexander Pope, an English contemporary of Voltaire, that this was the best of all possible worlds:

> All Nature is but Art, unknown to thee;
> All chance, direction which thou canst not see;
> All discord, harmony not understood;
> All partial evil, universal good:
> And, spite of Pride, in erring Reason's spite,
> One truth is clear, Whatever is, is right.

In *Candide* Voltaire satirized the disasters abounding in the best of all possible worlds, an argument made more telling because there had recently been a real disaster, the earthquake, tidal wave, and fire that engulfed Lisbon, the Portuguese capital, on November 1, 1755, and killed some 60,000 people.

Deism enabled Voltaire to reconcile a perfect God and an imperfect world by comparing God to a watchmaker who fashioned a delicate mechanism but assumed no responsibility for its operation once it started to run. Voltaire argued, however, that since only intellectuals were likely to accept deism, the great majority required a more exacting faith. "Man has always needed a brake," he observed, and he built a fine church for the tenants on his estate.

Some philosophes, however, argued that human beings did not require the external brake of religion because their very nature would act as an inner brake. La Mettrie (1709–1751), a French physician, published a book entitled *L'Homme Machine (Man a Machine)*, which contended that all the inhabitants of the world, both human and animal, are self-regulating mechanisms made from one universal substance and behaving as their natures compel them to behave. D'Holbach (1723–1789), a German baron residing in Paris, argued that "The virtuous man is one who has been taught by correct ideas that his self-interest or happiness lies in acting in a way that others are forced . . . to approve out of their own self-interest."* D'Holbach was the most outspoken atheist of the Enlightenment. He dismissed God

as a "phantom of the imagination," whose existence was denied by the shortcomings and miseries of the world. Such radical doctrines attracted few followers in France, which was not yet prepared to dispense entirely with traditional religion.

Political Thought

"In politics as in religion toleration is a necessity," said Voltaire. Tolerant Britain was his utopia, and he paid its unwritten constitution the most flattering compliment of an enlightened age by claiming that it "might have been invented by Locke, Newton, or Archimedes." A more detailed analysis of British political virtues was drawn up by Montesquieu (1689–1755), an aristocratic French lawyer and philosopher. In *The Spirit of the Laws* (1748), he asserted that no one system of government suited all countries because of their wide differences in climate, resources, and traditions. Republics were best suited to small and barren countries, limited monarchies to the middle-sized and more prosperous, and despotisms to vast empires. Accordingly, middle-sized and prosperous Britain was quite properly a monarchy limited by aristocracy. The hereditary nobility sat in the House of Lords, and the elected representatives, constituting a nobility of talent, sat in the House of Commons. All this seemed admirable to Montesquieu, who thought the masses "extremely unfit" for government. He found another reason for the political superiority of Britain in the play of checks and balances. In Parliament, Lords and Commons checked one another; in the government as a

Montesquieu: bust by Lemoyne.

---

* *Système de la Nature*, trans. L. G. Crocker, ed., in *The Age of Enlightenment* (New York, 1969), pp. 160–61.

whole, a balance was maintained by the separation of powers, legislative, executive, and judicial.

For Americans, Montesquieu and Locke were the most important thinkers of the Enlightenment and their ideas were reflected in the constitution of the new republic. For Europeans, the most important thinker was Rousseau, who inspired the radicals of the French Revolution. Rousseau's ideas proceeded from a sweeping generalization typical of the age: Whereas nature dignifies humanity, civilization corrupts it; humanity would be corrupted less if civilized institutions followed nature more closely. This theme lay at the heart of the educational reform proposed in *Émile*. In an earlier work, the *Discourse on the Origin of the Inequality of Mankind* (1755), Rousseau attributed the vices of civilization to private property:

> The first man who, having enclosed a piece of ground, bethought himself of saying, "This is mine," and found people simple enough to believe him, was the real founder of civil society. From how many crimes, wars, and murders, might not anyone have saved mankind, by pulling up the stakes and crying to his fellows: "Beware of listening to this imposter; you are undone if you once forget that the fruits of the earth belong to us all, and the earth itself to nobody."*

To protect private property men accepted laws and governors:

> They had too many disputes among themselves to do without arbitrators, and too much ambition and avarice to go long without masters. All ran headlong to their chains in hopes of securing their liberty. . . .†

Government was evil, Rousseau concluded, but a necessary evil. In *The Social Contract* (1762), he sought to make the necessity less evil by reconciling the liberty of the individual and the institution of government. This he proposed to accomplish through a revolutionary version of the contract theory of government. From the Middle Ages to John Locke, contracts had hinged on an agreement between the people to be governed and their governor or governors. In contrast to this political contract, Rousseau recommended a *social contract*, in which a whole society agrees to be ruled by its general will. "Each individual," Rousseau explained, "may have a particular will

contrary or dissimilar to the general will which he has as a citizen."‡ If the individual insists on putting self-interest above the interest of the community, he must be made to honor the general will. "This means nothing less than that he will be forced to be free."§ Thus the general will has a moral quality, for it represents what is *best* for the whole community, what the community *ought* to do.

Everyone must participate in formulating the general will, according to Rousseau. Executing the general will once it has been formulated, however, could rest with a smaller group. Like Montesquieu, Rousseau believed that the number of governors should vary inversely with the size and resources of the state—monarchy for the large wealthy state, aristocracy for the state of middling size and wealth, and democracy for the small and poor. Rousseau doubted, however, that any state was suited for the absolute form of democracy in which the people themselves executed the laws: "Were there a people of gods, their government would be democratic. So perfect a government is not for men."‖

Almost every radical political doctrine advanced during the two centuries since Rousseau's death has owed something to him. Socialists justify collectivism by citing his attacks on private property and his insistence that "the fruits of the earth belong to us all." Patriots and nationalists hail him for exalting "the dear love of country" and pleading in the final chapter of *The Social Contract* for the establishment of a "civil religion" that would free the state from competing with the Church for the allegiance of citizens.

Rousseau's "civil religion" and "general will" have also been interpreted as totalitarian concepts. Hostile critics see him as a man who worshiped the state and paved the way both for the French Revolution's Reign of Terror and the dictatorships of the twentieth century. This authoritarian interpretation, however, neglects both the strongly idealistic and democratic tone of Rousseau's writings and his personal hostility toward absolutist governments. It seems probable that by the general will Rousseau was simply trying to describe how a good citizen participated in decision-making and then accepted the final outcome. The process was rather like achieving "consensus" or determining the "sense of the meeting," and the concept of the general will attempts to explain the psychology of obedience

---

* *The Social Contract and Discourses* (New York: Everyman's Library, 1913), p. 192.
† Ibid., p. 205.

‡ Ibid., p. 15.
§ Ibid., p. 15.
‖ Ibid., p. 56.

to man-made laws. Finally, Rousseau's declaration—"Were there a people of gods, their government would be democratic"—has stirred champions of democracy ever since the French Revolution to find ways to make people more godlike. *Émile* showed how education could help, and the *Social Contract* implied that citizens might one day follow the general will naturally and would no longer have to be "forced to be free."

Enlightened Despotism

Some of the philosophes, however, sought a political alternative that could operate more readily within existing monarchical institutions. This was enlightened despotism, for which a hereditary monarchy seemed ideally suited. The monarch, as co-owner of all the territories under his rule, was in the unique position of having his personal interests coincide with the national welfare. Both aristocratic and democratic governments, on the other hand, suffered from a conflict of interests between the ruler's selfish concerns and the well-being of the nation. Only a king could follow the example of the reforming tyrants of ancient Greece and Renaissance Italy and permit the laws of nature to replace the hodgepodge of man-made laws that frustrated progress.

Thus it is scarcely surprising that in the eighteenth century self-proclaimed "enlightened" or "benevolent" despots occupied many thrones. They could claim to be the champions of reason and nature while pressing the age-old fight to make royal authority more absolute. What is more surprising, perhaps, is that some of the despots proved to be genuinely enlightened rulers, as the next chapter will show.

Critics of the Enlightenment

Most of the philosophes expected people to accept reason when it was pointed out to them and to give up the habits of centuries and to behave according to natural law. But people would not always accept reason and would cling to irrational customs and unnatural traditions. The French historian and philosopher, Mably (1709–1785), got at the central problem when he inquired: "Is society, then, a branch of physics?" The philosophes and their followers did indeed try to extend the mathematical methods used in the physical sciences to the unpredictable activities of humanity. The Physiocrats, for example, tried to reduce human economic activities to a few simple laws.

Hume, Rousseau & Kant

But not all the philosophes agreed that society was a branch of physics. David Hume (1711–1776), a brilliant Scot, while sharing the Enlightenment's criticism of existing institutions, was skeptical that anything could be achieved by appeals to nature and reason. Human conduct, he asserted, could not be analyzed "in the same manner that we discover by reason the truths of geometry or algebra."

> The ultimate ends of human actions can never be accounted for by *reason,* but recommend themselves entirely to the sentiments and affections of mankind, without any dependance on the intellectual faculties. Ask a man *why he uses exercise:* he will answer, *because he desires to keep his health.* If you then enquire, *why he desires health,* he will reply, *because sickness is painful.* If you push your enquiries farther, and desire a reason *why he hates pain,* it is impossible he can ever give any.[*]

The problems that troubled Hume also disturbed two of his contemporaries, Rousseau and Kant. Rousseau coupled a passionate defense of nature and natural law with a warning against relying on reason. "Too often does reason deceive us," he wrote in *Émile.* "But conscience never deceives us, . . . he who obeys his conscience is following nature and need not fear that he will go astray."[†]

Immanuel Kant (1724–1804), professor of philosophy at the University of Königsberg in East Prussia, advanced a similar argument in Platonic terms. While supporting many of the doctrines of the Enlightenment, Kant also believed in a higher reality rather resembling the Ideas of Plato. He called the eternal truths of the higher realm *noumena* (the Greek term for "things thought") in contrast to the *phenomena* (observations through the senses) of the material world. Knowledge of the world of noumena, Kant believed, reached men through reason—not the reason of common sense, however, but that of intuition. The highest expression of Kant's reason was the *categorical imperative,* the moral law within, the conscience implanted in man by God. When an individual confronted an ethical choice, he must follow the course that would serve as a universal precedent, not just the most expedient solution to his own dilemma.

[*] *An Enquiry Concerning the Principles of Morals,* ed. L.A. Selby-Bigge (Oxford, 1902), p. 293.
[†] (New York: Everyman's Library, 1911), pp. 249–50.

Pietists and Methodists

Other reactions against the rationalism of the Enlightenment came from the churches, especially those involved in the Protestant evangelical revival. The revival began with the German Pietists, who were the spiritual heirs of the sixteenth-century Anabaptists. Deploring the deists' stress on natural law and the growing formalism of the Lutheran establishment, they turned to the "evangel," the good news of Christ's teachings. They asserted that faith came from the heart, not the head, and that God was far more than the creator of the world machine. One Pietist leader was a German noble, Count Zinzendorf (1700–1760), who founded the Moravian Brethren and set up a model community based on Christian principles. Moravian emigrants to America planted a colony at Bethlehem, Pennsylvania, helping to give the "Pennsylvania Dutch" their reputation for thrift, hard work, and strict living.

In Britain the example of Zinzendorf and other Pietists inspired John Wesley (1703–1791), an Anglican priest who felt his own faith evaporating after the failure of his two-year ministry in the backward colony of Georgia (1736–1737). Pietism enabled Wesley to recover his faith through inner conviction. For more than fifty years he labored tirelessly to share his discovery, preaching in churches, in the fields, at the shafts of coal mines, and even in jails. He was such a charismatic preacher that crowds who came to scoff remained to pray. When he died, his movement had enrolled more than a hundred thousand

John Wesley in 1788.

adherents, termed Methodists because of their methodical devotion to piety and plain living. Though Wesley always considered himself a good Anglican, the Methodists eventually set up their separate nonconformist chapels ("Church" was reserved for members of the Church of England).

The new sect won its following almost entirely from among the lower and middle classes, among people who were seeking the religious excitement and consolation that neither deism nor the austere formalism of the Church of England could provide. The Methodists had in full measure the Puritan conscience of the nonconformists. They agitated against drunkenness, against the trade in slaves, and against the barbarous treatment of prisoners, the insane, and the sick. Wesley opened dispensaries for the poor in London and Bristol and established schools for coal-miners' children. Where the philosophes argued for public reform, the Methodists favored private charity. And where the philosophes sought to attack the *causes* of social evils, the Methodists, while accepting evil as part of God's plan, yet sought to ease its *effects*. On the practical level, the skepticism of the philosophes and the faith of the Methodists contributed to the long process of improving the institutions of society.

IV LITERATURE AND THE ARTS

Literature and the arts also shared in the great modern revolution. The seventeenth and eighteenth centuries witnessed the birth of the novel, the opera, the symphony, and other new media of expression. Writers and painters helped lower rigid social barriers by choosing more subjects from the middle and lower ranks of society. Yet a striking characteristic of these centuries was the extent to which Paris and Versailles served as the arbiters of taste and fashion for most of Europe. Although French military glory had lost its luster by the time Louis XIV died in 1715, Europeans still looked to France for guidance in how to behave at court, what clothes to wear, what to eat and drink, what diversions to pursue and dances to favor, and what books to read, plays to see, and music to hear.

French cultural imperialism depended on the fact that nearly everywhere on the Continent sovereigns, aristocrats, and intellectuals used

An illustration from Abraham Bosse's "Le Palais Royal" (1640) gives a picture of French fashions and taste.

French in preference to their native tongue. German, for example, came close to vanishing as the language of educated Germans, and it was ironic that one of the major heroes of German nationalism, King Frederick the Great of Prussia, habitually spoke and wrote in French. Although English suffered no such eclipse in its home islands, it did not begin to compete with French for international status until the heyday of British imperialism in the Victorian age. Even Shakespeare was as yet little appreciated beyond the English-speaking world because of the difficulty of translating his exuberant language into French. In the fine arts, however, many of the leading innovators were not French but Dutch, English, Spanish, and Italian. And while the greatest monument of neoclassical architecture was Versailles, many of the best examples of the more innovative baroque and rococo styles were to be found in Rome, Germany, Portugal, and even overseas, in Mexico and Peru. France was not an oasis in the midst of a cultural desert but the acknowledged capital of a vigorous culture that had flourishing outposts elsewhere in Europe and in the New World.

Literature

Just as Louis XIV and his predecessors imposed greater discipline on French politics, the classical writers of the seventeenth century disciplined the French language and French literature. They insisted on the observance of more rules, on the authority of models from classical antiquity, and on a more select vocabulary. Early in the 1600s the example of the new refinement was set by the marquise de Rambouillet, an aristocratic lady who held a *salon* (literally, a reception room) in her Paris town house. Later, proper behavior was standardized by the court ceremonial at Versailles and proper vocabulary by the great dictionary of the French language compiled by the experts of the Academy founded by Richelieu. Exaggerated notions of propriety outlawed from polite usage the French equivalents of *spit, vomit,* and dozens of other plain-spoken words. The result was a widening gap between classical French and the coarser language of the majority of French people.

The linguistic purge of the seventeenth century also brought important benefits, for without its discipline French could not have won its unique reputation for clarity and elegance. The great playwrights, Corneille (1606–1684) and Racine (1639–1699), obeyed all the do's and don'ts of classicism. These included the "unities" of Aristotle's *Poetics* which limited the actions of a drama to one place, one twenty-four-hour span of time, and one topic. Within this rigid form Corneille and Racine created moving portraits of

Painting of a Molière farce, with Molière himself shown at the far left.

individuals upholding exalted ideals of honor or crushed by overwhelming emotions. In psychological insights their classical tragedies rank with those of the ancient Greeks.

As a writer of comedies Molière (1622–1673), the other master dramatist of the age, was under less pressure to follow classical rules. He was able to create a gallery of characters who were at the same time distinct individuals and examples of social types. The gallery included the hypocrite *(Tartuffe),* the miser *(L'Avare),* the newly rich and self-important *(Le Bourgeois Gentilhomme),* and the pedantic ladies of the *salons (Les Précieuses Ridicules).* Like all good satires, those of Molière have more than a touch of moralizing. A more cynical evaluation of human nature appeared in the *Maxims* of La Rochefoucauld (1613–1680), which he phrased in prose of classic purity. Here are two of them: "We generally give praise only in order to gain it for ourselves." "We always find something not altogether displeasing in the misfortunes of our friends."*

Seventeenth-century English literature also had its cynics, notably Wycherley, Vanbrugh, Congreve, and the other playwrights who wrote the witty, bawdy, and disillusioned Restoration

* *The Maxims of La Rochefoucauld,* trans. F. G. Stevens (London, 1939), pp. 49, 173.

comedies. They reflected the violent swing in the pendulum of public taste after the restoration of Charles II against the moralistic Puritans, who had closed the theaters as dens of sinfulness. One Puritan, however, John Milton (1608–1674), who was the secretary of Oliver Cromwell, produced a truly major work of literature—*Paradise Lost,* the only English epic in the grand manner that still attracts many readers. Milton's complex style of writing and his profound belief in Christian humanism made him the last great figure of the English Renaissance rather than a pioneer of English classicism.

To attain classical status the English language needed to standardize its chaotic spelling and restrict the elaborate flourishes and flights of rhetoric favored by Shakespeare and other writers in the age of Elizabeth I and James I. Under the influence of John Dryden (1631–1700), English began to model itself on French, adopting its straightforward word order, its relatively brief sentences, and its concern for polish, neatness, and clarity. English letters then entered the Augustan Age, which lasted through the first half of the eighteenth century, when Britain boasted a group of talents comparable to those of Vergil, Horace, and Ovid in the days of Rome's Emperor Augustus. Addison and Steele made the *Tatler* and

Spectator vehicles for popularizing serious intellectual discussion, and Alexander Pope cast his philosophical and satirical essays in the poetic style of rhymed couplets. The greatest writer of the age was Jonathan Swift (1667–1745), author of the corrosive satire, *Gulliver's Travels*, whose pessimism and convictions about human depravity went far beyond the moderation of the classical spirit.

As the eighteenth century advanced, literature in the classical style lost ground to less inhibited and more emotional writings. In England, particularly, the simplification of the language enlarged the market for fiction. Two very early examples were by Daniel Defoe—*Robinson Crusoe* (1719) and *Moll Flanders* (1722), both novels, though masquerading as autobiographies, and both far removed from the refinements of classicism. In 1749 the London magistrate, Henry Fielding, published the first great social novel, *Tom Jones*, which portrayed very realistically both the toughs from London slums and the hard-riding hard-drinking squires of the countryside.

Fielding's contemporary, Samuel Richardson, a printer by trade, wrote three gigantic sentimental novels in the form of letters by the main characters. In *Clarissa Harlowe* (1748), 2,400 pages of small print record the misfortunes of the heroine, whose suitor was a scoundrel and whose greedy relatives were scheming to get hold of her valuable property. Although Richardson was prone to excess emotionalism and preachiness, his description of the struggles of passion and conscience carried such conviction that he won a large middle-class reading public for the novel of "sensibility."

In France the leading novel of sensibility was Rousseau's lengthy account of a conflict between love and duty, *La Nouvelle Héloïse* (1761). Because of the strict sexual morality preached (but not always practiced) by Rousseau, the new Eloise, unlike her medieval namesake in the affair with Abelard, died in time to avoid adultery. The retreat from classicism was also marked on the French stage by the popularity of "tearful comedies," a blend of laughter, pathos, and melodrama.

In Germany the dramas of Lessing (1729–1781) combined the middle-class appeal of Richardson with a moderation and tolerance more in tune with the classical spirit. In his romantic comedy, *Minna von Barnhelm*, the lively heroine pits her feminine values and charm against a Prussian officer in a fashion quite contrary to the stereotype of German militarism. In the 1770s young

German writers were associated in the movement called *Sturm und Drang* ("Storm and Stress") that focused on yearning, despair, and self-pity. Its great landmark was the short novel, *The Sorrows of Young Werther*, by the youthful Goethe (1749–1832). This lugubrious tale of a young tutor who falls in love with the mother of his pupils was immensely popular. Napoleon claimed to have read it seven times and wept when the hero shoots himself because the woman he loves is already married.

Architecture

The great palace that Louis XIV built at Versailles is an admirable introduction to the artistic styles competing in the seventeenth and eighteenth centuries. The exterior of the palace, with its emphasis on symmetry and its columns, followed the classical models of Renaissance builders. Neoclassicism extended to the gardens, with their geometrical layout, straight avenues, and carefully clipped trees and shrubs; only the fountains provided a touch of exuberance. Inside the palace, however, exuberance was everywhere—in the dramatic Hall of Mirrors (they created an illusion of great width); the majestic Staircase of the Ambassadors, designed to remind diplomats that the Grand Monarque was unique; and the acres of ceilings painted with smiling cherubs.

The theatricality and lavish embellishments inside Versailles were hallmarks of the style called *baroque*, a term derived from the Portuguese *barroco* (an irregular pearl). Baroque architects placed great emphasis on the vertical line and curves, and on striking effects to assert a building's dominance. A moderate example of baroque, still under classical restraints, is St. Paul's Cathedral in London, designed by Christopher Wren to replace a structure destroyed in the Great Fire of 1666. Even today, when London has a fair quota of skyscrapers, Wren's huge structure still dominates the City, the mile-square financial district. Examples of uninhibited baroque may be found in sites as far apart as Austria and Mexico and, above all, in Rome. Many of the Roman baroque monuments were the work of Bernini (1598–1680), who created the great open spaces and curving colonnades of St. Peter's Square as a most impressive entrance to the imposing basilica designed by Michelangelo. More grandiose than anything on the exterior of St. Peter's is Bernini's baldachin, a canopy over the main altar as high as an eight-story building and supported

Versailles.

by immense twisted columns of bronze, at once massive and restless.

In the early eighteenth century the baroque style evolved into the *rococo,* a term derived from the French word for seashells. Often employing a shell motif in its intricate ornamentation, rococo was lighter and more elegant than baroque, depending less on mass to create an effect and more on graceful lines and elaborate decoration. Some of the smaller European palaces and hunting lodges are charming examples of this style. So are the delicate chairs, tables, and other furniture called Louis Quinze (XV). Rococo taste for the dainty and exotic made Chinese objects extremely popular: scenic wallpaper, painted scrolls, delicate porcelains, and the other decorative items known collectively as *chinoiserie.* An eighteenth-century garden often boasted a pagoda, while the gardens themselves began to exchange the severely formal landscaping of Louis XIV for the more natural look of the English garden.

During the second half of the century, rococo was eclipsed by a neoclassical revival result-ing from the discovery of the well-preserved remains of Roman Pompeii, destroyed by the eruption of Vesuvius in A.D. 79. In Paris classical models were used for the strikingly well-proportioned buildings flanking the Place de la Concorde (then called the Place Louis XV). In Britain the Adam brothers adapted Roman models most skillfully to design some of the most elegant townhouses and country mansions ever built. In Virginia, George Washington's residence at Mt. Vernon was a modest example of the neoclassical style still flourishing in America today under the labels of "colonial" or "Georgian."

Painting

A baroque combination of the theatrical and the otherworldly had characterized the paintings of El Greco in late sixteenth-century Spain. Velázquez, the outstanding painter of seventeenth-century Spain, returned to the secular and realistic traditions of Renaissance art. He executed forty faithful portraits of the homely Hapsburg

St. Paul's Cathedral, London.

king, Philip IV, and some marvelous pictures of the royal children and court dwarfs. By painting what the eye sees at a glance, rather than all the details, Velázquez created what has been termed "optical realism."

In the Low Countries, the center of northern European painting in the 1600s, some artists also achieved optical realism in such themes as the painter at work in his studio and the well-to-do businessman and his household. But at least one operated in a thoroughly baroque manner and made painting a big business. Rubens (1577–1640) received handsome commissions from French and English royalty, ran a studio with two hundred students, and executed personally at least part of the brushwork on two thousand canvases, many of them very large. Rembrandt (1606–1669) displayed a more subtle baroque quality in his effort to involve the viewer directly in the action depicted. In successive sketches for *"Ecce Homo,"* when Pilate has the crowd choose between Christ and Barabbas, Rembrandt progressively eliminated the crowd, so that the beholder comes to realize that he is one of the multi-

tude choosing to release Barabbas. Rembrandt, who was a devout member of the Mennonite sect of Anabaptists, is the only great Protestant religious painter, an exception to the Protestant shunning of the visual arts.

In the eighteenth century, painting, too, evolved from the baroque to the rococo. Two French artists, Watteau (1684–1721) and Fragonard (1732–1806), often painted the flirtatious pampered favorites of the court. In England Sir Joshua Reynolds (1723–1792), the president of the Royal Academy, and his talented contemporaries—Romney, Gainsborough and Lawrence—produced handsome portraits of aristocrats and such prominent figures as the actress Mrs. Siddons. The leading innovator was William Hogarth (1697–1764), who accomplished in art what Defoe, Richardson, and Fielding achieved in the novel. Instead of catering to a few wealthy patrons, Hogarth won a mass market for the engravings he turned out in thousands of copies—"Gin Lane," "Marriage à la Mode," "The Rake's Progress," and other graphic sermons on the vices to be found at every level of British life.

Bernini's baldachin in St. Peter's, Rome.

Rubens' "Maria dé' Medici,
Queen of France, Landing in Marseilles."

Rococo architecture: the Amalien-
burg hunting pavilion at Nymphen-
burg, near Munich.

Velázquez "The Maids of Honor."

Rembrandt's "The Descent from the Cross."

Fragonard's "The New Model."

Reynolds' "Mrs. Siddons as the Tragic Muse."

Music

The seventeenth and eighteenth centuries were the formative period of classical music, when the opera and oratorio, the sonata, concerto, and symphony all made their debut. The first innovators were Italian, followed by Germans, Austrians, and English. In Venice Monteverdi (1567–1643) composed the first important operas, a baroque fusion of music and theater which became so popular that the city soon had sixteen opera houses. Later, operas degenerated into ramshackle vehicles in which "stars" could show off their vocal prowess. The stars themselves provided the final touch of unreality, since male roles were sung by women and female by *castrati* (male sopranos). From Italy Louis XIV imported Lully (1632–1687), musician, dancer, speculator, and politician who vied with Molière for the upper hand in directing the cultural life of the court.

Many techniques of baroque music were brought to perfection early in the next century by a German choirmaster, Johann Sebastian Bach (1685–1750). For the organ Bach developed the fugue, an intricate adaptation of the round in which each voice begins the theme in turn while the other voices repeat and elaborate it. For small orchestras he composed the Brandenburg Concertos, in which successive instruments are given the chance to demonstrate their charms. And for

Hogarth's "The Orgy": a scene from "The Rake's Progress."

choirs and solo voices he composed the Mass in B minor and two moving reenactments of the Passion of Christ, according to the gospels of Matthew and John.

In contrast to Bach's quiet provincial life was the stormy international career of his countryman, Handel (1685–1759). After study in Italy, Handel passed most of his adult years in England attempting to run an opera company. Although he wrote more than forty operas himself, he is best known for the *Messiah* and other sacred works arranged for large choruses and directed to a mass audience. These oratorios were an elaboration on the earlier and simpler Italian oratorios, designed for the tiny prayer chapels called oratories.

Although Bach and Handel composed many instrumental suites and concertos, it was not until the second half of the eighteenth century that orchestral music came to the fore. New instruments appeared, notably the piano, which had a much greater range than its ancestor, the harpsichord. New forms of instrumental music appeared, developed in particular by the Austrian Haydn (1732–1809). He wrote many piano pieces in sonata form, in which two contrasting themes are stated, developed, interwoven, repeated, and

finally resolved in a *coda* ("tail" in Italian). For orchestras Haydn grafted the sonata onto the Italian operatic overture to comprise the first movement of the symphony. At the same time, opera itself was making a revolutionary advance, thanks to another German composer, Gluck (1714–1787), who devised well-constructed musical dramas based on the heroes and heroines of classical mythology.

The concerto, symphony, and opera all reached a climax in the works of the Austrian, Mozart (1756–1791), a child prodigy whose versatility multiplied until he died at thirty-five, a debt-ridden pauper. Mozart added new solo instruments for concertos, such as the French horn and the bassoon. He carried one tradition of Italian comic opera to new heights with the light-hearted *Così Fan Tutte* ("Thus Do All Women"); *The Marriage of Figaro,* based on the great hit of the Paris theater in the 1780s, in which the valet outwits and outsings his noble employers; and *Don Giovanni,* a "black comedy" about the havoc wrought by Don Juan on earth before his descent to hell. The ballroom scene in *Don Giovanni* was both a tour de force and a social commentary, as three different tunes were played simultaneously for three different dances—a minuet for the aristocracy, a country dance for the middle class, and for the lower orders a waltz, then not yet accepted as appropriate for polite society.

Indications were multiplying in the eighteenth century that Europe was on the brink of a social revolution. Writers, artists, and musicians no longer had to depend almost entirely on the patronage of the powerful, the well-born, and the rich. In England the growing middle class bought the prints of Hogarth, the novels of De-foe, Fielding, and Richardson, and attended orchestral performances conducted by Haydn. It was symptomatic that Haydn exchanged the patronage of the immensely wealthy Hungarian family of Esterhazy for a successful independent venture with the popular concert audiences of London. Thus, a lively interest in culture was evident among the bourgeoisie when the French began their turbulent experiment with democracy in 1789.

READING SUGGESTIONS on The Great Modern Revolution Begins (Asterisks indicate paperback.)

General Surveys of the Seventeenth and Eighteenth Centuries

M. Ashley, *A History of Europe, 1648–1815* (*Prentice-Hall); M. S. Anderson, *Europe in the Eighteenth Century,* 2nd. ed. (*Longmans); R. J. White, *Europe in the Eighteenth Century* (*St. Martin's); L. Krieger, *Kings and Philosophers, 1689–1789* (*Norton). Introductory accounts designed for college classes.

The New Cambridge Modern History, Vols. IV–VII (Cambridge). Wide-ranging essays by many scholars covering the period from 1609 to 1763; uneven in quality but often dealing with topics and countries neglected in briefer surveys.

The Scientific Revolution

H. F. Kearney, *Science and Change* (*McGraw-Hill). A many-sided introduction.

H. Butterfield, *The Origins of Modern Science* (*Free Press). A lively and controversial interpretation minimizing the contributions of scientists before Galileo, notably Copernicus.

A. N. Whitehead, *Science and the Modern World* (*Free Press). An incisive critique of the implications of the scientific revolution by a celebrated English philosopher of the early twentieth century.

Martha Ornstein, *The Role of Scientific Societies in the 17th Century* (Arno, 1975). Reprint of a standard study of these important institutions.

J. E. King, *Science and Rationalism in the Administration of Louis XIV* (Johns Hopkins, 1949). Evaluation of the impact on France.

E. A. Burtt, *Metaphysical Foundations of Modern Physical Science* (Humanities, 1967). Reprint of an older study of the links between philosophy and science.

F. H. Anderson, *Francis Bacon: His Career and Thought* (Greenwood, 1978). An informative study of the celebrated English defender of inductive science; first published in 1962.

G. de Santillana, *The Crime of Galileo* (*University of Chicago). An assessment of the famous Italian scientist and the difficulties resulting from his innovative views.

F. Grayeff, *Descartes* (*British Book Centre). An assessment of the equally famous French mathematician and philosopher.

E. Mortimer, *Blaise Pascal* (Greenwood, 1976). Reprint of an older sympathetic study of a remarkable man.

F. Manuel, *A Portrait of Isaac Newton* (*New Republic); and E. Andrade, *Sir Isaac Newton* (Sharon Hill). Reprints of two informative studies of another remarkable man.

The Economic Revolutions

C. M. Cipolla, ed., *Fontana Economic History* (*Watts). Volume II of this introductory study covers the sixteenth and seventeenth centuries, and Volume III the industrial revolution.

S. B. Clough and R. T. Rapp, *European Economic History,* 3rd ed. (McGraw-Hill, 1975). Informative general textbook.

The Cambridge Economic History of Europe, Vols. V and VI. (Cambridge). More advanced scholarly essays by many experts.

T. S. Ashton, *An Economic History of England: The Eighteenth Century.* (*Methuen). A lucid introduction by an expert.

A. Redford, *Economic History of England, 1760–1860.* Another study of the leading innovator in economic revolution.

P. Deane, *The First Industrial Revolution,* 2nd ed. (*Cambridge). Up-to-date study of the British economy from 1750 to 1850, based on lectures to undergraduates at Cambridge University.

The Enlightenment and the Philosophes

P. Gay, *The Enlightenment: An Interpretation,* 2 vols. (*Norton). Comprehensive scholarly survey with extensive bibliographies. Gay has also published several other works on the Enlightenment.

I. Berlin, *The Age of Enlightenment: The Eighteenth Century Philosophers* (*Mentor). A lucid introduction.

N. Hampson, *The Enlightenment* (*Penguin). Another helpful introduction to eighteenth-century thought.

E. Cassirer, *The Philosophy of the Enlightenment* (*Princeton). Important study of the main principles of eighteenth-century thought.

C. Becker, *The Heavenly City of the Eighteenth-Century Philosophers* (*Yale). Delightful essays seeking to prove that the philosophes were less modern in their outlook than is generally believed.

R. Anchor, *The Enlightenment* (*University of California). A stimulating interpretation linking intellectual and social history.

L. Crocker, *An Age of Crisis* (John Hopkins, 1959). Study of the attitudes of eighteenth-century French thinkers toward humanity and the world.

D. Mornet, *French Thought in the Eighteenth Century* (Shoestring, 1969). English translation of an important older study by a French scholar.

C. Frankel, *The Faith of Reason* (Octagon, 1969). Reprint of an older study on the idea of progress in the French Enlightenment.

L. Bredvold, *The Brave New World of the Enlightenment* (University of Michigan, 1961). Highly critical assessment.

R. Darnton, *The Business of Enlightenment* (Harvard University, Belknap Press, 1979). A history of the trials of publishing the *Encyclopédie,* the great vehicle of enlightened ideas.

A. M. Wilson, *Diderot* (Oxford, 1972). The definitive biography of the influential editor of the *Encyclopédie.*

N. Torrey, *The Spirit of Voltaire* (Russell, 1968). Reprint of an older study of the celebrated defender of enlightened ideas.

B. R. Redman, *The Portable Voltaire* (*Penguin). A good sampler of his writings, with an introduction assessing the man himself.

L. Crocker, *J.-J. Rousseau,* 2 vols. (Macmillan, 1968, 1973). A detailed biographical study of this controversial figure.

For other assessments, see G. Havens, *J.-J. Rousseau* (Twayne, 1978); A. Cobban, *Rousseau and the Modern State* (*Allen & Unwin); J. Talmon, *The Origins of Totalitarian Democracy* (*Norton); and E. Cassirer, *The Question of J.-J. Rousseau* (*Indiana University). Useful editions of Rousseau's key writings are *The Social Contract and the Discourses* (*Dutton) and *Émile,* in a new translation by A. Bloom (*Basic Books).

Literature and the Arts

F. Artz, *From the Renaissance to Romanticism: Trends in Style in Art, Literature and Music* (*University of Chicago). A helpful introduction.

B. Willey, *The Seventeenth-Century Background* and *The Eighteenth-Century Background* (Columbia). Widely used studies of the relationship between English literature and the broader intellectual and cultural world.

W. P. Ker, *The Eighteenth Century* (Porter, 1978). Reprint of a useful survey.

A. R. Pugh, *From Montaigne to Chateaubriand* (*Humanities). Introduction to prose literature in France during the seventeenth and eighteenth centuries.

J. S. Held and D. Posner, *Seventeenth- and Eighteenth-Century Art* (Prentice-Hall, 1972). An informative comprehensive survey.

S. Faniel, ed., *French Art of the Eighteenth Century* (Simon and Schuster, 1957). Valuable for its coverage of the minor arts.

M. Bukofser, *Music in the Baroque Era* (*Norton, 1947). A survey down to 1750.

C. Rosen, *The Classical Style* (*Norton). Evaluates the contributions of Mozart, Haydn, and Beethoven.

CHAPTER ELEVEN

Politics And War:
1715-1789

Historians usually restrict the eighteenth century in Europe to the seventy-five years between the death of Louis XIV in 1715 and the outbreak of revolution in France in 1789. These were highly eventful years during which the pressures of the great modern revolution, especially the new economic and intellectual advances, undermined the Old Regime *(Ancien Régime).* This term referred not only to France but to many other European states as well, where society and politics were still based on institutions inherited from the Middle Ages. The beginnings of a new regime could be detected in England, where the upheavals of the seventeenth century had greatly modified the medieval inheritance. The British example helped to inspire the American colonies' revolt in 1776 and the more formidable French overturn of 1789.

By the second half of the eighteenth century many European rulers tried to devise a peaceful combination of the old and the new. Their "enlightened despotism" attempted to apply some of the reforms proposed by the Enlightenment in order to make monarchy more efficient and perhaps more popular but without sacrificing traditional royal authority. More dramatic than these experiments were the shifts in the international balance of power. Britain defeated France in the struggle for colonial supremacy, while two newcomers, Russia and Prussia, emerged as major players in the game of exerting influence and acquiring territory.

THE MAJOR POWERS IN EUROPE

The Old Regime

In the eighteenth century almost every European state retained the most characteristic feature of the Old Regime, the division of society into three estates of very unequal size. The smallest was the first estate, the clergy; next came the second estate, the nobility; and finally the third estate, the commoners, which included the vast majority of people, the peasants of the countryside and the workers and business and professional people of the urban centers. For members of the third estate, the Old Regime was less oppressive in Western Europe than in Eastern. The dividing line between the "two Europes" was the River Elbe, which rises in Bohemia (part of present-day Czechoslovakia), flows northwest across Germany, and reaches the North Sea near the port of Hamburg. In eastern Germany and in Hungary, Poland, and Russia, the majority of peasants were still serfs in 1715. In the west, notably in Britain, France, the Low Countries and in western Germany, the majority had been emancipated centuries earlier.

Almost everywhere in Europe, however, the titled aristocrats and landed gentry of the second estate still wielded substantial power, and it was only the commoners at the top of the third estate who exerted a significant influence on politics. Examples were the prosperous businessmen of Holland and Britain, and the lawyers and merchants in France who were wealthy enough to purchase government office. Every government in Europe represented chiefly the interests of the few, whether it was an absolute monarchy like France, a constitutional monarchy like Britain, or a republic like the Dutch United Provinces.

Great Britain

Aided by economic leadership and naval supremacy, Britain was becoming the wealthiest nation in the world. In the 1720s the London financial community, the City, recovered quickly from the South Sea Bubble and challenged Amsterdam's role as the capital of international trade and finance. As British merchants outdistanced their old Dutch rivals, they also took the lead over their new competitors, the French. Judged by the yardsticks of mercantilism—commerce, colonies, and seapower—Britain was the strongest state in Europe. Yet the British colonial empire did not follow all the teachings of mercantilism. The lax supervision of the Board of Trade, a policy described as "salutary neglect," promoted the prosperity and self-reliance of the colonies. By contrast, the rigid controls imposed by France and Spain on their possessions overseas favored the interests of the mother countries.

Although British warships were inferior in design to those of France and Spain, the British had a decisive lead over the French in the number of warships and merchant vessels. They also had the advantage of superior personnel, especially the naval captains who profited by many years of practical training. By contrast, the British army was inferior and its officers were reputed to be the poorest in Europe. Neglect of the army reflected both the relative safety of the British Isles from invasion and the fears of many Englishmen that a standing army might revive the absolutist policies attempted by Cromwell and James II in the preceding century. To fill the ranks in time of war Britain relied on mercenaries, such as the Hessians of the American Revolutionary War, who came from the German principality of Hesse-Cassel.

One of Britain's greatest assets was its parliamentary government. During the Glorious Revolution of 1688–1689, Parliament had approved the accession of William and Mary to replace James II. When Mary's sister, Anne, died in 1714 without leaving offspring (all her children had died young), Parliament again determined the succession. The crown passed to the Elector of the German state of Hanover, who was a great-grandson of James I. Under the first two Hanoverian kings, George I (1714–1727) and George II (1717–1760), the institution that would assure parliamentary control over the executive was gradually taking shape. This was the cabinet.

Today the British cabinet is a committee of the majority party in the House of Commons, headed by the prime minister, and it remains in office as long as it can muster the support of a majority in Commons. The cabinet dominates the executive branch of the government; the monarch

Europe in 1715

Legend:
- Brandenburg-Prussia
- Austrian Hapsburg lands
- Swedish possessions
- Venetian possessions
- Ottoman Empire
- Boundary of the Holy Roman Empire
- ■ Battle sites

Atlantic Ocean

SCOTLAND
Edinburgh
Berwick

North Sea

NORWAY
Oslo
S W
Stockholm

ULSTER
IRELAND
Drogheda
Boyne R.
Dublin
Limerick

DENMARK
Copenhagen

KINGDOM OF
GREAT BRITAIN

ENGLAND

London
Dover
Tor Bay

Hamburg
Bremen
Elbe R.
HANOVER
Fehrbellin

Baltic
B
SWEDISH
POMERANIA
Danzig
BRANDENBURG
Berlin
Oder R.

UNITED
NETHERLANDS
Ryswick
Utrecht
Nimwegen

WEST-
PHALIA
Göttingen
Halle
SAXONY

SILESIA

C. La Hogue
AUSTRIAN
NETHERLANDS
Oudenarde
Ramillies
Aachen
Rhine R.
THE
EMPIRE

Prague
BOHEMIA
MORAVIA

Malplaquet
Paris
Seine R.
Verdun
Metz
Toul
LORRAINE
Rastadt
Strasbourg
Blenheim
Augsburg

AUSTRIA
Vienna

Versailles

Nantes
Blois
Orléans
Loire R.

FRANCE

FRANCHE-
COMTÉ
ALSACE

SWITZERLAND

BAVARIA

STYRIA

CARINTHIA
TYROL
CARNIOLA

Bordeaux

Geneva

SAVOY
MILAN
Po R.
Venice
VENETIAN
REPUBLIC
Adriatic Sea
Ragusa

Avignon
(to the papacy)
Marseilles

Genoa
Florence
Leghorn
TUSCANY
PAPAL
STATES

PORTUGAL
Lisbon
Tagus R.
Burgos
Ebro R.
Madrid

S P A I N

Barcelona

Valencia

BALEARIC IS.

CORSICA
(to Genoa)

Rome

NAPLES

Naples

Guadalquivir R.
Seville
Granada

MINORCA
(Br.)

SARDINIA
(to Austria, 1714;
to Savoy, 1720)

Gibraltar
(Br.)

Mediterranean   Sea

ALGERIA

TUNIS

MALTA

Palermo

SICILY
(to Savoy, 1714;
to Austria, 1720)

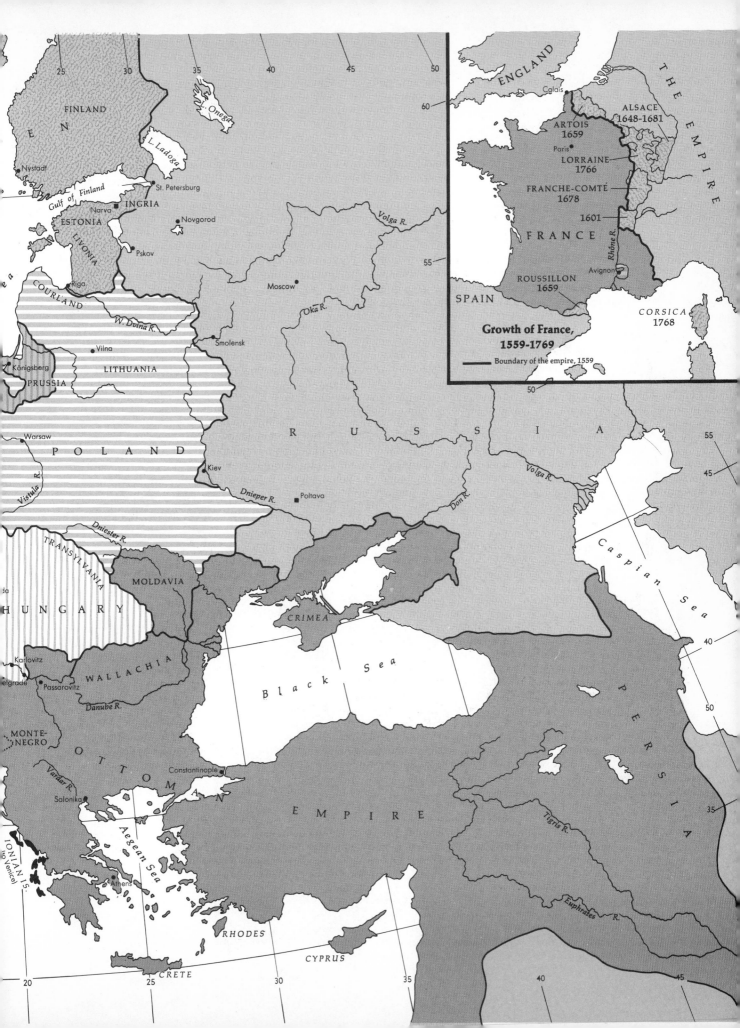

FINLAND

25   30   35   40   45   50

L. Onega

Nystadt

Gulf of Finland   St. Petersburg

INGRIA

Narva   Novgorod

ESTONIA

LIVONIA

Pskov

Riga

COURLAND   *W. Dvina R.*

Vilna   Smolensk   Moscow   *Volga R.*

Königsberg

PRUSSIA   LITHUANIA

R   U   S   S   I   A

55

Warsaw

Oka R.

P   O   L   A   N   D

Kiev

Vistula R.   *Dnieper R.*   Poltava   *Don R.*

Dniester R.   *Volga R.*

TRANSYLVANIA

MOLDAVIA

HUNGARY

Caspian Sea

55

45

40

CRIMEA

Karlovitz

WALLACHIA

B   l   a   c   k   S   e   a

50

Belgrade   Passarovitz

Danube R.

MONTE-
NEGRO

O   T   T   O   M   A   N

P   E   R   S   I   A

35

Vardar R.

Constantinople

Salonika

E   M   P   I   R   E

Tigris R.

Aegean Sea

IONIAN IS.
(to Venice)

Athens

Euphrates R.

RHODES

CYPRUS

20   CRETE   25   30   35   40   45

Inset map

ENGLAND

THE   EMPIRE

Calais

ARTOIS
1659

ALSACE
1648–1681

Paris

LORRAINE
1766

FRANCHE-COMTÉ
1678

1601

F   R   A   N   C   E

Rhône R.

Avignon

SPAIN

ROUSSILLON
1659

CORSICA
1768

Growth of France,
1559–1769

———— Boundary of the empire, 1559

50

merely reigns. Under George I and George II, the cabinet was only beginning to acquire this immense authority. Modern scholarship rejects the old view that the first two Hanoverian monarchs were so obsessed with their German interests and so ill at ease in England and with the English language that they were pleased to have the cabinet rule for them. They took a direct interest in the South Sea Bubble and other financial matters and frequently intervened in the conduct of war and diplomacy to a degree that would now be regarded as quite improper. They chose Whigs as cabinet ministers because it was the Whigs who had engineered the Glorious Revolution and arranged for the Hanoverian succession. George I and George II distrusted the Tories, some of whom were involved in futile Jacobite plots to restore to the throne the descendants of James II (Jacobite from *Jacobus,* Latin for James).

For two decades after the collapse of the South Sea Bubble, from 1721 to 1742, Robert Walpole, the Whig leader in the House of Commons, headed the cabinet. He was in effect prime minister, although the title was not yet official. In 1733 Walpole forced the resignation of ministers opposed to his radical fiscal reform, thereby taking a major step toward establishing cabinet unanimity on a crucial issue. It took all Walpole's

political experience to maintain his majority in the Commons, for party discipline was nonexistent. The terms "Whig" and "Tory" designated informal and shifting interest groups, not well-organized parties.

Under the first two Georges the Whigs were a coalition of landed and "funded" gentry—that is, of nobles and squires from the country and of business and professional men from London and the provincial towns. Walpole himself exemplified this coalition, for he was the son of a country squire and married the daughter of a timber merchant, who had served as lord mayor of London. As prime minister, Walpole promoted the interests of the City by ensuring political stability; he promoted financial stability through systematic retirement of the national debt. Family ties, a common reverence for property, and a common determination to frustrate the Jacobites and maintain the Hanoverian succession also linked the rural and urban Whigs.

While historians still debate the exact connotation of the terms *gentry, gentleman,* and *squire,* it is generally agreed that they referred to a class just below the titled nobility. The gentry included the younger sons of nobles, since the family title and a seat in the House of Lords descended only to the oldest son. The gentry also included other

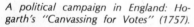

A political campaign in England: Hogarth's "Canvassing for Votes" (1757).

owners of landed estates, all of whom were addressed verbally as "Sir" and in writing as "Esquire" (the shieldbearer of a feudal knight). Though the gentry had always lived off the revenues of landed property, by the 1700s many of them also had a stake in the commercial revolution. Moreover, successful businessmen sometimes bought country estates, set themselves up as gentlemen, and were accepted as such by neighboring gentry.

Despite these examples of upward social mobility, the social and political structure of Walpole's England remained oligarchic. Only gentlemen could hope to rise in the professions, to become army and navy officers, lawyers, clergymen, and physicians. In local matters, the gentry monopolized the powerful office of Justice of the Peace. A justice not only presided over a court but also fixed wage scales, superintended relief of the poor, and provided for the maintenance of bridges and highways. The justices were fanatical defenders of the propertied classes, and their vigorous enforcement of the stringent laws against theft accounts for the saying, "As well be hanged for a sheep as for a lamb."

In the main, only gentlemen had the right to vote for members of Parliament. The small roster of voters in many constituencies encouraged corruption, particularly in the "rotten" or "pocket" boroughs where control of the votes resided in the pocket of some wealthy leader. The immensely rich Duke of Newcastle controlled elections in four counties and seven pocket boroughs. Voters were often bribed outright or promised places on the government payroll. Thus in Britain, as on the Continent, the ruling classes governed the voteless masses, who sometimes suffered more than their Continental counterparts, especially if they were victims of the agricultural enclosure movement. London was already facing some of the problems of a modern metropolis—the proliferation of slums and slum dwellers, crimes of violence, traffic jams—but with almost no police or fire protection.

The Whig oligarchy faced a threat when the first Hanoverian born and raised in England came to the throne in 1760. George III, king for sixty years, was virtuous as a person and devoted to his family, but stubborn, shortsighted, and ultimately unsuccessful as a monarch. He tried to wrest control of the House of Commons from the Whigs by copying their reliance upon patronage and bribery. It was easy at first for him to exploit the factional strife among the Whigs, which resulted in the resignation of William Pitt

the Elder, a highly effective prime minister from 1757 to 1761 during the Seven Years' War. As his successor, George chose Lord Bute, a close friend. But the king and prime minister found it hard to justify Britain's disappointment at the Peace of Paris that ended the Seven Years' War in 1763, particularly France's retaining the sugar-rich islands in the West Indies. The Commons ratified the treaty, but George dismissed Bute to appease the critics of British diplomacy.

The chief critic was John Wilkes, a member of Commons, who dubbed the Paris settlement "the peace of God, for it passeth all understanding." Wilkes's attack in his paper, the *North Briton,* infuriated the king, who persuaded Commons to order the offending issue burnt. Later, Wilkes ran for Parliament three times and won, but each time royal pressure made the Commons void his election. Riots took place in defense of "Wilkes and Liberty," and he became a popular hero before he finally took his seat in Parliament in 1774.

Meanwhile, after seven years of short-lived ministries (1763–1770), George III finally found a minister who would do the king's bidding—Lord North, who headed the cabinet for a dozen years (1770–1782). Under North, royal intervention in politics stiffened, then wavered, and at length collapsed in the face of the stubborn revolt by the thirteen North American colonies and the inept response of Great Britain. By 1780 George III's policies had become so unpopular at home that the House of Commons passed a resolution that "the influence of the crown has increased, is increasing, and ought to be diminished."

George III:
a portrait by Gainsborough.

The influence of the crown was indeed diminished. In 1782 Lord North finally persuaded the king to accept his resignation, and in 1783 William Pitt the Younger became prime minister. This son of the heroic Pitt, though only twenty-five, was already a seasoned veteran of parliamentary maneuvers. During his eighteen years in office, the influence of the professional politicians mounted, while that of the king declined. George III, who briefly contemplated abdication, accepted a more passive role, particularly because of recurrent spells of illness. (Recent medical research has determined that he suffered not from insanity, as had long been thought, but from porphyria, an inherited metabolic disorder.) The constitutional nature of the British monarchy was becoming more pronounced.

France

In almost every area where Britain was strong France seemed to be weak. During the long reign of Louis XV (1715–1774), France suffered particularly from the rigidity of its colonial policy, the inferiority of its navy, and the mediocre abilities of most of its statesmen. The Ministry of the Navy, which ruled the empire overseas, opposed any steps toward colonial self-government and applied the same regulations to colonies as different as the tropical islands of the West Indies and the wilderness of Canada. Innumerable controls stifled the initiative of the colonists, although they helped to double the commercial activity of Nantes, Bordeaux, and other ports in the mother country. French warships, while admirably designed, were inadequate in number, and the merchant marine was too small to supplement the fleet. French naval officers, rigorously trained in the classroom, lacked the practical experience of British captains.

The French army played a more vital role, for France was a land power, and its vulnerable northeastern frontier, along the Flemish plain, invited invaders. Except in size, however, the army of Louis XV scarcely maintained the great military traditions of Louis XIV. Troops were poorly trained, and their organization was top-heavy: one officer to fifteen men, while in the more efficient Prussian army the ratio was one to thirty-five. Both navy and army were revitalized later in the century after French defeats in the Seven Years' War. The number of warships was increased, the officer corps of the army was cleared of deadwood, and more aggressive military tactics were introduced. These measures helped to ex-

plain the excellent showing made by French participants in the American Revolutionary War, but they were too late to save the Old Regime.

The Old Regime was weakest at the very top. Louis XV and his grandson, Louis XVI, who succeeded him in 1774, were hardly worthy successors of Louis XIV. Few of their ministers approached the calibre of Richelieu and Colbert. The dissolute duke of Orléans, regent from 1715 to 1723, did attempt two significant experiments, but both soon failed. John Law's "system" collapsed, together with the Mississippi Bubble. Orléans set up ministerial councils composed of distinguished noblemen to replace the individual bourgeois ministers favored by Louis XIV. The experiment petered out after a three-year trial because of the endless squabbles between the councilors from the nobility of the robe and those from the nobility of the sword, "between the grandnephews of lawyers and the ever-so-great-grandsons of feudal lords."

The nobles, though unable to govern, were effective troublemakers. The strongholds of the nobility of the robe were the important courts called parlements in Paris and a dozen provincial cities; they were staffed by more than one thousand judges. The parlements took advantage of the regency to push a long-standing claim to register government edicts before they could be published and enforced. Many judges of the parlements had family ties with the influential Jansenists, whose doctrines were condemned by a papal bull. When the Parlement of Paris refused to register the bull, the regent held a *lit de justice* ("bed of justice," the reference is to the ceremonial seat of the monarch), a special royal session forcing the Parlement to yield. The strife between parlement and king continued, however, and was marked by repeated refusals of judges to carry on normal court business and by the exiling of judges from Paris as punishment for insubordination. In the 1760s the parlements succeeded in suppressing the Jesuits, the archenemies of the Jansenists. In the last years of his reign Louis XV tried to end the strife by suppressing the parlements and substituting new courts under close royal control. But the parlements were restored, more combative than ever, under his successor.

Meanwhile, French administrators confronted other problems. Soon after the end of Orléans' regency, the tutor of Louis XV, the aged Cardinal Fleury, became chief minister, a post he held from 1726 to his death in 1743 in his ninetieth year. Fleury did not remedy the injustices of French fiscal policy, but he did stabilize the coinage, put the farming of taxes on a more businesslike basis, and made loans more available by establishing state pawnshops in the principal cities. The administrative stability achieved by Fleury soon vanished after Louis XV began his personal rule in 1743. The king had neither the patience nor the interest required to supervise the details of government. He appointed and dismissed ministers on a personal whim or at the bidding of his mistresses and favorites. In thirty years he had eighteen different foreign secretaries and fourteen different controllers general (the chief fiscal officer).

Yet despite all these weaknesses, France remained a great power. French tastes and the French language retained the international preeminence they had won in the age of Louis XIV. The French army was the largest in the world, the navy the second largest, and France led the world in overseas trade until Britain forged ahead in the final quarter of the 1700s.

Spain and Italy

With the withdrawal of Sweden and the Dutch Republic from the international struggle for power, Spain was the only remaining state in Western Europe with a claim to great-power status. Spain suffered relatively little damage from the long war over the succession to the Spanish throne, a war fought mainly outside its own borders. The loss of Belgium and parts of Italy in 1713 reduced the unwieldy Spanish dominions to more manageable size. The new Bourbon kings were a marked improvement over the last Spanish Hapsburgs. Philip V (1700–1746), the first of the Spanish Bourbons, imported French experts schooled in the system of Louis XIV to reduce the endless formalities and delays of Spanish administrative routine. They reasserted the authority of the monarch over the traditionally powerful clergy and nobility. They also improved the tax system, encouraged industry, built up the navy, and fortified strategic sites in Spain's American empire.

These reforms, however, did not strike at the root causes of Spain's decline. Progress was hampered both at home and in the colonies by the restrictions of mercantilism, the greed of officials, and the remnants of power still resting with the reactionary nobles and clerics. Philip V himself was neurotic and dominated by his strong-willed second wife, the Italian Elizabeth Farnese. Since Philip's son by his first marriage would in-

herit the Spanish crown, Elizabeth was determined to find thrones in Italy for her own two sons. Her relentless pursuit of these maternal interests repeatedly threatened the peace of Europe.

In the readjustment of the European balance of power in 1713, Italy exchanged one foreign master for another, as the Austrian Hapsburgs took over the Italian possessions of their Spanish cousins. The political map of the peninsula showed Austria established in Lombardy, flanked to the east and south, respectively, by the decaying republics of Venice and Genoa. In the mountainous northwest was the small but rising state of Piedmont-Savoy, termed the Kingdom of Sardinia after it acquired that island in 1720. Farther down the peninsula the most important states were the Grand Duchy of Tuscany, the papal domains, and the Austrian-controlled Two Sicilies (the kingdom of Naples and the island of Sicily).

As Metternich would later remark, Italy was merely "a geographical expression," the components of which were manipulated by outsiders. In the 1730s the succession of the Two Sicilies was awarded to Elizabeth Farnese's elder son, Carlos, while the Austrians were compensated by the succession of Tuscany. Yet, though none of the Italian states was more than a minor power, Italian culture continued to be an important force in European life. Venice still produced fine painters such as Tiepolo and Canaletto; Naples was the schoolmaster of singers and musicians; and Lombardy, Tuscany, and Naples all contributed to the economic and intellectual advances of the Enlightenment.

Germany

Germany, also, with its three hundred states, large, small, and minute, appeared to be a geographical expression. Unlike Italy, however, Germany included two really major participants in the contest for power: Austria and Prussia. During the two decades preceding 1715, the Austrian Hapsburgs won a series of military and diplomatic victories. By the peace of Karlovitz (1699) they recovered Hungary from the Ottoman Turks. Though failing to keep the Spanish succession from going to a French Bourbon, they were generously compensated with Spain's Belgian and Italian lands.

Charles VI (1711–1740), aware that his impressive title of Holy Roman Emperor conferred little real authority, concentrated on the Hapsburg family possessions. He persuaded his noble subjects to ratify the Pragmatic Sanction, a solemn decree which directed that all his lands would pass to his daughter, Maria Theresa, in the absence of a son. Much still remained to be done to consolidate Hapsburg rule over territories that included many different nationalities. In three crucial areas—German Austria, Czech Bohemia, and Magyar Hungary—the nobles retained their medieval prerogatives. By their influence over local estates and diets they controlled the granting of taxes and the appointment of officials. The weakness of Charles VI's regime was dramatically illustrated by the fact that when he died the exchequer was nearly empty and the pay of the army and civil service was more than two years in arrears.

Where Austria possessed the appearances but not the realities of great-power status, Prussia showed few of the appearances but enjoyed many of the realities. Prussian territories, scattered across north Germany, consisted largely of sand and swamp with little value for agriculture. With fewer than three million inhabitants in 1715, Prussia ranked twelfth among the European states in population. Its capital city, Berlin, located on the minor river Spree, had none of the geographical advantages enjoyed by Istanbul, London, Paris, and other great capitals.

Since the fifteenth century, members of the Hohenzollern family had been the electors of Brandenburg, which lay between the Elbe and Oder rivers. In 1618 the elector of Brandenburg inherited East Prussia at the southeast corner of the Baltic Sea. It had been acquired first by the crusading order of the Teutonic Knights, whose last master had been a Hohenzollern. East Prussia, however, was separated from Brandenburg by Polish West Prussia. In northwest Germany, the

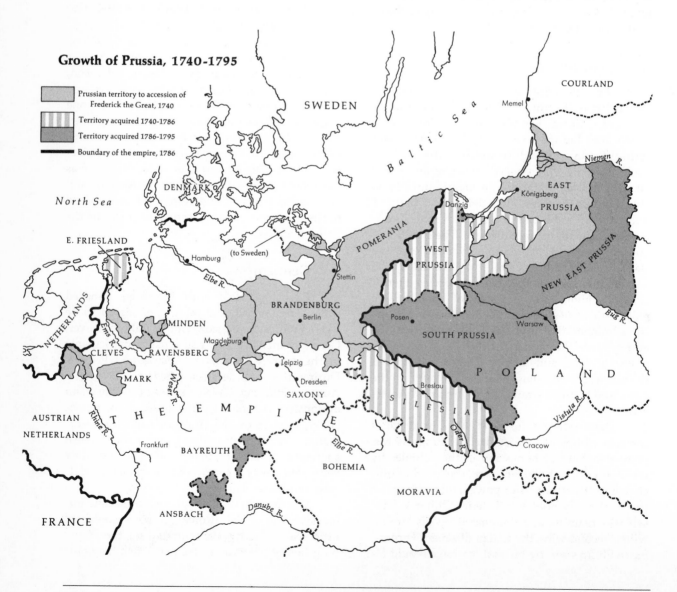

Growth of Prussia, 1740-1795

Prussian territory to accession of Frederick the Great, 1740

Territory acquired 1740-1786

Territory acquired 1786-1795

Boundary of the empire, 1786

Hohenzollerns had also acquired the small but strategically located states of Cleves and Mark. Thus, when Frederick William, the Great Elector (1640–1688), succeeded to the Hohenzollern inheritance, his lands consisted of Brandenburg as the center with separate outlying regions to the east and west. For the next two hundred years the rulers of Brandenburg-Prussia devoted themselves to expanding their holdings into a single block of territory.

The Great Elector found his domains wrecked by the Thirty Years' War. Farms were ruined, the population reduced by half, the army a rabble of a few thousand men. To replenish the population, he encouraged the immigration of Polish Jews and other refugees from religious persecution, notably twenty thousand skilled French Huguenots. He built a small but efficient standing army that enabled Prussia to command large foreign subsidies for participating in the campaigns for and against Louis XIV.

The Great Elector fixed the Hohenzollern pattern of militarized absolutism, a policy supported by the Lutheran state church, which taught the virtues of obedience and discipline. The Great Elector found that in all his territories the authority of the ruler was limited by the existence of estates, medieval assemblies representing landed nobles and citizens of the towns. He battled the estates for supremacy and won, thereby delaying for two centuries the introduction of representative government in the Prussian domains. He also acquired the crucial power of levying taxes, which he then assigned to the War Office and the army. Once the Great Elector had ended the independence of the aristocracy, he relied on aristocrats to assist him, particularly the *Junkers*, the landed gentry of East Prussia. He confirmed the Junkers' absolute authority over the serfs on their own estates and their ascendancy over the towns. He also encouraged them to serve the state, especially as army officers. Thus, in contrast to some other monarchies, the absolutism of the Hohenzollerns rested on the cooperation of the sovereign and the aristocracy, not on their antagonism.

The Great Elector's son, Frederick I (1688–1713), gained new prestige for his country by assuming the title "King in Prussia" (he was king only in East Prussia, which lay outside the boundaries of the Holy Roman Empire). Frederick I insisted on international recognition of his new status as the price for Prussia's entry into the War of the Spanish Succession against Louis XIV. The new royal dignity, however, nearly caused

bankruptcy, as Frederick spent lavishly on the trappings of monarchy and on subsidies to the intellectuals and artists he invited to Berlin. This departure from the Hohenzollern tradition of frugality ended with Frederick's death and the accession of his son, King Frederick William I (1713–1740).

Frederick William honored his father with a lavish funeral, but then dismissed most of the court officials and converted part of the royal palace into offices. He proclaimed a policy of *Ein Plus Machen* ("Make a surplus"), which reduced expenditures to a fraction of what they had been and enabled him to bequeath a full treasury to his son. To strengthen royal control over the government, he set up a small board of experts with the wonderfully explicit name of *Generaloberfinanzkriegsunddomänendirektorium* (General Superior Finance War and Domain Directory). Members of the Directory administered departments of the central government and also super-

One of the giant soldiers of Frederick William I.

vised activities in the outlying provinces. Although the arrangement was cumbersome, it brought provincial administration under closer royal control. The king treated the experts of the Directory as he did lower officials, paying them meagerly, fining them for lateness, and striking them with his cane as punishment for slovenly performance of their duties.

Frederick William doubled the size of the standing army but avoided a serious reduction of the labor force by assigning troops to work on farms nine months of the year. He set up state factories to supply guns and uniforms. The army prompted his only extravagance, a regiment of giant grenadiers recruited by scouts in other German states, often at high prices. The king cherished his army too much to risk a venturesome foreign policy. His only significant campaign was against Sweden, whereby Prussia obtained in 1720 part of Pomerania, to the northeast of Brandenburg, and the important Baltic port of Stettin.

European contemporaries called the Prussia of Frederick William "an armed camp" and a "gigantic penal institution." The king was so determined to economize that he refused pensions to soldiers' widows and allowed lawyers and judges such meager incomes that they turned to corruption on a grand scale. Despite these shortcomings, his regime worked very well in terms of power politics. The Junkers, who were intensely loyal to their Hohenzollern rulers, made excellent officers for an army that was the best drilled and disciplined in Europe. When Frederick William died in 1740, the Prussian David was ready to battle the Austrian Goliath.

Russia

Even more impressive than the rise of the Hohenzollerns were the gains made by Russia under Peter the Great, tsar from 1689 to 1725. Almost seven feet tall, extremely lively and intelligent, Peter became tsar at seventeen and was fascinated by military games. As a lad, he set up a play regiment, staffed it with full-grown men, and enlisted himself as a common soldier in its ranks. He discovered a broken-down boat in a barn and learned about rigging and sails from Dutch sailors living in the foreigners' suburb of Moscow. Married at age sixteen, Peter neglected his wife in favor of his military maneuvers, sailing, and relaxing with his comrades.

Peter and his cronies smoked huge quantities of tobacco, horrifying conservative Muscovites who believed it was forbidden by the biblical text that "what cometh out of the mouth defileth a man." They also made obscene parodies of church services when they were drunk and roared about Moscow late at night on sleighs. At more proper parties staid Moscow ladies, accustomed to haremlike seclusion, were forced to wear low-necked gowns in the Western style and to dance and drink. If a lady refused wine, Peter simply held her nose and poured it down her throat.

The young tsar had an insatiable appetite for new experiences, taking up carpentry, shoemaking, cooking, clockmaking, ivory-carving, etching, and even dentistry. Once he had acquired a dentist's instruments, he practiced on anyone who was handy—and those were the days before anesthetics! Wearing shabby clothes, driving his own horses, and paying little heed to court and church ceremonials, Peter was a total departure from Muscovite ideas of a proper tsar.

Peter's favorite after 1700 was Menshikov, a man of low birth, who reached high office, received the title of prince and a huge fortune, and, like many public servants at the time, was an unscrupulous grafter. Peter sent his first wife to a convent and later took on as mistress a girl who had already been involved with Menshikov and others. She bore Peter two children, and he finally married her in 1712. This was the Empress Catherine, a simple, hearty and affectionate woman who was able to control her difficult husband as no other human being could.

In 1696, anxious to try his hand at war, Peter sent a fleet of boats down the river Don with the help of Dutch experts and defeated the Turks at Azov, on an arm of the Black Sea. The project of forming an anti-Turkish league gave Peter an excuse for a trip abroad, the first undertaken by a Russian sovereign since the Kievan period. Fascinated by Western technology, he visited Holland and England to learn the latest methods of shipbuilding. He toured every factory, museum, and printing firm he could find, and hired several hundred technicians to work in Russia. The huge tsar, in all his vigor and crudity, made an unforgettable impression—as a common laborer on the docks in Holland, sleeping with a dozen followers on the floor of a tiny room in a London inn with no windows open, and in a drunken spree, wrecking the handsome house and garden of the English diarist John Evelyn. In 1698 Peter's trip was cut short by news of a revolt by the *streltsy*, a branch of the military with a long record of insubordination. He rushed

A contemporary caricature of Peter the Great cutting the beard of a boyar.

home and joined Menshikov in chopping off the heads of alleged plotters.

Peter was now more determined than ever to modernize his country and his countrymen. On the very day of his return, assisted by the court jester, he clipped off the beards of his courtiers with a great pair of shears. It was an action full of symbolism, for Orthodox tradition held that God was bearded, and that a man made in the image of God must have a beard or become a candidate for damnation. Peter decreed that Russian nobles must shave or pay a substantial tax for wearing beards. He also commanded that all boyars, members of the gentry, and the city population generally should adopt Western dress and abandon their long robes with flowing sleeves and tall bonnets. Again he took up his shears to cut off sleeves, and again his victims resented this assault on precious customs.

War remained Peter's greatest interest. Soon after he returned from his western trip, he made an alliance with Poland and Denmark to dismember the Baltic empire of Sweden. The allies' hopes were high, since the Swedish throne had passed to the fifteen-year-old Charles XII in 1697. They might have reconsidered had they seen Charles beheading at a single stroke apiece whole flocks of sheep driven down his palace corridors in single file. After Charles had already knocked Denmark out of the Great Northern War (1700–1721), Peter rushed unprepared into the conflict. Although Charles defeated a much larger Russian force at Narva (1700), he failed to exploit his advantage by invading Russia. Instead, he pursued the Polish king, Augustus the Strong; it took

seven years before Augustus would yield the Polish crown to the Swedish candidate, Stanislas Leszczyński. Peter used this reprieve to conquer the Swedish Baltic provinces nearest to Russia, Ingria and Livonia. In Ingria he founded the future Russian capital of St. Petersburg (1703).

In 1708 Charles swept far to the south and east into the Ukraine, where his exhausted soldiers were defeated by the Russians in the decisive battle of Poltava (June, 1709). Peter reinstated Augustus as king of Poland and then engineered a war between Russia and Turkey, where Charles had found refuge. When Peter invaded the Ottoman province of Moldavia (today part of Romania), Turkish forces obliged him to surrender (1711). The Turks could have made Peter their captive and taken him off to Istanbul, but they required him only to return Azov to Turkey and accept the creation of an unfortified zone between Russian and Ottoman territories. When Charles tried to provoke yet another Russo-Turkish War, the Turks expelled their firebrand visitor (1714).

The Great Northern War dragged on for seven more years, as Russia seized Finland and inflicted naval defeats on the Swedes. After Charles was killed in 1718, it took a Russian landing in Sweden itself to end hostilities. In a treaty concluded at the Finnish town of Nystadt (1721), Russia returned Finland to Sweden and made a substantial payment for the Swedish lands acquired along the eastern shore of the Baltic. These were Peter's famous "windows on the West," which enabled seaborne traffic to Russia to give up the long and difficult route around the far northern edge of Europe into the White Sea, an arm of the Arctic.

During the next two years (1722–1723) Peter undertook an inconclusive campaign against Persia (today known as Iran). At his death in 1725 Russia had been at war for virtually the whole of his thirty-five-year reign, with never-ending demands for men and money. More men died of disease, hunger, and the cold than at the hands of the enemy, but the survivors were a tough nucleus for a regular army. Although Peter built a Baltic fleet, Russia had as yet no real naval tradition, so that English and Dutch apprehensions about Russian seapower were premature.

To provide army officers and civilian officials, Peter rigorously enforced the rule by which all landowners owed service to the state. At the age of fifteen every male child of this "service class" was assigned to his future post in the army, the civil service, or the court. Peter often forced

Russian Expansion in Europe, 1689-1796

Acquired by Peter the Great, 1689-1725

Acquired 1730-1740

Acquired by Elizabeth, 1741-1762

Acquired by Catherine, 1762-1796

■ Battle sites

the gentry into posts they considered beneath their dignity. When a member of the service class died, the tsar required him to leave his estate to a single son, so that the land would not be divided anew in every generation. Thus the class of service nobility became completely dependent upon the tsar. The system did open the possibility of a prestigious career for talented men who possessed neither estates nor rank. Such men, when they attained a certain level in any branch of the service (for example, major in the army) automatically received lands and a noble title.

To raise money, Peter debased the currency, taxed virtually everything—including sales, rents, real estate, tanneries, baths, and beehives—and

exploited the government's monopolies over a bewildering variety of products, including salt, oil, coffins, and caviar. Since the tax on individual households did not produce enough revenue, Peter substituted a head tax on every male—the "soul tax." This innovation required a census, which produced a most important, though unintended, result. The census-takers classified as serfs a large number of floaters on the edge between freedom and serfdom; they and their descendants were permanently labeled as unfree.

Peter also created new administrative units: twelve provinces, each with its own governor and staff, who took over many functions previously discharged inefficiently by the central government. With the tsar often away from the capital, decentralization went so far that Russia seemed at times to have little central government. Eventually, Peter copied the Swedish central ministries and created nine "colleges"—for foreign affairs, army, navy, commerce, mines and manufactures, justice, income, expenditure, and control. The activities of each college were determined by the majority vote of an eleven-man *collegium,* or board of directors. This arrangement made corruption less likely since each member of a college could be checked by his colleagues, but the lengthy deliberations of directors often delayed decisions. Corruption still continued in high places, despite savage punishment of those who were caught. Yet the machinery Peter established to meet the immediate needs of his wars was superior to that of any previous Russian ruler.

Ever since 1703 Peter had been building the great city of St. Petersburg in the swamps seized from the Swedes. Remote from the rest of Russia, the new capital was frightfully expensive because food and building materials had to be brought over great distances. Peter commanded all members of the nobility to reside there, although they complained bitterly about leaving their beloved Moscow for this uncomfortable and costly city. Peter also set out to bring the Church under his domination. Knowing how the clergy loathed his regime, he failed to appoint a successor when the patriarch of Moscow died in 1700 and eventually extended the collegiate system of administration to the Church. He put it under an agency first called the "spiritual college" and later the Holy Directing Synod, headed by a procurator who was a layman and served as the tsar's agent.

The social and economic advances under Peter reflected his technological and martial inter-

The Cathedral of St. Peter and Paul within Peter the Great's fortress at St. Petersburg.

ests. Naval, military, and artillery academies were established for the education of future officers and civil servants. Peter continued the practice, begun long before him, of importing foreign technicians and artisans to practice their specialties and teach them to Russians. Industrial enterprises lagged, however, because they were often manned by serfs who had little incentive for this kind of work and whose products were inferior to those imported from abroad.

The records of Peter's secret police are full of complaints heard by his agents. Wives and children of peasants were deserted by their men, who were snatched away to fight on distant battlefields or to build the city that only Peter wanted. The number of serfs increased as a result of the soul tax and the grants of land to service men. Even the service men suffered their own kind of bondage, condemned to lifelong work for the tsar with few opportunities to visit their estates. Nobles of ancient families were treated no differently from upstarts of low birth. Conservative churchmen were convinced that Peter was the Antichrist as they observed the influx of foreigners and innovations from the hated West. Leaders of the noble and clerical opposition

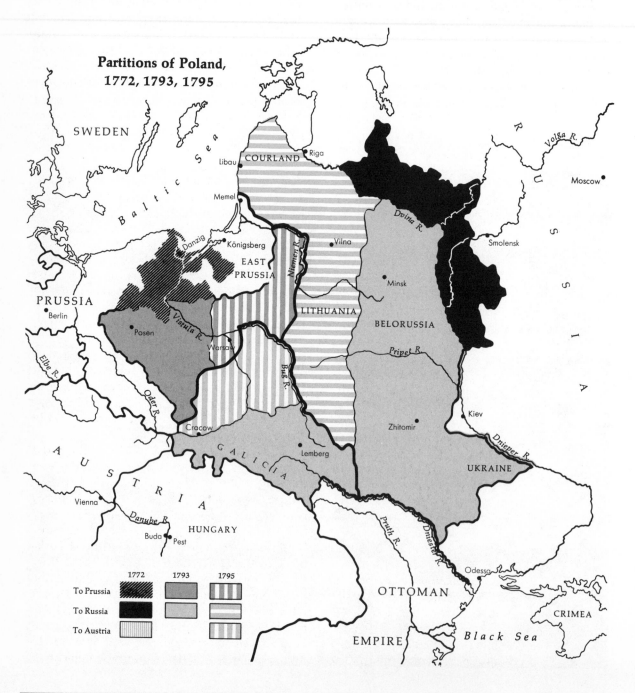

Partitions of Poland,
1772, 1793, 1795

	1772	1793	1795
To Prussia			
To Russia			
To Austria			

hoped that Alexis, Peter's son by his first wife and the heir to the throne, would stop the costly foreign wars and move back to Moscow. Alexis, an unstable alcoholic, fanned the hopes of the opposition. When he fled abroad, Peter lured him back with the promise of fair treatment and then made him the showpiece of an investigation that condemned many to death or exile. Alexis himself was tortured to death in his father's presence.

A century later, Russian intellectuals would express admiration for Peter because they felt he had turned his back on Russia's Slavic character and Byzantine heritage. In fact, however, Peter intensified many traditional Russian characteristics. He made a strong autocracy even stronger, a serf even more of a serf, and the demand for universal service ever more insistent. His fondness for foreign ways, his worship of advanced technology, and his wars all had their precedents under earlier tsars. Peter's true radicalism lay in manners and behavior. His attack on beards and dress, his hatred of ceremony and his fondness for manual labor were indeed innovations. And so were the vigor and passion of his actions. They were decisive in winning a revolutionary reputation for a monarch who in many aspects of his reign continued policies long since established.

Turkey and Poland

By the early eighteenth century, Russia was the only great power in Eastern Europe. While the Ottoman Empire and Poland still bulked large on the map, they were destined to lose land, for their evident decay stimulated the aggressive appetites of their stronger neighbors. The Ottoman Empire survived, albeit with diminished territory, thanks to its own long military tradition and to the rivalry between Russia and Austria. Poland disappeared as an independent power before the end of the century, the victim of partitions by Austria, Russia, and Prussia.

The Polish monarchy was elective: each time the throne fell vacant, the Diet chose a successor, sometimes a foreigner and usually the candidate offering the largest bribes. Once elected, the king was nearly powerless, for he was obliged to transfer the royal prerogatives to the Diet when he accepted the crown. The Diet was an assembly of aristocrats, each of whom was a power unto himself. The right of *liberum veto* allowed a single member to block a proposal by shouting "I do not wish it!" The Polish state had no regular army or diplomatic corps or central bureaucracy. Unlike the British gentry or Prussian

Junkers, the Polish nobles had no tradition of service to the crown or any kind of loyalty except to their own class. They helped destroy a once-flourishing urban middle class by persecuting Jewish shopkeepers and foreign merchants, and on their estates the lot of the serfs was harsher than it was in Russia.

II DIPLOMACY AND WAR, 1713–1763

The Rules of the Game

The conduct of diplomacy and war in the eighteenth century has been compared to an elaborate game, serious and sometimes bloody, yet governed by unwritten rules generally observed by the players and designed to keep their losses at a minimum. The chief players—monarchs, diplomats, generals, admirals—were usually aristocrats, who accepted a common code of behavior. Most of them understood and respected one another far more than they understood or respected the lower classes of their own countries.

The limited financial resources of the governments under the Old Regime permitted only limited warfare; no power could as yet afford the enormous armies or navies required for "total war." On the battlefield generals were reluctant to risk losing soldiers who represented a costly investment in training; they favored sieges, which made it possible to wear out an enemy by cutting off vital supplies. At the peace table diplomats were reluctant to destroy an opponent outright and generally awarded him a bit of territory or a minor throne to compensate for a greater loss. Like total war, "unconditional surrender" was not an eighteenth-century concept.

The powers' handling of the Turkish and Polish questions is a good example of the way the rules of the game operated. In the Austrian-Turkish War of 1716–1718 the Hapsburg emperor, Charles VI, recovered the part of Hungary still under Ottoman rule and secured other Turkish lands in the Danube valley. In the next Turkish war, 1735–1739, Austria was allied with Russia, but foreshadowing the later struggle of the two powers for control of the Balkans, they quarreled over dividing the spoils. In the end there was little to divide, and Charles VI had to hand back the Danubian lands annexed in 1718. In negotiating the Austrian-Turkish settlement of

1739, the Ottoman Empire had powerful support from France, which had been a Turkish ally since the 1530s and an enemy of the Hapsburgs even longer.

Meanwhile, France and Austria also supported opposing sides in a crisis over the Polish kingship. During the Great Northern War, Stanislas Leszczyński, the protegé of Charles XII of Sweden, had temporarily replaced Augustus the Strong as king of Poland. After Augustus recovered the Polish crown, the daughter of Stanislas, Marie Leszczyńska, was married to Louis XV of France. When Augustus died in 1733, French diplomats engineered the election of Stanislas to succeed him. But Austria and Russia disliked the idea of a French puppet on the Polish throne. Russia sent 30,000 troops into Poland and convoked a rump session of the Diet, which elected a rival king, Augustus III, son of Augustus the Strong. The stage was set for the War of The Polish Succession, 1733–1735: Stanislas, France, and Spain, France's Bourbon ally, against Augustus III, Russia, and Austria.

The main fighting, between French and Austrian armies, took place far from Poland in the Rhine valley and northern Italy. Then the diplomats worked out a settlement. To the satisfaction of Austria and Russia, Augustus III secured the Polish crown. Stanislas Leszczyński was compensated by acquiring the duchy of Lorraine on the northeastern border of France, which would go to his daughter Marie on his death and thence to the French crown. France thus moved one step closer to filling out her "natural frontiers." The duchy of Lorraine already had a duke, Francis, husband of the Hapsburg heiress, Maria Theresa. He was compensated for his loss by obtaining the Grand Duchy of Tuscany, where the old line of rulers conveniently died out in 1737. Finally, Elizabeth Farnese of Spain was awarded the throne of Naples for her son Carlos.

Jenkins' Ear and Austrian Succession

Throughout the period from 1713 to 1739, Britain and France took the lead in efforts to prevent any one power from upsetting the international applecart. They moderated their own traditional rivalry because their respective leaders, Walpole and Fleury, sought stability abroad in order to improve the economy at home. But neither of them could prevent a renewal of Anglo-French competition for commerce and empire. A worldwide war between Britain and the Bourbon monarchies broke out in 1739 and would last,

with many intervals of peace, until Napoleon's defeat in 1815.

The specific issue in the crisis of 1739 arose from British disappointment over the Asiento privilege, which gave Britain only a token share in the trade of the Spanish-American colonies. Captains of British merchant vessels resorted to smuggling, Spain retaliated by increasing patrols in American waters, and British smugglers complained of rough treatment by Spanish guards. One victim was Captain Jenkins who claimed that Spanish brutality had cost him an ear, which he duly produced, preserved in salt and cotton, when he appeared before Parliament in 1738. Walpole argued that protecting British smugglers against legitimate Spanish controls did not constitute a very strong case. But he could not restrain the anti-Spanish fever sweeping the country and the hawkish faction of "Boy Patriots" among his own Whigs. In October 1739, Britain began the War of Jenkins' Ear. France soon joined Spain to protect its own economic interests, since France supplied the bulk of the wares that cheaper British contraband was driving out of the Spanish colonial market.

In 1740 events linked the colonial war to a great continental conflict touched off by the death of the emperor Charles VI. The Hapsburg domains passed to his daughter, Maria Theresa, who was twenty-three years old and had little political experience. Expecting to take advantage of the new empress, the German princes ignored the Pragmatic Sanction guaranteeing her succession and planned to profit from a partition of the Hapsburg lands. The first to strike was Frederick the Great (reigned 1740–1786), who had just inherited the Prussian throne. In December 1740, with no warning, he invaded Silesia, a prosperous Hapsburg province in the Oder valley to the southeast of Brandenburg.

In this War of the Austrian Succession, Britain and Austria were ranged against France, Spain, and Prussia. Frederick the Great won a decisive victory in the campaigns on the continent, as the Prussian army surprised Europe by its long night marches, sudden flank attacks, and other tactics that violated the rules of the game. Frederick also antagonized his own allies by making peace arrangements with Austria behind their backs. The Anglo-Austrian alliance worked no better, since many Englishmen believed that George II was betraying true British interests by involving them in squabbles that affected only Hanover and other German states. Nevertheless, British preference for rule by a Hanoverian rather

*Maria Theresa with Francis I
and their children.*

than a Stuart was demonstrated once more when "Bonnie Prince Charles," the grandson of James II, landed in Britain with French backing (1745). He won significant recruits only among the chronically discontented highlanders of Scotland, where he was defeated in 1746 at the battle of Culloden, near Inverness.

Overseas the fighting of the 1740s was indecisive. New England colonists took Louisburg, the French naval base on Cape Breton Island commanding the approach to the St. Lawrence. On the other side of the world, the French took the port of Madras from the English East India Company. A treaty in 1748 restored both Louisburg and Madras to their former masters. In central Europe, by contrast, the War of the Austrian Succession was a decisive step in the rise of Prussia

to the first rank of powers. By appropriating Silesia, Prussia gained a large population, an important textile industry, and extensive deposits of coal and iron. Maria Theresa received little compensation for this serious loss. Although her husband, Francis, won recognition as Holy Roman Emperor, she had to surrender Parma in northern Italy to Elizabeth Farnese's second son, Philip.

The Seven Years' War

During the nominal peace before the outbreak of the Seven Years' War in 1756, Britain and the Bourbon monarchies continued their struggle in an undeclared war. The English and French East India companies fought each other at second hand by taking sides in the rivalries of native princes. In North America, English colonists from the Atlantic seaboard had already staked out claims to the wilderness between the Appalachians and the Mississippi River. The French, equally intent on occupying the same area, advanced south from Canada and established a string of forts in western Pennsylvania from Presqu'Isle on Lake Erie south to Fort Duquesne (later Pittsburgh).

A dramatic shift of alliances among the European powers immediately preceded the Seven Years' War. This "Diplomatic Revolution" was touched off in 1755 when the British concluded a treaty with Russia to insure the defense of Hanover. The treaty alarmed Frederick the Great, who feared an eventual showdown between Prussia and Russia for control of the Baltic Sea and of Poland. He therefore allied himself with Britain and agreed to defend Hanover, thereby disrupting the brief Anglo-Russian flirtation. The Austrian chancellor, Kaunitz, anxious to find a more effective military partner than Britain, seized the opportunity to ally Austria with France in the hope of regaining Silesia. Kaunitz persuaded Louis XV and his influential mistress, Madame de Pompadour, to drop the traditional Bourbon-Hapsburg rivalry. The last factor was added to the Diplomatic Revolution when the Russian empress Elizabeth (reigned 1741–1762), who hated Frederick the Great, joined the Franco-Austrian alliance. Thus in the new conflict the basic antagonisms were the same as in the old—Britain versus France, Prussia versus Austria—but the powers reversed their alliances.

The Seven Years' War (1756–1763), like the War of the Austrian Succession, was really two separate wars—one European, the other naval and colonial. In the European campaigns, Frederick the Great faced a formidable test. Prussia confronted the forces of Austria, France, and Russia, whose population was fifteen times greater; Britain, the only significant Prussian ally, supplied little military assistance, and its subsidies covered only a fraction of Frederick's expenses. The Prussian king resorted to drastic measures. To increase his supply of specie, he melted down Saxon, Polish, and Russian coins; to fill the depleted ranks of his army, he kidnapped men from Prussia's smaller neighbors, Saxony and Mecklenburg.

Perhaps the most important element in saving Frederick from defeat was the shakiness of the apparently formidable coalition opposing him. Russia's generals were timid, and those of France and Austria often incompetent; moreover, France lacked the resources for effective combat

in Europe and overseas simultaneously. The grand alliance engineered by Kaunitz began to disintegrate when Elizabeth of Russia died in January 1762. Her successor, Tsar Peter III, who admired Frederick as much as she had hated him, at once placed Russian forces at Frederick's disposal. In 1763 Austria accepted a peace settlement confirming Prussia's retention of Silesia.

In the fighting at sea and abroad, the British suffered major setbacks at first. They lost the important Mediterranean base of Minorca in the Balearic Islands. In North America, they gave up their outpost of Oswego on Lake Ontario and fumbled an attack against Louisburg. In India the nawab of Bengal, a French ally, jammed 146 British prisoners into a small stifling room; by morning only 23 had survived the "Black Hole" of Calcutta. The man who turned the tide in Britain's favor was William Pitt, the Elder, the grandson of a merchant who had made a fortune in India. Pitt had been a leader of the "Boy Patriots" protesting Walpole's peaceful policies and served as a member of Parliament from the notorious rotten borough of Old Sarum.

Pitt's great war ministry (1757–1761) ended the vacillation and weakness that had characterized the cabinets since Walpole's downfall in 1742. When deficits rose higher and higher, Pitt utilized his connections with the bankers of the City to secure government loans. He strengthened the alliance with Prussia by increasing the subsidies to Frederick and placing the English forces in Hanover under an able Prussian commander, who replaced a bungling son of George II. As Pitt dismissed other incompetent generals and admirals, Britain began to score victories. In 1759 the Royal Navy defeated both the Atlantic and the Mediterranean squadrons of the French fleet.

Command of the seas enabled the British to continue their prosperous trade abroad, while French overseas trade sank to a sixth of its prewar rate. Cut off from supplies and reinforcements, the French colonies began to fall. In India the British captured the chief French outposts in addition to punishing the nawab of Bengal for the "Black Hole" incident. In the West Indies the French lost most of their lucrative sugar islands. In North America the 65,000 French settlers, inadequately supplied and poorly fed, were no match for the million settlers of the thirteen colonies, fully supported by the mother country. In what the colonists called the French and Indian War, Fort Duquesne was taken and renamed Pittsburgh to honor the prime minister. In 1758, the English general Wolfe captured Louisburg,

North America and the Caribbean, 1763
Situation after the Seven Years' War

the key to Canada, and in the next year was killed as he led his forces to a great victory on the Plains of Abraham outside the city of Quebec. The fall of Montreal in 1760 sealed the doom of France's North American empire.

Pitt had won the war, but he was not allowed to make the peace. George III, who ascended the throne in 1760, soon dismissed Pitt because he feared such a strong and popular minister. In the Peace of Paris, 1763, Pitt's successors outraged British patriots by handing the sugar islands back to the French. However, Britain did acquire Canada and the lands between the Appalachians and the Mississippi. Spain, which had joined France late in the war, ceded its Florida

territories to Britain—East Florida, the peninsula, and West Florida, the coast of the Gulf of Mexico between the peninsula and the Mississippi. As compensation the Spaniards received from the French the city of New Orleans and the vast Louisiana territories west of the Mississippi. In India, France retained a few trading stations but was forbidden to fortify them or to manipulate native rulers. Except in the West Indies, the old French colonial empire virtually ended in 1763.

The Seven Years' War, although decisive in its results, by no means equaled the Thirty Years' War of the preceding century in destructive force. Few of the participants were fighting for a great cause, like Catholicism or Protestantism or national independence. And thanks to the widely observed rules of the game, the actual fighting had become less bloody. Soldiers were better disciplined, armies better supplied, troops less often forced to live off the land. The warfare of the eighteenth century reflected the order and reason characteristic of the Enlightenment.

III ENLIGHTENED DESPOTISM

The half-century preceding the French Revolution was the heyday of enlightened despotism. In Lisbon, Madrid, Florence, Vienna, Copenhagen, Stockholm, Berlin, and even St. Petersburg—in almost every Continental capital except Versailles—monarchs and statesmen claimed they were applying the prescriptions of nature and reason to cure the ills of the Old Regime. These enlightened or benevolent despots appreciated the favorable image to be gained by courting the approval of the philosophes. But, while pursuing the goals of a more modern and efficient state, they also sought to make their authority more absolute.

Frederick the Great

Of all eighteenth-century monarchs, Frederick the Great of Prussia seemed best attuned to the Enlightenment. He relaxed the drill-sergeant methods of his father, delighted in music (he played the flute), corresponded with the philosophes, and even persuaded Voltaire to reside for a time as his pensioner at Potsdam, outside Berlin. Frederick was an eloquent advocate of enlightened statecraft:

> . . . Kings are not clothed with supreme authority to plunge with impunity into debauchery and luxury. . . . [The ruler] should often remind himself that he is a man just as the least of his subjects. If he is the first judge, the first general, the first financier, the first minister of the nation, . . . it is in order to fulfill the duties which these titles impose upon him. He is only the first ser-

Frederick the Great leading a chamber concert at Sans Souci, his palace near Potsdam.

vant of the state, obliged to act with fairness, wisdom, and unselfishness, as if at every instant he would have to render an account of his administration to his citizens.*

Frederick was indeed "the first servant of the state," shunning luxury and ostentation, wearing stained and shabby clothing, and working long and hard at his desk. Yet, despite his pamphlet denouncing the immorality of Machiavelli's *The Prince,* he conducted his foreign and military policies in true Machiavellian style. His surprise invasion of Silesia in 1740 would have won the approval of the famous Florentine. In his Potsdam palace, where he conducted the business of state, he sometimes drove his subordinates like slaves.

To improve Prussian agriculture Frederick imported many innovations from Western Europe: the planting of clover and potatoes, the rotation of crops, and the use of the iron plow which turned over the soil more effectively than the traditional wooden plowshare. He opened new farmlands in Silesia and in the Oder valley, and to work them he brought in 300,000 immigrants, mostly from other areas of Germany. To repair the damage suffered by farms during the Seven Years' War, he gave peasants tools, stock, and seed. He also helped to establish the German tradition of scientific forestry.

The acquisition of Silesia, the expenses of two major wars, the maintenance of a large standing army, and the rapid expansion of the bureaucracy greatly increased the cost of government. This necessitated higher taxation, which fell particularly on the middle class, with an exception, however, for developers of new businesses who received what we would call "tax incentives." Frederick also attempted to strengthen the economy by applying mercantilist measures of cutting imports to the bone. He levied special duties on tobacco, coffee, and other popular commodities that could not be grown at home.

For Frederick the state was of overwhelming importance, and he treated his subjects accordingly. He had no use for the middle class as a whole and, as soon as the Seven Years' War was over, forced all bourgeois officers to resign from the army. Yet he did appoint those of its members he considered especially capable to civilian administrative posts. While the landed nobility and

gentry were Frederick's favorites, even they did not escape his penny-pinching. For example, he discouraged Junker officers from marrying in order to reduce the number of potential widows to whom the state would owe a pension.

Frederick was astute enough to realize the vital importance of the peasants for a state rooted in agriculture. He made no effort, however, to remove the shackles of serfdom binding many of them, especially in East Prussia. When he urged peasants to learn the 3 R's, he wanted them to acquire only a minimum of literacy; greater knowledge might make them dissatisfied with their position as "beasts of burden."

As a deist, Frederick prided himself on his tolerance. When Jesuits were expelled from Catholic states, he invited them to predominantly Protestant Prussia. He gave Prussia's Catholic minority, particularly important in Silesia, virtually full equality and urged them to build their church steeples as high as they liked. On the other hand, he treated the Jewish population harshly, declaring they were "useless to the state," subjecting them to special heavy taxes, and virtually excluding them from the professions and the civil service.

Frederick's enlightenment was perhaps most evident in his judicial reforms. He authorized his able minister, Cocceji, to introduce changes which freed the courts from political pressure and reduced the use of torture. The traditional bribery of underpaid judges was watered down by arranging that their "tips" be placed in a common pool from which each magistrate should draw only his fair share.

Frederick found it difficult to get along with people; he neglected his wife and quarreled repeatedly with Voltaire. He gave favorite dogs and horses special house privileges and directed in his will that he be buried alongside his dogs. "Such," remarked a French observer, "is the last mark of contempt he thought proper to cast upon mankind." This verdict has been sustained by many liberal historians who dismiss Frederick's enlightenment as a cynical attempt to clothe his naked absolutism with the decent intellectual garments of the age. It can be argued as well, however, that Frederick tried to fuse two largely incompatible philosophies—the Spartan traditions of the Hohenzollerns and the humane principles of the Enlightenment. The former, with its Calvinist conviction of man's sinfulness, prevented him from sharing the Enlightenment's optimism about the human potential. Frederick the Great was an enlightened despot only when the

---

* "Essai sur les Formes de Gouvernement et sur les Devoirs de Souverains," *Oeuvres Posthumes* (Berlin, 1788), VI: 64, 83–84. Our translation.

precepts of reason did not interfere with the imperatives of Prussian kingship.

Maria Theresa and Joseph II

Prussia's decisive victory in the War of the Austrian Succession convinced the empress Maria Theresa (1740–1780) of the urgent need to reform the weak structure of Hapsburg government. She often took as a model the institutions of her hated Hohenzollern rival, but unlike Frederick she depended heavily on capable ministers schooled in cameralism (see Chapter 10) which stressed raising revenues and increasing administrative efficiency. The empress and her experts required their non-German provinces to accept the German officials of Vienna and employ German as the language of administration. They strengthened the central government at the expense of local aristocratic assemblies and increased taxes, especially on the nobility. Though Maria Theresa did not force the nobles to free the serfs on their estates, she set an example by liberating serfs on the Hapsburg family holdings. Her concern for the welfare of her subjects led them to honor her as "mother of the country."

Catherine the Great, however, called her "Lady Prayerful" and mocked her devotion to the Church. Personal piety did not keep Maria Theresa from subjecting the Church to heavy taxation, confiscating some monastic property, and expelling the Jesuits. On the other hand, she had little respect for the Enlightenment, banned the writings of Rousseau and Voltaire in her domains, and forbade circulation of the Catholic *Index* lest its list of improper books arouse the curiosity of her subjects. Some historians question whether Maria Theresa was an enlightened despot, reserving that distinction for her eldest son, Joseph II.

Joseph became emperor after the death of his father in 1765 and ruled jointly with his mother until her death in 1780. Often thwarted by her when he attempted enlightened experiments, the impatient Joseph plunged into activity when she died. During his ten years as sole ruler (1780–1790), eleven thousand laws and six thousand decrees were issued from Vienna. The frenzied pace created the impression that the son's policies ran counter to his mother's. In fact, their goals were often the same, but Joseph's methods were much more drastic and less conciliatory.

Joseph did make real innovations in religious policy. For the first time in the history of Catholic Austria, Calvinist, Lutheran, and Orthodox Christians gained full toleration. The emperor also took measures to end the persecution of Jews, exempting them from special taxes and from wearing a yellow patch on their garments as a badge of inferiority. He intensified his mother's efforts to control the Church and insisted that he, rather than the pope, was the ultimate arbiter of ecclesiastical matters in Hapsburg territories. He encouraged what he believed to be socially useful in Catholicism and dealt ruthlessly with what he judged superfluous. He established hundreds of new churches in areas neglected by the clergy and at the same time suppressed 700 of the 2,100 monasteries and nunneries, sparing those active in educational or charitable work. Revenues from the properties of the suppressed establishments supported the hospitals that earned Vienna its reputation as a medical center.

In contrast to Frederick the Great, Joseph really believed in popular education and social equality. His government furnished the teachers and textbooks for primary schools, which were attended by more than a quarter of the schoolage children in Austria—the best record of any country in Europe at the time. A new legal code followed Beccaria's recommendations by abolishing capital punishment, limiting the use of torture, and prescribing equality before the law. Aristocratic offenders, like commoners, had to stand in the pillory and sweep the streets of Vienna as punishment. He freed the serfs and ended most of their obligations to manorial lords, who were deprived of their traditional right of administering justice to the peasantry.

Joseph also made a disastrous experiment with the Physiocrats' proposal of a single tax on land applied equally to the farms of the peasantry and the estates of the aristocracy. The opposition of the nobility was so violent that he had to revoke the decree a month after it was issued. Even the peasants, whose status he had so improved, keenly resented his reducing the number of religious holidays and meddling with other religious customs.

Not all Joseph's policies were enlightened. He followed the mercantilist tradition by maintaining high protective tariffs and supervising all aspects of the economy. He continued his mother's efforts to advance the German language and German officials. He also endeavored to terminate the autonomous rights of his non-German possessions, notably Bohemia, Hungary, and Belgium. But Hungary and Belgium rose in rebellion against his centralizing efforts and forced him to reconfirm their autonomous rights.

Joseph II worked himself to death, as a

Batoni's painting of Joseph II
with the future emperor Leopold II.

friend observed, "by governing too much and reigning too little." Unlike his mother, who used flattery and charm to disarm opponents, Joseph simply laid down the law. He died unshaken in the conviction that he had always pursued the proper course, yet believing that he had accomplished nothing. He was wrong on both counts.

Catherine the Great

Although most lists of enlightened despots include the name of Catherine the Great, Russian

Catherine the Great.

empress from 1762 to 1796, she had relatively few qualifications for this distinction. When she became empress, the Russian autocracy had been without an effective autocrat since the death of Peter in 1725. During the next thirty-seven years, Russia had seven rulers, mainly children or politically ineffectual women. At first, the old boyar families gained the upper hand with a program of revoking Peter's hated changes. But the military-service nobility, fearing a permanent boyar ascendancy, seized power with the help of the guards regiments established by Peter. The guards caused a series of palace overturns, one of which brought to the throne the daughter of Peter the Great, the empress Elizabeth (1741–1762).

Elizabeth inherited her father's lust for life but not his ability or interest in matters of state. Important state papers languished for days unread and unsigned. When she died in January, 1762, the succession passed to her nephew, Peter III, who was more German than Russian and who greatly admired Frederick the Great. His effort to apply rigid discipline on the Prussian model to the Russian army and his hatred of the guards regiments cost him the friends he needed most. A palace revolution in July 1762 transferred the throne to his wife Catherine, a German princess whom he had married in 1745. One of her lovers eventually murdered Peter; her own role in this overthrow remains obscure.

The Russia over which Catherine ruled had undergone many changes since Peter the Great. The military-service nobility freed itself from some of the demands imposed by Peter, shortening its term of service from life to twenty-five years and arranging that in every family with two or more sons one would be exempted from service to look after the family estate. The nobles also increased their authority over the serfs, who could no longer obtain freedom by enlisting in the army nor engage in trade or purchase land without written permission from their masters. Under Elizabeth, the right of owning serfs was restricted to those who were already nobles, and the class that had been open to new recruits under Peter the Great was closed by his daughter. Then, in 1762, Peter III decreed that the nobles no longer need serve in the army unless they chose to do so.

When Catherine II became empress, she was already accomplished in political maneuvering. Brought up in a petty German court, then transplanted to St. Petersburg as a mere girl, living with a husband she detested, she learned to deal with the intrigues surrounding the empress Elizabeth. She fancied herself an intellectual, wrote plays, edited a satirical journal, and devoured the literature of the Enlightenment. Since she anticipated the modern concern for public relations, she wanted leading spirits in the West to think well of her and also of conditions in Russia under her rule. Voltaire accepted her bounty and in return praised her as "the north star" and "the benefactress of Europe." To assist Diderot, the editor of the *Encyclopédie,* Catherine purchased his library, then allowed him to keep his books and added a pension.

There was something of the enlightened despot about Catherine's style, but as a woman, a foreigner, and a usurper who owed the throne to a conspiracy, she had to proceed very cautiously. Depending upon the good will of the nobility, she could not lay a finger on the institution of serfdom. And she had to reward her supporters with vast grants of state lands, inhabited by hundreds of thousands of state serfs, who now became privately owned and subject to sale by their new owners. Moreover, she was convinced that the vastness of Russia made autocracy the only possible form of government.

Once firmly established as empress, Catherine convoked a commission to codify the laws of Russia. With the help of advisers, she spent three years composing the *Instruction* to the delegates, a document based on arguments drawn from the writings of Montesquieu and Beccaria but revised to conform with her own convictions. The *Instruction* showed no intention to meddle with fundamentals but some concern for eliminating the worst abuses. The 564 delegates to the commission were elected by organs of the central government and by every social class in Russia except the serf peasants. Each delegate was charged to bring written documents from his neighbors presenting their grievances and requests for change.

Many of these documents survive and tell a great deal about the state of public opinion in Catherine's Russia. Although nobody seems to have been dissatisfied with the autocracy, each class of delegates was eager to extend its own rights. Free peasants wanted to own serfs; townsmen wanted to own serfs and be the only class allowed to engage in trade; nobles wanted to engage in trade and to have their exclusive right to own serfs confirmed. After 203 sessions lasting over a year and a half, Catherine ended the labors of the commission in 1768. Although it had not codified the laws, it was the sole effort to consult the Russian people as a whole for 138 years—until revolution summoned the first Duma into existence in 1906.

Catherine utilized the spadework of the legislative commission in her later reforms, which resulted from the great rebellion of the Cossacks led by Pugachev, 1773–1775. Pugachev roused the frontiersmen to revolt against Catherine's cancellation of their special privileges. Pretending to be tsar Peter III, and promising liberty and land to the serfs, he swept over a wide area of southeastern Russia and finally marched toward Moscow. His revolt revealed the existence of bitter discontent, not with the supreme autocrat but with landlords and local officials. The ramshackle provincial administration almost collapsed under the strain of this rebellion, and when the rebels were finally suppressed, Catherine reorganized local government, creating fifty provinces to replace the twenty old ones. The reform of 1775 gave the nobles the lion's share of provincial offices but subjected them to close supervision by the central government's representatives in each province.

Ten years later a charter completely exempted the nobles from military service and taxation and gave them absolute mastery over their serfs and their estates. A charter for the towns established the principle of municipal self-government, but it remained a dead letter because of the rigorous class distinctions in the urban centers. For the serfs there was no charter. Besides adding almost a million to their number by the gifts of state lands to individuals, Catherine gave proprietors the right to sell serfs without land. Serf families were broken up; serfs were gambled away at cards, given as presents, and mortgaged for loans. However, serfowners did made a distinction between field hands and household servants, who were often treated with kindness. Great landowners often had hundreds of the latter, some of whom were musicians or actors, tutors of children, and household poets and scientists.

In foreign policy Catherine was vigorous and unscrupulous. In 1763, the throne of Poland fell vacant, and Catherine secured the election of her former lover, a pro-Russian Pole, Stanislas Poniatowski. When Catherine joined Frederick the Great in a campaign to win rights for the persecuted Lutheran and Orthodox minorities in Catholic Poland, a party of Polish nobles resisted this foreign intervention. They secured the aid of France and Austria, which prevailed on Turkey to go to war with Catherine to distract her from Poland.

In the Russo-Turkish War (1768–1774), Catherine's forces won a series of victories that convinced Frederick the Great he must act quickly to keep Russia from seizing most of Poland. He arranged the first partition of Poland (1772), which reduced Polish territory by a third and the population by one half. Frederick's gain, though the smallest, included the strategic region linking East Prussia with Brandenburg. Russia obtained a substantial part of White Russia (today called Belorussia). And Maria Theresa, abandoning her Turkish and Polish allies, acquired the large province of Galicia.

Two years later, Russia imposed on Turkey the peace of Kutchuk Kainardji (1774). Catherine annexed much of the Ottoman lands along the Black Sea and obliged the Turks to yield their overlordship of the Tatar state of the Crimea, which became independent. Russia also secured freedom of navigation on the Black Sea and through the Bosporus and Dardanelles. A vaguely worded clause gave Russia rights to protect the Christian subjects of the sultan, thus providing an excuse for future Russian intervention in Turkish affairs. Catherine now dreamed of expelling the Turks from Europe and reviving the Byzantine Empire as a Russian protectorate. In preparation, she annexed the Tatar state of the Crimea, where she built a naval base at Sebastopol. In a second Russo-Turkish War (1787–1791), difficulties with Austria obliged Catherine to give up her Byzantine dream and be content with acquiring the remaining Turkish lands along the north coast of the Black Sea.

In 1793, the second partition of Poland gave Russia and Prussia two more generous slices of territory. A revolution attempted by the Poles against the reduction of their state to a foreign-dominated remnant resulted in the third and final partition (1795). Austria obtained the Cracow region; Prussia, the region of Warsaw; and Russia, Lithuania and other Baltic and east Polish lands. The spectacular successes of Catherine meant the acquisition of millions of people—Poles, Lithuanians, Belorussians—who loathed the Russians and left a legacy of trouble. By destroying useful Polish and Tatar buffers, Russia now had frontiers directly bordering two potential enemies, Prussia and Austria.

Pombal, Charles III and Leopold

Although Catherine was a most successful expansionist, she had less claim to the title of "enlightened despot" than did several of her contemporaries. In Portugal the marquis of Pombal, the prime minister of King Joseph I (reigned 1750–1777), made his reputation by the rapid and attractive rebuilding of Lisbon after the devastating earthquake in 1755. He also tried to diversify the Portuguese economy, making it less dependent on the export of a single commodity, the port wine shipped to Britain. He loosened the grip of the Catholic church on Portuguese life by ousting the Jesuits, extended religious toleration, and modernized the curriculum of the national university at Coimbra. He reduced the influence of the nobles by attacking their rights of inheritance but went far beyond the bounds of enlightenment by jailing thousands of them for alleged involvement in aristocratic plots against his regime.

In neighboring Spain, the crown passed to Elizabeth Farnese's son, Carlos, who became King Charles III (reigned 1759–1788). He had already struggled with the forces of feudalism and the Church during a long apprenticeship in Naples as king of the Two Sicilies. On returning to Madrid, he energetically advanced the progressive policies begun by his father, Philip V. He exiled the Jesuits, reduced the political influence of the Church and the aristocracy, and extended that of the crown. To stimulate the economy, he established banks and textile mills, built roads and

Charles III of Spain in hunting costume, by Goya.

canals, and aided the development of agriculture by extending irrigation and reclaiming wastelands. Spain's foreign commerce increased by a whopping 500 percent during his reign. Under his successors, however, Spain slipped back into its old lethargic ways.

The least of the enlightened states in size, the Grand Duchy of Tuscany was a leader in enlightened achievement during the reign of Grand Duke Leopold (1765–1790), a brother of Joseph II. Leopold made the administration more efficient, reformed the judicial system along the humane lines proposed by Beccaria, and increased commercial activity at Tuscany's thriving port of Leghorn. Unlike Joseph, Leopold actively enlisted the participation of his subjects in government. He was considering the creation of a representative assembly modeled on that of Virginia when he was recalled to Vienna in 1790 to succeed Joseph as Austrian emperor.

Two centuries after the peak of the Enlightenment, it requires some historical perspective to evaluate the achievements of the benevolent despots. They were not elected leaders publicly committed to supporting certain policies, but hereditary rulers or their agents who followed what they judged to be the best policies for their subjects but still more for themselves. On the whole, only a few lasting innovations and reforms were achieved by the despots. They expended much energy in pursuit of doctrinaire goals, or improving the ruler's image, or catering to the Old Regime values of the nobility. The fate of their policies in the future depended almost entirely on the rulers who inherited the crown; they proved to be unenlightened mediocrities. Consequently, the most enduring achievements of the Enlightenment were made not by the benevolent monarchs but by the revolutionaries in France and in America.

The Eighteenth Century

In the eighteenth century the grandiose extravaganzas of baroque yielded to lighter and more delicate artistic styles. In Italy, Guardi painted a series of landscapes that he termed "fantastic" with a dreamlike quality anticipating the romantic movement that would emerge at the end of the century, and Canaletto painted views of Venice with subtly colored clouds and sky, though the canals below were thronged with ordinary citizens going about their daily rounds. In France, the paintings of Watteau and Fragonard exemplified the spontaneity and intimacy of the style called *rococo* (from the popularity of motifs derived from rock formations and shells, espe-cially in interior decoration). Another development was the emergence of Britain and her former American colonies into artistic prominence thanks to a series of accomplished portraitists—Hogarth, Lawrence, Reynolds, Gainsborough, and Romney in the one, Gilbert Stuart and Copley in the other. For the most part, eighteenth-century painting reflected the aristocratic old regime at its most elegant and frivolous, but it also hinted at the more democratic subjects and the new concern with color and light that would revolutionize the arts in the century to come.

Fantastic Landscape, by Francesco Guardi.
The Metropolitan Museum of Art,
gift of Julia A. Berwind, 1953.

Scer
The

James Monroe, by Gilbert Stuart, 1817.
The Metropolitan Museum of Art, bequest of Seth Low, 1929.

IV THE AMERICAN REVOLT

The course of the American Revolution was followed closely by European rulers and statesmen. The breach between the thirteen colonies and the mother country became serious after the Seven Years' War. The vast territories in Canada and beyond the Appalachians acquired by Britain in 1763 brought added opportunities for profitable exploitation and added responsibilities for government and defense. Unrest among the Indians prompted the royal proclamation of October 1763, forbidding settlement west of a line running along the summit of the Allegheny Mountains between Virginia and New York. Colonists attacked the proclamation line as a deliberate attempt to exclude them from the riches of the West. They resented still more keenly British efforts to raise more revenue in North America.

The British had a strong case for increasing colonial taxes. Their national debt had almost doubled during the Seven Years' War, in part because the colonies were reluctant to recruit soldiers or levy taxes. In addition, the mother country faced the continued expense of protecting the frontier. But the first of the new revenue measures, the Sugar Act of 1764, alarmed the merchants of the eastern seaboard because customs officers required payment of duties on molasses, sugar, and other imports. This was an unpleasant departure from the comfortable laxity of "salutary neglect." Then the Stamp Act of 1765 imposed levies on legal and commercial papers, liquor licenses, playing cards, newspapers, among other items. Indignant merchants boycotted all imports rather than pay the duties, and delegates from nine colonies met in New York as the Stamp Act Congress (October 1765), which proclaimed the celebrated principle of no taxation without representation.

Although Britain did not yield on the principle, it did repeal the Stamp Act. In 1767, Parliament again tried to raise revenue, this time by duties on colonial imports of tea, paper, paint, and lead; again, there were boycotts by colonial merchants. In 1770, the duties were withdrawn except for the three-penny tariff on a pound of tea, retained as a symbol of parliamentary authority over the colonies. Three years later, the English East India Company, found it had a surplus of unsold tea and lowered its price in the colonies so that, duty included, its tea would be much

cheaper than the Dutch tea smuggled by colonists. On December 16, 1773, a group of Bostonians with a large financial stake in smuggled tea disguised themselves as Indians, boarded three East India Company ships in the harbor, and dumped overboard chests of tea worth thousands of pounds.

Britain answered the Boston Tea Party with the Quebec Act (1774), incorporating the lands beyond the Alleghenies into Canada, thus bolting the door to colonial expansion westward. The "Intolerable Acts" of the same year closed the port of Boston to trade, suspended elections in Massachusetts, and imposed still other restraints that outraged its inhabitants. In April 1775, the "embattled farmers" at Lexington and Concord fired the opening shots of the War of Independence. More than a year passed, however, before delegates to the Continental Congress at Philadelphia formally declared the independence of the colonies on July 4, 1776.

The crucial battle in the War of Independence took place at Saratoga, New York, north of Albany, in 1777. General Burgoyne was forced to surrender the British forces which had marched south from Montreal hoping to drive a wedge between New England and the other colonies. Burgoyne's surrender convinced the French that support of the American colonists would enable them to renew and win their "Second Hundred Years' War" with Britain. Entering the war in 1778, France gained the alliance of Spain and eventually secured the help, or at least the friendly neutrality, of most other European states. French intervention prepared the way for the victory of George Washington's forces and the final British surrender at Yorktown in 1781. In the peace signed at Paris in 1783, Britain recognized the independence of the thirteen colonies. Spain recovered East and West Florida as well as the strategic Mediterranean island of Minorca, but not Gibraltar.

The revolution did not command unanimous support from the colonists. Many of the well-to-do, including Southern planters and Pennsylvania Quakers, either assumed a neutral posture or actively backed the mother country. New York furnished more recruits to the forces of George III than to those of George Washington. Scholars, however, now believe that the traditional estimate—that only a third of the colonists actively backed the revolution—is too low. Revolutionary sentiment ran particularly high in Virginia and in New England, and also among frontiersmen and among certain religious sects, notably the Presbyterians and the Congregationalists.

At the Constitutional Convention in Philadelphia, 1787, the delegates founded the Constitution of the young republic on the separation of powers proposed by Locke and Montesquieu. Each of the three branches of government—executive, legislative, and judicial—had some power to check the other two. The president, for instance, might check Congress by a veto. Congress could check the executive and the courts by refusing to enact proposed legislation, by rejecting appointees to office and, in extreme cases, by impeachment. The Supreme Court could decide the constitutionality of presidential and congressional acts.

The first ten amendments to the Constitution (1791), adapted from England's Bill of Rights of 1689, guaranteed freedom of religion, freedom of speech, and other basic liberties. The democracy and liberty of the new republic, nevertheless were diluted by the legal recognition of slavery in many states and by the right of each state to determine who was eligible to vote. A majority of them imposed significant property qualifications, which were not to be lifted for a generation or more. But on the whole the Founding Fathers of the United States succeeded better than any other leaders of the age in adjusting the ideals of the philosophes to the realities of practical politics.

READING SUGGESTIONS on *Politics and War in the Eighteenth Century*
(Asterisks indicate paperback.)

General Works

Three volumes in the series, *The Rise of Modern Europe* (Harper), W. L. Langer, ed., available in many college libraries, provide a detailed survey of the century and have lengthy bibliographies: P. Roberts, *The Quest for Security, 1715–1740* (1947); W. L. Dorn, *Competition for Empire, 1740–1763* (1940); and L. Gershoy, *From Despotism to Revolution, 1763–1789* (1944).

M. S. Anderson, *Europe in the Eighteenth Century, 1713–1783* 2nd ed. (*Longmans) and R. J. White, *Europe in the Eighteenth Century* (St. Martin's). More recent and less detailed introductions by British scholars.

L. Krieger, *Kings and Philosophers, 1689–1789* (*Norton). A thoughtful survey by an American scholar.

A. Goodwin, ed., *The European Nobility in the Eighteenth Century* (Black, 1953). Very helpful essays on the still powerful artistocrats, arranged country by country.

P. Goubert, *The Ancien Régime* (Harper, 1973). A wide-ranging study of the Old Regime in France from 1600 to 1750, by a French scholar.

G. P. Gooch, *Courts and Cabinets* (Arno). A graceful introduction to the memoirs of some of the great personages of the time.

Britain

J. Plumb, *England in the Eighteenth Century* (*Penguin). A good, brief account by a British scholar who has also written studies of Walpole, Pitt, and the first four Georgian kings.

J. R. Jones, *Country and Court, 1658–1714* and W. A. Speck, *Stability and Strife, 1714–1760* (*Harvard U.). Two volumes in the recently published "New History of England."

L. B. Namier, *England in the Age of the American Revolution* (*St. Martin's). A controversial revision of traditional concepts of English political institutions in the eighteenth century.

R. Hatton, *George the First* (Harvard, 1978). A scholarly biography defending the importance and effectiveness of his rule.

J. S. Watson, *The Reign of George III* (Oxford). Enlightening general account of British history from 1760 to 1815.

G. Rudé, *Wilkes and Liberty* (*Oxford). Detailed analysis of the unrest in Britain during the early years of George III's reign.

H. Fielding, *Tom Jones* (*several editions). The greatest of the social novels on mid-eighteenth century England.

T. Smollett, *The Adventures of Roderick Random* (*Dutton). A realistic novel of life in His Majesty's Navy when George II was king.

France

A. Cobban, *A History of Modern France,* Vol. I (*Penguin). Informative survey from 1715 to 1799 by a British scholar.

C. B. A. Behrens, *The Ancien Régime* (*Harcourt Brace). Readable study of society in France, with copious illustrations.

F. Ford, *Robe and Sword* (Harvard, 1953). Instructive examination of the French aristocracy after the death of Louis XIV.

G. P. Gooch, *Louis XV* (Greenwood); and N. Mitford, *Madame de Pompadour* rev. ed. (Harper, 1968). Lively biographies of the king who refused to rule and of his enlightened mistress.

Spain

R. Herr, *The Eighteenth-Century Revolution in Spain* (Princeton, 1958). Important reappraisal of the effect of the enlightenment on Spain. More recently, Herr has published *A Historical Essay on Modern Spain* (*University of California).

Austria

A. Wandruszka, *The House of Hapsburg* (Sidgwick & Jackson, 1964). A useful history of the famous dynasty.

C. A. Macartney, *Maria Theresa and the House of Austria* (Verry, 1969); E. Crankshaw, *Maria Theresa* (Viking, 1969); Karl Roider, ed., *Maria Theresa* (*Prentice-Hall). Three informative studies of the famous empress.

Prussia

H. Holborn, *A History of Modern Germany,* Vol. II (Knopf, 1964). Succinct survey from 1648 to 1840.

F. L. Carsten, *The Origins of Prussia* (Oxford, 1954). Excellent monograph that carries the story through the reign of the Great Elector.

F. Schevill, *The Great Elector* (University of Chicago, 1947). Informative study of the founding father of Prussian despotism.

R. R. Ergang, *The Potsdam Führer* (Columbia, 1941). A splendid analysis of Frederick William I.

H. Rosenberg, *Bureaucracy, Aristocracy, Autocracy* (*Beacon). An interpretation of Prussian history, 1660–1815.

G. Craig, *The Politics of the Prussian Army, 1640–1945* (*Oxford). Splendid scholarly study ranging well beyond the limits of this chapter.

Russia

E. Schuyler, *Peter the Great* (Scribner's, 1884). Still a remarkably good study, by an American diplomat.

V. Klyuchevsky, *Peter the Great* (*Vintage). Another good older evaluation.

B. H. Sumner, *Peter the Great and the Emergence of Russia* (*Collier). Admirable brief account.

M. S. Anderson, *Peter the Great* (Thames & Hudson, 1978). Recent evaluation by an able British scholar.

M. Raeff, *Imperial Russia, 1682–1825* (Knopf, 1971). Informative survey of the Russian advance to the status of a great power.

A. Lentin, *Russia in the Eighteenth Century* (Heinemann, 1973). A fairly brief account, directed to students.

D. Merezhkovsky, *Peter and Alexis* (Putnam, 1905). A novel about the conflict between the great tsar and his son.

The Enlightened Despots

L. Krieger, *An Essay on the Theory of Enlightened Despotism* (University of Chicago, 1975). A scholarly evaluation.

J. Gagliardo, *Enlightened Despotism,* 2nd ed. (*AHM). Brief and informative.

W. Hubatsch, *Frederick the Great* (Thames & Hudson, 1977). Stresses his absolutism and administration.

G. Ritter, *Frederick the Great* (University of California, 1966). Well-balanced lectures by a German scholar.

L. Reniers, *Frederick the Great* (Oswald Wolff, 1960). A critical estimate.

H. C. Johnson, *Frederick the Great and his Officials* (Yale U., 1975). Examines an important aspect of his reign often neglected by scholars.

T. Blanning, *Joseph Second and Enlightened Despotism* (Longmans, 1970). Good brief introduction.

P. P. Bernard, *Joseph II* (Twayne, 1968). Appraisal by a scholar who has also written more detailed works on Joseph's reign.

S. K. Padover, *The Revolutionary Emperor,* 2nd. ed. (Shoestring, 1967). Highly enthusiastic about Joseph II, but not about Maria Theresa.

J. Haslip, *Catherine the Great* (Putnam, 1977); and V. Cronin, *Catherine: Empress of all the Russias* (Morrow, 1978). Recent biographies.

G. S. Thomson, *Catherine the Great and the Expansion of Russia* (*Collier). A sound brief appraisal.

L. J. Oliva, *Catherine the Great* (*Spectrum); and M. Raeff, ed. *Catherine the Great: A Profile* (*Hill & Wang). Informative studies of the empress.

The American Revolt

C. Becker, *The Declaration of Independence* (Peter Smith). Older scholarly study stressing the influence of the Enlightenment upon the Founding Fathers and other Americans.

G. Wills, *Inventing America* (*Vintage). A recent popular account of the Declaration.

B. Bailyn, *Ideological Origins of the American Revolution* (*Harvard) and J. Miller, *Origins of the American Revolution* (*Stanford). Illuminating scholarly studies of the background of the revolt.

E. S. Morgan, *The Birth of the Republic, 1763–1789,* rev. ed. (*University of Chicago); L. H. Gipson, *The Coming of the Revolution, 1763–1775* (*Harper); and J. R. Alden, *The American Revolution, 1775–1783* (*Harper). Standard scholarly accounts.

CHAPTER TWELVE

The French Revolution

The year 1789 is one of the great milestones of modern history, for it marked the beginning of the revolution in the most powerful state on the Continent of Europe. The revolutionary motto—*Liberté, Egalité, Fraternité* ("Liberty, Equality, Fraternity")— seemed to promise a new democratic regime. What it actually provided was a republic dependent first on the Reign of Terror, then on the less terrible but less democratic Directory, and finally on the autocracy of Napoleon, who transformed the First Republic into the First Empire. His determination to dominate the whole of Europe led to his ultimate defeat and the restoration of the Bourbons. But by then the ideology of liberty, equality, fraternity had attracted so many supporters not only in France but also among victims of the French expansion that a full restoration of the Old Regime was impossible.

THE DESTRUCTION OF THE OLD REGIME

In France, as in the thirteen American colonies, a financial crisis helped to trigger a revolution. There was not only a parallel but also a direct link between the revolutions of 1776 and 1789. The cost of French involvement in the War of Independence increased the already unmanageable French debt by more than a third, and the example of the new republic overseas convinced many philosophes that dramatic changes were possible in Europe as well. But the American Revolution only accelerated a French crisis that had long been under way. Just as the reasons for revolution were more deeply rooted and more complex in France, the revolution itself was more violent and more sweeping.

Behind the immediate French crisis of the 1780s lay many decades of financial mismanagement that reached back into the seventeenth century. The nobles and clergy, jealous of their traditional privileges, refused to pay their fair share of taxes. Resentment against unfair taxes and inefficient government built up among the unprivileged majority—the bourgeoisie, the workers, and the peasants. King Louis XV had refused to take decisive steps to remedy the abuses of the Old Regime, and what he would not do his grandson and successor, Louis XVI (reigned 1774–1792), could not do. The new king was honest, earnest, and pious, but also both stubborn and unpredictable; he was most at home hunting, eating, and working as an amateur locksmith. Joseph II, his brother-in-law, criticized him for treating petty intrigues with the greatest attention and neglecting important affairs of state. His queen, Marie Antoinette, the fifteenth of Maria Theresa's six-

Left: Marie Antoinette and her children, by Madame Vigée-Lebrun. Right: David's sketch of the queen on her way to the guillotine.

teen children, was poorly educated, extravagant, and isolated in the artificial little world of Versailles. To French patriots she was also a constant reminder of the ill-fated Bourbon-Hapsburg alliance in the Seven Years' War.

That the French government functioned at all was a credit to a relatively few capable administrators, notably the intendants, the royal officials who ran much of provincial France. But they could not codify the law to eliminate medieval survivals or overhaul the courts to make them act swiftly, fairly, and inexpensively. Many judges and lawyers, who had purchased or inherited their offices, regarded them mainly as an avenue to private wealth and admission to the nobility of the robe. Their great stronghold, the courts called parlements, had been suppressed by Louis XV toward the close of his reign then restored when Louis XVI gained the throne. Many Frenchmen applauded their revival as a check on royal absolutism but failed to realize that the parlements were also a formidable obstacle to needed social and economic reform.

The Three Estates

The social and economic foundations of the Old Regime were beginning to crumble. The first estate, the clergy, still controlled extensive property and performed many functions that are normally undertaken by the state today—running schools, recording vital statistics, and dispensing relief to the poor. But the Gallican Church, the semi-independent French Catholic institution, was a house divided. The bishops and abbots were usually recruited from the nobility and retained an aristocratic outlook. Although some of them took their duties seriously, dozens let subordinates run their bishoprics or monasteries, pocketing most of the revenues themselves and residing in Paris or Versailles. The lower clergy were drawn almost entirely from the third estate, and they were for the most part poorly paid and hard-working. These parish priests resented the wealth and arrogance of their superiors.

The worldliness of the Church aroused much criticism. Good Catholics deplored the declining number of monks and nuns; taxpayers hated the tithe levied by the Church and complained about the meager amount of the "free gift" the clergy voted to pay the government in lieu of taxes. On the whole the peasants remained moderately faithful Catholics and regarded the local priest with esteem and affection. In the cities and towns, however, many bourgeois accepted the anticlericalism of the Enlightenment and were eager to strip the Church of wealth and power.

The second estate, the nobles of the Old Regime, also enjoyed privilege, wealth—and unpopularity. Forming less than 2 percent of the population, they held about 20 percent of the land, were almost exempt from taxation, and monopolized commissions in the upper echelons of the army and navy. At the top of the second estate were the nobles of the sword, only a few of whom were descendants of medieval feudal lords; most came from families ennobled within the past two or three centuries. Ranking next were the nobles of the robe, including judges and a host of important officials, whose ancestors had risen to aristocratic status by buying their offices. By the late eighteenth century, intermarriage of the two noble groups was frequent, and the nobles of the robe were becoming more affluent as they invested in such business ventures as the Anzin coal mines and the Baccarat glassworks. The ablest defenders of special privilege in the dying years of the Old Regime were the rich judges of parlement, not the nobles of the sword who were elegant but ineffectual courtiers at Versailles.

Many noblemen, however, belonged neither to the sword or to the robe and were too poor to leave their estates. Hard pinched by rising prices, they insisted on the meticulous collection of their feudal and manorial dues and found old documents to justify levies long forgotten. Accordingly their peasants hated them. Not every noble, however, was a snobbish courtier, a selfish defender of the status quo, or a grasping landlord. Some of the grandest noble families produced enlightened spirits. The marquis de Lafayette returned from the American war to champion reform at home and in 1787 helped secure a partial emancipation of Protestants from the severe restrictions imposed by Louis XIV when he revoked the Edict of Nantes in 1685. Meanwhile, young bloods were applauding the ingenious valet, Figaro, when he outwitted his aristocratic employers in Beaumarchais' satire, *The Marriage of Figaro*, the great hit of the Paris stage in 1784.

In 1789 the first two estates represented only a small fraction of the French population, 98 percent of whom fell within the third estate. The great majority were peasants, whose status was in some respects more favorable in France than it was anywhere in Europe. Serfdom had largely disappeared, and it is estimated that in France three quarters of the peasantry held at least some land. The great problem was that their holdings were so small, less than a third of the total land in France, and in poor crop years the average landholder was threatened with starvation. The danger of local famines was increased by the restrictions on free movement of grain within France which had been imposed to keep local flour for local consumption but instead promoted hoarding and speculation. Peasants who held no land and were unable to find steady farmwork drifted to the cities or became brigands.

Prices rose in France throughout the eighteenth century, bringing prosperity to many towns but adding the hardships of inflation to the backward rural economy. The price of the products sold by farmers rose less swiftly than that of the goods they bought. To the Church the peasants paid the tithe, and to the nobility feudal and manorial dues. To the state they owed a land tax, an income tax, a poll tax, and still other duties, of which the most resented was the *gabelle*, the obligatory purchase of salt from government agents at a high price. Though there were no rural uprisings in France in the decades before 1789, unemployment and poverty fostered a revolutionary temper among the peasants. They wanted more land, if need be from the clergy and the nobility; they wanted an end to obsolete manorial dues and relief from taxation that bore hardest upon those least able to pay.

The other members of the third estate, the urban workers and bourgeoisie, had little reason to cherish the Old Regime. Labor, in the modern sense of a large body of industrial workers, hardly existed in prerevolutionary France, which had few large factories. Some villages and almost every town, however, had wage earners and apprentices employed in small businesses or workshops—for example, weavers and hatters. Although these workers were pinched by rising prices, they were unorganized and did not take a leading role in the revolution.

Leadership came from the bourgeoisie, a category that included Frenchmen of very divergent resources and interests—rich merchants and bankers; doctors, lawyers, and other professional men; storekeepers and many thousands of craftsmen who ran their own little businesses. Hostility toward the privileged estates and a warm response to the ideas of the philosophes cemented this sprawling middle class into a powerful political force. The bourgeoisie suffered fewer hardships than the peasants and workers but resented the abuses of the Old Regime even more keenly. Though they paid a smaller proportion of their income in taxes, they violently denounced the inequality of assessments. Enterprising businessmen profited by the rise in prices yet complained about guild regulations and other restraints on free commercial activity. They found it galling to be snubbed by nobles and excluded from posts of power in government, church, and army.

The men of the middle class took the leading part in formulating the grievances of the entire third estate, which were compiled in a large number of *cahiers* (notebooks) and submitted to the Estates General in 1789. A representative *cahier* supported freedom of the press, deplored the harshness of criminal laws, and recommended a "social contract" (the term was borrowed from Rousseau) between the monarch and his subjects to safeguard "the personal freedom of all citizens." It insisted upon the sanctity of private property but advocated a large measure of equality, proposing that "all Frenchmen should have the right and the hope of securing any state office . . . and all military and ecclesiastical dignities." Taxes should be levied on "all property without distinction as to owners, and to all persons without distinction of order and rank."[*]

The Financial Crisis

The chronic financial difficulties of the French monarchy strengthened the hand of the middle-class reformers. The government debt tripled between 1774 and 1789 until interest payments consumed over half of the state's revenues, and expenditures had to be met by deficit financing. When Louis XVI came to the throne in 1774, he named as chief minister Turgot, who sympathized with the Physiocrats and had a brilliant record as an intendant. Turgot reduced the deficit by imposing strict economies, particularly on expenditures of the court. He curtailed ancient guild monopolies, lifted restrictions on internal shipments of grain, and replaced the *corvée* (the work on roads demanded of peasants) with a tax affecting nobles and commoners alike. He hoped to restore the Edict of Nantes to bring the Huguenots back into French life and to liberalize the monarchy by setting up representative assemblies. The vested interests of the Old Regime were appalled at Turgot's innovations and, backed by Marie Antoinette, secured his dismissal in 1776. The ousted minister warned Louis XVI: "Remember, sire, that it was weakness which brought the head of Charles I to the block."

[*] The full text of this cahier is printed in B. F. Hyslop, *A Guide to the General Cahiers of 1789* (New York, 1936), pp. 318–26. Our translation.

Louis ignored Turgot's warning, and his officials continued to raise new loans until in 1786 bankers refused to make further advances. The government was now caught between the irresistible force of the third estate's demand for tax relief and the immovable object of the other estates' refusal to give up their fiscal privileges. Calonne, the finance minister in 1786, proposed to meet the crisis by reviving Turgot's reforms. Hoping that the first two estates would consent to pay more taxes, he convoked the Assembly of Notables, which included the chief aristocratic and ecclesiastical dignitaries of the kingdom. When the Notables rejected his program, Louis dismissed them and replaced Calonne. Then with surprising firmness, he decided to levy a uniform tax on all landed property without regard to the status of the holder. The clergy replied by reducing their "free gift" for 1788 to one-sixth of what it had previously been. The parlements declared the new tax illegal and asserted that only the nation as a whole assembled in the Estates General could make so sweeping a change. The king retreated, and in the summer of 1788 announced that the Estates General would meet the following spring.

The Estates General

In summoning the Estates General, Louis XVI revived an almost forgotten institution which did not seem likely to initiate drastic reforms. In the past the three estates, despite their enormous differences in numbers, had enjoyed equal representation and voting rights, so that the two privileged orders could outvote the commoners. The Estates General of 1789, however, was convened under unique circumstances. Its election and subsequent meeting took place during an economic crisis. Unemployed peasants searched for work in the cities, especially Paris, and inflation grew worse as prices rose at twice the rate of wages. Unemployment also mounted in some textile centers as a result of a trade treaty with England (1786) in which the French agreed to lift restrictions on importation of cheaper English textiles and hats in return for increased British importation of French wines and brandies.

Hail and drought reduced the wheat harvest of 1788, and during the harsh winter of 1788–1789 the Seine froze over at Paris, blocking barges carrying essential shipments of grain and flour. By the spring of 1789 the price of bread had al-

Making bread—the staple food for most of the population—in an eighteenth-century French bakery. The dough is kneaded in a wooden trough (Fig. 1), weighed (Fig. 2), formed into loaves (Figs. 3 and 4), and baked in an oven (Fig. 5). The illustration is from Diderot's "Encyclopedie."

most doubled—an extremely serious matter when the average worker normally spent almost half his wages on bread for his family. Although France had survived bad weather and poor harvests in the past without a revolution, the economic hardships of 1788–1789 were the last straw. Starving peasants begged, borrowed, and stole, poaching on the hunting preserves of great lords and attacking their game wardens.

The turbulence increased the sense of urgency pressing on the deputies to the Estates General, and so did the method of electing deputies themselves. The suffrage was wide, particularly in rural areas, where it extended to almost all adult males; in fact, more Frenchmen probably voted in 1789 than in any subsequent election or referendum during the revolutionary era. In each district of France, the third estate voted for electors at public meetings; the electors then chose the deputies who would go to Versailles. This procedure favored bourgeois orators over inarticulate farmers, so that lawyers and government administrators won control of the commoners' deputation. The reformers of the third estate found some sympathizers in the second estate and a great many in the first, where the discontented lower clergy were heavily represented. Moreover, in a departure from precedent, the king had agreed to "double the third," allotting it as many deputies as the other two estates combined. All told, a majority of the deputies were prepared to make drastic changes.

In past meetings of the Estates General, each order or estate had deliberated separately, with the consent of two estates and the crown required for passage of a proposal. In 1789 the king and the privileged orders favored retaining this "vote by order," but the third estate demanded "vote by head," with the deputies from all three orders deliberating together. The question of procedure became crucial soon after the Estates General convened on May 5, 1789, at Versailles. A campaign for vote by head was led by Siéyès, a priest, and Mirabeau, a renegade nobleman, both sitting in the third estate. On June 17, the third estate accepted Siéyès' invitation to proclaim itself the National Assembly. When it invited the deputies of the other estates to join its sessions, a majority of the clerical deputies, mainly parish priests, accepted; the nobles refused. The king then barred the commoners from their usual meeting place, whereupon they assembled at an indoor tennis court on June 20 and swore not to disband until they had given France a constitution. Louis XVI responded to the Tennis-Court Oath by ordering

each estate to resume its separate deliberations, but the third estate and some deputies of the second balked. In a few days Louis gave in and ordered the first two estates to join the National Assembly. The nation, through its representatives, had successfully challenged the king and the vested interests; the revolution had begun.

The Death of the Old Regime

As the National Assembly started work, a great wave of rioting swept over France. During the summer of 1789, unemployment increased and bread seemed likely to remain scarce and expensive until after the harvest. Meantime, suspicion grew that the king and the privileged orders might attempt a counterrevolution, especially after large concentrations of troops appeared in the Paris area early in July. Suspicion deepened into conviction after Louis dismissed Necker, the popular Swiss Protestant financier who had been serving as chief royal adviser. On July 12 and 13, in reaction to Necker's dismissal, the men who had elected the Paris deputies of the third estate formed a new municipal government and a new militia, the National Guard, both of them loyal to the National Assembly. Crowds roamed the streets, parading busts of Necker draped in black and demanding cheaper bread.

On July 14, in search of arms, they broke into the Invalides, the great military hospital, and found one arsenal. A few hours later, hoping to find another arsenal, an armed group several hundred strong stormed the Bastille, a fortress in the eastern part of the city. They killed part of the garrison and suffered many casualties themselves. The legend, cherished by defenders of the Old Regime, that the assault was the work of a "mob" or "rabble" has been exploded by the facts. An official list of "conquerors of the Bastille" carefully compiled some time after the event showed that the great majority were respectable craftsmen and tradesmen from the district of the city close to the Bastille. Although only seven prisoners, all meriting a term in jail, were found in the Bastille, the conquest of the fortress had immense symbolic significance for its capture and subsequent demolition virtually insured the destruction of the Old Regime. No wonder the Fourteenth of July became the French equivalent of the American Fourth of July.

Late in July, rioting spread to much of France, as the provinces reacted to the news from Paris. In town after town the local counterpart of the Bastille was attacked, officials were forced to step down, taxes went unpaid, and valuable records were destroyed. Rural districts scattered over France experienced the "Great Fear." Rumors spread from village to village that "brigands" were coming, toughs hired by the aristocrats who would destroy crops and villages and thus force the National Assembly to preserve the status quo. Although there were no organized brigands, only an occasional starving farmhand trying to steal food, peasants in many districts grabbed hoes and pitchforks to defend themselves. When the brigands did not appear, they attacked the chateaux of their landlords, breaking into any building that might house hoarded grain or the hated documents justifying collection of manorial dues. Some nobles gave the peasants what they wanted, others saw their barns and archives burned, and a few were lynched.

The Great Fear had the important result of prompting the National Assembly to abolish by law what the peasants were destroying by fire. In a session begun on the evening of August 4, the clergy gave up its tithes, and the nobles gave up their immunity to taxation and their right to levy manorial dues and to maintain game preserves. The Assembly then made it a clean sweep by abolishing serfdom, forbidding the sale of justice or of judicial office, and decreeing that "all citizens, without distinction of birth, can be admitted to all ecclesiastical, civil, and military posts and dignities." When this memorable session ended at two o'clock on the morning of August 5, the Old Regime was dead, even though the deputies later awarded the nobles compensation for their losses.

The "October Days," the final popular outburst of a momentous year, again demonstrated the weakness of Louis XVI and the power of his aroused subjects. The wheat harvest of 1789 had been good, but a late summer drought crippled the watermills that ground flour. When autumn came, Parisians still queued for bread and looked with suspicion at the royal troops stationed in the area. Reports of the queen's behavior intensified concern, particularly the rumor that on hearing people had no bread she remarked: "Let them eat cake." While false, this was widely accepted as accurate. It was true, though, that army officers cheered the queen when she made a dramatic appearance at a banquet with the dauphin, the heir to the throne, in her arms.

On October 5, 1789, a column of determined women—coarse marketwomen and fishwives, neatly dressed milliners, middle-class ladies—marched in the rain from Paris to Versailles, a dozen miles away. They disrupted the National Assembly, extracted kisses from Louis XVI, and might have lynched Marie Antoinette if she had not taken refuge in the king's apartment. This bizarre demonstration had very significant political consequences. On October 6, the women marched back to Paris, escorting "the baker, the baker's wife, and the baker's boy"—the royal family—who took up residence at the Tuileries Palace in the center of the city. Later, the National Assembly also moved to Paris. The most revolutionary place in France had captured both the head of the Old Regime and the herald of the new.

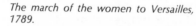
The march of the women to Versailles, 1789.

II THE CREATION OF A NEW REGIME

Six weeks before the women's march, on August 26, the National Assembly had formulated the goals of the new regime in the Declaration of the Rights of Man. It stated that "Men are born and remain free and equal in rights," which it specified as "liberty, property, security, and resistance to oppression." Property was defined as "inviolable and sacred" and liberty as the "exercise of natural rights" subject to the limits "determined by law." The Declaration defined law as "the expression of the general will. All citizens have the right to take part, in person or by their representatives, in its formation." It stated further that "Any society in which the guarantee of rights is not assured or the separation of powers not determined has no constitution."* Thus the Declaration incorporated some of the catch phrases of the Enlightenment and also reflected the economic and political concerns of the middle class. It committed the French to the kind of constitutional liberalism already affirmed by the English in 1688–1689 and extended by the Americans in their Constitutional Convention in 1787.

Finance and the Church

The National Assembly found no magic formula to translate the ideals of the Declaration into practice. The belief that all Frenchmen should be taxed equally did not solve urgent financial problems, for the new land tax imposed by the deputies simply could not be collected. Tax collectors had vanished in the liquidation of the Old Regime, and naïve peasants thought they now owed the government nothing. Once more the state borrowed but soon exhausted its credit. In desperation, the National Assembly, declaring that "the wealth of the clergy is at the disposition of the nation," ordered the confiscation of church lands (November 1789). Acquisition of this immense asset permitted the issuing of paper notes called *assignats* to pay the government's debts. The assignats temporarily eased the financial crisis, but as the state sold off parcels of confiscated clerical land it reduced the amount

* G. Lefebvre, *The Coming of the French Revolution* (Princeton, 1947), Appendix.

of property backing the assignats. Theoretically, the number of assignats in circulation should have been reduced accordingly; in practice, the temptation to keep assignats circulating was irresistible and the result was more inflation.

Property seized from émigrés, aristocrats who fled France, was auctioned along with that of the Church. The beneficiaries were well-to-do peasants and bourgeois seeking a stake in land; the National Assembly did nothing to help the poor and landless peasants who could not afford to buy land. This was, in effect, a recognition of the doctrine of laissez-faire, which the Assembly also followed in abolishing the restrictive guilds and the tariffs and tolls on trade within France. In the name of laissez-faire it also forbade both labor unions and strikes.

The suppression of tithes and the seizure of ecclesiastical property deprived the Church of revenues. The Assembly therefore agreed to finance clerical salaries, an arrangement that virtually nationalized the Gallican Church. Its decision to restrict monasteries and convents caused little difficulty, since many of them were already decayed. But an uproar arose over the Civil Constitution of the Clergy (July 1790) which altered the status of the secular clergy (bishops and priests). The Civil Constitution reduced the number of bishoprics by about one-third making their boundaries coincide with those of the new civil units, the departments. It made bishops and priests civil officials, not only paid by the state but also elected by the citizens of the diocese or parish, including non-Catholics. The Civil Constitution required new bishops to take an oath of loyalty to the state and forbade the traditional application to the pope for confirmation. These drastic changes led the pope to denounce the Civil Constitution, whereupon the National Assembly required every member of the French clergy to take a special oath supporting the Constitution. When only seven bishops and fewer than half the priests complied, it was evident that a breach had opened between the revolution and a large segment of the population. Good Catholics, from Louis XVI down to humble peasants, rallied to the nonjuring clergy, as those who refused the special oath were termed.

The Constitution of 1791

A year later, the National Assembly completed its political blueprint, the Constitution of

1791. To replace the hodgepodge of provincial units that had multiplied under the Old Regime the Assembly devised a neat and orderly system. It divided the territory of France into eighty-three *départements* of approximately equal size; each department was compact enough for its chief town to be within a day's journey of outlying towns. The departments were subdivided into *arrondissements* (districts) and the arrondissements into *communes* (municipalities). In communes and departments, elected officials and councils exercised considerable self-government, so that in principle the administration of the new France was to be far more decentralized than the Old Regime had been.

In reconstructing the central government, the Constitution of 1791 replaced the parlements and other tribunals of the Old Regime with courts staffed by elected judges. It vested legislative authority in a single elected chamber; and, conforming to the separation of powers, it made the ministers of the executive branch responsible only to the king, not to the chamber. The king headed the executive, but his authority was limited by the requirement that his ministers must approve his decisions. The king had only a suspensive veto, which could block legislation for a maximum of four years. Louis XVI, no longer the absolute "king of France," received the new title "king of the French."

The new constitution included other measures of reform favored by the Enlightenment. It made punishments less severe, declared marriage to be a contract rather than a sacrament, and transferred to the state the old ecclesiastical functions of recording vital statistics and providing charity and education. The constitution promised a system of free public schools, a promise realized only in part later in the revolution. It also promised a new uniform code of law, achieved a dozen years later under Napoleon.

The Constitution of 1791 went a long way toward instituting popular government but stopped short of full democracy. It limited voting to "active" citizens, whose annual taxes amounted to three days' wages for unskilled labor in the locality. About a third of the male population fell short of this requirement and were designated as "passive" citizens. Even active citizens did not vote directly for deputies but for a series of electors, who chose the deputies and were required to have substantial wealth. The decentralized and limited monarchy established by the Constitution of 1791 was too radical to suit the king and most of the aristocracy and not radical

enough for many bourgeois, who began to demand a republic. The majority in the National Assembly who supported the constitution would suffer the fate commonly experienced by political moderates in a revolution: they would be squeezed out by the extremists.

The extremists of 1791 were the Jacobins, members of a political club quartered in a former Jacobin (Dominican) monastery in Paris. The Jacobins accepted the constitution only as a stopgap until the monarchy was replaced by a republic based on universal suffrage. The Jacobins mastered pressure group techniques. They sponsored rabble-rousing articles in the lively revolutionary press and manipulated the crowds of volatile spectators at the sessions of the National Assembly. The network of Jacobin clubs, which extended throughout the departments, was the only nationwide political organization; it soon dominated most of the new department and commune councils. In local elections, as in the election of the Estates General, a determined minority prevailed over a largely illiterate and politically inexperienced majority.

Defenders of the Old Regime also played into the hands of the Jacobins. From the summer of 1789 on, alarmed prelates and nobles, including the two brothers of Louis XVI, fled France. Many of these émigrés, hoping to secure Austrian and Russian support for a counterrevolution, gathered in the German Rhineland. The king, who was deeply disturbed by the Civil Constitution of the Clergy, made a disastrous attempt to join them. In June, 1791, three months before the assembly completed work on the Constitution of 1791, Louis and Marie Antoinette left the Tuileries disguised as a valet and governess. But along the route the king was recognized from his portrait on the assignats, and at Varennes in northeastern France a detachment of troops forced the royal party to return to Paris. The royal couple were now widely viewed as potential traitors and lived in the Tuileries under virtual house arrest.

The Legislative Assembly and the Outbreak of War

Thus the experiment in constitutional monarchy was already in deep trouble before the newly elected Legislative Assembly met on October 1, 1791. The seating of deputies set a pattern later adopted by most Continental European assemblies. Supporters of constitutional monarchy made up the Right because they sat to the right of the presiding officer as he faced the deputies;

the radical Jacobins formed the Left; and uncommitted deputies made up the Center, nicknamed the Plain because they occupied the lowest seats in the assembly. The Jacobins soon won support from many of the uncommitted, thereby augmenting the problems facing the constitutional regime.

Jacobin leadership rested with the Girondins, so named because some of them came from Bordeaux in the department of Gironde. The Girondins were not an organized faction but a loose affiliation of men who shared certain ideas. They pictured France as the intended victim of a reactionary conspiracy, led at home by the royal family and the nonjuring clergy. The conspirators abroad were the émigrés, supported by a league of monarchs headed by the Austrian emperor, Leopold II, the brother of Marie Antoinette. The Austrian threat mounted after the sudden death of Leopold in March, 1792, and the accession of his less cautious son, Francis II. The war fever in France forced Louis XVI to name a ministry dominated by Girondins.

On April 20, 1792, the Legislative Assembly declared war on Austria, a war that would continue for the next twenty-three years. French mobilization was slowed because many veteran officers had emigrated. Prussia soon joined Austria, and in June morale on the home front received a blow when the king dismissed the Girondin ministers for proposing to banish nonjuring priests. Spirits revived in July when national guardsmen from the departments paused on their way to the front to celebrate Bastille Day in Paris. The Marseilles contingent introduced the patriotic song that was to become the national anthem of republican France, the Marseillaise. On July 25, the Prussian commander, the duke of Brunswick, issued a manifesto drafted by an émigré threatening Paris with vengeance if the Tuileries should be attacked and violence attempted against the royal family.

The Birth of the First Republic

The duke of Brunswick expected that his manifesto would terrify the French; instead, it stiffened the determination of republicans to do away with the monarchy. The Jacobins won the support of army recruits, national guardsmen, and the rank and file of Parisians, who were angered by the depreciation of the assignats and the high price and scarcity of food. One by one, the forty-eight *sections* (wards) of the city came under Jacobin control, and on the night of August

9–10, 1792, leaders of the sections ousted the incumbents from the Paris city hall and installed a new Jacobin commune. On the morning of August 10, forces supporting the new commune attacked the Tuileries and massacred the king's Swiss guards, while the royal family took refuge with the Legislative Assembly. By then, however, the Assembly was little more than the errand boy of the new commune. With most deputies of the Right and the Plain absent, the Assembly voted to suspend the king from office, place the royal family in prison, and arrange for the election of a constitutional convention. Until the convention met, the government was to be run by an interim ministry staffed in part by Girondins but dominated by Danton, a Jacobin opportunist who was minister of justice.

The next few weeks were filled with crisis and tension. The value of the assignats depreciated by 40 percent in August alone, alarming Parisians who were already stirred up by the capture of the Tuileries. Additional excitement was created by Jacobin propagandists led by Marat, a frustrated and embittered physician turned journalist. Then news came that Prussian troops had invaded northeastern France. Danton won immortality by urging patriots to respond with *de l'audace, encore de l'audace, toujours de l'audace* ("boldness, more boldness, always boldness"). For five days, beginning on September 2, bloodthirsty Parisians moved from prison to prison, holding impromptu trials and executing alleged traitors and enemy agents. Neither the Paris commune nor the interim ministry could check the hysterical wave of lynchings that claimed over a thousand victims. They included ordinary criminals and prostitutes as well as aristocrats and nonjuring priests who were often innocent of the treason charged against them. Later in the month, "the miracle of Valmy," in reality a rather minor victory, turned the duke of Brunswick's forces back from the road to Paris and reassured French patriots.

Gironde and Mountain

In theory the election of deputies to the National Convention marked the beginning of political democracy in France since the polls were opened to both active and passive citizens. But only 10 percent of a potential electorate of seven million voted; the great majority abstained or were turned away from the polls by Jacobin watchdogs. The result was a landslide for republicans, with Girondin deputies forming the Right and the more radical Jacobins the Left, or Mountain (so designated because their seats were high up in the meeting hall). Both Gironde and Mountain were composed of men from the middle class, steeped in the ideas of the philosophes. And both were viewed with distrust by citizens lower down the economic ladder, now frequently termed the *sans-culottes,* because they wore the long baggy trousers of the worker, not the *culottes* (knee breeches) of the well-to-do. Politically, the term "sans-culottes" soon designated enthusiastic supporters of the revolution, particularly the activists of the Paris sections.

When the Convention met, Gironde and Mountain united to declare France a republic (September 21, 1792) and then split on other issues. The Girondins sought a breathing spell in revolutionary legislation and championed "federalism," which meant a national government limited by checks and balances, with more authority vested in local units and less in Paris. The leaders of the Mountain denounced federalism and advocated an all-powerful central government. Their spokesman was Maximilien Robespierre (1758–1794), an earnest young lawyer who looked deceptively unrevolutionary, for he powdered his hair neatly and wore the light-blue coat and knee breeches of the Old Regime. In fact, he was a political fanatic whose speeches were lay sermons delivered in the language of a new revelation based on Rousseau's *Social Contract.* He was confident that he knew the "general will" of Frenchmen and that it demanded a Republic of Virtue. Should Frenchmen fail to be free and virtuous voluntarily, then they would be "forced to be free."

Robespierre and the Republic of Virtue triumphed. In January 1793, after a hundred hours of continuous voting, the Convention declared "Citizen Louis Capet" guilty of treason. By a narrow margin, he was sentenced to the guillotine (named after Dr. Guillotin, who invented this new device for beheading to replace the less reliable axe). On January 21, 1793, Louis XVI died bravely. Some Girondin deputies voted against subjecting him to the death penalty. They made a courageous defense of the humanitarian principles of the Enlightenment but opened themselves to charges of counterrevolutionary activity.

Events soon destroyed the Gironde. In February 1793, the Convention rejected the Girondin constitution drafted by Condorcet, and in the same month it declared war on Britain, Spain, and the Netherlands. The French now faced a formidable coalition, for Austria and Prussia re-

Jacques Louis David's
"The Death of Marat."

mained in the war. In March, the army under the Girondin Dumouriez was defeated in the Low Countries, and in April Dumouriez deserted to the enemy. When Marat, the Jacobin extremist, denounced all associates of Dumouriez as traitors, Girondin deputies called for his impeachment, but he was triumphantly acquitted. A few weeks later (July 13, 1793), Marat was assassinated by Charlotte Corday, a young woman who was convinced that she was a new Joan of Arc called to deliver France from Jacobin radicalism; to the Jacobins, however, Marat was a martyr.

Meantime, the Girondins' devotion to laissez-faire made it difficult for them to cope with the problems of unemployment, high prices, and shortages. The Paris sections demanded price controls and food requisitioning and also the expulsion of Girondins from the Jacobin clubs and the Convention. On June 2, 1793, a vast crowd of armed sans-culottes invaded the Convention and forced the arrest of twenty-nine Girondin deputies. Backed by these armed Parisians, the Mountain intimidated the deputies of the Plain, and the arrested Girondins were sentenced to the guillotine. The Convention then voted a constitution granting universal manhood suffrage and assigning supreme power, unhampered by Girondin checks and balances, to a single legislative chamber. Though the Constitution of 1793 was overwhelmingly approved in a referendum (August 1793), less than 25 percent of the potential voters

French aristocrats imprisoned in the Conciergerie.

actually participated. Two months later, the initiation of the new constitution was postponed indefinitely.

The Reign of Terror

France was now under the dictatorship of the Mountain; the Reign of Terror had begun. Robespierre justified it in a famous speech:

> To establish and consolidate democracy, we must first finish the war of liberty against tyranny. We must annihilate the enemies of the republic at home and abroad, or else we shall perish. If virtue is the mainstay of a democratic government in time of peace, then in time of revolution a democratic government must rely on virtue and terror. Terror is nothing but justice, swift, severe, and inflexible; it is an emanation of virtue.*

Under the Terror, the governing force was the twelve-man Committee of Public Safety, composed of Robespierre and other stalwarts from

* Condensed from *Le Moniteur Universel* (February 7, 1794). Our translation.

the Mountain. Though nominally responsible to the Convention, it exercised a large measure of independent authority and acted as a war cabinet. Never under the dominance of any one individual, it functioned as a genuine committee and was remarkably effective.

A second committee, that of General Security, supervised police activities and turned suspected enemies of the republic over to the new Revolutionary Tribunal. The sixteen judges and sixty jurors of the tribunal were eventually divided among several courts to speed the work of repression. Special local courts supplemented the grim task of the tribunal, and local Jacobin clubs purged unreliable officials from department and commune administration. To make doubly sure that all parts of France toed the line, the Mountain sent out reliable members of the Convention as its agents, the "deputies on mission." It also steadily reduced the activities of the Paris sections, which have been likened to forty-eight independent republics or town meetings in continuous session. The Terror was the most effective centralized regime in French annals.

The "swift, severe, and inflexible justice" demanded by Robespierre is estimated to have taken the lives of nearly twenty thousand French men and women, including Marie Antoinette and

Robespierre, having ordered the execution of all the rest of France, now guillotines the executioner: a contemporary cartoon.

her son, "Louis XVII," the Bourbon heir. The number of victims is nearly doubled if one adds those who died in prison or by procedures separate from the Revolutionary Tribunal and the special local courts. The Terror fell with the greatest severity on the clergy, aristocracy, and Girondins, but the rank and file of the third estate also suffered. Many victims came from the Vendée, a strongly Catholic and economically depressed area in western France, which had risen in revolt. Prisoners from the Vendée were among the two thousand victims drowned at Nantes, where the accused were set adrift chained to leaky barges on the River Loire.

The wartime hysteria that produced the Terror also inspired a very practical patriotism. On August 23, 1793, the Convention issued a decree enlisting the entire population in the service of the nation:

> Young men will go into combat; married men will manufacture arms and transport supplies; women will make tents and uniforms and serve in the hospitals; children will make old linen into bandages; old men will be carried into the public squares to arouse the courage of the soldiers, excite hatred for kings and inspire the unity of the republic.*

In a pioneering measure of universal conscription, the army drafted all bachelors and widowers between the ages of eighteen and twenty-five. By the close of 1793, the forces of the republic had driven foreign troops from French soil by recapturing the naval base at Toulon on the Mediterranean, which had surrendered earlier to the British. The French success could scarcely have been possible without the new democratic spirit that allowed men of the third estate to become officers and made the army the most enterprising and perhaps the most idealistic in Europe.

Total mobilization demanded equality of economic sacrifice. To combat shortages, the government rationed bread and meat, and to check inflation it put a *maximum* (ceiling) on prices and wages. In theory, wages were not to rise more than 50 percent above the wage rates prevailing in 1790, and prices were not to exceed those of 1790 by more than 33 percent. In practice, these ceilings were ineffective. Parisians rejected attempts to enforce the maximum on wages. The ceiling on prices, though temporarily checking the depreciation of the assignats, also drove many articles onto the black market. Early in 1794 the Convention passed the Laws of Ventôse (the name of a month in the new revolutionary calendar) recommending the distribution to landless Frenchmen of properties seized from émigrés and other enemies of the republic. The socialistic implications were diluted when a spokesman for the Committee of Public Safety explained that "the properties of patriots are sacred, but the goods of conspirators are there for the unfortunate."* In fact, the Laws of Ventôse were never enforced.

The most revolutionary aspect of the Terror was its drastic program of social and cultural innovations. The Convention abolished slavery in French colonies. It outlawed the tradition of addressing men as *Monsieur* and women as *Madame* or *Mademoiselle* with their undemocratic deference to lord and lady, and substituted *Citoyen* and *Citoyenne* (citizen, citizeness). Knee breeches and elaborate gowns were to be avoided as symbols of idleness and privilege. Robespierre excepted, good republican men became sans-culottes, and women wore high-waisted dresses adapted from the republican Rome of antiquity. Indeed, Rome served as a model: children were named after its heroes, Brutus, Cato, and Gracchus; theaters staged stilted dramas glorifying Roman heroes;

---

* *Le Moniteur Universel* (August 24, 1793). Our translation.

* *Le Moniteur Universel* (February 27, 1794). Our translation.

and cabinetmakers produced sturdy neoclassical furniture decorated with Roman symbols.

In a sweeping change the first day of the republic, September 22, 1792, initiated the Year I, and later years were designated by Roman numbers. The months, however, lost their Roman names and received natural ones: for example, Ventôse (the month of wind) replaced that of Mars (March), Thermidor (the month of heat) replaced July (that of Julius Caesar); and Brumaire (the foggy month) replaced November, the Roman ninth month. Each month had three ten-day weeks, each day ten hours, and the five days left over at the end of the year (six in leap years) were designated sans-culottides and dedicated to Genius, Labor, Noble Deeds, Awards, and Opinion. Although the revolutionary calendar was a worthy product of the Enlightenment, it was too abstract and also antagonized workers, who resented having to labor nine days out of ten. It never really took root, and Napoleon scrapped it a decade later.

Another reform was more successful: the metric system. A special committee of distinguished scientists devised new weights and measures based on decimals rather than the haphazard accumulations of custom. The meter became the standard unit of length, the liter that of volume, and the gram of weight. Uniform prefixes indicated larger and smaller units, from kilo- (1,000) down to milli-(1/1000). Although the Convention did little to advance the revolutionary ideal of universal education, it did convert parts of the inheritance from the Old Regime into the foundations for such great Paris institutions as the Louvre Museum, the National Archives, and the National Library.

The Terror attempted to destroy traditional religion and substitute a new faith. Many churches were closed or turned into barracks or administrative offices, their medieval glass and sculpture often destroyed. Some were converted into "temples of Reason," but Robespierre argued that the Republic of Virtue should acknowledge an ultimate author of morality. The Convention therefore decreed (May 1794) that "the French people recognize the existence of the Supreme Being and the immortality of the soul." Robespierre presided at a great festival where he set fire to figures representing Vice, Folly, and Atheism, and from the embers a statue of Wisdom emerged, smudged with smoke because of a malfunction. The mishap was symbolic, for this new cult of deism was too contrived to gain popular support.

The Thermidorean Reaction and the Directory

Indeed, the Republic of Virtue was too abstract in ideals and too violent in practice to retain popular support. By June 1794, Robespierre was pressing the Terror so relentlessly that even members of the Committees of Public Safety and General Security feared they might be the next victims. Robespierre lost his following in the Convention, where more and more deputies favored moderation. The crucial day was the ninth of Thermidor, Year II (July 27, 1794), when his attempts to speak were drowned out by shouts of "Down with the Tyrant!" The Convention ordered Robespierre's arrest, and he went to the guillotine the next day. The sans-culottes of Paris made no move to rescue him, for only a few days before the government had made a new effort to enforce the unpopular maximum on wages.

The leaders of the Thermidorean Reaction, many of them former Jacobins, dismantled the machinery of Terror. They put an end to the Revolutionary Tribunal, recalled the deputies on mission, and deprived the Committees of Public Safety and General Security of their independent authority. They closed the Paris Jacobin club and invited the surviving Girondin deputies to resume their seats in the Convention. The press and the theater recovered their freedom, and pleasure-seekers again flocked to Paris, as life became more normal. The Thermidorean Convention set up institutions for advanced training, such as the École Polytechnique for engineers. In each department it established a central school to provide a secondary education of good quality at relatively low cost to students.

But the return to normality also exacted its price. In southern and western France, a counter-revolutionary "White Terror" claimed many victims. Acute inflation followed the suspension of the economic legislation of the Terror; the price of some foods, no longer checked by the maximum, rose to a hundred times the level of 1790, and the assignats sank so low that many businessmen refused to honor them. Hungry and desperate Parisians staged several demonstrations against the Thermidoreans in 1795 demanding bread and lower prices, but with no success.

The Thermidorean Reaction concluded when the Convention adopted the Constitution of 1795. Since the Thermidoreans sought a republic dominated by propertied citizens, the constitution denied the vote to the poorest fourth of the nation and required that candidates for public

The closing of the Hall of Jacobins during the night of 9–10 Thermidor.

office own substantial property. It established two legislative councils, the Elders and the Five Hundred, patterned after the Areopagus and the Five Hundred of ancient Athens. The Elders had to be at least forty years old and either married or widowers, and both councils were to be elected piecemeal following the United States' example of renewing a third of the Senate every two years. The Council of Five Hundred nominated, and the Elders chose five directors to head the executive Directory, which was almost totally independent of the legislative councils. It soon turned out that the separation of powers did not function well in a country still at war.

The Directory suppressed with ease a "conspiracy of the equals" (1796–1797) headed by Gracchus Babeuf, who has come down in socialist legend as the first communist but who seems to have been a utopian dreamer without practical organizing skill. The Directory had greater diffi-

culty with the recurring plots of royalists and Jacobins and the repeated clashes between the directors and the legislative councils. The councils dismissed directors before their terms were completed, and the directors refused to permit duly elected councilors to take their seats. On the other hand, the new regime made a vigorous attack on economic problems. It was helped by good harvests, which eased food shortages, and by the loot from France's victorious military campaigns. It destroyed the plates used to print assignats, made tax collection more efficient, and reduced the crushing burden of national debt by repudiating two-thirds of it.

The Directory pursued the war with vigor. By the close of 1795, French troops occupied Holland; and France had annexed Belgium, the German Rhineland, Savoy, and Nice, thereby securing the "natural frontiers" of the Alps and the Rhine sought by Louis XIV. The first anti-French coalition disintegrated because of the friction between Austria and Prussia resulting from the final partition of Poland. Prussia was the first to withdraw and by the Treaty of Basel (1795) ceded to France the scattered Prussian holdings west of the Rhine with the understanding that compensation might be sought elsewhere in Germany. With Spain and Holland also defecting, only Austria and Britain remained at war with France.

General Bonaparte

To lead the attack against Hapsburg forces in northern Italy, the Directory picked a young general, born Napoleone Buonaparte in Corsica (1769), soon after the French acquired the island from Genoa. As a boy of nine Napoleon entered military school in France. Though he now spelled his name in the French style, he was snubbed as a foreigner by his fellow cadets, and concentrated on his studies and reading (Rousseau was his favorite). When the revolution began, the young artillery officer helped to overthrow the Old Regime in Corsica and later returned to France where he resumed his military career. He commanded the artillery when the forces of the Convention recovered Toulon at the close of 1793. After Thermidor he was suspected of being a terrorist, then regained favor when his "whiff of grapeshot" dispersed a royalist riot in Paris (October 5, 1795), shortly before the Thermidorean Convention was succeeded by the Directory. Napoleon advanced his career by marrying Josephine de Beauharnais, a widow six years his senior, whose contacts with the ruling clique of the Directory helped him to secure the supreme command in the Italian campaign (1796).

Major General Bonaparte, still in his twenties, drove the Austrians from their strongholds in Italy and made them sue for peace. He perfected the famous strategy of striking at his opponents before they had time to consolidate their defenses. He also showed a gift for propaganda and public relations. He encouraged the patriotic fervor of his underpaid and underfed French soldiers and appealed also to the nationalism of Italians with promises of liberation from Austria and guarantees of orderly conduct by the French army. He himself negotiated the Treaty of Campoformio (1797), in which Austria accepted the loss of Belgium and recognized the puppet republics Napoleon set up in northern Italy: the Ligurian (Genoa) and Cisalpine (south of the Alps), formerly Austrian Lombardy. Austria was compensated by acquiring the Italian lands of the Venetian Republic and by a secret French assurance that Prussia, despite the French promise of 1795, would not be permitted to annex lands in Germany.

Only Britain now remained at war with France. Napoleon decided to attack it indirectly through Egypt, a semi-independent vassal of the Ottoman Empire. He talked grandly of digging a canal across the isthmus of Suez to give French merchants a new short route to India and exact belated retribution for Britain's victory in the Seven Years' War. Sharing the enthusiasm of the Enlightenment for science and antiquity, he took with him over a hundred archaeologists and other experts, who founded the study of Egyptology. They discovered the Rosetta Stone, the first key to the translation of ancient Egyptian hieroglyphics, and established in Egypt an outpost of French cultural imperialism, vestiges of which still survive today.

From the military standpoint, however, the campaign failed. Napoleon landed in Egypt in July 1798 and easily defeated its old-fashioned defense forces. But disaster struck on August 1, when the British admiral Nelson destroyed the French fleet anchored at Abukir Bay off the Mediterranean coast. Nelson's victory prevented the French from receiving either supplies or reinforcements. After a year of futile campaigning in Palestine, Napoleon deserted his remaining forces in August 1799 and returned to France.

There he found the situation ripe for a decisive political stroke, as the Directory was badly shaken by a vigorous revival of Jacobinism. The legislative councils demanded a forced loan from the rich and passed the Law of Hostages threatening that, if émigrés engaged in activities hostile to the French Republic, their relatives in France would suffer reprisals. Moderates feared a new Reign of Terror might soon be unleashed. Abroad, too, the Directory faced difficulties, for a second great coalition had been formed against the French by Britain, Austria, and a newcomer, Russia. Catherine the Great's successor, her son Paul, tsar from 1796 to 1801, feared that France would frustrate his dream of establishing a Russian foothold on the Mediterranean. In the campaign of 1799, Russian troops defeated the French repeatedly in Italy and Switzerland, and by August the French were expelled from Italy.

Napoleon got a rousing reception on his return to France and was soon involved, along with two of the five directors, in a plot to overthrow the Directory. On November 9 and 10, 1799 (18 and 19 Brumaire in the revolutionary calendar), the plot was executed. The three directors not involved resigned, and Bonaparte attempted to persuade the legislative councils that he should join the two remaining directors in drafting a new constitution. Napoleon nearly failed. In the Elders, he mumbled about "volcanoes, tyrants, Jacobins, Cromwell," and in the Five Hundred, where there were many Jacobin deputies, he was greeted with cries of "Outlaw him!" After being pummeled, he scratched his face until he drew blood, and then fainted. Luckily, his brother Lucien was the presiding officer of the Five Hundred and saved the day until troops loyal to Napoleon arrived and expelled the hostile deputies.

III CONSULATE AND EMPIRE

Napoleon and France

The Constitution of the Year VIII, drawn up after the coup of Brumaire, represented the fourth attempt in less than ten years to endow France with an enduring political framework. It created a very strong executive composed of three consuls, of whom only Napoleon, as first consul, really counted. Four separate bodies had a hand in legislation: (1) the Council of State proposed laws; (2) the Tribunate debated them but did not vote; (3) the Legislative body voted them but did not debate; (4) the Senate had the right to review and veto legislation (the Consulate, Tribunate, and Senate were all named after institutions of the ancient Roman Republic). The members of all four bodies were either appointed by the first consul or elected indirectly by a process so complex that Bonaparte had ample opportunity to manipulate candidates. The core of the system was the Council of State, which served both as a cabinet and as the highest administrative court. The other three bodies were expected to enact whatever the first consul decreed but sometimes got out of hand. The Tribunate so annoyed Napoleon that he abolished it in 1807.

Napoleon steadily enlarged his own authority. In 1802 he got the legislators to drop the ten-year limit on his term of office and make him first consul for life, with power to designate his successor and amend the constitution at will. France was again a monarchy in all but name. In 1804, he prompted the Senate to declare that "the government of the republic is entrusted to

an emperor"; and on December 2, a magnificent coronation was staged at Notre Dame cathedral in Paris. Napoleon characteristically seized the imperial crown from the pope and placed it on his own head.

Each time Napoleon made an antirepublican move, he also made the republican gesture of submitting the change to the electorate. Each time—in 1800, 1802, and 1804—the referendum was overwhelmingly favorable. Although considerable official pressure was exerted on voters, the great majority of Frenchmen unquestionably supported Napoleon. His military triumphs appealed to their growing nationalism, and his policy of fostering stability at home seemed to insure them against further revolutionary crises and changes.

Napoleon wiped out the last vestiges of local self-government inherited from the early years of the revolution. He replaced elected officials with his own appointees—prefects in departments, subprefects in arrondissements, mayors in communes; all were instructed to enforce compliance with the emperor's dictates. He staffed the imperial administration with men from every political background, from ex-Jacobins to former émigrés, thereby demonstrating that the consulate and empire rested on a broad political base.

Napoleon paid officials well; and with the establishment of the empire, he rewarded many of them with noble titles, creating dukes by the dozen and counts and barons by the hundred. He raised outstanding generals to the rank of marshal and invited other officers and civilian officials into the Legion of Honor. "Aristocracy always exists," he observed. "Destroy it in the nobility, it removes itself to the rich and powerful houses of the middle class."[*]

Bonaparte revived some of the glamor of the Old Regime, but not its glaring inequalities. The series of legal reforms generally designated as the Code Napoléon (1804–1810) declared all men equal before the law without regard to their wealth and rank. It extended to all the right to follow the occupation and profess the religion of their choice. It gave France the single coherent system of law demanded by the philosophes but did not incorporate the full judicial reform program of the Enlightenment. It took from ancient Roman law whatever strengthened the authority of the empire, placed the interests of the state above the rights of the individual, and permitted

[*] Quoted in H. A. L. Fisher, *Napoleon* (New York, 1913), Appendix I.

Jean-François Bosio's "A Parisian Salon in 1801" depicts the new aristocracy created by the Revolution.

some resort to torture in trial procedure. Judges were no longer elected but appointed by the emperor; his prefects selected jurors. Although Napoleon confirmed revolutionary legislation permitting divorce by mutual consent, his code canceled revolutionary laws protecting women, minors, and bastards, and allowed the man of the family to regain his traditional dominance.

Expediency determined Napoleon's attitude toward civil liberties. He welcomed former political opponents into his administration, but if conciliation failed he turned to force. In the western departments, where royalist uprisings had become chronic since the revolt in the Vendée, he massacred rebels who declined his offer of amnesty. When it was rumored that royalist conspirators had chosen the duke of Enghien to recover the throne of France, he had the duke kidnapped from the neutral German state of Baden and then

executed, even though he had learned that the duke was innocent. He had no use for freedom of speech, subjecting both the press and the theaters to censorship.

Political considerations determined Napoleon's decisions on religion. "I do not see in religion the mystery of the incarnation," he said, "but the mystery of the social order. It attaches to heaven an idea of equality which prevents the rich man from being massacred by the poor."* Because French Catholics detested the anticlericalism of the revolution, Napoleon sought reconciliation with Rome. In 1801 he negotiated with Pope Pius VII the kind of settlement between the church and lay rulers known as a *concordat*. The Concordat of 1801 canceled the most contro-

* Quoted in H.A.L. Fisher, *Napoleon* (New York, 1913), Appendix I.

versial feature of the Civil Constitution of the Clergy when Napoleon agreed to suppress the popular election of bishops and priests. Bishops were to be nominated by the French government, then consecrated by the pope; priests were to be appointed by bishops. By declaring Catholicism as the faith of "the majority of the French people" rather than the state religion, the concordat implied toleration of Protestants and Jews.

Napoleon also made the activities of the church in France subject to "police regulations," which he appended to the concordat without consulting the pope. These regulations gave the French government final authority to oversee the publication of papal bulls, the activities of priestly seminaries, the contents of catechisms, and a long list of other details. The concordat did not please everybody, though millions of French Catholics welcomed it. Anticlericals in the legislative bodies of the Consulate were so hostile that it took all Bonaparte's pressure to secure ratification of the concordat. The pope objected to Napoleon's high-handed conduct, and when the emperor converted the papal states into a French satellite, the pope was exiled from Rome and became a French prisoner.

Politics also determined Napoleon's approach to education and economics. In 1802 he abolished the secondary central schools opened by the Thermidorean Convention and replaced them with a smaller number of *lycées,* named after the Lyceum where Aristotle taught in ancient Athens. The lycées, which were elitist in character, aimed to produce capable and loyal administrators. They accepted only the relatively few students who could afford the high tuition or received state scholarships. Napoleon did almost nothing to improve primary education but took care to bring all schools, lay and clerical, under the supervision of a hierarchy of government officials with the misleading title of "university."

Napoleon sought to promote French national unity by catering to the interests of his most important subjects. He knew that the peasants wanted to be left alone to consolidate the gains they had made since 1789; he seldom disturbed them except to raise recruits for the army. The middle class wanted a balanced national budget and an end to revolutionary experiments with paper currency and with a government-controlled economy. Napoleon continued the sound money of the Directory, established a private institution—the Bank of France—to act as the government's financial agent, and balanced the budget thanks to the immense plunder from his military campaigns. He intensified the restrictions imposed on labor by earlier revolutionary legislation by ordering every worker to carry a *livret* (booklet) listing the jobs he had held and the employers' rating of his performance and reliability. Generous war contracts and government subsidies kept employment and profits at a high level except in seaports, which were depressed by the decline in French overseas trade.

Thus the domestic policies of Napoleon had something in common with those of other famous rulers. Like Julius Caesar, Napoleon rendered lip service to a republic while subverting republican institutions; he used prefects to impose centralized authority as Louis XIV had used intendants; and, like modern dictators, he scorned free speech. Yet a strong case can be made that Napoleon was also the greatest of the enlightened despots. Parts of his law code would have delighted the philosophes, and he ended French civil strife without sacrificing the redistribution of land and the advances in equality gained earlier in the revolution.

Napoleon and Europe

Napoleon had barely launched the Consulate when he set off on another campaign, crossing the Alps with much fanfare in the spring of 1800. After defeating the Austrians in Italy, he negotiated the Treaty of Lunéville (1801), whereby Austria recognized the various French satellites in Italy and agreed that France should take part in reorganizing Germany. Once more only the British remained at war with France. By 1801 they had nearly won the worldwide colo-

Unfinished portrait of Napoleon by David, 1798.

nial and naval contests by capturing former Dutch and Spanish colonies and expelling the French from Egypt and Malta. The British cabinet was confident that it had a strong bargaining position, but in the Peace of Amiens (1802) the British agreed to surrender some of their colonial conquests and received nothing in return. France refused to reopen the Continent to British exports or to relinquish Belgium, which Napoleon called "a loaded pistol aimed at the heart of Britain."

"Boney" (the English nickname for their enemy) alarmed British exporters by imposing higher tariffs. He also threatened British interests in the Caribbean by a grandiose project for a colonial empire based on Haiti and on the vast Louisiana territory which Spain had returned to France in 1800. In Haiti, the hopes of the black majority had risen when the Convention abolished slavery in the colonies; the blacks now revolted against the restoration of slavery by subsequent French governments. Stubborn black resistance under Toussaint L'Ouverture and Jean Jacques Dessalines and an epidemic of yellow fever took a heavy toll of French troops and forced Napoleon to abandon the American project. In 1803 he sold the Louisiana territory to the United States for $16,000,000 (a bargain price for land that would form parts of thirteen states). In 1804 Haiti became the first sovereign black nation in the New World, with the former slave, Dessalines, as emperor.

By then France and Britain were at war again. Napoleon prepared to invade England, assembling over 100,000 troops and 1,000 landing barges in French ports on the English Channel. He sent the French fleet to the West Indies to lure Nelson and the British fleet away from European waters and thus enable the barges to cross the Channel. Nelson, however, tailed the French fleet, which put in at a friendly Spanish port when it returned to Europe instead of heading directly for the Channel as Napoleon had ordered. Nelson engaged the combined French and Spanish fleets off Cape Trafalgar at the southwest corner of Spain (October 1805). He lost his life but not before he had destroyed half of the enemy fleet without losing a single vessel of his own. Britain's undisputed control of the seas blasted French hopes of a cross-channel invasion.

By the time of Trafalgar, Austria and Russia

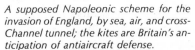

A supposed Napoleonic scheme for the invasion of England, by sea, air, and cross-Channel tunnel; the kites are Britain's anticipation of antiaircraft defense.

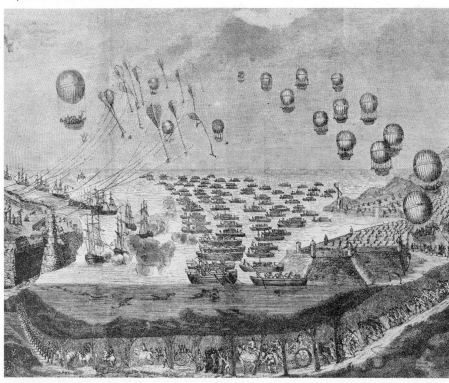

had joined Britain in the third coalition. Austria was alarmed by Napoleon's German projects, which began in 1803 with the liquidation of more than a hundred German states, mainly small ecclesiastical principalities and city-states. The chief beneficiaries were the south German states of Baden, Württemberg, and Bavaria, with which Napoleon intended to form a "third Germany" dominated by France (Austria was the "first Germany" and Prussia the second).

Bonaparte routed the Continental forces of the third coalition in the most dazzling campaign of his career. He captured 30,000 Austrians on the upper Danube in October 1805, then marked the first anniversary of his coronation by defeating the remainder of the Austrian army and the main Russian force at Austerlitz (December 2, 1805). He forced the Hapsburg emperor, Francis II, to sign the Treaty of Pressburg, which awarded the Austrian Tyrol to Bavaria and Venetia to the Napoleonic satellite kingdom of Italy. Next it was the turn of the Prussians, who joined the third coalition because of Napoleon's involvements in Germany. The French overwhelmed the main Prussian forces in the twin battles of Jena and Auerstädt (October 1806). After a setback, Napoleon finally defeated his only remaining Continental opponent, Russia, at Friedland (June 1807).

The French Empire at Its Peak

The war against the third coalition marked the peak of French military success. Conscription furnished the army with an average of 85,000 new recruits a year. They were quickly toughened by being assigned in small batches to veteran units—a process called the *amalgame* that had been developed by the revolutionary regime in the war against the first coalition. French officers were promoted on the basis of ability rather than seniority or influence, and they were more concerned with the morale of their men than with strict discipline. Bonaparte seldom risked an engagement unless his forces were the numerical equal of the enemy's; then he staked everything on a dramatic surprise.

Yet even Napoleon's seemingly invincible army had defects. The medical services were inadequate, so that a majority of deaths resulted from disease or improperly treated wounds. Pay was low and often delayed, and it was Napoleon's policy to have men and horses live off the land as much as possible to cut costs and avoid waiting for supplies to arrive.

After the victory at Friedland, Napoleon met Tsar Alexander I on a raft in the Niemen River at Tilsit on the frontier between East Prussia and Russia. The two emperors drew up a treaty in which the tsar acknowledged France's dominance over Central and Western Europe, and Napoleon recognized Eastern Europe as the sphere of Russia. Bonaparte demanded no territory from the defeated tsar but insisted on a commitment to cease trading with Britain and join the war against her.

The Prussian king, Frederick William III (reigned 1797–1840), lost almost half his domains. Prussia's Polish provinces became the Grand Duchy of Warsaw, assigned by Napoleon to the king of Saxony, a French ally; Prussia's lands west of the Elbe River went to Napoleon to dispose of as he wished. Napoleon lowered the maximum strength of the Prussian army to 42,000 men and stationed troops of his own on Prussian soil.

This latter-day Caesar divided almost all Europe into three parts: the French Empire; its satellites; and states forced by defeat to become France's allies: Austria, Prussia, and Russia. Only Britain, Turkey, and Sweden remained outside the Napoleonic system. The French Empire at its most extensive (in 1812) included Belgium and Holland; the sections of Germany west of the Rhine and bordering the North Sea; the Italian lands of Piedmont, Genoa, Tuscany, and Rome; and, detached from the rest, the Illyrian provinces along the Dalmatian coast, taken from Austria in 1809. These annexed territories were usually subdivided into departments ruled by prefects, just like those of France proper.

The roster of French satellites included Switzerland, the Grand Duchy of Warsaw, and large sections of Italy and Germany. The kingdom of Italy consisted of all the lands in the north and center of the peninsula not directly annexed by France; it was governed by a viceroy, Napoleon's stepson, Eugène de Beauharnais. In Naples Bonaparte deposed the Bourbon king in 1805 and bestowed the crown first on his brother, Joseph, and then on Joachim Murat, husband of his sister Caroline. Napoleon's project of a "third Germany" led him to decree a further reduction in the number of German states and to arrange for the formal dissolution of the antiquated Holy Roman Empire (1806). In its place Napoleon created the Confederation of the Rhine, including almost every German state except Prussia and Austria. At its heart Napoleon carved out for his brother Jerome the kingdom of Westphalia, incorporating the lands west of the Elbe seized from Prussia at Tilsit.

In the territories annexed by France and in the satellites, Bonapartist rule curbed the power of the Church, abolished serfdom, built roads, and introduced the metric system and the Code Napoléon. But it also exacted a heavy toll of tribute and subjugation. Napoleon flooded his relatives with instructions on governing their states and brought them to heel whenever they showed signs of putting local interests above those of France. When his brother, Louis, king of Holland, disobeyed the imperial orders, his kingdom was annexed to France (1810).

Napoleon longed to give dignity and permanence to his creations. It was not enough that his brothers and his in-laws occupied thrones; he himself must found a dynasty, must have the heir so far denied him in fifteen years of childless marriage. He divorced Josephine and in 1810 married Marie Louise, the daughter of the Hapsburg emperor, Francis II. She bore him a son, the "king of Rome," who was destined never to rule in Rome or anywhere else.

The Continental System

Napoleon tried, and failed, to regulate the economy of the whole European Continent. The defeat of the third coalition gave him the opportunity to experiment with economic warfare on a grand scale. His Continental System began with the Berlin Decree (November 1806), which forbade all trade with the British Isles and all commerce in British merchandise. Britain replied by requiring that neutral vessels trading with France put in first at a British port and pay duties, so that Britain might share in the profits of neutral shipping. Napoleon retaliated with the Milan Decree (December 1807), ordering the seizure of all neutral ships that complied with Britain's requirements. French seizure of American vessels in European ports strained Franco-American relations. But British restrictions also alienated Americans, who were further disturbed by the impressment of American seamen into British service on the pretext that they were deserters from the Royal Navy. These concerns, together with the designs of American expansionists on Canada, set off the indecisive Anglo-American War of 1812.

The Continental System failed almost totally. A few French enterprises did benefit from it: the cultivation of sugar-beets, for example, was stimulated by the difficulty of securing cane sugar from the West Indies. But the general decline of overseas trade depressed French Atlantic ports, and the shortage of cotton and other raw materials resulted in widespread unemployment and a rash of bankruptcies. Since the new French markets on the Continent did not compensate for the loss of older ones overseas, the value of French exports fell by more than a third between 1805 and 1813.

The Continental System did confront the British with a severe economic crisis. The uncertain markets for British exports, the reduction of food imports, and the rapid rise of prices caused widespread hardship. Britain's economic and naval leadership, however, enabled her to ride out the storm. Every tract of land that might grow food was brought under the plow, and British exporters developed lucrative new markets abroad and smuggled goods to old customers on the Continent. Even the French army could not get along without certain British cloth and leather products, and Napoleon violated his own decrees by authorizing secret purchases from Britain.

The Downfall of Napoleon

The political and military consequences of the Continental System formed a decisive and disastrous chapter in Napoleonic history. In 1807 the emperor decided to impose the system on Portugal, a traditional ally of Britain. The Portuguese expedition gave Napoleon an excuse for occupying neighboring Spain, where he replaced the Bourbon monarch with his brother, Joseph. The installation of a foreign monarch, the attempts to enforce the Continental System, the suppression of the Inquisition, and the curtailment of noble and clerical privileges aroused Spanish nationalism. While an anti-French rising in Madrid was soon repressed, the guerrilla tactics of Spaniards in the ensuing Peninsular War proved extremely effective. The guerrillas were supported by a British expedition commanded by Sir Arthur Wellesley, later duke of Wellington. Napoleon assigned more than 300,000 men to the Peninsular War, but in 1813 Joseph was forced to flee from Madrid, and Wellington's army invaded southern France.

Meantime, a nationalist reaction was beginning among the traditionally disunited Germans. When Austria reentered the war in 1809, it attempted a total mobilization comparable to that decreed by the French Convention in 1793. The new spirit enabled the Austrians to make a better showing, although they were defeated by a narrow margin at Wagram and had to accept another peace dictated by Napoleon. The Treaty of

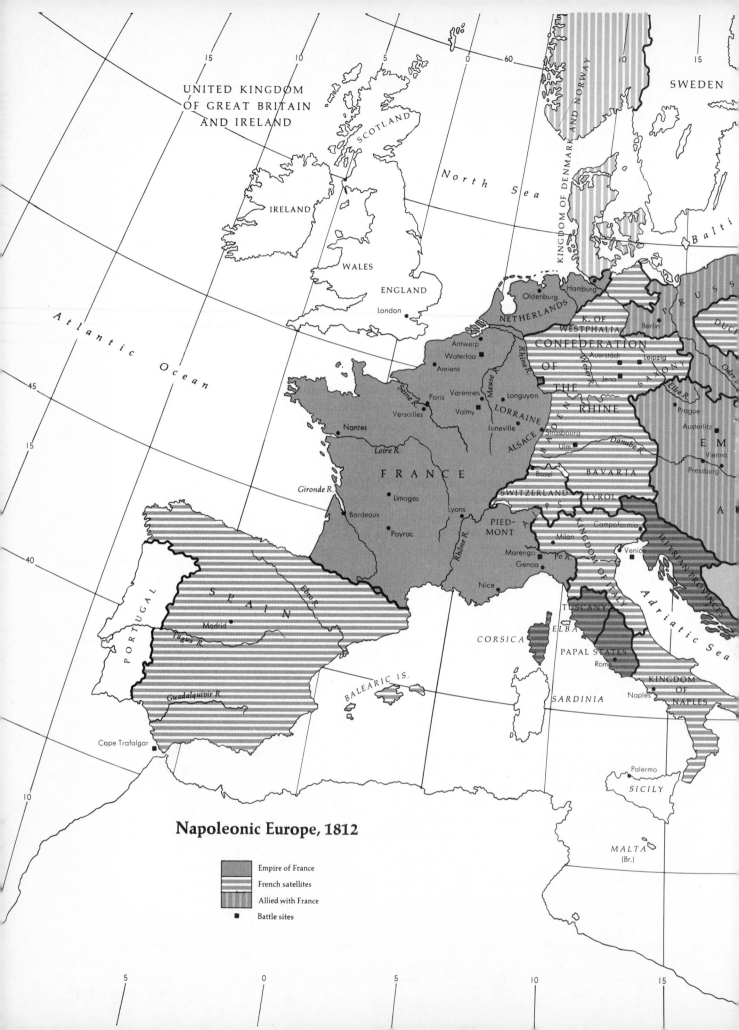

Napoleonic Europe, 1812

Empire of France
French satellites
Allied with France
■ Battle sites

FINLAND

L. Ladoga

Gulf of Finland

30
35
40

Moscow
55

W. Dvina R.
Vitebsk
Oka R.

Tilsit
nigsberg
Smolensk

Friedland
Vilna
Niemen R.

Napoleon's route, 1812

Warsaw

F WARSAW

Kiev

Dnieper R.

Vistula R.

Dniester R.

RUSSIA

IRE OF

STRIA

HUNGARY

Morava R.
Danube R.

Black Sea

Don R.

Volga R.

45

Caspian Sea

40

MONTE-
NEGRO

Vardar R.

O
T
T
O
M
A
N

E
M
P
I
R
E

PERSIA

35

IONIAN IS.
(Br.)

Aegean Sea

Euphrates R.

Tigris R.

CRETE

CYPRUS

Mediterranean Sea

ARABIA

Abukir Bay
Alexandria

Cairo

EGYPT

20
25
35
40
45

GREAT
BRITAIN

P
R
U
S
S
I
A

RUSSIA

GERMANY

BATAVIAN
REPUBLIC

F R A N C E

SWITZ.

AUSTRIA

CISALPINE REP.

LIGURIAN REP.

SPAIN

CORSICA

OTTOMAN
EMPIRE

Western Europe, 1798

Extent of French influence

PARTHENOPEAN
REPUBLIC

50

Schönbrunn (1809) stripped them of the Illyrian provinces and assigned their Polish territory to the Grand Duchy of Warsaw. Francis II was obliged to give his daughter in marriage to Bonaparte and to become the unwilling ally of France.

Leadership in the German revival passed to Prussia, which had been aroused to action by the shock of Jena and Tilsit. The able general Scharnhorst relaxed the severe discipline of the Prussian army; the ceiling of 42,000 troops imposed at Tilsit was evaded by assigning recruits to the reserves after brief intensive training and then calling up another set of recruits. Social and administrative reorganization began under the energetic Baron Stein. He won support from middle-class Prussians by granting cities a degree of self-government, and he also sponsored an edict abolishing serfdom (October 1807). The liberated serfs received no land, however, and the Junkers retained both their large estates and their feudal rights of justice over the peasantry. The Hohenzollern state was not so much reformed as restored to the efficient absolutism of the Great Elector and Frederick the Great.

The event that led the Germans to reenter the struggle against Napoleon was the disaster suffered by the French in Russia. French actions after Tilsit soon convinced Tsar Alexander that Napoleon was intruding on Russia's sphere in Eastern Europe. French acquisition of the Illyrian provinces in 1809 raised the prospect of French domination over the Balkans, and the simultaneous transfer of Galicia from Austria to the Grand Duchy of Warsaw suggested that this Napoleonic satellite might attempt to take over Russia's Polish territories. The breach between France and Russia was widened by Napoleon's insistence that Russia enforce the Continental System and by French annexations in northwest Germany that wiped out the duchy of Oldenburg, where Alexander's uncle had been the reigning duke.

For the invasion of Russia in 1812, Napoleon assembled the Grand Army of nearly 700,000 men, a majority of whom were not Frenchmen but conscripts in the service of a foreign master. When the army crossed Russia's western frontier, the supply system broke down, and the Russian scorched-earth policy made it very hard for soldiers to live off the land and impossible for horses, many of which had to be destroyed. As the Grand Army advanced, one of Napoleon's aides reported: "There were no inhabitants to be found, no prisoners to be taken, not a single straggler to be picked up. . . . We were like a vessel without a compass in a vast ocean, knowing noth-

ing of what was happening around us."[*] Napoleon marched all the way to Moscow without striking a knockout blow, then remained in the burning city for five weeks (September–October 1812) in the vain hope of forcing the tsar to make peace. Russian stubbornness and the shortage of supplies forced Bonaparte to begin a retreat that became a nightmare, as his soldiers suffered horribly from sudden Russian attacks and from the onslaughts of "General Winter." Less than a quarter of the Grand Army survived.

In 1813 almost every state in Europe joined one more coalition against the French. Napoleon raised a new army but could not replace the equipment squandered in Russia. He lost the "Battle of the Nations" at Leipzig in eastern Germany (October 1813), and by the spring of 1814 the forces of the coalition occupied Paris. Faced also with mounting unrest at home, the emperor went into exile as ruler of the small island of Elba off the western coast of Italy.

The statesmen of the victorious coalition met at the Congress of Vienna to draw up terms of peace. The Bourbons returned to France in the person of Louis XVIII, a younger brother of Louis XVI, who established a conservative constitutional monarchy. Then, on March 1, 1815, Bonaparte pulled his last surprise by landing on the Mediterranean coast of France. For a hundred days, beginning on March 20, when he reentered Paris, the French Empire was reborn. The emperor promised the French genuine elections and a real parliament but had little time to show whether he would follow through. On June 18, 1815, the British under Wellington and the Prussians under Blücher delivered the final blow at Waterloo, near Brussels. Again Napoleon went into exile, this time to the remote British island of St. Helena in the South Atlantic. There he died in 1821.

IV THE AFTERMATH

The Vienna Settlement

By the time of Waterloo the peacemakers at Vienna had nearly completed their work. Most major decisions were made by four men—Metternich, Castlereagh, Talleyrand, and Tsar Alexander. Prince Metternich, Austrian foreign minister and host of the congress, came from the German

[*] A.A.L. de Caulaincourt, *With Napoleon in Russia* (New York, 1935), p. 62.

Rhineland, where his family had suffered losses as a result of the French Revolution. He also believed that the boost given to liberalism and nationalism by the revolution threatened a loose-jointed multinational state like the Austrian Empire. Viscount Castlereagh, the British foreign minister, was less concerned with punishing the French for their sins than with preventing the appearance of new Robespierres and Napoleons. "To bring the world back to peaceful habits" was his aim, and the method he proposed was a restoration of the balance of power, with no major state either too strong or too weak. Talleyrand, the foreign minister of Louis XVIII, had a remarkable ability to scent which way the political winds were blowing. Originally one of the worldliest bishops of the Old Regime, he was among the very few bishops who accepted the Civil Constitution of the Clergy; he later served as Napoleon's foreign minister but turned against him after Tilsit. This supremely adaptable diplomat soon maneuvered himself into the inner circle at Vienna, where he was an expert at exploiting the differences among the victors.

Tsar Alexander multiplied these differences by proposing a partial restoration of the Polish state, with himself as king; Austria and Prussia would lose the Polish lands they had seized in the partitions. Alexander won Prussian approval by backing Prussia's demand to annex Saxony, whose king had remained loyal to Napoleon. Metternich did not want Prussia to gain so much, and both he and Castlereagh were disturbed by the prospect of a Russian-dominated Poland. Talleyrand made the most of his chance to fish in troubled waters by joining Metternich and Castlereagh in threatening Prussia and Russia with war unless they moderated their demands (January 1815). A settlement resulted immediately: Prussia received half of Saxony, and Alexander accepted a smaller Poland, while Prussia and Austria kept part of their loot from the partitions.

The Congress then turned to other dynastic and territorial questions. By what Talleyrand called "the sacred principle of legitimacy," thrones and frontiers were to be reestablished as they had been in 1789. Legitimacy benefited chiefly the Bourbons, who regained the crowns of France, Spain, and Naples. The Congress did not attempt to revive the republics of Genoa and Venice or most of the hundreds of German states that had vanished since 1789. France was to return to the boundaries of 1790, substantially those of the Old Regime plus Avignon, acquired early in the revolution. The French were to return

Talleyrand.

Napoleon's art plunder to the rightful owners, pay the victorious allies an indemnity of $140,000,000 (an immense sum in those days), and finance a temporary allied occupation of seventeen forts on French soil.

In Germany, the Congress provided for thirty-nine states joined in a loose confederation that came close to reviving the weak Holy Roman Empire. Beside annexing part of Saxony, Prussia enlarged the scattered Hohenzollern lands in western Germany into the Rhine province, incorporating the Napoleonic kingdom of Westphalia. Austria yielded Belgium, which was joined with the kingdom of the Netherlands to strengthen the northern buffer against France. Austria was compensated by retaining Venetia and recovering Lombardy and the Illyrian provinces. Control of these territories together with the close family ties between the Hapsburgs and the rulers of smaller Italian states enabled Austria to dominate Italy. The only truly independent Italian state was the kingdom of Piedmont-Sardinia in the northwest, which annexed Genoa as a buffer against French expansion.

Another buffer against France was the enlarged republic of Switzerland. Elsewhere, the Congress of Vienna confirmed the earlier transfer of Finland from Sweden to Russia. As compensation to Sweden, Norway was shifted from Danish to Swedish rule, a move that also punished the Danes for supporting France. Great Britain retained the strategic Mediterranean island of Malta and the former Dutch colonies of Ceylon and the Cape of Good Hope. Beside strengthening

France's neighbors to discourage any future French aggression, the "big four"—Britain, Austria, Prussia, Russia—joined in the Quadruple Alliance (November 1815) to insure that the French adhered to the Vienna settlement.

Public opinion, however, especially in the English-speaking countries, often confused the Quadruple Alliance with Tsar Alexander's Holy Alliance (September 1815). Though criticized as reactionary, this Alliance was little more than a vaguely phrased proposal that "the policy of the powers ought to be guided by the sublime truths taught by the eternal religion of God our Saviour." Most rulers in Europe subscribed to the document, though few took it seriously. Castlereagh termed it "a piece of sublime mysticism and nonsense," and Britain declined to participate. So did the pope, who remarked that the Vatican did not welcome interpretations of Christian doctrine by the laity.

At the next meeting of the Quadruple Alliance in 1818, the allies agreed to end their occupation of France, which had paid up the indemnity imposed by the Vienna settlement. Then Tsar Alexander upset the applecart by proposing an international union with the contradictory goals of promoting constitutional monarchies everywhere, repressing revolution, advancing disarmament, and creating an international army to maintain the status quo. Austria and Britain rejected this effort "to endow the transparent soul of the Holy Alliance with a body," as Castlereagh put it.

The Legacy of the Revolution and Napoleon

Despite the widening rifts among the victorious allies, the Vienna settlement of 1814–1815 proved more effective than either of its predecessors—Westphalia (1648) and Utrecht (1713)—or its successor, the Paris settlement of 1919–1920. Victors have seldom treated a defeated aggressor with the generosity shown to France in 1815. There was to be no war involving several great powers until the second-rate Crimean conflict of the 1850s, and no major struggle embroiling the whole of Europe until 1914.

The enlightened statesmanship at Vienna could not prevent the survival of an important legacy from the tumult created by revolutionary and Napoleonic France. Bonapartism did not die at Waterloo or with Napoleon himself in 1821. A Napoleonic legend remained, fostered by the emperor and his circle on St. Helena, glossing over his faults and depicting him as the champion of liberalism and nationalism. It paved the way for the advent of another Napoleon in 1848.

A more potent legacy was bequeathed by the great revolutionary motto—Liberté, Egalité, Fraternité—which would inspire later generations of revolutionaries in France and elsewhere. While French institutions in 1815 did not always measure up to the Liberty promised in the Declaration of the Rights of Man of 1789, the ideals had been stated and the effort to apply them in practice was to be the main theme of French domestic history in the nineteenth century. The achievements of Equality by 1815 were more impressive. The Code Napoléon ended any possibility of reviving the worst legal and social inequalities of the Old Regime, and Protestants, Jews, and freethinkers secured toleration both in France and the French satellites. The revolutionary and Napoleonic regimes established the principle of equal liability to taxation. They opened more economic opportunities for the third estate by removing obstacles to business enterprises and breaking up the landed estates of the clergy and nobility. These benefits were not shared equally, however, for they were enjoyed largely by the urban bourgeois and well-to-do peasants.

Fraternity, the vaguest component of the revolutionary motto, had the greatest latent power. It encouraged the inhabitants of France to feel superior to all other nations, and it turned this feeling to a practical purpose in the Convention's decree of total mobilization on August 23, 1793. The Napoleonic Empire then showed how nationalism on an unprecedented scale could lead to imperialism of unparalleled magnitude. Half a century later, Alexis de Tocqueville, the great French student of democracy, would write:

> The French Revolution was a . . . political revolution, which in its operation resembled a religious one. It had every characteristic feature of a religious movement; it not only spread to foreign countries, but was carried by preaching and by propaganda. It roused passions such as the most violent political revolutions had never before excited. This gave to it that aspect of a religious revolution which so terrified contemporaries, or rather it became a kind of new religion in itself—a religion imperfect it is true, without a God, without a worship, without a future life, but which nevertheless poured forth its soldiers, its apostles, and its martyrs over the face of the earth.*

* Condensed from A. de Tocqueville, *The Old Regime and the Revolution* (London, 1888), Part I, Chapter 3.

Works treating events both in France and in other countries.

G. Lefebvre, *The French Revolution,* 2 vols. (*Columbia Univ.) and *Napoleon,* 2 vols. (Columbia Univ., 1969). English translations of comprehensive surveys by a distinguished French historian.

G. Rudé, *Revolutionary Europe, 1783–1815* (*Torch). Brief introduction by a leading expert on the period.

C. Brinton, *A Decade of Revolution, 1789–1799* (*Torch) and G. Bruun, *Europe and the French Imperium 1799–1814* (Harper, 1938). Though first published more than forty years ago, these two volumes in the series, *The Rise of Modern Europe,* are still worth reading because of their clear and instructive interpretations of events.

R. R. Palmer, *The Age of the Democratic Revolution,* 2 vols. (*Princeton Univ.). A detailed study arguing that the French Revolution was the largest link in a chain of democratic revolutions. Particularly useful for its excellent accounts of the Directory in France and of the upheavals in some of the smaller European states.

Works concentrating on events in France:

J. M. Roberts, *The French Revolution* (*Oxford Univ. Press). Recent brief and informative study, with an uptodate critical bibliography.

N. Hampson, *The French Revolution, A Concise History* (Scribner, 1975). Helpful overview by the author of the excellent *Social History of the French Revolution* (*Univ. of Toronto) and two studies of revolutionary leaders: *The Life and Opinions of Maximilien Robespierre* (*Duckworth) and *Danton* (Holmes & Meier, 1978).

A. Soboul, *The French Revolution, 1787–1799* (*Random House). By a very capable Marxist, the author also of *The Parisian Sans-Culottes and the French Revolution, 1793–1794* (Greenwood, 1979), an English translation of part of his extensive studies based on police records.

M. J. Sydenham, *The First French Republic, 1792–1804* (Univ. of California, 1974). A good survey of the Convention, the Directory, and the Consulate; by the author of an important re-evaluation, *The Girondins* (Greenwood), demonstrating that they were not a coherent political party.

G. Lefebvre, *The Coming of the French Revolution* (*Princeton Univ.). Masterly account of the momentous events of 1789 and their background. Lefebvre's detailed study, *The Great Fear,*

is also available in English translation (*Random House).

A. de Tocqueville, *The Old Regime and the Revolution* (*Anchor). A celebrated study stressing the continuities between the old and new regimes, written more than a century ago. It may be compared with the equally celebrated hostile critique by Edmund Burke: *Reflections on the Revolution in France,* Everyman ed. (Dutton, 1910).

L. Gershoy. *The French Revolution and Napoleon* (Appleton, 1964). Reprint of a sympathetic and lucid survey by an American expert.

J. M. Thompson, *The French Revolution* (2nd ed., Blackwell, 1962). Another lucid older survey by the author of *Robespierre and the French Revolution* (*Collier).

G. Rudé, *The Crowd in the French Revolution* (*Oxford Univ.). Important reassessment of the participants in the great revolutionary demonstrations.

R. R. Palmer, *Twelve Who Ruled* (*Princeton Univ.). Very readable collective biography of Robespierre and his colleagues in the Committee of Public Safety.

Three informative older studies by American historians are available in reprinted editions:

G. Bruun, *Saint-Just: Apostle of the Terror* (Shoe String). The career of the youngest and most radical member of the Committee of Public Safety.

L. Gottschalk, *Jean-Paul Marat* (Univ. of Chicago). Biography of the famous rabble-rousing journalist.

C. Brinton, *The Jacobins* (Russell). Reassessment of their activities in both Paris and the provinces.

Napoleon

Recent biographies and evaluations:
F. Markham, *Napoleon* (*Mentor) and *The Bonapartes* (Taplinger, 1975).
A. Horne, *Napoleon: Master of Europe* (Morrow, 1979).
C. Barnett, *Bonaparte* (Hill & Wang, 1978).
A. Castelot, *Napoleon* (Harper, 1971).
R. Ben Jones, *Myth and Man* (*Holmes and Meier, 1977).
M. Hutt, *Napoleon* (Oxford Univ. Press, 1965).
W. & A. Durant, *Napoleon* (Simon & Schuster, 1975).
O. Connelly, *The Epoch of Napoleon* (*Krieger) and *Napo-*

leon's Satellite Kingdoms (*Free Press).
D. Chandler, *The Campaigns of Napoleon* (Macmillan, 1973).
R. B. Holtman, *The Napoleonic Revolution* (*Lippincott).

Useful older publications
J. Thompson, *Napoleon Bonaparte, His Rise & Fall* (Oxford Univ., 1952).
H. Butterfield, *Napoleon* (*Collier).
H. Fisher, *Napoleon* (reprinted by Folcroft).
A. Caulaincourt, *With Napoleon in Russia* and *No Peace with Napoleon* (reprinted by Greenwood). Fascinating memoirs by one of his chief aides.
J. C. Herold, ed. *The Mind of Napoleon* (*Columbia Univ.). Illuminating autobiographical documents.

The Congress of Vienna

H. Nicolson, *The Congress of Vienna* (*Harcourt Brace). A classic by a celebrated English diplomat.
E. V. Gulick, *Europe's Classical Balance of Power* (*Norton). Places the work of the congress in a larger perspective.
H. Kissinger, *A World Restored* (*Houghton Mifflin). Appraisal of efforts to restore the European balance; doctoral dissertation by an ardent admirer of Metternich's policies.

Fiction

Anatole France, *The Gods Are Athirst* (Queens House). English translation of an excellent novel about a fanatical Jacobin.

Charles Dickens, *A Tale of Two Cities* (*many editions). Deficient in historical accuracy but unsurpassed in colorful episodes.

Victor Hugo, *Ninety-Three* (Harper, 1874). The last novel by the famous French Romantic author; conveys some of the drama of the year when the Terror began.

P. Weiss, *The Persecution and Assassination of Jean-Paul Marat as Performed by the Inmates of the Asylum of Charenton under the Direction of the Marquis de Sade* (*Atheneum). Dramatic depiction of the intensity of the revolutionary experience.

L. Tolstoy, *War and Peace* (*several editions, often abridged). The epic novel about Napoleon's Russian campaign.

CHAPTER THIRTEEN

Industry And Democracy:
1815-1870

Two major elements in the great modern revolution made important advances during the quarter century between the capture of the Bastille and the downfall of Napoleon. The political upheavals in France and its satellites marked an early stage in a long journey that would lead to democracy after many twists and turns. The invention of machines and the building of factories enabled modern industry to "take off," first in Great Britain and a generation or two later in Western Europe and North America. This economic revolution reinforced the push toward democracy. As goods became cheaper and more plentiful, so did popular expectations—and frustrations. Workers in the new industrial societies faced frequent unemployment, dangerous conditions in factories and mines, and unhealthy and inadequate housing. They responded by pressing for the right to strike and to organize in unions, and they followed the example of their employers by seeking a voice in politics. Their successes and failures down to 1870 are recorded in this chapter and the next.

Britain Takes Off

Although the term "industrial revolution" has long been part of the modern vocabulary, some historians and economists question its accuracy on the ground that the changes it describes were too gradual to be termed revolutionary. But other historians and economists defend the old term because industrialization advanced at a rapid pace with revolutionary results. The American scholar, W. W. Rostow, borrowed the aviation term, "take-off," to describe the stage when production expanded rapidly and the economy moved into a long period of sustained growth. Britain, during the two decades after 1783, was the first to take off.

The relative abruptness of Britain's take-off contrasted with the centuries of slow preparation that preceded it. This preparatory stage has been traced back to the discipline of medieval monasteries which assigned monks specific tasks at specific times and thus served as a model for organizing the labor force in a mine or a mill. Other factors that prepared the way were the expansion of banking in the late Middle Ages and the acquiring of colonial empires in the sixteenth and seventeenth centuries. The growing competition among rival states, the Protestant stress on hard work, and the attack on tradition by scientists and philosophers also paved the way for innovations.

Britain was the first to take off, Rostow contends, because "with its political, social, and religious revolution fought out by 1688" it "alone was in a position to weave together cotton manufacture, coal and iron technology, the steam engine, and ample foreign trade. . . ."* Britain had extensive deposits of coal and iron plus a large reservoir of manpower, filled by English farmers who were victims of the enclosure movement and by emigrants from overcrowded Ireland. The self-confidence and drive of Englishmen multiplied after their victories over the Spaniards in the sixteenth century, over the Dutch in the seventeenth, and the French in the eighteenth. The commercial and naval leadership of Britain accelerated the search for raw materials and new markets; in turn, profits from abroad nourished investment in industry at home. The long war against revolutionary and Napoleonic France

* W. W. Rostow, *The Stages of Economic Growth* (Cambridge, 1960), p. 33.

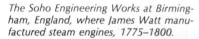

The Soho Engineering Works at Birmingham, England, where James Watt manufactured steam engines, 1775–1800.

stimulated the demand for metal goods and the invention of new machines. It also led to the construction of vast docks along the lower Thames, thereby strengthening London's position as the economic capital of the world.

The British textile industry pioneered in the use of power-driven machinery, starting with the spinning jenny of the 1760s and followed by a mechanical loom for weaving cotton thread into cloth. At first the new techniques depended on water power, an unreliable source during dry spells. In 1768 the Scot James Watt invented the steam engine, but difficulties in procuring exactly fitting parts delayed mass production of this new device. British engineers solved the problem by studying the precision techniques of watchmakers and developing a lathe that produced screws and other parts of perfect regularity. The American, Eli Whitney, made two important contributions to the advance of industry. His cotton gin (1793), a machine that removed the seeds from the fibers of raw cotton, enabled one slave to do what had previously required the labor of fifty slaves. In 1800 he experimented at his Connecticut factory with the making of standardized parts, later to become a basic ingredient of modern mass production.

By the early 1800s the market for coal in Britain expanded with the popularity of the steam engine and the growth of the metallurgical industry which converted coal into coke, used in the smelting of iron. Smelting became much more efficient after the development of the blast furnace (1828), in which fans provided a blast of hot air to intensify the action of the coke on iron. As yet, however, there was no inexpensive method of securing the long, intense heating needed to remove most of the carbon from iron, thereby converting it to the stronger metal called steel. Finally in 1856, Bessemer, an Englishman of French extraction, invented the converter, which removed impurities from molten iron by shooting jets of compressed air into it. A decade later, Siemens, a German living in England, devised the open-hearth process of making steel; it used scrap as well as new iron and handled larger amounts of metal than the converter could.

By the mid-nineteenth century the railroads were major consumers of iron and later shifted to steel when it became less expensive. One mile of track required 300 tons of rail. The revolution in transport began early in the century when many hundreds of miles of canal were dug in Europe and North America, and highways were improved by the durable surface of broken stones

named for its creator, the Scot McAdam. But only the railroad made possible the inexpensive overland shipment of heavy items like coal and iron. In Britain, during the 1820s, George Stephenson and others put the steam engine on wheels and created the locomotive. The railroad boom was soon in full swing: Britain had 500 miles of track in 1838, 6,600 in 1850, and 15,500 in 1870.

Meantime, after Robert Fulton's steamboat made a successful voyage on the Hudson River (1807), paddle-wheel steamers plied the inland waterways of the United States and Europe. Ocean-going steamships were hampered by the inefficiency of marine engines, which required so much coal that it took up almost half the cargo space on a transatlantic voyage. In mid-century most freight was still carried by sailing ships, such as the beautiful American clippers. The improvement of marine engines in the 1860s and the substitution of the screw propeller for the cumbersome paddle wheel eventually made the commercial sailing vessel obsolete.

The most dramatic lowering of the barriers of distance occurred in communications, beginning with the British penny post of 1840, which reduced the cost of sending a letter to a fraction of what it had been. In 1844 the first telegraph message, from Baltimore to Washington, demonstrated that electricity could provide virtually instantaneous communication. Then came the first submarine cable, under the English Channel (1851); the first transatlantic cable (1866); and the first telephone (1876).

New inventions attracted capital from many sources. The slave traders of Liverpool financed the cotton mills of Manchester and other towns nearby; the tobacco merchants of Glasgow provided the funds that made their city the industrial hub of Scotland; and tea merchants in London and Bristol assisted the iron smelters of South Wales. Bankers played such an important role that Disraeli, Queen Victoria's favorite politician, listed the Barings of London and the Rothschilds among the great powers of Europe. In the early 1800s, each of the five Rothschilds, sons of a German Jewish banker, established himself in an important economic center—London, Paris, Frankfurt, Naples, and Vienna. They promoted international investment—the Paris Rothschild, for example, arranging for British capital to underwrite the construction of French railroads in the 1840s.

During the Napoleonic wars, British banks issued paper money to supplement the meager supply of coins. But whenever a financial crisis occurred, local banks failed and their banknotes became worthless. Parliament therefore encouraged the stronger banks to take over the weaker, and in 1844 it gave the Bank of England a virtual monopoly over the issuance of banknotes. Meantime, the requirement of unlimited liability discouraged investment in business enterprises: when a company went bankrupt all the assets of its shareholders were liable to seizure to pay off its creditors. Beginning in the 1850s Parliament passed legislation providing for limited liability (indicated by the "Ltd." after a company's name), which restricted a shareholder's liability according to the number of shares he held, thus diminishing the risk of investment.

International Repercussions

By the mid-nineteenth century, the signs of British economic dominance were evident on every hand—on the teeming London docks; in the thriving financial houses of the City of London; and in the mushrooming factory and mining towns of the Midlands, the North of England, and Scotland. American trains ran on rails rolled in British mills and on money from British inves-

tors. Lancashire cotton goods clothed a sizable part of the world's population. Support for Britain's claim to be the "workshop of the world" was provided by the Great Exhibition of the Works of Industry of All Nations, opened by Queen Victoria in London's Hyde Park on May 1, 1851. Britain's latest mechanical marvels were displayed in the Crystal Palace, a remarkable structure of iron and glass that stretched like a mammoth greenhouse for a third of a mile.

Britain was the industrial leader, but it never monopolized inventive skills. Frenchmen devised the chlorine process of bleaching cloth and perfected the Jacquard loom for weaving intricate patterns. German technicians led the world in agricultural chemistry and in utilizing the valuable by-products of coal. And the United States had an impressive list of inventors, in addition to Eli Whitney: Morse and the telegraph, Singer and the sewing machine, and McCormick, whose reaper (1834) was the first of many farm machines developed in America.

The whole North Atlantic world, both European and American, was becoming a single vast economic community. As Britain's economy matured, other members of the community reached

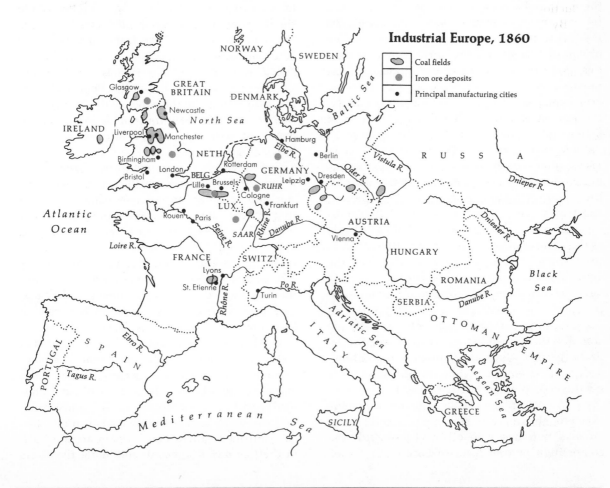

Industrial Europe, 1860

Coal fields
Iron ore deposits
Principal manufacturing cities

the take-off stage. In the vanguard were France, Belgium (which had close ties with British industry), and the northeastern and middle western American states. Some of the German states began to take off about 1850 and consolidated their success with the triumphant unification of the German Empire in 1871. By the end of the century, the economies of Japan and Russia were nearing take-off and threatening to reduce the advantages of the head start enjoyed by the North Atlantic community.

While the industrial revolution made nations more interdependent, it also increased international tensions by inspiring a fierce competition for markets and raw materials. It sharpened the differences between the champions of relatively free international trade, the British above all, and the economic nationalists who demanded protective tariffs. It added to the outburst of expansionist energies in the half-century preceding 1914 that brought so much of the world under Western imperialist domination.

The Impact on Agriculture

The industrial revolution gave agriculture the tools and chemicals that enabled fewer and fewer farmers to produce more and more. The steel plow and the reaper permitted the opening of vast new areas, like the North American prairies, that could hardly have been touched if the pioneers had had to rely on hand labor. International trade in farm products increased rapidly, the annual export of wheat from the United States and Canada, for instance, rising from 22 million bushels in the 1850s to 150 million in 1880. Britain relied increasingly not only on imported flour but also on mutton from Australia, beef from Argentina, and cheese, eggs, butter, and bacon from Denmark and the Netherlands.

Germany now took over Britain's old role as the pioneer of scientific farming. By the 1840s the German scientist Liebig was publicizing the agricultural uses of organic chemistry, particularly the importance of nitrogen, potassium, and phosphorus in fostering the growth of plants. Liebig's warning that these elements must be restored to the soil led to the increased use of fertilizers, particularly potash, nitrate (from Chile), and guano (from the nesting islands of sea birds off the west coast of South America).

The new phase of the agricultural revolution brought unprecedented prosperity to some growers but misery to others. Faced with the competition of beet sugar in Europe, the cane-

growing islands of the West Indies entered a prolonged depression from which some of them have never recovered. The southern American states and Egypt, with their dependence on the export of cotton, seemed doomed to the colonial role of supplying raw materials for industry and buying manufactured goods from their customers. So, too, did Argentina, which depended on shipping beef and wool to Britain.

The Impact on Society

In Britain itself farming was no longer the principal occupation of Englishmen, and land was no longer the measure of wealth and power. The manufacturers and merchants scored a decisive victory over the landed gentry in 1846 when Parliament repealed the Corn Laws, which had restricted the importation of grain from abroad. By this time the population was growing so rapidly that self-sufficiency in foodstuffs was no longer possible. Despite substantial emigration, the number of inhabitants in England and Wales rose from 9 million in 1800 to 32.5 million in 1900. Scholars are still debating whether or not the industrial revolution was responsible for this population explosion. Some demographers attribute the increase not to a higher birth rate but to the lower death rate resulting from improved food and sanitation, along with the availability of cheap, washable cotton materials. Others claim that neither diet nor sanitation improved until the second half of the nineteenth century, and that in the first half the population increased mainly in rural areas, while death rates were high in urban centers.

Controversy surrounds the question of whether the industrial revolution improved the standard of living. Incomplete statistics suggest that starting about 1820 the purchasing power of British workers increased very gradually as cheaper goods became more plentiful. And although both the workers' chance for a steady job and the opportunity to master new skills improved, the frequent ups and downs of the business cycle caused many people to believe that their standard of living was declining.

There is little debate, however, about the truly revolutionary changes that industry brought to the structure of the population. Mines and factories urbanized large areas of rural England, and by mid-century a similar transformation was under way in the lowlands around Glasgow, in the northern French plain around Lille, in the German Rhineland, and along the rivers

"Over London by Rail": An 1872 engraving after Gustave Doré showing the living conditions of the working class.

of the northeastern United States. This urbanization caused a rise in the numbers and influence of the two classes that form the backbone of an industrial society—business and labor. Captains of industry, bankers, investors, and promoters joined the already established capitalists and professional men to form the modern middle class, or bourgeoisie. Millhands, railroad men, miners, clerks, and a host of other recruits swelled the ranks of wage-earning laborers.

Both businessmen and workers had their grievances and their hopes. In Britain the new industrialists of the 1810s and 1820s had little chance to make national policy, for such booming centers as Manchester and Birmingham sent not a single member to the House of Commons. A high proportion of businessmen were Nonconformists (Protestants who were not members of the Church of England) and therefore subject to discrimination when it came to holding public office or sending their sons to Oxford or Cambridge. Later segments of this chapter will show how the French and Belgian bourgeoisie made important political gains in 1830, and the British in 1832. Elsewhere in Europe, it took the middle

classes longer to win the place in the sun they felt they deserved.

For workers progress was slower still. By the 1830s most white males in the United States had gained the vote, but most blacks had to wait until the next century. In 1848 both Switzerland and France inaugurated universal male suffrage, but the French soon went back to a discrimination like that between active and passive citizens during the great revolution. Germans first gained universal male suffrage in the late 1860s, and in most of the other European states it was not granted until the first two decades of the twentieth century. Though most members of the industrial working force in Britain obtained the vote in 1867, it took another half century for all adult males to obtain the franchise. By contrast, Britain was the first to ease the restrictions on labor unions and their activities (in the 1820s), but it was not until the last third of the century that unions in Britain and elsewhere acquired the right to strike.

For many workers the drive for legal and political rights was a marginal matter compared to the pressing need to find jobs and make ends

"Hurrying Coal": A girl drawing a loaded wagon of coal weighing between two hundred and five hundred pounds underground in a Yorkshire mine, 1842.

meet. The industrial revolution speeded up the business cycle, with its recurrent slumps and substantial layoffs of workers. Many of the new factories made no attempt to maintain a steady level of employment. Machines and men were worked to capacity until a batch of orders was filled, and the factory then shut down until more orders came in. Even laborers with steady jobs earned such low wages that a family man might have to put both his wife and children to work.

Humanitarian tradition probably exaggerates the extent to which women and children were exploited in factories or mines and makes an extreme example an average instance. But inhuman exploitation did occur, as evidenced by the testimony of a British factory worker before a parliamentary committee in 1831:

> At what time in the morning, in the brisk time, did those girls go to the mills? *In the brisk time, for about six weeks, they have gone at 3 o'clock in the morning, and ended at 10, or nearly half-past, at night.*
>
> What intervals were allowed for rest or refreshment during those nineteen hours of labour? *Breakfast a quarter of an hour, and dinner half an hour, and drinking a quarter of an hour. . . .*
>
> Had you not great difficulty in awakening your children to this excessive labour? *Yes, in the early time we had them to take up asleep and shake them when we got them on the floor to dress them, before we could get them off to their work; but not so in the common hours.*
>
> What was the length of time they could be in bed during those long hours? *It was near 11 o'clock before we could get them into bed after getting a little victuals, and then . . . my mistress used to stop up all night, for fear that we could not get them ready for the time. . . .*

So that they had not above four hours' sleep at this time? *No, they had not.*

For how long together was it? *About six weeks it held; it was only done when the throng was very much on; it was not often that.*

The common hours of labour were from 6 in the morning till half-past eight at night? *Yes. . . .*

Were the children excessively fatigued by this labour? *Many times; we have cried often when we have given them the little victualling we had to give them; we had to shake them, and they have fallen to sleep with the victuals in their mouths many a time.*

Did this excessive term of labour occasion much cruelty also? *Yes, with being so very much fatigued the strap was very frequently used.*

What was the wages in the short hours? *Three shillings a week each.* [73 U.S. cents]

When they wrought those very long hours what did they get? *Three shillings and sevenpence halfpenny.* [88½ U.S. cents]

For all that additional labour they had only sevenpence halfpenny a week additional? *No more.* *

Few plants had safety devices to guard dangerous machinery, and cotton mills kept heat and humidity at high levels because threads broke less frequently in a hot damp atmosphere. After facing hazards at work many laborers went home to the greater perils of contaminated water, primitive sewage facilities, and overcrowded housing. Fantastic numbers of human beings were jammed into the slums of London, Manchester, Liverpool, and Lille. Londoners living near the Thames were reluctant to open windows because of the stench from the river. It was estimated in the 1840s that

* Bland, Brown, and Tawney, *English Economic History: Select Documents* (London, 1915), pp. 510–13.

the life expectancy of a boy born to a working-class family in Manchester was only half that of one born to rural laborers. At the same time, illiteracy was also commonplace. In the 1840s, records noted that a third of the men and half the women married in England could not sign their names on the marriage register and simply made a mark. A Sunday school was often the only place where a millhand's child could learn the ABCs, and only a millhand with great perseverance would attend the adult evening classes in "mechanics' institutes." In all the industrial countries educational facilities remained grossly inadequate until provisions were made for free schooling during the last third of the century.

II BRITAIN TO 1870

In the seventeenth century the English had been regarded as the most revolutionary people in Europe because they had executed one king and sent another into exile. In the nineteenth century they became famous as the most stable and law-abiding people in Europe. Britain was envied as the only great power able to combine traditional monarchy and modern democracy without a revolution.

The Road to Reform

In 1815 the British Parliament was still very far from being a democratic institution. The House of Lords, which except for money bills had equal power with the Commons, was composed of the small privileged class of hereditary peers plus a few new peers created by the crown from time to time. The House of Commons, its members unpaid, was recruited largely from the country gentry, the professional classes, and unusually successful businessmen. It was elected by less than one-sixth of the adult male population. Both the working classes in town and country and the average prosperous men of the middle class were generally denied the franchise. The largely rural south, once the most populous area of the kingdom, now had more representatives in Commons than it merited, including a large contingent from depopulated "rotten boroughs," while the teeming new industrial centers of the north, such as Manchester, Liverpool, and Sheffield, usually had no representation at all.

Proposals to modernize Parliament had come close to success in the late eighteenth century. But the wars with revolutionary France made reform impossible, and in the postwar years even moderate reformers were still denounced as Jacobins. In August 1819, a nervous Tory government permitted soldiers to break up a peaceful mass meeting at St. Peter's Field near Manchester to hear speeches on parliamentary reform. In this "Peterloo massacre" eleven were killed and several hundred wounded. Repression reached a peak in December 1819 when Parliament passed the Six Acts, curtailing freedom of speech and of assembly and invading other civil rights. Fortunately, the governments of the 1820s, led by such enlightened Tories as George Canning and Robert Peel, restored civil rights and sponsored other reforms. The Combination Acts, outlawing unions and strikes, were modified to permit laborers to organize, and the antiquated criminal code, with its severe penalties, was eased. The seventeenth-century Test Act, which, though no longer enforced, legally excluded Nonconformists from public life, was repealed. Also repealed were the laws that really did exclude Catholics from public life.

Parliamentary reform began in 1832. The Whig Lord Grey gained Tory support for reform of the House of Commons, but the Tory House of Lords blocked the bill. Grey persuaded King William IV (reigned 1830–1837) to threaten the creation of hundreds of new Whig peers who would put the reform through the Lords. The threat, combined with fears of a run on the Bank of England and alarm over popular violence (it had already broken out in Bristol), resulted in passage of the bill on June 4, 1832.

The First Reform Bill and Its Consequences

The First Reform Bill is often cited as the most celebrated act of legislation ever passed by Parliament. Yet, while it was a most important beginning, it did not bring political democracy to Britain. It did wipe out more than fifty rotten boroughs and awarded seats in the Commons to more than forty previously unrepresented industrial centers. The number of voters was increased by about 50 percent and included virtually all the middle class, but the property qualifications for voting excluded the great mass of workers.

The immediate sequel to the 1832 bill was a series of reforms that helped make over British economic and social life. Inspiration for these reforms came from a small but influential middle-class group of "Philosophic Radicals." These disciples of the Enlightenment believed that men, once they were properly educated, would be guided by rational self-interest and would therefore do what was best for themselves and most useful for their fellows. They followed the teachings of Jeremy Bentham (1748–1832), who based his social teachings on the concept of utility.

"Nature," Bentham wrote, "has placed mankind under the governance of two masters, pain and pleasure," and so the community will regard as useful anything that enhances pleasure and averts pain. Ordinarily, he believed, the government would safeguard the well-being of a community most effectively by keeping its hands off social and economic matters. But it would be justified in intervening when the pursuit of self-interest by some individuals worked against the best interests of others. If the pains suffered by the many exceeded the pleasures enjoyed by the few, then the state would be justified in acting to defend the general welfare.

Under the utilitarian influence of the Philosophic Radicals, England's local government and legal system were simplified and made more efficient by eliminating much of the red tape that had accumulated over the centuries. For instance, legal procedures, which had become so complicated that the Chancery Court was many years behind in its backlog of cases, were gradually speeded up. The Municipal Corporations Act of 1835 assigned the basic authority in most towns and cities to elected councils, which supervised professional civil servants. Among the latter were the recently established uniformed policemen, who got their nickname "bobby" from their par-

liamentry sponsor, Robert Peel. On the whole, however, the middle-class radicals kept government intervention to a minimum. They believed in education, but not in compulsory education; private initiative, they argued, would do better what government would do poorly and tyrannically. Private initiative did indeed sponsor mechanics' institutes and support the new universities at London, Manchester, and other cities that ended the centuries-old monopoly of Oxford and Cambridge. The latter, however, with their colleges of medieval stone, enjoyed vastly more prestige than did the "red brick" newcomers.

The utilitarian reform that aroused the most controversy was the New Poor Law of 1834, which altered a complex system of "public relief" ("welfare" is the American term) dating back to the Elizabethan era. Under the old "outdoor relief" the poor could supplement low wages and obtain support for their children with payments from the parishes, the smallest units of local government. Under the new system of "indoor relief," the able-bodied poor were no longer assisted in their homes but sent to formidable workhouses in which the sexes were rigorously separated. The theory behind this heartless change, which outraged humanitarians, was that recipients of poor relief should be made as uncomfortable as decency would permit in order to prod them out of laziness and into becoming self-supporting.

Parliament recognized that evils could exist in private business as well as in public relief, and began to regulate the exploitation of workers in factories and mines. The Factory Act of 1833 forbade child labor below the age of nine and restricted it to nine hours a day for children under thirteen and twelve hours for those between thirteen and eighteen. Since many industrialists had ignored earlier efforts to regulate child labor, the Act of 1833 put "teeth" into its requirements by authorizing salaried inspectors to see that the law was enforced. Together with thorough investigations by parliamentary committees, which were published as "blue books," a precedent was set for later legislation regulating mines as well as factories and protecting adult workers of both sexes in addition to children.

Victorian Reforms, 1837–1870

During the long, eventful reign of Queen Victoria (1837–1901), the pace of reform slowed at first, but the gradual democratization of Britain continued. Victoria never thought of herself as

Jeremy Bentham, 1823.

a mere figurehead and frequently advised her ministers on questions of policy. Nevertheless, she reigned rather than ruled, for it was established practice that basic decisions were taken by the Parliament and cabinet, not by the crown. In the mid-nineteenth century, the two major political parties were coming to be known as Liberal and Conservative instead of Whig and Tory. They were quite different from the loose and quarrelsome factions of the eighteenth century, more disciplined by party "whips" in Parliament, and more concerned with issues affecting the masses of people. It is important to note that Liberals and Conservatives did not by any means take opposing positions on all the great issues of the day. While the Liberals put through the First Reform Bill in 1832, the Conservatives sponsored the Second Bill of 1867.

Agitation for the second bill began soon after the passage of the first. Workingmen wanted the right to vote for members of Parliament in order to press for legislation easing the hardships of the industrial revolution. Their demands were drawn up in the "People's Charter." It called for universal manhood suffrage, a secret ballot to replace the tradition of voting in public, the abolition of property requirements for members of Parliament, the payment of members, and equal electoral districts. The Chartists greatly alarmed conservative Britons. They were strongest among urban industrial workers and had many supporters among intellectuals. In 1839 they presented to Parliament a monster petition, with more than a million signatures, urging adoption of the charter. Parliament never considered the petition, and did not respond to further peaceful Chartist initiatives in 1842 and 1848. Although Chartism petered out after 1848, all of its major demands were destined to become law within the next two generations.

By the 1860s the ground swell for more parliamentary reform was so powerful that Disraeli (1804–1881), the Conservative leader in the Commons, decided that if his party did not sponsor reform the Liberals certainly would. The Conservatives should get the credit and might well also get the votes of newly enfranchised workingmen. As it turned out, the first general election after the new reform brought the Liberals in! The Reform Bill of 1867, like that of 1832, was a piecemeal change that made electoral districts more nearly uniform and equal, but left them still divided into boroughs and shires (counties), as in the Middle Ages. It doubled the number of voters by extending the franchise in the boroughs to householders owning or renting dwellings. But it did not widen the franchise significantly in rural areas. Four more reform bills were needed before male suffrage became universal in 1918.

Free Trade and Ireland

Another policy to which both Liberals and Conservatives contributed was free trade. Traditionally, the Tories had supported tariffs to protect British agriculture from foreign competition, notably the Corn Laws restricting the import of food grains from abroad ("corn" in Britain means any grain, while "maize" or "Indian corn" designates what Americans know as corn). Businessmen with Liberal sympathies supported the Anti-Corn-Law League, a pressure group that wanted Britain to adopt free trade and argued that cheaper food from abroad could be paid for by exports of British manufactured goods.

Their case was helped by a blight that ruined the Irish potato crop in 1845 and resulted in a disastrous famine. In the face of the urgent need for cheap foreign grain, the free traders won their victory in 1846 when they persuaded the Conservative Peel to abandon Tory protectionism. Free trade came too late, however, to prevent more than twenty thousand Irish from dying of starvation and hundreds of thousands more from succumbing to typhus and cholera. The British government failed to provide prompt and efficient measures of relief; nor was there as yet an international organization like the Red Cross to step in. Hundreds of thousands of Irish emigrated from their overcrowded island, mainly to the

Disraeli Measuring the British Lion: Cartoon from "Punch," 1849, on the state of the nation three years after the repeal of the Corn Laws.

United States where they organized anti-British pressure groups.

The terrible famine intensified Irish hatreds centuries old. In Ireland an English minority and, in the northern province of Ulster, Scottish immigrants were privileged Protestant landowners in the midst of a much larger population of Catholic peasants. In 1801 Ireland had been incorporated into the United Kingdom of England and Scotland, thereafter called the United Kingdom of Great Britain and Ireland. Irish members were admitted to Parliament only if they were Protestants. Beginning with the Catholic Emancipation Act of 1829, Catholics could sit in Parliament and hold other public offices.

The Irish then pressed for more thorough changes and eventually for "home rule." They sought land reforms to break the economic dominance of the Protestant minority. And they demanded disestablishment of the Anglican Church in Ireland—that is, abolition of a state church which served only a minority of the population but was supported by taxes levied on Catholics and Presbyterians as well as Anglicans. The Liberals disestablished the Anglican Church in 1869, and in 1870 passed the Irish Land Act, which tried to protect tenants from "rack-renting" (rent-gouging) by landlords. But reform moved too slowly to satisfy the Irish, who were motivated not only by questions of land and religion but also by an intense nationalism.

Empire and Dominions

Overseas, meantime, the British also confronted outbreaks of incipient nationalism which took the form of stubborn resistance to dictation from London. In the early 1840s they went to war with China when it attempted to restrict the importation of opium from British India. The Opium War resulted in the British acquisition of Hong Kong as a crown colony. It also paved the way for Western powers to obtain "treaty ports," Chinese cities opened to foreign commerce. They also secured for their citizens rights of "extraterritoriality," making them subject to the laws of their own countries rather than to those of their Chinese hosts. Such concessions were a blow to Chinese sovereignty and national pride.

In India British supremacy was shaken by the Sepoy Rebellion of 1857. The Sepoys, who were native soldiers in the service of the East India Company, mutinied in part because of rumors that bullets issued to them were greased with beef fat, repugnant to Hindus, or with pork fat, repugnant to Muslims. Above all, the Sepoys feared that the imposition of alien ways would destroy their own traditions. Once the rebellion was put down (1858), the British government took over the lands and responsibilities of the East India Company. The British now ruled directly about two-thirds of the Indian subcontinent, including the most densely populated areas, and supervised the nominally independent native states in the remaining third.

Britain's Chinese and Indian policies marked one aspect of the British imperialism that would reach its heyday during the generation preceding World War I. But there was a more attractive aspect, first evident when Britain outlawed the slave trade in the early 1800s and later emancipated the slaves in its colonies (1833). These actions were the result of a vigorous campaign by British abolitionists. The antislavery measures greatly irritated the Boers of Dutch and French Huguenot descent in the Cape Colony, at the southern tip of Africa, acquired by Britain during the French revolutionary wars. Disturbed also by the arrival of English colonists, many Boers set out in covered wagons (1835) on a "Great Trek" to the vast open spaces farther north. There they founded the Transvaal Republic and the Orange Free State, both recognized as independent by Britain yet both destined to be at the core of British-Boer tensions later in the century.

Half a world away, in Canada, events led Britain to a precedent-setting experiment that encouraged the peaceful loosening of ties binding colonies to the mother country. In the early nineteenth century, Canada was composed of five separate units—the three maritime colonies of Nova Scotia, New Brunswick, and Prince Edward Island; Lower Canada (the old French region of Quebec); and Upper Canada (the newer English and Scottish settlements of Ontario). In 1837 rebellions in both Lower and Upper Canada led to the appointment of a young Whig, Lord Durham, as governor general. In 1839 Durham made a report to Parliament recommending the union of Upper and Lower Canada and the granting of substantial self-government to the new entity.

The Durham Report led ultimately to the British North America Act of 1867, which approved the joining of the Maritime Provinces with Quebec and Ontario to form the nearly independent Dominion of Canada, only loosely tied to the mother country. As Canadian lands farther west attracted settlers, new provinces were admitted to the Dominion, much as new states gained admission to the United States. Meanwhile, the principles of the Durham Report were applied to Australia and New Zealand, the other major territories of white settlement. But nearly a hundred years would pass before Britain could contemplate extending dominion status to nonwhite populations.

III FRANCE

The Bourbon Restoration

France, like Britain, moved toward a more democratic government, but in a much more dramatic fashion, punctuated by revolutions and coups d'état. The Bourbon restoration got off to an uncertain start under Louis XVIII (reigned 1814–1824). Although the king would have preferred to rule as an absolute monarch, he was sensible enough to realize that a complete return to the Old Regime was impossible, especially since he was aging and in declining health. He settled, instead, for ambiguous policies, well illustrated in the constitutional charter he issued in 1814. While asserting that "authority resides in the person of the king," the charter set up a legislature composed of a Chamber of Peers appointed by the king and a Chamber of Deputies elected on a very restricted suffrage that allowed fewer than a hundred thousand of France's thirty millions to vote. Though the chambers had no formal right to confirm the king's choice of ministers, Louis tended to appoint men acceptable to majority opinion in the legislature. Thus France acquired a backhanded parliamentary government. More important, the charter confirmed many of the decisive changes instituted by the great revolution of 1789–1814. These included religious toleration, equality before the law, equal eligibility to civil and military office, the Napoleonic Code, and the revolutionary redistribution of noble and clerical property.

The charter greatly irritated the noble and clerical émigrés returning to France. The Ultraroyalists, grouped around the king's brother and heir, the count of Artois, were determined to recover both the privileges and the property they had lost during the Revolution. When the Ultras won control of the Chamber of Deputies in the election of 1815, the victorious opponents of France in the Napoleonic Wars insisted that Louis

XVIII dismiss the Chamber. A new election returned a less extreme majority in 1816 and enabled Louis to install a moderate ministry. Events, however, soon strengthened the Ultras' influence. Fear of a new revolution swept France in 1820 following an uprising against the Bourbon king of Spain and the assassination in Paris of the king's nephew, the duke of Berry. The assassin hoped to extinguish the Bourbon line, but the widowed duchess gave birth to a son seven months later. The Ultras won control of the Chamber of Deputies, clamped controls on the press, and passed a law giving extra weight to the votes of the wealthiest 25 percent of the electorate. They also sent French troops to help restore the authority of the Spanish king.

The tempo of reaction quickened when Louis died and Artois, the Ultra leader, became King Charles X (reigned 1824–1830). Charles encouraged Jesuit activities, though the order was still legally banned in France, and appointed clerics to posts in the state school system. He sponsored a law granting special annuities to returned émigrés as compensation for property lost during the revolution. This measure lifted the threat of confiscation hanging over those who had acquired émigré property. But, together with Charles's clericalism, it infuriated many well-to-do citizens who believed, incorrectly, that the government was financing the annuities by simultaneously lowering the interest it was paying on its other obligations.

In 1829 Charles further antagonized his subjects by naming as his chief minister the prince of Polignac, an Ultra extremist, who claimed to have had visions in which the Virgin Mary promised him success. Hoping to bolster the prestige of the king by a victory abroad, Polignac sent an expedition to Algeria. The assault followed an incident in which the ruler of this Ottoman vassal state, already notorious for his support of the Barbary pirates, struck the French consul with a fly whisk. The capture of the city of Algiers (July 5, 1830) laid the foundation of the French Empire in North Africa. But it did not diminish attacks on Polignac's policies in the Chamber of Deputies, where the liberals had just won a majority after a national election.

The Revolution of 1830

On July 25, 1830, without the approval of the chamber, Charles and Polignac issued four ordinances muzzling the press, dissolving the recently elected chamber, ordering a new election, and imposing voting limitations to disfranchise the bourgeois voters who were the mainstay of the parliamentary opposition. The king and his minister expected the recent victory in Algiers to rally public opinion in their favor. Instead, the citizens of Paris, aroused by the protests of liberal journalists, staged a riot that became a revolution. During the "three glorious days" of July 27, 28, and 29, they threw up barricades, captured the city hall, and hoisted the tricolor atop Notre Dame. When Charles X saw the revolutionary flag through a spyglass from his suburban retreat, he abdicated in favor of his grandson (the duke of Berry's posthumous child) and sailed to exile in England.

It has often been claimed that the July Revolution was almost bloodless; in fact, it took the lives of eighteen hundred insurgents and two hundred soldiers. It has also been claimed that most of the revolutionaries were the poor and downtrodden, victims of the unemployment, bank failures, and high food prices prevailing in the France of 1830. In fact, the barricades of 1830 were manned chiefly by tradesmen and skilled artisans, essentially the same social groups who had conquered the Bastille forty-one years earlier.

The revolutionaries of 1830, like those of 1789, were not agreed on the kind of regime they wanted. Some favored a democratic republic and rallied to Lafayette, now an aged symbol of revolution. Others, particularly well-to-do bourgeois, preferred a constitutional monarchy with a narrow suffrage. These moderates were headed by the elderly but still astute Talleyrand, by the wealthy banker Laffitte, and by two cautious young liberals, Thiers and Guizot. Thiers edited a newspaper opposing Charles X and had written a history of the Great Revolution stressing its peaceful, constructive achievements. Guizot, too, had written history, a survey of civilization focused on the rise of the bourgeoisie. He had also been active in an organization—whose motto was "Heaven helps those who help themselves" (*Aide-toi, le Ciel t'aidera*)—that rallied voters against the Ultras.

In 1830 the moderates had the brains, they had the money, and they had the support not only of parliamentary opponents of Charles X but also of Napoleonic officials who hoped to recover the posts they had lost under the restoration. The moderates also proposed a strong candidate for the throne, Louis Philippe, the duke of Orléans, a cousin of Charles X. His father had participated in the Paris demonstrations of 1789, assumed the revolutionary name of Philippe

Egalité (equality), and voted for the execution of Louis XVI before being sentenced to the guillotine himself. Louis Philippe had fought in the revolutionary army at Valmy in 1792 and later emigrated before the peak of the Terror. He claimed to have little use for the pomp of royalty and dressed and acted like a sober businessman. Having won over the gullible Lafayette by feigning republican sympathies, he then accepted the crown at the invitation of the chamber that had been elected in May of 1830.

The July Monarchy

Louis Philippe's regime, the July Monarchy, lasted for eighteen years. Its constitution was Louis XVIII's charter of 1814 as revised by the Chamber of Deputies. It granted the legislature more initiative and implied that the charter was no longer a grant by the monarch but a pact between him and the nation. Following the precedent of 1791, it designated Louis Philippe as king of the French rather than king of France; the tricolor also replaced the white flag of the Bourbons. While the number of voters doubled, the suffrage was still restricted to the large rural landowners and well-to-do business and professional men who paid a tax of at least 200 francs ($40 in U.S. currency of the 1830s), 166,000 Frenchmen all told. The France of Louis Philippe, rather like eighteenth-century Britain, functioned on the narrow social base of landed and funded gentry.

Alexis de Tocqueville, author of the celebrated *Democracy in America* and later a member of the Chamber of Deputies, remarked that "Government in those days resembled an industrial company whose every operation is undertaken for the profits which the stockholders may gain thereby." The stockholders of the July Monarchy were the social and economic elite who had the vote. They included former Napoleonic officials who became prefects and diplomats after the sweeping change in personnel following the July Revolution. Demands for liberalization of the suffrage were met with Guizot's curt recommendation, "get rich" (*enrichissez-vous!*) to qualify for the vote. The government banned labor organizations; and its harsh repression of demonstrations by working people was symbolized by the massacre of the rue Transnonain (April 1834) in a poor quarter of Paris, when soldiers killed fourteen residents of a house thought to be harboring a sniper. In eighteen years the July Monarchy introduced only two measures helping workers—

an extension of state aid to primary schools, and a laxly enforced law limiting child labor.

Nationalistic Frenchmen were dismayed by Louis Philippe's failures in foreign policy, particularly after the return of Napoleon's ashes from St. Helena in 1840, which dramatized the contrast between the great days of Bonaparte and the humiliating present. In that same year Thiers was dismissed as prime minister because of the collapse of his Egyptian policy. Thiers had vigorously supported the ambitious empire-building of the governor of Egypt, Muhammad Ali, who took advantage of the weakness of his overlord, the Ottoman emperor, to seize control of Syria and Palestine. He might have taken Anatolia as well had not Russia made a defensive alliance with Turkey in 1833 and secured in return special rights to navigate the straits linking the Black Sea with the Aegean. These encroachments on Ottoman sovereignty alarmed the British, who bombarded the Syrian coast in 1840, forced Muhammad Ali to relinquish his gains, and persuaded Russia and France to subscribe to an international convention closing the straits to all warships in peacetime.

Guizot dominated the French ministry from 1840 to 1848, while Thiers headed the loyal opposition. More determined opposition came from the advocates of a republic, whose numbers mounted with the growth of literacy and political awareness among the working class (by 1847 two-thirds of the men mustered into the army could read). Discontent deepened after 1845 when the potato blight ravaging Ireland spread to France, and starvation threatened after the failure of the grain harvest in 1846. The food crisis was compounded by an industrial depression, touched off in 1847 by the collapse of a boom in railroad construction which put more than half a million Frenchmen out of work.

The Revolution of 1848

In the summer of 1847 republicans and members of the loyal opposition joined in a series of political banquets throughout France demanding a wider suffrage and the resignation of Guizot. The campaign appeared relatively harmless until an enormous banquet was scheduled for Paris on February 22, 1848. When the Guizot ministry forbade the banquet, the Parisians substituted a huge demonstration. Louis Philippe dismissed Guizot and prepared to entrust the ministry to Thiers, but his concessions came too late. Supported by workers, students, and the more radical

republican leaders, the demonstration of February 22 turned into a riot on February 23, which resulted in more than fifty casualties.

On February 24, Louis Philippe abdicated, and the July Monarchy gave way to a provisional government set up by the Chamber of Deputies. The provisional government invited a few radical reformers to join its ranks in the hope of checking the popular unrest resulting from widespread unemployment. Among the newcomers was Louis Blanc, an advocate of "social workshops" that the workers themselves would own and manage with the financial assistance of the state. As a gesture toward the "right to work" sought by the jobless, the provisional government sponsored "national workshops" in Paris. They fell far short of the social workshops projected by Louis Blanc, however, and were only a temporary means of relief organized on semimilitary lines. The national workshops enrolled more than a hundred thousand of the unemployed, about ten thousand of whom earned two francs (40 cents) a day by working on municipal improvements, while the great majority received a dole of one franc a day.

On April 23, 1848, elections were held for the National Assembly, which would draw up a constitution for the Second Republic (the First Republic had lasted from 1792 to 1804). All adult males were entitled to vote—nine million as compared with the 250,000 who had the franchise during the last years of the July Monarchy. In this momentous election—the first in a major European state with universal manhood suffrage—84 percent of the electorate participated. The conservative peasants, who comprised the bulk of the population, approved the demise of the July Monarchy but feared that efforts to promote the "right to work" would threaten their own property. Of the nearly nine hundred deputies elected to the National Assembly, the great majority were either monarchists or conservative republicans; only about a hundred sympathized with the Paris radicals.

The radicals, however, refused to accept the decision of the country. On May 15, a huge crowd of noisy, unarmed demonstrators invaded the National Assembly to demand its dissolution and the formation of a new provisional government at the Paris City Hall. This echo of the bloody August days of 1792, when the capture of the City Hall had toppled Louix XVI's constitutional monarchy, thoroughly alarmed the moderates in the National Assembly. The assembly arrested the leading radicals and arranged for the orderly

"The Uprising, 1848," by Daumier.

closing of the national workshops on the ground that they were attracting too many economically desperate citizens to the capital. Those enrolled in the workshops were given the alternative of enlisting in the army or accepting work in the provinces.

From June 23 to June 26, 1848, the poor districts of Paris rose in an insurrection until they were subdued by troops brought in by General Cavaignac, the energetic minister of war. Later, socialists would claim that these "June Days" were a landmark in modern history, the first great confrontation between the rich and the poor. It seems probable, however, that most of the insurgents came from the ranks of the unemployed who had sought vainly to enroll in the workshops. At the end of their tether, they seem to have been motivated by desperation rather than the hope of attaining a socialist republic. Among them were men of the new industrial age—mechanics, railroad men, stevedores—as well as tradesmen and craftsmen of the type who had been prominent in the attack on the Bastille.

The threat of a social upheaval, though it may have been remote, terrified the propertied classes. Tocqueville reported that "peasants, shopkeepers, landowners, and nobles" were pouring into Paris on the new railroads to quell the uprising. The atmosphere of panic accounted

for the severe repression of the insurgents of the June Days. About ten thousand were killed or wounded, and about the same number were later deported, chiefly to Algeria. All clubs and newspapers accused of socialist activities were padlocked, as republican France became a virtual military dictatorship under General Cavaignac.

The Second Republic

The fears of the moderates were reflected in the formal constitution of the Second Republic completed by the National Assembly in November 1848. The Assembly declared property to be sacred and rejected a motion to list the right to work among the fundamental rights of French citizens. In other respects the constitution seemed to be a daring venture in representative democracy by establishing both a strong presidency and a powerful legislature. Yet it was not so daring as it appeared, since the election of April 1848 had shown that universal suffrage could be a weapon against radicalism. The legislature was a single chamber, to be elected by universal male suffrage every three years; a new president was to be chosen by popular election every four years.

In the presidential election of December 1848, the three genuinely republican candidates

Portrait of Napoleon III by Chappel.

together received only half a million votes, General Cavaignac won a million and a half, and Louis Napoleon Bonaparte swept to victory with five and a half million votes. The new president, the son of the great Napoleon's troublesome brother, Louis, was not a very impressive figure. He spoke haltingly in heavily accented French (the result of boyhood exile in German-speaking Switzerland), and he was notorious for his associations with disreputable people and involvement in ill-conceived projects. But in 1848 he staged a clever campaign to identify himself with order and stability, volunteering, for example, to serve as a constable in London when the British expected a massive Chartist demonstration. Above all, he had the asset of bearing the magical Bonaparte name. In 1848, as in 1792, a revolution established a republic that would soon be transformed into a Napoleonic empire.

The new president soon quarreled with the Legislative Assembly elected in May 1849, where monarchist sentiment, either Legitimist (pro-Bourbon) or Orléanist, outweighed Bonapartism. The Assembly refused to amend the Constitution of 1848 so that Louis Napoleon might serve a second term as president. It also deprived about

three million Frenchmen of the vote, thus enabling him to appear as the champion of persecuted popular democracy. On December 2, 1851, he staged a coup d'état, artfully timed for the anniversaries of Napoleon I's coronation and his great victory at Austerlitz. Controlling both the army and the police, Louis Napoleon arrested prominent anti-Bonapartists, including sixteen members of the Assembly. Street fighting in Paris, which broke out the next day, resulted in hundreds of casualties, mostly bystanders fired upon by panicky soldiers. Louis Napoleon now posed as the champion of order against an alleged socialist plot; his massive arrests sent twenty thousand citizens to prison or into exile.

Toward the end of December 1851, the prince-president restored universal suffrage for a plebiscite which, by 7,500,000 votes to 640,000, authorized him to draw up a new constitution. Some of his opponents simply abstained from voting; others voted "Yes" because they were frightened by the specter of socialism raised by the June Days of 1848, and still others were drawn to Bonaparte by the magic of the Napoleonic legend. The new constitution of January 1852 copied the consulate of Napoleon I in setting up an authoritarian regime with a republican facade. Within the year the facade crumbled when another plebiscite authorized the prince-president to assume the title of Emperor Napoleon III. ("Napoleon II," the son of Napoleon I and Marie Louise, died in 1832 without ever having ruled.) The Second Empire had succeeded the Second Republic.

The Second Empire

The experiment with another Bonapartist dictatorship began with the installation of Emperor Napoleon III on December 2, 1852. The emperor insisted that he would introduce genuine reforms, undertaking great public works at home and promoting international understanding abroad. He sponsored the rebuilding of the capital and many provincial cities, providing them with large public markets and spacious boulevards and promenades. Urban France still bears the stamp of the Second Empire, especially in Paris, where the emperor's prefect, Haussmann, cut through the medieval maze of streets to create broad straight avenues with splendid vistas. These avenues could easily be swept by gunfire, thus making street fighting much more difficult. The Second Empire also promoted new housing and encouraged mutual societies that financed improvements in the living conditions of working people. Nevertheless, the standard of living reached by French workers in the growing industrial centers remained lower than that of their British and German counterparts.

The bourgeoisie gained the most under the Second Empire. They profited greatly from funds supplied through the government-sponsored *Crédit Foncier* and *Crédit Mobilier,* which promoted investment in real estate and movable property, respectively. The government also aided the advance of industry, improved banking facilities, and fostered the extension of railroads by state subsidies. However, many Frenchmen still rejected the industrial revolution, preferring their traditional ways of doing business—small family enterprises and luxury trades based on handicraft skills rather than on machinery. In consequence, the industrial growth of France remained slower than that of the leading economic powers. The French also lagged in population growth, perhaps in part because so many of them were small proprietors determined to avoid the division of modest inheritances among several heirs.

On the international scene the Second Empire played an active but often overly ambitious role. The Paris Exposition of 1855, a counterpart of the London Exhibition of 1851, was a great success. The French, however, gained little by joining Britain and Turkey in the inglorious Crimean War against Russia (1853–1856), although Paris did have the honor of being host to the subsequent peace congress. Partly through a romantic interest in "oppressed nationalities," partly from motives of prestige, Napoleon III joined Piedmont in a war with Austria for the liberation of Italy. In the spring of 1859, French armies won narrow victories at Magenta and Solferino ("Magenta" was soon exploited by the Paris fashion trade as the name of a new color). But they did not force the Austrians out of the war, and in the summer of 1859, sickened by the bloodshed on the battlefields and fearful that Prussia might come to Austria's assistance, Napoleon III suddenly made a separate peace. The Austrians agreed to give up Lombardy but not Venetia.

In 1860 the disappointed Italians sought compensation by seeking to incorporate Rome into a unified Italy. Since this would have put an end to the pope's territorial power, Napoleon stationed a French garrison in Rome to safeguard papal rule. He did recognize the unification of most of Italy under the leadership of Piedmont. In return, France annexed two small but strategically important Piedmontese territories—the French-speaking area of Alpine Savoy and the Mediterranean city of Nice and its hinterland.

In its adventures overseas, the Second Empire almost unnoticed took the city of Saigon (1862), thereby establishing the first French foothold in Indochina. A year earlier, Louis Napoleon began a more disastrous and highly publicized intervention in Mexico. He used the Mexican government's failure to make payments on its foreign debt as a pretext for taking over the country. In 1861 a French expedition invaded Mexico and in 1864 installed the Austrian prince Maximilian as emperor. Maximilian had some support from the Mexican upper class, which, like its counterparts in most Latin American countries, was strongly attracted to French culture. But the rank and file resented the intruder, and Maximilian had to rely on French armed support to penetrate to Mexico City. The United States protested this infraction of the Monroe Doctrine and, as soon as the Civil War ended in 1865, pressed France to withdraw. The Mexican republican leader Juárez then defeated the forces of Maximilian, who died before a firing squad in 1867.

At home, meanwhile, Napoleon III did not retain for long the nearly unanimous public support suggested by his one-sided victories at the polls in 1848, 1851, and 1852. French nationalists questioned the wisdom of promoting the unification of Italy, which would create an important new power on France's southeastern frontier. French Catholics were alarmed by the reduction of the pope's political role in Italy. They also mistrusted the emperor because of his earlier record of anticlerical sympathies, even though in 1853 he had married a Spanish aristocrat and a devout Catholic, the Empress Eugénie. Conservatives were alarmed by the radical implications of the emperor's efforts to improve the lives of the working class.

Louis Napoleon's response to these developments was, perhaps, the most remarkable feature of his unorthodox career. Instead of tightening his authoritarian regime, he gradually permitted it to assume some of the features of a constitutional monarchy. Throughout the 1860s he increased the powers of the once impotent legislature and permitted the development of competing political parties. When the election of 1869 brought some champions of a republic into the Legislative Assembly, he granted the assembly the right to propose laws and to criticize and vote the budget. The Liberal Empire, as this new phase was called, reached its peak in May 1870 when a plebiscite overwhelmingly approved the recent changes.

It is possible that the Second Empire might have gone on to become a parliamentary regime on the British model with legislative control over the ministries. Yet the changes had been wrung from an ailing and vacillating emperor by popular agitation, notably when the Liberal Empire relaxed the ban on strikes first imposed by the National Assembly in 1791. So, it is also possible that a radical republican ground swell might have submerged the empire completely. In any event, the Franco-Prussian War, into which Napoleon III was maneuvered in July 1870 by Bismarck, the Prussian prime minister, abruptly ended the experiment of the Liberal Empire.

The sluggish mobilization and overconfidence of the French gave the Prussians a decisive head start. Within six weeks on September 2, 1870 Napoleon III and a large French army surrendered at Sedan, near the Belgian border. Two days later, rioting Parisians forced the remnant of the Legislative Assembly to decree the fall of the Second Empire. Napoleon III went into captivity in Germany and eventually to exile in Britain, where he died in 1873. Defeated France faced a prolonged crisis over establishing a new regime, resolved only in part by the formation of the Third Republic in 1875.

IV OTHER LEADERS OF PROGRESS

Europe

Belgium

Among the smaller European states of the mid-nineteenth century, the leaders in progress were Belgium and Switzerland. The union of Belgium and the Netherlands, decreed by the peacemakers of 1815, worked fairly well economically because Holland supplied markets for the textile, glass, and other manufactures of Belgium. Politically, however, King William I of the Netherlands soon alienated his newly acquired Belgian subjects. He denied their plea for fuller representation in the States-General, where "Dutch arithmetic" alloted the same number of seats to the Belgian provinces (population three and a half million) and to the Dutch (population two million). He refused to recognize the special position of the Roman Church in Catholic Belgium and insisted that the education of priests come under state supervision. These grievances and many others created a fragile Belgian nationalism made up of French-speaking Walloons in Brussels and the industrial provinces to its south and the Flemings in the northern provinces who spoke a dialect of Dutch.

The Belgian revolution of 1830, which broke out in Brussels on August 25, was inspired by the example of the French and perhaps incited by French agents. By the end of September Dutch rule collapsed. Most of the fighting was done by students and industrial workers, but it was the better-organized leaders from the middle class who gained control of the revolutionary movement and predominated in the national congress convened in November 1830. This congress proclaimed the independence of Belgium and made it a constitutional monarchy. A new constitution put rigorous limitations on the monarch's power and permitted extensive local self-government, thereby allowing Belgian towns to resume their centuries-old traditions of partial independence. Although it did not establish universal suffrage, the financial qualifications for voting were lower in Belgium than in either France or Britain. As the most liberal of Europe's written constitutions (Britain's was unwritten), the Belgian model would be copied many years later when Ottoman Turkey, Persia, and Egypt attempted to set up limited monarchies.

The congress's first choice as king of the Belgians was a son of Louis Philippe, who withdrew after the British protested strongly against bringing Belgium into the orbit of France. The second choice, the German princeling Leopold of Saxe-Coburg, had close connections with British royalty and was admirably prepared for the exacting role of constitutional monarch in a brand-new kingdom. Since he tactfully married a daughter of Louis Philippe, both France and Britain assisted the Belgians against Dutch attempts to recover their country. Prolonged negotiations led to official Dutch recognition of Belgian independence in 1839. Representatives of Britain, France, Prussia, Austria, and Russia guaranteed the neutrality of Belgium in a document that Germany would term "a scrap of paper" when it invaded Belgium in 1914.

Switzerland

Switzerland, the perennial neutral in Europe, went through a crisis in 1847. A miniature civil war broke out between the conservative, rural Catholic cantons and the liberal, urban Protestant cantons. The Catholic forces were soon defeated, and in 1848 the victorious Protestants sponsored a constitution that enlarged the authority of the traditionally weak central government of the Swiss Confederation and reduced that of the twenty-two separate cantons. It also established universal male suffrage which remained undiluted, unlike that of the Second Republic in France. However, the Swiss would lag in extending the voting privilege to women, which was not granted until the 1970s.

The Americas

Latin America

In the Western Hemisphere only the United States and Canada made impressive progress toward more democratic regimes between 1815 and 1870. The Latin American states won full independence from Spain and Portugal between 1806 and 1825. They took advantage of the upheavals in their mother countries resulting from the Napoleonic wars, and they also gained the support of the United States and Britain. American assistance took the form of the Monroe Doctrine, pre-sented to Congress by President Monroe in December, 1823, warning European powers to keep hands off developments in the western hemisphere. A more effective deterrent to European involvement was the knowledge that the British fleet was prepared to defend the new Latin American entities against foreign intervention.

Independence brought neither stable nor democratic regimes to Central and South America. Brazil was a monarchy, and most of the other states were in theory constitutional republics but in fact dictatorships, subject to frequent miniature "revolutions" when power changed hands. Latin America also suffered from its difficult geography. The Andes Mountains were a greater barrier to communications than the North American Rockies. And the vast basin of the Amazon River, with its formidable jungles, was hostile to civilized settlement, in contrast to the prairies of the Mississippi-Missouri basin of the United States. Most islands of the West Indies remained under colonial rule—Spanish, British, French, Dutch, and Danish. The only exception was Hispaniola, divided between the unstable warring republics of Haiti and Santo Domingo.

The United States

Favorable geography and a very small population of native Indians enabled the United States to expand rapidly during the first half of the nineteenth century. The Louisiana Purchase of 1803 added to the new republic vast territories stretching from New Orleans to Montana. Two wars with Mexico (1836, 1846–1848) led to the acquisition of Texas, New Mexico, and California. In 1848 the republic had virtually reached the boundaries of the forty-eight contiguous states today. The simultaneous development of the railroad and telegraph greatly assisted the incorporation of these lands into the federal union. The rapid growth of the republic also had its seamy aspects: the military campaigns that forced Mexico to yield the lands that filled the southwestern quarter of the United States, and the ruthless slaughter of Indians and seizure of their lands as if they were nonpersons.

At the same time the federal republic had the enormous advantage of a constitution at once enlightened and flexible. It preceded any European state in making the suffrage democratic. By the time Andrew Jackson became president in 1829, most of the states had established universal male suffrage, except for Indians and slaves. The existence of slavery led to the greatest crisis ever faced by this republic, remembered by the North as the Civil War and by the South as the War between the States. In 1861 the southern states, led by South Carolina, decided to secede from the federal union and proclaimed their own independent Confederacy in what proved to be an abortive nationalist revolution.

The South was predominantly agricultural with a society based on plantation slavery. Its chief products, cotton and tobacco, were exported to the northern states and to Europe. The North, by contrast, was entering the stage of industrial takeoff, and its society was based on free labor and independent farm owners. The differences in economic interest were heightened by a conflict in culture and ideals, centered on the institution of slavery, which was believed by most Southerners to be ordained by nature, but seemed immoral to many in the North.

The North entered the war enjoying many advantages, both in industrial resources and in the number of potential soldiers, while the South had a smaller population and dared not use blacks in its army. Yet the Confederacy won victories at first, aided by its very able corps of army officers and by the overconfidence of the North. In the long run, however, the North thwarted the

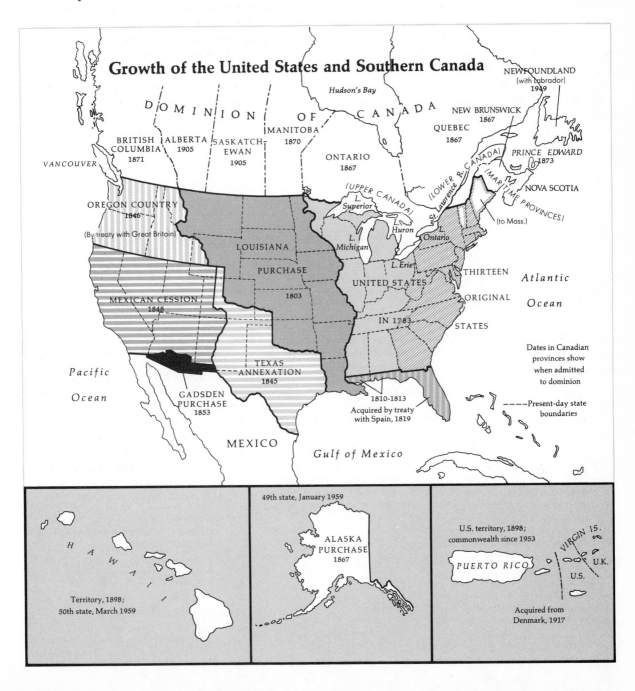

Growth of the United States and Southern Canada

efforts of Confederate diplomats to secure British assistance and was able to enforce a naval blockade that made it impossible for the South to import essential war materials.

Measured in terms of casualties relative to total population, the Civil War remains the deadliest of American wars. It was also very decisive. Reunion was not easy, however, for the assassination of President Lincoln in 1865 removed a great moderate leader who might have curbed the vengeance demanded by northern radicals. The South was occupied by northern soldiers and "carpetbaggers" (salesmen in search of quick profit), and illiterate emancipated blacks were given the suffrage. Yet there were no wholesale reprisals and executions. Jefferson Davis, the president of the Confederacy, after two years in prison was released to live quietly for another thirty, despite the wartime Northern song, "We'll hang Jeff Davis to a sour apple tree." The soldiers of the South returned to devastated homes and lost fortunes, but they went back under amnesty.

Ten years after the war ended, Northern vengeance had run its course, and Southerners regained control of their states. Slavery, abolished by Lincoln's Emancipation Proclamation of 1863, was never restored, but the blacks were deprived of the vote and "white supremacy" reigned in the South. The South began to build up its own industries and partly freed itself from dependence on cotton, while the North went full speed ahead in industrial expansion. Those were the days when government regulation of industry scarcely existed, and "robber barons" along with "rugged individualists" of higher principles made great fortunes. At times American democracy seemed likely to be engulfed by the predominance of the profit motive. In the last two decades of the century, however, both federal and state governments began a mild regulation of private industry, preparing the way for the "trust-busting" of President Theodore Roosevelt in the early years of the next century.

READING SUGGESTIONS on Industry and Democracy

Introductions:

C. Breunig, *The Age of Revolution and Reaction, 1789-1850*, 2nd. ed. (*Norton) and N. Rich, *The Age of Nationalism and Reform, 1850-1880.* (*Norton). Brief reviews of major European developments.

W. Langer, *Social and Political Upheaval, 1832-1852* (*Torch). Full account of 20 years particularly important in the development of industry and experiments with more democratic governments.

E. Hobsbawm, *The Age of Revolution, 1789-1848* (*Mentor). Argues that the Industrial Revolution was even more significant than the French Revolution.

The Industrial Revolution:

D. Landes, *The Unbound Prometheus* (*Cambridge University Press). Discusses the linkage of technological change and industrial development in Western Europe.

E. Hobsbawm, *The Pelican Economic History of Britain*, vol. 3: *Industry and Empire* (*Penguin). By a leading British Marxist.

W. W. Rostow, *Stages of Economic Growth*, 2nd ed. (*Cambridge Univ.). Essay on the timetable of industrialization and the reasons for Britain's head start; by a non-Marxist American scholar.

P. Deane, *The First Industrial Revolution*, 2nd ed. (Cambridge Univ., 1980); T. S. Ashton, *The Industrial Revolution*

1760-1830 (*Oxford Univ.). Clear informative introductions.

W. O. Henderson, *The Industrial Revolution in Europe, 1815-1914* (*Times Books). Stresses France, Germany and Russia.

A. Briggs, *From Iron Bridge to Crystal Palace* (Thames & Hudson, 1979). The impact of the industrial revolution on Britain's economy and society.

E. P. Thompson, *The Making of the English Working Class* (*Random House). Detailed sympathetic study of the effects of the French and Industrial Revolutions.

S. Pollard & C. Holmes, ed., *The Process of Industrialization, 1750-1850* (St. Martin's, 1968); R. Pike, ed., *Human Documents of the Industrial Revolution in Britain* (*Allen & Unwin); P. Stearns & D. Walkowitz, ed., *Workers in the Industrial Revolution* (*Transaction Books). Source materials on the impact of industrialism on people.

Britain

A. Briggs, *The Age of Improvements, 1783-1867* (Longman, 1959); G. Kitson Clark *The Making of Victorian England* (*Atheneum); N. Gash, *Aristocracy and People: Britain, 1815–1865* (Harvard U., 1980). Helpful introductions to Britain's gradual political revolution.

G. M. Young, *Victorian England: Por-*

trait of an Age (*Oxford Univ.). Celebrated analysis of a changing society.

C. Woodham-Smith, *The Great Hunger* (Harper, 1963) and *The Reason Why* (*Dutton). Examination of two famous disasters: the potato famine in Ireland and the charge of the Light Brigade in the Crimea.

C. Woodham-Smith, *Queen Victoria* (Knopf, 1972); E. Longford, *Queen Victoria* (Harper, 1973); N. Gash, *Peel* (Longman, 1976); R. Tames, *Disraeli* (Viking, 1976); P. Magnus, *Gladstone* (*Dutton). Biographies of important actors in British political life.

France

A. Cobban, *A History of Modern France, vol. 2: 1799-1871* (*Penguin) and G. Wright, *France in Modern Times*, 2nd ed. (Rand). Very good general surveys.

G. Bertier de Sauvigny, *The Restoration* (Univ. of Pennsylvania, 1966). Sympathetic account of the reigns of Louis XVIII and Charles X.

M. Leys, *Between Two Empires* (Longman, 1955). Brief survey of French social and political history, 1814-1848.

T. Howarth, *Citizen-King* (Eyre & Spottiswoode, 1961). Biography of Louis Philippe.

D. Pinkney, *The French Revolution of 1830* (Princeton Univ., 1972). Important reassessment.

D. Johnson, *Guizot* (Routledge, 1963) and R. Albrecht-Carrié, *Adolphe Thiers* (Twayne, 1977). Biographies of two important figures in the July Monarchy.

G. Duveau, *1848: The Making of a Revolution* (*Vintage). By a leading French scholar.

J. M. Thompson, *Louis Napoleon and the Second Empire* (*Norton) and T. Zeldin, *The Political System of Napoleon III* (*Norton). Two highly regarded studies of a regime that was both democratic and autocratic.

A. Guérard, *Napoleon III: A Great Life in Brief* (Greenwood). Sympathetic biography by a Franco-American scholar.

A. Brodsky, *Imperial Charade* (Bobbs, 1978) and D. Duff, *Eugénie & Napoleon III* (Morrow, 1978). More recent evaluations of the enigmatic emperor and his wife.

The United States

R. B. Morris, ed., *Encyclopedia of American History,* 5th ed. (Harper, 1976), and *Harvard Guide to American History,* revised ed. (Harvard Univ., 1974). Standard volumes of reference.

S. E. Morison, *The Oxford History of the American People,* 3 vols. (*Mentor). Revision of a popular book by a distinguished American historian.

H. Commager, *The Blue and the Gray,* 2 vols (*Mentor). The Civil War as viewed by another distinguished historian.

Alexis de Tocqueville, *Democracy in America* (*Anchor). The celebrated pioneering study by the young Frenchman who visited the U.S. in the 1830s.

R. Hofstadter, *The American Political Tradition* (*Vintage). Very perceptive study.

Historical Fiction

C. Dickens, *Hard Times* (*several editions). An unforgettable picture of Coketown, a raw industrial city, and its inhabitants.

E. Gaskell, *Mary Barton* (*Everyman). A sympathetic picture of working class life in Manchester during the "hungry forties."

A. Trollope, *The Prime Minister* (*Oxford Univ.). Many critics rate this as the best political novel ever written.

E. Zola, *Germinal* (*Signet). Dramatic account of a strike by French coal miners in the 1860s; earthier than its English counterparts.

M. Mitchell, *Gone with the Wind* (*Avon). The Civil War portrayed through a mist of Confederate nostalgia.

M. Kantor, *Andersonville* (*Signet). Grimly realistic account of life in a military prison during the Civil War.

CHAPTER FOURTEEN

Nationalism And Reform:

Southern, Central And Eastern Europe

For more than forty years after the Vienna Congress few significant political advances were recorded in southern, central and eastern Europe. Revolutions failed almost everywhere: in Spain (1820-1823); in Naples (1820-1821); in Russia (1825) and Russian-dominated Poland (1830-1833); and in Italy, Germany and the Hapsburg Empire during the great wave of revolt in 1848-1849. The only exceptions were the modest advances recorded in Portugal and Greece during the 1820s, made possible by the help of outside powers.

Between 1859 and 1870 the tempo of change quickened dramatically. The forces of nationalism, which had slowly been gaining strength since the Napoleonic era, at last scored impressive victories. The Italian states, with military support from France and Prussia, were merged into a single kingdom. Prussia, without outside help, fused more than three dozen German states into a new empire. Austria, after losing its Italian lands and its traditional role as the dean of German states, tried to shore up its disintegrating empire by belated concessions to its restless Hungarian subjects. Even the sluggish Russian autocracy felt the groundswell of reform as the tsar at last liberated the serfs (1861) and set up the building blocks for a more representative government.

SOUTHERN EUROPE

Spain, Portugal and Naples

The first outbreaks of revolution after 1815 occurred in the Iberian, Italian and Balkan peninsulas. In Spain, during the war against Napoleon, representatives from the liberal middle class of Cadiz and other commercial towns had framed the constitution of 1812. It granted wide authority to the Cortes (parliament) elected on a broad suffrage, and it also deprived the Spanish church of some of its lands and privileges. This constitution faced great difficulties in traditionalist Spain. It was suspended by the Bourbon king, Ferdinand VII, when he assumed the throne in 1814. He also restored the social inequalities of Spain's old regime, and reestablished the Jesuits and the Inquisition. These reactionary measures alienated intellectuals and army officers, who organized a liberal opposition. They were joined by merchants, who faced ruin as the revolt of Spanish colonies in the New World destroyed their protected market. To crush the colonial rebels, Ferdinand assembled a motley collection of warships at Cadiz. This pathetic "armada" never sailed for on January 1, 1820 a mutiny broke out at Cadiz, led by the liberal Colonel Riego. The mutineers rallied enough support in Madrid, Barcelona, and other Spanish cities to force restoration of the Constitution of 1812.

The Spanish example was soon followed by Portugal and Naples. A Portuguese army faction seized control of the government in Lisbon and set up a constitution on the Spanish model of 1812. In Naples, the capital of the Two Sicilies, the revolution was the work of the Carbonari (charcoal burners), a secret society with more than fifty thousand members. The Carbonari had opposed French reforms during the heyday of Napoleon; now they sponsored a vaguely liberal program inspired by the French Revolution. King Ferdinand I of the Two Sicilies, the uncle of Spain's Ferdinand VII, agreed to introduce a constitution on the Spanish model.

Of these revolutionary regimes only the Portuguese survived, largely because it had the backing of Portugal's traditional "big brother," Great Britain. Elsewhere the revolutionary regimes collapsed because of foreign intervention and the mounting unpopularity of their inexperienced leaders. Since the Neapolitan revolution threatened Austria's dominance over Italy, Metternich sent a Hapsburg army to Naples (1821), where Ferdinand I resumed his reactionary policies. In Madrid, the new regime was weakened by a split among the revolutionaries. The *Moderados* (moderates) wanted to retain the Constitution of 1812, while the *Exaltados* (extremists) led by Colonel Riego proposed to establish a strongly anticlerical republic. Although both *Moderados* and *Exaltados* alienated the Spanish rank and file, it took intervention by French troops to restore the absolute authority of the monarch (1823). Ferdinand VII executed Riego and hundreds of his followers and again discarded the Constitution of 1812.

Serb and Greek Independence

In southeastern Europe most of the Christian Balkan peoples were still under Ottoman rule when the nineteenth century began. Their yearning for independence was stimulated by the French Revolution and by the reforms that Napoleon's officials had introduced in the Illyrian provinces.

The Serbs (today the largest of the many nationalities composing Yugoslavia) were the first of the Balkan peoples to rebel (1804). They turned for help to Russia, which shared their Orthodox religion, Slavic language, and Cyrillic alphabet (named for Cyril, the Christian apostle to the Slavs in the ninth century). With Russian assistance a Serbian prince won recognition of a small autonomous Serbia (1830). This was a major step toward eventual independence, even though the prince had to pay tribute to the Ottoman authorities, and Turkey still maintained a garrison in the Serb capital, Belgrade.

Meanwhile, the Greeks launched their own rebellion against the Turks (1821). The Island Greeks, based on the islands in the Aegean Sea, already dominated trade in the Near East and had important outposts in European cities. They revived not only the Greek mercantile tradition but also the old Greek zeal for self-government. Their countrymen joined in a campaign to restore the classical Greek language of antiquity by eliminating Turkish and Slavic words that had later entered the language.

In 1821 Greek nationalists began a war for

independence by launching an uprising among the peasants in the Morea (the ancient Peloponnesus). The Ottoman government responded to the slaughter of Turkish landlords by executing the Greek patriarch in Constantinople and killing or selling into slavery thirty thousand Greeks from the prosperous island of Chios (Scio). To repress the uprising the Ottoman emperor relied on help from his powerful vassal, Muhammad Ali, the governor of Egypt. By 1827 it appeared likely that the Egyptian expeditionary force would recapture the last rebel strongholds. Throughout the Western world Philhellenic (pro-Greek) committees won wide popular support for their demand that the powers intervene.

Intervention hinged on the attitude of Russia, which was strongly committed to the Greek cause; yet, as Metternich reminded the tsar, it was also committed to the suppression of revolution. When the tsar prepared to help the Greeks directly, Britain and France felt obliged to act in order to keep Russia from gaining mastery over the whole Near East. Therefore, a three-power joint intervention seemed the only course that would both rescue the Greeks and check the Russians. Neither aim was fully achieved.

In October, 1827, Russian, British, and French warships sank the Turkish and Egyptian vessels anchored at Navarino, in the southwest Morea, and thus destroyed the chief Ottoman base. The subsequent Treaty of Adrianople (1829) arranged that the Turkish Danubian provinces, Moldavia and Wallachia (today part of Romania), should become a virtual Russian protectorate. The European powers recognized the existence of an independent Greek kingdom of very modest size. Many Greeks remained within the Ottoman Empire, and Greek patriots schemed for the day when they might enlarge the boundaries of their new kingdom. Meanwhile, Philhellenes everywhere were disillusioned by Greek politicians who threatened the stability of the infant kingdom by continuing the bitter feuds that had divided them in the midst of their struggle for independence.

Italy: Hopes and Disappointments, 1831-1849

After 1830 the focus of activity in southern Europe shifted to Italy, where excitement over the July Revolution in France set off a few revolutionary fireworks but soon fizzled out. In 1831, the Carbonari took over the duchies of Parma and Modena in north central Italy plus nearby papal territories, including the important city of Bologna. Among the participants was Louis Napoleon Bonaparte, the future Napoleon III. The insurgents counted on securing French assistance, but the new July Monarchy had no intention of risking war by trespassing on an area that the Hapsburgs regarded as their special preserve. Again, as in 1821, Metternich sent troops to restore legitimacy in Italy.

New movements for Italian liberation eventually replaced the discredited Carbonari. One group, based in Piedmont, expected to take the lead in freeing Italians from Austrian domination. At its head was Count Cavour (1810–1861), a wealthy landowner who admired the cautious liberalism of Britain and France and edited an influential newspaper in Turin, the capital of Piedmont. The name of his paper, *Il Risorgimento* ("resurgence" or "regeneration"), soon extended to the whole movement for unification, which Cavour would later advance toward completion. Meanwhile, he faced the competition of two other groups.

One of these was led by a priest, Gioberti, and took the title of Neo-Guelf, because, like the Guelf political faction of the Middle Ages, it sought to end the control of Italy by a Germanic emperor. Gioberti declared that the pope should head, and the army of Piedmont should defend, a federation of Italian states, each with its own monarch and a cautiously liberal constitution. In contrast Young Italy, the third group, proposed to make the whole of Italy into a single democratic republic. It was "young" because only men under the age of forty were eligible for membership. Its founder was Mazzini (1805–1872), who hoped to create an organization more effective than the Carbonari. He failed in this attempt, but he was to enjoy his moment of glory in the revolution of 1848 and win an enduring reputation as the great democratic idealist of modern Italy. Mazzini was a good European, as well as an ardent Italian nationalist, and inspired the formation of Young Germany, Young Poland, and similar groups, all joined together in a federation called Young Europe.

The prospects for Italian nationalism brightened with the election of Pope Pius IX (1846–1878). He appeared to promote liberal changes by releasing political prisoners and beginning to modernize the antiquated administration of the Papal States. Actual revolution, however, began not in Rome but in the kingdom of Naples, where an uprising in January 1848 forced King Ferdinand II to grant a constitution modeled on the

French charter as revised in 1830. The grand duke of Tuscany soon followed Ferdinand's example; he was joined by King Charles Albert of Piedmont and Pope Pius IX after news arrived of the revolution in Paris.

The spotlight then shifted to the Hapsburg possessions of Lombardy and Venetia, where the ideas of Mazzini's Young Italy had won a substantial following. Ever since New Year's Day, 1848, citizens of Milan, the capital of Lombardy, had been boycotting cigars to protest the Austrian tax on tobacco—a maneuver suggested by a professor's lecture on the Boston tea party. Reports that a revolution had begun in Vienna (March 12–13) touched off heavy fighting in Milan. Its citizens made barricades of pianos, sentry boxes, and omnibuses as well as the traditional paving blocks. The Austrians withdrew their forces and also pulled out of Venice, which proclaimed itself the Republic of St. Mark.

The rapid collapse of Hapsburg rule inspired an Italian crusade against the Austrians, led by Charles Albert of Piedmont who commanded forces including contingents from Tuscany, Naples, and the Papal States. But he refused the help offered by the provisional government in France with the ill-fated prediction, *Italia farà da sè* ("Italy will do it alone"). Only for a moment did it seem possible that the Piedmontese and Neo-Guelf forces would work together long enough to gain a total victory.

When Piedmont annexed Lombardy, Parma, and Modena, other Italian states began to fear Piedmontese expansion more than they desired national unification. The Neo-Guelf cause received a fatal blow at the end of April when Pius IX declared that his "equal affection" for all peoples obliged him to take a neutral position and withdraw the papal contingent from the fighting. He was disturbed by the increasing radicalism of the Roman population and by the threats of Austrian and German bishops to proclaim an antipope. In May the king of Naples, who had scrapped the constitution granted earlier, withdrew his military units. The Austrian forces, taking the offensive, reconquered Lombardy and then defeated the army of Charles Albert (July 1848). Italy had not been able to do it alone.

A few months later, the Italians made one more try. In Rome adherents of Young Italy staged an uprising (November 1848) that led Pius IX to take refuge on Neapolitan territory. The Papal States became the democratic Roman Republic, with Mazzini himself in charge. Next, radicals in Turin forced Charles Albert to renew the war with Austria (March 1849), which promptly defeated the Piedmontese once more. In August 1849, the Austrians put an end to the Republic of St. Mark after a long bombardment of Venice, which also suffered severely from famine and an epidemic of cholera. A month earlier, Mazzini's Roman Republic had surrendered to French troops sent by President Bonaparte to assist the pope and win the gratitude of French Catholics.

Except for the presence of the French garrison in Rome, Italy returned to its prerevolutionary status. With both the Neo-Guelf and Young Italy movements discredited, Piedmont emerged as the leader of Italian nationalism. Despite two defeats by the Austrians, it won credit for trying; it also had the distinction of being the only Italian state to retain the constitution granted in 1848.

The Risorgimento Triumphant

Three men now led the Risorgimento to a great victory. One was the new king of Piedmont, Victor Emmanuel II (reigned 1849–1878), who inherited the crown after Charles Albert abdicated. The second was Garibaldi (1807–1882), a romantic adventurer who had participated in the Young Italy movement, won a reputation as a formidable guerrilla fighter in South America, and made a gallant though unsuccessful effort to defend Mazzini's Roman Republic against French troops in 1849. And the third, and most important, was Cavour, the architect of the Risorgimento, who became Victor Emmanuel's chief minister. Cavour sponsored the development of banks, railroads, steamships, and industries to strengthen Piedmont's economy. He was also a great expert in *Realpolitik,* the realistic diplomacy needed to gain the support of stronger powers in his campaign for Italian unity.

Cavour's first move was to have Piedmont join Britain and France in the battlefields of the Crimean War (1855). While Piedmont gained no territory, it appeared to win the gratitude of its new allies. Cavour was dismayed when the British rebuffed his overtures to gain support for the Risorgimento because they were unwilling to offend Austria. He had better luck with Napoleon III, whom he convinced that Austrian retention of Italian lands was an affront to the principles of nationalism.

In 1859 France joined Piedmont in fighting Austria, then withdrew after two inconclusive battles. At a conference in July 1859, Napoleon III and the Hapsburg emperor Francis Joseph

A camp of the 5th Dragoon Guards during the Crimean War.

agreed that Piedmont should annex Lombardy but leave Venetia under Austrian control. Cavour resigned from office in protest, but he had already won a great victory. During the war four states in north central Italy—Tuscany, Parma, Modena, and the Romagna (the northern province of the papal domains)—had experienced nearly blood-

Right Leg in the Boot at Last: English cartoon of 1860 commenting on Garibaldi's retirement after having given Italy to Victor Emmanuel.

less revolutions. Plebiscites demanding annexation by Piedmont soon followed. Early in 1860 Cavour returned to office in order to manage the annexations and to pay off Napoleon III by ceding Nice and Savoy to France.

Next the rapidly developing situation in southern Italy put Cavour's skill in *Realpolitik* to the test. In May 1860, an expedition outfitted in ports under Piedmont's control, but not acknowledged by Cavour's government, set out to liberate Sicily and Naples. The thousand "redshirts" under Garibaldi's command took over Sicily with ease and then crossed over to the toe of the Italian boot where they began a march northward. Cavour, who feared Garibaldi might try to set up an independent republic, welcomed with relief Garibaldi's declaration of loyalty to King Victor Emmanuel. By then the victorious redshirts were attracting many new recruits and winning wide support abroad. Even cautious Britain indicated that its fleet might act to block any efforts by outsiders to intervene against the redshirts.

Cavour's worries were not yet over, for he feared that Garibaldi might advance north from Naples and offend Catholic powers by attacking the city of Rome, which was still defended by

Unification of Italy, 1859-1870

French troops. To prevent this, he stationed Piedmontese troops in the papal territories adjoining Rome. Again a crisis was defused, as Victor Emmanuel joined forces with Garibaldi near Naples and assured the success of Cavour's policy. In the autumn of 1860 Sicily, Naples, and the papal territories outside the area of Rome voted to unite with Piedmont. In March 1861, the kingdom of Italy was officially proclaimed, with its capital at Florence and Victor Emmanuel as its monarch. A few months later Cavour died, his work almost complete.

To complete the Risorgimento two more important territories were needed—Venice and Rome. The new Italian kingdom acquired Venetia in 1866 after joining Prussia in a successful war against Austria (the success was exclusively Prussian, for both the army and navy of Italy suffered humiliating defeats). Rome was added in 1870 when the outbreak of the Franco-Prussian War forced the withdrawal of French troops from the city. The Italian capital moved from Florence to Rome, and the whole of Italy was now unified except for two small areas retained by Austria:

the port of Trieste at the head of the Adriatic, and the area around Trent in the mountains north of Venice. To Italian nationalists they constituted *Italia Irredenta*—unredeemed Italy.

The new kingdom started life under serious handicaps. The pope, calling himself the "prisoner of the Vatican," refused to acknowledge the legitimacy of the new kingdom and forbade Italian Catholics to participate in political life. While actual relations were not so tense as this might suggest, the "Roman Question" sharpened the conflict between Catholics and anticlericals. Except in Piedmont, Italians had little experience with parliamentary government, and most of them were excluded from participation in politics by the restricted suffrage. The most fundamental problem of all was the contrast between north and south, even more serious and deeply rooted than that in the United States. Northern Italy resembled the progressive prosperous states of northern Europe and took little interest in the problems of the south. These were enormous, for southern Italy was almost entirely agricultural, overpopulated, and still almost medieval in its culture. Even today, more than a century later, the problems of the south remain unresolved.

II THE UNIFICATION OF GERMANY

The pattern of unification in Germany roughly paralleled that of Italy. During the three decades following the Vienna settlement of 1815, Austria easily suppressed amateurish efforts to liberalize and consolidate the German states. The revolution of 1848 brought a more determined attempt to establish both a liberal and a unified German entity, but it soon collapsed in the face of continued Austrian opposition. Success was ultimately achieved by Bismarck, the Prussian counterpart of Cavour, who engineered victorious wars against Austria and France, which led to the proclamation of the German Empire in 1871.

But there were also important differences between the Italian and German experiences. Prussia was already a first-rate power, larger and stronger than Piedmont, with deeply rooted autocratic and military traditions. Bismarck outdistanced Cavour in the practice of Realpolitik, but he did not share Cavour's commitment to moderate liberalism and economic progress. The German Empire proved to be a much more formidable institution than the kingdom of Italy.

"Animated Sleepwalking," 1815–1847

The poet, Heine, exaggerated only a little when he characterized early German efforts to promote change as "animated sleepwalking." During the years after 1815, political agitation came mainly from a small minority of intellectuals—writers, journalists, university professors, and students. In October 1817, the *Burschenschaft* (students' union) celebrated the three-hundredth anniversary of Luther's Ninety-five Theses and the fourth anniversary of the battle of Leipzig. During a rally at the Wartburg, the castle where Luther had translated the Bible into German, students from the University of Jena burned a diplomat's wig, a Prussian officer's corset, and books by reactionary writers. When a Jena student later murdered a reactionary journalist, Metternich got the Diet of the German Confederation to approve the Carlsbad Decrees (September 1819). They stiffened press censorship, curtailed academic freedom, and dissolved the Burschenschaft, which later reorganized underground.

In the early 1830s, inspired by the July Revolution in France, a few German states granted constitutions. Excited by these successes and by the arrival of refugees from Poland, many thousands of revolutionary sympathizers gathered at Hambach in the Rhineland, (May 1832). The participants toasted Lafayette and demanded the union of German states under a democratic republic. In 1833 some fifty academic radicals tried in vain to take over the city of Frankfurt, the capital of the German Confederation. The insurgents, together with hundreds of students accused of illegal Burschenschaft activities, received harsh sentences from the courts in Prussia and other states.

In the 1840s German liberals and nationalists found a new hero in the Prussian king, Frederick William IV (1840–1861). Though attractive and cultivated, he was also an enthusiastic believer in divine-right monarchy. He promised to give Prussia a constitution and an elected assembly, then refused to carry out his promises. The only substantial Prussian contribution to German unity before 1848 was not political but economic: the *Zollverein* (customs union). In 1818, Prussia had abolished internal tariffs within its scattered territories and initiated a uniform tariff schedule for imports. Small neighboring states were the first to join the Zollverein, followed by almost

"Storming the Arsenal": Wood engraving depicting the revolutionary outbreaks in Berlin in 1848, from an English newspaper.

all the other German states except Austria. The Zollverein liberated Germany from outdated local tolls and taxes and cleared the way for the remarkable German industrial development later in the century. It also suggested that the state fostering economic unity might also take the lead in political unification.

The Abortive Revolution, 1848–1850

Unification seemed almost certain in 1848. Stimulated by the example of Paris, German revolutionaries forced the rulers in some western German states to adopt more liberal policies. Demands for constitutions, civil liberties, and strengthening of the German Confederation then spread eastward. By the middle of March most of the smaller German states had yielded to these demands. In Berlin, where demonstrators erected barricades, Frederick William accepted some liberal changes and appealed for calm. But before his appeal could be publicized, violence erupted and more than two hundred rioters, chiefly workingmen, were killed. Survivors broke into the

royal palace and forced the king to salute the corpses of the victims. Humiliated and terribly upset, the king accepted the major reforms proposed by liberals and nationalists. He summoned an assembly to draw up a constitution, declared Prussia "merged in Germany," and proclaimed himself "king of the free regenerated German nation."

Drastic reform of the German Confederation now began. In May 1848, a constitutional convention held its first session in the Church of St. Paul at Frankfurt. Its 830 members came from every corner of Germany but were often chosen by electoral colleges or under suffrage restrictions that made the results fall short of a genuine popular mandate. While doctors, lawyers, judges, professors, businessmen, and clergy were generously represented, there were only four artisans and a single dirt farmer among the 830.

The Frankfurt Assembly had to define the geographical limits of Germany. The existing Confederation included Austria proper but excluded most of the non-German Hapsburg lands as well as the eastern provinces Prussia had acquired from the partitions of Poland. The Austrian question divided the assembly into two camps. The "Big Germans" favored the inclusion of Austria and Bohemia, with its large Czech population, in the projected German state; the "Little Germans" opposed the idea. When Austria objected to the Big German proposal, the assembly adopted the Little German alternative. On the question of Prussian Poland, the assembly voted by a large majority to include in the new Germany some areas where Poles formed a majority of the population. One ardent nationalist declared that a German minority had a natural right to rule the Poles, who had "less cultural content."

The constitution finally drawn up by the Frankfurt Assembly for a federal Germany (March 1849) was decidedly liberal and drew heavily on American and British precedents. The federal legislature would consist of a lower house, elected by universal male suffrage, and an upper house chosen by the governments and legislatures of the various states. Ministers responsible to the legislature would form the federal executive; a German emperor would preside as a constitutional monarch. The assembly elected the king of Prussia as emperor, but Frederick William, ignoring his earlier promises and alarmed by Austrian opposition, rejected the offer. No monarch by divine right, he asserted, could accept "a crown from the gutter."

This insult sealed the doom of the Frankfurt Assembly. It had never gained recognition by foreign governments, never raised a penny in taxes or exerted real sovereignty over Germany. The couplet mocking the academic deputies for their lack of practicality had been justified:

> *Hundert fünfzig Professoren!*
> *Lieber Gott, wir sind verloren!*

> (A hundred and fifty professors!
> Good Lord, we're sunk!)

German liberalism, as well as nationalism, had suffered a major defeat. After the initial euphoria over the revolutions wore off, the professional and business classes became alarmed by the radicalism of workers and artisans. The German princes either revoked or abridged the constitutions they had granted, and Frederick William and his conservative advisers repeatedly modified the work of the Prussian constitutional assembly.

The Prussian Constitution of 1850 established a bicameral legislature: a hereditary upper house, including nobles and royal appointees, and a lower house elected in a most undemocratic way. Voters were divided into three classes according to the taxes they paid. In the top bracket, 4 percent of the electorate chose a third of the representatives; in the next bracket, 14 percent chose another third; and the remaining 82 selected the last third. Moreover, many men who were judged "not economically independent" were denied the vote. Except for the right to approve the budget, the lower house had little authority. Questions of policy were decided either by the upper house or directly by the king and his advisers. Thus the king and the Junkers continued to dominate Prussia.

Bismarck Creates a New German Empire

Even the very diluted liberalism of the 1850 constitution soon proved too much for the divine-right sentiments of Frederick William IV, who adopted repressive policies violating the constitution. In 1858 the king's emotional instability obliged him to step aside in favor of his brother, who served as regent and then as King William I (1861–1888). William's conviction that he must honor the constitution led Prussian liberals to salute the "new era." At the same time, the number of liberals in the lower house of the Prussian legislature increased. The prosperous businessmen who paid heavier taxes now qualified for advancement into the top electoral bracket and became the chief beneficiaries of Prussia's weighted voting.

The new era was short-lived. Prussian mobilization for possible intervention to support Austria against France in the war of 1859 revealed weaknesses requiring a larger and more expensive army, according to Prussian military leaders. Their program triggered a prolonged political crisis when the lower house of parliament refused to approve the budget increasing military outlays. As the crisis continued, King William decided in 1862 to appoint as prime minister the only man who could outwit parliament. This was Otto von Bismarck (1815–1898).

A Junker, with all the devotion of his class to the Prussian crown, Bismarck was a master of Realpolitik who exploited every opportunity to advance the "Little German" solution excluding Austria from a united Germany. In the 1850s and early 1860s, he had valuable diplomatic experience as Prussia's representative to the Diet of the German Confederation and then as minister to St. Petersburg and to Paris. When he left Paris to become prime minister in Berlin, he began to collect and spend revenue for the army, alleging that a "gap" in the constitution permitted the government to collect taxes even when the lower house had not approved the budget. Again and again he dissolved the parliament, only to face another hostile house after new elections. Bismarck was able to get away with his illegal procedures because of the dazzling successes he scored in foreign policy.

Since Bismarck intended to overthrow the existing German Confederation, he blocked Austrian efforts to reform it and kept Austria out of the Zollverein. He cultivated the friendship of the Russians during a Polish rebellion in 1863 by allowing them to pursue Polish fugitives on Prussian territory. Also in 1863, Bismarck exploited the question of Schleswig and Holstein, two duchies at the base of the Danish peninsula. They were ruled by the Danish king but were independent of Denmark proper. Holstein, to the south, was mainly German in population and a member of the German Confederation. Schleswig, to the north, of mixed Danish and German population, was not a member. In 1863 Denmark tried to annex Schleswig, despite a long-standing guarantee that the two duchies would never be separated.

When the duchies resisted Danish annexation, Bismarck seized the opportunity to raise Prussia's prestige among German nationalists and to obtain the valuable port of Kiel in Holstein. He maneuvered Austria, which had no real interest in the duchies, into joining Prussia in a brief, victorious war with Denmark (1864). An agreement in 1865 assigning Schleswig to Prussia and Holstein to Austria gave Bismarck an excuse to nag Vienna about its administration of Holstein. He also made a secret military agreement with Italy against Austria. When Austria took the Schleswig-Holstein question to the German Confederation, Bismarck sent Prussian troops into Holstein, thereby provoking war with Austria (1866).

In this seven-weeks' war, Austria was supported by the four other German kingdoms (Bavaria, Württemberg, Saxony, and Hanover) and most of the lesser German states. The Austrians, however, were fatally weakened by the need to fight on two fronts, German and Italian, even though they eventually defeated the Italians. By skillful use of railroads, the telegraph, and superior weapons, Prussian forces quickly overran northern Germany and invaded Bohemia, where they defeated the Austrians at Sadowa. Prussia annexed the states of Hanover, Hesse-Cassel and Nassau together with Schleswig-Holstein and the free city of Frankfurt.

Bismarck overrode both the generals and King William, who wished to punish Austria severely. He insisted on the wisdom of treating Austria gently so that it might eventually become an ally of a unified Germany. Except for the transfer of Venetia to Italy, Austria suffered no territorial losses but had to accept the liquidation of the old German Confederation. Germany north of the River Main was to form a new North German Confederation sponsored by Prussia. The South German states (Bavaria, Württemberg, and Baden), though supposedly free to join a union of their own, were linked to Prussia by treaties of alliance.

The victory over Austria enabled Bismarck to settle his long-standing disagreement with the Prussian parliament. He asked for an "indemnity" to legalize his unconstitutional collection and expenditure of revenues during the preceding four years. Dazzled by the feats of Prussian arms and Prussia's enormous territorial gains, the deputies voted not only the indemnity but also a gift of $300,000 to Bismarck personally. To disarm the liberal opposition, Bismarck approved universal suffrage for the North German Confederation. But his constitutional draft for the Confederation provided that the king of Prussia should be its president and the future parliament, the *Reichstag*, would have little power over the budget and none at all over the ministers. A federal council, the *Bundesrat*, made up of delegates chosen by the sovereigns of the member states would make policy decisions in secret and have veto power over measures passed by the Reichstag. A chancellor would preside over the Bundesrat and countersign measures taken by the Prussian king in his presidential capacity. Since Prussia commanded not only its own votes in the Bundestag but also those of the newly annexed states, Bismarck's plan made it possible for the king of Prussia to run Germany.

Bismarck's success in 1866 shocked Napoleon III, who had expected that the Austro-Prussian War would reach a stalemate enabling France to act as referee and obtain in return a choice morsel of territory, perhaps Belgium or Luxembourg. As the French press demanded "revenge for Sadowa," tension was increased by a dispute over filling the throne of Spain, which became vacant in 1868. One of the candidates for the throne was a Hohenzollern prince from the South

German Catholic branch of the family, whom Bismarck backed secretly by bribing influential Spaniards. Napoleon, fearful that a Hohenzollern king of Spain would expose France to attack on two fronts, exerted diplomatic pressure on King William, who persuaded his cousin to withdraw (July 12, 1870).

The French now rubbed salt in the wound of Hohenzollern pride by demanding that William promise he would never sanction a revival of the candidacy. On July 13, when the king was at Ems, a spa in the Rhineland, he courteously rejected the French demand. He then sent a telegram to Bismarck describing his interchange with the French ambassador. Bismarck released to the press a doctored version of the Ems telegram making it appear that William had thoroughly snubbed the ambassador for being "provocative." As Bismarck hoped, the French reacted by declaring war (July 19, 1870).

Within six weeks the Germans had advanced into France, bottled up one French army at Metz, in Lorraine, and defeated another at Sedan, near the Belgian frontier, where Napoleon III was captured. Paris fell early in 1871 after a long siege. Defeated France ceded to Germany the rich province of Alsace, of mixed French and German heritage. It also gave up two-fifths of the predominantly French province of Lorraine, desired by the German military as a buffer against

Unification of Germany, 1866-1871

Prussia before 1866

Annexed by Prussia, 1866

Other states that joined Prussia to form North German Federation

••••••••• Boundary of North German Federation, 1866

States joining confederation to form German Empire

Territories annexed by Treaty of Frankfurt

■■■■ Boundary of the German Empire, 1871

■ Battle sites

possible French attack. France had to pay a billion-dollar indemnity and support German occupying forces until it was paid.

Meantime, German unification was triumphantly completed as the South German allies, who had supported Prussia in the war, joined the North German Confederation in forming the Second Reich (the Holy Roman Empire had been the first Reich). The birth of the German Empire provided little comfort to those who hoped that Germany would now cultivate liberalism and democracy. The constitution of the empire was modeled on that of the North German Confederation. King William of Prussia was proclaimed emperor in Louis XIV's Hall of Mirrors at Versailles (January 18, 1871) in a ceremony of princes and soldiers but without any participants from the Reichstag.

III THE HAPSBURG EMPIRE

The Revolutions of 1848–1849

Germany and Italy might have achieved unification earlier if the Hapsburg revolutions of 1848 had immobilized the government in Vienna for a long period. But a counterrevolution won out in the Hapsburg Empire and gave Austria a temporary reprieve.

The outcome of the Hapsburg revolutions was closely linked to the complex national groupings within the empire:

Nationality	Percentage of Total Population in 1848
German	23
Magyar (Hungarian)	14
Czech and Slovak	19
South Slav (Yugoslav)	
Slovene	4
Croat	4
Serb	5
Pole	7
Ruthenian (Little Russian)	8
Romanian	8
Italian	8

These national groups were not always neatly arranged in compartments. The Hungarian part of the empire contained important numbers of Slovaks, Romanians, Serbs, Croats, and Germans; together they slightly outnumbered the dominant Magyars. Throughout the empire, moreover, German bureaucrats and tradesmen predominated in most cities and towns.

In 1848 nationalism was strongest among the Italians in Lombardy-Venetia, the Czechs in Bohemia, and the Magyars and Croats in Hungary. Magyar nationalism had won an important victory in 1844 when Hungarian replaced Latin as the official language in the eastern half of the empire. The fervent nationalists, whose spokesman was the spellbinding orator Louis Kossuth, viewed this linguistic reform as the first in a series of projects to cut all ties with the Vienna government. They bitterly opposed any satisfaction of the growing national aspirations of their non-Hungarian subjects. The most discontented were the Croats, whose national awakening had begun when their homeland became the Illyrian province of Napoleon's empire.

The antagonism between Croats and Magyars revealed an all-important fact about the nationalistic movements within the Hapsburg Empire. Some minorities—Italians, Magyars, Czechs, Poles—resented the German-dominated government in Vienna. Others, notably Croats and Romanians, were not so much anti-German as anti-Magyar. Here was a situation where Vienna could apply the policy of "divide and conquer," as it had already done in 1846 to suppress a revolt in Galicia, the province acquired by Austria in the partitions of Poland. When the Polish landlords in Galicia revolted, their exploited Ruthenian peasants rose against them with full backing from Vienna.

Liberalism also had an important role in the Hapsburg revolutions, particularly in Vienna. The expanding middle class desired civil liberties, a voice in government, and the lifting of mercantilist restrictions on business activity. In Vienna, as in Berlin and Paris, some workers demanded more radical democratic reforms.

From 1815 to 1848, except for the linguistic concession to Hungary, the Hapsburg government virtually ignored the grumblings in almost every corner of the empire. If Prince Metternich had had his way, he would probably have made additional liberal and nationalistic reforms. But he was blocked by the emperors—the bureaucratic Francis I (1792–1835) and the feeble-minded Ferdinand I (1835–1848)—and by the vested interests of the aristocracy.

The news of the February revolution in Paris shook the empire to its foundations. Four separate revolutions erupted in March 1848—in Milan and Venice, in Hungary, in Bohemia, and in Vienna itself. In Hungary, Kossuth and his supporters forced Emperor Ferdinand to accept the March Laws, which gave their country political autonomy. The March Laws provided for a parliamentary government with an elected legislature replacing the feudal Hungarian diet. They also abolished serfdom and ended the exemption of nobles and gentry from taxation. But they rode roughshod over the rights of non-Magyars by making proficiency in the Hungarian language a requirement for election as a deputy to the legislature.

In Vienna, on March 12, university students excited by the Hungarian revolt demonstrated together with workers who faced mounting unemployment. The next day, Prince Metternich resigned from the post he had held for thirty-nine years and fled to Britain. A constitution granted by the government did not satisfy the insurgents in Vienna, where rioting continued. Authority passed to a revolutionary coalition of students and national guards called the "committee of safety." This distant offspring of the French revolutionary Committee of Public Safety was to be in charge until the meeting of a constituent assembly in July.

Meanwhile, in Prague, the capital of Bohemia, Czech nationalists were demanding rights similar to those Hungary had obtained in the March Laws. Czech discontent mounted with the news that the "Big German" faction in the Frankfurt Assembly planned to include Bohemia in a German federation. A Pan-Slav Congress, composed largely of Czechs, assembled to resist German encroachments. During the demonstrations accompanying its meeting, the wife of Prince Windischgrätz, the commander of the Austrian garrison in Prague, was accidentally killed (June 12, 1848). Five days later, Windischgrätz forced the Czech revolutionaries to disperse; he then set up a military government in Bohemia. The counterrevolution had begun.

In July, the Austrian army defeated Piedmont; in September, the Vienna Constituent Assembly, representing all the units of the empire except Italy and Hungary, produced a democratic constitution that would never be enforced. The only lasting achievement of the assembly was the emancipation of the peasants from their last servile obligations, notably the requirement to work for their landlords. The peasants, the core of the Hapsburg population, having achieved their main goal, refused to support further revolutionary measures.

The time was ripe for the policy of "divide and conquer." In Hungary, the Germans, Slovaks, Romanians, Serbs, and Croats, all outraged by the discrimination against them in the March Laws, rose up against the Magyars. In September 1848, the imperial government authorized the governor of Croatia, the Croat Baron Jellachich, to invade central Hungary. While belligerent Magyars held off his forces, the radicals in Vienna revolted in support of the Magyars and proclaimed Austria a democratic republic. The armies of Jellachich and Windischgrätz returned and crushed the Viennese revolution (October 31). The brother-in-law of Windischgrätz, the energetic and unscrupulous Prince Schwarzenberg, became the chief minister of the Hapsburgs.

Schwarzenberg arranged for the abdication of the incompetent Ferdinand and the accession of his eighteen-year-old nephew, Francis Joseph (reigned 1848–1916). Declaring that promises made by the old emperor did not legally bind his successor, Schwarzenberg shelved most of the projects of the Austrian Constituent Assembly except for the emancipation of the peasantry. His high-handed policies infuriated the Magyars, who declared Hungary an independent republic and named Kossuth its chief executive (April 1849). Austria received an offer of military assistance from Tsar Nicholas I, who feared that the revolutionary contagion might spread to Russian Poland unless it was checked. Schwarzenberg accepted the offer, and in August 1849 Russian troops helped demolish the Hungarian Republic.

The Dual Monarchy

Although the Hapsburg monarchy put its humpty-dumpty realm back together after the upheavals of 1848, the defeats later suffered by Austria in the wars of 1859 and 1866 made it evident that more was needed than another application of old remedies. Little initiative could be expected from Emperor Francis Joseph, who was very conservative and inflexible, diligent in reading and signing state papers but indifferent to newspapers and books on current problems. The most pressing issue was the mounting discontent of the minorities, especially the Magyars, who were still smarting from the suppression of their republic in 1849.

In 1860 Francis Joseph agreed to a cautious experiment in decentralization by granting more authority to the noble-dominated parliaments in Hungary and Bohemia. The Magyars thought this concession was too small, but the German bureaucrats felt it conceded too much. In 1861 they persuaded the emperor to remove power from the provincial parliaments and concentrate it in a central imperial legislature. The scheme had to be abandoned when Magyars, Czechs, and Poles boycotted the central legislature. At last Francis Joseph agreed to negotiate with the Magyars. After the war of 1866, their talks led to the *Ausgleich* (compromise) of 1867, which set up the Dual Monarchy and enabled the Hapsburg realm to survive for another half century.

The Ausgleich made Austria and Hungary distinct though not fully independent partners in government. Both halves of the Dual Monarchy were united in the person of the emperor, who was crowned king of Hungary in a special ceremony at Budapest. Joint ministers appointed by the emperor unified the partners' foreign, military, and fiscal policies. A common budget was to be determined by "delegations" from the Austrian and Hungarian parliaments.

Otherwise, Austria and Hungary went their separate ways. As king of Hungary, Francis Joseph could appoint professors and bishops as well as government ministers and civil servants. Hungary had its own legislature with an upper house of hereditary peers and a lower house that represented only the tiny fraction of the population that met the economic and linguistic requirements for voting. In Austria the Constitution of 1867 made the authority of the emperor rather like that of other constitutional monarchs, with the important exception that he could dissolve parliament at his pleasure and decree legislation himself when it was not in session.

The creation of Austria-Hungary appeased the Magyars but did not settle the grievances of other minorities. The Constitution of 1867 promised all nationalities in the Austrian part equal rights, including the use of their languages in education, administration, and public life; the Hungarian parliament enacted comparable legislation in 1868. The trouble was that these pledges were not honored in either half of the Dual Monarchy. Discrimination and persecution were to plague Austria-Hungary for the rest of its existence.

IV AUTOCRACY AND REFORM IN RUSSIA, 1796–1866

Paul and Alexander I, 1796–1825

Russia, the third of the great eastern empires, also felt the first stirrings of reform and revolutionary activity. When Catherine the Great died, her son became Tsar Paul (reigned 1796–1801). Although Paul was the best-educated Russian ruler to date, his mother's fear that he might become involved in a conspiracy to unseat her had kept him from participating in the government. Upon inheriting the throne, therefore, Paul was determined to undo his mother's work. But he himself was undone by his own eccentric behavior and by his tough attitude toward the nobility. He exacted compulsory service once more, and in the provinces forced nobles to meet the bills for public buildings, pay new taxes on their lands, and be subject to corporal punishment for crimes. Paul, like Peter III, wanted to make army officers more like the strictly disciplined Prussians, thereby alienating the guards regiments. In 1801 a conspiracy of guardsmen led to the murder of Paul and the accession of his son, Alexander I (reigned 1801–1825).

It appeared possible that the new tsar might undertake a fundamental reform of the Russian autocracy. He gathered around him a small "unofficial committee" of young men, including one who had been active in the Paris Jacobin club and two others who greatly admired the English system of government. The committee had as its self-appointed task the preparation of a constitution for Russia. But its discussions amounted to little more than the after-dinner talk of pleasant well-born young men.

In the interval of peace between the Tilsit settlement and Napoleon's invasion (1807–1811), Alexander had as his chief mentor Michael Speransky. The son of a priest, Speransky was intelligent, well-educated, and conscientious. Following Montesquieu's principle of the separation of powers, he drafted for Alexander a constitutional project that would have made Russia a limited monarchy. A series of elected assemblies, from the smallest administrative subdivision up through districts and provinces, would have culminated in a great national assembly, the Duma. The Duma would approve laws decided on by the tsar and would function as a genuine Russian parliament. His proposals represented a real advance, even though the voting arrangements favored the nobility and excluded the serfs. If enacted, they might have altered the whole course of modern Russian history; Alexander, however, refused to carry out Speransky's plan.

Following Napoleon's invasion, Alexander fell under the influence of Madame de Krüdener, a Baltic baroness who persuaded the tsar that he was chosen by destiny to overthrow Bonaparte and inaugurate a new Christian order. The tsar's religious enthusiasm brought about his sponsorship of the Holy Alliance and convinced him that as the bearer of a sacred mission all he needed to do was follow the promptings of his inmost feelings. Many Orthodox clerics were displeased by the new piety, which included elements from Protestant Pietism, Freemasonry, and eccentric Russian sects.

After 1815 the most important figure at Alexander's court was Count Arakcheev, a competent but brutal officer, who once bit off the ear of one of his men as a punishment. Arakcheev directed the hated system of "military colonies," the drafting of the male population of whole districts to serve in regiments. While not drilling or fighting, the soldiers were to work farms in the district. By the end of Alexander's reign, almost 400,000 soldiers were living in these colonies, which were virtual concentration camps.

As king of Poland under the Vienna settlement, by contrast, Alexander gave the Poles an advanced constitution along with their own army, their own Polish officials, and the free use of their own language. In Finland, too, after its annexation by Russia in 1809, he allowed the Finns to keep their own law codes and their traditional forms of local government. The "liberal tsar" was liberal only outside Russia.

The Decembrist Revolt

Nevertheless, liberal ideas continued to penetrate Russia. They were imported by Freemasonic lodges that awakened the humanitarian impulses of some nobles and gave them the opportunity to talk with men of lower status. Moreover, the contrast between the relatively enlightened West and backward Russia made a deep impression on officers who had served in the campaigns against Napoleon. In the last years of Alexander's reign, high-ranking officers at St. Petersburg secretly formed the Northern Society. They hoped to make Russia a limited, decentralized monarchy, with the various provinces enjoying rights somewhat like those of the states in the American republic. The serfs would receive their freedom but no land, and the whole series of reforms would be achieved by peaceful means.

A second secret organization, the Southern Society, with headquarters at Kiev, in the Ukraine, included many relatively impoverished officers among its members. Its leader was Colonel Pestel, a Jacobin in temperament and an admirer of Napoleon. In every respect the program of the Southern Society was more radical than that of the Petersburg group. Pestel advocated a highly centralized republic, the granting of land to liberated serfs, and the assassination of the tsar. Pestel planned to install a dictatorship, supported by secret police, as a temporary government between the overthrow of the tsarist regime and the advent of the republic. The program of Pestel's Southern Society may be viewed as an early blueprint for the revolutionary regime that would rule Russia after the Bolshevik uprising of 1917.

Both the Northern Society and the Southern Society tried to exploit the political confusion following the death of Alexander (December, 1825). Since Alexander left no son, the crown would normally have passed to his younger brother, Constantine, his viceroy in Poland. Constantine, however, had relinquished his rights to a still younger brother, Nicholas, but in a document so secret that Nicholas never saw it. After Alexander's death, Constantine declared that Nicholas was the legal tsar, and Nicholas declared that Constantine was!

While the two brothers were clarifying their status, the Northern Society summoned the St. Petersburg garrison to revolt against Nicholas. Throughout the day of December 26, 1825, the Decembrist rebels stood their ground until troops loyal to Nicholas subdued them. Two weeks later, the Southern Society launched a movement that was doomed from the start because Pestel had already been arrested. Nicholas was so alarmed by the Decembrists' revolt that he had five of them executed and more than a hundred exiled to Siberia, where many of them helped to improve local government and education. The Decembrists had become the first in the long line of modern Russia's political martyrs.

The Polish Revolution, 1830–1833

The new tsar, Nicholas I (reigned 1825–1855) soon faced a revolution in Poland. The liberal constitution introduced by Alexander I had proved difficult to apply in practice, particularly since many of the men he selected for official posts in Poland were not acceptable to the Poles. Censorship and police intervention appeared during the last years of his reign, and the accession of the highly conservative Nicholas increased political friction. Meantime, many students at the universities of Warsaw (in Poland) and Vilna (in Lithuania) were converted to nationalist doctrines. The Polish nationalists demanded the re-

Tsar Nicholas I, by Landseer.

Russia under Nicholas I

At home Nicholas gained popularity by dismissing Arakcheev and ending the hated experiment with military colonies. But he continued to rely on the secret police and on censorship to insulate Russia from the subversive Western ideas that had inspired the Decembrists. To strengthen the autocracy he added several sections to his personal secretariat, including the notorious "third section," charged with political police work. Since the rapid enlargement of the tsar's own staff was not matched by any reduction in the older organs of government, bureaucratic confusion, incompetence, and injustice multiplied.

In this less-than-efficient police state, no effective insulation from Western ideas was possible. They continued to be circulated by publications, universities, and the conversations of the men and women comprising the intelligentsia. Discussions among these intellectuals centered on the question of whether or not Russia was or should be a part of Western culture. The Westerners insisted that Peter the Great had tried to set Russia on the right course, and that it was now time to catch up with Western constitutional monarchy. But the Slavophiles, the champions of Slavic traditions, deplored Peter's efforts to crush the unique Russian spirit founded on the peasants' devotion to the Orthodox Church. They also deplored the materialism and anticlericalism of the Enlightenment, and wanted to return to the patriarchal, benevolent monarchy they believed had prevailed before Peter the Great.

Defense of the Orthodoxy cherished by Nicholas I and the Slavophiles was a factor in Russia's involvement in the disastrous Crimean War (1853–1856). The war resulted from a squabble between Nicholas and Napoleon III about the respective rights of Orthodox and Catholic clergy over the Holy Places, notably the Church of the Holy Sepulcher in Jerusalem and the Church of the Nativity in Bethlehem. Britain became involved out of fear that Russia would use protection of the Orthodox peoples in the Ottoman Empire as a pretext for acquiring a dominant influence in Turkish affairs. British interests in the Near East would be threatened in consequence. The main event of the fighting was the prolonged British and French siege of the Russian naval base at Sebastopol on the Crimean peninsula that juts into the Black Sea. After both sides committed many blunders, including the futile charge of Britain's Light Brigade, the Russians eventually

turn to Poland of provinces that had belonged to the Polish state before the partitions of the late eighteenth century—Lithuania, Belorussia, and the Ukraine. Secret societies modeled after the Italian Carbonari were formed in these provinces as well as in the kingdom of Poland.

In November 1830, a secret society of army cadets in Warsaw launched a revolution. It never won wide popular support, for the nobles who soon dominated the revolutionary government still had all the traditional aristocratic contempt for peasants and townspeople. Radicals in Warsaw and other cities rose against the new government, which collapsed in September 1831. Polish misery was intensified by an epidemic of cholera, the first outbreak of this terrible Asian disease in Europe.

By 1833 Russian forces regained control. Tsar Nicholas scrapped the Polish constitution, imposed permanent martial law, and shut down the universities at Warsaw and Vilna. To escape the tsar's vengeance several thousand revolutionaries and intellectuals fled the country. They found asylum in the West, where Paris became the capital of Poles in exile.

had to yield. The Black Sea clauses of the Peace of Paris (1856) inflicted severe humiliation by forbidding Russia to maintain a fleet in that sea or to fortify its coast.

The Reforms of Alexander II

When peace came, Russia had a new tsar, Alexander II (reigned 1855–1881). While almost as conservative as his father, Nicholas, Alexander resolved to take the revolutionary step of abolishing serfdom to calm the mounting unrest among the serf population. In addition, serf labor was proving to be increasingly inefficient and unproductive both in agriculture and in the factories that were beginning to appear in Russia. In 1861 a statute freed the serfs. It assigned each newly free peasant family the land they had tilled for their own benefit under serfdom, but not the lands they had cultivated for their lord.

This statute, liberating more than forty million human beings, has been called the greatest single legislative act in history. Yet, while it was an immense moral stimulus to peasant self-respect, it also created grave difficulties. The emancipated peasants had to pay the state not only taxes but also redemption payments over forty-nine years that would compensate their former lords for the loss of land. Peasant mobility was not significantly increased, and in general peasants received too little land, were required to pay too much for it, and were denied a share of important forest and pasture lands. Even so, the settlement was surprisingly liberal, despite the problems it failed to solve and despite the agrarian crises that its inadequacies would provoke in the future.

The emancipation of the serfs ended the landlords' rights to police their own estates and dispense justice to the inhabitants. This, in turn, required a major reform of local administration. In 1864 a statute created provincial and district assemblies called *zemstvos*, whose members were chosen by an elaborate electoral process. Voters were divided according to their class—nobles, townspeople, and peasants. In practice, no one class dominated the zemstvos, and the peasants had substantial representation. The zemstvos made great advances in promoting primary schooling and improving public health. They also dealt with local finances, the maintenance of roads, and the development of scientific agriculture.

Cities gained municipal assemblies, with duties much like those of the zemstvos in the countryside. Legal procedures and the whole system of justice were completely overhauled. For the first time in Russian history, juries were introduced, cases were argued publicly, and all classes were made equal before the law. Censorship was relaxed, the universities were freed from the restraints imposed by Nicholas I, and the antiquated and often brutal system of military service was modernized and made less severe.

Tens of thousands of Russians expected that these reforms would culminate in the creation of a central parliament, the Duma. But the liberalism of Alexander had already been stretched to the limit when the first attempt to assassinate him was made in 1866. The Duma was not granted, and the regime shifted from reform toward the reactionary policies that would prevail in Russia during the last third of the nineteenth century.

READING SUGGESTIONS on Nationalism and Reform: Southern, Central and Eastern Europe

Books Covering Most of Europe

F. B. Artz, *Reaction and Revolution, 1814–1832*; W. L. Langer, *Political and Social Upheaval, 1832–1852*; R. C. Binkley, *Realism and Nationalism, 1852–1870*. Meaty volumes in the series, "The Rise of Modern Europe" (*Torchbooks).

C. Breunig, *The Age of Revolution and Reform, 1789–1850*, 2nd ed.; N. Rich, *The Age of Nationalism and Reform, 1850–1890* (*Norton). More recent brief surveys.

J. Droz, *Europe between Revolutions, 1815–1848* (Harper, 1967). Review by a French scholar stressing social and economic forces.

P. Stearns, *1848: The Revolutionary Tide in Europe* (*Norton). Helpful analysis of the factors in its ebb and flow.

P. Robertson, *Revolutions of 1848* (*Princeton). Lively social history, stressing the role played by individuals.

L. B. Namier, *1848: The Revolution of the Intellectuals* (*Anchor). Essay criticizing "liberals" for their illiberal attitudes, particularly in Germany.

A. J. P. Taylor, *The Struggle for the Mastery of Europe, 1848–1919* (Oxford, 1954). Crisp and provocative; a volume in the Oxford History of Modern Europe.

The Revolutions in Southern Europe

R. Carr, *Spain 1808–1939* (Oxford, 1966). Good scholarly survey.

P. Sugar, *Southeastern Europe under*

Ottoman Rule (U. of Washington, 1977). Analysis of the background of modern Balkan history.

M. Petrovich, *A History of Modern Serbia, 1804–1918* (Harcourt Brace, 1976). Assesses the role played by the leading Balkan Slavic state.

C. M. Woodhouse, *The Greek War of Independence* (Russell, 1952) and *Modern Greece: A Short History* (*Faber & Faber). By a leading British expert.

D. Dakin, *The Struggle for Greek Independence* (U. of California, 1973). Definitive scholarly study of events between 1821 and 1833.

D. Mack Smith, *Italy: A Modern History,* revised edition (Univ. of Michigan, 1969). By a ranking expert on the subject, author also of *Cavour and Garibaldi* (Cambridge, 1954) and *Garibaldi* (Knopf, 1956).

S. Woolf, *A History of Italy, 1700–1860* (Methuen, 1978). Discusses both the 19th-century revolution and its 18th-century background.

A. J. Whyte, *The Evolution of Modern Italy* (*Norton). Sound introduction.

G. Romani, *The Neapolitan Revolution* (Northwestern U., 1950). Detailed account of the events of 1820–1821.

G. Salvemini, *Mazzini* (Stanford U., 1957). Sympathetic appraisal by a fellow champion of Italian democracy. May be supplemented by selections from Mazzini's writings: I. Silone, ed., *The Living Thoughts of Mazzini* (Greenwood, 1972).

German Unification

T. S. Hamerow, *Restoration, Revolution, Reaction* (*Princeton). Scholarly appraisal of economic and political developments in Germany, 1815–1871.

R. H. Thomas, *Liberalism, Nationalism, and the German Intellectuals* (Cambridge, 1952). Careful study of the period 1822–1847.

W. O. Henderson, *The Zollverein,* 2nd ed. (Cass, 1968). The standard work on German economic unification.

O. Pflanze, *Bismarck and the Development of Germany* (Princeton, 1963). Scholarly study down to 1871.

E. Eyck, *Bismarck and the German Empire* (*Norton). Condensation of a longer study by a German scholar.

A. J. P. Taylor, *Bismarck: The Man and the Statesman* (*Vintage). An often hostile evaluation by a maverick British scholar.

F. Stern, *Gold and Iron* (*Vintage). Recent study of how Bismarck built the German Empire.

G. O. Kent, *Bismarck and His Times* (*Southern Illinois). Another recent study.

The Hapsburg Empire

R. J. Rath, *The Viennese Revolution of 1848* (Univ. of Texas, 1957). Good detailed account.

Peters, Carsten et al., ed., *The Hapsburg Empire, 1835–1918*, 2 vols. (Barnes & Noble, 1979). Volume I treats Austria and Bohemia; Volume II covers Hungary.

C. A. Macartney, *The Hapsburg Empire, 1790–1918* (Macmillan, 1969). By a recognized expert in Hapsburg politics.

A. J. P. Taylor, *The Hapsburg Monarchy, 1809–1918* (*Univ. of Chicago). Spirited brief survey.

Russia and Poland

H. Seton-Watson, *The Russian Empire, 1801–1917* (Oxford, 1967), and *The Decline of Imperial Russia, 1855–1914* (Praeger, 1952). By a highly respected expert in the field.

A. G. Mazour, *The First Russian Revolution* (*Stanford U.) and M. Raeff, *The Decembrist Movement* (Prentice-Hall, 1966). Valuable studies of the aborted revolution of 1825.

N. V. Riasanovsky, *Russia and the West in the Teaching of the Slavophils* (Harvard, 1953) and *Nicholas I and Official Nationality in Russia, 1825–1855* (*California). Informative studies.

W. E. Mosse, *Alexander II and the Modernization of Russia* (*Collier). Brief survey of an important period in Russian reforms.

R. F. Leslie, *Polish Politics and the Revolution of 1830* (Athlone, 1956). Detailed account of the internal factors that doomed the revolution.

CHAPTER FIFTEEN

The Ideas And Culture Of The Nineteenth Century

The nineteenth century recorded not only many shifts in the structure of politics and the balance of power but also significant changes in the way people looked at themselves and expressed their hopes for the future. The Romantic movement of the early nineteenth century strengthened the forces of nationalism and revived interest in the emotional and spiritual qualities of human beings. But the hardships resulting from the industrial revolution led to demands for a better distribution of wealth. Blueprints for change ranged from the step-by-step liberalism of John Stuart Mill and the Christian democrats to the unreal utopias of the early socialists and the total revolution demanded by the communists and the anarchists. While new advances in science promised a brighter future for humanity, Darwin's theory of evolution touched off prolonged debates about the fundamental nature of men and women. On the whole, philosophers, psychologists, poets, novelists, and playwrights took a cautious or gloomy view of humanity. It was the musicians and even more the painters who responded with exuberance as they found new doors to expression opened by the advances in science.

THE ROMANTIC RETREAT FROM THE ENLIGHTENMENT

In 1790 Edmund Burke, a Whig member of the British Parliament, published an eloquent attack on the French Revolution and on the enlightened ideas that had helped precipitate it. Burke's *Reflections on the Revolution in France* challenged the validity of the philosophes' appeals to natural rights and simple natural laws. Contrary to the Enlightenment, he argued that "the nature of man is intricate; the objects of society are of the greatest possible complexity." Therefore social and political institutions, constructed so painstakingly over the centuries, should be changed only gradually and with the greatest caution.

Earlier, Burke had defended the American Revolution because it developed from a glorious tradition established by the mother country in 1688. But he condemned the French revolutionaries of 1789 because their rage and frenzy "pull down more in half an hour than prudence, deliberation and foresight can build up in a hundred years." "Society is indeed a contract," he wrote, but not the "social contract" cherished by disciples of Rousseau:

> The state ought not to be considered as nothing better than a partnership agreement in a trade of pepper and coffee . . . taken up as a little temporary interest. It is to be looked upon with other reverence. . . . It is a partnership in all science, in all art. . . . As the ends of such a partnership cannot be obtained in many generations, it becomes a partnership between those who are living, those who are dead, and those who are to be born.*

Burke's *Reflections* are a good introduction to one aspect of the Romantic movement that flourished during the first third of the nineteenth century. Many Romantic writers joined Burke in deploring the naïve optimism of the Enlightenment and its reliance on simple laws of nature. Because life was so complex, men and women needed to draw on the experience gathered over the centuries by established religious and monarchical institutions. They also needed to draw on their own emotions and sense of conscience.

Literature

Emotion and conscience were very important elements in the Romantic literature that emerged during the middle decades of the eighteenth century. Examples were the novels of feeling, then often called "sensibility," such as Richardson's *Clarissa* and Rousseau's *La Nouvelle Héloïse.* In the 1770s and 1780s, the German "Storm and Stress" movement contributed Goethe's tearful *Sorrows of Young Werther.* As the century ended, another representative of the movement, Schiller (1759–1805), wrote highly colored dramas about heroes and heroines of the past—William Tell, founder of the Swiss republic; Joan of Arc; Mary, Queen of Scots; and Wallenstein, the ambitious general of the Thirty Years' War.

Despite the self-pity of *Werther,* Goethe (1749–1832) was in some respects an eighteenth-century man of reason, deeply interested in natural science. Comfortably settled at the enlightened court of the small German state of Weimar, he was almost untouched by the political passions of the revolutionary and Napoleonic era. Yet Romantic values were at the core of his masterpiece, *Faust,* a long philosophical and poetic drama. According to legend, the aging Faust, weary of books and yearning for eternal youth, sold his soul to the devil. He recovered the joys of youth for an allotted time and then was cast into the everlasting fires of Hell. Goethe revised the legend. Faust makes his compact with Mephistopheles, who stresses the emptiness of intellectual pursuits: "Grey, dear friend, is all theory, but the golden tree of life is green!" Faust is saved when he gives up indulgence of self to promote the welfare of others. A drama of human sinning, striving, and redemption, *Faust* is a reaffirmation of Christian values.

Romantic writers rediscovered the vigor and color of the Bible, Homer, and Shakespeare. In England two young poets, Wordsworth (1770–1850) and Coleridge (1772–1834), jointly published *Lyrical Ballads* (1798). Their aim was to create "new and striking images." Coleridge's *Rime of the Ancient Mariner* related the curse afflicting a sailor who killed an albatross; his *Kubla Khan* has been compared to the hallucinations of a drug addict:

---

* Condensed from Burke, *Reflections on the Revolution in France* (New York: Dutton, 1910), p. 93.

In Xanadu did Kubla Khan
A stately pleasure dome decree:
Where Alph, the sacred river, ran
Through caverns measureless to man,
  Down to a sunless sea.

This imaginary realm was far removed from the Newtonian world machine, which did not recognize the existence of "measureless caverns" or "sunless seas."

Wordsworth urged his readers to learn directly from nature, not from the printed page:

One impulse from a vernal wood
May teach you more of man,
Of moral evil and of good,
Than all the sages can.

Sweet is the lore which Nature brings;
Our meddling intellect
Mis-shapes the beauteous forms of things:—
We murder to dissect.

Enough of Science and of Art;
Close up those barren leaves;
Come forth, and bring with you a heart
That watches and receives. *

For Wordsworth nature was a mysterious vital force that had to be experienced directly by the individual; it was not something that could be analyzed and reduced to scientific laws.

Nation and History

Romantic thinkers viewed a nation as a natural organism, slowly growing from birth to youth and then to maturity. They viewed the Middle Ages, so despised by the Enlightenment, as an exciting era of youthful national awakening. The German Herder (1744–1803) declared that each nation had its own particular personality, or *Volksgeist* ("folk spirit"). It could be measured by the literature it produced—poetry in youth, prose in maturity. Herder fostered the rediscovery of the popular ballads expressing the *Volksgeist* of medieval Germany. He also sponsored the publication of the *Nibelungenlied* ("Song of the Nibelungen," 1782), a mythological saga from the remote past that would later inspire Wagner's operatic cycle, *The Ring of the Nibelung.* Herder thus helped to free the German literature of his own day from its bondage to French culture. But he was no narrow nationalist and insisted that a cultivated individual should study cultures other

* *The Tables Turned,* II. 21–32.

than his own. He promoted German translations of *Don Quixote,* the plays of Shakespeare, and ancient Sanskrit writings from India.

In Britain, Sir Walter Scott (1771–1832) collected medieval ballads and made historical fiction enormously popular. Of the more than thirty novels he wrote, the best known is *Ivanhoe,* set in the time of the Crusades when Richard the Lion-Hearted was king of England. In Russia the poet Pushkin (1799–1837) wrote the first major works in the Russian vernacular, which began to replace the archaic Slavonic of the Orthodox Church as the national literary language. Pushkin took subjects from the past, such as the tempestuous rule of Boris Godunov,which inaugurated Russia's "Time of Troubles" at the close of the Middle Ages.

In France the literary revolution arrived like a pistol shot in 1830 at the first night of Hugo's *Ernani,* a tragedy set in early sixteenth-century Spain. Victor Hugo (1802–1885) deliberately flouted the rigid classical rules of writing drama based on the Aristotelian unities. When one of the characters in *Ernani* recited a line of verse that ended in the middle of a word, traditionalists in the audience started a riot. The furore continued at the theater and in the press for weeks afterward. In the next year Hugo published his historical novel, *Notre Dame de Paris* (better known as "The Hunchback of Notre Dame"), set in the final years of Gothic France when Louis XI was on the throne.

Music and the Arts

Romantic musicians also adapted popular ballads and tales from the national past. Composers of opera and song turned to Shakespeare's plays, Scott's novels, and the poems and tales of Goethe and Pushkin. Concert music experienced a revolution of its own with the addition to the orchestra of the double bass, more wind and percussion instruments, and, above all, the piano. Beethoven (1770–1827) was the first to exploit the opportunities for more color and passion in composition. Beethoven's contemporary in Vienna, Schubert (1797–1826), combined the piano and the human voice in more than six hundred *Lieder* (songs), many of them set to poems by Goethe. Weber (1786–1826) created a truly German opera, taking an old legend as the libretto for *Der Freischütz* ("The Freeshooter"), with choruses and marches borrowed from traditional folksongs.

The most spectacular and inventive Roman-

Berlioz in 1845:
engraving from a French newspaper.

tic composer was the Frenchman Berlioz (1803–1869). He explored the theatrical potentialities of music in his *Fantastic Symphony*, said to have been inspired by Goethe's *Werther*. He also made a symphonic adaptation of *Romeo and Juliet*; and composed a symphonic opera, *The Damnation of Faust*. Berlioz's *Requiem* required a full orchestra, a great pipe organ, four brass choirs, and a chorus of two hundred voices. The Romantic passion for bigness also led to a precedent-setting performance of Bach's oratorio *The Passion According to Saint Matthew*. Conducted by Mendelssohn in

1829, it utilized a full orchestra and a chorus of hundreds, many times the number of participants Bach himself had employed.

In the fine arts, however, Romanticism scored few triumphs. The neoclassicism of the eighteenth century continued into the nineteenth under the virtual dictator of European painting, the Frenchman David (1748–1825). David headed the Paris Jacobin club, served on the Committee of General Security during the Terror, and organized many of the great revolutionary ceremonies. His paintings provide a capsule history of the rise and decline of revolutionary fervor. Before 1789 he chose Roman republican heroes and victims of aristocratic persecution like Socrates; then he turned to such contemporary events as the Tennis Court Oath and the assassination of Marat. Following the Brumaire coup, he painted Napoleon crossing the Alps and his coronation as emperor, doctoring the actual events to create the effect the publicity-conscious Bonaparte desired.

No matter what the subject, David stressed the neoclassical concern for line, form, and perspective. The works of his Spanish contemporary, Goya (1746–1828), were much closer to the Romantic spirit with their warmth and passion, and their excursions into the grotesque. Goya's outraged Spanish patriotism inspired his painting called "The Third of May, 1808," depicting French reprisals against the insurgents who had fought the French the day before. Goya's fellow

David's "The Death of Socrates."

Francisco Goya's "The Third of May, 1808."

Eugéne Delacroix's "The Massacre of Scio."

The Houses of Parliament, London.

Spaniards claimed he must have made his preliminary sketches in the blood of the executed patriots whose agonies he recorded.

In 1824 Romantic painting at last won official approval when a Paris exhibition included the works of two pioneers, Constable and Delacroix. Constable (1776–1837), an Englishman, took painting out of the studio and into the world of nature. His peaceful landscapes stressed light and color and paved the way for the impressionist revolution later in the century. Delacroix (1798–1863), a Frenchman, also championed light and color and added a large element of drama. He urged young painters to study the flamboyant canvases of Rubens, deplored by David and the neoclassicists, and asserted that the purpose of art was "not to imitate nature but to strike the imagination." His "Massacre of Scio," depicting the Turkish vengeance against the inhabitants of the island during the Greek war of independence, seems almost tame today. In 1824, however, it was denounced as "barbarous, drunken, deliri-

The library of the University of Virginia, designed by Thomas Jefferson.

ous—the massacre of painting." French painting was soon divided between the Romantic followers of Delacroix and the still influential school of David.

Architecture, too, was split between two flourishing schools during the first half of the nineteenth century—the neoclassical and the more Romantic neo-Gothic. Many architects mastered both styles, designing buildings of classical proportions then adding an external shell and decoration borrowed from medieval Gothic cathedrals. The Houses of Parliament in London, rebuilt after a disastrous fire in the 1830s, seem very Gothic at first glance with their spires and towers; a longer look also reveals a classical symmetry of design.

In France the revolutionary enthusiasm for Roman buildings reached its peak in Napoleonic Paris. The great landmark, the Arc de Triomphe, was patterned on the huge triumphal arches of Roman emperors. The Church of the Madeleine was an enlarged copy of a surviving Roman temple, the Maison Carrée ("square house") at Nîmes in southern France. In America the versatile Thomas Jefferson adapted the same temple for the Virginia capitol at Richmond. At Charlottesville, about 1820, Jefferson provided the University of Virginia with an elegant academic setting. Its centerpiece is a circular library, derived from the Pantheon in Rome, which presides over a large lawn bordered by two rows of smaller structures, each recalling a different Roman temple and connected by colonnades.

By the second quarter of the nineteenth century, neo-Roman was yielding place to the Greek Revival style, an offshoot of Philhellenic enthusiasm. London's British Museum and Philadelphia's Girard College are two of many splendid examples.

Meantime, especially in Britain, the Gothic Revival was also gaining ground, stimulated by the wealth of architectural lore in Scott's novels. At least a touch of Gothic, was applied to every kind of structure from the Houses of Parliament and churches on down to elaborate villas and modest cottages. The fad for furniture bristling

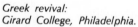

Greek revival:
Girard College, Philadelphia.

with spikes prompted one wag to warn that the occupant of a neo-Gothic room would be lucky to escape being "wounded by some of its minutiae." Though the Gothic Revival created some monstrosities, it also inspired the restoration of magnificent medieval structures damaged by neglect and vandalism.

Religion and Philosophy

Neo-Gothic architecture was one aspect of the Christian revival that accompanied the Romantic movement. Another was the papal reestablishment of the Jesuit order (1814), which had been suppressed during the Enlightenment. Most Romantic writers were horrified by the religious skepticism of the philosophes; the outspoken atheism of the English poet Shelley was an isolated exception. In Germany, Catholicism and Protestant Pietism gained new converts among Romantic writers. In Britain, Wordsworth, who had spent part of his youth in revolutionary France, became disillusioned with rational reform and in his later years wrote sonnets honoring the Church of England. And Coleridge introduced to his countrymen the German philosophers of idealism who were building on the work of Kant.

Foremost among these idealists was Hegel (1770–1831), a professor at the University of Berlin, who rejected as superficial the view of human nature and human history taken by the Enlightenment. To Hegel history was a record of human struggles to achieve goodness as part of the gradual unfolding of God's plan for the world. Hegel asserted that history was a *dialectical* process—that is, a series of conflicts between the *thesis,* the established way of life, and the *antithesis,* the challenge to this old order. Out of the struggles between thesis and antithesis there emerged the *synthesis,* a new and better way of life, another step in humanity's slow progression toward the good. In time the dialectic would resume as the synthesis broke down and a new antithesis confronted the thesis.

The death throes of the Roman Republic provided Hegel with an example of the dialectic at work. The thesis was represented by the decaying republic and the antithesis by "oriental despotism," the tradition of the autocratic monarchies in Egypt and the Near East. The new synthesis was the strong regime of Julius Caesar and his successor, Augustus. Hegel explained that "This important change must not be regarded as a thing of chance; it was *necessary,*" a part of God's grand design. Hegel called Caesar a "hero," one

of the few "world-historical individuals," like Alexander the Great and Napoleon, who "had an insight into the requirements of the time" and understood "what was ripe for development." This Hegelian concept of the hero as the agent of a cosmic process is another characteristic of the Romantic outlook. Hegel's philosophy of history also helped shape the dialectical materialism of Karl Marx, in which the worker is the hero.

II PRESCRIPTIONS FOR SOCIAL AND ECONOMIC CHANGE

Remedies for the hardships created by the industrial revolution ranged from the laissez-faire attitude of Adam Smith and his followers all the way to the revolutionary proposals of Marxists and anarchists. Our examination of these remedies begins with the defenders of laissez-faire who argued that the patient must learn to cure himself.

The Classical Economists

The champions of laissez-faire liberalism in the nineteenth century are known to history as the "classical economists." To their critics, however, they were the advocates of the "dismal science." Their doctrine of free trade did bring some improvements in living standards, such as the cheaper bread available to the British after the repeal of the Corn Laws. In the main, however, the classical economists refused to meddle with things as they were. They opposed the first legislation brought before the British parliament to safeguard public health: "Suffering and evil are nature's admonitions; they cannot be got rid of; and the impatient attempts of benevolence to banish them from the world by legislation . . . have always been productive of more evil than good."*

This attitude of do-nothing-lest-bad-matters-become-worse derived in part from the teachings of Thomas Malthus (1766–1834). His *Essay on the Principle of Population* (1798) warned that the human species might well breed itself into starvation. Malthus contended that population increased by a geometric progression (2:6:18:54) while the food supply grew only by an arithmetic

*he Economist (May 13, 1848).

progression (2:4:6:8). Malthus predicted that the unchecked increase in human numbers would intensify human misery:

> When the wages of labour are hardly sufficient to maintain two children, a man marries and has five or six. He of course finds himself miserably distressed. He accuses the insufficiency of the price of labour to maintain a family. . . . He accuses the partial and unjust institutions of society. . . . He accuses perhaps the dispensations of Providence, which have assigned to him a place in society so beset with unavoidable distress. . . . In searching for objects of accusation, he never adverts to the quarter from which his misfortunes originate. The last person that he would think of accusing is himself, on whom in fact the whole of the blame lies. . . .†

The reduction of the birth rate was the only hope that Malthus held out to suffering humanity. It was to be achieved by late marriage and by "chastity till that period arrives."

The predictions of Malthus lost most of their credibility during the second half of the nineteenth century because of the rapid increase in agricultural output and the simultaneous emigration of many Europeans who settled abroad. But one hundred years later, interest in Malthusian doctrines revived in the light of the immense difficulties faced by the newly independent states of Africa and Asia in feeding their ever-growing population.

Malthus was the first professional economist. He made his living by teaching future administrators of the East India Company at its training school in Britain. His influential friend, David Ricardo (1772–1823), was an economist with a more practical background. The son of a Jewish immigrant, Ricardo became a millionaire banker and won election to the House of Commons. After an early retirement from business, he published *On the Principles of Political Economy* (1817), which gave a new dimension to Malthusian pessimism. Ricardo forecast that the diminishing output from mines and farms combined with a growing population would increase the cost of coal, food, and other necessities. This in turn would force the wages of laborers to a very low level, since an ever larger portion of the "economic pie" would go to the men who owned mines and farmland.

Ricardo regarded this prediction as a probability but not a certainty, since new factors might

† *Essay on the Principle of Population,* Book IV, Ch. 3.

enlarge the dimensions of the economic pie. On the other hand, some of his followers believed that the "Iron Law of Wages" bound workers to a cycle from which there was no escape. Higher wages would promote bigger families, thereby increasing the supply of laborers. The increasing competition for jobs would then reduce wages. Workers contended that, if these were the natural laws of economics, the state should intervene to make the laws more humane. The demands of the Chartists (see Chapter 13) reflected their keen sense of grievance, and so did the more radical doctrines of the emerging socialists and communists. Since the classical economists were against letting the state tamper with sacred natural laws, more sensitive economists stepped in to modify the "dismal science" of laissez-faire orthodoxy.

The Retreat from Laissez-Faire

The earliest modification of the "dismal science" came from the English Utilitarians, who claimed to support whatever policy would insure the greatest good for the greatest number of people. In practice, however, their recommendations often fell wide of the mark, notably in the controversial New Poor Law of 1834 (discussed in Chapter 13). In education, the Utilitarian attempt to force children to memorize details of scientific information they were too young to understand triggered Dickens' satirical attack on M'Choakumchild's school in *Hard Times* (1854).

The man who humanized laissez-faire and Utilitarian teachings was John Stuart Mill (1806–1873). His father, James Mill, was closely associated with Ricardo and Jeremy Bentham, the founder of Utilitarianism. Mill was a child prodigy—studying Greek at the age of three, writing history when he was twelve, and organizing a "Utilitarian Society" at sixteen. At twenty the overworked youth suffered a breakdown. To escape from being a "mere reasoning machine" he sought new outlets in music and in the poetry of Wordsworth and Coleridge. He fell in love with Harriet Taylor, whom he married twenty years later, following the death of her husband. Mill credited Mrs. Taylor with supplying the warmth and humanity he gave to his liberal creed.

Mill rejected the "Iron Law of Wages" in his very successful textbook, *The Principles of Political Economy*:

> By what means, then, is poverty to be contended against? How is the evil of low wages to be remedied? If the expedients usually recommended for

the purpose are not adapted to it, can no others be thought of? Is the problem incapable of solution? Can political economy do nothing, but only object to everything . . . ?*

Mill expressed sympathy with the French national workshops of 1848. He proposed that British workers should be free to join trade unions and form consumers' cooperatives; in addition, they should receive higher wages and might well deserve to share in a company's profits. Mill believed that many of his proposed changes could be realized within the framework of private enterprise, but he recognized that some problems were so pressing that the state would have to intervene. After reading the reports of parliamentary investigations of child labor, he recommended legislation to protect children and to improve intolerable living and working conditions.

Mill argued that all men deserved the vote and the educational opportunities that would enable them to make intelligent use of the ballot. He contended that women deserved the same rights and published a pioneering study, *The Subjection of Women* (1869), inspired by the great respect he had for his wife. He also recommended proportional representation in elections to the House of Commons, so that political minorities would not be overwhelmed by the two major parties. Some critics believe, however, that Mill seemed to express distrust of majority opinions and to favor those of an intellectual elite.

Mill's fears of excessive state power and the hopes he placed in enlightened individuals were firmly in the nineteenth-century liberal tradition. He made protection of fundamental human rights the basis for a celebrated essay, *On Liberty* (1859). "The worth of a state," he asserted, "is the worth of the individuals composing it. . . . A state which dwarfs its men, in order that they may be more docile instruments in its hands even for beneficial purposes will find that with small men no great thing can really be accomplished."

Christian Socialism and Christian Democracy

In his later years Mill called himself a socialist. In practice, however, he stopped well short of the genuine socialist's conviction that the production of goods should be transferred from the control of individuals to that of the whole community. The same reservation applied to the small group of Anglican clergymen known as Christian Socialists. In the mid-nineteenth century they urged the Church of England to put aside disputes over questions of theology and direct its efforts to ending social abuses. A leading Christian Socialist was Charles Kingsley (1819–1875), who published a long novel, *Alton Locke*, and a vigorous pamphlet, *Cheap Clothes and Nasty*, both denouncing the sweatshops where tailors and seamstresses worked long hours for meager pay, usually under appalling conditions. Kingsley helped to launch the Working Men's College in London and to promote programs that led to the organization of the Young Men's Christian Association. The Christian Socialists relied far more on private philanthropy than on assistance from the government.

The Catholic counterparts of the Christian Socialists called their reform programs of Christian Democracy or Social Christianity. Christian Democracy arose from the crisis that confronted the Church during the second half of the nineteenth century. A thousand years of papal rule over central Italy ended in 1870 when Rome became the capital of unified Italy. Anticlerical legislation threatened traditional Catholic strongholds in Italy, France, and parts of Germany. The materialism of the industrial revolution and the new ideologies of science, nationalism, and socialism all competed for the allegiance of Catholic workingmen.

Pope Pius IX (1846–1878), whose flirtation with liberalism ended in 1848, sought refuge in the past. In 1864 he issued *The Syllabus of Errors*, which condemned social theories and institutions not consecrated by centuries of tradition. While Pius rejected the materialism of laissez-faire economics, many thoughtful Catholics were disturbed by his apparent hostility to democracy and to labor unions. They were dismayed by the statement in the *Syllabus* that it was an error to think that the pope "can and ought to reconcile and harmonize himself with progress, liberalism, and modern civilization."

The next pope, Leo XIII (1878–1903), recognized that if the Church continued in this vein it would suffer serious losses. As a papal diplomat, he had seen the rapid changes resulting from science and technology in the industrial regions of Belgium, France, and Germany. He knew also that Catholicism was flourishing in the American democracy. Moreover, his studies of the writings of St. Thomas Aquinas convinced him that the Church had much to gain by following the mid-

---

* *The Principles of Political Economy* (Boston, 1848), Book II, Ch. 13.

dle-of-the-road social and economic policies recommended by that great medieval thinker.

In 1891 Pope Leo issued the encyclical *Rerum Novarum* (concerning new things), which criticized vigorously both the defects of capitalism and the socialists' doctrine of class war. He pronounced it a great mistake to believe "that class is naturally hostile to class, and that the wealthy and the workingmen are intended by nature to live in mutual conflict." Leo urged the economic man to act as a Christian man of good will:

> Religion teaches the laboring man . . . to carry out honestly and fairly all equitable agreements freely entered into; never to injure the property, nor to outrage the person, of an employer; never to resort to violence. . . . Religion teaches the wealthy owner and the employer that their work-people are not to be accounted their bondsmen; that in every man they must respect his dignity and worth as a man and as a Christian; that labor is not a thing to be ashamed of, . . . but is an honorable calling, . . . and that it is shameful and inhuman to treat men like chattels to make money by, or to look upon them merely as so much muscle or physical power.*

The state might regulate child labor, limit the hours of work, and insist that Sundays be free for religious activities and for rest. But workers must also help themselves, and *Rerum Novarum* concluded with a fervent appeal for the formation of Catholic trade unions. Although these unions have remained a minority in organized labor, the Christian democracy preached by Leo XIII eventually became a significant factor in the political life of Germany, Italy, and other European states.

Utopian Socialism

What is socialism? For Mill and Kingsley it meant helping the unfortunate and the underprivileged, with relatively little reliance on action by government. Later, it meant that at a minimum the state acts as the trustee of the whole community and nationalizes basic industries like mining, railroads, and steel. Socialism in its most complete form involves public ownership of all the instruments of production, including farmlands, thus virtually eliminating private property.

Since the Bolshevik Revolution of 1917, the term *communism* has often replaced *socialism*. Socialism describes the gradual shift of property from private to public ownership by regular political procedures with compensation for private owners. Communism describes the swift collectivization of property through revolution and outright confiscation without compensation. Although the final goals of communism and socialism are similar, the means of achieving them may be worlds apart. This highly significant difference developed long before 1917, as two divergent schools of socialist thought emerged in the mid-nineteenth century. These were Utopian Socialism and Marxian Socialism.

The Utopian socialists were children of the Enlightenment. They believed that if people applied reason to solving the problems of an industrial economy, manmade inequalities would be wiped out. The great natural law of brotherhood would operate freely, and Utopia, named after the imaginary island of Sir Thomas More's sixteenth-century book, would be realized.

The first Utopian socialist was Saint-Simon (1760–1825). Although he came from a French noble family that claimed descent from Charlemagne, he insisted that positions of power must be filled on the basis of talent, not birth. Saint-Simon wanted supreme political authority delegated to a Parliament of Improvements composed of ten industrialists and five each of artists, philosophers, chemists, physiologists, physicists, astronomers, and mathematicians. He also projected a federation of European states, beginning with the union of Britain and France under a "Council of Newton" and culminating in the establishment of a European parliament. Some of Saint-Simon's proposals for international improvements were more practical. The most famous of them was the Suez Canal, completed

Saint-Simon

* *The Great Encyclical Letters of Pope Leo XIII* (New York, 1903), pp. 218–19.

in 1869 and engineered by one of his followers, Ferdinand de Lesseps.

Saint-Simon's fellow Frenchman, Fourier (1772–1837), also drew up elaborate plans for improving the human situation. As a young man, he was shocked when he visited the textile center of Lyon and saw the wealth of the silk manufacturers and the misery of their workers. In Paris he was dismayed to find that a single apple cost as much as a hundred apples did in the countryside. Clearly, something was very wrong about a society that permitted such fantastic differences, and he claimed that the historical importance of his apple would be on a par with Newton's. Just as Newton discovered the force holding the heavenly bodies in a state of mutual attraction, so Fourier claimed to have discovered the force binding the individuals of human society in a state of mutual attraction.

This force he called *l'attraction passionnelle:* human beings are drawn to one another by their passions and feelings. Fourier drew up a list of passions—sex, companionship, food, variety, luxury, and some eight hundred more. Since existing institutions frustrated the satisfaction of these passions, he proposed to rearrange society into units that he called *phalanges.* Each phalanx would have four hundred acres of land and support five hundred to two thousand individuals. Volunteers would form a phalanx by setting up a community company and agreeing to divide its profits three ways—five-twelfths to workers, four-twelfths to managers, and three-twelfths to those who furnished the capital.

Each phalanx would supply most of its members' needs from its own fields, orchards, and workshops. Those who had the most unpleasant tasks would receive the highest pay, and the work environment would be made as cheerful as possible. Everyone was to reside in the "phalanstery," a communal apartment hotel with a central kitchen to provide the meals, and contingents of little boys (who loved dirt, according to Fourier) would take care of the garbage and other refuse. The phalanstery would encourage full satisfaction of the passions; Fourier advocated complete sexual freedom and recommended marriage only for the elderly.

Fourier asserted that a worker's "enthusiasm cannot be sustained for more than an hour and a half or two hours in the performance of one particular operation." Therefore members of a phalanx should change jobs eight times a day. They would work from four or five in the morning to eight or nine at night, enjoying five meals plus snacks. The variety of work would be so invigorating that people would require only five hours of sleep, and everyone would live to the age of 140 and enjoy such good health that physicians would be unnecessary. A Utopia indeed!

The most famous of the Utopian socialists was the self-made British businessman, Robert Owen (1771–1858). When still in his twenties, Owen took over a large cotton mill at New Lanark

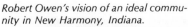
Robert Owen's vision of an ideal community in New Harmony, Indiana.

in Scotland, where the working force was largely composed of children recruited from orphanages in Edinburgh. Appalled to find many of the children "dwarfs in body and mind," Owen set out to demonstrate that he could improve the welfare of all the workers and at the same time increase profits. He converted New Lanark into a model industrial village and gave working children time for schooling. He raised the minimum age for employment to ten, hoping later to fix it at twelve.

When Owen found that few businessmen followed his example, he drew up plans for an idealized version of New Lanark, very much like Fourier's phalanx. His Parallelogram (so named from the arrangement of its buildings) was to be a voluntary organization, neatly balanced between farming and industry, and committed to loosening conventional ties of marriage and family. In the 1820s Owen visited America to establish a Parallelogram at New Harmony, Indiana. After this project failed, he promoted the association of all workers in one giant union (also a failure) and the organization of consumers' cooperatives to lower the cost of basic necessities (a great success). He offended many of his contemporaries by his advocacy of "free love," his attacks on conventional religion, and his own enthusiasm for spiritualism.

Both Owen and Fourier attracted followers in the United States. The American Fourierists included Whittier, the poet, and Horace Greeley, the crusading editor. They established more than thirty phalanxes, the best known being Brook Farm near Boston. But most of them, along with half a dozen Owenite experiments, soon vanished. The few that survived eventually returned to conventional ways of individual profit-taking and family life.

In contrast to the Utopians' reliance on private initiative, the French socialist Louis Blanc (1811–1882) advocated intervention by the state. "What workers need," he wrote in 1839, "is the instruments of labor; it is the function of government to furnish these. If we were to define our conception of the state, our answer would be that it is the banker of the poor."* The government should finance and supervise "social workshops" and then withdraw once the workshops were well established. As workshops multiplied, socialist enterprise would replace private enterprise and laborers would become the only class in society.

* "L'Organisation du Travail" (1839), in *The French Revolution of 1848*, ed. J. A. Marriott (Oxford, 1913), I: 144. Our translation.

Thus Louis Blanc was the first to move socialism from the philanthropists to the politicians, a shift that would be exploited by Karl Marx and his followers.

Marxian Socialism

Whereas the early socialists had expected a gradual and peaceful evolution toward utopia, Karl Marx (1818–1883) forecast a sudden violent revolution. The workers would take over governments and make them the instruments to turn society upside down. Marx's enormous self-confidence and the fact that he had been born in the Prussian Rhineland earned him the nickname of "The Red Prussian."

Marx was convinced that three basic laws would dictate the future of humanity. *Economic determinism* was the first law: economic conditions determined the nature of all other institutions, not only society and government but also religion and art. The second law was the *class struggle:* history was a dialectical process, a series of conflicts between warring economic groups. In Marx's day the war was between the "haves," the property-owning bourgeoisie, and the "have-nots," the workers who constituted a *proletariat* because they possessed nothing except their working skills. The third law was, the *inevitability of communism:* the class struggle was bound to produce the final upheaval that would raise the victorious proletariat in triumph over the defeated bourgeoisie.

Karl Marx.

Both grandfathers of Marx had been rabbis, while his father was a deist and a skeptic who introduced his son to the ideas of the Enlightenment. Marx himself has been called "a great secular rabbi" because of his intense belief in the natural laws of economic determinism and class struggle. He and his followers were convinced that only their brand of socialism was scientific and dismissed the Utopian socialists as mere Romantics. The young Marx was greatly impressed by the materialism of the anti-Christian philosopher Feuerbach, who proclaimed that *Man ist was er isst* ("One is what one eats"). Yet it was the Romantic philosophy of Hegel that contributed more to the intellectual structure of Marxism.

Although Hegel had died in 1831, his influence still dominated the University of Berlin during Marx's student days (1836–1841). For Hegel the nature of the real world was determined by the "Idea," God's plan for humanity. "With me, on the other hand," Marx later wrote, "the ideal is nothing else than the material world reflected by the human mind, and translated into forms of thought. . . . The mystification which dialectic suffers in Hegel's hands, by no means prevents him from being the first to present its general form of working in a comprehensive and conscious manner. *With him it is standing on its head.* It must be turned right again, if you would discover the rational kernel within the mystical shell."*

On leaving the University of Berlin, Marx worked for a newspaper at Cologne but was exiled when his atheistic articles alarmed the Prussian authorities. In 1843 he moved to Paris and two years later to Brussels after his antibourgeois propaganda had irritated the government of Louis Philippe. Meantime, Marx read widely in the writings of economists and talked with socialists and other radicals. He became more convinced than ever that the capitalistic order was unjust, rotten, and doomed to fall.

In the 1840s Marx also began his long friendship and collaboration with Friedrich Engels (1820–1895), the son of a German textile manufacturer and the representative of the family business in Liverpool and Manchester. Unlike Marx, who was utterly preoccupied by his economic studies except for his devotion to his wife and children, Engels loved sports and high living. But he also hated the evils of industrialism and wrote a bitter study, *The Condition of the Working*

Class in England (1844), based on his first-hand knowledge of the appalling situation in Manchester.

In 1847 the Communist League, a small international group of radical workingmen, requested Engels and Marx to draw up a program for their organization. The end product, published in January 1848, was *The Communist Manifesto*, the few dozen pages of which are the classic statement of Marxian socialism. "The history of all hitherto existing society," it asserts, "is the history of class struggle." Changing economic conditions determined that the struggle should develop successively between "freeman and slave, patrician and plebeian, lord and serf, guildmaster and journeyman." The guild system gave way to manufacturing by small capitalists and then to "the giant, modern industry," which will inevitably destroy bourgeois society.

Modern industry creates economic pressure by producing more goods than it can sell. It creates social pressure by narrowing the circle of capitalists to fewer individuals and forcing more people down to the level of the proletariat. These pressures mount to the point where they touch off a revolutionary assault on private property. Landed property will be abolished outright; other forms of property will be liquidated gradually by the imposition of heavy income taxes and the abolition of inherited wealth. Then social classes and tensions will vanish, and "we shall have an association in which the free development of each is the condition for the free development of all."

The *Manifesto* furnishes only this vague forecast of the nature of a postrevolutionary society. Marx defined political authority as "the organized power of one class for oppressing another," and he apparently expected that, in his famous phrase, "the state would wither away" once it had created a regime without classes. He seems to have assumed also that the great dialectical process of history, having achieved a final synthesis, would cease to operate in its traditional pattern.

The Communist Manifesto assigned propaganda a very important role in the communist movement. It supplied the catch phrases that became the hallmark of Marxism—the constant sneering at bourgeois morality, bourgeois law, and bourgeois property, and the dramatic references to communism as the "specter haunting Europe" and to the proletarians who "have nothing to lose but their chains." The *Manifesto* emphasized the importance of a party in forging the proletarian revolution. The communists were a spear-

---

* Preface to the second edition of *Capital* (New York: Modern Library, n.d.), p. 25. Our italics.

head, "the most advanced sections of the working-class parties of every country," who "have over the great mass of the proletariat the advantage of clearly understanding the line of march . . . and the ultimate general results of the proletarian movement."

The *Manifesto* also clearly established the line separating communism from the other forms of socialism. Marx's unshakable conviction that he alone had all the answers and his belief in total revolution made his brand of socialism a thing apart. He scorned and pitied the Utopian socialists. They were about as futile, the *Manifesto* proclaimed, as "organizers of charity, members of societies for the prevention of cruelty to animals, temperance fanatics, hole-and-corner reformers of every kind."

Age neither mellowed Marx nor greatly altered his outlook. From 1849 to his death in 1883, the Marx family lived in London, at first in a slum where three of the five Marx children died. Later, Marx acquired a modest income from the generosity of Engels and from his own writings, notably a weekly article on British and international affairs for Horace Greeley's *New York Tribune.* He spent his days in the British Museum, reading the reports of parliamentary investigating committees and piling up evidence of the conditions of miners and factory hands. He used this material for his massive economic study, *Das Kapital.* The first volume appeared in 1867; two further volumes, pieced together from his notes, were published after his death.

Capital developed at length the doctrines of the *Communist Manifesto.* It spelled out Marx's labor theory of value, according to which the worker created the total value of a commodity that he or she produced yet received as wages only a part of the sale price of the commodity. The difference between the sale price and the worker's wages constituted *surplus value,* created by labor but appropriated by capital as profit. It is the nature of capitalism, Marx insisted, to diminish its own profits by replacing human labor with machines, thus choking off the source of surplus value. The result will be the crises of overproduction and underconsumption predicted by the *Manifesto.*

Marx's Competitors

Marxian socialism was not the only new ideology at work in Europe. It had significant competition from the ideas of his French contemporary, Proudhon (1809–1865). "What is prop-

erty?" Proudhon inquired in a famous pamphlet published in 1840; "property is theft"—not all property but unearned income, the revenues gained by individuals from investment rather than from their own labor. The worst form of unearned income was the "leprosy of interest," and the most deplorable of capitalists were the moneylenders. Under existing conditions only those who were rich could afford to borrow, but in Proudhon's utopia everyone would be able to secure loans without interest from a People's Bank and become a producer.

Thus, where Marx predicted a revolution in ownership of the means of production, Proudhon predicted one in financing production, a "revolution of credit." And where Marx anticipated the liquidation of the bourgeoisie by the proletariat, Proudhon proposed raising the proleterians to the bourgeois level by making every worker an owner. His utopia was an association of individuals, guided by *mutualism.* Economically, mutualism would foster associations of producers in agriculture and industry. Politically, it would promote *federalism,* a loose federation of associations that would replace the centralized state, somewhat like the cantons of the Swiss Confederation.

Extremists intensified Proudhon's attack on the all-powerful state in the movement called *anarchism.* The anarchists rejected all governments as instruments of oppression to be eliminated by acts of terrorism. They assassinated three heads of state—Carnot, the president of France (1894); King Humbert of Italy (1900); and the American president McKinley (1901). Otherwise, they accomplished little except to provide the stereotype of anarchists as bearded, wild-eyed bomb-throwers.

Another kind of terrorism was promoted by the French firebrand, Auguste Blanqui (1805–1881). His activities as a professional revolutionary forced him to spend more than half his life as a prisoner. He took as his utopia the Jacobin Reign of Terror and claimed that the imposition of a dictatorship by a small vanguard of conspirators would be sufficient to make a new revolution.

The First and Second Internationals

In 1864 Karl Marx was one of the founders of the First International Workingmen's Association, an ambitious attempt to organize workers from every country and of every radical ideology. A loose federation rather than a well-organized political party, the First International soon began to disintegrate. Increasing persecution by hostile governments helped to bring it to an end in 1876. And so did the internal wrangling by communists, anarchists, and terrorists, to which Marx himself contributed by his ineptitude in practical politics and his inability to tolerate disagreement with his views.

In 1889 the Second International was launched. It was more effectively organized than the First and represented the Marxian or Social Democratic parties, which were becoming important forces in European politics. Yet factionalism continued to weaken the International. Orthodox Marxists opposed any cooperation between socialists and bourgeois political parties. "Revisionist" Marxists disagreed, for they believed in cooperation between social classes rather than in a struggle to the death between them. They expected that intelligent people, working through democratic governments, could avert class war. This departure from Marxian orthodoxy foreshadowed the split between communists and socialists early in our own century.

III A NEW REVOLUTION IN SCIENCE

Marx's claim that his radical socialism was "scientific" supplied one more piece of evidence that the scientific advances of the nineteenth century greatly affected Western politics, religion, and culture. In the scientific revolution of the seventeenth and eighteenth centuries, mathematics and astronomy had led the way. In the new scientific revolution, leadership came from physics, chemistry, and, above all, biology.

The invention of the steam engine encouraged the study of thermodynamics, a branch of physics dealing with heat and power. Physicists formulated the first law of thermodynamics, which suggested that energy was everlasting, transforming itself from heat into power and then back again to heat. Soon, however, a second law concluded that the quantity of useful energy was slowly being exhausted. The American intellectual, Henry Adams (1838–1918), was greatly disturbed by the possibility that the sun might gradually lose its heat, the earth might get colder, and the whole universe would slow down.

Physicists' studies of electricity and magnetism revealed that these two closely related forces seemed to behave as continuous waves. When light itself also seemed to act as a wave, it was argued that the apparently empty spaces in the universe must be filled with a medium through which light waves could travel. This substance was called the ether. Although the idea of ether seemed to contradict the idea of space, the wave theory of light led many physicists to question Newton's contention that light was composed of minute separate particles. Humanity appeared to live in a world of waves and therefore of continuity, not separateness.

Other scientists still believed in a universe of particles, of untold numbers of atoms. In chemistry, this view was strengthened by the discovery that atoms of two elements might combine to form a molecule, as hydrogen and oxygen join to produce water. In biology, the counterpart of the atomic theory was the idea that all plant and animal structures were made up of living units called cells. The medical counterpart was the theory of germs, later refined into viruses and bacteria. This was a great advance over the older belief that disease was caused by a mysterious "spontaneous corruption," as in the designation of tuberculosis as "consumption."

Medicine Takes Off

The German biologist Koch (1843–1910) discovered the organisms that caused tuberculosis and cholera. The American doctor Walter Reed (1851–1902) found that the virus of yellow fever was transmitted by a mosquito, and that careful mosquito control greatly lowered the incidence of the fever among the construction workers on the Panama Canal. The British physician Lister (1827–1912) demonstrated that germs caused wounds to become infected. The application of rigorous antiseptic measures significantly lowered the mortality rate among patients who had undergone surgery and soldiers injured on the battlefield. In France the chemist Pasteur (1822–1895) developed a vaccine for inoculating victims of rabies and devised the famous process of "pasteurization" to sterilize milk.

By 1900 Western medicine, surgery, and public health were at the point of takeoff that would increase the average life expectancy in North America and Europe by twenty to thirty years. Yet in historical significance the wonders achieved by these great heroes of science were overshadowed by the theory of evolution put forward by Charles Darwin (1809–1882), which sent

Charles Darwin in 1840; a portrait by George Richmond.

a shock wave through the religious and intellectual communities.

Darwin and Evolution

In 1859, after three decades of fieldwork and study, Darwin published *On the Origin of Species by Means of Natural Selection.* His explanation of the origin of species agreed with the scientific facts far more readily than the biblical explanation. The Book of Genesis stated that all forms of life were created in the space of a single week by a Creator about six thousand years ago. All existing humans and animals were descended from one pair of each species preserved in Noah's ark during a great universal flood. But the materials assembled by geologists showed that organic life had been present on earth for millions of years, during which time thousands of plant and animal species had appeared, developed, and sometimes disappeared.

Darwin found one clue in Malthus' contention that organisms, including human beings, multiplied to a point where many of them would perish in the intense competition for food. This gave Darwin the idea of the *struggle for existence.* He next asked what determined that certain individuals would survive while others died. It was clear from observation that individuals of a given species are not identical. Variations appear that make some sturdier, more aggressive, fitter for competition. Here is the second of Darwin's key phrases, the *survival of the fittest.* The organism with the variations best suited to getting food and shelter lives to produce young that will tend to inherit these favorable variations. The variations are slight, but over many generations they are

cumulative. Finally an organism is produced so different from the distant ancestor that it represents a new species. The new species has *evolved by natural selection.*

Darwin's theory has undergone later modification as scientists have found that variations important in the evolutionary process are probably not the numerous tiny ones stressed by Darwin but bigger and much less frequent ones called *mutations.* And a much-disputed geological theory holds that sudden catastrophic movements of the earth's crust in the past have so radically altered the environment that they have wiped out whole species and hastened the evolution of others.

The first edition of *The Origin of Species* sold out the day of its publication; what Darwin himself considered a book of interest only to students and specialists became a best seller. The major reason was the challenge that orthodox Christians found in the book, a new phase of what President Andrew White of Cornell University termed "the warfare of science with religion." For more than a century geologists had been insisting that the evidence of fossils demonstrated that the earth must be a great deal older than the biblical six thousand years. Although the doctrine of God's special creation of each species had also been challenged earlier, Darwin won attention because he identified a process—evolution—and an agent—natural selection. He also gained notoriety because of the unfair accusation that he made the monkey the "grandfather" of the human race. Later, in *The Descent of Man* (1871), Darwin pointed out that *Homo sapiens* is descended not from any existing ape or monkey but from a very remote common ancestor.

The Origin of Species caused fundamentalists, both Protestant and Catholic, to denounce Darwin and hold fast to Genesis. But the Catholic Church and many Protestant sects eventually adopted a more neutral attitude. They viewed Darwinism as a scientific theory that was not necessarily right or wrong but was also quite separate from religion. Many Christians eventually accepted Darwinism and denied any supernatural intervention in the planning and running of the universe.

Social Darwinism

More important than the theological conflict was the appeal made to Darwin's basic concepts and vocabulary in debates over moral, economic, and political issues. The term *Social Darwinism* covers these transfers from biology to the social sciences and human relations. The central idea taken over from Darwin was that competition also applied to human individuals and groups. In their struggle for existence the variations that counted were those that brought success in economic competition.

Darwin's findings seemed to confirm the middle-class conviction that the universe was designed to reward hard work, thrift, intelligence, and self-help, and to punish laziness, waste, stupidity, and reliance on charity. Therefore, attempts by private philanthropy or state intervention to take from the well-to-do and give to the poor were futile efforts to reverse the course of evolution. Herbert Spencer (1820–1903), an ardent British supporter of evolution, claimed that the "ultimate result of shielding men from folly is to fill the world with fools." Spencer rejected all attempts by government to provide social security or welfare; he even opposed a law requiring city dwellings to be connected with sewers.

Yet even Spencer could not have stood by while the unemployed and their families starved to death. He could not transfer to the human struggle for existence the ruthless freedom of the jungle that the poet Tennyson called "Nature red in tooth and claw." The Social Darwinists faced the dilemma posed by the Darwinian struggle within the human species on the one hand, and on the other the evidence that humanity seldom lets the unfit fall by the wayside and perish.

To escape from this dilemma Social Darwinists lifted the human struggle from the biology of the individual to the politics of the group. For example, they argued that the struggle that counts is not that within the community of Englishmen but the rivalry between Great Britain and competing powers. The competitors were nation-states or groups of states, such as the "Nordic" or "Latin" countries. They might also include whole families of people, such as the white "Caucasians" in competition with colored peoples, yellow, brown, or black. The group that defeated another group in war demonstrated that it was superior and had the evolutionary right to seize the lands of the vanquished and settle them with its own "fitter" human beings. Social Darwinism thus reinforced the idea of a Chosen People and intensified the international struggle for power.

The men who preached this kind of political evolution assumed that superior groups had certain traits that could not be transmitted to their inferiors. They were, in short, racists who believed humanity had already evolved into sepa-

rate species. For these racists a black skin was a sign of innate inferiority, and blacks were doomed to go the way of dinosaurs into extinction. Meantime, inferior peoples should serve their masters by carrying out menial tasks as "hewers of wood and drawers of water." Darwin himself never accepted the racist ideas of social Darwinists, which have long been dismissed as thoroughly unscientific.

Science and Philosophy

Darwinism, however, did contribute to a major change in the way people looked at the universe. It helped to replace the static universe of Newton with a much more dynamic and evolving universe. Darwin's biology strengthened the concept of progress in human history already advanced by Herder and the Romantic historians.

Even before the publication of *The Origin of Species,* the new discoveries of science provided the basis for a program to improve the intellectual, political, and economic qualities of humanity. The program was called *positivism,* and it was promoted in the writings of a Frenchman, Auguste Comte (1798–1857). Comte identified three stages in peoples' attitudes toward the world. The infant period of human history was the age of theology, when people were in awe of nature and sought to placate the gods that controlled it. In the adolescence of humanity, supernatural or metaphysical concepts such as Plato's "Ideas" replaced the gods as the controlling forces of the world. As people matured, science would enable them to understand the world of nature without recourse to theology or metaphysics. They would be able to undertake positive actions to manipulate the world to their advantage. The positivist age was at hand.

Comte also ranked according to maturity the sciences that enabled humanity to reach this positive age. He awarded seniority to mathematics and astronomy, put chemistry and physics next, then biology and psychology, and last—and youngest—sociology, the science of society. Sociology would give people the key to the positive age. Realizing that the French revolutionary attempt to build a new society had ended in terror and dictatorship, Comte argued that Utopia could be reached peacefully through the teachings of dedicated champions of science. He called them preachers of a new "religion of humanity." His critics, on the other hand, argued that these scientists were a new set of priests, propagandists of a positivist dogma that might be more intolerant than old religious dogmas.

The popularity of doctrines advocating leadership by an elite grew with the Darwinist stress on the human will as an active force in the struggle for existence. The term *will* became a favorite in the titles of philosophical studies—*The World as Will and Idea* by the German, Schopenhauer (1788–1860); the *Will to Power* by another German, *Nietzsche* (1844–1900); and *The Will to Believe* by the American, William James (1842–1910). The will appeared slightly disguised as the "vital force" *(élan vital)* in *Creative Evolution* by the Frenchman, Bergson (1859–1941). The cult of the will was an intensified expression of the Romantic protest against the eighteenth-century cult of reason.

The antirationalists—the opponents of reason—in the late nineteenth century may be divided into two groups, moderates and extremists. The moderate antirationalists tried to salvage what they could of the eighteenth-century belief in human reason. Psychologists like William James and Sigmund Freud (1856–1939) sought to aid human reason by pointing out the difficulties under which it must work. For them reason is limited by the individual's "drives" or instincts, the biological inheritance of the human animal. Reason is also limited by humanity's inheritance of tradition and custom, emphasized by Burke and by many historians. Moderate antirationalists, using a metaphor of John Locke, regarded human reason as a flickering candle which they wanted to keep burning as brightly as possible.

By contrast, the extreme antirationalists wanted to extinguish the candle. Reason seemed to them a wrong turning made by evolution from which humanity must retrace its steps to a sounder life based on instinct, emotion, and faith. Many of the extremists turned violently against democracy, which they thought rested on a false estimate of human rationality. Nietzsche denounced parliamentary governments as "the means whereby cattle become masters" and proposed a new aristocratic regime run by "supermen." His followers insisted that Nietzsche's supermen were to be spiritual aristocrats, rising far above the materialism and nationalism of the middle class. His critics, citing his approval of "blond beasts," asserted that his supermen were simply German warriors.

Even the defenders of democratic values were troubled by antirationalist doubts. They were not at all sure that people were naturally good or that Adam Smith's "invisible hand" of laissez-faire economics operated in a reasonable manner. The English economist, Walter Bagehot (1826–1877), who was greatly influenced by Darwin, published *Physics and Politics* (1869—"Biology and Politics" would have been a more appropriate title). Bagehot emphasized how hard it was to persuade people to break "the cake of custom" and to change their accumulated habits and traditions and make rational innovations.

IV LITERATURE AND THE ARTS

The Novel and Drama

The popularity of science and the growth of industry promoted the development of realism in literature. Some of the leading realistic novelists exposed the selfishness of the middle class and its exploitation of the workers with all the exaggeration and preaching of their Romantic predecessors. This was particularly true of the Frenchman Balzac (1799–1850), the Englishman Dickens (1812–1870), and the Russian Dostoevsky (1821–1870).

More controlled, almost "scientific" in its objectivity, was the prose of three other realists: the Frenchman Flaubert (1821–1880), the Englishman Trollope (1815–1882), and the Russian Turgenev (1815–1882). In *Madame Bovary* Flaubert not only analyzed the longings and frustrations of a small-town doctor's wife but also went to great pains to achieve scientific accuracy. He al-

Dostoevsky: an oil painting of 1872.

ways sought the *mot juste,* the exactly right word. Trollope wrote many novels about Victorian politicians, clergymen, country gentlemen and heiresses. He never exaggerated, as did Dickens, but strove to give his readers exact information as, for example, the annual incomes that enabled his characters to be waited upon by a retinue of servants.

In *Fathers and Sons,* Turgenev portrayed the clash between the fading Romantic generation and the rising realists. Its hero was Bazarov, a brash young student, a nihilist to whom nothing was sacred, no matter how sanctified by tradition, unless it was validated by science. Turgenev also drew a portrait of Bazarov's mother—old-fashioned, pious, superstitious, and devoted to her son and to her doctor husband. He then commented with the irony of the realist: "Such women are not common nowadays. God knows whether we ought to rejoice!"

During the last third of the century, a new generation of writers complained that the realists were not realistic enough. These were the *naturalists,* often described as realists with an ideology. Their leader, the Frenchman Émile Zola (1840–1902), was much influenced by the Darwinian revolution. He sought to discover laws of human development much as the biologist arrived at laws of organic development. To show what people were like and why, he wrote twenty novels about a family during the Second Empire of the 1850s and 60s. Each focused on some problem—prostitution, alcoholism, the hardships of the peasants, the sufferings of striking coal miners. He sought also to link the failings of individuals with qualities inherited from their parents. *Nature,* in Zola's writing, was very different from eighteenth-century ideas of natural innocence; nature seemed to make people greedy, selfish, combative, lecherous, and stupid.

Naturalism inspired the "problem play," pioneered by Ibsen (1828–1906) in Norway and then developed by Brieux (1858–1932) in France and Shaw (1856–1950) in England. Ibsen shocked his contemporaries with *A Doll's House,* depicting the heroine's rebellion against the doll-house existence imposed on her by her husband. Along with Mill's *Subjection of Women,* it was an early defense of women's rights. Later, Ibsen's *Ghosts* and Brieux's *Damaged Goods* upset many theatergoers by bringing to the stage the problem of venereal disease. Shaw, too, was denounced for dramatizing the career of a prostitute in *Mrs. Warren's Profession.*

Poetry and Music

Poetry and music were influenced, though hardly revolutionized, by the economic and scientific upheavals of the nineteenth century. Poetry, while no longer the dominant form of literature as it had been in the Romantic era, remained very popular for the rest of the century. Victor Hugo in France, Tennyson in England, and Longfellow in New England still developed the Romantic themes of love, death, legend, and nature. However, the spiritual crisis resulting from the scientific revolution was mirrored in Tennyson's *In Memoriam* and with greater despair in Matthew Arnold's *Dover Beach:*

> *And we are here as on a darkling plain*
> *Swept with confused alarms of struggle and flight,*
> *Where ignorant armies clash by night.*

The horrors of the industrial revolution inspired a poetic protest in Thomas Hood's *Song of the Shirt,* published in the Christmas issue of the English magazine *Punch* in 1843. It was prompted by a press report of a seamstress arrested for stealing from her employer. Her maximum earnings were seven shillings ($1.75) a week, out of which she was to support her two young children as well as herself. Here is the last stanza:

> *With fingers weary and worn,*
> *With eyelids heavy and red,*
> *A Woman sate in unwomanly rags,*
> *Plying her needle and thread—*
> *Stitch! stitch! stitch!*
> *In poverty, hunger, and dirt,*
> *And still with a voice of dolorous pitch,*
> *Would that its tone could reach the Rich!*
> *She sang this "Song of the Shirt"!*

A more cheerful note was sounded by the enormous popularity of vocal music among the middle and working classes. Small towns as well as cities had their opera houses and music halls, which provided a welcome change from the tedium of factory and office. Yet many of the leading composers of the middle and later nineteenth century followed in the paths established by the Romantic generation. Their works are still mainstays of the repertoire today: the operas of Verdi, Gounod, and Bizet, and the symphonies and concerti of Brahms and Tchaikovsky, for example.

An ambitious attempt to break with tradition was made by the German, Richard Wagner

Wagner in 1868.

(1813–1883). Wagner converted opera into "music drama," seeking to create an immense synthesis of plot, scenery, and sound. He discarded the usual showy arias that interrupted the dramatic and aesthetic line. Instead, he provided the *Leitmotiv,* a recurring musical theme in which the human voice blended with the orchestra rather than rising above it in the conventional way. He shunned the flimsy operatic plots, replacing them with epic themes from the past: the Holy Grail in *Parsifal;* a legend of ill-fated love from the days

of King Arthur in *Tristan and Isolde;* and, most ambitious of all, the four operas of *The Ring of the Nibelung,* based on the mythical gods of the ancient German epic.

Wagner's reputation has long suffered because of the extraordinary length and heaviness of his most celebrated operas. Later, his works fell out of favor because of their popularity with Hitler and the Nazis. Wagner was an ardent German nationalist, but it is only fair to note that he also considered himself a left-wing liberal and was exiled to Switzerland for thirteen years because he had participated in an abortive revolt against the king of Saxony in 1848. His music dramas later contributed to the development of "program music," which attempted to express literary, social, and even philosophical themes.

Toward the close of the century Wagner's countryman, Richard Strauss (1864–1949), wrote program music in the form of "tone poems." He took as subjects the adventures of Don Quixote, the writings of Nietzsche, and the cares and humors of family life. The Frenchman, Debussy (1862–1918), refined the tone poem in his impressionist compositions. Greatly influenced by the delicacy and exoticism characteristic of Far Eastern music, he sought to express the ever-changing sounds of the moment, much as the contemporary impressionist artists sought to record the constant shifts in light and color.

Daumier's "The Uprising, 1848."

Courbet's "The Woman in the Waves."

The Fine Arts

The impressionist revolution in painting developed from the rebellion against academic painting launched in the Romantic era. In England the rebellion was continued by Turner (1775–1851), whose experiments in recording the fast-changing phenomena of light and mist were more daring than those of Constable. He called his picture of a moving train "Rain, Steam, Speed," all considered unpaintable by conventional artists.

In France, Daumier (1808–1879) exploited new advances in technology that made mass production of prints inexpensive. He won a wide audience for his savage attacks on the selfish and repressive judges and politicians of the July Monarchy. His favorite target was Louis Philippe, whose pear-shaped figure invited caricature. Daumier recorded with compassion the victims of the king's regime—a casualty of the massacre in the rue Transnonain, and the nameless participants in the "Uprising, 1848," who look almost like ghosts. Daumier's countryman, Courbet (1819–1877), portrayed people considered unworthy subjects by academic painters, such as wrestlers, stonecutters, and nudes quite unlike the idealized women of classical art. In 1863 when Courbet's followers were excluded from exhibiting their work at the annual Paris salon, they organized their own *salon des refusés* ("exhibition by the rejected") and won the backing of Napoleon III.

Among the rejected artists was Edouard Manet (1833–1883) who, a few years later, painted the controversial "Death of Maximilian," the unfortunate emperor of Mexico. Manet challenged traditional ideas of perspective by placing the firing squad almost on top of its victim. He further abandoned factual accuracy by dressing them in the uniforms of French soldiers. Manet

Manet's "The Death of Maximilian."

Monet's "Water-Lilies, Giverny."

Monet devoted most of his long career to demonstrating that light, as physicists came to realize, was constantly changing because it depended on the vision of the human eye. To prove his point he painted the same subjects again and again—the cathedral at Rouen, the lily pond in his own garden. The results varied greatly depending on the time of day. Monet broke light and shadow into their component colors, using thousands of little dabs of pure color. At close range his paintings were a formless mesh of color, but viewed from a proper distance they were magically transformed into recognizable scenes flooded with light.

The impressionists further shook the artistic establishment by following Courbet's precedent of taking subjects from everyday life rather than from the limited world of the studio. Milliners, prostitutes, ballerinas, circus and cabaret performers, and peasants peopled the canvases of Renoir, Toulouse-Lautrec, Degas, and Van Gogh.

Some impressionists moved on to other experiments that led them to be termed "postimpressionists." Their leader was Cézanne (1839–1906), who reacted against the obsession with light which, he felt, neglected the geometry and architecture that existed in nature. He used color to dramatize the basic geometric forms of a landscape. In looking at "Mont Sainte Victoire," a subject that Cézanne painted again and again, the viewer feels that the outer layers of the landscape have been peeled off to reveal nature's scaffolding and building blocks beneath.

In contrast to painting, the other fine arts waited until the new century to complete their

asserted that a realist painted what he himself saw, which did not have to agree with the image recorded by a camera.

In 1872 another shock hit the art world of Paris when Claude Monet (1840–1926) put on view a misty painting of Le Havre (the port at the mouth of the Seine) with the title "Sunrise: Impression." Hostile critics dismissed his way of painting as mere "impressionism," a label that was soon assumed proudly by other innovators.

Degas's "The Dancing Class."

Toulouse-Lautrec's "In the Circus Fernando: The Ringmaster."

great leap forward. During most of the 1800s statuary remained within the limits of neoclassical statues, sometimes a little romanticized. In the century's final decades, however, the French sculptors Rodin (1841–1919) and Maillol (1861–1944) began to strengthen and sometimes to exaggerate the contours of their men and women to make them appear more realistic.

Most architects continued to venerate the past. They adapted the Romanesque and Gothic styles of the Middle Ages for university buildings and copied palaces and châteaux of the Renaissance for city halls and other public edifices. In the last years of the century, monumental structures acquired a more disciplined and classical look under the influence of the School of Fine Arts in Paris. This Beaux-Arts style was employed for the buildings of Chicago's Columbian Exposition of 1893, including the Art Institute which still stands today.

Also in Chicago, even before 1893, signs of an impending revolution in architecture appeared with the use of structural steel to support the first skyscrapers. And at the very end of the century, a gifted young architect, Frank Lloyd Wright (1869–1959), introduced a radical departure from the usual Victorian house. Inspired by the simplicity of Japanese dwellings, Wright's "prairie houses" in Chicago stressed planes and spaciousness rather than height and intricate detail. The stage was set for the "functional" and "organic" architecture of our own century.

Renoir's "Mme Charpentier and Her Children."

Cézanne's "Mont Sainte Victoire."

Maillol's "The Mediterranean."

The Nineteenth and Twentieth Century

During the past hundred and fifty years an aesthetic revolution has created a modern art that leaves literal representation to the photographer and experiments with new ways of expressing the fundamentals beneath surface appearances. In painting, a high point of the revolution was reached in the 1870s and 1880s with the French impressionists, who took their name from a canvas by their leader, Claude Monet (*Impression: Sunrise*). In a sustained scientific experiment Monet painted the same subjects over and over in varying lights—Rouen Cathedral, the lilies in his own garden pond—applying many little dabs of pure color and leaving it to the eye of the viewer to fuse and focus them into a recognizable scene.

The impressionists were by no means the only revolutionaries. Earlier, the leading French painter of the romantic era, Delacroix, who claimed that the purpose of art was "not to imitate nature but to strike the imagination," employed raw colors, such as the reds, blues, and greens in *The Abduction of Rebecca*, which illustrates an episode in Scott's romantic novel, *Ivanhoe*. A French contemporary of Monet, Edouard Manet, made another departure from the realism of the camera with portraits of boldly outlined individuals against an indistinct background, as in *Torero Saluting*. Manet was influenced by pictures he saw in Madrid, among them works by Goya, the most original genius of the romantic era, who often chose subjects from the lower depths or the disreputable fringes of Spanish society, as in his *Majas*. Whistler, an American contemporary of Monet, converted a rowdy London resort, *Cremorne Gardens*, into a dreamlike vision.

The color plates illustrate works by other ranking artistic revolutionaries. Cezanne restored to landscapes the basic architecture of nature, which he thought the impressionists' obsession with color had neglected. Matisse captured the fundamentals of life by reducing colors and figures to a minimum in a joyous though frenzied series of paintings, *The Dance*. Picasso moved from the expressionism of his early "blue period," in which the dominant color underscores the mood of the subject (*The Blind Man's Meal*), to the more radical experiments discussed in Chapter 33. After World War II the abstract expressionists sought to convey a mood nonrepresentationally, by color and design alone; the American Jackson Pollock hurled paint on huge canvases with his "spatter" painting. Finally, in the 1960s, pop art, reacting against the alleged social irrelevance of abstractionism, employed a mixture of painting and other media to illustrate what it termed the "everyday crap" of our standardized machine-dominated society, as in Marisol's *Women and a Dog*.

Water-Lilies, by Claude Monet.
Formerly in the Museum of Modern Art, New York. Robert S. Crandall from the Granger Collection.

Women and Dog, by Marisol.
Wood, plaster, synthetic, polymer paint, and miscellaneous items, 1964. 72 x 82 x 16 inches.
Gift of the Friends of the Whitney Museum of American Art.
Collection Whitney Museum of American Art, New York.

Rodin's "Balzac."

READING SUGGESTIONS on The Ideas and Culture of the Nineteenth Century

Introductory Works

F. B. Artz, *Reaction and Revolution, 1814–1832;* W. L. Langer, *Political and Social Upheaval, 1832–1852;* R. C. Binkley, *Realism and Nationalism, 1852–1870;* C. Hayes, *A Generation of Materialism, 1871–1900.* These four volumes in "The Rise of Modern Europe" series (*Torch) have substantial sections on ideological and cultural developments.

W. H. Coates and H. V. White, *The Ordeal of Liberal Humanism* (*McGraw Hill). Informative survey of intellectual developments since 1789.

R. N. Stromberg, *European Intellectual History since 1789,* 2nd. ed. (*Prentice-Hall). Another useful introduction.

A. Castell, *An Introduction to Modern Philosophy* 3rd ed. (Macmillan, 1976) and J. Collins, *Interpreting Modern Philosophy* (*Princeton). Helpful surveys of a challenging subject.

H. D. Aiken, ed., *The Age of Ideology* (*Mentor). Selections from 19th century philosophers with informative comments by the editor.

The Romantic Retreat

H. Hugo, ed., *The Romantic Reader* (*Penguin). Imaginatively arranged anthology.

J. R. Halsted, ed., *Romanticism* (Walker, 1968). Another good anthology.

Lilian Furst, *Romanticism,* 2nd ed. (*Methuen). Helpful interpretation.

K. Lowith, *From Hegel to Nietzsche* (*Anchor). Analysis of nineteenth-century thought, particularly in Germany.

K. Clark, *The Gothic Revival* (*Harper). Entertaining essay, focused on Britain.

Henry-Russell Hitchcock, *Architecture: Nineteenth and Twentieth Centuries* (Penguin, 1958) and F. Novotny, *Painting and Sculpture in Europe, 1780–1880* (Penguin, 1960). Comprehensive volumes in the series, "The Pelican History of Art."

W. Friedlaender, *David to Delacroix* (Harvard, 1952). Good study of neoclassical and romantic painting in France.

T. Prideaux, *The World of Delacroix* (Time-Life Books, 1966) and R. Schickel, *The World of Goya* (Time-Life Books, 1968). Studies of important artistic pioneers.

R. M. Longyear, *Nineteenth-Century Romanticism in Music,* 2nd. ed. (Prentice-Hall, 1973); A. Einstein *Music in the Romantic Era* (Norton, 1947). Very helpful analyses.

J. Barzun, *Berlioz and His Century* (Peter Smith). How the innovative French composer exemplified the Romantic attitude.

Prescriptions for Social Change

R. Heilbroner, *The Worldly Philosophers* (*Touchstone). Popular introduction to laissez-faire economics.

J. Schumpeter, *Capitalism, Socialism, and Democracy.* (*Torch). Thoughtful scholarly survey.

T. R. Malthus, *Population: The First Essay* (*Ann Arbor). The original essay of 1798 expressing Malthusianism in its most extreme form.

J. S. Mill, *Principles of Political Economy* (Univ. of Toronto, 1965); *Autobiography* (several editions); *On Liberty* (several editions); *On the Subjection of Women* (*M.I.T.); *Utilitarianism* (several editions). Major writings of the great Victorian liberal.

H. Cranston, *J. S. Mill* (*British Book Center); M. S. Packe, *The Life of John Stuart Mill* (Peter Smith, 1954). Good conventional biographies.

B. Mazlish, *James and John Stuart Mill* (Basic Books, 1975). An analysis of father and son by a psychohistorian.

Pope Leo XIII, et al., *Seven Great Encyclicals* (*Paulist Press). Basic statements of Christian Democracy.

A. Fried and R. Sanders, *Socialist Thought: A Documentary History* (*Anchor). A compilation of source materials.

E. Wilson, *To the Finland Station* (*Anchor). A sympathetic study of socialism.

F. E. and F. P. Manuel, *Utopian Thought in the Western World* (Harvard, 1979). Detailed survey of socialist pioneers.

K. Taylor, ed., *H. Saint-Simon, Selected Writings,* (Holmes & Meier, 1975); N. V. Riasanovsky, *The Teaching of Charles Fourier* (California, 1969); J. Harrison, *Quest for the New Moral World: Robert Owen and the Owenites in Britain and America* (Routledge, 1969). Introductions to key utopians.

R. C. Tucker, ed., *Marx-Engels Reader* (*Norton) and L. S. Feuer, ed., *K. Marx, and F. Engels: Basic Writings on Politics and Philosophy* (Peter Smith). Selections from the publications of the joint founders of communism.

I. Berlin, *Karl Marx: His Life and Environment* 4th ed. (*Oxford); D. McLellan, *Karl Marx: His Life and Thought.* (*Harper); S. Avineri, *The Social and Political Thought of Karl Marx* (*Cambridge). Three good studies of this major figure.

E. Hobsbawm, *Revolutionaries* (*New American Library). Sympathetic study of leftist thinkers.

A. B. Spitzer, *The Revolutionary Theories of Auguste Blanqui* (Columbia, 1970). Appraisal of the famous firebrand.

Science

W. Wightman, *The Growth of Scientific Ideas* (Greenwood, 1951). An enlightening interpretation.

Charles Darwin: *Autobiography* (*Norton); *Voyage of the Beagle* (*Anchor); *On the Origin of Species* (*several editions). Three key works for understanding Darwin's ideas.

C. Gillispie, *The Edge of Objectivity* (*Princeton). Appraises Darwin and other nineteenth-century innovators. Gillispie is also the author of a study on the tension between science and religion prior to Darwin: *Genesis and Geology* (*Torch).

L. Eisley, *Darwin's Century* (*Anchor). Analysis of the doctrine of evolution and the men who formulated it.

G. Himmelfarb, *Darwin and the Darwinian Revolution.* (*Norton). Excellent critique. For a different assessment consult M. Ghiselin, *The Triumph of the Darwinian Method* (*California).

J. C. Greene, *The Death of Adam* (*Iowa State). Appraises the impact of evolution on western thought.

R. Hofstadter, *Social Darwinism in American Thought* (*Beacon). Thoughtful study of the use and abuse of science.

Literature and the Arts

G. M. Young, *Victorian England: Portait of an Age,* 2nd. ed. (*Oxford); W. Houghton, *The Victorian Frame of Mind, 1830–1870* (*Yale). Excellent introductions to the English literary scene.

J. H. Miller, *The Disappearance of God* (Harvard, 1976). Five significant English writers: De Quincey, Robert Browning, Emily Brontë, Matthew Arnold, Gerard Manley Hopkins.

H. House, *The Dickens World* (*Oxford). Appraises the celebrated romantic realist.

H. Levin, *The Gates of Horn: A Study of Five French Realists* (*Oxford). Discusses Stendhal, Balzac, Flaubert, Zola, and Proust.

A. Cockshut, *Anthony Trollope* (*New York Univ.). A critical study of the great Victorian realist.

V. S. Pritchett, *The Gentle Barbarian* (*Vintage). The life and work of Turgenev, the great Russian realist.

E. Wilson, *Axel's Castle* (*Scribner's). Stimulating study of imaginative literature during the late 1800s and early 1900s.

G. H. Hamilton, *19th and 20th Century Art* (Prentice-Hall, 1972). Encyclopaedic survey, copiously illustrated.

J. C. Sloan, *French Painting between the Past and the Present* (*Princeton). Stresses the years 1848 to 1870, which marked the birth of modern painting.

P. Courthion, *Impressionism* (*Abrams). Well-illustrated introduction to the painters of light and color.

P. Schneider, *The World of Manet* (Time-Life, 1968); B. Petrie, *Claude Monet* (Dutton, 1979); R. Murphy, *The World of Cézanne* (Time-Life, 1968). Good analyses of three important painters.

H. McKinney and W. Anderson, *Music in History,* 3rd ed. (American Book, 1966) and D. J. Grout, *A History of Western Music* (Norton, 1973). Informative surveys.

CHAPTER SIXTEEN

Prelude, Theme, And Coda:

1870-1919

The half-century between 1870 and 1920 saw the great powers prepare for and fight the first of the twentieth century's fantastically destructive wars, World War I (1914–1918). But the period between 1870 and 1914 was far more than a mere preparation for the explosion.

In this chapter we begin with an account of the internal development of Great Britain, France, and other Western European parliamentary states. We turn next to Germany, Austria-Hungary, Russia, and Turkey—the Eastern European empires—and then to the world outside Europe, the colonial empires old and new, the United States, and China and Japan.

We will be discussing mostly peace and progress, industrialization, increasing prosperity, improvement in social conditions, the growth of political parties. Yet even domestic developments point to the troubles ahead.

We shall observe the political instability and passions of France, the cynical militarism of Germany under Bismarck and especially under William II, the incompetence of Russian imperial government, the agitation of minorities in the

Hapsburg Empire, and the spreading view that no power could have national prestige without large overseas colonies.

Moreover, what at first looks like progress can often be viewed as the reverse. The more people won the vote, the more politics became a matter of raw appeal to the masses. The more the state had to manage and control the new technology, and pay for and run programs of social welfare, the more individualism suffered and collectivism gained. After 1870 the liberalism of the mid-nineteenth century was attacked from the left by the socialists and from the right by conservatives who used nationalistic ideas for their own purposes. This was especially true of the continent of Europe, but even in England the phenomenon was a striking one.

THE NATIONS OF EUROPE AT HOME, 1870–1914

Britain

During the last third of the nineteenth century, Britain continued to set an example of steady peaceful progress. William E. Gladstone (1809–1898), leader of the Liberal Party and four times prime minister between 1868 and 1894, personified the Victorian virtues of sobriety, hard work, piety, and moral earnestness.

Gladstone with Queen Victoria.

By the Education Bill of 1870, the first Gladstone ministry (1868–1874) accepted the idea that it was the responsibility of government to provide a literate electorate. State money now went to church-affiliated schools, which were made liable to inspection, and so improved in quality. Local education boards also received money to establish nonsectarian primary schools open to all.

The government, defying the vested army interests, abolished the sale of officers' commissions in the army (1871). The new emphasis on merit helped prepare the way for military success in the colonial warfare that lay ahead.

Gladstone's picturesque and brilliant rival, the Conservative leader Benjamin Disraeli (1804–1881), a converted Jew and a successful novelist, served briefly as prime minister (1868) and put through the Second Reform Bill (see p. 387). His second and last ministry (1874–1880) passed the first laws authorizing towns to build public housing for workers, a clear example of his interest in allying the landed gentry with the industrial workers against the commercial middle class.

Disraeli appealed also to nationalist sentiment by rejecting the "Little England" idea and embracing imperialism. He made Victoria empress of India. He got the majority of the shares of the Suez Canal Company for England, ensuring control of the route to India.

After Disraeli's death in 1881, the Conservatives dropped the cause of social reform which the Liberals took up. They had become convinced that one could not allow the economy and society to take care of themselves, but that the state must work out ways to make the rich help the poor.

In his second ministry (1880–1885), Gladstone put through the Third Reform Bill (1884). It further extended the franchise in rural districts, giving the vote to most adult males and raising the total number of voters from three million to about five. A companion bill (1885) set up single-member parliamentary districts that were nearly uniform in population.

Trade unions now grew as Parliament lifted restrictions on picketing and other union activities. By 1900 the unions were industrywide and included both skilled and unskilled workers. In the early years of the new century, a working men's political party developed, the Labour party.

The Labourites favored a gradual, evolutionary socialist program. This moderate position reflected its leaders' religious and humanitarian sentiments. Highly influential were the "Fabians," a group of intellectuals that included Bernard Shaw, H. G. Wells, and Beatrice and Sidney

Webb. The Fabians took their name from the Roman general, Fabius Cunctator, "the delayer."

Before 1914 Labour never won as many as 10 percent of the seats in a parliamentary election. But the Liberals came to depend on the votes of Labour members. So they put through much legislation in the interest of the working man: the sanctity of trade-union funds, employers' liability to compensate for accidents, peaceful picketing, minimum-wage-fixing procedures (1906), and modest, state-financed old-age pensions (1908).

The expense of these programs, and still more the costs of a big navy, impelled Lloyd George, the Liberal chancellor of the exchequer, to present in 1909 a budget increasing income taxes in the higher brackets and raising death duties (inheritance taxes). The Conservatives, especially in the House of Lords, were opposed, and the Lords rejected the budget. This set off a political crisis, since traditionally the Lords had approved all money bills passed by the Commons.

When the Liberals won two closely contested elections in 1910, the Commons set out to prevent a recurrence of such action by the Lords. King George V was pressured into using the weapon that had allowed the triumph of the Reform Bill of 1832. By threatening to create enough new Liberal Lords to control their house, he forced the Lords to vote the Parliament Act of 1911. This "Fourth Reform Bill" denied the Lords' right to veto a money bill, and limited their veto over other bills to two years.

Women still had no vote, and some "plural" voters had the right to vote more than once. But by 1911 democracy was far advanced in Britain. The National Insurance Act (1911) introduced health and unemployment insurance jointly financed by employers, workers, and the state.

But the Liberals clung to the traditional doctrines of free trade, advantageous only so long as British industrial development was the most advanced in the world. As American and German industrial competition became severe in the later nineteenth century, the advantage disappeared, and economic stagnation threatened. Agitation for protective tariffs was led by Joseph Chamberlain (1836–1914), a self-made businessman who had served as reforming mayor of the industrial city of Birmingham in the 1870s.

Chamberlain believed in strengthening all of Britain's imperial ties, and he had broken with the Liberals in the 1880s, when Gladstone endorsed home rule for Ireland. Between 1895 and 1903 Chamberlain served as colonial secretary in a Conservative cabinet and tried to put through mercantilist measures. He sought to make the empire a compact economic unit by imposing tariffs on imported goods, thus assuring the mother country both markets for exports and supplies of raw materials. The program failed but would be revived after World War I.

Ireland remained a grievous problem throughout the period. The Liberals disestablished the Anglican Church in Ireland (1869), no longer requiring the Catholic majority to support a Protestant state church. They tried to protect Irish tenants from extortionate rents imposed by their landlords, who were usually English. But the Irish nationalists wanted home rule.

In Parliament, their leader, Charles Stewart Parnell, agitated brilliantly on their behalf. In 1886, Gladstone proposed a home-rule bill that would have given Ireland her own parliament, though leaving control over foreign policy to London. It failed in Parliament, and the Conservatives now put through measures that enabled Irish tenant farmers to buy their own farms on easy terms.

Irish nationalism was now nourished by a remarkable literary revival. Romantically harking back to the glorious Irish Celtic past, rediscovering Irish myth, and emphasizing the Gaelic language, now spoken only in the remote parts of Western Ireland, W. B. Yeats and J. M. Synge wrote plays and poems. George Russell (AE) and others combined literary achievement and political agitation for complete independence.

The Liberals passed a new home-rule bill in 1914. It could not be enforced because the predominantly Protestant population of Ulster in northern Ireland so feared submersion in a Catholic state that they organized an illegal militia to prevent any loosening of the ties with Britain. As World War I broke out, violence was threatening; Ulstermen who were officers in the British army were planning mutiny, and Irish nationalists were planning to resist them by force.

France

Bitterness and division characterized French political life in the decades between 1871 and 1914. In 1871 a patriotic minority even wanted to continue the war against the Germans, while the majority in the newly elected National Assembly reluctantly accepted the necessity of signing a peace treaty that ceded Alsace and part of Lorraine to the new German Empire.

In March 1871 the minority revolted, seized control of Paris, and installed the Commune, designed to revive both the name and the patriotic vigor of the revolutionary city government of 1792. Karl Marx hailed the Commune as a true socialist regime, but it was rather Jacobin and anarchist. It lacked a social or economic program but intended to make France a republic and end defeatism. Civil war broke out between the Commune and the Assembly, and in May 1871 the Commune was suppressed. Twenty thousand French lives were lost, about as many as the victims of the Terror.

In the victorious Assembly, the Monarchists had a majority. They were split between the Legitimists, who supported the count of Chambord, grandson of Charles X, and the Orléanists, who supported the count of Paris, grandson of Louis Philippe. If the count of Chambord, who had no son, had agreed to make the count of Paris his heir, and had accepted the tricolor flag, which Louis Philippe had done in 1830, a compromise would have been possible. But Chambord insisted on the Bourbon white flag and its golden lilies, symbol of the Old Regime. So the

Orléanists settled for a republic under the presidency of Adolphe Thiers (1797–1877), once prime minister under Louis Philippe.

By the Constitution of 1875 France received a two-chamber legislature, with the Senate elected indirectly and the Chamber of Deputies directly by universal male suffrage. Together the two chambers elected the president, who, though chief executive, had to have all his orders countersigned by a member of the council of ministers or cabinet.

In 1877, President MacMahon, a Legitimist, precipitated a crisis. He forced the cabinet to resign so he could choose ministers he liked better. But the Chamber of Deputies would not support him, and new elections returned a majority of republican deputies. MacMahon had to accept a cabinet of their choosing. This affair decided the question for the entire history of the Third Republic. Down to 1940, no president would again dissolve the chamber. French presidents were powerless constitutional figureheads. The real power lay in a cabinet (or ministry) headed by a prime minister (or premier).

There were a dozen or more French political

Barricades in Paris during the Commune, 1871.

parties, so each ministry necessarily represented a coalition, working together only temporarily, and subject to collapse at short notice. Such cabinet crises studded the history of the Third Republic. The average life of a ministry was less than a year. Yet many of the crises involved only a few shifts in ministerial personnel. The professional civil servants continued to run the country while the politicians argued. Government by coalition forced politicians to avoid extremes, to look for the middle ground, and to compromise.

The enemies of the republic, however, hated compromise. The Legitimists yearned for a king. After the crisis of May 1879, the republic took an anticlerical turn; it made divorce possible, curtailed the activities of religious orders, and banned religious instruction from the state school system. Clerical Catholics also became irreconcilable. Supported by Royalists and clericals, and also by left-wingers, General Georges Boulanger, minister of war in 1886–1887, started a coup d'état in 1889 but lost his nerve.

The Dreyfus Affair

In 1894 a more severe crisis began when Alfred Dreyfus, a French army captain of Jewish origin, was accused of passing military information to the Germans. Dreyfus protested his innocence but was convicted and sent to prison on Devil's Island off the coast of French Guiana in South America. An investigation showed that Dreyfus had been convicted on the basis of forged evidence, and that the real traitor was a Major Esterhazy.

The French high command tried to hush this up. They did not want to admit their blunder,

Boulanger as General Bonaparte: An English cartoon comment on Boulanger's return as deputy by a huge electoral majority in 1889.

and it suited them to have a Jew as the villain. In January 1898 Esterhazy was acquitted by a military court. Two days later, the novelist Émile Zola published an open letter accusing the military leaders of sacrificing an innocent man. The forged evidence was publicly exposed, the forger committed suicide, and Dreyfus obtained a new trial. But a military court found him guilty again, "with extenuating circumstances" (1899). This absurd verdict meant only that the army would not admit his innocence. The president of the Republic pardoned him. In 1906, when the excitement had died down, Dreyfus was formally acquitted, restored to the army, and promoted to major.

The *affaire Dreyfus* had ripped French society apart. The heirs of the revolution of 1789—intellectuals, leftists, anticlericals—mostly lined up behind Dreyfus. Their opponents—royalists, clericals, the army—mostly lined up against him. There were exceptions: some left-wingers assumed his guilt because he was a rich bourgeois; some Catholics championed him because they were convinced that he was innocent. Anti-Semitism played a major role.

When the crisis was over, the army was purged, and new anticlerical laws were passed dissolving Catholic teaching orders and closing some twelve thousand Catholic schools. In 1905 Napoleon's Concordat of 1801 was abrogated, and the Catholic Church lost its privileged position as a state-supported institution. Since then, the French Church has been a private, self-supporting organization.

In social and economic matters, the leaders of the Third Republic before 1914 made fewer concessions to labor's demands for social security and improved conditions than their opposite numbers in England or Germany. Unions found the government ready to use force against strikers, and their own members reluctant to pay dues or accept discipline. A Marxist but evolutionary Socialist party gained steadily at the polls, winning a sixth of the vote in 1914.

The French economy was well balanced between farm and factory. But in France industrialization lagged behind England and Germany, and French farmers and businessmen clung to old-fashioned ways of doing things. Yet neither political strains nor slow economic growth proved a severe handicap in the war of 1914–1918. Frenchmen might hate the Republic but they all loved France. The desire for revenge against the Germans and recovery of Alsace and Lorraine united them all.

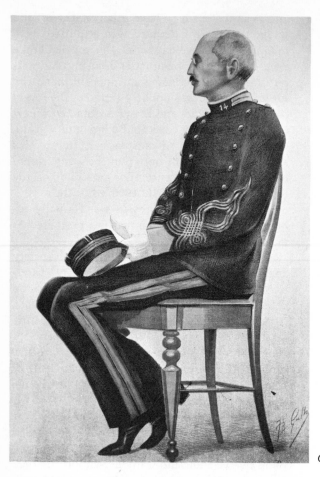

Captain Alfred Dreyfus, 1899.

Italy and the Smaller Western States

Like the French, the Italians were divided on religious issues. The clericals supported the popes in their refusal to accept the end of papal political authority and the annexation of Rome by the kingdom of Italy. Economically, despite the lack of coal and iron deposits, Italy made significant advances by exploiting hydroelectric power. The industrial north progressed at the expense of the predominantly rural south, however, which was exploited by its absentee landlords and neglected because of its differing historic traditions. This problem continues unsolved even today. After 1890, mass emigration to North and South America relieved the problems of overpopulation and underemployment. Parliamentary government had difficulty in functioning because of the lack of a strong democratic tradition and the flourishing of corruption in the south. In 1912, suffrage was extended to all males of thirty, whether or not they could read.

As a result of a war with Turkey in 1911–1912, Italy began at last to acquire a colonial empire, annexing Libya in North Africa and the Dodecanese Islands off the Turkish coast. This eased the memory of earlier failures in Tunisia, taken by the French in 1881, and in Ethiopia, where a native army defeated the Italians in 1896. The continued Austrian possession of *Italia Irredenta,* however, was a chronic source of nationalist frustration.

Elsewhere in Western Europe the familiar forces were at work in familiar ways. Belgium, Spain, and Portugal were the scene of strife between clericals and anticlericals. Industrial growth promoted the development of trade unions and socialist parties. Socialists generally moved away from a strict Marxian revolutionary program, because most workers wanted immediate reforms and social gains rather than violence and civil strife. Political trends generally moved toward liberal democracy. The suffrage was broadened for the parliaments elected in the Low Countries, Switzerland, and the Scandinavian states. In Italy, Spain, and Portugal, on the other hand, poverty, class antagonism, and regional discontent hampered the advance of liberalism.

Germany

Except for the small Balkan states, Central and Eastern Europe consisted of four empires: the German, the Hapsburg, the Russian, and the Ottoman. These were the lands of autocratic monarchies, conservative in social and political traditions, with relatively powerless parliaments appearing relatively late.

The German imperial constitution provided for a federal union of German states under the kaiser (emperor), who was the king of Prussia. The federal legislature consisted of a lower house, the Reichstag, elected by universal male suffrage, and an appointed upper house, the Bundesrat, which Prussia dominated. But neither house had much control over the chief minister, the chancellor, who was responsible only to the emperor.

In practice, William I, emperor until 1888, left most decisions to Bismarck, chancellor until 1890. Germany was an authoritarian, militaristic, efficient regime. During the Bismarckian decades it enjoyed extraordinary industrial development, which brought its coal and steel production up to or past the English levels by 1900. Alsace and Lorraine had brought new resources. Unification brought single railway and monetary systems. Business and technology cooperated in the new chemical and electrical industries. German efficiency and aggressiveness kept standards high and competition keen; German workers worked longer hours and for lower pay than their English counterparts.

Politically, Bismarck distrusted the patriotism of the Catholics because of their support for the dogma of papal infallibility and their con-

"Visiting Grandmamma": Cartoon by John Tenniel on William II's visit to England in 1889. "Now, Willie dear," says Queen Victoria to the emperor, "you've plenty of soldiers at home; look at these pretty ships, I'm sure you'll be pleased with them."

tacts with such potential adversaries of Germany as the French, the Austrians, and the Poles. Moreover, their Center party in Germany challenged the ascendancy of the Protestant Prussian aristocracy and middle classes. In the early 1870s Bismarck put through laws expelling the Jesuits, forbidding clerical criticism of the government, and closing the schools run by religious orders. By the late 1870s Bismarck had begun to move against the socialists and sought Catholic support against them.

The German socialists alarmed Bismarck by polling 10 percent of the vote in the election of 1877. In 1878 the Reichstag made the Social Democratic party illegal, banned its meetings, suppressed its newspapers, and made its members liable to expulsion from their homes by the police. Individual Social Democrats, however, were still allowed to run for the Reichstag. During the 1880s Bismarck's government put through accident and unemployment insurance and old-age pension laws in order to deprive the socialists of their chief arguments. But in 1912, the last election before the war, the Social Democrats polled a third of the votes.

William II (1888–1918), a grandson of William I, impulsive and erratic, was resolved to rule Germany himself. He disagreed with Bismarck's policies of friendship with Russia and opposition to the socialists, and in 1890 secured his resignation. William's own policies were strongly militarist; he nearly doubled the size of the army,

Otto von Bismarck.

which reached the figure of 900,000 by 1913. In the late 1890s he began to develop a major navy and thus aroused British alarm.

The dangers of his policies were underscored by the interview he gave in 1908 to the London *Daily Telegraph,* in which he protested his friendship for Britain but complained that the British had never shown him proper gratitude for giving them the military advice that brought them victory in the Boer War (see p. 458), a claim as fantastic as it was untrue. The English were disturbed by the interview. There was much protest in Germany, too. But William II's power remained unlimited.

The Hapsburg Monarchy

In the Hapsburg Empire, the autocrat was the conscientious but rigid and unimaginative Francis Joseph (1848–1916). The Ausgleich of 1867, which set up the dual monarchy of Austria-Hungary, eased tensions between Austrians and Magyars, but in both halves of the empire minority problems made political life difficult.

In Austria, the Czechs of Bohemia wanted rights like those the Magyars had won, and agitated for a triple rather than a dual monarchy. The German minority in Bohemia bitterly opposed them. Culturally and industrially the most advanced of the Slavic peoples, the Czechs often let their thwarted national ambitions paralyze the work of the Austrian parliament. The Polish minority, mostly landowners in Galicia, enjoyed a flourishing cultural life and were better off than those Poles who lived under German or Russian rule. But their peasants, who were mostly Ruthenian (Ukrainian), suffered severe repression. The small minority of Italians wanted union with Italy.

In Hungary, the minority problem was still worse. The Magyars numbered only a little more than half the population yet tried to impose the Magyar language in all schools and state services. Slovaks, Romanians, and South Slavs (Serbs and Croats) living in Hungary remained bitterly discontented. The Romanians of Transylvania wanted to unite with independent Romania across their borders. In the south Slav province of Croatia, a special Ausgleich was worked out in 1868. But it failed to satisfy many nationalistic Croatians and only alienated the Serbs. Both within Hungary and in Croatia, Serbs and Croats often agitated for union with independent Serbia.

Conditions were still more explosive in the provinces of Bosnia and Herzegovina, inhabited by Serbs and Croats. These remained under Ottoman rule until 1878 and were then administered for thirty years from Vienna, though technically remaining part of the Ottoman Empire. When Austria-Hungary annexed the two provinces outright in 1908, it deeply distressed independent Serbia, which had hoped to take them over. In the years just before the outbreak of World War I, Bosnian students began to take potshots at the Hungarian governors of Croatia, as the Serbs looked on sympathetically. These were ominous rehearsals for the crime that set off the war itself.

Austrian society was characterized by a high-living and frivolous aristocracy owning large estates, and a peasantry with small holdings and low standards of living and literacy. Between them a relatively small urban middle class included many Jews, who made large contributions to the music and cultivation of the "Viennese" way of life, and to medicine and science.

Some Jews were assimilated but many were not. The influx of poorer Jewish shopkeepers from elsewhere in Eastern Europe helped fan serious anti-Semitism among the urban lower middle classes, who favored anti-Semitic politicians. This led some Jews to found the Zionist movement for a Jewish state in Palestine.

Among Austrian political parties, the Christian Socialists, loyal to the monarchy and strongly Catholic, won support among the peasantry, the small businessmen, and the Catholic clergy. Their leader was the violently anti-Semitic Karl Lueger, perennial mayor of Vienna (d. 1910), who deeply impressed the young Hitler. The Social Democrats, founded in 1888, were gradualist socialists, usually led by intellectuals, many of them Jewish, but winning an increasing number of working-class supporters. They favored democratic federalism as a solution to the minorities problem and wanted to allow each nationality its own schools and free cultural expression.

Socially, Hungary was characterized by a landowning aristocracy with huge estates and by a more numerous group of "gentry" landowners whose holdings were smaller but who exercised great political influence. The towns, traditionally German and Jewish, became steadily more Magyar. In Hungary anti-Semitism was never as important politically as in Austria.

In Hungary, Catholicism was the faith of only 60 percent instead of 90 percent of the population, and a strong Catholic party like the Austrian Christian Socialists never arose. Austria had a liberal franchise before 1907 and universal manhood suffrage thereafter, but Hungary continued to restrict the vote to about 6 percent of the population. Hungarian political life thus degenerated into sterile bickerings on petty issues involving the prestige of Hungary within the dual monarchy.

Russia

The reforms of Alexander II of Russia (see p. 416), though sweeping, failed to satisfy the malcontents or to silence the opposition. Instead, they stimulated new demands and greater restlessness. A few articulate intellectuals transformed the old debate between Slavophiles and Westerners (see Chapter 14) that had raged under the oppressive Nicholas I into something far more serious.

Like Alexander Herzen (1812–1870), who began his career as a Westerner and became a revolutionary socialist and Slavophile after witnessing the failure of the Paris Revolution of 1848, others, too, preferred action to argument.

Michael Bakunin (1814–1876) spent much of his career participating in revolutions and in and out of European jails. He expected a great revolution to start in the Slavic world and spread everywhere, destroying all institutions. In the 1860s Bakunin and other senior Russian revolutionaries were living in exile in Switzerland.

One of them, Lavrov (1823–1900), argued that all Russian intellectuals owed a great historic debt to the peasantry. Peasant labor alone had made possible their leisure and education, and they should pay it by going among the peasants and educating them. Another, Tkachev (1844–1886), felt that the masses were ineffective and that only a tight, dedicated elite could touch off a truly revolutionary movement.

Listening to these men and others in Switzerland were many Russian students who had christened themselves "nihilists," those who believe in nothing. They liked to think of themselves as hard-boiled and intensely practical. They favored only the useful in art and literature,

The assassination of Alexander II, March 13, 1881.

and the abolition of old moral values like marriage and the family tie. In his novel *Fathers and Sons* (1862), Ivan Turgenev drew a convincing picture of a nihilist: obstinate, rude, and arrogant.

Real people imitated the fictional hero. The nihilist students in Switzerland, prompted by the teachings of Lavrov and the others, returned to Russia in the early 1870s as "populists," determined to "go to the people" and teach them how to improve their lot and prepare themselves for revolution. Populism failed partly because these idealists did not know how to talk to peasants, who often betrayed them to the police. After two great public trials of populists in the 1870s, those who had stayed out of jail formed a revolutionary organization. Its more radical wing, called The People's Will, turned in 1879 to terrorism.

For two years they tried to kill Alexander II, eventually (March 1881) succeeding on the very day when he had signed a document that summoned a commission to consider further reforms. His successor, Alexander III (reigned 1881–1894), refused to summon the commission, smashed The People's Will, and embarked on a period of reaction that would last through the first ten years of the reign of his son, the last tsar, Nicholas II (reigned 1894–1917).

During the reaction the government made elections to the zemstvos much less democratic. "Rural leaders" appointed from the capital replaced the elected justices of the peace in the countryside. The minority peoples—Finns, Poles, Ukrainians, Armenians, and Jews—were subjected to discriminatory "russifying" policies ranging from suppression of their own institutions in the case of the Finns to outright massacre in the case of the Jews.

A peasant bank did make credit easier to obtain, and some legislation helped the urban workers. Russian industrialization boomed. The Donets coalfields and the Baku oil wells came into production; steel output soared. A self-made railroad expert, Serge Witte, who served as minister of finance from 1892 to 1903, supervised the great expansion of the railroad network, which doubled with the building of the Trans-Siberian line. Working conditions in industry were probably the worst in Europe.

Marxism now made its first real impact in Russia, as the younger generation of revolutionaries formed the Social Democratic party (SDs) in 1898. One of their leaders was a young intellectual from the upper middle class named Vladimir Ilyich Ulyanov (1870–1924), who used the penname Lenin. Sometimes he prefixed the initial N, a Russian abbreviation for "nobody," in order to tell his readers that he was using a pseudonym (his first name was *not* Nikolai).

Soon the SDs began to quarrel among themselves: should the party operate under a strongly centralized directorate, or should each local group be free to agitate for its own ends? Following Bakunin and Tkachev, Lenin insisted on the tightly knit directorate. At a party congress held in Brussels and London in 1903, the majority of delegates voted with him. Lenin's faction took the name *Bolshevik* ("majority"), and their opponents called themselves *Menshevik* ("minority"). Unlike most of the socialist parties in Europe, the Bolsheviks were not gradualist or evolutionary.

As Marxists, the SDs were interested chiefly in the urban worker, still a small class numerically in Russia. The direct heirs of the populist tradition, on the other hand, were interested in the peasant as the future revolutionary. They too organized a political party, the Social Revolutionaries, or SRs, who wanted more land for the peasantry, and who continued the terrorist program of their predecessors.

A third political grouping, neither SD nor SR but mostly moderate liberal intellectuals, veterans of the zemstvos, also came into being and called itself Constitutional Democrats—KDs or Kadets. They favored a constitution for Russia and the creation of a national parliament or *duma*. The tsar's government, however, made no distinction between its violent and its moderate opponents.

The period of reaction culminated with the Russo-Japanese War of 1904–1905. Rivalry between the two nations in the Chinese province of Manchuria and in Korea and the weakness of China were the underlying causes. The Russians forced the Chinese to let them build a railroad line across Manchuria to get a shortcut to their own Far Eastern province. In 1897 they took the Chinese harbor at Port Arthur, which they had earlier kept out of Japanese hands (1895). Adventurous Russians intrigued for concessions in Korea, and Russian politicians who thought war would silence political dissent at home secured the dismissal of the sagacious and cautious Witte.

The Japanese began hostilities by a surprise attack on Russian ships in Port Arthur (1904). Though holding their own on land, the Russians suffered a severe defeat when their fleet, which had sailed all the way from the Baltic, was destroyed by the Japanese at Tsushima (May 1905).

Both sides accepted President Theodore Roosevelt's offer to mediate. In the Treaty of Portsmouth (1905), Russia recognized a Japanese protectorate over Korea and ceded Port Arthur and the southern half of Sakhalin Island to Japan, but retained a substantial role as a power in the Far East.

The Revolution of 1905 and the Dumas

In Russia itself revolution was breaking out. The SRs fomented peasant riots and assassinated the minister of the interior. A police agent of the government, planted in the factories of the capital to combat SD activities among the workers, organized a parade to petition the tsar for an eight-hour day, the right to strike, and a national assembly. But Nicholas ordered the troops to fire on the peacefully marching workers. About a thousand of them were killed on "Bloody Sunday" (January 22, 1905). The massacre infuriated the entire opposition. Moderates joined radicals in demanding concessions. The timid, vacillating, and unintelligent tsar hesitated, strikes multiplied, vital services were paralyzed, and the SDs

among the printers formed the first *soviet,* or workers' council. Witte told Nicholas II that he must either impose a military dictatorship or summon a national legislative assembly, a duma.

By the October Manifesto of 1905, Nicholas promised full civil liberties and the election of a duma by universal manhood suffrage. Not until troops returning from the Far East proved to be loyal to the government, however, could left-wing violence be suppressed after several days of fighting (December 1905). The Duma was duly elected.

Before it could meet, Witte secured a French loan, making the government financially independent, and passed a set of "fundamental laws" that the Duma could not change. These left all matters of finance and foreign policy in the hands of the tsar, and empowered him to dissolve the Duma and to legislate when it was not in session. He did have to set the date for new elections, and any interim law of his own would have to be approved by the Duma. The Duma marked a major attack on traditional Russian autocracy.

The tsar soon dissolved the first Duma because it demanded radical agrarian reforms that

Bloody Sunday (January 22, 1905): demonstrators and soldiers in Petersburg.

would have given the peasants lands belonging to the state, the church, and some private owners. The second Duma was also dissolved (1907). Now the government illegally altered the election laws, reducing the number of deputies from the peasants and the national minorities and increasing those from the gentry. Thus the government obtained a majority, and the third Duma (1907–1912) and the fourth (1912–1917) lived out their five-year terms. Unrepresentative and limited in power though these Dumas were, they were still useful forums for the airing of national issues. The initiative in governing, however, rested with the executive.

From 1906 to 1911 the executive was dominated by the intelligent conservative chief minister, Stolypin. Towards revolutionaries Stolypin was ruthless, but towards the peasants he was generous and imaginative. He put through laws that enabled them to free themselves from the village commune, to which they had remained attached after the emancipation of 1861. A man wishing to detach his property could demand that he receive a single tract of land rather than the scattered plots previously assigned to him. Stolypin called this program the "wager on the strong and sober." He was betting on the ability of individual peasants to function on their own as small farmers.

The government came close to winning the wager. Between 1906 and 1917 about a quarter of the peasant households in European Russia seceded from the communes. Only war and revolution kept the process from going further and perhaps satisfying the perennial land hunger that made peasants support the SRs and other radicals.

Rasputin.

The assassination of Stolypin in 1911 was a disaster for the tsarist regime. The government now drifted into a purely reactionary policy, spreading a vast web of police spies to trap SD and SR agitators, yet never succeeding in catching them all. The tsar and his family fell under the domination of Rasputin, a half-mad, wholly evil, dirty, ignorant, and power-hungry monk from Siberia. Rasputin had the ability, perhaps hypnotic, to stop the dangerous bleeding spells of the tsar's only son, who suffered from hemophilia. Rasputin became the real ruler of Russia, to the horror of loyal supporters of the dynasty and the detriment of the rational conduct of affairs.

The Ottoman Empire

The Ottoman Empire also underwent a partial revolution—the Young Turk uprising of 1908. The Young Turks were the more vigorous heirs of the ineffectual Ottoman reformers of the mid-nineteenth century. They wanted the modern industrial achievements of the West, they wanted its liberal political apparatus, and they wanted to have Turks respected and feared as members of a modern *nation*.

The Young Turks opposed the ultrareactionary policies of Sultan Abdul Hamid II (1876–1909), and they hated the weakness of the Ottoman Empire, which had already lost large parts of its European possessions and continued to lose its African territories. The dominant element in the population was Turkish in nationality and Muslim in religion, but important minorities—the Christian Greeks and Armenians, and the mainly Muslim Arabs—wanted a status equaling that of the privileged Turks.

When Young Turk army officers rebelled in 1908, they promised to inaugurate a new era. Abdul Hamid was to become a constitutional monarch. The minorities, who had often been promised equality, were to secure it now under a new cosmopolitan concept of Ottoman nationality. In general, decrepit Turkish institutions were to be revitalized by the influence of the West. But the promising concept of an Ottoman nationality failed. Both the minorities and the Young Turks themselves were too nationalistic. The Young Turks increasingly favored an intolerant policy of "turkification" very like the "russification" of Tsar Alexander III.

From 1911 to 1913, Turkey was involved in disastrous wars with Italy and the Christian states of the Balkans. In this deteriorating situation three Young Turk officers established a dicta-

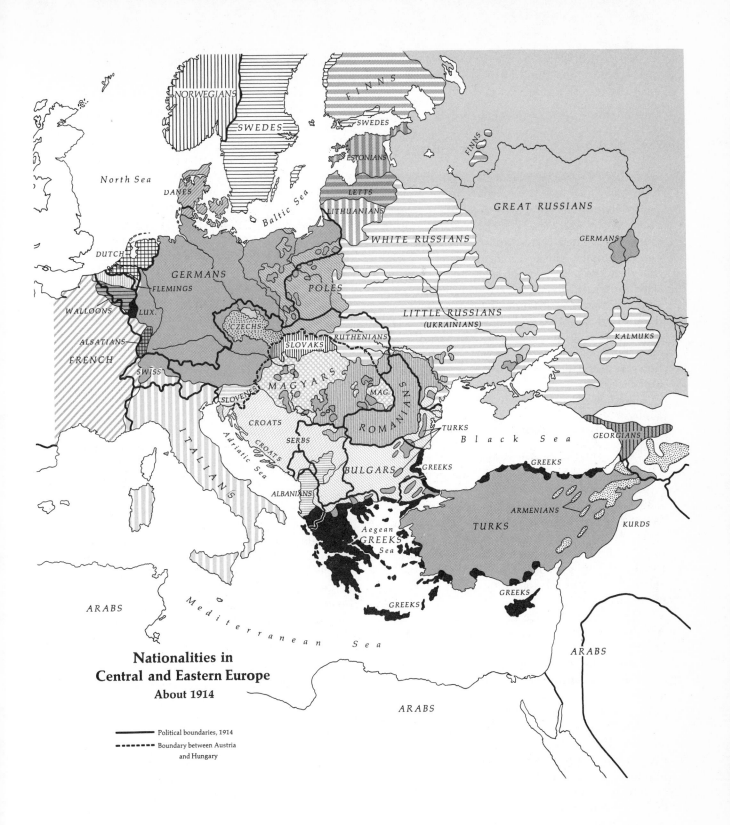

**Nationalities in
Central and Eastern Europe**
About 1914

———————— Political boundaries, 1914

--------------- Boundary between Austria
and Hungary

torship (1913). Thus the Ottoman Empire, like the Hapsburg and the Russian, was unready to meet the test of World War I.

II THE WORLD OVERSEAS

Between 1870 and 1914, Britain and France acquired new colonies, and Italy, Germany, Belgium, the United States, and Japan joined the race for empire. The governments seemed to feel that only the possession of colonies could make a nation great. Mixed with nationalism and racism there was an element of religious and humanitarian impulse. As free trade gave way to a revived mercantilism, businessmen and politicians also sought colonies to enlarge the market for home manufactures and to provide fresh fields for investment.

The British Empire

By 1914 the British controlled more than a third of Africa and three-fifths of its population. After a French company had built the Suez Canal (1869), Egypt became more important than ever as the key to the voyage between Europe and India. As we saw, Disraeli bought for England in 1875 the shares of Suez Canal stock held by Ismail, ruler of Egypt. Ismail was deposed in 1879, and in 1882 England sent troops to put down a nationalist uprising.

Egypt now became a British protectorate. A British resident directed the policies of the Egyptian government. Egyptians felt that even the Aswan Dam (1902), improving irrigation, was only an effort to perpetuate their colonial economic function of supplying raw materials. National feeling grew stronger.

South Africa provides a contrasting imperialist case history. Here the discovery of gold and the growth of the diamond industry in the Boer Republic of the Transvaal brought a new wave of immigration in the 1880s. To the Boers these new arrivals were intruders. Cecil Rhodes, imperialist-minded prime minister of the Cape Colony, protected the immigrants. In 1895, a follower of Rhodes, Dr. Jameson, led a raid into the Transvaal, which the immigrants were expected to assist by an armed uprising. But the plan failed.

Kaiser William II then sent an open telegram congratulating President Kruger of the Transvaal,

infuriating English public opinion. Tensions arising from the Jameson raid culminated in the Boer War (1899–1902) between Britain and the Boer republics of Transvaal and the Orange Free State. As the Boers held out for three years, many English Liberals and most foreigners sympathized with them as underdogs. British prestige suffered.

But the peace of 1902 brought British rule and the promise of ultimate self-government, fulfilled in 1910, when the Boer republics and the British Cape Colony and Natal were joined in the Union of South Africa. This self-governing dominion had both Afrikaans (the Boer dialect) and English as official languages. But Boer resentment continued to smolder. South African whites were outnumbered four to one by the black Africans, the "coloreds" (people of mixed blood), and immigrants from India.

In 1877 Queen Victoria was proclaimed empress of India, an act that symbolized the wealth and size of the subcontinent with its mixture of castes, languages, and religions. By 1914 the British had built thousands of miles of railroads and telegraph lines in India, had founded schools and universities, using English as the language of instruction, and had established hospitals and seaports. British capital financed textile and other industries.

Gradually Indians were achieving public and private positions of greater and greater responsibility. But the Indian middle class longed for more white-collar jobs. Indian nationalists were impatient with the slow growth of literacy and disapproved of British toleration for the native princes and their fantastically luxurious style of life side by side with peasant misery. Although many British civil servants in India were unselfishly devoted to India and the needs of Indians, the physical and spiritual climate of India imposed great hardship. And many Indians regarded the British as overbearing even when they strove not to be.

British West, Central, and East African territories, Malaya and Hong Kong in Asia, many islands in the West Indies, and British Honduras and British Guiana on the mainland of Tropical America were all run as colonies. But in the early twentieth century South Africa, Australia, and New Zealand followed the precedent of Canada and became self-governing dominions. Australia and New Zealand were sparsely populated, partly because they excluded Asians and had to compete with the United States for European immigrants. But by 1914 they had developed distinctive and contrasting national personalities: New Zealand,

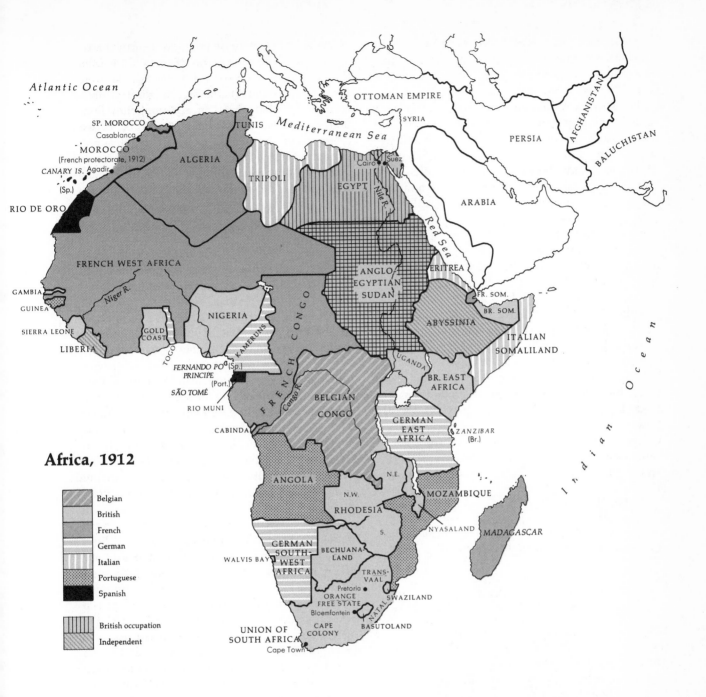

Africa, 1912

Belgian
British
French
German
Italian
Portuguese
Spanish

British occupation
Independent

very "English" but far more egalitarian; Australia, individualistic, boisterous, and often anti-English.

All the dominions followed the British system of prime minister and cabinet controlled by parliament. By 1914 all enjoyed full control over their internal affairs, could levy tariffs, even on British goods, and had the beginnings of their own armies. Not legal subjection, but strategic, economic, cultural, and emotional ties bound them to Britain. This unique relationship would be further systematized in the 1920s and 1930s.

The Other Empires

In 1914 France controlled the second largest colonial empire. In Asia the French ruthlessly dominated Indo-China (present-day Vietnam), which grew rice and rubber. In Africa, they ruled vast tropical areas: much of the West African bulge, equatorial Africa to the south of the bulge, and Madagascar off the east coast. In North Africa Algeria had been French since 1830, and France now acquired Tunisia (1881) and Morocco (1911), both as protectorates.

The mild climate of North Africa attracted substantial numbers of European immigrants, the *colons,* Italians and Spaniards as well as Frenchmen. They occupied some lands belonging to the native Muslim Arabs and Berbers, who often resented their presence deeply. French colonial administrators worked to assimilate these native populations and make Muslim Frenchmen out of them. Many North Africans benefited by French education and some became assimilated. But most remained indifferent if not hostile.

Newcomers to colonial competition, the Germans, led by businessmen seeking new contracts and nationalists seeking new glory, exhibited greed and violence. In Africa by 1914 they had acquired Togoland and the Cameroons, South-West Africa, and Tanganyika. In the Pacific they had some small islands and part of New Guinea. None of these colonies contributed much to the German economy. Everywhere the Germans were brutal to the inhabitants.

In Africa Italy held only Libya and two colonies bordering Ethiopia—Eritrea and Somaliland. The Belgian king Leopold II (1865–1909), however, came off with the great area of the Congo. Early grandiose plans for civilizing missions vanished in horrifying scandals over slavery and exploitation involving the king himself.

The United States

In these decades the United States also embarked on imperialism. After the Spanish-Ameri-

President Theodore Roosevelt on a steam shovel in Panama during the construction of the canal.

can War, touched off by the sinking of the battleship *Maine* in Havana harbor (February 15, 1898), the Americans won control of the Spanish colonies of Cuba and Puerto Rico in the Caribbean and of the Philippines. In addition, the United States annexed the Pacific islands of Hawaii (1898), and in 1903 supported a revolution in Panama, then a part of Colombia. This assured direct American control of the zone of the Panama Canal that would soon be constructed.

The acquisition of an empire delighted some Americans, notably Theodore Roosevelt, president from 1901 to 1909, but aroused others to indignation as a betrayal of democratic principles. By 1914 the United States had become a great industrial nation, with a highly mechanized agriculture and with financial resources so great that, as a banking center, New York was a serious rival to London. The influx of European immigrants supplied tremendous amounts of manpower.

Critics of the era then and since have pointed to its crass materialism, its political bossism, and the prevalence of robber barons in its business life. Yet despite loud argument, Americans agreed on political fundamentals. The South completed its difficult "road to reunion." It suffered from greater poverty and illiteracy than other regions. Its white population remained committed to the maintenance of white supremacy.

Government now began to intervene in economic affairs, setting minimum wages and limiting child and female labor. Here the lead was taken by individual states, notably Wisconsin. Crusading journalists helped expose corrupt practices. Public opinion readied itself to accept federal regulation: a "square deal" for labor (Theodore Roosevelt's term), and the "busting" or at least policing of the trusts that were gaining monopolistic control over important economic areas. The Standard Oil Company was broken up. Though some of its children grew bigger than the parent, American business was no longer allowed to operate on the principle of "The public be damned!" voiced by the nineteenth-century railroad magnate William Henry Vanderbilt.

The Far East

When the American Commodore Perry "opened" Japan in 1854 and ended her two centuries of self-imposed isolation, he stimulated the Japanese themselves to move toward modernization. The feudal oligarchy that ruled the country was not only greedy but ineffectual. A political

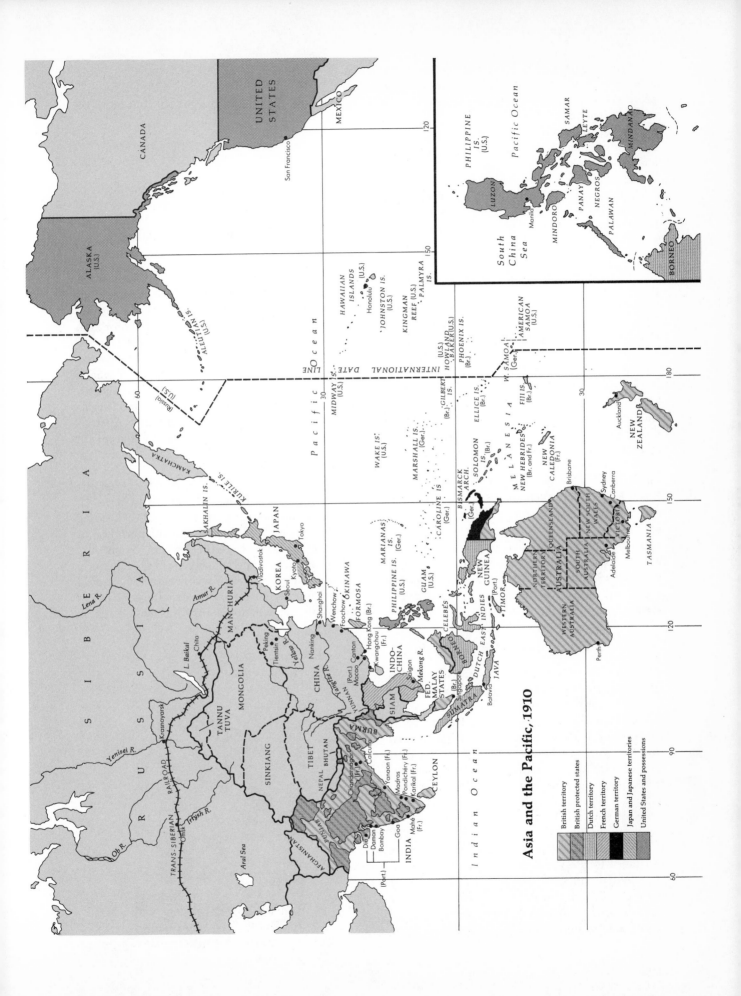

Asia and the Pacific, 1910

British territory
British protected states
Dutch territory
French territory
German territory
Japan and Japanese territories
United States and possessions

CANADA

UNITED STATES

MEXICO

San Francisco

ALASKA (U.S.)

ALEUTIAN IS. (U.S.)

Pacific Ocean

HAWAIIAN ISLANDS (U.S.)
Honolulu
JOHNSTON IS. (U.S.)
KINGMAN REEF (U.S.)
PALMYRA IS.

INTERNATIONAL DATE LINE

MIDWAY IS. (U.S.)
WAKE IS. (U.S.)

HOWLAND (U.S.)
BAKER (U.S.)
PHOENIX IS. (Br.)
W. SAMOA (Ger.)
AMERICAN SAMOA (U.S.)

GILBERT IS. (Br.)
ELLICE IS. (Br.)
FIJI IS. (Br.)

SIBERIA

RUSSIA

(Russia) (U.S.)

KAMCHATKA

KURILE IS.

SAKHALIN IS.

JAPAN
Tokyo
Kyoto
KOREA
Seoul
Vladivostok

MANCHURIA

MONGOLIA

L. Baikal
Chita

Lena R.
Amur R.

TRANS-SIBERIAN RAILROAD

Yenisei R.
Krasnoyarsk

Ob R.
Irtysh R.
Omsk

Aral Sea

TANNU TUVA

SINKIANG

TIBET

NEPAL
BHUTAN

AFGHANISTAN

PAMIR

INDIA
Bombay
Daman
Diu
Goa
Mahé (Fr.)
Madras
Pondichéry (Fr.)
Karikal (Fr.)
Yanaon (Fr.)
Chandarnagar (Fr.)
Calcutta

CEYLON

Indian Ocean

BURMA

SIAM

CHINA
Peking
Tientsin
Yellow R.
Nanking
Shanghai
Yangtze R.
Wenchow
Foochow
Canton
Kwangchou (Fr.)
Hong Kong (Br.)
Macao (Port.)

OKINAWA
FORMOSA

MARIANAS (Ger.)

GUAM (U.S.)

PHILIPPINE IS. (U.S.)

MARSHALL IS. (Ger.)

CAROLINE IS. (Ger.)

YUNNAN
INDO-CHINA
Saigon
Mekong R.

FED. MALAY STATES
Singapore

SUMATRA

BORNEO (Br.)

CELEBES

DUTCH EAST INDIES

JAVA
Batavia

TIMOR (Port.)

NEW GUINEA (Ger.)

BISMARCK ARCH. (Ger.)

SOLOMON IS. (Br.)

NEW HEBRIDES (Br. and Fr.)

NEW CALEDONIA (Fr.)

MELANESIA

Brisbane

NORTHERN TERRITORY
WESTERN AUSTRALIA
SOUTH AUSTRALIA
QUEENSLAND
NEW SOUTH WALES
VICTORIA
AUSTRALIA
Perth
Adelaide
Melbourne
Sydney
Canberra

TASMANIA

NEW ZEALAND
Auckland

Inset

PHILIPPINE IS. (U.S.)

LUZON
Manila
MINDORO
PANAY
NEGROS
PALAWAN
SAMAR
LEYTE
MINDANAO

South China Sea

Pacific Ocean

BORNEO

revolution beginning in 1868 benefited chiefly the urban merchants, the craftsmen, and the samurai, professional military retainers in the lower ranks of the aristocracy.

Using the almost forgotten emperor, and endowing his office with a sacred authority, these ambitious middle-class people moved into the center of power, both economic and political. From the overpopulated countryside they easily recruited cheap manpower for the new industries. In 1889 the emperor granted a constitution. It established a bicameral Diet. But neither peasants nor urban workers could vote, and the cabinet was responsible only to the emperor and so to the ruling clique.

With modernization came Japanese imperialism, primarily at the expense of China. In 1904 the defeat of Russia gave Japan a free hand in Manchuria and in Korea (annexed in 1910). Japanese imperialists longed to control all of China, but other powers were also scrambling for it. In 1899 John Hay, the American secretary of state, sought to obtain international recognition for the Open Door policy, whereby all foreign goods could be marketed in China on even terms.

To all this the Chinese responded by forming an antiforeign secret society, the Boxers. The Boxer Rebellion in 1900 caused two hundred foreign deaths, mostly among missionaries, and led to the dispatch of foreign troops, including United States Marines, and to the extraction of a huge indemnity from the Chinese government. In 1911–1912 a new Chinese revolution would break out (see p. 500) and open a new era in the history of the Far East.

The Balance Sheet of Imperialism

The Boxers well illustrate the victims' discontent with imperialist practices. Egyptian and Indian nationalists echoed their arguments and would have enjoyed ousting the foreigners by force. Indeed, Western ideas of self-determination and human equality were making converts among colonial peoples. Equality threatened the traditional bases of their own cultures at least as much as it did the Western interlopers. The introduction of law and order, the extension of communications, the advances in health—all Western contributions—ironically enough made resistance to the West easier and more popular.

When colonies supplied home industry with cheap and abundant raw materials, they were often a well-paying proposition. But the seamy side of imperialism gave liberals at home

a chance to denounce and advertise its hypocrisies. And colonial rivalries among the powers in Africa and Asia made a large contribution to the outbreak of World War I.

III THE FIRST WORLD WAR

The Road to War: Triple Alliance and Triple Entente

England and Germany were rivals in trade, empire, and navies. The French wanted revenge on Germany for 1871. Russians and Austrians competed to dominate southeastern Europe, as the Austrians feared that the Russians would arouse their own Slavic minorities. These were the obvious tensions that culminated in war in 1914. When war broke out, two great alliances—the Triple Entente of France, Britain, and Russia, and the Triple Alliance of Germany, Austria-Hungary, and Italy—stood toe to toe. Except for the defection of Italy, they fought the war in this alignment.

The road to 1914 began in 1871. After the defeat of France, Bismarck designed a series of alliances for Germany, in the hope of keeping the French isolated. He tried to distract France from any plan for war with Germany by encouraging French imperial adventures, especially those—like that in Tunisia—where they would annoy another power, in this case Italy. The German-Austrian alliance of 1879 was made possible

"Peace": Daumier's view of the European situation after 1871.

by Bismarck's lenient treatment of Austria after the defeat of 1866. It lasted down to 1918 and was the cornerstone of his system. In 1882 Italy was brought into the alliance.

Russian-Austrian friction over Ottoman territory in the Balkans gave Bismarck his gravest problem. In 1877 Russia supported the rebellious Christians of Bosnia and Bulgaria and defeated the Ottomans. In 1878 the Russians dictated the peace of San Stefano. They broke their earlier promises and tried to create a new "Big Bulgaria" that the powers, especially Austria, believed would become a mere Russian satellite.

The Congress of Berlin (1878), with Bismarck presiding, drastically revised the San Stefano arrangements. The new Bulgaria was reduced by two-thirds. The congress awarded Bosnia and Herzegovina to Austria, Cyprus to Britain, and Tunisia to future French domination. Deprived of their gains, seeing the other powers grabbing Ottoman territories for which Russia had done the fighting, the Russians grew so resentful that Bismarck feared they might ally themselves with France and "encircle" Germany.

Bismarck strove to prevent this by promoting a secret "Three Emperors' League" of Germany, Austria, and Russia in 1881. When the Russians withdrew, he concluded a secret Reinsurance Treaty (1887) between Germany and Russia alone, but he let the Russians know of his obligations to Austria, to discourage any Russian aggression. Probably even Bismarck could not have kept up these acrobatics indefinitely.

And when William II dismissed him (1890), the kaiser soon afterwards "cut the wire" to Russia by refusing a Russian request to renew the Reinsurance Treaty. Bismarck's nightmare of encirclement now came true: in 1894, France and Russia reached an alliance, despite the mutual dislike of the autocratic tsar and the French republican politicians.

The next major step came a decade later when Britain decided to move out of isolation and toward alignment with France and Russia. The old colonial rivalry with France flared up in 1898 when French and English forces competed for possession of Fashoda in the disputed Sudan. Russia and England were rivals for concessions both in the Far and Near East. But these tensions were less important than the threat posed to the British by the rapid German naval building program.

Traditional British isolation disappeared with the conclusion of the Anglo-Japanese alliance of 1902, designed to check Russia's Far Eastern ambitions. The Russo-Japanese War hastened British negotiations with France, leading to the *Entente Cordiale* of 1904, by which England gave France a free hand in Morocco in exchange for a free hand in Egypt and the Sudan. The two powers began such close collaboration that it amounted to alliance. An Anglo-Russian agreement followed in 1907, never so intimate as that with France, but easing imperial rivalry.

Crises over Morocco and the Balkans

In the last decade before 1914, crisis after crisis shook Europe. Two of them arose over Morocco. The first came in 1905, when the kaiser made a visit to Tangier as a sign that he did not accept French predominance in Morocco. This was settled by the Algeciras conference (1906). In 1911 the kaiser rashly sent a gunboat to the Moroccan port of Agadir as an anti-French gesture. This second crisis was settled only when France ceded part of the French Congo to Germany in exchange for German recognition of French hegemony in Morocco.

Between the two Moroccan crises came a more important one in the Balkans. The Austrians responded to the Young Turk revolt of 1908 by annexing outright Bosnia and Herzegovina, which they had been administering since 1878. The annexation dealt a crushing blow to the Serbian hope that these provinces would eventually become part of Serbia. This outraged the Russians, who regarded themselves as protectors of the Serbs. Moreover the Austrians had promised to assist the Russian effort to lift the ban on Russian warships passing through the Turkish straits and into the Mediterranean, and now broke the promise.

In 1912 the Balkan states, backed by Russia and encouraged by Italian victories over the Ottomans, themselves attacked the Ottoman Empire. Bulgaria, Serbia, and Greece won the First Balkan War (1912–1913). But Austria refused to let the Serbs have the outlet to the Adriatic that they had won, and instead sponsored the new state of Albania. Bulgaria refused to compensate the Serbs for their loss by giving them part of their own territorial prizes. So Serbia, Greece, Romania, and the recently defeated Ottomans turned on Bulgaria in the Second Balkan War (1913).

The Crisis of 1914

All these crises had been successfully contained, but the next could not be. On June 28,

Princip immediately after his assassination of Archduke Francis Ferdinand at Sarajevo.

1914, a Serbian student, Gavrilo Princip, assassinated the heir to the Hapsburg throne, Archduke Francis Ferdinand, and his wife in the streets of the provincial capital of Bosnia, Sarajevo. Determined to end Serbian agitation among their south Slav subjects, and convinced that the Serbian government had known about Princip's plot in advance, the Austrians consulted the German government. Germany promised to support any Austrian action against the Serbs.

On July 23, Austria sent Serbia a forty-eight-hour ultimatum, designed to be unacceptable. The Serbs refused to let Austrian civil or military officials participate in the investigation of Princip's plot. To the world it seemed as though Austria was bullying the Serbs. Probably, however, Serbia already had a promise of help from Russia if war should come. Serbian rejection of part of the ultimatum brought an Austrian declaration of war on July 28, 1914.

The kaiser and his civil advisers, resisting their own generals, now tried to persuade Austria to accept a compromise. William II telegraphed Tsar Nicholas II, and Russia temporarily agreed to substitute a partial mobilization for the full mobilization that had already been ordered. But Russia was a country of long distances and poor communications, and her generals feared that the enemy would get the jump on them. On July 30 they took the fateful decision to resume full mobilization.

On August 1, Germany declared war on Russia, and on August 3 against France, Russia's ally. Possibly Britain would have been brought into the war by the closeness of her ties with France. What made British entry certain was Germany's violation of Belgian neutrality, which both Britain and Prussia had in 1839 agreed to guarantee. On August 2, Germany notified Belgium that German troops would cross Belgian territory on their way to France. Belgium resisted and appealed to the other guaranteeing powers. On August 4, Britain declared war on Germany.

The German chancellor, Bethmann-Hollweg, remarked that Britain had gone to war just for a "scrap of paper." This cynical phrase for the 1839 treaty solidified British opinion in favor of the war. It also played a big part in the charge of war guilt later laid against Germany.

In all the European countries, of course, public attitudes ranged from ultramilitarism to ultrapacifism. Yet in each country there was a prevailing opinion. In Germany the kaiser set the tone. His efforts to prevent war came only in the last hectic week of July 1914. Before that he had been consistently warlike and noisy.

In Germany ambition and envy had produced an intense hatred of Britain, mixed with a sense of inferiority. Especially the English upper classes, perfectly tailored, serene in effortless superiority, seemed to the Germans the favored children of fortune. In the years before the war

German naval officers would drink to *Der Tag*, the day of reckoning against England. Few Englishmen returned the hate, but many believed that the Germans should be taught a lesson. The expensive naval race with Germany, the kaiser's hostility in incident after incident, and the growing competition from German industrial goods in world markets all contributed to the feeling.

In France, the characteristic attitude was the embittered patriotism of the losers of 1870–1871, though many, like the socialists, were committed in theory to pacifism. From 1871 onward, the statue representing Strasbourg, capital of Alsace, among the cities of France in the Place de la Concorde in Paris was perpetually draped in black.

Among the other warring powers too, the decision of the governments to fight was not unwelcome. Germans and Magyars in Austria-Hungary welcomed the chance to punish the troublesome Slavs. Russians believed that God and the right were on their side. The war could not have been waged by the emperors, frock-coated diplomats, and military "brass hats" had not the people of Europe welcomed it.

Strength of the Belligerents

The war was fought between the Central Powers (Germany and Austria-Hungary, later joined by Turkey and Bulgaria) and the Allies (France, Russia, Britain and its dominions, Serbia, and Belgium, joined in 1915 by Italy and in 1917 by the United States). From the first, the Central Powers were weaker in manpower and material resources than the Allies, yet it took the Allies four years to win. Why?

The very name "Central Powers" suggests one reason: Germany and Austria were Central European neighbors and spoke the same language. They had interior lines of communication so they could quickly move troops from one front to another. Britain and France, on the other hand, were cut off from Russia because Germany blocked the Baltic route and Turkey the Black Sea route. Russia could be reached only by the long Arctic journey to Archangel on the White Sea or by the long Pacific journey to Vladivostok.

Language separated each of the three major Allies from the other. They were recent partners and had no long tradition of cooperation. France and Britain were democracies, whose populations, though capable of great sacrifice, found it hard to accept the firm military controls demanded by war. Only in 1918 did they, with the United States, consent to a unified command on the Western front under the French Marshal Foch.

France was slow to mobilize her economic resources; Britain was a naval power, with a small army, and relied on volunteers, postponing a draft until 1916. Russian distances, bad communications, and low industrial output hampered the operations of the immense Russian army, whose morale had not recovered from the defeat by Japan. The revolution of 1905 and the increasing corruption and inefficiency of the tsarist government distressed the public. By contrast, Germany was the only power really ready for war in 1914. The army was efficiently organized and German industry was easily put on a war footing. Germany also had the psychological advantage of the offensive.

The Fighting Fronts

The invasion of Belgium, at the very beginning of the war, was a vital part of the Germans' plan for a quick victory on two fronts. First they would concentrate on the West and win a decision there before Russia could even complete mobilization and threaten in the East. The Germans poured through Belgium and into northern France, but the French rallied and checked them outside of Paris in the first battle of the Marne River, September 1914.

Later the Germans failed in an attempt to capture the French Channel ports and cut the short cross-Channel communication lines to Britain. The opposing armies in France dug trenches along a line from the Channel to Switzerland. Bloody trench warfare on the Western front continued in a long deadlock. Here, four years later, the Allies, by then including the Americans, would finally break through and win.

The other fronts ate up German men and resources. On the Eastern front, a Russian advance into East Prussia was halted at Tannenberg in August 1914. Thereafter the Germans kept enough troops in the East to help their hard-pressed Austrian allies. They held the Russians off, but could not knock them out. The defeat of a major Russian offensive against Austria in 1916 led to the Russian revolutions of 1917. The new Bolshevik regime had to sign the Peace of Brest-Litovsk dictated by the Central Powers. The western provinces of Russia fell under German-Austrian domination.

After the Allies bought Italian intervention by promising Italy Italia Irredenta and the Dalmatian coast and other territories, an Italian front

*Allied soldiers trying to keep warm,
near Ypres in Flanders, 1914.*

was opened in 1915 in the mountains along the Austro-Italian border. In the autumn of 1917 the Germans routed the Italians at Caporetto, but the Austro-German advance was slowed by shortages of supplies.

In southeast Europe the Central Powers gained the adherence of Bulgaria (1915), still smarting from its defeat in the Second Balkan War, and overran Serbia. Winston Churchill, first lord of the British Admiralty, worked out a plan to take advantage of Turkish weakness, to strike at the Central Powers through the Balkans, and to open up the Black Sea route to Russia. He mounted a naval attack on the Gallipoli peninsula, along the European shore of the Dardanelles. Other Allied leaders were skeptical and refused to allot all the men and equipment requested. The landing was bungled, and the plan failed late in 1915.

Allied promises of Hungarian territory lured Romania into the war. In 1916 the Central Powers overran Romania, left exposed by Russian defeats. Not until the Allies forced Greece into the war on their side (1917) and landed troops who marched northward in the late summer of 1918 did they score successes in the Balkans. Then they knocked Bulgaria out, liberated Serbia, and threatened to destroy Austria-Hungary.

In the Middle East, the eccentric English colonel T. E. Lawrence assisted a "revolt in the desert" against the Turks by discontented Arabs. In 1917 Jerusalem fell, and in 1918 Turkish resistance collapsed. The Arabs hoped for a Middle East made up exclusively of Arab states. But in 1917 the British government, trying to rally Jews throughout the world to the Allied cause, issued the Balfour Declaration (named for the foreign secretary) favoring "the establishment in Palestine of a national home for the Jewish people." Zionist aspirations and Allied promises thwarted Arab hopes.

The War at Sea and on the Home Fronts

At sea the German and British surface navies fought the inconclusive battle of Jutland

Europe, 1914-1918

Allied and Associated Powers
Central Powers and their allies
Neutrals
—— Political boundaries, 1914
—·—·— Boundary between Austria and Hungary
▬▬▬ Greatest advance by Central Powers
•••••• Greatest advance by Allies
■ Battle sites

(1916) in the North Sea. Although German losses in tonnage were only half those of the British, the German fleet never dared put to sea again. In 1918, when ordered to make a last stand, German sailors mutinied and helped touch off the German revolution that led to the Armistice of 1918.

German submarines were far more dangerous. In May 1915 one of them torpedoed the British liner *Lusitania,* with the loss of more than a thousand lives, including about a hundred Americans. In the still neutral United States public opinion was outraged. In January 1917 the Germans announced unrestricted submarine warfare. They knew that sinking neutral ships carrying nonmilitary cargoes to the Allies might bring the United States into the war. But they hoped they would sink so many vital cargoes of food and raw materials that Britain would be starved into surrender before America could mobilize.*

Indeed, by the time the United States declared war (April 6, 1917), submarine action had reduced British food reserves to barely one month's supply. Counterattack by depth charges, antisubmarine patrols, and the system of convoying merchant ships with armed escorts were developed only at the eleventh hour. But soon the Allies turned the weapon of blockade against Germany. As time went on the Germans suffered increasingly from malnutrition.

On the home front, all the governments eventually imposed censorship, introduced the draft, set priorities in industry, and rationed scarce commodities. Britain began these measures in 1916, when the dynamic Lloyd George became prime minister. France achieved tight homefront organization only late in 1917, under George Clemenceau as premier.

Despite the German reputation for technical superiority, the German home front was never effectively organized. A better system of rationing would have reduced malnutrition. By 1918 the Allies were winning the battle of production. In Germany the home front was ready to collapse under any unusual pressure from the battlefields.

Decision on the Western Front

In an effort to break the deadlock in the West, both sides had long tried airplanes, useful in spotting targets for artillery and also in scouting against submarines, but not yet effective bombers or fighters. The Germans also used lighter-than-air craft, the Zeppelins, which dropped some bombs on London but not enough to cause serious damage. On the ground the Germans tried poison gas, but learned that a shift in the wind might blow the gas back on their own troops. The Allies had the protection of gas masks and retaliated. The British almost won with the first tanks, a pet project of Winston Churchill. But they went into action prematurely in 1916 when the Allies did not have enough of them.

The weapons of trench warfare were the repeating rifle, the machine gun, and fast-firing artillery. All were accurate and deadly, mowing down hundreds of thousands of victims. In 1916

the Germans lost 350,000 men in a vain attempt to capture Verdun, the fortress at the eastern end of the French line, and the French lost the same number in defending it. In the same year the British lost over 50,000 men in a single day.

Armies could not indefinitely endure such appalling casualties. In April and May of 1917, French soldiers mutinied and were savagely put down, the innocent being shot with the guilty. The entry of the United States in April 1917 helped revive the morale of the Allies who were facing the withdrawal of revolution-torn Russia from the war.

The end finally came in the West. A last desperate German offensive was checked in the Second Battle of the Marne during the summer of 1918. The French, British, and Americans counterattacked, laying down a massive artillery barrage and using tanks in the actual assault. The exhausted German soldiers, needing supplies and reinforcements which the demoralized home front could no longer furnish, gave ground.

Facing certain defeat in the field and a rapidly mounting threat of revolution at home, the German government requested an armistice. It was signed on November 11, 1918. By then William II had abdicated, and a republic had been proclaimed. Germany was in the throes of revolution.

IV THE POSTWAR SETTLEMENTS

A World in Turmoil

The German revolution was only one of many disturbances that swept the world after the Armistice and deeply influenced the diplomats who assembled at Paris in January 1919 to make the peace. Bolshevism, already in control in Russia, was an acute issue. The Allies landed detachments at Archangel and Vladivostok to help the anti-Bolshevik "whites" in civil war against the "reds" (see Chapter 17).

Communist uprisings occurred in Germany during the winter of 1918–1919. In Bavaria a Soviet republic was proclaimed in April 1919. In Hungary a communist dictatorship was established in the spring of 1919 under Bela Kun, who had worked with Lenin in Russia. All of these proved to be short-lived, but the peacemakers did not know this in advance.

---

* American public opinion was further aroused by the State Department publication on March 1, 1917, of the "Zimmermann telegram," an intercepted message showing that the German government was encouraging the Mexican government to attack the United States.

In the Middle East, Zionists, Arabs, British, and French were at odds over the future of Palestine and other portions of the defeated Ottoman Empire. The Greeks, dreaming of a restored Byzantium, landed at Izmir (Smyrna) on the coast of Asia Minor and marched inland, touching off a fierce and eventually successful Turkish resistance.

In India, nationalists organized a campaign of disorder to win greater autonomy from Britain. As strikes and riots mounted, a British general ordered his troops to fire on an unarmed mob crowded in a small enclosure at Amritsar. Sixteen hundred people were killed or wounded (April 1919). Liberal opinion throughout the world shared the Indian feeling of outrage. As Russia struggled in civil war, Japan renewed her old aggression against northern China. The American troops sent to Vladivostok went less to oppose the Bolsheviks than to watch the Japanese.

The Fourteen Points —and Other Points of View

The world was in turmoil. Obviously the peacemakers could not satisfy everyone. Yet idealists everywhere expected that they would do so. Large sections of public opinion regarded the war as a "war to end war," a "war to make the world safe for democracy." These idealists found

One of the last photographs of President Wilson.

their spokesman in President Woodrow Wilson and their program in his Fourteen Points, advanced in an address to Congress, on January 8, 1918.

Some of the Fourteen Points dealt with specific issues: Belgium "must be evacuated and restored" (Point VII), Alsace-Lorraine returned to France (Point VIII), and the frontiers of Italy readjusted "along clearly recognizable lines of nationality" (Point IX). Wilson favored national self-determination, promising the minority peoples of Austria-Hungary and the Ottoman Empire "the freest opportunity of autonomous development" (Points X and XII). There was to be an independent Polish state once more, enjoying "free and secure access to the sea" (Point XIII).

The Fourteen Points also contained Wilson's diagnosis of the underlying causes of the war and his prescription for dealing with them. Point I condemned by implication the old secret diplomacy of the Triple Alliance and Triple Entente. It demanded "Open covenants of peace, openly arrived at" and declared that "diplomacy shall proceed always frankly and in the public view." Point III urged the "removal of all economic barriers" among nations, and Point IV recommended that armaments be reduced to the lowest amount "consistent with domestic safety." In Point XIV, finally, Wilson mentioned his favorite project, the League of Nations:

> A general association of nations must be formed for the purpose of affording mutual guarantees of political independence and territorial integrity to great and small states alike.*

Wilsonian idealism, however, had to contend with an array of violent emotions: the wild nationalism of minorities freed from alien rule, fierce anti-German feeling, selfish opportunism. The Allies had allowed both Arabs and Jews to believe that Palestine would be theirs, both Italians and South Slavs to believe that they could get Dalmatia. Allied propaganda, widely believed by the British and French peoples, had promised that Germany would be made to suffer for her war guilt and be made incapable of future aggression. Above all—and this was a favorite British theme—Germany must pay for the war through payments called *reparations.* Many Frenchmen wanted reparations and also the restoration of French leadership in Europe. Many Americans

---

* Woodrow Wilson, *War and Peace: Presidential Messages, Addresses, and Public Papers,* ed. R. S. Baker and W. E. Dodd (New York, 1927), I: 159–61.

were determined to withdraw from the corruption of the Old World and return to the purity and isolation of the New.

The Process of Peacemaking

The peacemakers of 1919 met in the suburbs of Paris—at Versailles to settle with the Germans, at St. Germain to settle with the Austrians, at the Grand Trianon (in the park of Versailles) with the Hungarians, at Neuilly with the Bulgarians, and at Sèvres with the Turks. The separate treaties are usually bracketed together as the Versailles or Paris settlement. Nearly thirty nations sent delegates to the conference, but neither the Russians nor the Central Powers were represented. The principal Allied powers were in no mood to invite the Bolsheviks, and they simply told the defeated states to sign the finished treaties. The Germans, in particular, resented the re-

fusal of the Allies to negotiate terms with them and were soon referring to the *Diktat*—the dictated peace—of Versailles.

Idealists hoped that the enthusiastic welcome given to Wilson in Europe would make possible a peace conference operating according to his principle of "open covenants openly arrived at." They expected a kind of international town meeting that would reach decisions by majority vote after discussion by all the delegates. The conference, however, soon fell into the pattern of traditional diplomacy, very like the Vienna Congress of 1815.

The "Big Three"—Clemenceau, Lloyd George, and Wilson—did most of the negotiating and deciding, irritating not only the small and middle-sized nations, but also their own technical staffs. These bright young experts in economics, history, and political science expected their recommendations to be followed. When their chiefs

Paris, December 1918. Seated, from left to right: Orlando, Lloyd George, Clemenceau, and Wilson.

failed to take their advice, they spoke out angrily and helped discredit the conference among liberal intellectuals.

The settlement of 1919 represented a series of compromises between the Wilsonian idealism and the material demands of the powers. In resolving territorial issues, the peacemakers had to balance the claims of the victors and allow for the land hunger of the new nations arising from the disintegrating Hapsburg, Russian, and Ottoman empires. And they had to do this without violating too obviously the Wilsonian principle of national self-determination, which could not be practically applied in Central and Eastern Europe. The diplomats tried, however, and in so doing created new nation-states with new discontented minorities.

Territorial Changes

Austria-Hungary was totally dismembered. The heart of its German-speaking area became the small republic of Austria, which was forbidden to unite with Germany. The heart of the

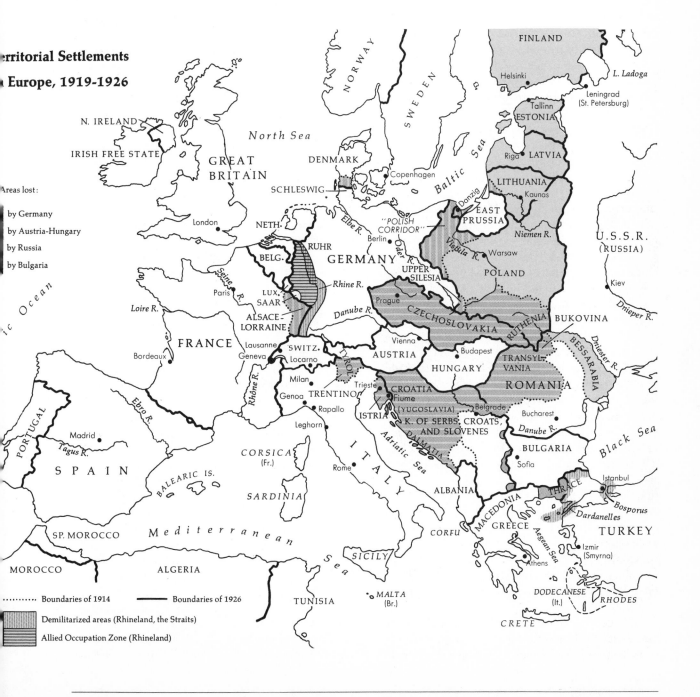

Territorial Settlements in Europe, 1919-1926

Magyar-speaking area became the small kingdom of Hungary. The Czech lands of Bohemia and Moravia, formerly ruled by Austria, were joined with Slovakia, formerly ruled by Hungary, in the republic of Czechoslovakia. This included a large and potentially troublesome minority of "Sudeten" Germans and another of Ruthenians (Ukrainians).

The south Slav lands of both Austria and Hungary joined Serbia to become the "Kingdom of the Serbs, Croats, and Slovenes," later Yugoslavia. Romania obtained Transylvania, formerly Hungarian, and Bessarabia, a province of tsarist Russia, thereby doubling its territory. New republics of Estonia, Latvia, and Lithuania were created from Russian Baltic lands taken by Germany at Brest-Litovsk.

A new independent Poland included all the lands that Prussia, Austria, and Russia had grabbed in the eighteenth-century partitions. Access to the sea was secured through the "Polish Corridor," a narrow strip of land that separated East Prussia from the rest of Germany and ended on the Baltic at the wholly German city of Danzig, which the Allies made a Free City. Germans traveling to and from East Prussia had to cross the corridor in sealed trains. The new Poland contained important minorities of non-Polish peoples—Germans, Ukrainians, and Jews.

Italy received Trieste and the Trentino, including sizable Slavic and German-speaking minorities, and eventually in 1924 also got the former Hungarian Adriatic port of Fiume. The Allies, however, reneged on an earlier promise to Italy and gave Dalmatia to the new Yugoslav state, thus poisoning Italo-Yugoslav relations.

France recovered Alsace-Lorraine. In addition, Clemenceau wanted the Saar Basin of Germany, rich in coal, to compensate for French coal mines destroyed by the Germans during the war. He also wanted to detach from Germany all lands on the left (west) bank of the Rhine and set up a Rhineland republic that would become a French satellite. British and American opposition obliged the French to settle for a fraction of what they wanted. The Saar was separated from Germany as a ward of the League of Nations for fifteen years, when a plebiscite would determine its future status. Meantime, its coal output was to go to France. The Rhineland remained part of Germany, though demilitarized and subject to Allied occupation.

Greece received eastern Thrace, the only European territory remaining to Turkey aside from Istanbul. The Greeks were also allowed to occupy for at least five years the territories they had invaded around Izmir in western Anatolia. But before the treaty could go into effect a group of Turkish army officers led by Mustafa Kemal revolted against the government in Istanbul and galvanized the Turkish people into a new national life. Kemal's forces drove out the Greek invaders and set up a Turkish republic with its capital at Ankara in the heart of Anatolia. In 1923, by the Treaty of Lausanne, Kemal recovered both eastern Thrace and the area of Izmir. All Orthodox Christians in Turkey were to be exchanged for Muslims in Greek territory. More than two million people were later exchanged.

The Arab lands of the Ottoman Empire and the former German colonies were distributed as "mandates." The League of Nations awarded each to a mandatory power to prepare the population for self-government and eventual independence. Britain obtained the mandates for Palestine, Transjordan, and Mesopotamia (Iraq). France got those for Syria and Lebanon. German East Africa (Tanganyika) went to Britain. South-West Africa went to the Union of South Africa. Cameroon and Togo were divided between Britain and France. In the Pacific, Australia got the mandate for the German portions of New Guinea, and Japan that for most of the other German islands. Japan treated its mandates as a device for annexation, illegally fortifying the Pacific islands. Otherwise the mandatory powers did the job assigned to them.

The Punishment of Germany

The settlement required Germany to hand over many of her merchant ships to the Allies and to make large deliveries of coal to France, Italy, and Belgium over a ten-year period. The Germans also had to promise reparation for all the damage done to Allied civilian property during the war. The annual payment was to be $5 billion, a huge sum in those days, until a final total could be agreed upon. This total obviously would be so great that Germany could pay it only in goods. This in turn depended on the prosperity of German industry which a weak and divided country could not achieve.

The Versailles Treaty limited the German army to 100,000 men. The western frontier zone, extending to a line fifty kilometers east of the Rhine, was to contain neither fortifications nor soldiers. The Allies could keep armies of occupation on the left bank of the Rhine for fifteen years. Germany was forbidden to have either submarines or military planes and was severely limited with respect to surface warships. Finally, by Article 231 of the Treaty of Versailles Germany accepted

> the responsibility for causing all the loss and damage to which the Allied and Associated Governments and their nationals have been subjected as a consequence of the war imposed upon them by the aggression of Germany and her allies.

This was the "war guilt" clause.

The Settlement in Retrospect

The Treaty of Versailles also incorporated Wilson's blueprint for a better world, the covenant of the League of Nations. The capital of the League was to be the Swiss city of Geneva. A permanent secretariat administered it. It also had an assembly in which each member state had one vote, and a council which had permanent seats for the "Big Five" (Britain, France, Italy, Japan, and the United States) and four seats to be occupied in rotation by lesser powers. The way was left open for Russia and Germany to join, and they later did. But the League failed to promote disarmament or to prevent and punish aggression.

Liberals and idealists found the whole peace settlement deeply disappointing. To the Germans it supplied a chronic national grievance that Hitler would play upon. Yet, compared to the German-dictated Treaty of Brest-Litovsk, the Treaty of Versailles was generous. Like the Utrecht and Vienna settlements before it, it had both merits and faults.

It had the merit of recognizing that the long-frustrated nationalities of Central and Eastern Eu-rope must secure satisfaction, even though this meant the "balkanization of Europe" by the creation of more small, competing political units. One of its faults was surely that it humiliated Germany but allowed Germany to remain a first-class power.

Some argue that the trouble with the 1919 settlement lay in the failure of the powers to enforce it. The United States rejected the settlement, largely as a result of the antagonism between a Republican Congress and an inflexible Democratic president. Isolationist sentiment and postwar disillusionment were also involved. In the elections of 1918 the Republicans won control of both House and Senate. But Wilson did not take a bipartisan delegation to Paris with him in 1919. He rejected modifications in the Versailles Treaty that might have met some Republican objections. So the Senate refused to ratify the treaty or to authorize American participation in the League of Nations. It also refused to approve a defensive alliance of France, Britain, and the United States that Wilson reluctantly agreed to as part of the price for France's giving up annexation of the Saar and establishing a Rhineland republic.

When Britain also withdrew from the alliance project, France created a system of alliances with the states on the eastern side of Germany: Poland, Czechoslovakia, Yugoslavia, and Romania. The British at first worried that the French were going to dominate the Continent. But in fact the war had weakened the French too greatly for that. The world of peace settlements was not the brave new world for which the idealists had hoped. Instead it was very like the bad old world that had fought the war. And within a decade it faced new threats that it did not yet understand.

READING SUGGESTIONS on Prelude, Theme, and Coda: 1870–1919 (Asterisks indicate paperback.)

General Works

A. J. P. Taylor, *The Struggle for Mastery in Europe, 1848–1918* (1954). A detailed, useful survey.

L. C. B. Seaman, *From Vienna to Versailles* (*Colophon). A brief sketch, the latter portion of which deals with the period of this chapter.

C. J. H. Hayes, *A Generation of Materialism, 1871–1900;* and O. Hale, *The Great Illusion, 1900–1914* (*Harper Torch-books). Two consecutive volumes in The Rise of Modern Europe series that cover the years to the outbreak of World War I.

Barbara Tuchman, *The Proud Tower* and *The Guns of August* (*Bantam). Well-

W. L. Langer, *European Alliances and Alignments, 1871–1890* (*Knopf), and *The Diplomacy of Imperialism, 1890–* written popular volumes dealing with Europe on the eve of World War I and on the war itself. Good reading, but not always reliable as scholarship.

1902 (*Knopf). Comprehensive and masterly accounts of international diplomacy.

Britain

R. C. K. Ensor, *England, 1870–1914* (Clarendon, 1936). A comprehensive survey in The Oxford History of England.

C. Cross, *The Liberals in Power, 1905–1914* (1964); M. Bruce, *The Coming of the Welfare State* (1961); R. E. Barry, *Nationalism in British Politics* (1965). Useful studies of the great changes after 1870.

P. Magnus, *Gladstone* (*Dutton); R. Blake, *Disraeli* (*Anchor); R. Jenkins, *Asquith* (*Dutton); and M. Gilbert, ed., *Lloyd George* (*Prentice-Hall). Valuable biographical accounts of the major leaders of the period.

F. S. L. Lyons, *Ireland since the Famine* (*Fontana). A splendid detailed study.

France

D. W. Brogan, *The Development of Modern France,* 2 vols. (*Harper Torchbooks). Detailed and remarkable for its wit; not for beginners.

D. Thomson, *Democracy in France since 1870* (*Oxford). A brilliant study, brief and suggestive.

T. Zeldin, *France, 1848–1945,* 2 vols. (1973, 1976). Highly original and controversial recent work that breaks new ground.

R. L. Williams, *The French Revolution of 1870–1871* (1969). The Franco-Prussian War and the uprising culminating in the Commune. Very good.

G. Chapman, *The Dreyfus Case: A Reassessment* (1955); and G. Johnson, *France and the Dreyfus Case* (1966). Two scholarly treatments.

E. Weber, *Peasants into Frenchmen* (1976). A fine and original study of social change in the period before 1914.

Italy

C. Seton-Watson, *Italy from Liberalism to Fascism, 1870–1925* (1967). A detailed scholarly study.

D. Mack Smith, *Italy: A Modern History* (1959). Emphasizes the recent period.

D. Beales, *The Risorgimento and the Unification of Italy* (1971). A reliable account.

Germany

E. J. Passant, *A Short History of Germany, 1815–1945* (*Cambridge); K. Pinson, *Modern Germany: Its History and Civilization* (1954). Sound textbooks.

A. Rosenberg, *Imperial Germany* (*Beacon). A shorter account that emphasizes the period of William II.

A. J. P. Taylor, *The Course of German History* (*Capricorn); and *Bismarck: The Man and the Statesman* (*Vintage). Two lively works with anti-German overtones that are nonetheless hard to dispute.

F. Meinecke, *The German Catastrophe* (*Beacon). A thoughtful analysis by a distinguished German historian. An antidote to Taylor's work.

T. Veblen, *Imperial Germany and the Industrial Revolution* (*Ann Arbor). A very old book but a brilliant one, by a noted American sociologist.

The Hapsburg Monarchy

R. A. Kann, *The Multinational Empire,* 2 vols. (1950). The most authoritative and detailed study in English, treating each nationality separately.

A. J. May, *The Hapsburg Monarchy, 1867–1914* (*Norton). A shorter but more pedestrian general study.

A. J. P. Taylor, *The Habsburg Monarchy, 1809–1918* (*Harper Torchbooks). Lively and biased, as usual with Taylor's work.

O. Jászi, *The Dissolution of the Habsburg Monarchy* (1929). An old but still valuable study viewed from the standpoint of a liberal Magyar.

R. W. Seton-Watson, *German, Slav, and Magyar* (1916). By the leading English scholar of Eastern Europe of the generation of World War I.

C. E. Schorske, *Fin de Siècle Vienna* (1980). A new and brilliant original cultural study of the architecture, music, painting, literature, politics, and psychology of the imperial capital in the period immediately before the Old World blew up. Difficult, but rewarding.

Russia

H. Seton-Watson, *The Decline of Imperial Russia, 1855–1914* (*Praeger). A valuable and solid study of almost the entire period dealt with in this chapter.

N. Riasanovsky, *Nicholas I and Official Nationality in Russia, 1825–1855* (*California). A good monograph of the ideology of this important reign.

B. Pares, *The Fall of the Russian Monarchy* (*Vintage). An excellent account of the period between 1905 and 1917 by an English scholar who was in Russia during much of the time.

G. T. Robinson, *Rural Russia under the Old Regime* (*California). A classic study of the peasant problem.

Martin Malia, *Alexander Herzen and the Birth of Russian Socialism* (*Universal Library). Sets one of the most important Russian thinkers in his proper place in European thought.

J. Joll, *The Anarchists* (*Universal Library). Includes good chapters on Bakunin and Kropotkin.

B. D. Wolfe, *Three Who Made a Revolution* (*Beacon). A triple study of Lenin, Trotsky, and Stalin, chiefly in the period before 1914.

I. Deutscher, *The Prophet Armed: Trotsky, 1879–1921* (*Vintage). The first volume of a three-volume biography of Trotsky by a learned sympathizer.

The World Overseas

R. Koebner and H. D. Schmitt, *Imperialism: The Story and Significance of a Political Word* (*Cambridge). An important study covering the period 1840–1900.

D. K. Fieldhouse, *The Colonial Empires* (*Dell). A solid survey from the eighteenth century onward.

A. P. Thornton, *Doctrines of Imperialism* (*Wiley). The ideas of the imperialists.

J. A. Schumpeter, *Imperialism and Social Classes* (*Macmillan). By a famous economist; not for beginners.

Lenin, *Imperialism: The Highest Stage of Capitalism* (*International). The Bolshevik leader's theories on the subject.

T. Geiger, *The Conflicted Relationship* (*McGraw-Hill). Deals with the impact of the West upon Asia, Africa, and Latin America.

C. E. Carrington, *The British Overseas: Exploits of a Nation of Shopkeepers* (*Cambridge). A detailed, favorable account.

M. Beloff, *Imperial Sunset: Vol I, Britain's Liberal Empire, 1897–1921* (1970). Reliable study.

H. Brunschwig, *French Colonialism: Myths and Realities, 1871–1914* (1966). An informative work by a Frenchman.

M. E. Townsend, *The Rise and Fall of Germany's Colonial Empire* (1930). Still the standard general account; see also W. O. Henderson, *Studies in German Colonial History* (1963).

J. W. Pratt, *America's Colonial Experiment* (1950). A valuable survey.

E. Robinson, and J. Gallagher, *Africa and the Victorians* (*Anchor). Useful.

R. R. Betts, *The Scramble for Africa* (*Heath). A collection of opinions on the international race for colonies.

J. Duffy, *Portugal in Africa* (*Penguin); H. R. Rudin, *Germans in the Cameroons, 1884–1914* (1938). Good special studies.

K. S. Latourette, *China* (*Prentice-Hall). A good introduction by a noted authority.

E. O. Reischauer, *Japan, Past and Present* (*Knopf). A brief introduction by the leading American expert.

The First World War and the Postwar Settlements

L. Lafore, *The Long Fuse* (*Preceptor). A good summary of the varying causes of the war.

S. B. Fay, *Origins of the World War,* 2 vols. (*Free Press); B. Schmitt, *The Coming of the War,* 2 vols. (1930). Two older studies with highly divergent emphases.

E. R. May, *The World War and American Isolation, 1914–1917* (*Quadrangle), and *The Coming of War, 1917* (1967). How did we get in? Two balanced and reliable treatments.

C. Falls, *The Great War* (*Capricorn); H. Baldwin, *World War I* (*Evergreen); and B. H. Liddell Hart, *The Real War, 1914–1918* (*Little, Brown). Three useful, short, complete treatments.

R. M. Watt, *Dare Call It Treason* (*Simon and Schuster); A Morehead, *Gallipoli* (1956); and A. Horne, *The Price of Glory: Verdun, 1916* (*Colophon). Three more specialized studies.

H. Nicolson, *Peacemaking, 1919* (*Universal Library). A good short work by a British diplomat and politician.

T. A. Bailey, *Woodrow Wilson and the Lost Peace* and *Woodrow Wilson and the Great Betrayal* (*Quadrangle). What went sour in Paris and in Washington after the war.

J. M. Keynes, *The Economic Consequences of the Peace* (*Harper Torchbooks). The most famous of the attacks on the peace settlement by an influential economist; should be read with E. Mantoux, *The Carthaginian Peace, or the Economic Consequences of Mr. Keynes* (*Pittsburgh), which emphasizes the harm that Keynes's attack did.

CHAPTER SEVENTEEN

Interlude And Repetition:
The Years
Between The Wars
And World War II

In this chapter we deal with the period between the end of World War I and the end of
World War II. For Russia, this began with the
Revolution of 1917. We begin with a description
and analysis of the Revolution and a discussion
of the ensuing communist regime, through its
own period of civil war, New Economic Policy,
and Stalin's dictatorship in domestic and foreign
affairs down to the Hitler-Stalin Pact of August
1939.

Next, we move to a discussion of fascism,
triumphing in postwar Italy in 1921. We consider
Mussolini as a political theorist and fascist boss
and trace his regime down to the moment when
war was imminent. Post-World War I Germany
passed through some fourteen years of the Weimar Republic before it too went fascist. We examine the political and economic troubles of the
Republic and analyze the rise to supreme power
of Hitler and the Nazis. Then we consider the
six turbulent years of Nazi rule in Germany
(1933–1939), until in 1939 Hitler precipitated the
Second World War.

Third, we turn to the victorious Allies of

World War I, and discuss the troubled interlude between the wars from the points of view of Britain, France, the United States, Japan, China, India, and the Middle East. And finally, having reached the fateful year 1939 and the outbreak of World War II itself, we begin by retracing international efforts to keep the peace and their failure, and close by reviewing the complex history of the war itself on its many fronts until 1945, when Hitler, Mussolini, and the Japanese had been defeated by America, Britain, and the U.S.S.R.

I COMMUNIST RUSSIA, 1917–1941

In 1917 Russia was a backward agricultural country with a tiny urban proletariat. Marx would have said revolution was impossible there. Yet Russia had the first successful Marxist revolution. Why?

Marx underestimated the revolutionary force latent in the Russian peasantry and lacked the imagination to conceive such a brilliant, ruthless, and lucky tactician as Lenin. Also, the Russian Revolution was not wholly Marxist. It temporarily retreated into a kind of capitalism. Then it produced Stalin, a brutal dictator in whose rule nationalism and lust for personal power was more important than Marxism. At untold expense in human lives, Stalin's programs created the U.S.S.R., an industrial state fed by a collectivized agriculture. With much outside assistance, the U.S.S.R. eventually repelled the savage attack that came from Adolf Hitler's Germany in June 1941.

The March Revolution and the Provisional Government

In World War I Russia suffered almost four million casualties in the first year alone. Munitions manufacture and supply were inefficient. After 1915 the tsar was at the front and the Duma not in session. So the empress and her favorite, Rasputin, controlled the government. Adventurers and profiteers speculated in commissions, draft deferments, and commodities.

Conservative patriots denounced the scandals, and in December 1916 they murdered Rasputin. Strikes and defeatism spread, while the armies bled to death at the front. The tsar re-mained apathetic and refused all appeals to create a responsible ministry to clean up the mess.

Between March 8 and 12, 1917, a "leaderless, spontaneous, and anonymous revolution" took place in Petrograd (the new Russian name given to the capital city of St. Petersburg during the war). The troops of the Petrograd garrison refused to fire on striking workers, and joined the strikers. A soviet (council) of workers and soldiers with a fifteen-man executive committee took over the revolution, installed itself across the hall from the Duma, which was now in session, and asked that the Duma temporarily run the country.

In consultation, Duma and Soviet created a "provisional government," composed mainly of Kadets (Constitutional Democrats; see Chapter 16), headed by a liberal, Prince Lvov. A prominent member was Alexander Kerensky, a radical labor lawyer and member of both Soviet and Duma. Nicholas II abdicated and was arrested.

Between March and November 1917, the provisional government struggled against enormous difficulties. Its members had no experience in government. They felt that they must continue the war and simultaneously democratize the huge, unwieldy Russian Empire. The Soviet had the instruments of power, but would accept no responsibility.

The provisional government could not suppress its opponents. In the provinces, local peasant-elected soviets sprang up. The peasants wanted land immediately. But the provisional government believed in legality and refused to approve peasant seizures of land. Russians wanted peace, but the provisional government continued the war. While waiting for a constituent assembly to be elected to give Russia a new constitution, the provisional government granted complete political liberty.

Lenin and the November Revolution

Bolsheviks and other exiles began to return to Russia and to political life. The German general staff thought that the return of Lenin from Switzerland would help disrupt the Russian war effort; so they permitted him to travel across Germany to the Baltic in a sealed railway car (April 16, 1917). Most Social Democrats believed that a bourgeois parliamentary republic would have to precede a socialist revolution, but Lenin favored an alliance between workers and peasants in an immediate social revolution from which the Bolsheviks would eventually emerge supreme.

Lenin regarded himself as chief of the elite inner group of the Bolshevik party, which in turn would command the working class. The brilliant intellectual Leon Trotsky, who understood Lenin's dictatorial tendencies, believed that the working class could seize power without waiting for the establishment of a bourgeois republic.

Lenin now returned to Russia and called for the immediate seizure of power by the soviets, much to the surprise of all but a very few of the SDs. Demanding the immediate confiscation of estates and an immediate end to the war, he echoed the popular cries for land and peace. The army, the police, all government officials must go, and a republic of soviets must rise. Lenin galvanized the Bolsheviks into a truly revolutionary group that was waiting only for the moment to seize power.

When an offensive on the front collapsed in July, and some troops rioted in the capital, Kerensky became premier. General Kornilov, commander in chief of the army, rallied conservative support for a coup to disperse the Soviet. But railroad and telegraph workers sabotaged his movements, and his troops would not obey him. By September 14, Kornilov had been arrested. The only result of his efforts was increased pro-Bolshevik sentiment. The army mutiny got out of hand and peasant disorders mounted.

Late in October, the Bolsheviks seized control of a military revolutionary committee originally chosen to defend the capital against the Germans but now transformed by Trotsky into a general staff for the revolution. On November 7, with little bloodshed, the Bolsheviks took over Petrograd. Adopting the program of the SRs (So-

The first mobilization of Moscow workers in the spring of 1918.

Russian peasants carrying banners bearing Stalin's 1929 slogan "Liquidation of the kulaks as a class."

cial Revolutionaries), Lenin abolished landlords' property rights, proposed an immediate peace, and set up the Council of People's Commissars with himself as president.

Trotsky was foreign commissar. A young Georgian named Joseph Djugashvili, who called himself Stalin, became commissar of nationalities. With varying speed, as most provincial garrisons helped them, the Bolsheviks seized power in Moscow and in most of the provinces. Georgia, however, went Menshevik. Kornilov and some Duma politicians took refuge in Rostov-on-Don in southern Russia.

The Russian people were not pro-Bolshevik. When Lenin permitted elections for a constituent assembly, the first and last free elections in Russian history, the Bolsheviks polled only about 25 percent of the vote. The other socialist parties, chiefly the SRs, polled 62 percent. Lenin permitted the new assembly to meet only once (January 18, 1918). He dissolved it the next day by decree, and sent guards with rifles to disperse it.

Thus Lenin nullified the popular will. Russia did not have the high literacy rate, the tradition of debate, the respect for individual rights, or the large middle class usually associated with successful constitutional government. But it was Lenin's arbitrary use of force that ended the chance for true parliamentarism in Russia.

Civil War and Foreign Intervention, 1917–1921

For the next three years, to the end of 1920, civil war raged in Russia, while foreign powers intervened to assist the enemies of the Bolsheviks, who changed their name to Communists and in 1918 shifted the capital to Moscow. At first the Communists believed that world revolution would soon begin in Germany and then engulf other nations; so they regarded foreign affairs as unimportant.

By 1920, they completed the nationalization of all banks and all industrial enterprises employing more than ten workers. They requisitioned

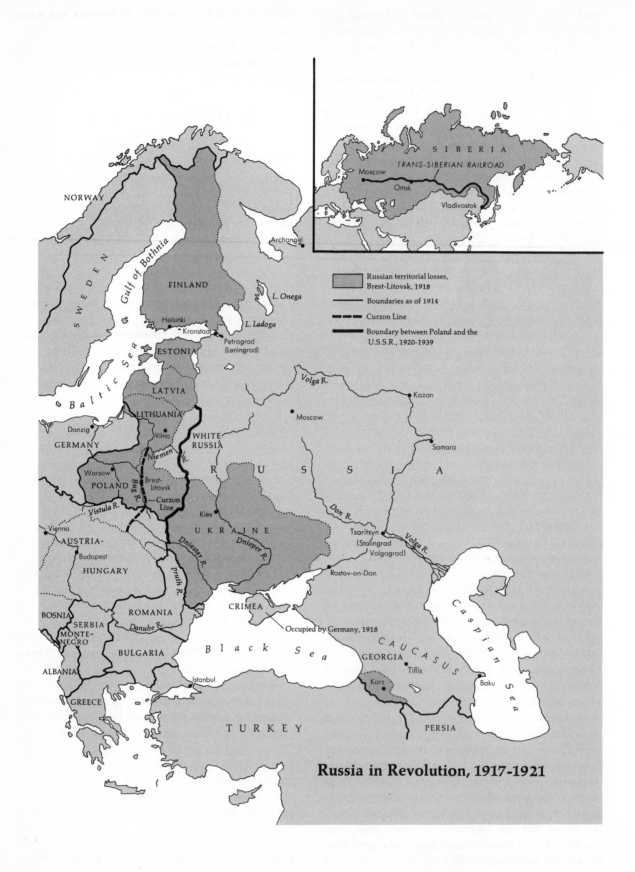

Russia in Revolution, 1917-1921

Legend:
- Russian territorial losses, Brest-Litovsk, 1918
- Boundaries as of 1914
- Curzon Line
- Boundary between Poland and the U.S.S.R., 1920-1939

SIBERIA
TRANS-SIBERIAN RAILROAD
Moscow
Omsk
Vladivostok

NORWAY

SWEDEN

Gulf of Bothnia

FINLAND

Archangel

L. Onega

Helsinki

L. Ladoga

Kronstadt

Petrograd (Leningrad)

ESTONIA

Baltic Sea

LATVIA

LITHUANIA

Volga R.

Kazan

Danzig

Vilna

Moscow

GERMANY

Niemen R.

WHITE RUSSIA

Samara

Warsaw

Bug R.

Brest-Litovsk

R U S S I A

POLAND

Curzon Line

Vistula R.

Kiev

Don R.

Vienna

Dniester R.

UKRAINE

Dnieper R.

Tsaritsyn (Stalingrad Volgograd)

Volga R.

AUSTRIA-HUNGARY

Budapest

Pruth R.

Rostov-on-Don

Caspian Sea

BOSNIA

ROMANIA

CRIMEA

Occupied by Germany, 1918

SERBIA

Danube R.

C A U C A S U S

MONTE-NEGRO

BULGARIA

B l a c k   S e a

GEORGIA

ALBANIA

Istanbul

Tiflis

Kars

Baku

GREECE

T U R K E Y

PERSIA

food from the peasants. They mobilized the poorer peasants against the richer (*kulak,* meaning "fist," and implying hard-fisted usuriousness). They set up a secret police (the *Cheka,* from the initials of the words meaning "extraordinary commission"). Early in 1918, they signed the Treaty of Brest-Litovsk with Germany giving away a third of Russia's population, 80 percent of its iron, and 90 percent of its coal.

The civil war started when a brigade of Czech soldiers, mostly deserters from the Hapsburg armies, was sent east across Siberia by rail so that they could proceed by ship to the western front. The Czechs quarreled with Hungarian prisoners on a Siberian railway siding. When the Soviet regime tried to punish them for killing a Hungarian, they seized some towns in western Siberia. The local SRs were sympathetic to them, and local anti-Bolshevik armies sprang up. Under threat from one of them in July 1918, a local soviet decided to execute the tsar and his entire family rather than lose possession of them. All were murdered.

British, French, Japanese, and American forces landed in Vladivostok in August 1918, after the Czechs had overthrown the local soviet. British and Americans also landed at Archangel. In Siberia there were three different anticommunist governments of varying complexions.

Trotsky took the lead in organizing a Red Army, three million strong by 1920. When the German western front collapsed, the Soviet government repudiated the Brest-Litovsk treaty, and the Reds moved back into part of the Ukraine. After severe fighting, the Red Army defeated its three main "White" enemies: General Denikin moving north from Rostov and the Caucasus, Admiral Kolchak operating from Omsk in Siberia, and General Yudenich in the Baltic region.

In 1920 the Poles drove the Reds from Warsaw with the help of the French chief of staff, General Weygand. At the peace in October 1920, Poland obtained a large area of the Ukraine and White Russia.

The Reds won the civil war in part because the Whites could not unite on a political program beyond the mere overthrow of the Reds. The White forces were located on the outer edge of the huge Russian territory, whereas the Reds had internal lines of communication, greater manpower, and more of the weapons inherited from the tsarist armies. The Whites never gained the support of the peasantry. Indeed they often restored the landlords.

Allied intervention on the White side was ineffectual and amateurish. It enabled the Reds to pose as defenders of the nation against foreign invaders. It may at least have prevented the Reds from sponsoring successful revolutions in other countries.

The NEP, 1921–1928

By the end of the civil war, all vital services had broken down in Russia. Famine was raging. Agricultural and industrial output had fallen disastrously. Anarchist revolts broke out, notably at the naval base of Kronstadt (March 1921), and were suppressed with much bloodshed. But they frightened Lenin into a change of policy.

The "New Economic Policy" (always called NEP), adopted in 1921 and lasting until 1928, marked a temporary retreat from communist programs. Its chief aim was reconstruction. At home the communists appeased the peasants. Abroad, since there had been no world revolution, they sought the resources of capitalist states. The government no longer seized the whole of a peasant's crop above the minimum necessary to keep him alive. He paid a very heavy tax in kind, but could sell his crop to a private purchaser if he wished. Peasant agriculture became capitalist again. The kulaks grew richer, while poor peasants often lost their land and hired out their labor.

The state controlled heavy industry, banking, transportation, and foreign trade—what Lenin called the "commanding heights"—but allowed private enterprise in domestic trade and light industry. The partial return to capitalism brought economic recovery by 1926–1927.

Many leading communists hated NEP. Government officials often subjected businessmen or farmers to petty persecution. Those who wanted to abolish NEP, wipe out those who profited by it, and advance world revolution were called "Left deviationists." They included Trotsky. Those who wanted to push the NEP program still further were the "Right deviationists." Their chief spokesman was Nikolai Bukharin. The question agitated the communist leaders, especially during and after Lenin's last illness (1922–1924).

Stalin's Rise to Power

The two leading contenders to succeed Lenin were Trotsky and Stalin. Toward the end of his life Lenin himself urged that Stalin be deprived of power. It was only Lenin's death that saved Stalin's career. To defeat Trotsky, Stalin first allied himself with Bukharin and argued for

Lenin and Stalin in 1923.

a kind of gradualism: peasant cooperatives but not collectives, no forced industrialization program, limited cooperation with capitalist states. Once he had deprived Trotsky of influence, Stalin adopted many of his ideas.

Stalin, finding that agricultural production was not keeping pace with industry, came out in 1927 for collectivization. He favored rapid industrialization, which he knew required huge investments of capital. Trotsky argued that socialism in a single country could not succeed until world revolution brought communism to the industrial nations, making their skills available to the cause. Stalin maintained that "socialism in one country"—Russia—could succeed. His argument reflected his own Russian nationalism as well as his bid for popularity with the rank and file.

Stalin's victory, however, had less to do with the merits of the rival theories than with his personal power. As commissar of nationalities he managed the destiny of almost half the population of the new Russian Soviet Republic and of all the Asians in the "republics" that he created. In 1922 he sponsored the formation of the U.S.S.R. (Union of Socialist Soviet Republics). Moscow firmly controlled war, foreign policy, trade, and transport, and coordinated finance, economy, food, and labor. But in theory the separate republics administered their own justice, education, and agriculture. A Council of Nationalities—with equal numbers of delegates from each ethnic group—became a second chamber, the Supreme Soviet being the first. Together the chambers appointed the administration, the Council of People's Commissars.

As chief of the Workers' and Peasants' Inspectorate, Stalin could send his men anywhere in the government to eliminate inefficiency or corruption. He was also a member of the Politburo, the tight little group of Communist party bosses. He managed the party, prepared the agenda for meetings, transmitted orders, controlled party patronage, maintained files on individuals' loyalty and achievement. Stalin had quietly got hold of the real reins of power.

Trotsky was much more glamorous: minister of war, creator of the Red Army, a cultivated intellectual. But Stalin and two Bolshevik collaborators sent Trotsky's supporters to posts abroad, prevented the publication of Lenin's attacks on Stalin, and gradually deprived Trotsky of his positions. In 1927 Stalin had Trotsky expelled from the party and deported to Siberia. It was the first stage in a long exile that eventually brought Trotsky to Mexico, where an emissary from Stalin murdered him with an ice-axe in 1940.

Stalin in Power: Collectivization

The same congress that expelled Trotsky in December 1927 brought NEP to an end, and announced a "new socialist offensive" for 1928. Stalin became supreme. The years between 1928 and 1941 would bring the collectivization of agriculture, forced industrialization, the great political purges, and the building of an authoritarian state apparatus.

In 1929 Stalin declared war on the kulaks. He virtually ended individual farming in Russia, proclaiming immediate full-scale collectivization. In exchange for locating and turning over to the state hidden crops belonging to the kulaks, the poorer peasants were promised places in collective farms to be made up of the kulaks' land and equipped with their implements. There were about two million kulak households in Russia, perhaps ten million people in all. Now they not only lost their property but they were refused a place in the new collectives.

Peasants were gunned into submission, kulaks deported to Siberia or allowed to starve. Rather than join collectives peasants often burned their crops, broke their plows, and killed their cattle. Between one-half and two-thirds of the livestock in Russia were slaughtered. Famine took millions of human lives. In March 1930 Stalin blamed local officials who had been "dizzy with success" for the tragedy.

In one year 50 percent of Russian farms had been thrown into collectives. Thereafter the pro-

Tractor production in the Soviet Union, 1937. In the foreground is one of the first caterpillar tractors. Previously the Russians had produced only the wheeled tractors shown in the background.

cess was more gradual and there were fewer excesses. By 1941 virtually all Russian farms had been collectivized. There were 250,000 collectives *(kolkhoz),* 900,000,000 acres in extent, supporting 19,000,000 families.

The *artel,* or cooperative, in which each family *owned* its homestead, some livestock, and minor implements, soon became the predominant type of collective farm. On the collectively managed land, the peasants labored under brigade commanders and were rewarded according to their output, measured by the artificial unit of the "labor day."

Every kolkhoz turned over to the government a fixed amount of produce at fixed rates. The sum total of food collected was supposed to guarantee the feeding of the urban population, especially industrial laborers and members of the army. The kolkhoz also paid taxes for local purposes. Surpluses might be sold by the peasant directly to a consumer, but private resale was punished as speculation.

In the years after 1934 at least two-thirds of the government revenue came from resale on the market at a large profit of food acquired cheaply from the kolkhoz. The government profit was called the "turnover tax." By controlling the supply of farm machinery to the kolkhoz through the establishment of Machine Tractor Stations (MTS), the government could maintain surveillance over farm operations and make or break any individual kolkhoz manager.

The Five-Year Plans

In industry, 1928 saw the first of the five-year plans, setting ambitious goals for production over the coming five years. Stalin appropriated ever bigger sums for capital investment and often demanded impossibly high rates of growth. He wanted to mechanize the new large-scale farms by the rapid production of tractors and by building power stations. But he also wanted to create the mass industrial working class that Marxism taught was necessary for socialism.

Stalin was determined to make socialism in Russia secure against outside attack, which he was sure threatened from all directions. The goals of the first five-year plan were not attained by 1932. Fulfillment was announced just the same, and the second plan for 1933–1937 went into effect. The third followed in due course, and was interrupted only by German invasion in 1941.

The five-year plans emphasized heavy industry: steel, electric power, cement, coal, oil. Between 1928 and 1940 steel output went up four-and-one-half times, power eight, cement more than two, coal four, and oil almost three, with similar rises in chemical and machine production. Russia did in about twelve years what the rest of Europe had taken three-quarters of a century to do.

The government whipped up enthusiasm by publicizing awards to especially productive workers. The hardships were great. Inexperience and inefficiency produced a heavy drain. Housing the workers, moving whole industries, and opening up new resources cost hundreds of thousands of lives.

The state managed the economy directly. *Gosplan* (the state planning commission) drew up the plans and supervised their fulfillment. *Gosbank* regulated capital investment. The iron and steel trust, for example, had its own mines, blast furnaces, and rolling mills. In each plant, as on each kolkhoz, the manager was consulted on setting production targets and was held responsible for meeting the goals.

By 1940 Russia had one-third of its people living in cities. Moscow and Leningrad (the former Petrograd and, before that, St. Petersburg) almost doubled in size, and smaller towns grew even faster. The whole social picture had been changed.

The prerevolutionary privileged classes had disappeared. The middle class, temporarily reprieved by NEP, vanished after 1928. Most of the old intelligentsia, unable to stomach the dictatorship, emigrated. Those who stayed were forced into line with the new Soviet intellectual movements, and were expected to concentrate their efforts on technological advances.

Stalin's new system of incentives rewarded the small minority of skilled laborers, bureaucrats, and kolkhoz bosses, together with writers, artists, and entertainers, who formed the new elite. Although Soviet propaganda predicted the withering away of the state and reasserted that true communism was still the goal, the U.S.S.R. created no Marxist equality but a new caste system.

Stalin's Dictatorship

Opposition to Stalin's ruthlessness existed, of course, but he imagined it to be everywhere.

In 1934 the famous and mysterious purges began. Unlike the Jacobin Terror in France, these did not begin until seventeen years after the onset of the revolution. Unlike Robespierre, Stalin survived. The murder of the party boss of Leningrad, Sergei Kirov (December 1, 1934), touched off the first purge. Kirov apparently had urged Stalin to relax his pressures, and Stalin probably arranged his murder.

At intervals until 1938 a series of trials, some of them secret, and many executions without trial led to the death of every member of Lenin's Politburo except Stalin himself. Most of the Soviet diplomatic corps, fifty of the seventy-one members of the Communist party's Central Committee, judges, two successive heads of the secret police, and the prime ministers and chief officials of the non-Russian republics of the U.S.S.R.—all were murdered or disappeared without a trace.

It was doubtful whether any of the victims had actually conspired with Hitler, as some were accused of doing, though many of them certainly hated Stalin. Some who confessed publicly probably felt so deep a loyalty to the communist system that they sacrificed themselves for Stalin's Soviet state. Some doubtless hoped to save their families or even themselves. Some may have hoped that their confessions were so ridiculous that nobody would believe them. Despite the upheaval, no breakdown in the system took place. New bureaucrats quickly replaced the old.

In 1936, while the purges were going on, Stalin proclaimed a new Soviet constitution. It purported to extend civil liberties, but these were a sham. Only the Communist party organizations had the right to nominate candidates for office. Any citizen might apply for party membership to a local branch, which voted on the application after a year of trial. Party organizations existed not only in every territorial subdivision but in every factory, farm, and office. At every level, agitation and propaganda, organization and training were carried on. Government policy was party policy. Stalin was chairman of the Council of People's Commissars (the cabinet, appointed by the Supreme Soviet), chairman of the Politburo (the supreme governing body of the party, appointed by the Central Committee), and general secretary of the party, as well as commissar for defense. Similar overlapping of party and government posts was the regular practice. In 1936 and 1940 new republics were added to the U.S.S.R., making the grand total sixteen, each with its government patterned on that of the Soviet Union itself.

Between 1928 and 1941, there was a wholesale retreat from many of the ideas of the revolution. In the army traditional ranks were restored. Russia's national past was officially rediscovered and praised. The family, attacked by the old Bolsheviks who had made divorce and abortion easy, was rehabilitated. Stalin stressed the sanctity of marriage, made divorce more difficult to get, and encouraged children to obey their parents. In education, the authority of the teacher over the schoolroom was reaffirmed after a long period of classroom anarchy. But education became indoctrination, as newspapers, books, theaters, movies, music, and art all plugged the party line.

Censorship under Stalin outdid censorship under Nicholas I, since it prescribed that all artists constantly praise the system. Even the traditional militant atheism of the Bolsheviks was modified in 1937, as church-going no longer constituted reason for persecution or arrest. All these measures were designed partly to retain popular loyalty during the disruptive purges of the party, and also to prepare for a German attack. Whatever the shift in views, Stalin dictated and managed it.

Soviet Foreign Policy

Although world revolution did not happen, the Soviet regime kept helping communists everywhere to bring it about. In 1919, Lenin founded the Third International (Comintern) for the purpose. This operated alongside the Soviet Foreign Office, but sometimes in seeming contradiction to it, giving Soviet foreign policy a peculiar dual nature.

The Foreign Office concluded treaties that promised not to stir up revolutions in England and other European countries. By the Treaty of Rapallo (1922) with defeated Germany, Russia obtained technical assistance from the Germans while giving them an opportunity secretly to defy the Treaty of Versailles by building arms and aircraft factories in Russia. The Comintern meanwhile tried but failed to install communist regimes in Italy, Bulgaria, Germany, Poland, and China. By 1928, with Stalin in full control, the Comintern was brought into line with the Soviet Foreign Office in order to avoid further foreign-policy conflict.

Stalin himself had little real interest in foreign communists. His attack on Social Democrats as the worst enemies of communism helped the triumph of Hitler and the Nazis in Germany. He joined the League of Nations (1934) only because he saw Hitler liquidating German communists and feared a German attack on Russia. In 1935, he made pacts with France and Czechoslovakia.

Now the Comintern suddenly shifted its line. It embraced the Social Democrats it had been attacking, and urged the formation of "popular fronts" against fascism. "Popular Front" regimes came to power in France and Spain. Many individuals in the West fell for the new communist line. But Stalin's killing his own party hierarchy in the purges led others to doubt the effectiveness of Russia as an ally.

Hitler repeatedly declared his intention of eventually attacking the Soviet Union. Western appeasement of Hitler and neutrality in the Spanish Civil War, which we treat later in this chapter, convinced Stalin that the Western European nations only intended to turn Hitler full force against Russia. Not until 1939 did the British and French reluctantly conclude that their security demanded a firmer alliance with the U.S.S.R. By then Stalin was negotiating with the Germans. The Soviet-German pact of late August 1939 freed Hitler to attack first Poland and then the West. Stalin hoped this would give him time to prepare Soviet defenses. But he got less than two years. In June 1941 came the full-scale German assault on the U.S.S.R.

II FASCISM, 1918–1939

By 1939 right-wing governments, generally called *fascist,* were in firm control of Italy, Germany, Spain, and all the countries of Eastern Europe except Russia and Czechoslovakia. Fear of communist revolutions played a large role in bringing them to power. So did economic depression. The fascists preached a violent—often mystical—nationalism, and usually offered a vaguely radical program to win mass support.

All fascist movements had colored shirts, private armies, special salutes and war cries, mass hypnotism in special ceremonies, and a vast program of eventual conquest. All of them opposed democracy, liberalism, and parliamentary institutions as much as they did communism. In fact they were like the communists in hating constitutional governments and despising individual human beings. Censorship, political police, concentration camps, the rule of the bludgeon, the end of legal protection—all these characterized both fascism and communism. The circumstances that brought fascists to power varied widely from country to country.

Italy

Italy suffered many casualties in World War I, and a postwar slump bred discontent. The Allies had broken their promise to give the Italians Dalmatia. Young men released from the army and with no job to go to drifted restlessly ready for politicians to exploit their grievances.

Gabriele d'Annunzio, romantic nationalist poet, gathered a band of black-shirted followers brandishing daggers. They captured the Adriatic port of Fiume and hysterically threatened to move on Rome and thence conquer the world. The Italian government threw them out in 1920, but Benito Mussolini (1883–1945) imitated d'Annunzio in building the fascist movement between 1918 and 1922.

Mussolini had been a radical socialist, a pacifist, antimonarchist, atheist, and antinationalist. He now swung to the opposite positions. He attacked communism, became a mystical nationalist, and rabid militarist. He was consistent only in his hatred for parliaments, his love of violence, and his yearning for power.

In 1919 he founded the first *fasci di combattimento* ("groups for combat") and soon put himself forward as the protector of Italy against communism. Mussolini's bands went around beating up communists and socialists and indeed anybody in workmen's clothes. The government, frightened of revolution, gave him army trucks, gaso-line, and weapons. Between 1920 and 1922 the fascists killed perhaps two thousand people. They entered the Italian parliament as a political party (1921). Important people in the royal family and among officers and industrialists backed them. In October 1922 came the fascist "March on Rome." Mussolini himself arrived by sleeping car after the king had invited him to form a government.

Parliament granted Mussolini temporary dictatorial powers, and he took over the administration of Italy. A fascist militia owed allegiance to him alone. The army took an oath of personal loyalty to him. He got the electoral laws changed. Now the political party obtaining the largest number of votes (provided that it won at least 25 percent of the total) would capture two-thirds of the seats in parliament.

By April 1924 the cabinet was wholly fascist. Mussolini's bully-boys murdered a socialist member of parliament, Matteotti (June 1924), but Mussolini weathered the scandal. Control over the press, arrests of political opponents, a law providing the death penalty for action against Mussolini, the abolition of nonfascist political parties—all strengthened the dictatorship. Like Stalin, Mussolini was both chief of the party *(Duce)* and chief of the government *(Capo di Governo)*. His fascist Grand Council of Twenty-four corresponded to the Soviet Politburo.

Mussolini claimed that representation in the

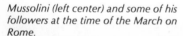

Mussolini (left center) and some of his followers at the time of the March on Rome.

government should be based on economic interests organized in "syndicates," a theory advanced before World War I by the French revolutionary syndicalist Georges Sorel. But while Sorel believed in government by syndicates of workers only and in class warfare, Mussolini believed in producers' syndicates as well as workers' and in capitalism and class collaboration. In April 1926 the state officially recognized both producers' and workers' syndicates in industry, agriculture, commerce, transportation, and banking, with a separate syndicate of intellectuals.

Each syndicate could bargain and reach contracts, and could assess dues on all those engaged in their own fields. Strikes and lockouts were forbidden. In 1926, Mussolini became minister of corporations, the boss of the syndicate system, and the architect of a much-publicized "corporative state." In 1928 he decreed that parliamentary representation would be by syndicate. Eventually the old Chamber of Deputies declared itself replaced by a Chamber of Fasces and Corporations. Mussolini remained firmly in personal control.

During the 1930s the fascists strove to make Italy self-sufficient in agriculture. They subsidized shipping and air transport and protected Italian industry by high tariffs. They undertook public works, drained marshes, attacked malaria, and extended the hydroelectric system. But Italy could not overcome its deficiencies in coal and iron.

Mussolini made emigration a crime. He encouraged large families in order to swell his armies and bolster his claim that overpopulated Italy must expand abroad. At the age of six, children joined the fascist youth movement. School textbooks, newspapers, books, plays, and films all spouted fascist propaganda. The secret police hunted down all those suspected of opposition. Mussolini recognized the Vatican City as independent and Catholicism as the state religion (Lateran Treaty, 1929). Yet friction persisted between government and papacy.

In foreign affairs, as we shall see, Mussolini undertook a policy of adventure that led Italy from aggression to aggression: against Greece (1923), Ethiopia (1935), the Spanish Republic (1936–1939), and Albania (1939). He allied himself with his fellow fascist, Hitler, and pressed claims against the French for Corsica, Tunisia, Nice, and Savoy.

The German alliance also led to a new domestic policy: anti-Semitism. Italy had only seventy thousand Jews, most of them long residents and thoroughly Italian in sentiment. Some were fascist. But in 1938 Hitler persuaded Mussolini to expel Jews from the Fascist party, to forbid them to teach or attend school, to intermarry with non-Jews, or to conduct business.

Germany

The Early Years of the Weimar Republic

After World War I, Germany lived for fifteen years under a democratic government, the Weimar Republic, named after the constitution adopted in Weimar in 1919. The immediate postwar years, down through 1923, were very difficult. Economic disorders grew and both the left and the right threatened political stability.

The defeat in World War I surprised the German people, who had never been given the true news from the battlefields. Seeing their armies come home intact, many Germans simply could not believe they had lost the war. The Allies did not force the defeated German generals to surrender, and the generals insisted that they had been sold out. So the legend of the "stab in the back" grew up. Civilians, democrats, liberals, socialists, communists, and Jews had betrayed the armies—according to the monarchists, agrarians, industrialists, and militarists. The "war-guilt" clause in the Versailles Treaty obliged Germany to assume full responsibility for the war. This made it harder for the Germans to accept defeat. Many of them denied guilt, hated their enemies, blamed the wrong people, and eagerly schemed for a second chance.

The Social Democrats, who proclaimed the republic two days before the armistice of November 11, 1918, followed a moderate policy. They did not attack large landed estates or attempt to nationalize industry, and they concluded collective bargaining agreements with the industrialists. To their left, communists and fellow travelers tried in the winter of 1918–1919 to stage a revolution on the Russian model, but the Social Democrats used the army to stop it.

A Soviet republic emerged briefly in Bavaria. It was liquidated in May 1919. Bavaria became the home of a permanent red-scare. Local Bavarian authorities steadily encouraged right-wing intrigues. Here former soldiers banded together in rabidly antidemocratic "Free Corps" units, specializing in violence and assassinations. Here Hitler got his start.

Besides the Social Democrats, the parties accepting the republic were the Catholic Center, which favored moderate social legislation; the

Democrats, a middle-class group; and the People's party, which included the moderate industrialists. On the right, the antirepublican Nationalists commanded the support of many great industrialists, bureaucrats, and members of the lower middle classes. The parties supporting the Republic won 75 percent of the seats in the elections for a constituent assembly in 1919.

By the Weimar Constitution, the president had powers that made dictatorship a real possibility. For example, he could temporarily suspend civil liberties and take whatever measures he might deem necessary to restore order. Voting by proportional representation for entire party lists of candidates encouraged small splinter parties to multiply.

The first president, the Social Democrat Friedrich Ebert, overcame a coup *(Putsch)* from the right in 1920 by calling a general strike that paralyzed Germany. A communist uprising in the Ruhr followed, and when German troops entered the area, demilitarized by the Treaty of Versailles, the French intervened. Extremists were further encouraged by the huge bill for reparations (132 billion gold marks) presented by the Allies (April 1921).

Moderate politicians who tried to prove German good will by fulfilling German obligations were murdered: the Catholic Erzberger (1921) and the Jew Rathenau (1922). Amidst the disorders the National Socialist Party of the German Workers (Nazis), a group founded by an expatriate Austrian and frustrated artist, Adolf Hitler (1889–1945), came into being.

Hitler drew on pseudoscientific race theories of "Nordic" and "Aryan" supremacy as enunciated by Gobineau (1816–1882) and others. His hero was the anti-Semitic Karl Lueger, mayor of Vienna in his youth. Hitler favored the elimination of Jews from all aspects of German life. He put forth a radical economic program that included the confiscation of war profits, nationalization of trusts, and land grants to the peasants.

Endowed with hypnotic oratorical gifts, Hitler made himself absolute leader (*Führer:* compare Mussolini's title, *Duce*) of his party. He

Nazi party membership card No. 1, held by Hitler.

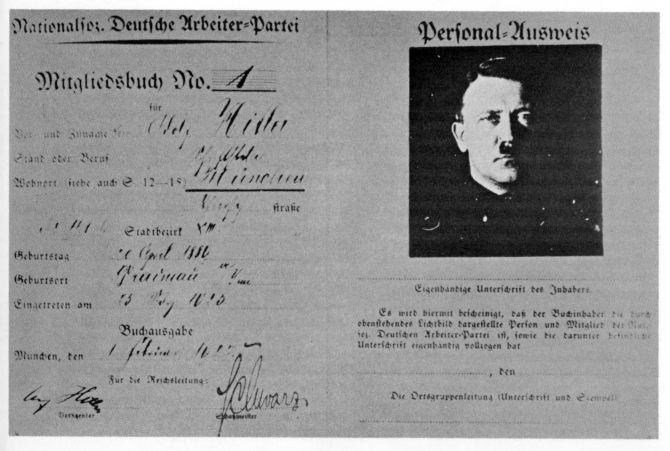

Berliners selling discarded tin cans to a sidewalk scrap merchant during the inflation of 1923.

founded a brown-shirted corps called the SA (*Sturmabteilung,* "storm troops") wearing swastika armbands. Like the Italian fascists, the SA illegally got access to government supplies of arms. At first, however, the Nazis were unimportant politically.

Inflation, Fulfillment, and Depression

In 1922 and 1923 Germany suffered from a runaway inflation, caused in part by the failure of the wartime government to pay the expenses of the war through taxes. Having expected to win and extract the costs from the losers, the kaiser had simply borrowed from the banks and repaid them with paper money not backed by gold. Prices rose, and wages followed. The inflationary spiral was intensified by the reparations payments. When the Germans failed to make payments, the French occupied the Ruhr (January 1923), intending to recoup their loss by the products of this industrial region. The German government ordered the Ruhr workers to quit their jobs.

To finance this passive resistance and support the idle workers, the government rapidly printed huge amounts of increasingly worthless money. The mark, normally worth 4.2 to the dollar, had dropped to 8.4 in 1918. It finally sank to the fantastic low of several trillions to the dollar. Lifetime savings were wiped out overnight, real property took on fantastic value, and speculation flourished.

Industrialists took advantage of the inflation to pay off their indebtedness in worthless marks. Workers suffered as the purchasing power of wages vanished. The middle classes suffered too, particularly those living on fixed incomes. In class-conscious Germany they could not join with the working-class parties. Instead they turned away from the moderate republican parties to the Nationalists and to Hitler's Nazis.

In the autumn of 1923 Gustav Stresemann, leader of the People's party and chancellor, ordered passive resistance ended and work resumed in the Ruhr. In Munich, the capital of Bavaria, Hitler announced in a beer hall the beginning of a "national revolution." Troops stopped this premature Nazi effort and Hitler went to jail. He was sentenced to five years, mild enough for high treason, but spent only eight months in a comfortable cell writing *Mein Kampf* ("My Battle"), the famous bible of the Nazis.

The title page of the first edition of "Mein Kampf." The subtitle, "Eine Abrechnung," means "a settling of accounts."

In the last months of 1923 economic experts took over. They stopped printing the old currency and opened a new bank to issue new marks. These were given the prewar value of 4.2 to the dollar. Not gold but an imaginary mortgage on all of Germany's agricultural and industrial wealth backed this currency. One trillion old marks might be exchanged for one new one.

These measures restored confidence, but at the cost of further hardships. The government proclaimed rigorous economies and increased taxes. As prices fell, overexpanded businesses collapsed. Unemployment rose, wages stayed low, and hours of work remained long.

The Allies helped end the crisis. By the Dawes Plan (1924), the French were to leave the Ruhr, and a special bank would receive reparations payments. These would be financed for the first five years by an international loan. Within Germany a moderate coalition accepted the terms over right-wing protests.

From late 1924 to late 1929, the Weimar Republic was politically stable. It fulfilled the Versailles Treaty requirements and enjoyed economic prosperity. Production rose. "Vertical trusts," like those in the U.S.S.R. but privately owned, brought together all processes from mining to the finishing of the product. Prosperity depended in part upon a big armaments program. Reparations were paid with no damage to the German economy, as foreign investments, especially American, more than balanced the outflow.

The election of the wartime commander Marshal von Hindenburg as president in 1925 created some dismay abroad, but until 1930 Hindenburg acted constitutionally. Prosperity brought political moderation. Abroad, Germany joined the European system of security, signing the Locarno Pact (1925, see p. 503), joining the League of Nations (1926), and in 1929 signing the Kellogg-Briand Pact, which outlawed aggressive war. In 1929 the Young Plan reduced the original total of reparations demanded by the Allies and established lower rates of payment. The Allies evacuated the Rhineland in 1930, three years earlier than the date set by the Treaty of Versailles.

But the worldwide depression that began in 1929 knocked the props out from under the Weimar Republic. Foreign credit was no longer available. Unemployment, hunger, and want reappeared. The middle classes, with no unemployment insurance, were the hardest hit. Hitler, whose fortunes had fallen low in the years of fulfillment, reaped the harvest. As moderate politicians faltered, intrigues on the right grew more sinister. Nazis and communists both gained in the elections of 1930. They fought each other in the streets but collaborated in the Reichstag. The eighty-year-old Hindenburg narrowly defeated Hitler for the presidency in 1932. But Hindenburg himself became the tool of a scheming political soldier, von Schleicher.

The only barrier against the Nazis was a tricky right-centrist nobleman, von Papen. In November 1932, having persuaded the Allies to forgive all reparations, he called for new elections, and the Nazi vote fell. The Nazis were slipping, money was drying up, and Hitler was desperate. Schleicher, however, spoiled Papen's success. Schleicher had no political following but became chancellor himself for eight weeks and then gave way to Hitler. Papen now backed Hitler, and the industrialists were again ready to subsidize him. On January 30, 1933, Hitler took office. The Weimar Republic was doomed.

Germany under Hitler, 1933–1939

In February 1933, the Reichstag (the parliament building in Berlin) burned down in a sensational fire. Hitler probably ordered it himself in order to blame the communists and make himself dictator. After the fire, President Hindenburg used his emergency powers to suspend freedom of speech and the press. The SA used terror freely.

In March 1933 a newly elected Reichstag voted an Enabling Act suspending the constitution. On January 30, 1934, all those members of the Nazi party who might embarrass Hitler were killed, including many SA leaders and radicals. Hitler stripped the state governments of their individual powers and made Berlin supreme. He assumed the office of president when Hindenburg died (1934), and he dissolved other political parties.

Anti-Semitism inspired much of Hitler's legislation. The Jews of Germany numbered about 600,000 in a country of 60,000,000. They had become leading members of the professions. Most of them were patriotic Germans, and many would have followed Hitler in everything but his anti-Semitism. By the Nuremberg Laws (September 1935), no person with a single Jewish grandparent might be a German citizen, marry a non-Jew, fly the national flag, write or publish, act on stage or screen, teach, work in banks, give concerts, sell books or antiques, or receive unemployment insurance or charity. The names of Jews who had died for Germany in World War I were erased from war memorials.

In November 1938 a Jewish boy of seventeen, in despair at the persecution of his parents, shot and killed a diplomat in the German embassy in Paris. This was the signal for a systematic and organized pillage of Jewish shops in Germany, and for new rules including special dress and names for Jews. These measures, designed to make life impossible for Jews, were only the prelude to their actual physical extermination during World War II. Few non-Jews in Germany protested. Hitler's government encouraged "Nordic" purity by favoring early marriages and many children, and by introducing sterilization for the "racially impure."

Hitler created a new system of "people's courts" to try all cases of treason. He appointed all the judges. Concentration camps were established for enemies of the regime. His Gestapo (*Geheime Staatspolizei*, "Secret State Police") opened private mail, tapped wires, and spied on the citizenry.

In economic policy the Nazis protected large estates, but fixed farm production goals as well as farm prices and wages. Preparing for war, Hitler spurred a drive toward agricultural self-sufficiency, which, except for fats and coffee, was 83 percent successful by 1937.

Imitating Stalin, Hitler embarked on industrial planning, with a four-year plan in 1933 and

Hitler and Mussolini in Venice, 1933.

a second in 1937. The first, by means of labor camps, public works, and armament manufacture, reduced unemployment. The second was designed to make Germany blockade-proof in the event of war. Output of raw materials was increased and their allocation strictly controlled. War industry got first priority. Germany produced new synthetic rubber and motor fuels and set up an enormous vertical iron and steel trust. The Nazi Labor Front replaced all labor unions and employers' organizations. Workers could not change jobs without the state's permission. All men and women of working age might be drafted for labor.

Some Nazis favored a return to the worship of old German pagan gods. But they had to deal with Christian churches. They took over the Lutheran national synod and appointed their own bishop. With the Catholics Hitler reached a concordat in 1933, guaranteeing freedom of worship and permitting religious instruction in the schools. But the Nazis often broke their promises, insulting or persecuting individual priests. Millions of Protestants and Catholics alike gave complete support to Hitler.

In the arts, Hitler's own vulgar tastes became standard. In education, Nazi doctrine and the great past achievements of Germany were stressed. A school's purpose was to develop strong bodies and the military spirit.

The Nazis preached that Germany was entitled to all territories inhabited by Germans: Austria, the western borders of Czechoslovakia, Danzig, the Polish corridor. Germans were also entitled to the rest of Eastern Europe as living space (Lebensraum), since Germans were superior to all Eastern European peoples.

Hitler called the medieval German Empire the First Reich and Bismarck's Empire the Second. His own would be the Third Reich and would last a thousand years. He would punish decadent Britain and France and bring them into line. Lesser states would disappear; Germany would occupy the "heartland" of Eurasia and thus dominate the world. When Hitler put this program into effect, he eventually brought about World War II.

Spain

Fascism triumphed in Spain as well as Italy and Germany. Spanish politics was deeply affected by regionalism and economic backwardness, by the close association between the Catholic Church and the propertied classes, and by

the Spanish affection for anarchist revolutionary ideas. Spain had missed not only most of the Enlightenment and the French Revolution, but even the Reformation and the Renaissance. Spanish conservatism had a sixteenth-century flavor, rather than eighteenth or nineteenth.

Neutral during World War I, Spain entered the postwar period under Alfonso XIII, a constitutional monarch ambitious for power. Between 1923 and 1930, a military dictatorship under General Primo de Rivera governed with Alfonso's approval. The dictator depended on the support of the landlords. He failed to carry through constitutional reform, although he did try to woo the workers from anarchism.

After his death in 1930, the elections of 1931 brought in a large republican majority. Alfonso XIII left the country. A republican constitution of 1931 provided for a responsible ministry and a single-chamber parliament. But the republic lacked the support of army, Church, and landowners on the right and of anarchists on the extreme left.

The republic was weakened by an anarchist uprising (1933) and a coalminers' revolt (1934) supported by anarchists and socialists both. In putting down the miners, the government used Moors from North Africa commanded by the new minister of war, General Francisco Franco. The left, united in a "Popular Front," won the elections of 1936. But extreme leftists soon tried to start revolution.

For the first time the Communist party emerged as a strong element. On the right the *Falange* ("Phalanx") now appeared. This was a fascist party on the Italian pattern. It favored aggression in Africa and against Portugal, and had its own youth groups and private army.

In July 1936 General Franco, supported by the right, led a military coup against the government. This touched off a civil war that lasted three years and cost a million Spanish lives. Decisively aided by Mussolini and Hitler, Franco's forces eventually captured the republican strongholds of Madrid and Barcelona in 1939 and won the war.

The Popular Front government was unable to suppress terror in the areas it controlled. Anarchists and communists murdered each other. The Western democracies did not help the republic, but the fighting in Spain became a deeply emotional issue for many in the West who were strongly anti-Franco. They looked for help to Stalin, inventor of the "Popular Front" idea. But he sent to Spain chiefly Stalinist agents who

Pablo Picasso's "Guernica" (1937): the artist's protest to the Spanish Civil War.

fought the Trotskyites and anarchists. The triumphant Franco regime depended on the landowners, the army, and the Church.

Eastern Europe

In Eastern Europe fascism triumphed too, helped by the lack of a firm parliamentary tradition, the fear of Bolshevism and the failure to solve economic problems after the depression of 1929. Observing the success of Mussolini and Hitler, little "Führers" put on uniforms and screamed their hatred of neighboring states. Especially in the Balkan countries, whose agricultural economy complemented the German industrial economy, German economic pressure after the depression led to German domination of foreign trade and increasing Nazi political influence.

After the peace settlement had broken the vast Hapsburg Empire into small pieces, Austria became a small German state. The imperial capital, Vienna, with its huge population was cut off from the lands on which it had always depended economically. Union with Germany was forbidden by the Allies. The rival Christian Socialist and Social Democratic parties, almost evenly balanced in parliament, organized private armies of their own. After 1930 the Christian Socialists became steadily more fascist in outlook.

When Hitler came to power in Germany in 1933, many Christian Socialists became openly Nazi. Engelbert Dollfuss, the Christian Socialist chancellor, resisted the Nazis, but could not join the Social Democrats in a common anti-Nazi coalition. Instead, he banned all parties except a new one of his own. He raided Social Democratic headquarters and bombed newly built workers' apartment houses in which the Social Democratic leaders were hiding (February 1934). Dollfuss had become an anti-Nazi fascist dictator. The Nazis assassinated him in July 1934. Only Mussolini's troop concentrations on the frontier prevented Hitler from annexing Austria then.

Dollfuss's successor, Schuschnigg, was committed to the same policies. But as Mussolini and Hitler drew closer together Schuschnigg lost ground. Hitler demanded and obtained privileges for the Nazis. When Schuschnigg announced that Austria would hold a plebiscite (national referendum) on the question of independence, Hitler marched in (March 1938) and installed a Nazi chancellor. Schuschnigg went to jail. The Nazis had now incorporated Austria into the German Reich without Italian opposition.

In 1919 Hungary, the other partner in the former Dual Monarchy, had a brief and terrible communist experience under Lenin's agent, Bela Kun. Kun put through revolutionary nationalization decrees and slaughtered many peasants. This spurred a Romanian invasion, expelling Kun. Under French protection a counterrevolutionary regime was formed in 1920 under Admiral Horthy, a member of the gentry class. He remained as chief of state through World War II. Horthy presided over a "White Terror" directed largely against Jews, but also against workers and peasants.

Between the wars the chief political issue in Hungary was the passionate wish of the upperclass Magyars to regain the provinces lost in the peace settlement: Transylvania to Romania, Slovakia to Czechoslovakia, and Croatia and other south Slav areas to Yugoslavia. Most Hungarians, however, cared as little about this as they had about politics in the past. The magnates and gentry retained their traditional dominance.

Always a dictatorial government operating behind a parliamentary screen, the Hungarian regime became more and more fascist in character after the depression. Political organizations like the Nazi "Arrow Cross" sprang up. After the annexation of Austria, Hitler had Hungary in his pocket. When he broke up Czechoslovakia in March 1939, he gave Hungary the westernmost portion, Ruthenia. Hungary passed anti-Semitic laws to please Hitler. He did not put the Arrow Cross in power until near the end of World War II.

The Kingdom of Serbs, Croats, and Slovenes, consisting of the former independent kingdom of Serbia and the Hapsburg south Slav lands, took the name Yugoslavia in 1929. Yugoslavia became a dictatorship because it could not satisfy the hopes of both Serbs and Croats. Many Serbs felt that they should dominate the new state, ruled by their own king and from their own capital of Belgrade. The Croats, with their different tradition, their Latin alphabet, and Catholic religion, wanted much more independence within a federalized, not a centralized, Yugoslavia. The mass of the peasant population deeply loved freedom but had little experience with Western parliamentary forms.

Corruption and assassination led first to the dictatorship of King Alexander (1929). Then a Croatian fascist subsidized by Mussolini assassinated Alexander in 1934. The Serb royal dictatorship continued, and Croat demands for autonomy were not satisfied until the summer of 1939, only weeks before World War II. In 1941 Hitler split the country into its old provinces, turning each over to native fascists or foreign occupying forces.

Elsewhere in Eastern Europe, the story varied from country to country, but the outcome was similar. In Poland, Marshal Pilsudski's coup (1926) against a democratic government, created a military dictatorship founded on the support of the landowners and industrialists.

In Romania, corruption, anti-Semitism, and economic dislocation brought fascism. When the leading fascist party, the Iron Guard, began a program of assassination in the 1930s, King Carol, to head off a coup, adopted much of its program as his own (1938). In 1940, when Stalin and Hitler both seized Romanian territory, Carol fled. The government fell into the hands of Hitler's ally, Marshal Ion Antonescu. In Bulgaria and Greece, too, fascist regimes took over.

In Eastern Europe dictatorship did not rest on popular support as it did in Italy and Germany. It relied on the police, the bureaucracy, and the army. The liberal constitutions were only pieces of paper, especially after the depression. In the 1930s extremes of left and right became popular. Fear of communism, combined with the propaganda of fascism, brought victory to the right.

III

THE DEMOCRACIES BETWEEN THE WARS

Disappointed in their hopes that democracy would take root in the new Europe of the World War I peace settlement, Britain, France, and the United States found themselves the only democracies among the major powers. The crisis grew steadily blacker after the depression and the advent of Hitler.

When World War II came in 1939, it was clear that the years since 1919 had been only a truce. The dictatorships bore the major responsibility for unleashing the new war. But the democracies' preoccupation with domestic problems and their hatred of war itself gave the dictators the leeway to make aggressive moves. The democracies also faced the developing nationalism of the colonial peoples. This did not reach its full height until after World War II, but by 1934 it already posed severe problems for Britain, France, and the United States.

Britain

In World War I Great Britain suffered 750,000 killed and 1,500,000 wounded, including many of the most promising young men of an entire generation. It lost 40 percent of the merchant fleet. The national debt multiplied tenfold. Many British investments abroad had to be liquidated. The system of international trade that had produced a prosperous Britain could not be quickly restored. The war had stepped up the industrial production of the United States, Canada, and even India. All now competed with that of Britain. By the 1920s German industry was also back in competition. Britain, the pioneer in the industrial revolution, had lost its former lead.

British workers, however, were in no mood to accept a lower standard of living. They had been led to believe that the defeated enemy would pay the costs of the war and give Britain a new start. Reparations fell far short. By 1921 there were almost one million unemployed, living from payments on unemployment insurance: the *dole.* The Welsh coal-mining regions were hit the hardest.

As a result, the Liberal party almost disappeared. The Conservatives still commanded the votes of the upper and middle classes, who favored a minimum of government intervention. Trade unionists and intellectuals of all classes who wanted more government intervention in the economic problems of the day supported the Labour party. In 1922 for the first time Labour polled more votes than the Liberals and became the opposition party to the Conservatives in power.

To increase the sales of British goods abroad the Conservatives wanted to make private industry more efficient. But American tariffs, the uncertainties of trade with Russia, and the drive for industrialization everywhere stood in the way. So the Conservatives more and more called for tariffs and imperial preference agreements, with the dominions and colonies supplying the raw materials and Britain the manufactured goods. But Canada and Australia wanted their own industries and rejected this revival of Joseph Chamberlain's mercantilism (see Chapter 16).

The Labour Party wanted the government itself to buy and run transportation, power, coal, steel and other major industries: nationalization. Some who favored this nationalization were socialists who believed that private profits meant exploitation of the workers. Others believed nationalization would result in the increased efficiency necssary for Britain to compete in international markets. Labour politicians also argued that British workers would become more productive if they thought of themselves as owners of their industries.

In 1924 and in 1929 Labour came to power briefly. But it never had enough votes in Parliament to permit it to nationalize any industry. The Conservatives' program, on the other hand, was blocked by their own internal disagreements and by the ambitions of dominion and colonial countries. As a result, there was no radical change in Britain between the wars, least of all in traditional attitudes and behavior.

In 1926, 2.5 million workers briefly tried to tie up all vital services in a general strike. But thousands of men from the middle and upper classes drove trucks or operated locomotives or ran telephone switchboards to keep essential services operating. Britain was a land where the parliamentary decencies dominated even the class struggle that the Marxists insisted was going on. Politically Britain became more democratic. In 1918 all the old exceptions to universal male suffrage were swept away, and women over thirty were given the vote. In 1928 this remnant of inequality vanished, and women too could vote at twenty-one.

Never having attained full economic recovery, Britain was hard-hit by the depression. In 1931 a coalition of Conservatives, Liberals, and right-wing Labourites cut the dole and social services, abandoned the gold standard, and allowed the pound to decline in value. New protective tariffs and stopping payments on war debts helped stem the depression. After the coalition won the election of 1935, the Conservative, Stanley Baldwin, became prime minister. But economic and social questions appeared less urgent in the face of threats of a new war from Mussolini and Hitler.

Even during World War I the Irish question had caused Britain much anxiety. In 1916, with German help, Irish nationalists staged an armed rising in Dublin. By putting down this "Easter rebellion" the British made new martyrs. By the end of the war the nationalist organization, the Sinn Fein (Gaelic, "ourselves alone") was demanding complete independence. Between 1919 and 1921 guerrilla warfare raged and revolution was in full swing.

One wing of the Sinn Fein, under Arthur Griffith and Michael Collins, was willing to accept a compromise, making Catholic southern Ireland a self-governing dominion but leaving Protestant Ulster under British rule. The other wing, under Eamon de Valera, insisted on republican status for the entire island. In 1921 the British accepted the moderates' terms. Southern Ireland became the Irish Free State, with its own parliament, the Dail, and complete self-government under the crown.

The de Valera wing attempted civil war but the public was tired of violence. De Valera himself brought his fellow republicans into the Dail in 1927. In 1933 the oath of loyalty to the crown was abolished. In World War II Ireland was neutral. In 1949 Britain recognized the Republic of Eire. Ulster remained under British rule as part of the United Kingdom of Great Britain and Northern Ireland.

Elsewhere on the globe British lands obtained a still greater measure of self-government. In the Statute of Westminster of 1931, a long historic process reached its culmination. Britain and the dominions were recognized as "autonomous communities . . . equal in status . . . united by a common allegiance to the crown and freely associated as members of the British Commonwealth of Nations." Any dominion that wished to secede from the Commonwealth might do so, and southern Ireland did just that.

In 1939 all the others freely decided to enter the war on Britain's side. Only the Union of South Africa, where many Afrikaners sympathized with Hitler, hung back. But the pro-British General Smuts brought South Africa, too, to join the war against Germany.

France

In World War I French suffering was even greater than British. Two million Frenchmen were killed or incapacitated; 300,000 houses and 20,000 factories were destroyed. As in England, a generation of potential leaders in every field had been wiped out. The psychological life given by victory did not heal the wounds caused by the horrible four-year struggle. No wonder that the French concentrated on extracting every possible cent in reparations, and on denying the Germans the means to fight again. The two policies were contradictory because in order to pay, Germany needed to recover industrially. French occupation of the Ruhr in 1923 gained nothing, as German passive resistance closed down industry there.

In the 1920s France suffered inflation because the government kept taxes low but had to pay for a big army and reconstruction. New taxes, new economies, and the improvement of trade overcame inflation, but the value of the franc did fall from twenty American cents to two, and was stabilized at about four in 1928. Those hurt worst were the middle-class bondholders and those living on fixed incomes or dependent on savings. Political and social tensions increased and were worsened by the depression, in full swing by 1932.

The old political conflict between the anticlerical republican left and the royalist, or authoritarian, right still divided France. On the left, socialists and communists demanded a "welfare state." Workers, civil servants, and intellectuals tended to vote left. But the communists followed the Moscow line, while the socialists did not. The major labor union organization, the CGT (Confédération Générale du Travail, "General Confederation of Labor") was similarly split.

On the right were the wealthy, many of them monarchist and clerical, who opposed the very existence of the republic. They were supported by conservative peasants and small businessmen who opposed all new welfare-state measures. In social legislation France lagged behind Britain, Germany, and Scandinavia. Between right and left was a republican party of the center that was very slow to accept social and economic reforms, and was very misleadingly named the Radical Socialists.

A major political crisis began in December 1933. A certain Stavisky, a shady speculator with highly placed connections, was caught sponsoring a fraudulent bond issue. He committed suicide or was murdered. The ensuing scandal rocked France. The royalists, organized as the *Action Française,* had strong-arm squadrons called the *Camelots du Roi* ("King's Henchmen"). They joined a rightwing fascist-style veterans' organization, the *Croix de Feu* (Cross of Fire), in street fighting against communists and in riots against the government (February 1934).

The left called a general strike. The immediate crisis was met only by a coalition of all parties except the royalists, socialists, and communists. But when the new government tried to meet a new crisis of the franc, Radical Socialists, socialists, and communists, backed by the CGT, formed a Popular Front. The Popular Front won the election of 1936 and came to power under socialist premier Léon Blum.

The Popular Front victory reflected a strong wish for increased social welfare measures like those of the American New Deal. A major target was the Bank of France, stronghold of the conservative financial solution to all social problems. The bank, a private institution, was dominated by the "two hundred families" alleged to control the French economy.

Many Frenchmen, too, were alarmed at the unchecked advances of Mussolini and Hitler and at the rearmament of Germany. The U.S.S.R. instructed communists to cooperate in the Popular Front. But the bitter political division of France made it a bad time for a French New Deal. Blum introduced a program for a forty-hour week, partial nationalization of the Bank, the railroads, and the arms industry, and compulsory arbitration of labor disputes.

On the left, the communists were unwilling to let Blum have the credit for making these measures work. Their sit-down strikes frightened businessmen. On the right, the conservatives would not pay income taxes or buy government bonds unless Blum called a halt to the reform measures, which he did in March 1937. The Popular Front then collapsed.

The left-right split was now worse than ever. The left resented the abandonment of social welfare measures. Only the army prevented a general strike in 1938. The right resented the fact that the Blum experiment had even been tried at all. "Better Hitler than Blum" was their slogan. The middle-of-the-road Radical Socialist premier, Daladier, kept France aligned with Britain in opposition to Hitler and Mussolini. In 1939 France was deeply divided and unprepared in every way for the approaching war.

The United States

In World War I the United States, with a population three times that of France, lost fewer than a tenth as many men. In material terms the United States gained from the war. Allied war orders stimulated heavy industry. New York was outstripping London as the financial center of the world. The dollar had begun to replace the pound. Until 1933 the United States collected some interest on the war debts of the Allies. When payments stopped prematurely in the early 1930s, the stimulation given American industry as a result of the loans outweighed the losses. Despite American victory and prosperity, however, the national revulsion against the war in 1919 and later years was as great as that in Europe. In the presidential election of 1920, the Republicans ousted the Democrats, who had been in control since 1913, and repeated their victory in 1924 and 1928. This was the era of the Republican presidents Harding (1921–1923), Coolidge (1923–1929), and Hoover (1929–1933).

American public opinion underwent a strong wave of isolationist sentiment. The Senate repudiated both the Treaty of Versailles and the League of Nations. If Wilson had made more con-

cessions to the Republicans, he might perhaps have gotten the two-thirds majority he needed in the Senate. Or some major Republican leader might have put through the idea of a bipartisan foreign policy. But many Americans felt they had done enough by beating the Germans, and wanted no more to do with Europe.

Isolationism was reflected in high tariffs. The Fordney-McCumber Tariff of 1922 and the Smoot-Hawley Tariff of 1930 set increasingly high duties on foreign goods. These laws, designed to protect American high wage-scales against competition from cheaper foreign labor, made it impossible for the European debtor nations to earn dollars in the American markets and so to repay their debts. Congress did consent to lower the obligations of defeated Germany. But it tended to agree with President Coolidge's remark about the Allied debts: "They hired the money, didn't they?"

Isolationism expressed itself also in a reversal of the traditional American policies of free immigration. In 1924 immigrants from any country were limited to an annual quota of 2 percent of the number of nationals of that country resident in the United States in 1890. Since the heavy immigration from Eastern and Southern Europe had come mainly after 1890, the choice of 1890 was designed to reduce the flow from those areas to a trickle.

But America did not retreat into its shell altogether. In 1928, Frank B. Kellogg, the secretary of state, submitted to the European powers a proposal for the renunciation of war. Similar proposals came from the French foreign minister, Aristide Briand. Together they were incorporated as the Pact of Paris (Kellogg-Briand Pact, August 1928), eventually signed by twenty-three nations including the United States. Of course, the pact did not actually prevent World War II. But at least the United States had shown its concern for the peace of the world. American businessmen, American money, and American goods were now everywhere. In the Far East in 1922, the United States took the lead in a Nine-Power Treaty, committing them all, including Japan, to respect the sovereignty and integrity of China.

At home, prosperity ruled throughout the Coolidge era of the 1920s. Almost everybody played the stock market. Liquor was illegal ("Prohibition"), and bootleggers flourished. It was the Jazz Age, the age of short skirts, of the Charleston, and "sex appeal," Clara Bow, the red-haired "It" girl of the movies, Henry Ford, the enormously successful pioneer in the automobile in-

A Sunday afternoon in St. Louis,
Missouri, in the 1920's.

dustry, Al Capone, the gangster who made millions out of Prohibition and turned crime into big business, Calvin Coolidge himself, the sober, unimaginative business-minded president—each in his or her way was a symbol of the twenties. High standards of living were steadily spreading; America had more human comfort for more human beings than any other society had ever before supplied.

The stock market crash of 1929 ended it all. Millions of speculators had been buying stocks on margin, paying only a fraction of their cost in cash and often borrowing even the fraction. Credit had swollen beyond the point of safety, and the shrewdest speculators started to sell in the belief that the bubble would burst. Values began to drop disastrously in October 1929, and continued to fall almost without pause until 1933.

Yet the crash was only the immediate cause of the depression. Coolidge prosperity had been distributed unevenly all the time. Agriculture had been in a kind of permanent depression through-

out the 1920s. Farmers had expanded their production and borrowed to finance the expansion, believing that the great demand and high prices of wartime would continue and increase. But the foreign market dried up, the home market shrank, farm prices fell, and farm mortgages began to be foreclosed. Workers, too, went into debt to raise their standard of living. It was business, especially big business, that had made the greatest gains of the Coolidge era.

The Great Depression was worldwide, but nowhere more serious than in the United States. In the early 1930s sixteen million Americans, a third of the national labor force, were unemployed. Between 1929 and 1933 the value of the gross national product fell almost 50 percent. A few intellectuals turned to Marxism, but there was no organized movement for revolution. People continued to put their trust in established American institutions. Local authorities and private charities helped soften the worst suffering.

In 1932 President Hoover established the RFC (Reconstruction Finance Corporation) to re-

A soup kitchen in New York City, 1931.

lease frozen assets, but generally clung to the belief that things would take care of themselves. In the election of 1932, those who wanted a more vigorous government attack on economic problems voted for the Democrats, electing Franklin D. Roosevelt president.

The New Deal

President Roosevelt (1933–1945) took office in the midst of a financial crisis that had closed banks all over the country. He summoned Congress to an emergency session and declared a bank holiday. The action boosted national morale. Gradually the sound banks reopened, and the government enacted a series of measures called the New Deal, in part aimed at immediate problems but in part designed to change American society permanently.

Often the men who sponsored the measures were not sure in their own minds which motive was the stronger or what they were really trying to do. The New Deal brought to the United States social welfare measures like those we have al-

ready encountered in Victorian and Edwardian Britain and in Bismarckian Germany. The New Dealers abandoned the gold standard in order to lower the price of American goods in world markets no longer tied to gold. By a large-scale program of public works they aimed to relieve unemployment. They extended the activities of the RFC and created new government lending agencies in order to unfreeze credit. They safeguarded bank deposits and regulated stock market speculation through the Federal Deposit Insurance Corporation and the Securities and Exchange Commission. These were immediate measures.

The long-term measures included the Social Security Act of 1935, introducing unemployment insurance, old-age pensions, and other benefits. Increased federal taxation led to a somewhat more even distribution of the national wealth. Agricultural legislation regulated crops and prices to an unprecedented degree. New laws dealing with labor relations increased the power of organized labor. In the Tennessee Valley Authority, the government created a regional planning board that wholly changed the economic life of a relatively backward area by checking erosion, instituting flood control, and providing cheap electric power from government-built dams.

These measures were hotly debated. Each of them made some Americans protest that the government was interfering with their rights. The New Deal changed American society. Government now tried to prevent the wasteful exploitation of natural resources. To some degree it regulated the distribution of wealth. More of the very poorest people were helped into the middle class. The gross national product began to mount once more.

The strength of American institutions and the resilience of the American people, reinforced by the New Deal, began to pull the United States out of the depression. In 1939, when war came in Europe, Americans mostly hoped to remain neutral. But they were not tired or cynical like the French. Republicans often bitterly attacked "that man in the White House" and all his works. But Republicans and Democrats were not like the French left and right. In America neither side ever dreamed of attacking the basic framework of the nation. When the great international crisis came in 1939–1941, Americans were divided but found little difficulty in closing their ranks for war.

The Loosening of Imperial Ties

Before World War I (see Chapter 16), native nationalist movements occasionally made trouble for a colonial power. The war speeded the growth of such nationalism. Non-Western peoples had rendered important services to the colonial powers. The Arabs had raised armies. The Allies had fought the war in the name of self-determination, and Wilson put the "interests of the populations" of colonial areas on the same level with the interests of the colonial powers.

After the war the Allies kept their colonies. And they added to their territories by the mandate system whose very terms called for gradual emancipation. During the years between the wars, it was in the Far East that old imperial ties were most decisively loosened.

Japan, the only non-Western industrialized nation, gave the vote to all men after World War I. Political parties and labor unions came into existence. But European-style parliamentary democratic institutions lost out to a clique of powerful army officers, hostile to civilian government. Supported by business interests, they used the emperor as spokesman for their views. They systematically assassinated their political enemies and by the 1930s had begun to erect a military dictatorship.

Elections were held, but their results were disregarded. State Shinto, a cult of emperor worship designed to win popular support for an aggressive foreign policy, was cooked up by the military for mass consumption. In Japan the "thought police" played the role of the Gestapo in Hitler's Germany. Like fascists or Nazis, the Japanese militarists claimed to be a have-not nation. They urged an increase in their already too-large population, and planned a program of aggressive expansion abroad, chiefly against China.

Exploited by Japanese and Europeans (see Chapter 16), China in 1911 underwent a revolution. It was patterned in part on Western ideas and examples, though directed against Westerners and pro-Western Chinese. And it overthrew the emperor, Pu-yi. One faction of the revolutionaries, the Nationalists (Kuomintang), led by Sun Yat-sen, wanted a democratic parliamentary republic of China that would adapt industrialism to the old Chinese family and village structure. Their rivals, led by Yüan Shih-k'ai, favored a regime that would modernize China by dictatorial methods. By 1914, Yüan had won and become president. But the defeated Sun has remained the hero of the revolution.

During World War I, Yüan died (1916) and authority fell into the hands of rival warlords. Even before that, Japan had secretly presented "twenty-one demands," virtually requesting a protectorate over China. The feeble Chinese Republic saved itself only by declaring war on the Central Powers and so winning Allied protection.

At the end of the war, the Allies, especially the United States, moved to check the ambitions of Japan. At the Washington Conference of 1922, Japan signed the Nine-Power Treaty guaranteeing the independence of China. Frustrated in their Chinese ambitions, the Japanese warlords blamed the United States. Their hostility would culminate with the attack on Pearl Harbor in 1941.

In the years between the wars, the Kuomintang came under the leadership of Chiang Kai-shek, an army officer trained in Japan, the brother-in-law of Sun Yat-sen. He never succeeded in putting down the warlords and establishing an effective central government. The communists competed with the Kuomintang for the loyalty of almost five hundred million Chinese,

An American newspaper cartoon of 1931 on the Japanese seizure of Manchuria.

mostly illiterate peasants. The Japanese waited for their opportunity to intervene.

In September 1931, Japan invaded Manchuria to seize its resources of coal and iron. In 1932 they proclaimed the puppet state of Manchukuo under the nominal rule of the last of the Manchu emperors, Pu-yi, who had been dethroned as a boy in 1912. The Chinese began to boycott Japanese goods, and the Japanese attacked the great Chinese port of Shanghai. The League of Nations proved unable to give more than moral support.

In July 1937, the Japanese launched a full-fledged invasion designed to conquer all of China. They seized the strategic ports of the coastal area and the heavily populated lower river valleys. Chiang withdrew his government and his army inland, establishing his capital at Chungking. When the United States became involved in World War II, it assisted Chiang by road and air from India and Burma. Chiang's government survived the Japanese defeat in World War II.

But Chiang's ineffectual rule and the corruption of his government and his officers prevented the Kuomintang from winning the loyalty of all the Chinese. The communists eventually would succeed in China where the Kuomintang

had failed. Encouraged from Moscow in the 1920s, the communists had begun as the left wing of the Kuomintang, accepted at first by Sun Yat-sen and even by Chiang.

In 1926, however, Chiang opened a campaign against the communists, and they were then expelled from the Kuomintang. The Chinese communists got no help from Stalin, who believed the time was not yet ripe for a proletarian regime in China. Led by Mao Tse-tung, the communists withdrew on the "long march" to the distant northern province of Yenan and established a base among the peasantry there.

Throughout the Japanese occupation, the communists organized a network of armies and councils in and around the Japanese positions. As Mao himself put it, they were the fish that could live in the water that surrounded them. By 1945 they were prepared to come to grips with Chiang.

India and the Near East

India's role in World War I, along with Allied propaganda in favor of self-determination, contributed to the Indian demand for self-government. In India the Muslims loathed the Hindu worship of many gods and the portrayal of these divinities in human form, and resented the caste system with its assertions of Brahmin superiority. The Hindus felt horrified and insulted by the Muslim disregard of Hindu feelings of reverence for the cow.

In the west (the Indus basin, the Punjab) and in a part of Bengal in the east the Muslims were a majority. Elsewhere Muslims lived scattered among Hindus. The Muslims were primarily peasants. More Hindus engaged in industry and were financially successful. Their mutual dislike led to the foundation of two movements to oust the British, the Indian National Congress, among Hindus, and the All-India Muslim League.

The Indian National Congress gained vast influence in India and worldwide fame through the leadership of Mahatma Gandhi (1869–1948), educated in law at Oxford and with political experience as a member of the Indian minority in South Africa. His simple and austere personal life, with its fasts and spinning, endeared him to his own people. His invention of "nonviolent noncooperation" as a political technique appealed to Hindus, who generally disliked force.

Gandhi used the boycott and the voluntary hunger strike against the British. Many of his followers used agitation that was hard to distinguish from violence. The British gave concession after concession. The Indians won experience in provincial government jobs as well as in the civil service. When the Second World War broke out, dominion status for India seemed just around the corner. But mutual antagonism between Muslim and Hindu would later lead to the creation of two new dominions instead of one.

After the Ottoman Empire collapsed at the end of World War I, the Arab territories were administered as mandates. The French took over Syria and Lebanon, the British Palestine, Transjordan, and Iraq. Saudi Arabia, occupying the bulk of the desert peninsula, was welded into a personal kingdom by Ibn Saud (1880–1953). These arrangements left the Arab nationalists dissatisfied.

Arab leadership was disunited but agreed on one thing: hostility to the immigration of Jews into Palestine and to the prospect of a Jewish "national home." In 1925 and 1926, the French used force against rebellions in Syria. The British were gentler. In 1922, for example, Egypt was proclaimed an independent kingdom, although Britain retained the right to station troops there. The Second World War exacerbated Arab nationalism. This wrecked the British effort to lead the Arabs toward independence and retain their friendship at the same time. Meanwhile, Western oil companies were developing the oilfields in Iran and Iraq and along the Persian Gulf.

The Turkish core of the old Ottoman state was revitalized by the revolutionary impulse of

Mahatma Gandhi, 1921.

the nationalist leader Mustafa Kemal (1881–1938, see Chapter 16). His Republic of Turkey had a Western-style constitution, and Kemal proceeded to a rapid and sometimes ruthless westernization of Turkish life. He abolished the red fez of the men, a traditional symbol of the old regime, and emancipated women, at least in principle. He forced the Turks to write their language in the Latin alphabet instead of the Arabic. For the first time mass literacy in Turkey became feasible.

Kemal strove to turn society away from the conservative influence of Islam. He called himself "Atatürk," Father of the Turks. Westernization moved more slowly than Kemal would have liked. After his death it became safer to defend the old system, and much reactionary sentiment has persisted into our own times.

Far less successful was the effort at modernization made in Iran (the name officially taken by Persia in 1935). The small class of wealthy landlords and the millions of poor peasants and restless tribesmen gave no appropriate social base for political westernization. Reza Shah, an army officer who seized the throne in 1925, tried feverishly but erratically and vainly to modernize Iran. When he supported Hitler in the Second World War, the old rivals in Persia, England and Russia, sent troops to force his abdication. Imperial ties were thus loosened but by no means dissolved.

IV THE SECOND WORLD WAR

Efforts to Keep the Peace

In the Locarno Treaty (October 1925), Germany, France, and Belgium agreed on a mutual guarantee of their frontiers, and Britain and Italy agreed to punish any power that might violate this treaty. The "Locarno spirit" led to Germany's admission to the League of Nations (1926) and signing of the Kellogg-Briand Pact (1928). The French withdrew the last of their Rhineland occupation forces (1930) well before they were obliged to do so.

Though not a member of the League of Nations, the United States helped further disarmament. At the Washington conference of 1921–1922, the naval powers agreed not to build any new battleships or heavy cruisers for a period of ten years, and set the ratio of tonnages for such warships at 5 for the United States and Brit-

ain, to 3 for Japan, and 1.67 for France and Italy. But a second conference in London in 1930 failed to reach agreement on further naval limitations. A disarmament conference sponsored by the League at Geneva 1932 failed because the Germans were asking equality in armament, and France refused.

Of course the depression, which sapped the morale of the democracies and played a major role in Hitler's success in Germany, lay behind the growth of international suspicion. The international atmosphere was also poisoned by the Soviet Union, openly dedicated to the fomenting of communist revolutions abroad by any means. The United States' withdrawal into isolationism helped make French policy unrelenting. French fear of Germany led not only to insistence on the enforcement of every provision of the Versailles Treaty that sought to keep Germany weak, but also to France's new alliances with Poland and with the "Little Entente" (Czechoslovakia, Yugoslavia, and Romania), all of which were anti-German.

To the British, however, French fear looked much like a renewed French ambition to dominate the Continent, a thing they had fought against for centuries. The British themselves were isolationist, unwilling to make firm commitments in Europe. The divergence between France and Britain greatly weakened the League of Nations.

Britain rejected a "Geneva protocol" (1924) that would have bound its signatories to settle their international disputes by arbitration. And the League was powerless when Mussolini bombarded and occupied the Greek island of Corfu (1923) after five Italians working for the League in marking out a new frontier between Greece and Albania had been assassinated. If France and Britain had not been in disagreement over the French occupation of the Ruhr, they could have seen to it that the League punished Mussolini.

The Road to War

What eventually made war inevitable was the dictators' policy of aggression, of which the Corfu affair was merely a warning. Step by step during the 1930s, with the League unable to stop them, Japan, Italy, and Germany upset the peace of the world. The Japanese seizure of Manchuria in 1931 was the first step. Henry L. Stimson, the American secretary of state, declared that the United States would recognize no gains made by armed force; but the other democracies failed to follow his lead. An official report to the League of Nations branded the Japanese as aggressors, but no nation seemed interested.

In October 1933 Hitler withdrew Germany from the League. On March 16, 1935, he denounced the Versailles limitations on German armaments and openly began to rebuild the German armies. In April the League condemned this action, but Hitler went on rearming. In May France hastily concluded a treaty of alliance with the U.S.S.R. against German aggression. Hitler continued rearming. In June the British signed a naval agreement with Germany, limiting the German navy to one-third the size of the British and the German submarine force to 60 percent of the British.

To the French these actions by the British seemed like treachery. In March 1936 Hitler sent German troops into the Rhineland, the zone demilitarized by the Treaty of Versailles. Once again he met with nothing but verbal protests. A united British-French show of force against this violation of Germany's obligations would have ended Hitler's career then and there.

In 1934, Mussolini demanded Ethiopia for Italy. The British and the French tried to appease him by offering economic and political concessions in Ethiopia, but they did insist that Ethiopia remain independent, for it was a member of the League. But Mussolini invaded Ethiopia in October 1935, avenging with planes, tanks, and poison gas the humiliating defeat inflicted on Italy by the Ethiopians in 1896. The king of Italy became emperor of Ethiopia.

The Ethiopian emperor, Haile Selassie, denounced the aggression before the League. A majority of League members voted to invoke Article 16 of the Covenant to impose economic sanctions against a member that had gone to war in violation of its pledges. But sanctions failed. Oil was not included among the forbidden articles, and the Italians continued to buy it freely. Britain and France did nothing to check the movement of Italian troops and munitions through the Suez Canal. The failure of the sanctions against Italy finished the League as an instrument in international politics. Italy withdrew from the League in 1937.

In July 1936 came the Franco coup against the Spanish Republic and the start of the Spanish Civil War, in which Hitler, Mussolini, and Stalin all intervened, while the Western democracies failed to send arms to the legal government as sanctioned by international law. The fascist success in Spain increased their appetites as well as their boldness. In October 1936 Mussolini signed

with Hitler the pact formally establishing a Rome-Berlin "Axis." Early in 1938 Hitler began a violent newspaper and radio propaganda campaign against the Austrian government. He summoned Chancellor Schuschnigg to his Bavarian retreat in Berchtesgaden, screamed abuse at him, and moved the German armies into Vienna. He had swallowed Austria.

Hitler's next target was the Czechoslovak republic, the only Central or Eastern European state where parliamentary democracy had succeeded, thanks to a rich and well-balanced economy and to the enlightened policies of the first president, Thomas Masaryk. But Czechoslovakia also included a minority of 3.4 million Germans, who felt contempt for the Slavs and tried to sabotage the republic. Hitler supported the agitation of these "Sudeten" Germans and in the spring of 1938 demanded autonomy for them. The Czechs counted on their alliance with France to protect them against the dismemberment of their country. But neither the French nor the British were willing to run the risk of a military showdown with Hitler.

By September 1938 Hitler was screaming against the Czechs. A full-fledged European crisis broke out. Twice the British prime minister, Neville Chamberlain, personally pleaded with Hitler to moderate his demands. Then, at Munich (September 19, 1938), Hitler and Mussolini met with Chamberlain and the French premier, Daladier. Though allied with France, the U.S.S.R. was not invited to Munich. Stalin concluded that the Western powers were interested only in turning Hitler's armies east against him, and that he had better make what terms he could.

At Munich, Hitler won the consent of the democracies to the dismemberment of Czechoslovakia. The Czechs were forced to give in. The Germans took over the Sudeten lands along with the mountain defenses of the Czech border. Poland received small border areas. Slovakia received autonomy, Hitler guaranteed the remainder. But, after a six-months' lull, Hitler marched his forces into Prague. This was the last straw. Finally, Chamberlain was convinced that Hitler could never be counted on to keep his word. The "peace with honor" that Chamberlain had proudly announced he had won at Munich proved to have been neither.

The British now (April 1939) guaranteed assistance to Poland, next on Hitler's schedule. And Mussolini, who had been trying vainly to bully France into ceding Nice, Savoy, Corsica, and Tunisia, found an enemy he could intimidate and

Europe on the Eve of World War II, August 1939

Neutral countries

The Axis Powers

Areas annexed by Germany 1935-1939

Areas made "protectorates" of Germany, 1939

Annexed by Italy, 1939

attacked the backward little Balkan state of Albania (April 1939).

From the first, appeasement of Hitler was hopeless. All along he had intended to destroy Czechoslovakia and move against Poland. Contemptuous of the French and British, he was prepared to fight them if he could avoid a two-front war. To this end he opened negotiations with Stalin, who was already convinced that the Soviet Union could never depend on Britain and France.

On August 23, 1939, to the horror of the West, Germany and Russia reached a nonaggression pact. They agreed secretly on a new partition of Poland. When the Germans invaded Poland a week later, the British and French declared war on Germany. The victorious Allies of the First

"Rendezvous": Low cartoon comment on the Hitler-Stalin pact, August 1939.

World War had with extreme reluctance abandoned their defensive position. World War II was under way.

Early Successes of the Axis

World War II was truly global. Major fighting took place in the Mediterranean, in Russia, in the Pacific, as well as on Western European fronts. Planes became major weapons on land and sea. Bombing from the air brought populations of the cities into the front lines. Experts were surprised at the bravery with which civilians stood up to the attacks, even those from the pilotless planes and rockets used by the Germans near the end of the war. In the final act of warfare (August 1945) the United States dropped the first two atomic bombs on two Japanese cities. These two blasts killed more than 100,000 people. The human race had now learned to destroy itself altogether, and prevention of atomic war became its most pressing problem.

World War II began with Hitler's rapid conquest of Poland. By agreement Stalin took over eastern Poland and the Baltic states of Latvia, Estonia, and Lithuania. In November 1939, the Russians attacked Finland to gain military and naval bases on its soil. It took the huge Russian armies four whole months to defeat the Finns. Hitler noted the Russian weakness. Throughout the fall and winter of 1939–1940, Hitler made no military move on the Western front. This "phony war" created a false sense of security.

In April 1940, however, Hitler suddenly invaded Denmark and Norway. Norwegian resistance, helped by token forces from Britain, lasted only a couple of weeks. On May 10, Hitler followed up this victory by a lightning attack on Holland, Luxembourg, and Belgium, and moved on into France, supported by fierce aerial bombardment.

Outflanking the French fortifications, the Germans swept to the Channel, separating the British armies from the French. In London, Neville Chamberlain was now replaced as prime minister by Winston Churchill, long an outspoken enemy of appeasement, who would rise to heroic stature as the war continued.

The Belgians surrendered in early June 1940. The British evacuated 215,000 of their own and 120,000 French troops from Dunkirk. In late May Hitler drove on to Paris, which the French evacuated without fighting on June 13.

Hoping that the French would continue the fight from southern France or from North Africa, Churchill now offered France political union with

Hitler in Paris, 1940.

Britain after the war. But French politicians who wished to surrender installed as premier the aged hero of World War I, Marshal Pétain. Pétain surrendered on the exact spot where the Germans had signed the Armistice of November 1918. Too late to affect the outcome, Mussolini now declared war on France, a "stab in the back" that greatly distressed American opinion, already disturbed by the Nazi success.

By the new armistice terms, the Germans occupied the northern three-fifths of France, including the Channel and Atlantic coasts. Pétain and a group of pro-German politicians led by Pierre Laval governed the rest of France from Vichy. The Vichy regime adopted "Labor, Family, Fatherland" instead of "Liberty, Equality, Fraternity" as the slogan of France.

General Charles de Gaulle, with a few followers, flew to London. With British help he established a "Free French," or "Fighting French," movement. Inside France, underground resistance groups formed to harass the occupiers. French North Africa came under Vichy control, but the French colonies south of the Sahara provided a base for anti-German activities.

Turning Points

Hitler expected that the British would make a separate peace, leaving him in control of Europe, but they did not. He then hoped a submarine blockade would starve them out, but overrated its possibilities. He thought of landing troops in England, but he had not made proper preparation. In August 1940 he decided to try to bomb the British into submission.

In the decisive "Battle of Britain" the Royal Air Force, using the new detection apparatus called radar, managed to shoot down more bombers than Hitler could afford to lose. By late September 1940 the Germans had been forced to switch from daylight to night bombing. But they could neither knock out British industrial production nor terrorize the British people into submission. By winter Hitler had met his first real defeat, although it was not so clear at the time.

In October 1940 Mussolini, without consulting Hitler, invaded Greece from his base in Albania. The Greek army drove the Italians northwards and held them on a front stretching across the Albanian mountains. Soon Mussolini needed help. Hitler lined up with the Balkan nations of Romania and Bulgaria.

In Yugoslavia, however, a Serb-led military coup unseated a government that would have given the Germans permission to cross their soil to go to Mussolini's aid. So in the spring of 1941, the Germans had to use precious time and troops to invade and dismember Yugoslavia, and to conquer Greece. They drove a British expeditionary force from Greece and finally captured the island of Crete in a spectacular glider and parachute operation.

In June 1941 Hitler launched his invasion

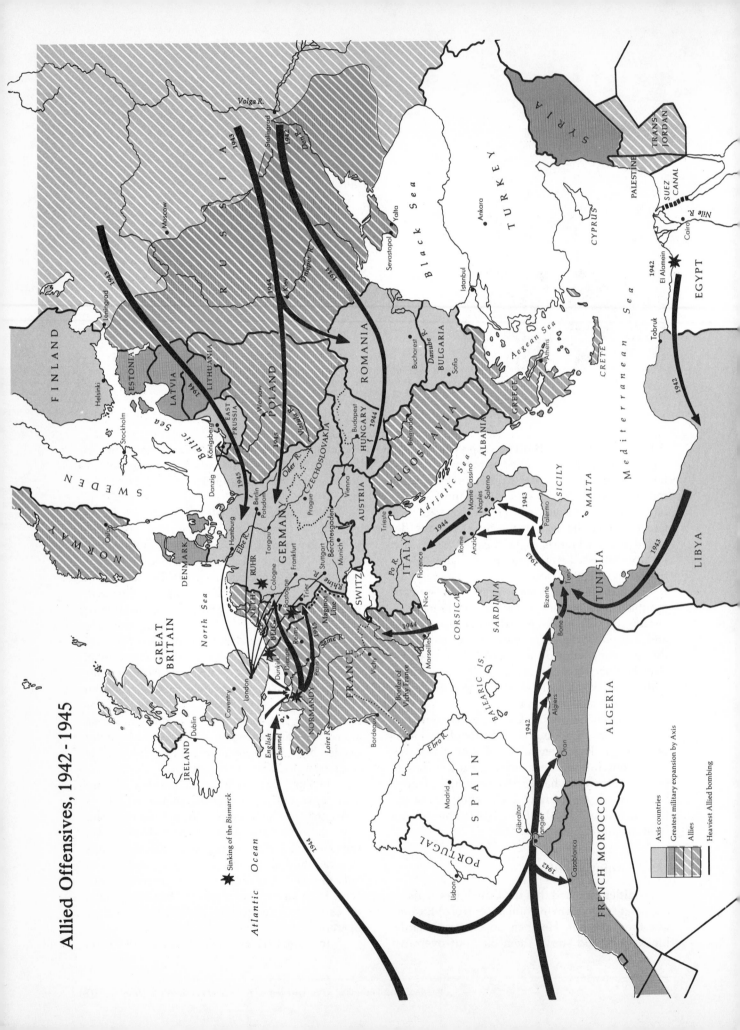

Allied Offensives, 1942 - 1945

Volga R.

R U S S I A

1943

1943

Moscow

Stalingrad

1942

Don R.

Leningrad 1943

FINLAND

Helsinki

1944

LITHUANIA

Dnieper R.

LATVIA

ESTONIA

Stockholm

Baltic Sea

EAST PRUSSIA

Königsberg

Kiev

1944

1944

SWEDEN

Oslo

NORWAY

Danzig

1945

Warsaw

Vistula R.

POLAND

1945

Berlin

Potsdam

Oder R.

Prague

CZECHOSLOVAKIA

Vienna

Budapest

1944

HUNGARY

ROMANIA

Bucharest

Danube R.

BULGARIA

Sofia

Belgrade

Yalta

Sevastopol

Black Sea

Istanbul

Ankara

T U R K E Y

CYPRUS

SYRIA

TRANS JORDAN

PALESTINE

SUEZ CANAL

Nile R.

Cairo

DENMARK

Hamburg

Elbe R.

Torgau

Frankfurt

Munich

Stuttgart

GERMANY

AUSTRIA

Trieste

YUGOSLAVIA

ALBANIA

GREECE

Athens

Aegean Sea

CRETE

1942

El Alamein

EGYPT

Tobruk

1942

Mediterranean Sea

GREAT BRITAIN

North Sea

Coventry

London

Dover

Dunkirk

Dieppe

NETH.

RUHR

Cologne

Bastogne

BEL.

Trier

Reims

1945

Seine R.

Berchtesgaden

Maginot Line

Rhine R.

SWITZ.

NORMANDY

FRANCE

Paris

Vichy

Border of Vichy France

Po R.

Monte Cassino

Salerno

Naples

Anzio

Rome

ITALY

Florence

1944

1944

Adriatic Sea

SICILY

Palermo

1943

MALTA

1943

IRELAND

Dublin

English Channel

Loire R.

Bordeaux

Nice

Marseilles

1944

CORSICA

SARDINIA

BALEARIC IS.

SPAIN

Madrid

Ebro R.

Lisbon

PORTUGAL

Gibraltar

Tangier

Oran

Algiers

1942

Bizerte

Bone

Tunis

TUNISIA

1943

1943

LIBYA

ALGERIA

FRENCH MOROCCO

Casablanca

1942

Atlantic Ocean

1944

Sinking of the Bismarck

★ Sinking of the Bismarck

Axis countries

Greatest military expansion by Axis

Allies

Heaviest Allied bombing

of the U.S.S.R. For him the Russian plains, with their wealth of natural resources had always been Germany's "living space." He was sure he could quickly defeat the Russians and then finish off Britain. He almost succeeded.

Within two months the Germans were besieging Leningrad. By October they had conquered the entire Ukraine and were closing in on Moscow. But winter was also closing in, and the months lost in the Balkans the previous spring could not be regained. The Soviet government had transferred some of its heavy industry far to the east, and American supplies were beginning to arrive.

The German armies had not been equipped for a winter of war in Russia. If they had given decent treatment to the anti-Stalinist Ukrainian people they had overrun, they could have found much support. Instead they were brutal conquerers and had to hold down their conquest by force. Soviet counteroffensives between December 1941 and May 1942 pushed the Germans back.

By then Hitler was also at war with the United States. When World War II began in 1939, there was a vocal body of isolationist sentiment in the United States, and there were a few Axis sympathizers. But much public opinion opposed Hitler from the first. The fall of France and the Battle of Britain strengthened these views. Between June 1940 and December 1941, the Roosevelt administration with the consent of Congress took a series of measures "short of war" to aid Britain and then Russia.

In exchange for Atlantic naval bases in British colonies, the United States gave the British fifty overage destroyers. Washington sent arms to Britain and used the American navy to assure delivery. The "Lend-Lease Act" (March 1941) authorized the president to supply war materials to any country whose defense he deemed "vital to the defense of the United States." When Hitler attacked the U.S.S.R., American supplies were sent.

Hitler had legal justification for regarding American actions as warlike. But it was his commitments to Japan that eventually got him into the war with the United States. After the fall of France, the Japanese militarists had stepped up their program of expansion in Asia, moving into French Indo-China (later Vietnam) and pushing ahead in China itself. The United States government froze Japanese credits, strove to shut off Japanese access to raw materials, and pressed the Japanese to withdraw from China and Indo-China.

While Japanese and American officials were discussing these matters, the Japanese without warning attacked the American fleet in Pearl Harbor with carrier-based planes (December 7, 1941). Though the attack did severe damage, it did not knock out the American navy, but it galvanized American opinion. The United States (with a single representative in Congress dissenting) declared war on Japan.

Thereupon Hitler and Mussolini declared war on the United States. The Americans increased lend-lease aid and actively helped the struggle against German submarines. In the Pacific the Japanese overran Guam, Wake Island, and the Philippines. By the spring of 1942 they had also taken Malaya—including Singapore—from the British and Indonesia from the Dutch. In control of Southeast Asia, they seemed poised for an attack on Australia.

Against Japan the first turning point came in the battle of the Coral Sea in May 1942. Carrier-based American planes dispersed a Japanese fleet aiming at the conquest of Port Moresby, Papua, on the big island of New Guinea. Against the European Axis, the United States and Britain landed in Morocco and Algeria in November 1942, overcoming brief opposition from the Vichy French. The plan was to crush the Germans and Italians holding Libya between these new Anglo-American forces moving eastward and British armies in Egypt moving westward.

The Vichy regime delivered Tunis to the Germans and enabled them to reinforce their armies in North Africa. But this only delayed the successful closing of the Allied vise. In May 1943 the Allies took the last Axis strongholds in Tunisia and accepted the surrender of 300,000 Axis troops under the German general Rommel, "the desert fox." The victory was not decisive, but allied morale soared.

More decisive was the successful Russian defense of Stalingrad in the summer and autumn of 1942, which turned into an offensive in November. Hampered by shortages of gasoline and by their very long communication lines, the Germans never quite reached the Russian oilfields in the Caucasus. By early 1943 the Russians were beginning the great push westward that eventually took them to Berlin two years later. Less spectacular, but perhaps most important, was the gradual victory over German submarines in the Atlantic. Convoys, plane patrols, and radar slowly cut down the sinkings that in 1942 had threatened to keep American supplies from getting to Europe.

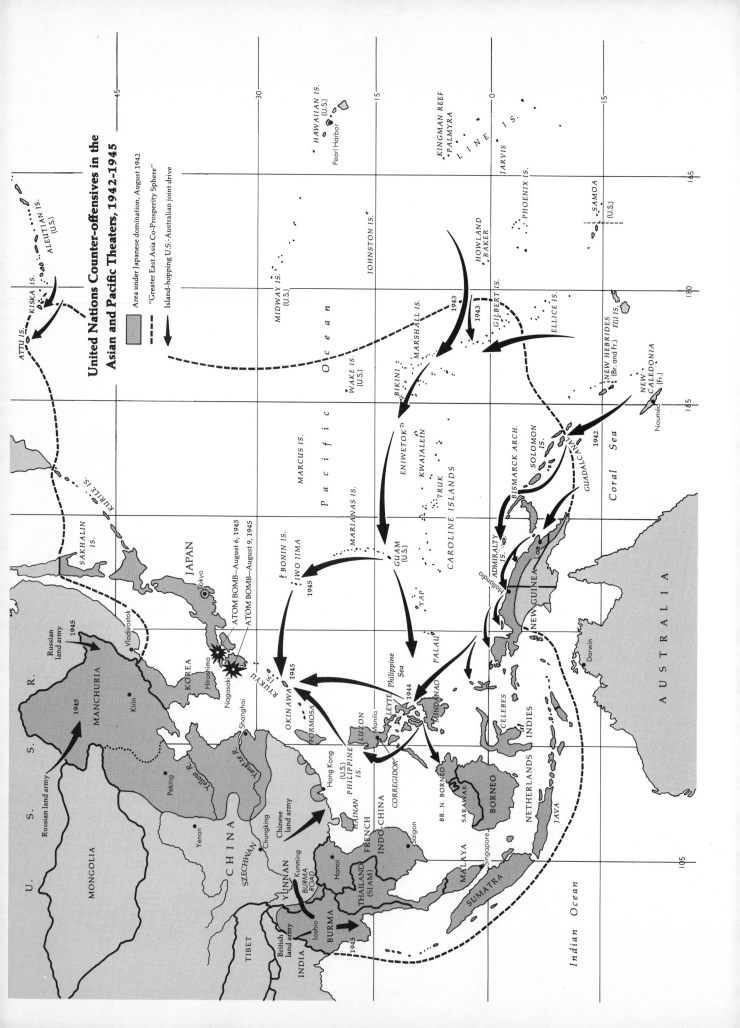

United Nations Counter-offensives in the Asian and Pacific Theaters, 1942-1945

Area under Japanese domination, August 1942

"Greater East Asia Co-Prosperity Sphere"

Island-hopping U.S.–Australian joint drive

ATTU IS.

KISKA IS.

ALEUTIAN IS. (U.S.)

HAWAIIAN IS. (U.S.)

Pearl Harbor

KINGMAN REEF

PALMYRA

L I N E

JARVIS IS.

PHOENIX IS.

SAMOA (U.S.)

JOHNSTON IS.

MIDWAY IS. (U.S.)

HOWLAND
BAKER

GILBERT IS.

1943

1943

ELLICE IS.

NEW HEBRIDES (Br. and Fr.)

Fiji IS.

NEW CALEDONIA (Fr.)

Nouméd

WAKE IS. (U.S.)

BIKINI

MARSHALL IS.

P a c i f i c   O c e a n

MARCUS IS.

ENIWETOK

KWAJALEIN

TRUK

CAROLINE ISLANDS

BISMARCK ARCH.

SOLOMON IS.

GUADALCANAL

1942

Coral Sea

MARIANAS IS.

GUAM (U.S.)

YAP

PALAU

ADMIRALTY IS.

Hollandia

NEW GUINEA

Lae

AUSTRALIA

Darwin

BONIN IS.

IWO JIMA

1945

ATOM BOMB—August 6, 1945

ATOM BOMB—August 9, 1945

JAPAN

Tokyo

Hiroshima

Nagasaki

KOREA

RYUKYU IS.

OKINAWA

1945

FORMOSA

Philippine
Sea

LEYTE

1944

LUZON

Manila

PHILIPPINE IS.

CORREGIDOR

MINDANAO

CELEBES

NETHERLANDS
INDIES

JAVA

U. S. S. R.

Vladivostok

SAKHALIN IS.

KURILE IS.

Russian
land army

1945

MANCHURIA

Kirin

1945

Shanghai

Hong Kong (U.S.)

HAINAN

BR. N. BORNEO

SARAWAK

BORNEO

SUMATRA

MALAYA

Singapore

MONGOLIA

Peking

Yenan

Yellow R.

C H I N A

SZECHWAN

Chungking

Yangtze R.

YUNNAN

Kunming

BURMA ROAD

Hanoi

Saigon

FRENCH INDO-CHINA

THAILAND (SIAM)

BURMA

Lashio

1945

British
land army

INDIA

TIBET

Chinese
land army

Indian Ocean

45

30

15

0

15

165

180

165

105

The Allied Victory

After this series of turning points, the Allies took the offensive everywhere. Allied bombers hit at German factories producing ball-bearings and jet-aircraft, at oil refineries and locomotives. Planes rained fire on the flimsily built Japanese cities. The Americans and British moved north from Tunis to Sicily (July 1943) and six weeks later onto the Italian mainland.

High Italian officers and dissident fascists organized a coup leading to Mussolini's fall and imprisonment. The Allies negotiated with a new government under Marshal Badoglio. But a special detachment of German troops rescued Mussolini (September 1943) and set him up once again as head of a "Fascist Republic" in the north. In 1945 he was caught and executed by communist

guerillas. The Allied military campaign moved slowly northwards. Rome did not fall until June 1944. When the Germans finally collapsed early in 1945, a front still stretched across Italy from a point north of Florence to Rimini.

At a conference in Teheran (December 1943), Churchill, Roosevelt, and Stalin decided that the main Allied war effort would be in France. Landings under the command of the American general Eisenhower began in Normandy (June 6, 1944). Landing craft, amphibious vehicles, and artificial harbors, superiority in the air, surprise, and a well-organized supply system enabled Eisenhower's men to hold a beachhead and then break out.

Led by General Patton's Third Army, the Allies swept the Germans eastward. A second landing was launched in the south of France and

Corpses of Nazi victims, Belsen concentration camp, 1945.

Allied troops moved easily northward. The French resistance assisted the advance. The population generally welcomed the invaders, who included de Gaulle's Free French troops. Paris was liberated before the end of August. Hitler survived an attempted assassination (July 1944) by a group of conservative and military conspirators. He kept his grip on the German state and armies and continued to fight.

Patton's troops ran out of gasoline. German pilotless planes and rockets fell on England and denied to the Allies the use of the key port of Antwerp. The German armies escaped into Germany. From the east, the Russians had driven Hitler's forces out of Russia, and to the south had swept to a junction with a Yugoslav communist resistance movement led by Tito. The Russians crossed Poland by early 1945, and by March were threatening Berlin.

In February the Western Allies broke the German fortifications and entered the heart of Germany. At Yalta (February 1945), Roosevelt, Churchill, and Stalin reached a new agreement avoiding a race between the Soviet Union and the West for German territory and outlining plans for military government of Germany. At Yalta it was decided that the Russians would be given the honor of taking Berlin. This and many other decisions reached at Yalta would later be severely criticized.

When the Russians entered a Berlin smashed by Allied bombing, Hitler committed suicide on a Germanic funeral pyre in his underground headquarters. President Roosevelt died in April 1945 and was succeeded by Vice-President Harry S Truman. On May 8 Churchill and Truman proclaimed victory in Europe.

The Allied advance into Germany revealed the full horror of the concentration camps. Here slave laborers from conquered countries, political opponents, and "inferior" peoples such as Slavs and Jews had been immured. Thousands of living skeletons, piles of emaciated corpses, told only part of the story. The Nazis had used gas ovens

Chiang Kai-Shek, 1931.

to exterminate literally millions of human beings, chiefly Jews. This was the Holocaust, an episode of such cruel insanity that a generation and more later it still haunts the human race.

Against the Japanese, the American forces began by "island hopping," clearing out Japanese bases in the South and Central Pacific, from Guadalcanal and the Solomons to New Britain and New Guinea and the Philippines; from Tarawa to Eniwetok to Kwajalein to Iwo Jima; and then from the Philippines and Iwo Jima to Okinawa. In the China-Burma-India theater, the Americans, with the British, supplied Chiang Kai-shek by air and kept Chinese forces in the fight against Japan.

Air raids on Japan proper had done immense damage. But the American government was sure that a major campaign against the Japanese home islands was still necessary to end the war. President Truman and his advisers decided that only the use of the newly developed atomic bomb could bring a quick decision. The United States had only two bombs. On August 6, 1945, its planes dropped one on Hiroshima, and three days later another on Nagasaki. Two days after the first bomb was dropped on Hiroshima, the Russians declared war on Japan (August 8, 1945) and began a large-scale invasion of Manchuria. On September 2, the Japanese surrendered. American military occupation under General Douglas MacArthur began.

Unsolved Problems

World War II had been an extraordinary effort. During the war the alliance against the Axis had come to call itself the United Nations. All of Latin America had joined. Exiled governments of states occupied by Hitler and Mussolini were active members. But the coalition was actually managed by Churchill and Roosevelt and Stalin.

Four months before Pearl Harbor, Roosevelt and Churchill met off Newfoundland and issued the Atlantic Charter (August 14, 1941), calling for the abandonment of aggression and the restoration of the rights of conquered peoples. Other top-level meetings during the war culminated in Potsdam (July-August 1945).

On the military side, the Americans and English avoided some of the tensions that had characterized the First World War by organizing completely intermeshing staffs; in this way, an American in command always had a British second and vice versa. The plan worked well. Anxious not to repeat another mistake of 1918, the Allies insisted that Germany would have to surrender "unconditionally." There would be no new German myth about a stab in the back. Many argued that the demand for "unconditional surrender" stiffened the German will to resist.

The British and Americans agreed on unconditional surrender but were inconsistent and disagreed on how much political purity they should demand of those who offered to assist them. Churchill favored the postwar restoration of kings in Italy and Greece. Roosevelt idealistically hoped for democratic republics everywhere. Churchill was more ready than Roosevelt to assist the communist Yugoslav, Tito. Roosevelt suspected de Gaulle and dealt readily with Vichy France. Churchill wholeheartedly supported de Gaulle.

More complicated was the question of Soviet influence in Eastern Europe. At Yalta, the U.S.S.R. promised to allow free elections in Poland, Hungary, Czechoslovakia, and the Balkan countries. The Western Allies accepted the assurance. Perhaps the West should have realized that by "free" elections the Russians meant elections that would return a procommunist majority. Perhaps it was foolish of the British and Americans to let the Russians advance so far west.

At the time, however, the United States and Britain wanted to keep the Russians actively in the war. Since nobody yet knew whether the atomic bomb would work, the Allies feared a long and bloody war with Japan. Churchill suspected that the Russians would try to communize Eastern and Southeastern Europe but was ready to run the risk. Except for Czechoslovakia, no prewar Eastern European state had been democratic anyhow.

After the war ended there was no peace. In Asia "colonial" peoples struggled against "imperialism." In Europe important issues remained unsolved. On both continents Stalin's Russia succeeded Hitler's Germany as the menace to Western peace and stability.

General Works

G. A. Craig, *Europe since 1914* (*Holt). A good textbook account.

H. Arendt, *Origins of Totalitarianism* (*Meridian). A philosopher's studies of some basic ideas underlying the totalitarian regimes.

E. Wiskemann, *Europe of the Dictators, 1919–1945* (*Little, Brown). By a leading expert on Central Europe, but equally good on other areas.

J. R. Western, *The End of European Primacy, 1871–1945* (*Colophon); and F. Gilbert, *The End of the European Era, 1890 to the Present* (*Norton). Both these books begin at an earlier point than this chapter, but the basic argument that Europe was ousted from its central position in the world by World War I is thrashed out during the discussions of our period in this chapter.

R. J. Sontag, *A Broken World, 1919–1939* (*Harper Torchbooks). Stops with the outbreak of World War II, but is very useful on the years between the wars.

Communist Russia

W. E. Chamberlin, *The Russian Revolution*, 2 vols. (*Universal Library). First published in 1935, but still in its present revised form the standard single work on the revolution itself.

B. Moore, Jr., *Soviet Politics: The Dilemma of Power* (*Harper Torchbooks). The relationships between communist ideas and Soviet practice as discussed by a sociologist.

M. Fainsod, *How Russia Is Ruled,* 2nd ed. (1963). Preferable to the more recent edition for its discussion of the period before very recent times.

M. Fainsod, *Smolensk under Soviet Rule* (*Vintage). A fascinating case-study of a single important city and its government in the late 1930s from captured original documents.

R. V. Daniels, *The Nature of Communism* (*Vintage), a fine study; and *The Russian Revolution* (*Prentice-Hall), a fine selection of source materials with excellent brief commentaries.

D. Shub, *Lenin* (*Mentor, abridged). A good biography of Lenin.

I. Deutscher, *The Prophet Unarmed* and *The Prophet Outcast.* Volumes II and III of the best, though highly favorable, biography of Trotsky. See Chapter 16 for the listing of Volume I. See also his *Stalin: A Political Biography* (*Galaxy).

A. B. Ulam, *Expansion and Coexistence* (*Praeger). Soviet foreign policy from 1917 to 1967. See also the same au-

thor's *The Bolsheviks: The Intellectual and Political History of the Triumph of Communism in Russia* (1965); *Lenin* (1970); and *Stalin, the Man and His Era* (1973).

R. F. Tucker and S. F. Cohen, eds., *The Great Purge Trial* (*Universal Library). The transcript of the major purge trial of 1938, with good notes.

S. Alliluyeva, *Twenty Letters to a Friend,* trans. P. J. MacMillan (1967). Stalin's daughter, who defected to the United States, writes her memoirs.

Fascism

H. Rogger and E. Weber, eds., *The European Right: A Historical Profile.* A good collection of scholarly essays on right-wing political movements in the various countries of Europe.

A. Coggan, *Dictatorship: Its History and Theory* (1939). A good early study.

P. Viereck, *Metapolitics: From the Romantics to Hitler* (*Capricorn); G. Mosse, *The Crisis of German Ideology: Intellectual Origins of the Third Reich* (*Universal Library); and F. Stern, *The Politics of Cultural Despair* (*Anchor). Three complementary studies of German fascist backgrounds.

E. Nolte, *Three Faces of Fascism* (1965). Considers France, Italy, and Germany.

G. Megaro, *Mussolini in the Making* (1938). A still unequalled biography.

H. Finer, *Mussolini's Italy* (*Universal Library). Good survey by a political scientist.

G. Salvemini, *Under the Axe of Fascism* (1936) and *Prelude to World War II* (1954). Two fine studies by a leading antifascist intellectual in exile.

A. Hitler, *Mein Kampf* (*Sentry). The basic bible of Nazism in English translation.

S. W. Halperin, *Germany Tried Democracy* (*Norton); and E. Eyck, *History of the Weimar Republic* (Science Ed.). Two studies of the Weimar Republic.

A. L. C. Bullock, *Hitler* (*Harper Torchbooks). The best of several biographies in English.

J. Wheeler-Bennett, *Wooden Titan* (1936) and *Nemesis of Power* (1954). The first is a useful book about Hindenburg, the second deals with the German army in politics from 1918 to 1945.

K. D. Bracher, *The German Dictatorship* (1970). By a German scholar, and probably the best single work on Hitler's regime.

F. L. Neumann, *Behemoth: The Structure and Practice of National Socialism*

(*Harper Torchbooks). A thorough analysis by a left-wing German exile.

A. Speer, *Inside the Third Reich,* trans. R. and C. Winston (1970). The memoirs of Hitler's chief city-planner and architect provide a valuable picture of life among the Nazis.

F. von Papen, *Memoirs* (1953). Apologies of the right-wing politician who was in some measure responsible for Hitler's coming to power, and who was acquitted at the Nuremberg trials.

H. Thomas, *The Spanish Civil War* (*Colophon). The most comprehensive single study of the subject.

H. Seton-Watson, *Eastern Europe between the Wars, 1918–1941* (*Harper Torchbooks). Deals with all the Eastern European countries except for Greece and Albania; expert and unbiased.

The Democracies between the Wars and the Loosening of Imperial Ties

C. L. Mowat, *Britain between the Wars, 1918–1940* (*Beacon). Good survey of the years covered in this chapter.

R. Graves and A. Hodge, *The Long Weekend* (*Norton). A lively review of social conditions in England between the wars.

H. Pelling, *Britain, 1885–1955* (*Norton). The book, with a strong emphasis on the labor movement, includes our era.

G. E. Elton, *The Life of James Ramsay MacDonald* (1939); K. Middlemas and J. Barnes, *Baldwin* (1970); and K. Feiling, *The Life of Neville Chamberlain* (1946). Useful biographies of leading politicians.

N. Greene, *From Versailles to Vichy* (*Crowell). Brief, useful survey of interwar France.

D. Brogan, *France under the Republic,* Vol. II (*Harper Torchbooks). A good political survey of France from 1909 to 1939.

R. Albrecht-Carrié, *France, Europe, and Two World Wars* (1961). Sets the troubles of France skillfully against the European background.

S. Hoffman et al., *In Search of France* (*Harper Torchbooks). A good collection of essays, as is J. Joll, ed., *The Decline of the Third Republic* (1959).

D. Thomson, *Democracy in France since 1870* (*Oxford). One of the best efforts at interpretation.

A. M. Schlesinger, Jr., *The Age of Roosevelt,* 3 vols. (*Sentry). A still incomplete but detailed, sympathetic survey of the New Deal years.

W. Leuchtenburg, *Perils of Prosperity, 1912–1932* (*Chicago) and *Franklin D.*

Roosevelt and the New Deal (*Harper Torchbooks). Good general accounts.

J. K. Galbraith, *The Great Crash* (*Sentry). By an economist who writes for the general public.

F. L. Allen, *Only Yesterday* and *Since Yesterday* (*Harper). Lively social histories of the twenties and thirties in America.

F. Perkins, *The Roosevelt I Knew* (*Colophon); and R. E. Sherwood, *Roosevelt and Hopkins* (*Universal Library). By close associates of President Roosevelt.

E. O. Reischauer, *The United States and Japan* (*Compass). Very good on the period between the wars, as is J. K. Fairbank, *The United States and China* (*Harvard).

E. Erikson, *Gandhi's Truth* (*Norton); by a learned psychoanalyst; R. Duncan, *Gandhi's Selected Writings.* Good books for beginners about India's prominent leader.

B. Lewis, *The Emergence of Modern Turkey* (Oxford); and G. Antonius, *The Arab Awakening* (*Capricorn). Both are useful basic introductions.

The Second World War

W. S. Churchill, *The Second World War,* 6 vols. (*Bantam). Splendid history by the great British prime minister and war leader, full of drama.

C. de Gaulle, *The Complete War Memoirs* (*Simon and Schuster). Beautifully written first-hand account of General de Gaulle's experiences.

Department of the Army, *United States Army in World War II* (1947). The department's official history in many volumes. It is matched by S. E. Morison, *History of United States Naval Operations in World War II,* 15 vols. (1947–1962), which has the advantage of being written by a single highly professional historian with a fine style.

E. H. Carr, *The Twenty Years' Crisis* (*Harper Torchbooks); A. J. P. Taylor, *Origins of the Second World War* (*Premier); A. Wolfers, *Britain and France between Two Wars* (*Norton). Three general surveys of the approaches to war, the first two provocative and controversial.

J. Wheeler-Bennett, *Munich* (*Compass); and T. Taylor, *Munich* (1978). The former a less detailed study of the last effort to appease Hitler, the latter a beautifully written but extremely detailed account by an American lawyer, general, and participant in the postwar Nuremberg trials of the Nazis.

G. Wright, *The Ordeal of Total War* (*Harper Torchbooks). An expert evaluation of Europe's involvement in World War II.

R. Wohlstetter, *Pearl Harbor* (*Stanford). A good study.

H. Feis, *Churchill, Roosevelt, and Stalin* (*Princeton). A good study of the relationship between the three top Allied leaders.

NOTE: General Eisenhower, General Montgomery, and President Harry S Truman are three other major leaders whose memoirs make excellent reading on the war years.

CHAPTER EIGHTEEN

The Cold War And Great-Power Domestic Policy:

1945-1970

",...FOR THE U.S.S.R. SOCIALISM IS SOMETHING ALREADY ACHIEVED AND WON..." STALIN

The twenty-five years immediately following World War II, between 1945 and about 1970 have a unity all their own. After 1970 the familiar patterns dissolved, and a new period seems to have begun. In this chapter and the next we deal with events through 1970. Here we discuss very generally the "cold war": the break in the World War II alliances between the West and the U.S.S.R., and the American-Soviet rivalry that replaced them. We then turn to a brief account and estimate of the domestic affairs of the major Western nations and of the Soviet Union.

In the next chapter we examine Soviet foreign policy and its relationship to international affairs in general, and then move on to the cold war in action and the clash between the U.S.S.R., China, and the United States in Asia. Finally, we deal with the emerging nations of Africa, the Middle East, and Latin America, viewed both from within and from the point of view of great-power politics. The two chapters are divided only for convenience and belong together.

Since 1945 the world has managed to avoid a war between the great powers for a much longer period than the twenty-one years that separated the end of World War I from the beginning of World War II. The existence of atomic weapons that would probably kill off much of the human race in another great war has held the powers back. Several times during the troubled years since 1945, world war seemed inevitable. But, despite much terrible localized fighting, it did not happen.

During World War II, most people expected that when the shooting stopped there would be a general peace conference, as there had been after all the earlier modern general wars. But differences in outlook between the Soviet Union and its Western allies, and the tensions that arose between them during the war itself, made a peace conference impossible. So the problems left by World War II had to be solved one by one if at all.

The devastation wrought by the war greatly exceeded even that in World War I: at least forty million dead, more than half of them civilians, and more than $2,000 billion in damage. Despite a sharply rising birth rate and vast programs of economic reconstruction, such losses could never be fully repaired. New and terrifying problems arose. Atomic weapons, hydrogen bombs, and the development of guided missiles threatened that a new general war might exterminate humanity or relegate it to another Stone Age.

The United States and the U.S.S.R. at first were the only powers that could launch or carry on atomic warfare. Leninist teaching and Stalin's own suspicious and vengeful character led the Russians to regard the Americans as their rivals for control of the world. The Americans quickly began to see the Soviet Union in the same light. The postwar history of international politics thus became in large part a history of Soviet-American rivalry: the cold war.

By 1945 German attack and occupation had caused incalculable devastation inside the Russian borders. Russia's capitalist ally, the United States, had remained intact and had invented and used atomic weapons. Stalin knew that if he had been the sole possessor of the atomic bomb, he would have used it against the capitalist world. He assumed the Americans would follow the strategy that he himself would have followed.

Stalin felt that all the technological efforts of the U.S.S.R. to catch up to the industrialized West had now been wiped out by the American development of the atomic bomb. It took Stalin four years (1945–1949) to catch up again by making his own atomic bomb. Scientific information given the Russians by agents and spies doubtless made some contribution to this achievement. But only the high level of Soviet science and technology and the Soviet capacity to concentrate their investments made it possible at all.

A Divided World: Germany and China

Before the U.S.S.R. could join the United States as an atomic power in 1949, the two had engaged in a series of tests of will in Europe and Asia. More and more clearly there emerged a boundary between a Russian sphere of influence and an American sphere of influence. After 1949 the confrontation continued. In Iran, in Greece, in Berlin, in Korea, the lines were drawn, tested, and redrawn, sometimes after bloodshed. The Soviet Union and its former Western allies did reach agreements on peace treaties with Italy and with Hungary, Romania, and Bulgaria (all of which had been Hitler's allies). However, no such treaties could be concluded with Germany or Japan.

The United States occupied Japan alone. But defeated Germany was divided into four zones—American, British, French, and Russian. The U.S.S.R. occupied Eastern Germany, bordering on Poland and extending considerably west of Berlin. As the former capital, Berlin was also divided into four occupation zones, one for each of the Allies.

This arrangement was designed for temporary military occupation. It continued in effect because no treaty could be reached. It was extremely dangerous because Berlin had become an island surrounded by Soviet-dominated territory, yet it was an island composed of zones to which the three Western allies were entitled to have access. The failure to reach any settlement over Germany left the most serious problem in Europe without a solution.

In 1949, the three Western powers allowed their respective zones to unite in the Federal Republic of Germany, called West Germany, with its capital at Bonn. The Russians responded by creating the communist German Democratic Republic—East Germany—with its capital at Pankow outside Berlin.

Many if not most West Germans were eager for reunion with their fellow Germans in the East.

Yet the Russians believed a reunion of Germany under Western capitalist auspices would mean a revival of German aggression. An all-communist Germany was equally intolerable to the Western powers. Indeed, few Frenchmen or Englishmen were anxious to reunite Germany. Although more Americans hoped reunion might some day be possible, all responsible American officials understood that the United States alone could not even consider trying to reunite Germany.

In Asia—with Japan under American occupation—the most grievous problem remained that of China. The communists, who had challenged Chiang Kai-shek's ruling Kuomintang (Nationalist) party for power, kept their forces in being during the years of Japanese occupation. The United States tried in 1946–1947 to bring about an agreement between Chinese Nationalists and communists that would end the civil war. The effort failed, and the civil war continued.

By 1949, the communists had defeated Chiang Kai-shek, who took refuge on the off-shore island of Formosa (Taiwan). The communists could not follow because they had no fleet. By then Chiang had lost his hold over the Chinese people. The morale of his own forces was low. Inflation ravaged the economy, already ruined by the long Japanese occupation.

By 1950, mainland China had gone communist and was now part of the Soviet bloc. Only Chiang's government in Taiwan remained a part of the American bloc. American foreign policy had suffered a major defeat. Some Americans blamed the failure on a conspiracy by a few pro-communist Americans. But the change was too great, too many millions of Chinese were involved for that.

Elsewhere too the Soviet Union pursued its goal of turning the whole world communist through the agencies of individual Communist parties. In virtually every country a Communist party

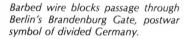
Barbed wire blocks passage through Berlin's Brandenburg Gate, postwar symbol of divided Germany.

existed, sometimes strong—as in France or Italy—sometimes weak—as in Britain or the United States. These parties varied in their willingness to take orders from the Communist Party of the Soviet Union (CPSU) and the Soviet government. But they were usually eager to act as the domestic agent for Soviet interests and policies. By contrast, the United States had no such disciplined and reliable supporters in most of the world.

The Two Coalitions

The Soviet Union thus had a certain advantage in the competition between the two superpowers for the support of the rest of the world. Each became the leader of a large coalition, whose members were attached more or less tightly by bonds of self-interest to the senior partner.

In 1945 the members of the loose American coalition included the Western hemisphere, Great Britain, Western Europe, Japan, the Philippines, Australia, and New Zealand. The Soviet coalition included the countries of Eastern Europe and, by 1949, China. The border between the two coalitions in Europe was called the Iron Curtain by Winston Churchill in 1946. It ran along a north-south line from Stettin on the Baltic to Trieste on the Adriatic. Yugoslavia lay in the Soviet sphere, and the frontier resumed again with the border between the Balkan communist countries (Albania, Yugoslavia, Bulgaria) and Greece, which was pro-western.

Turkey belonged to the Western coalition, and portions of the Middle East and of Southeast Asia were also linked to the Western coalition by a network of pacts. The dividing line between North and South Korea, with the U.S.S.R. occupying the north and the United States the south, represented an Asian extension of the long frontier between the two coalitions. Along the frontier the U.S.S.R. probed aggressively, causing crises and sometimes wars.

Repeatedly the United States tried and failed to ease the relationships between the two coalitions. In 1946 Stalin refused to join in a United Nations atomic energy commission, or to have anything to do with international control of atomic weapons. In 1947, the United States proposed an international plan of massive American economic aid designed to speed up European recovery from the ruin of the war—the Marshall Plan, so called for George C. Marshall, then secretary of state. The Soviet Union refused to accept the aid for itself and would not let its satellites participate. The Marshall Plan nations subsequently formed the nucleus of the North Atlantic Treaty Organization (NATO) in 1949.

In 1947, the Soviet coalition founded the Cominform (Communist Information Bureau) as a successor to the former Comintern, "abolished" during the war. In 1955 it created the Warsaw Pact, binding Eastern Europe together, as an answer to NATO. In the 1950s and 1960s the United States and Britain sought by a variety of means to prevent the spread of atomic weapons. The plan called for a joint Multilateral (Nuclear) Force (1968) in which the Germans would participate. France rejected it and in 1966 withdrew French forces from NATO and forced the withdrawal of NATO headquarters from France to Belgium.

In the Near East, the Baghdad Pact and its successor, the Central Treaty Organization (CENTO), proved no more than a series of agreements among the United States, Britain, Turkey, Iran, and Pakistan. With the withdrawal of Iraq in 1959, no direct alliances linked the Arab world with the West. In the Far East, on the other hand, the Southeast Asia Treaty Organization (SEATO) gave the United States the solid backing of Australia, New Zealand, the Philippines, and Thailand.

Outside the coalitions remained the neutral nations. Some, like Switzerland or Sweden, were simply maintaining their traditional policies of not aligning themselves with any grouping of powers. But most belonged to the new nations that were now emerging as independent, having discarded their formal colonial status. Of these India was the most influential, taking from both coalitions much-needed economic assistance.

As economic aid became an instrument in the cold war, neutral nations tried, often with success, to play the Americans off against the Russians. Not too subtly they would suggest that if Washington deprived them of something they wanted, they might regretfully have to go communist. Not until the 1960s did the United States learn to regard neutrality as often positively helpful to its interests.

The United Nations

Through the years of cold war, and the occasional outbreaks of something hotter, the United Nations—formed during World War II from among the opponents of the Axis and chartered in 1945 at San Francisco—served as an international organization where members of both coalitions and neutrals alike could meet in peaceful discussion. As the direct successor to the League of Nations, it inherited the League's duty of keeping the peace, but like the League it lacked independent sovereignty or authority over its members.

To deal with threats to the peace, its charter created a Security Council with eleven member states, five of which—the United States, the Soviet Union, Great Britain, France, and China—held permanent memberships. The other six were elected to rotating two-year terms by the General Assembly, to which all member states belonged. The secretary general, elected by the Security Council, could exert great personal influence in international affairs.

But each of the members of the Security Council had a veto over any substantive question. Therefore, decisions had to be unanimous before the UN could act. As a result, the Security Council often could not act because of a veto. Of the eighty vetoes cast between 1945 and 1955, the U.S.S.R. cast seventy-seven.

In the mid-1950s new nations joined the UN; some pro-Western, like Austria and Italy, some pro-Soviet, like Romania, Bulgaria, and the other former Axis satellites in Eastern Europe, and some neutral, mostly former colonies, like Ceylon or Libya. Japan joined in 1956. As former colonies obtained their independence during the late 1950s and early 1960s, each joined the United Nations, where the "Afro-Asian bloc" came to command a majority in the General Assembly.

Germany remained outside the UN, but both East and West Germany had their observers there. For twenty years the United States successfully opposed the seating of the Chinese communists. Until 1971 the permanent Chinese seat on the Security Council remained in the possession of Chiang Kai-shek's representative. The first three secretaries general were the Norwegian Trygve Lie, the Swedish Dag Hammarskjold, and the Burmese U Thant.

Though the UN could not "settle" the cold war, or bring about the international control of

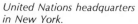

United Nations headquarters in New York.

atomic weapons, it often helped prevent small wars from becoming big ones. The League of Nations had never been able to put its own forces into the field. The UN did so. In Korea in 1950–1952 the American army fought under the sponsorship of the UN because the Soviet representative was absent from the Security Council and failed to veto the Council's decision to intervene. On the Arab-Israeli frontiers (1956–1967), in the former Belgian Congo, and in Cyprus, UN forces helped maintain peace.

The UN also helped governments initiate new development plans, controlled epidemics, and provided experts on modern farming techniques. Some Americans disliked the organization's spectacular buildings in New York and wished that it had never left Switzerland. With its successes and its failures the UN reflected both the diversity and the elements of unity in the world of which it was the forum.

II THE MAJOR FREE-WORLD STATES

The United States

Instead of turning inward as it had after 1918, the United States led in organizing both the United Nations and its own coalition. It spent vast sums for the Marshall Plan and to help the newly emerging countries of the former colonial world. Some of the money went for military assistance, but most of it went for economic development. Both Democrats and Republicans supported these programs despite some grumblings. The American government did not cut foreign aid much for twenty years until the Vietnam War began to strain the U.S. economy.

In fact, Republicans and Democrats were not far apart on domestic policies either. Most people would have said that the Democrats were the more liberal and radical of the two parties and the Republicans the more conservative. But in 1952 when the Republicans elected a president for the first time in twenty years, he was not a politician, but General Dwight D. Eisenhower, a popular hero because of his record in World War II.

And during eight years (1953–1960), the Eisenhower administration not only did not repeal the measures of the Roosevelt and Truman years (1932–1952) but even expanded the system of social security. An occasional Republican politician threatened to sell the Tennessee Valley Authority to private companies, but no Republican leader ever tried to do so. In foreign policy Eisenhower's secretary of state, John Foster Dulles, spoke of "rolling the Russians back" and "liberating" their satellites in Eastern Europe. But when the Russians invaded Hungary in 1956, Dulles did nothing—exactly what the Democrats would have done.

During the early 1950s, responding to the cold war, Senator Joseph McCarthy of Wisconsin accused a large number of American civil servants of being communists. Although some American communists had obtained government posts and had in some cases given information to the Russians, McCarthy never located a single communist in high places. Instead, he attacked many innocent persons on the flimsiest evidence or none at all. Bad as it was, the McCarthy period was no Reign of Terror. No blood was shed, the prisons were not filled. Brave men opposed McCarthy, and in 1954 he was condemned by his fellow senators 67 to 22 for abuse of his powers. The spectacle of McCarthy bullying witnesses on television—then a new device—helped arouse the public against him.

In 1946, the U.S. government "freed" the Philippine Islands, which became a sovereign state. Puerto Rico, a colony in 1952, became a free associated state, or commonwealth, with its own constitution and its own government. In 1958 Alaska and in 1959 Hawaii became states of the Union.

Between 1945 and 1970 the United States was generally prosperous and productive, with occasional recessions and readjustments. The gross national product grew steadily. The economy responded to measures recommended by experts. Some people felt that the Americans had learned how to avoid depression altogether.

But the wealth did not reach the poorest members of society. In the presidency of the Democrat Lyndon Johnson (1963–1968), a series of progams to assist the poor was proposed. But much of the planned effort had to be abandoned because of the war in Vietnam. The war created increasing domestic unrest, inflation, and rising unemployment. All these continued to mount after the Republican Richard M. Nixon succeeded Johnson in 1969.

Many of the poor in the United States were black. This racial division made America's worst social problem still worse. Gifted blacks had won recognition in the arts, in sports, in the field of

A "Freedom Rider" bus, sent into the South in 1961 to test segregation laws, firebombed on entering Alabama.

entertainment, and often in business and the professions. But American society still did not give blacks equal opportunities for education and for jobs.

In the South, more agricultural than the North, memories of slavery and the Northern victory in the Civil War were still fresh. Here some whites had bitter antiblack prejudice and refused to permit black people to advance themselves. In the cities of the North, too, where hundreds of thousands of blacks had flocked to live, their lives were often miserable and seemingly hopeless.

In 1954 the Supreme Court unanimously declared that the existence of separate compulsory schools for blacks was unconstitutional. This major decision, of course, immediately affected chiefly the South. Here "separate but equal" education for the two races had been the rule, but the separate black schools had usually been inferior. In any case, the Court declared, separate education could not be equal education.

The years that followed saw a struggle over the new requirements. Most parts of the South tried to disobey the Court or to admit only token numbers of black students to white schools. But after much controversy, black students began to study with whites in every state of the Union. By 1970 in the border states and in some cities

of the Deep South, such as Atlanta, the number was large. Southern state universities were also desegregated.

But the existence of black "ghettos" in the Northern cities and the prevalence of neighborhood schools everywhere meant that public education in New York or Boston was often as segregated as it was in Mississippi. Northern whites often opposed bussing children out of their home neighborhoods to school just as vigorously as Southern whites opposed desegregation. Many predominantly white universities strove to find and admit qualified black students. Colleges previously black began to worry about losing their most talented pupils. In the election of 1968, Nixon had much Southern white support. He owed a political debt to Southern politicians. The federal government therefore slowed down efforts to enforce desegregation. In 1970 the problem of equal education for blacks remained serious.

The drive to improve conditions for blacks extended beyond education. In the late 1950s and early 1960s Northern whites and blacks worked to increase the registration of black voters in the South and to liberalize real estate practices to enable blacks to buy houses wherever they wished. Both drives made considerable headway.

But some blacks felt that justice could never

be gained by gradual means. These turned away from such organizations as the National Association for the Advancement of Colored People (NAACP), which preferred to work by persuasion, and favored more militant groups. The Reverend Martin Luther King, a nonviolent black minister from the South, had sponsored a successful black boycott of busses in Montgomery, Alabama. He forced the bus lines to end segregation. But even he lost some of his following to militants preaching "Black Power."

During the summers of 1965, 1966, and 1967, severe rioting broke out in the Watts district of Los Angeles and in Newark, Detroit, and other Northern cities. Blacks burned large portions of their own neighborhoods, looted shops, and engaged in gunfights with the police. A federal Civil Rights Act was passed in 1965, and discrimination in real estate transactions was banned. But this did not calm the storm.

Black violence naturally enraged those whites who opposed any advance for blacks. But even moderates who favored black progress hated the riots, and grew more and more anxious about public order. This anxiety helped Nixon win the election of 1968.

By this time the Black Panther party appeared to be the most influential of the black militant movements. Its founder, Eldridge Cleaver, had published his autobiography, *Soul*

Martin Luther King, his wife, Coretta King, and an estimated 10,000 civil rights marchers on last leg of Selma-to-Montgomery March, March 3, 1965.

on Ice, a fierce and shocking document that aroused both sympathy and horror among its readers, white and black. It outdid the earlier *Autobiography of Malcolm X,* the Black Muslim leader assassinated by a rival faction. Under a prison sentence, Cleaver fled the United States to Algiers. At home Panthers preached and practiced violence. In the cities the conflict often narrowed down to one between Panthers and police. Local tensions mounted.

The new wave of violence in American life derived not only from the race question. In 1960 the Democrat John F. Kennedy, the first Roman Catholic to be elected president, defeated Nixon and succeeded Eisenhower. Kennedy was a young man of intelligence, personal elegance, and charm. His "New Frontier" planned federal medical care for the aged, tax reform, civil rights, and antipoverty measures. But Kennedy was assassinated in 1963 by a psychopathic killer with a rifle. Televised details of the crime came into every American home, as did the fantastic subsequent murder of the assassin by another psychopath.

The death and destruction in the summer riots of 1965, 1966, and 1967, the murder of Martin Luther King—also by rifle—in 1968, and the murder by pistol of President Kennedy's brother, Senator Robert F. Kennedy of New York, while he was campaigning to secure the Democratic nomination for the presidency in 1968, all sickened the American public. But Congress would not forbid the easy procurement of guns. Crime grew to be a major issue in politics.

Lyndon Johnson's administration successfully put through much of the Kennedy social program. But the gains were outweighed by the cost of life and money of the war in Vietnam and by the rising discontent with a society with such extremes of wealth and poverty.

City life, in particular, seemed to degenerate as rapidly as prosperity increased. Racial tension and crime, pollution of air and water, the pile-up of motor traffic belching poisonous fumes, strikes by sanitation employees, teachers, and air-traffic control officers made urban life a nightmare.

Garbage often festered in the streets. Children did not get the public education for which their parents were paying. Nobody felt safe walking home at night. It was hard to leave town by car or plane, and the railroad system had apparently suffered a total breakdown. Food and drink grew increasingly poisonous. And many city governments were both corrupt and bankrupt. Taxes rose faster than income. In the suburbs, neat lawns and good public schools did not hide what some felt to be a cultural desert. Others fought to preserve what they had so recently acquired from encroachments and looming threats.

By the late sixties pampered children of the well-to-do were "opting out" of the society in large numbers. Some took drugs. Marijuana ("pot"), they claimed, was no worse than the booze their parents indulged in. Far more dangerous were heroin, or LSD, or "speed." Many dropouts left home, congregated in special places (San Francisco's Haight-Ashbury district, New York's East Village), living from hand to mouth, dressed in American Indian feathers or beads, getting "into" Zen. They spoke a special dialect. They proclaimed their love for everybody, which often looked uncommonly like hate. These were the "hippies" of the late 1960s. The mindless Manson murders in California committed by a roving group of dropouts focused public attention on the growing number of young men and women self-outlawed from American society, who had apparently crossed the line into a new, mad universe.

Other young people actively rebelled against the institutions of their immediate world, the university or the draft board. Some took as their heroes Mao Tse-tung or the Cuban guerrilla leader Ché Guevara, killed in Bolivia. Starting at the University of California in Berkeley and Columbia University in New York, and moving then to other institutions small and large, student radical violence erupted in 1968 and 1969. Sit-ins or building seizures were often accompanied by the disruption of classes, the theft of documents from files, violence against teachers or administrators. Usually student radicals had a list of "demands." Some were local: abolish ROTC. Others were national: build more housing for the poor, get out of Vietnam, which the universities as such could not comply with.

Some violent students wanted to overthrow American society altogether. "Tear it all down first, and then discuss what should be put in its place" was an argument that Bakunin would have approved. Whenever university authorities summoned the police or the National Guard to quell violence, they turned moderate students into radicals. In 1970 the National Guard fired into a student demonstration at Kent State University in Ohio, killing four students, all white, and within a few days police in Mississippi killed two more, this time black. A cry of outrage arose on all university campuses.

National Guardsmen hurl tear gas at students of Kent State University, May 4, 1970.

On the far left fringe of the student radical movement were those who used bombs against university buildings, banks, or public buildings. In response, outraged Americans of older generations and of all social classes grew more militant. The construction workers, or "hard hats," the police in some communities, those who believed in seeking political and economic goals by peaceful means: all shared the revulsion. The most militant among them found their spokesman in Nixon's vice-president, Spiro Agnew, who regularly denounced rebellious youth.

Exploding in many Western European countries as well as in America, the rebellion of the children of the rich resembled the Russian nihilist and anarchist movements of the nineteenth century. The Russian "establishment" of the nineteenth century never understood that it could isolate the extremists among the rebels by embracing the moderates. Twentieth-century Americans often seemed equally dense.

Race relations, public order, the crisis of the cities, the disaffection of the young had combined in 1970 to create domestic crisis. As the Vietnam War continued, prosperity was shaken, inflation grew worse, and the stock market fell. Movements for the "liberation" of women and homosexuals added a new note to the chorus. Outraged by their inability to obtain equal pay for equal work, these militants sometimes sounded determined to end the human family as an institution.

Canada

After 1945, Canada enjoyed an economic growth and prosperity proportionately even greater than that of the United States. American capital poured in, and much was raised at home and in Britain. Though still producing vast amounts of raw materials from farm, mine, and forest, Canada came now to be a great industrial nation with vast hydroelectric resources and oil and mineral wealth.

In the mid-1950s Canada took the lead in carrying out a long-discussed canal from the Great Lakes to the lower St. Lawrence that would accommodate ocean-going ships and also produce hydroelectric power. The canal was opened in 1959. Many Canadians had begun to worry over what they felt was undue cultural and economic dependence on the United States.

Until the 1960s Canada was politically one of the stablest of Western nations. Except for the Conservative years of 1957–1963, the federal government remained under the control of the Liberals, who depended for their support on collaboration between the English-speaking provinces and the French-speaking province of Quebec. Minority parties—New Democrats, to the left, and Social Credit, favoring unorthodox but not socialist economic ideas—faded in importance as French-Canadian nationalist feeling rose in Quebec.

The few thousands of French left in Canada in 1763 had multiplied to some seven million. After World War II they enjoyed a vigorous economic growth and increasingly high standards of living. Their unrest was in part a demand for a greater share in the Canadian managerial and financial worlds. It was also a demand for greater cultural participation in dominion life. Especially they wanted recognition of the French language as equal to English in all of Canada and as the primary language of Quebec. Many people in the rest of Canada opposed their demands. French extremists who proposed to secede and set up an independent Quebec were still small in number. A federal commission on biculturalism was set up.

Into this somewhat tense situation the French president de Gaulle—with typical drama and concern for French *"grandeur"*—intruded in 1967, on a state visit to Canada. By shouting *"Vive le Québec libre!"* ("Long live free Quebec!") to an enthusiastic crowd, he seemed to be sponsoring secession. The Canadian federal government strongly objected. But de Gaulle tried to open French cultural and economic relations with Quebec. It all reflected de Gaulle's eagerness to make trouble for all "Anglo-Saxons," and all friends of the United States. The Canadians responded by producing a brand new political leader, a previously unknown Liberal, Pierre Elliott Trudeau.

Trudeau won a smashing electoral victory in 1968. Half-French, bilingual, handsome, and intelligent, he now had a free hand. He began to cut back on Canada's international commitments in an effort to achieve a "just society" for the Canadian people. Showing independence from U.S. policy, he established diplomatic relations with communist China. The Official Languages Act established French as the equal of English but did not satisfy the separatists. In 1970 one group of terrorists kidnapped a British diplomat and freed him only when they were allowed to go to Cuba. Others kidnapped and murdered a Quebec government official and got away. Trudeau proclaimed martial law and calmed the immediate crisis.

Western Europe

After 1945 the nations of Western Europe made real attempts to organize a "free Europe"

on a level above that of the national state. In 1952, as a first step, France, West Germany, and Italy joined Belgium, the Netherlands, and Luxembourg ("Benelux") in setting up the European Coal and Steel Community, a free market area of all six nations. A joint administrative body could make certain final and binding decisions without the participation of any government officials. Each nation had given up some part of its sovereignty, and the plan was a success.

In 1957, these six countries, by the Treaty of Rome, established the European Economic Community (EEC), better known as the Common Market, under a central administration made up of delegates from each partner. It was agreed that gradually, according to a schedule, the Common Market would get increasing powers over trade, production, and immigration. By the 1970s, it was planned, there would be in effect one common trading and producing society, free from internal tariffs. It would have a population of about 180 million, as many as the United States. Each partner would have a "mixed economy"—free enterprise under government regulation—with equal economic skills and experience.

The years after 1957 saw progress toward this goal. Tourists could now pass from one country to another by car or rail almost as easily as they crossed state lines in the United States. Yet difficulties arose in carrying out the schedule.

Twice France vetoed Britain's proposed entry into the EEC, insisting on specific provisions favoring French farmers in the Common Market. Not until de Gaulle left French politics in 1969 did the possibility of British entry into the Common Market revive. As for the British, many regarded themselves as primarily part of the Commonwealth and not as Europeans. In 1959 Britain set up the European Free Trade Association (the "Outer Seven") that included Britain, Sweden, Norway, Denmark, Austria, Switzerland, and Portugal. Each member could set its own external tariffs. This protected British "imperial preference" in favor of Commonwealth countries.

Great Britain

In the British election of July 1945, after the war had ended in Europe, Churchill and the Conservative party were defeated. For the first time the Labour party had an absolute majority in the House of Commons. The new prime minister was Clement Attlee, a middle-class social worker.

The new socialist government took over the coal industry, the railroads, and some parts of commercial road transportation; it also began to nationalize the steel industry. Britain's already well-developed system of social insurance was now capped by a system of socialized medical care. The educational system was partly reformed in an effort to lengthen the required period of compulsory education. Some parts of the old empire were given independence and others dominion status: national independence within the Commonwealth.

Although much more socialist than before, the British economy was still "mixed." The nationalized coal mines and railroads did not become state trusts run by bureaucrats on the Russian model, but public corporations not unlike private industries, run by boards not dominated by bureaucrats or politicians. Broad sectors of the economy remained in private hands.

In 1951 the Conservatives, with Churchill still at their head, returned to power and remained there for twelve years. They halted the nationalization of steel. Otherwise they kept intact the "socialism" of their opponents, including the National Health scheme. Churchill was succeeded by Anthony Eden (later Lord Avon), and Eden in turn by Harold Macmillan.

In the postwar years British industry fell behind its rivals. In the 1950s, for example, it lost much of its share of the world market for automobiles to the Germans, with their inexpensive, standardized light car, the Volkswagen. These losses of markets had an ironic side. Because the British had been the *first* to industrialize, their plants were the first to become obsolete. British management, too, was old-fashioned, slow to adopt new ways, and uninterested in research. British workers were suspicious of any change in methods and regarded management as its enemy.

Even in apparent prosperity, Britain remained in economic trouble. The pound, still standard along with the dollar, was always in danger. Its value, reduced in 1940 from $4.85 to $4.00, was after 1949 pegged at $2.80. But continued pressure on the pound in the 1960s repeatedly required help from Britain's allies to maintain this value.

This weakness of the pound reflected an unfavorable balance of trade. The British people were buying more from the rest of the world than they could sell to it. In the 1950s and 1960s, in what was called the "brain drain," some distinguished British scientists and engineers emigrated to the United States, Canada, or Australia.

Under Harold Wilson, a clever politician often called an opportunist, the Labour party returned to power in 1964 and governed until 1970.

In 1966, Wilson froze wages and prices in an effort to restore the balance between what the British spent and what they produced. His own Labour party disliked such measures as exploiting the poor to support the rich. Wilson had to devalue the pound once again, to $2.40.

By 1969 the deficits had disappeared, but inflation was severe. Prices were rising so fast that the workers' gains from higher wages were unsatisfactory. Yet more and more English workingmen bought cars and took vacations. The National Health scheme and education for working-class mothers led to vastly improved children's health care.

An increasing number of new universities sprang up to offer young people of all classes the educational opportunities that had traditionally been available only to the upper and middle classes. Oxford and Cambridge now admitted large numbers of working-class young men and women on state scholarships.

Labour created a major political issue by its plan to "democratize" secondary education by a new program of "comprehensive" schools. Many Labourites themselves feared that this scheme would penalize the ablest students. The Conservative opposition to the idea was headed by an articulate woman, Margaret Thatcher, who would eventually become prime minister in 1979.

In the 1950s the race problem for the first time became serious in Britain. Indians, Pakistanis, West Indian and African blacks—Commonwealth subjects with British passports—freely came to England in large numbers to take jobs in factories, public transportation, and hospitals. White racism rose markedly and affected both political parties. Despite its antiracist protestations, the Wilson government was forced to curtail immigration sharply. But the loudest warnings were sounded by the Conservative politician Enoch Powell. Powell predicted bloody race riots—and a few took place—unless black immigration was halted and all blacks already in England deported. Many working-class people, lifelong Labourites, supported Powell.

Closely related to the race issue at home was the question of official British relations abroad with South Africa and with the new white-dominated African state of Rhodesia. The Labour government refused to sell arms to South Africa because of South African racial policies. For similar reasons the Labour government did not recognize Rhodesia and imposed an economic boycott on it. Many deplored these policies, and charged that Labour had forgotten England's true interests.

The Irish problem also arose again in the late 1960s. The six counties of Ulster, Northern Ireland, with a Protestant majority, were still part of the United Kingdom. In this depressed industrial area, the Catholics were the first to lose their jobs in bad times. Cherishing their age-old feelings as the oppressed, they were outraged when the Protestant extremists (the "Orangemen") insisted on marching in annual parades to celebrate the anniversaries of William III's victories in the 1690s that had ensured Protestant domination. Provocatively shouting contemptuous slogans in Catholic districts, the Orangemen in the summer of 1969 set off disorders that began in Derry (Londonderry) and spread to Belfast and other areas. The regular police—the Royal Ulster Constabulary, or RUC—were accused by the Catholics of being mere tools of the Protestant oppressor and had to be disarmed. The British army intervened to keep order.

Members of the outlawed IRA, behind a barricade in Londonderry, North Ireland. They are masked to prevent identification.

Extremist voices, both Catholic and Protestant, were loud in Ulster. Their mutual hatred often sounded more like the sixteenth century than the twentieth. The government of the Republic of Ireland to the south took a strong interest and suggested that the UN be given responsibility for Ulster. The Northern Irish and British governments regarded the matter as altogether an internal problem.

When violence resumed in 1970, the British army was reinforced. The extremists of the south, the Irish Republican Army (IRA), had always claimed the northern counties for a united Ireland. They now revived their activities. But the IRA itself was now split between a relatively moderate wing and the Provisionals ("Provos"), anarchists dedicated to indiscriminate bombing.

In June 1970, to the general surprise, the Conservative party won a majority of forty seats in Parliament, and its leader Edward Heath became prime minister. Inflation, racism, and the Labour education program all helped to unseat Wilson. Both parties were pledged to push the entry of Britain into the European Common Market, and the Conservatives reopened discussions. But Powell and many Conservatives openly opposed British entry. So did many Labourites. So did many who were primarily English and loyal to the existing economic preference arrangements for the Commonwealth. Others disliked Europeans generally. And many feared that food prices would rise sharply if England should join. The issue would be decided in 1971 and 1972 in a dramatic debate discussed in Chapter 20 below.

Beginning with the enormous popularity of the four pop-singing Beatles in the late fifties, England for a decade set the international styles for young people in other countries. Long hair for men, the "unisex" phenomenon in dress, the popularity of theatrical and peculiar clothes, all the "mod" fashions that spread across the Atlantic and the Channel started in England. "Swinging London," Carnaby Street, Twiggy, and Mick Jagger and the Rolling Stones all became the fashion.

The international dominance of English styles was connected with a new and extremely important cultural and social development. Class distinction in England, the traditional home of social inequality, was gradually withering away. The Beatles were all working-class in origin, and all spoke (or sang) with a pure lower-class Liverpool accent. All the English pacesetters of the new styles in song, dress, and behavior among the young of the 1960s were lower class too. And these styles spread not only abroad but among the middle and upper classes of young people in England. It was the beginning of another English peaceful revolution.

France

World War II inflicted deep psychological wounds on the French. Defeat by the Germans, a brutal German occupation and economic exploitation, much French collaboration with the enemy, all this was followed by liberation. But, in spite of the part played by the Fighting French and the French Resistance movement, liberation was the work of American and British and, indirectly, of Russian arms.

For more than a century France had lapsed behind the leading industrial nations in production, in finance, in population growth. But by the late 1940s population had begun to grow again. This meant that hundreds of thousands of French men and women deliberately decided to have children.

In 1944 the French government-in-exile, led by General de Gaulle, easily reestablished in liberated France the old republican forms of government. Frenchmen called this state the Fourth Republic. But in 1946 de Gaulle, unable to attain real power in a state still ruled by unstable parliamentary coalitions of "splinter parties," retired from politics. Now the Fourth Republic began to look exactly like the Third. The average cabinets lasted only a few months. The Communist party, openly dedicated to revolutionary change, had new strength. The problems of the old empire, now known as the French Union, seemed insoluble. Its peoples were in ferment.

After nine years of war, Vietnam (Indo-China) was lost in 1954 in a great defeat at Dienbienphu. In the same year an active rebellion began against the French in Algeria, which France regarded not as a colony but as an overseas portion of France itself. Morocco and Tunisia were both lost in 1956, and the crisis deepened.

In 1958 General de Gaulle took power again. Financial instability, inflation resulting from the wars in Indo-China and Algeria, and popular disgust with the "politicians" all combined to overthrow the Fourth Republic. On May 13, 1958, a rightist military coup d'état took place in Algeria. De Gaulle then announced that he was willing to come out of retirement. The leaders of the

ICELAND

UNITED
KINGDOM

EIRE

NETH.
BEL.
L.
FRANCE
SW.

PORTUGAL SPAIN

MOROCCO
IFNI

SPANISH
SAHARA

MAURITANIA

SENEGAL
GAMBIA
PORT.
GUINEA

SIERRA LEONE
LIBERIA
IVORY COAST
GHANA
TOGO
DAHOMEY

NORWAY

SWEDEN

FINLAND

DEN.
E.
GER.
GER.
AUST.
SW.
ITALY

POLAND
CZECH.
HUN.
YUG.
ALB.

ROM.
BUL.

GREECE
TUNISIA

ALGERIA

LIBYA

MALI

NIGER

CHAD

SUDAN

UPPER
VOLTA

GUINEA

NIGERIA

CAM.

GABON

DAHOMEY CABINDA

OF
CONGO

CENTRAL
AFRICAN
REPUBLIC

GUINEA

UGANDA
RWANDA

ZAIRE

BURUNDI

TURKEY

LEBANON
ISRAEL
JORDAN

EGYPT

SYRIA

IRAQ

SAUDI
ARABIA

YEMEN
SOUTHERN YEMEN

AFARS & ISSAS
TERRITORY

ETHIOPIA

SOMALI REPUBLIC

KENYA

U.S.S.R.

IRAN

AFGHAN.

PAKISTAN

KASHMIR

TIBET

NEPAL

INDIA

BHUTAN

BANGLA-

BURMA

CEYLON

MONGOLIA

CHINA

N. KOREA
S. KOREA

JAPAN

TAIWAN

THAI.

CAM. VIETNAM

PHILIPPINE IS.

MALAYSIA

INDONESIA

NEW GUINEA

WEST IRIAN

PAPUA

TANZANIA

ANGOLA

ZAMBIA

MALAWI

MOZAM-
BIQUE

MALAGASY
REPUBLIC

MAURITIUS

Indian Ocean

AUSTRALIA

SOUTH
WEST
AFRICA

BOTS-
WANA

RHOD.

SWAZILAND

REPUBLIC OF
SOUTH AFRICA

LESOTHO

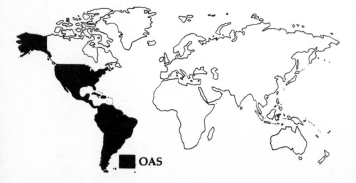

■ OAS

■ SEATO ■ ARAB LEAGUE

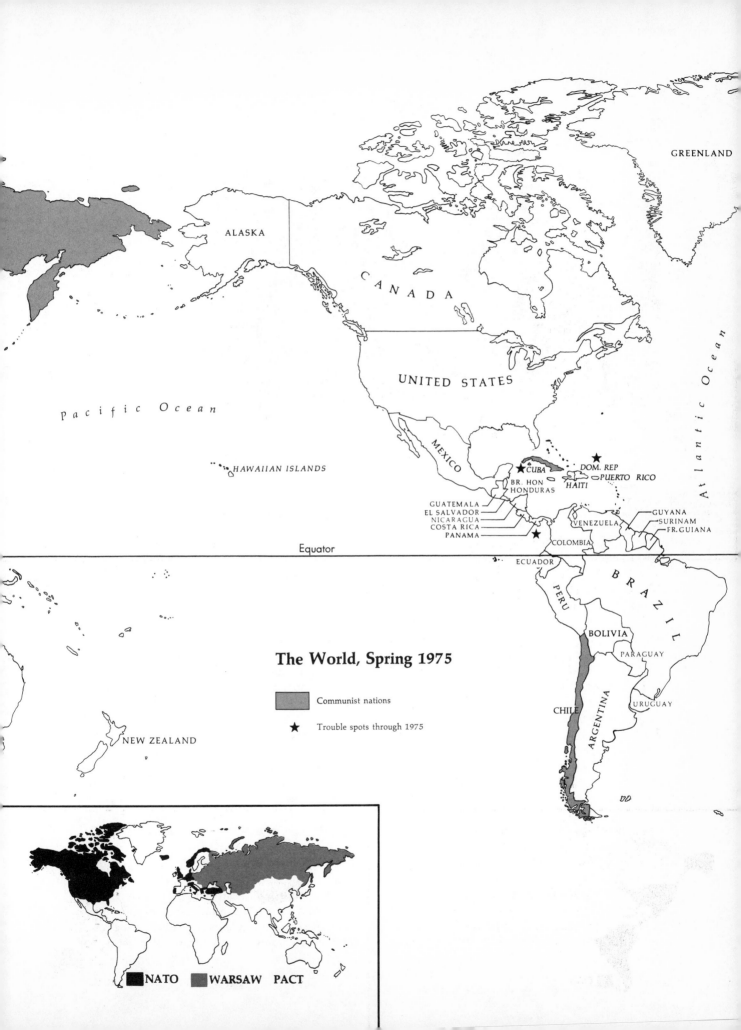

The World, Spring 1975

Communist nations

★ Trouble spots through 1975

GREENLAND

ALASKA

C A N A D A

UNITED STATES

Pacific Ocean

HAWAIIAN ISLANDS

MEXICO

★ CUBA
DOM. REP
PUERTO RICO
HAITI
BR. HON
HONDURAS
GUATEMALA
EL SALVADOR
NICARAGUA
COSTA RICA
PANAMA
GUYANA
SURINAM
VENEZUELA
FR. GUIANA
COLOMBIA

Equator

ECUADOR

PERU

Atlantic Ocean

B R A Z I L

BOLIVIA

PARAGUAY

URUGUAY

CHILE

ARGENTINA

NEW ZEALAND

NATO WARSAW PACT

General de Gaulle campaigning for the constitution that established the Fifth Republic, 1958.

coup wrongly believed that he would carry out their policies for keeping Algeria French.

In France a popular referendum (plebiscite) confirmed the change. The constitution of the new Fifth Republic provided for a president of France, to be elected for a seven-year term by direct popular vote. If an absolute majority was not achieved in a first election, there was to be a runoff between the two candidates with the greatest number of votes. Elected outright in 1958, de Gaulle was reelected to a second term in 1965 after a runoff.

The president appointed the premier, who could dissolve the legislature and order new elections at any time after the first year. Thus the new constitution gave the executive more power, the legislature less. Those who disliked the new constitution complained that it made the legislature a mere rubber stamp.

De Gaulle's enemies called him a dictator. Cartoonists enjoyed drawing him as Louis XIV, the *roi soleil,* with wig and silk stockings, the personification of French haughtiness and superiority. He was certainly obstinate and opinionated, but he was no Napoleon III or Pétain. Frenchmen still enjoyed freedom of speech, of the press, of public assembly. French journalists could say as nasty things about their president as American journalists could say about theirs. Yet the regime did control radio and television. In the general election of 1965 it yielded to the pressure of public opinion and consented to give de Gaulle's opposition candidates some time (not "equal time") on the air.

The French ruling classes believed that their colonial subjects, especially the Algerians, could be persuaded to want to become real Frenchmen. But most of the Muslim nine-tenths of the Algerian population disagreed. Against the wishes of those who had brought him to power, and in the face of terrorist incidents in France itself, de Gaulle in 1962 worked out a settlement that made Algeria independent but left France some "influence" and some rights over Saharan oil. The right regarded this as treason. Most of the leftists, on the other hand, never gave him even grudging credit for it.

Starting with the Marshall Plan aid in 1947, a great series of economic and social changes began in France. Unlike the United States, Britain, and Germany, France had hitherto preserved much of the small-scale, individualistic methods of production and distribution characteristic of the period before the industrial revolution. Now there began a full-scale reorientation of the economy in accordance with the usual practices of modern industry. Helped by foreign investment, especially American, France began to experience a real boom.

The growth rate in the 1960s was about a steady 6 percent per year, ahead even of West Germany. Inflation, though a problem, had until 1966 or 1967 been held down to 3 percent. Prosperity meant that for the first time the French people by the hundreds of thousands got their first cars, television sets, and hi-fi's. They traveled in ever-growing numbers. They enjoyed fearful traffic jams and incredible highway accidents. Many of those who found the new ways unsettling blamed all the changes, like Coca-Cola, *le drugstore,* and blue jeans, on the Americans.

In foreign policy, de Gaulle was a deeply committed old-fashioned nationalist Frenchman. His whole life had been a love affair with France and he identified personally with his country. He never forgot a slight, and a slight to him was a slight to France, to be repaid in due course. The way Churchill and Roosevelt treated him during World War II he could never forget. When he came to power he retained a healthy personal dislike of *les Anglo-Saxons.*

De Gaulle hated the idea of the Common Market, NATO, and other bodies that would rob France of her sovereignty even to a small degree. Still worse was the talk of a United States of Europe. De Gaulle spoke instead of a "Europe of fatherlands" that would include Russia—at least the European part—with all its historic European associations. And within this Europe, France would, of course, take the lead.

To do this France must have her own atomic weapons. Therefore de Gaulle refused to join the U.S., U.K., and U.S.S.R. in a treaty barring atomic tests. France continued to test nuclear weapons in the atmosphere, exploding her first hydrogen bomb in 1968 and continuing annually thereafter. She must also have her own *striking force* capable of delivering atomic weapons to their targets, and so of deterring an enemy.

Vigorously opposed to communism at home, de Gaulle nonetheless worked out a rapprochement with Russia. The U.S.S.R., he argued,

French newspaper headlines announcing the rejection of President de Gaulle's referendum, April 28, 1969.

in the 1960s no longer represented the threat to the general peace that it had represented in the 1950s. Now—in balancing the scales against the industrial and military power of the United States and its special friend, Britain—France needed to be friends with Russia. De Gaulle spread abroad his message that France would be the leader of Europe.

In the spring of 1968, however, Paris erupted unexpectedly. The French universities, so overcrowded that there were no classrooms for students to use and no way of their listening to their lecturers, had been disregarded by the regime in a period when the young everywhere were full of resentment against the society their parents had brought them into. Led by anarchists and others, the students occupied university buildings, fought the police, and eventually drew a reluctant Communist party into the fray.

In order not to lose the support of the French workers, who had already begun to strike in sympathy with the students, the Communist leadership had to support what looked for a few days like the beginning of a new French Revolution. De Gaulle assured himself of army support, and in new elections won a great victory obtaining a larger majority in the legislature than before.

Thereupon he dropped his prime minister, Pompidou, the chief organizer of the election victory. De Gaulle launched a new economic and social program calling for *participation* by the workers not only in the profits of industry but in its management. His new minister of education radically decentralized the educational system. De Gaulle had secured himself in power with the strong support of the right—as in 1958. He was also appeasing the left—again, as in 1958. Perhaps he would have to slow down his military and foreign programs, but nobody believed he would abandon them.

De Gaulle's political career ended suddenly and unexpectedly. He staked his political future on a comparatively unimportant political issue set before the public in a referendum, and lost. As he had done before, he withdrew into private life. His death in 1970 marked the disappearance of the last survivor—except for Tito—of the great men of World War II. His followers won the 1969 elections, and Pompidou became president of France. He continued de Gaulle's policies but pursued them much more quietly.

West Germany

In West Germany the wartime destruction of the industrial plant turned out to be an advantage: the new plant was built with the latest technological equipment. The Western Allies gradually abolished controls over German industry, save for atomic energy and some military restrictions. It advanced economic aid and scaled down prewar German debts. By the early 1950s West Germany had a favorable balance of trade. Industrial growth rose to 10 percent annually.

Gross national product mounted from $23 billion in 1950 to $103 billion in 1964, with no serious inflation. Prosperity spread through all classes of society. New buildings rose everywhere. The superhighways Hitler had built had to be widened and extended.

Politically, the Allies required "de-Nazification." At the Nuremberg trials in 1946, seventy-four top Nazi leaders were convicted of war crimes. Ten were hanged, after two had committed suicide. One was sentenced to life imprisonment, others to shorter terms; and three were acquitted. If the Allies had dismissed all civil servants who had held posts under the Nazi regime, they would have had nobody to administer the country. They did weed out prominent Nazis, though not enough to satisfy many anti-Nazis.

The West German constitution provided for a bicameral legislature. The lower house represented the people directly and the upper house represented the states *(Länder)*. The president, elected by a special assembly for a five-year term, was largely a ceremonial figure. Real executive leadership was vested in the chancellor, a prime minister dependent on a parliamentary majority.

The old multiparty system did not return to plague the new republic. The Christian Democrats, distant heirs of the old Catholic Centrist party, held power for twenty years until 1966. Until 1961 the chancellor was Konrad Adenauer, a Rhineland Catholic, conservative and pro-French. He retired only because of age and made life difficult for his successor, Ludwig Erhard, a Protestant.

The Christian Democrats were challenged chiefly by the Social Democrats, roughly similar to the British Labour party. They governed some of the states and cities, notably West Berlin, whose popular mayor, Willy Brandt, ran unsuccessfully for the chancellorship against Erhard in 1964. A small pro-Nazi group continued to exist but never won many votes. More of a threat were militant organizations of war veterans and of refugees from Germany's former eastern territories now lost to Poland, the U.S.S.R., or Czechoslovakia.

Communist-dominated East Germany, with

a population about 30 percent that of West Germany's, raised special problems. Could the two Germanies be reunited? If so, how and when? Meanwhile neither state recognized the other.

For fifteen years the East Germans had been attracted by better West German living conditions and had crossed the border by the tens of thousands. So in August 1961 the East German government began building a wall between the two parts of Berlin. Though on special holidays families in West Berlin were allowed to cross into East Berlin briefly to visit relatives and friends, the Berlin wall still stood in 1970 as the visible symbol of a divided Germany and a closely guarded frontier.

Early in the 1950s the Western Allies permitted West Germany to rearm and join NATO. By 1970 West Germany had a modern army, navy, and air force. Government and people supported the armed forces, but old German militarism did not revive. Access to the atom bomb was not included in German rearmament.

In the late autumn of 1966 a major political crisis arose. Chancellor Erhard was governing in coalition with a small right-wing party, the Free Democrats, antisocialist conservatives. There was friction with some of the high command of the armed forces. It was hard to support American policies in Europe and keep close relations with de Gaulle. Some feared a recession as economic growth slowed down. In November 1966 the Free Democrats refused to support Erhard's proposals for higher taxes, and the government fell.

Kurt George Kiesinger, a Christian Democrat, now formed a "grand coalition" with his major opponents, the Social Democrats. Willy Brandt became vice-chancellor and foreign minister. Some members of both parties disapproved, but the grand coalition lasted until the elections of 1969.

In these, the Christian Democrats lost for the first time. Willy Brandt became chancellor and formed a coalition in his turn with the Free Democrats. Brandt's major interest lay in the question of East Germany. He moved slowly and cautiously. The chief stumbling block was the Soviet fear of West Germany.

So the first step was a treaty, signed in 1970, between West Germany and the U.S.S.R., in which both renounced the use of force and recognized all existing European frontiers. Of course the Germans could still hope that changes might some day be negotiated.

The next step was an agreement with Poland, and this, too, Brandt achieved during 1970.

The East Germans would be next. For the first time, West German technical and industrial skills were available in Moscow. Washington, which had encouraged Brandt, now began to worry about his successes.

The Other Western Countries

In 1946 a referendum showed that 54.3 percent of the Italian voters favored a republic. Neither monarchists nor fascists had much influence in parliamentary politics. A Catholic party with a liberal reform program, the Christian Democrats regularly held power with support from other groups. Its leaders, in order, were Alcide de Gasperi, Amintore Fanfani, Aldo Moro, and Mariano Rumor.

The Christian Democrats broke up the large landed estates in the south and redistributed the land. De Gasperi was challenged chiefly by a very strong Communist party, the largest in the West. The Socialists were split. The larger faction under Pietro Nenni allied itself with the Communists. The smaller under Giuseppe Saragat participated in the government.

In the 1960s a series of complicated negotiations began a process the Italians called the "opening to the left." The Christian Democrats won over some Socialist support. And in 1966 the Socialists reunited as one party.

The Italians themselves called Italy's economic growth between 1953 and 1966 an "economic miracle," achieved with some government ownership and with much government regulation and planning. Milan began to look like another Chicago. Rome had perhaps the most desperate traffic problem of any great city in the world. Membership in the Common Market gave Italian enterprise opportunities that it had never had before.

The government attacked the problems of the southern part of the peninsula and the islands of Sardinia and Sicily. Money was invested, old-age pensions were provided. Surplus workers were encouraged to find jobs in the north or in Germany or Switzerland. An income of about $1 billion annually from tourists helped the Italian balance of payments.

Yet in the late 1960s Italian political stability began to crumble. Inside the governing Christian Democratic party personal feuds among politicians made cooperation more and more difficult. The Socialists were anticommunist on the national level, but in the towns they often cooperated with the communists. This hurt Christian

Democratic political power locally and caused bitterness inside the government.

As in other Western countries, inflation struck, but Italy, with its large poor population and its lack of any tradition of social welfare, suffered more. Strikes occurred sporadically and unpredictably but often. A prolonged political crisis ended temporarily in 1970 when an experienced economist, Colombo, formed a cabinet.

The smaller states of "free Europe" shared the general prosperity and the common problems. Belgium enjoyed great material well-being. But the old quarrels between the Dutch-speaking Flemings, the Catholic majority, and the French-speaking Walloons, the Protestant minority, grew so bitter that they threatened the very existence of the country.

In Spain, Franco continued to rule. The country advanced toward economic modernization. The tourist trade boomed, but low wages, especially in the depressed coal mining areas of the north, kept discontent alive. So did the failure to give any concessions to the separatist ambitions of Catalans and Basques. Franco arranged that after his death the monarchy would be restored under Prince Juan Carlos, grandson of Alfonso XIII.

Portugal, under the rigidly conservative Salazar, dictator since 1932, lagged well behind Spain. In 1968 because of illness, the replacement of Salazar promised to open a new chapter, though the expenditure of men and money involved in holding onto the Portuguese colonial empire drained the national resources. In Greece, the takeover of the government in the 1960s by a group of army officers ("the colonels") led to a ruthless repression of political opposition but not to a fascist state.

III THE COMMUNIST BLOC: THE U.S.S.R. AT HOME

Alone among the leaders of the Big Three of the war years, Stalin remained in power immediately after the war. His remaining years, 1945–1953, marked a continuation and even a sharpening of all his familiar policies. Some four years of political uncertainty followed his death, but in 1957 Nikita Khrushchev emerged as supreme and held onto power until 1964. He was succeeded by two co-chiefs, Brezhnev and Kosygin, who remained on top in 1970.

Stalin's Last Years

Facing the devastation caused by the war, and what he regarded as the immediate threat of American atomic weapons, Stalin ordered that austerity continue into the postwar years. The Communist party was still his docile instrument. He purged it regularly to prevent any relaxation. It dominated political life, with the constant assistance of the secret police. The army, still mobilized at high strength and performing occupation duties abroad, was the third Soviet institution with power of its own.

In 1952 Stalin created a new Presidium that would include the ten Politburo members and fifteen additional high-ranking Soviet officials. But he did not live to announce the membership of the new body or to summon a meeting of it. After his death, the new Presidium simply replaced the old Politburo, with the same ten members. Khrushchev later declared that, in enlarging the membership and changing the name of the Politburo, Stalin was planning to kill all ten existing members.

The fourth five-year plan (1946–1950) and its successor the fifth (1951–1955) continued to emphasize investment in heavy industry. Financial measures—the raising of prices, the wiping out of savings by the establishment of a new currency—kept the population under severe economic pressure. Reparations exacted from Germany and industrial loot from the Eastern European countries helped Soviet reconstruction.

The U.S.S.R. made its first atomic bomb (1949). The Volga-Don canal was built. The regime now decided to reduce the number and increase the size of collective farms. In 1951, Nikita Khrushchev, the leading party agricultural expert, proposed the creation of large agricultural cities *(agrogoroda)* to concentrate farm labor and abolish rural backwardness.

The cultural policy of the regime matched the bleak austerity and terror of these years. The cultural boss, Andrei Zhdanov, decreed that literature had to take an active role in the "engineering" of human souls. The official school of "socialist realism" was the only permissible line for a writer to follow. Zhdanov denounced Mikhail Zoshchenko for a witty story relating the adventures of a monkey accidentally set free by a bomb and hinting that life in a cage in a zoo was better than life among the Soviet people. Anna Akhmatova, a sensitive lyric poet, lamented in verse her feeling of loneliness. This was unpatriotic and she was silenced. Violent anti-Western propaganda filled Soviet books and resounded from the Soviet stage in such plays as *The Unfortunate Haberdasher,* in which President Truman was cast as Hitler.

With the attack on the Western nations went a constant drumbeat of new claims for Soviet, or at least Russian, "firsts" in every intellectual and artistic field. All scholarly writing began with quotations from Stalin, the great teacher, the leader of all scientific advance. Stalin endorsed a biologist, Lysenko, who argued that communism would change the human species biologically and that "new Soviet man" would be biologically superior.

Stalin also attacked the Jews, accusing Jewish doctors of plotting to poison him. When Stalin died, the stage seemed set for a full-scale anti-Semitic drive reminiscent of Hitler. In fact, many Soviet leaders were personally anti-Semitic and felt that the population would welcome anti-Semitism at a moment when there was little else in the government policies to cheer about. Official Soviet anti-Semitism would wax and wane in the 1950s and 1960s.

The Soviet Succession

By the early 1950s everyone in the West was wondering whether the Communist party, or the secret police, or the army would win out in a future struggle for succession. Would the world see a new bitter rivalry like the struggle between Stalin and Trotsky for the succession to Lenin? If so, would the Soviet government be weakened?

When Stalin died in March 1953, Georgi Malenkov succeeded him as premier but surrendered his Communist party secretaryship to Nikita Khrushchev. Clearly no one man would immediately inherit all of Stalin's power. Soon the regime began to denounce the "cult of personality" (Stalin's one-man rule) and proclaimed a "collegial" system (government by committee). The dreaded chief of the secret police, Presidium-member Beria, was executed for treason.

But no free-for-all among the remaining members of the inner circle followed. Malenkov vanished from the top post of premier and was succeeded by the political general, Bulganin; but Malenkov was simply demoted to a lower cabinet post and remained in the Presidium. When Malenkov confessed error, he took responsibility for the failure of the agrogoroda, which were actually Khrushchev's idea. Khrushchev was certainly very powerful, but his fellow members on the

Politburo had great influence and showed no outward signs of fearing him as they had Stalin. On the whole, it appeared that the transfer of power had actually gone quite smoothly.

Early in 1956 at a party congress, Khrushchev emotionally denounced Stalin. He listed ghastly acts of personal cruelty. When the details of the speech were leaked out to the Soviet public, there was some distress at the smashing of the idol they had worshiped so long. But no doubt many of them had all along suspected that Stalin was ruthless. The speech aroused no public disorder in the U.S.S.R.

Abroad, however, the speech led to turmoil in the Soviet satellites in Europe. So Khrushchev's opponents at home united against him. Within the Presidium they had a majority. But Khrushchev rallied to his support the larger body of which the Presidium was the inner core, the Central Committee of the Communist party of the U.S.S.R.

A veteran party worker, Khrushchev had installed his own loyal supporters in all key party posts, repeating Stalin's performance after the death of Lenin. So he emerged from this test with his powers greatly strengthened (June 1957). Now the Soviet press denounced his enemies: the "antiparty group" of Malenkov, Molotov, and Kaganovich.

In Stalin's day this would have meant their death. Khrushchev, however, merely expelled them from the Presidium and gave them positions far from Moscow. In 1958 Bulganin followed them into the discard. Khrushchev's succession to Stalin's position now seemed complete.

Domestic Policies under Khrushchev and His Successors
Bureaucratic Problems

Yet there were certain differences. Already in his sixties, Khrushchev could not hope for a quarter-century of dictatorship like Stalin's. He had also deprived himself of some of the instruments available to Stalin. After 1953 he had released millions of captives from prisons and slave-labor camps. Within a year or two, Soviet society at every level except the very top of the bureaucracy had absorbed these sufferers from tyranny.

The secret police was no longer powerful enough to challenge the party or the army. Khrushchev himself had denounced its terror. Individuals could still be persecuted by terrorist

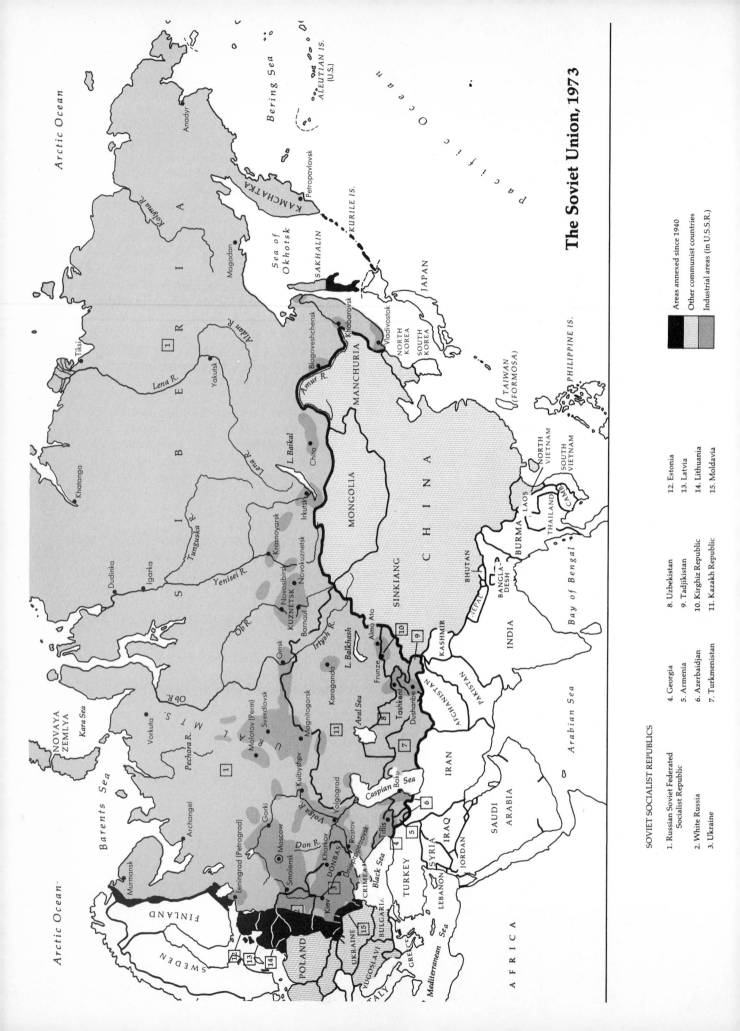

The Soviet Union, 1973

Arctic Ocean

Bering Sea

ALEUTIAN IS. (U.S.)

KAMCHATKA

Anadyr

Kolyma R.

Petropavlovsk

KURILE IS.

Sea of Okhotsk

SAKHALIN

Pacific Ocean

JAPAN

Vladivostok

NORTH KOREA

SOUTH KOREA

TAIWAN (FORMOSA)

PHILIPPINE IS.

Khabarovsk

Blagoveshchensk

Amur R.

MANCHURIA

Aldan R.

Lena R.

Yakutsk

S I B E R I A

Tiksi

Khatanga

Igarka

Dudinka

Tunguska R.

Yenisei R.

Ob R.

L. Baikal

Chita

Irkutsk

Krasnoyarsk

Novosibirsk

KUZNETSK

Novokuznetsk

Barnaul

Omsk

MONGOLIA

C H I N A

SINKIANG

Irtysh R.

L. Balkhash

Alma Ata

Karaganda

Aral Sea

Frunze

Tashkent

Dushanbe

KASHMIR

AFGHANISTAN

PAKISTAN

INDIA

NEPAL

BHUTAN

BANGLA-DESH

BURMA

THAILAND

LAOS

NORTH VIETNAM

SOUTH VIETNAM

CAMB.

Bay of Bengal

Arabian Sea

IRAN

Caspian Sea

Baku

Tiflis

TURKEY

IRAQ

SYRIA

LEBANON

JORDAN

SAUDI ARABIA

Mediterranean Sea

GREECE

BULGARIA

YUGOSLAVIA

ITALY

POLAND

UKRAINE

ROMANIA

Novaya Zemlya

Kara Sea

Barents Sea

Vorkuta

Pechora R.

U R A L M T S.

Molotov (Perm)

Sverdlovsk

Magnitogorsk

Kuibyshev

Volgograd

Gorki

Moscow

Smolensk

Leningrad (Petrograd)

Murmansk

Archangel

Arctic Ocean

FINLAND

SWEDEN

Kama R.

Volga R.

Don R.

Rostov

Dnepropetrovsk

Kharkov

Kiev

DONBASS

Dnieper R.

CRIMEA

Black Sea

AFRICA

Ob R.

U. S. S. R.

AFRICA

SOVIET SOCIALIST REPUBLICS

1. Russian Soviet Federated Socialist Republic
2. White Russia
3. Ukraine
4. Georgia
5. Armenia
6. Azerbaijan
7. Turkmenistan
8. Uzbekistan
9. Tadjikistan
10. Kirghiz Republic
11. Kazakh Republic
12. Estonia
13. Latvia
14. Lithuania
15. Moldavia

Areas annexed since 1940

Other communist countries

Industrial areas (in U.S.S.R.)

means, but Stalin's mass terror as a system of government had disappeared.

Khrushchev put through a series of bureaucratic changes. He gave the Russian Republic, by far the largest and most populous of the republics, a separate administration and took complete control of its personnel. In 1963 he did the same for Central Asia and the Transcaucasus. Khrushchev was trying to improve efficiency, output, and morale. Under Stalin, centralization had become unbearable.

But how far could one decentralize so huge an operation as the Soviet economy and still retain control over local operations? How far could one centralize and still keep local loyalty and increase production? Between 1953 and 1957 Khrushchev transferred responsibility for many heavy industries from the ministries of the central government to those of the individual republics. In May 1957 he abolished many central ministries, and transferred their duties to 105 newly created regional economic councils (sovnarkhoz).

Regionalism—devotion to regional interests as against national ones—replaced devotion to one industry ahead of others. But patriots for Armenian industry against other regions were no more satisfactory than patriots for the cement industry against other industries.

By 1960 a process of recentralizing had begun. By the end of 1962, the sovnarkhozes were reduced from 105 to about 40, and new state committees appeared to oversee their work. These committees greatly resembled the old ministries. Before long they were reorganized as ministries. The pendulum had swung back. All lower levels of the party were divided into agricultural and industrial wings, to make the political functionaries serve the economy more efficiently.

In mid-October 1964, Khrushchev was suddenly removed from power. L. I. Brezhnev replaced him as first secretary of the Central Committee of the Communist party, and A. N. Kosygin as premier. Both were "Khrushchev men": Brezhnev, aged fifty-eight, a metallurgist, had held posts in the Ukrainian, Moldavian, and Kazakhstan Communist parties. Kosygin, aged fifty, an engineer, had been premier of the Russian Republic throughout World War II, went into eclipse shortly before Stalin died, and re-emerged as a member of the Presidium only in 1957.

Official publicity spoke of Khrushchev's ill health and advanced age. But obviously he had not resigned of his own accord. How had Brezhnev and Kosygin managed it? And what did they stand for? Khrushchev had not kept constant watch over his associates. The plotters acted in his absence. They lined up the members of the Central Committee so that Khrushchev could not appeal over the head of the Presidium as he had done in 1957. Until his death in 1971 Khrushchev continued to live in retirement. No large-scale purge followed his removal.

Khrushchev was responsible for major agricultural failures at home and much more serious Soviet setbacks abroad, as we shall see. Yet he might have continued in office had it not been for his personal rudeness. The announcement of his fall referred to his "hare-brained scheming," to "half-baked conclusions and hasty decisions and actions, bragging and bluster, and a wish to be the best." Apparently Khrushchev was personally too hard to live with.

Industry and Agriculture

Like all Soviet leaders, Khrushchev had to choose between consumer goods and heavy industry. Temperamentally more interested in providing consumer goods than Stalin or Malenkov, Khrushchev also chose to emphasize the means of production. The sixth five-year plan (1956–1960) set more ambitious goals than ever before. However, huge expenses involved in the Polish and Hungarian outbreaks forced the Soviet government to shelve the plan.

At the end of 1958, a new seven-year plan was announced to run until 1965. Starting from base figures of 500 million tons of coal, 55 million tons of steel, and 113 million tons of oil, output by 1964 had reached 554 million tons of coal, 85 million tons of steel, and 224 million tons of oil. In 1966, the regime returned to the system of five-year plans.

Most spectacular were the successes achieved in the field of rocketry and space. The U.S.S.R. successfully launched the first earth satellite (Sputnik, 1957) and first reached the moon with a rocket (1959). Heavy Russian payloads soared aloft before American engineers could get their lighter ones off the ground. Spurred to some degree by the Soviet technical advance, the United States embarked on an intensive program of research and development in space. By the mid-1960s the United States had caught up in most aspects of space technology; and the American landings of manned space vehicles on the moon beginning in 1969 overshadowed Soviet accomplishments.

Agriculture continued to baffle the Soviet planners. Khrushchev's "virgin lands" scheme

The U.S. program to put a man on the moon, begun by President Kennedy, culminated in July 1969 with the flight of Apollo 11, whose astronaut Edwin Aldrin is shown here.

(1953) was a crash program to plow under more than 100,000 acres of prairie. Drought and poor planning led to failure by 1963. By 1964 the number of collective farms was down to about 40,000 from an original 250,000, and the average size of the new units was far larger, perhaps about 5,000 acres. By 1965, the government recognized that many collectives were now too big.

To increase incentives, the regime in 1958 abolished compulsory deliveries of farm products, the worst of the peasants' burdens, and raised agricultural prices. The government also gradually abolished the MTS's (Machine Tractor Stations) and sold the tractors to the individual collectives. In 1964, the government extended old-age and disability pensions to agricultural laborers. It removed the ceilings on the size of plot and number of cattle an individual peasant in a collective might own. Yet yields continued low.

After Khrushchev's fall from power in 1964, the Soviet authorities publicly discussed the best way to revise the statutes governing the collective farm. They ordered the collective farms to guarantee the individual farmers a monthly sum in cash for their work, and also to pay for produce actually received. Some argued for the introduction of a free market economy; others vigorously defended centralized planning. The Soviet authorities were recognizing the importance of "capitalist" incentives in agriculture. Yet they never could solve the problems of supply and production. The regime itself often publicly denounced failures caused by stupidity and bad management.

Education and the Arts

In 1958 Khrushchev abandoned the goal of a ten-year general education program for all, and emphasized vocational training and on-the-job experience. By the mid-1960s almost all children in the U.S.S.R. finished the first four years of school (ages seven to eleven). Illiteracy had virtually disappeared. Almost all went on through the second four years (ages eleven to fifteen), now made more "practical." In 1964, the next three years (ages fifteen to eighteen), usually taken by about 40 percent of Soviet youth, were reduced to two.

In the field of arts and letters Khrushchev partly relaxed Stalinist rules. It took Soviet writers some time to realize that they were freer. However, convinced Stalinists lay in wait to attack any departure from the old ways; and Khrushchev kept artists and writers uncertain about new purges. The dangers of self-expression continued great indeed.

But self-expression appeared, for example in Vladimir Dudintsev's novel *Not by Bread Alone* (1956). Its hero, a competent and enthusiastic engineer, was thwarted at every turn by bureaucrats. Government-controlled writers' agencies denounced Dudintsev, who apologized and for six or seven years was forced to earn his living by translation only.

Boris Pasternak's *Dr. Zhivago* (1958) created a stir throughout the world. Pasternak, a brilliant poet, took advantage of the "thaw" to produce a novel about a doctor who affirmed the freedom of the human soul through all the agonies of the First World War and the Russian Revolution. Accepted for publication in Russia, the novel was also sent to Italy to be published. Then the Soviet censors changed their minds and forced Pasternak to ask for the return of the manuscript in Italy. The Italian publisher refused. Versions appeared abroad in Russian, Italian, English, and other languages. In 1958 the Nobel Prize Committee awarded Pasternak the prize for literature. He accepted. But then the Khrushchev regime threatened him with exile if he accepted the prize. As a patriotic Russian he then declined it.

In the same week that a Soviet physicist accepted the Nobel Prize for physics, the regime called the Nobel Prize for literature a capitalist invention. And a few years later, Mikhail Sholokhov, a personal friend of Khrushchev, accepted

Yevgeny Yevtushenko with the composer Dmitri Shostakovich, 1963.

the Nobel Prize for literature. In his memoirs, Khrushchev admitted that he had been wrong in the Pasternak case.

In the 1960s the spirit of individualism found new and more vigorous expression among poets and novelists. The young Ukrainian poet Yevtushenko denounced Soviet anti-Semitism in his *Babi Yar* (the name of the ravine near Kiev in which the Nazis had massacred thousands of Jews), and declared his identity with the murdered human beings. In another very popular poem he begged the government to triple the guard over Stalin's tomb,

> *So that Stalin may not rise*
> *And, with Stalin the past.*
>
> *. . . the ignoring of the people's welfare*
> *The calumnies*
> *The arrests of the innocent. **

In the early sixties Soviet writers showed a deep interest in the terrible days of Stalin's labor camps and in the suffering of their inmates.

*Pravda (October 21, 1962).

Alexander Solzhenitsyn's novel, *A Day in the Life of Ivan Denisovich,* was the most famous. Khrushchev worried over the flood of fiction about the camps. He tried to remind the younger generation of the glorious revolutionary past through which their elders had triumphantly lived. He declared that even under full communism it would never be possible to give complete liberty to the individual, who would continue "like a bee in a hive" to make his contribution to society.

After Khrushchev's ouster in 1964, his successors tightened the reigns of censorship and repression. In September 1965 two writers, Andrei Sinyavsky and Yuli Daniel, were arrested. Writing under the penname Abram Tertz, Sinyavsky, in *The Trial Begins,* gave a frank and horrible picture of the life of the Soviet leaders under Stalin. His novel *The Makepeace Experiment* dealt with a one-man revolt against communism in a small Russian town. Under the penname Nikolai Arzhak, Daniel wrote a fantasy, *Moscow Calling,* in which the Soviet government set aside one day on which murder was allowed. In 1966, despite the protests of many young people, Sinyavsky and Daniel were tried and condemned to prison.

In 1967 Stalin's daughter Svetlana Alliluyeva defected to the United States and published her candid autobiography. The Soviet press said it was all a plot arranged by American agents to spoil the celebrations planned for the fiftieth anniversary of the Revolution of 1917. More arrests of writers and more protests gave the signal that Stalinist "social realism" was once again the only approved style.

Solzhenitsyn's somber and gripping novels *The First Circle* and *Cancer Ward* convinced many Western readers that Russian humane values had found a new spokesman of the stature of Tolstoy or Pasternak. In 1970 he was expelled from the party's Union of Writers and silenced. He was awarded the Nobel Prize in 1970 and accepted it, but explained that he could not come to Stockholm to receive it because he might not be permitted to return to Russia. He was denounced as a "spiritual emigrant" from the U.S.S.R. Before very long he would be a physical emigrant too. Protesters in the arts and sciences were ruthlessly dealt with, and hackwork of the old Stalinist type was still rewarded. In 1970 the regime was having trouble controlling its "intelligentsia," perhaps 20 percent of the Soviet working population.

READING SUGGESTIONS on The Cold War and Great-Power Domestic Policy

See the list at the end of Chapter 19.

CHAPTER NINETEEN

Great-Power Foreign Policy And The Emerging Nations: 1945-1970

SOVIET FOREIGN POLICY

The Last Years of Stalin, 1945–1953

*Eastern Europe, Iran,
Greece, and Berlin*

When World War II ended, the Soviet Union joined in putting through the Allied plan for dividing and ruling Germany. The four occupying powers together tried the chief surviving Nazi leaders at Nuremberg in 1946. In February 1947 came the peace treaties with Italy, Romania, Bulgaria, Hungary, and (for the U.S.S.R.) Finland. The U.S.S.R. annexed Romania, Bessarabia and northern Bukovina, Finnish border territories, part of former East Prussia, and the extreme easternmost portion of Czechoslovakia.

In Poland, Romania, Hungary, and Bulgaria, the U.S.S.R. sponsored new "people's republics" under communist governments. In each country the Russians eliminated all political groups that could be accused of collaboration with the Germans. They formed coalitions of "progressive" parties, and they destroyed all noncommunist elements in each party. First they split off a small fragment that would collaborate unquestioningly with the communists and then denounced and persecuted the remainder. Despite the promise at Yalta, elections were accompanied by intimidation and atrocities. Western protest uniformly failed. These four states became true Soviet satellites.

Yugoslavia organized its own communist government and had Albania as its own satellite. Soviet troops occupied the eastern third of Germany, where they organized the communist-ruled satellite of East Germany. The Russians handed over to their Polish satellite the section of Germany lying east of the line formed by the Oder and Neisse rivers. Here a wholesale transfer of population removed the Germans and replaced them with Poles.

Finland kept its prewar political institutions but became part of the Soviet defense system. The four Allied powers detached Austria from Germany and divided it, like Germany, into four occupation zones. The presence of Soviet troops in Hungary and Romania was specifically guaranteed to "protect" the communication lines between Russia and its occupying forces in Austria.

In 1948, the communists took over Czechoslovakia by a coup d'état, and ousted the government of Edward Beneš, a brave enemy of Hitler in 1938, betrayed now for a second time. Within each satellite the communists aped Soviet policies, moving with all speed to collectivize agriculture, impose forced-draft industrialization, control cultural life, and govern by terror.

As early as 1946 the U.S.S.R. refused to withdraw its forces from northwest Iran and yielded only to pressure from the United Nations. A more alarming probe came in Greece. Here during World War II a communist-dominated guerrilla movement had already attempted to seize control and had been thwarted only by British troops. In 1946, the Greek communists tried again, backed this time by the communist governments of Albania, Yugoslavia, and Bulgaria to the north. Simultaneously, Stalin exerted pressure on the Turks for concessions in the straits area.

In response, President Truman proclaimed that countries facing the threat of communist aggression could count on help from the United States. Under this "Truman Doctrine," he sent American military aid to Greece and Turkey. The threat to the Turks evaporated. By 1949, after severe fighting, the Greeks had put down the communist uprising with the help of American advisers.

In Germany, the Russians began in 1948 one of the most bitter phases of the cold war. By shutting off the land routes from the West into Berlin, they attempted to force the Western Allies to turn Berlin wholly over to them. The Allies stood firm, however, and in the next six months flew more than 2.3 million tons of coal, food, and other necessities into West Berlin. The Russians then gave up and reopened the land routes, but remained determined to oust the Western powers from Berlin.

The Yugoslav Rebellion

In 1948 Yugoslavia, the most pro-Soviet of all the new communist states of Eastern Europe, rebelled against Moscow. Yugoslavia had overthrown a pro-German government in 1941. Throughout World War II Yugoslav guerrilla action against the Germans and Italians had been constant.

There were two main groups of guerrillas. The Chetniks, led by General Mikhailovich, a Serb officer, represented Serb royalist domination. The Partisans were led by the Croatian-born communist Joseph Broz, better known by his underground name, Tito. The communist-dominated Partisans gained ground against the Chetniks, who preferred to wait for a Western Allied landing and compromise with the German and Italian occupying forces.

By 1943, Prime Minister Churchill decided to send supplies to Tito, who was killing more Germans, and the United States followed suit. When the Russians entered Belgrade in October 1944, they helped put their fellow communist Tito in control. Once in power, Tito installed his own communist government, abolished the Yugoslav monarchy, and for three years adopted all the standard Soviet policies. Yet in June 1948 the U.S.S.R. quarreled with Yugoslavia and expelled Tito's regime from the Cominform. The Soviet satellites broke their economic agreements with Yugoslavia, unloosed great barrages of anti-Tito propaganda, and stirred up border incidents.

Soviet arrogance and insistence on putting their own agents into the Yugoslav army and security organizations aroused Yugoslav national feeling. Stalin believed that he could bully the Yugoslavs into submission. "I will shake my little finger," he said, "and there will be no more Tito."

But Tito remained in power, accepting the aid that was quickly offered him by the United States. Washington saw that a communist regime

A cargo plane leaves Tempelhof Air Base during the Berlin blockade of 1948–1949.

hostile to Stalin was a new phenomenon that would deeply embarrass the Russians. Gradually Yugoslav communism evolved a modified ideology of its own. Tito declared that Stalin was a heretic, and that his own followers were the only true Leninists.

Tito decentralized the economy, beginning in the factories. Workers' committees began to participate actively in the planning. Decentralization spread to local government, then to the central government, and finally to the Yugoslav Communist party, rechristened the League of Yugoslav Communists. The regime admitted its past outrageous excesses, but the police continued to be a powerful force. Tito gradually abandoned agricultural collectivization, which, as always, was most unpopular with the peasants. Communist Yugoslavia, however, remained suspicious of the Western capitalists who were helping it.

Afraid that this new "national" communism would spread, the Soviets directed the other Eastern European regimes in a series of ferocious purges. Leading communists were executed for alleged "Titoism." When Stalin died in 1953, his heirs gave high priority to healing the breach with Yugoslavia, and eliminating the weakness it had created in their European position.

Asia: The Korean War

When balked in Europe, tsarist Russian governments had often turned to Asia. In the same way after failures in Greece and Berlin, the Soviet Union embarked on new Asian adventures. Here, communists had tried and failed to win power in Indonesia, Burma, Malaya, and the Philippines, and had succeeded in China. The Korean War, which broke out in June 1950, was certainly prompted in Moscow. The Russians limited their own contribution to support and sympathy, and allowed their Chinese ally to take the military lead.

Korea, a peninsula at the eastern extremity of Asia bordering on Manchuria and Siberia and close to Japan, had been a target of Russian interest in the late nineteenth and early twentieth centuries. The Japanese defeat of the Russians in

American marines retreating from North
Korea during the winter of 1950–1951.

1905, however, led to Japanese annexation of the
country in 1910. In 1945, at the close of World
War II, Russian troops occupied the northern part
of Korea and American troops the southern part.
The country was divided in the middle by a line
along the 38th parallel of latitude.

A communist-inspired People's Democratic
Republic of Korea was set up in the north, and
an American-inspired Republic of Korea in the
south. When all American forces except for a
few specialists were withdrawn from South Korea, the North Koreans marched south to unite
the nation under communist control.

Probably the communists thought the operation was safe. Official American pronouncements referred to Korea as outside the American
"defense perimeter." But when the invasion began, the United States—with UN approval (the
vote was taken in the absence of the Russians)—
at once moved troops into Korea. They halted
the North Korean drive, and pushed the enemy

back well north of the 38th parallel, almost to
the Yalu River, the frontier of China.

At this point, Communist China entered the
war. Chinese troops joined the North Koreans
in pushing the Americans southward again. By
1951, the line of battle had been stabilized
roughly along the old boundary between North
and South Korea. After prolonged negotiations,
an armistice was finally concluded in July 1953.
Stalin had been dead since March.

The Korean settlement did not end the tension between Communist China and the United
States. Serious friction developed over Taiwan
(Formosa) and two small offshore islands, Quemoy and Matsu, now in the hands of Chiang
Kai-shek. The Korean settlement was a compromise. After all the fighting, the United States
managed to hang on to the devastated southern
portion of the country, and the communists had
been driven back to the north, which they governed undisturbed. Neither side won.

Stalin's Heirs

Stalin's heirs realized that any attack that threatened the vital interests of the United States might bring atomic war. The policy of probing had already led to the Korean War. Continued tension between the two superpowers required the U.S.S.R. to continue to devote its resources to guns rather than butter. To relax the tension would theoretically have meant more butter, but might endanger the Soviet position as leader of world communism. China might seize the leadership, at least in Asia, and would denounce the Russians as old and tired, no longer true Leninists. Khrushchev could not hold these threats in balance. The choices he had to make led to a major split in the communist world.

Eastern Europe

In Eastern Europe, Khrushchev worked to repair the break with Tito. In May 1955 he went in person to Belgrade. He publicly apologized for the quarrel, taking the blame upon the U.S.S.R.. He also said that "differences in the concrete forms of developing socialism are exclusively matters for the people of the country concerned," echoing Tito's own claim. Relations between Tito and Moscow were temporarily improved, although the Yugoslavs never abandoned their ties to the West.

Khrushchev even declared that many prominent victims of the "Titoist" purges had been executed wrongly. He abolished the Cominform. But in healing the quarrel Stalin had started, Khrushchev had opened the door to new troubles.

His speech of 1956 denouncing Stalin and admitting so many past injustices led to trouble in the European satellites. Anticommunist riots by workers in Poznán, Poland, in June 1956, were followed by severe upheavals in the rest of that country. The Polish uprising remained under the control of one wing of the Communist party led by Wladislaw Gomulka, who had been purged for alleged Titoism in 1951. Not even the presence in Warsaw of Khrushchev himself and other members of the Soviet Presidium prevented the rise of Gomulka to power. Because the new government in Poland was, after all, a communist government, the Russians let it stay in power.

In Hungary, however, the upheaval went farther. It began, as in Poland, with an anti-Stalinist movement within the Communist party, and brought Imre Nagy, a communist like Gomulka, into office as premier. But popular hatred for communism and for the Russians then exploded. Young men and women flew to arms in

The Hungarian Revolt: head of a statue of Stalin toppled in downtown Budapest, 1956.

Budapest in the hope of ousting the communists and of taking Hungary altogether out of the Soviet sphere. They denounced the Warsaw Pact, the Russian alliance of Eastern European satellites set up by Moscow to oppose NATO.

Then Khrushchev ordered military action. In November 1956 Soviet tanks and troops put down the revolution in blood and fire. A puppet government led by Janos Kadar was installed. More than 150,000 Hungarian refugees fled to Austria to be resettled in various Western countries. The Russians charged that Western "imperialists" and "fascists" were responsible, but in fact, the West had played no part at all, not daring to help the Hungarians for fear of starting a world war.

Tito denounced the Soviet intervention, though he was frightened by the anticommunist character of the Hungarian revolt. Relations between Moscow and Tito were patched up again in the summer of 1957. But when Tito still insisted that each communist nation should make its own decisions freely, the quarrel was renewed for the third time. Khrushchev's efforts had failed.

Khrushchev's final choice of force reflected Chinese influence. The Chinese wanted to take a lead in formulating world communist ideology, and favored Stalinist repression. By the spring of 1958, the Chinese and Khrushchev himself had declared that Stalin's original denunciation of the Yugoslavs back in 1948 had been correct after all. In June 1958 the Soviet government executed Imre Nagy and other leaders of the Hungarian uprising, in violation of solemn promises of safe-conduct.

All the Eastern European satellites were bound together in the Council for Mutual Economic Aid (Comecon), established in 1949. Comecon worked to standardize machinery and coordinate economic policies, and denounced Western European efforts at cooperation like the Common Market. Yugoslavia never was a member.

In 1958–1959, Comecon called for a "specialization" plan: the more developed countries would concentrate on heavy industry, and Romania in particular on the production of raw materials (chiefly food and oil). The Romanian communist government protested.

By 1961 the Romanians, like the Yugoslavs, were assuming a more independent position within the communist bloc. They increased their trade with the noncommunist world. They remained neutral in the growing Soviet-Chinese quarrel. Although the Russians in 1963 gave in and approved Romania's efforts to build a steel industry, the disagreement widened under Khrushchev's successors. The Romanians successfully resisted a Russian plan to integrate the Danube region. They even dared to demand the return of the provinces of Bessarabia and northern Bukovina, annexed by the U.S.S.R. in 1940. Their skillful premier, Ceauşescu, collaborated with Tito and avoided being swallowed by the U.S.S.R.

In the 1960s terror was relaxed in Hungary. Increased tourism, wider trade with the West, a new agreement with the Vatican concerning the Hungarian Church made life easier. In Poland, however, Stalinist harshness reappeared in economic planning, in agriculture, in education, in religious policies, even in a return to anti-Semitism. A sudden rise of prices announced by the government in 1970 led to serious riots, suppressed with heavy loss of life. The Gomulka government fell. Edward Gierek became premier. The brittleness of communist control of Eastern European peoples had again been demonstrated.

In Czechoslovakia, liberalization began in the middle 1960s, beginning before Khrushchev's ouster and continuing after it. But the communist bureaucracy's economic failures in a formerly prosperous industrial state and a particularly brutal party leadership aroused great discontent. In 1968 this would explode and produce an international crisis (see below).

Berlin Again

In East Germany (D.D.R., the Deutsche Demokratische Republik), the U.S.S.R. had created its most industrially productive European satellite, now fully geared into the Comecon. Except for a workers' riot in East Berlin in 1953, the German communist puppets had silenced protest against Soviet and communist rule. Control over East Germany enabled the Russians to keep Poland surrounded, helpless to achieve more than a token autonomy.

But deep in the heart of the D.D.R., the United States, Britain, and France each retained a zone of occupation in Berlin, and accessible by subway from East Berlin. Every year, thousands of East Germans showed how they felt about communism by escaping into West Berlin. The East German population declined by two million between 1949 and 1961. For those who stayed behind in the D.D.R., West Berlin provided an example of prosperity and free democratic government more impressive than propaganda.

This situation accounted for Khrushchev's determination to get the Western powers out of Berlin. The method he proposed in 1958 and later was thoroughly Stalinist. He threatened to sign a peace treaty with the puppet D.D.R. never recognized by the West; to give the D.D.R. all communications to Berlin; and to support it in any effort it might make to cut these communications and force the Western powers out. This led to a prolonged diplomatic crisis during 1959.

The West could not allow the U.S.S.R. to force a repetition of the airlift of 1948. Nor could the West believe the Russian suggestion that, once Western troops were removed, Berlin would be a "free city." Defenseless and surrounded by communist territory, Berlin and its two million "free" citizens, it feared, would soon be swallowed up.

The U.S.S.R. was further proposing that after Western withdrawal, the D.D.R. would "confederate" with the West German Federal Republic. How could a state that was a full member of the Western system of NATO federate with one that belonged to the Soviet system's Warsaw Pact? How could a state that stood for free capitalist development federate with one completely communized? How could a parliamentary state with a multiparty system federate with a communist totalitarian state?

Obviously Khrushchev did not believe in the possibility of the confederation he was proposing. He expected that any possible union of the Germanies would be discredited, while the D.D.R., in full control over Berlin, would become a permanent Soviet satellite. The danger to West Germany and to NATO would be immense.

U-2, The Berlin Wall, Testing, Cuba

While the Berlin threat persisted, President Eisenhower and Khrushchev agreed to exchange visits, and Khrushchev actually toured the United States. When the leaders of the great powers held a summit meeting in Paris (May 1960), however, tension between Moscow and Washington was severe. A Soviet missile had brought down a lightweight, extremely fast American plane called a "U-2" that had been taking high-altitude photographs of Soviet territory. The Russians had captured the pilot unharmed. President Eisenhower had to admit the truth of the charge. The incident ended both the summit meeting and the plans for Eisenhower's visit to the U.S.S.R.

When Eisenhower's successor, John F. Kennedy, met Khrushchev in Vienna (June 1961), Khrushchev insisted that the U.S.S.R. would sign

Kennedy and Khrushchev at the Vienna summit meeting, 1961.

the treaty with East Germany before the end of the year. The number of refugees fleeing East Berlin rose to a thousand a day. On August 13, East German forces cut the communications between East and West Berlin and began to build a barrier—the Berlin Wall—to prevent further departures. The United States realized that it could not prevent the East Germans' closing their own border.

The U.S. protested and sent Vice-President Lyndon Johnson to reassure the West Berliners of America's resolve. The wall became the symbol of a government that had to imprison its own people to keep them at home. Occasional hair-raising escapes, captures, and shootings continued to take place along the wall. But Khrushchev had not carried out his threat to tear up the Berlin treaties by himself.

In August 1961 Khrushchev announced that the U.S.S.R. would resume atomic testing in the atmosphere, which had been stopped by both powers in 1958. In the two months that followed, the Russians exploded thirty huge bombs, whose total force considerably exceeded all previous American, British, and French explosions. Kennedy decided that, unless Khrushchev would agree to a treaty banning all tests, the United States would have to conduct its own new tests. Khrushchev refused, and the American tests began in late April 1962.

During the summer of 1962 Khrushchev placed Soviet missiles with nuclear warheads in Cuba, where an American-sponsored landing directed against the procommunist regime of Fidel

Castro had failed dismally at the Bay of Pigs the year before. Castro may not have asked for the missiles, but he did accept them. Soviet officers were to retain control over their use. Their installation would have doubled the Soviet capacity to strike directly at the United States.

But the mere presence of these weapons ninety miles from Florida would shake the confidence of other nations in the American capacity to protect even the United States. It would enable Khrushchev to blackmail America on the question of Berlin. American military intelligence photographed the missiles from the air. Khrushchev announced that the Soviet purpose was to help the Cubans resist a new invasion from the United States.

But Kennedy could not allow the missiles to stay in Cuba. At first, the only course of action seemed an air strike, which might well have touched off a new world war. Instead Kennedy found a measure that would prevent the further delivery of missiles—a sea blockade ("quarantine") of Cuba. He combined this with the demand that the missiles already in Cuba be removed. He thus gave Khrushchev a way to avoid world war and a chance to save face. After several days of almost unbearable tension, Khrushchev backed down, and agreed to remove the missiles.

The U.S.S.R. and U.S.
after the Missile Crisis;
Czechoslovakia

Kennedy exploited the American victory only to push for a further relaxation. In July 1963 the United States, the U.S.S.R., and Great Britain signed a treaty banning nuclear weapons tests in the atmosphere, in outer space, or under water. More than seventy nations later signed, although France and China refused. A "hot line" communications system was installed between the White House and the Kremlin so that the leaders of the two countries might talk to each other in case of need.

During the administration of President Johnson there was no new Soviet-American crisis as acute as that over the missiles. But relations remained tense and suspicious. The war in Vietnam made a real relaxation of tension impossible. The two powers were also opposed in the Middle East. Kosygin's meeting with Johnson at Glassboro, New Jersey, in 1967 accomplished little. In 1968 the United States and the U.S.S.R. agreed on a treaty to prevent the spread of atomic arms to nations that did not already have them. Soviet

intervention in Czechoslovakia in the summer of 1968 delayed Senate approval.

The most Stalinist of the Eastern European governments, the Czech regime, was unpopular. Soviet exploitation and Czech communist incompetence had crippled the once flourishing Czech economy. In 1968 Alexander Dubček became first secretary of the Czech Communist party. Dubček ended censorship of the press. The pent-up protests of years now filled its columns. It seemed as though the regime might even allow opposition political parties. Some army officers wanted to change the Warsaw Pact, which allowed the U.S.S.R. to hold military exercises in the territory of any member state. Yugoslavia and Romania encouraged the Czech "socialism with a new face."

Czechoslovakia had long frontiers with both East and West Germany. The Czechs' radical liberalization worried the Russians and the East Germans. The U.S.S.R. moved from denunciation of the Dubček regime to intimidation and bullying, and finally to armed intervention.

Soviet and satellite tank divisions swept into the country. The Soviet attack—as in Hungary in 1956—was directed against a population in armed rebellion. There was little bloodshed. But there was great shock. Those who believed that the U.S.S.R. had outgrown Stalinism were proved wrong. The French and Italian Communist parties joined the Yugoslav and Romanian in condemning the invasion.

The Soviet government kidnapped the Czech leaders. The Russians could at first find no one who would govern as a puppet, and so lend support to the Soviet claim that their armies had only acted on an invitation from Czechs and Slovaks who feared counterrevolution. In the end the Russians restored Dubček and his colleagues, but only after extracting promises from them that the liberalization would be reversed. Soviet military occupation continued.

The return of Stalinism to Czechoslovakia was gradual. Dubček, a broken man, was ousted from government and party. His followers were powerless. The Czech government once more became a mere Soviet puppet. A purge of Czech intellectuals threatened the country's cultural institutions. The Russians had been so alarmed by the Czech ferment that they threw away whatever international goodwill that they had.

For the third time in thirty years—in 1938, 1948, and 1968—it was demonstrated that democratic nations would sympathize with the sufferings of the Czechs at the hands of Nazis or Com-

German cartoon commenting on the Russian invasion of Czechoslovakia, August 1968. Mao is briefing his troops, saying ". . . and if the Russians complain, simply say that somebody called you."

munists but would do nothing to help. In 1969 and 1970 discussions between the United States and the U.S.S.R. on arms control resumed. Both powers hoped to reduce their huge expenditures on weapons.

II THE U.S.S.R., CHINA, AND AMERICA IN ASIA, 1956–1970

The Soviet-Chinese Quarrel

Until 1956, Chinese-Soviet relations were friendly. The Russians returned Port Arthur and Dairen to China in 1955. But when Khrushchev denounced Stalin, the Chinese disapproved. They attacked Tito as a "revisionist" and tried to block Khrushchev's reconciliation with him. They also wanted far more economic aid than the U.S.S.R. would give, especially aid in developing nuclear weapons.

In 1957 Mao briefly relaxed censorship ("Let one hundred flowers bloom") but soon reversed his policy. He announced a new rapid industrialization, the "great leap forward," with backyard blast furnaces and a mass collectivization of the "people's communes." It failed. The Russians dis-

approved, and hidden disagreement between the two communist giants began to show.

In 1959 Khrushchev told Peking that the U.S.S.R. would not furnish China with atomic weapons and tried unsuccessfully to oust Mao. The Chinese bombarded Quemoy and Matsu, conquered Tibet, invaded Indian territory, all without consulting the U.S.S.R. The Russians declared themselves neutral between China and India. In 1960 Khrushchev recalled all Soviet technicians from China.

China next picked up a European satellite: Albania, smallest and poorest of the Balkan countries. The Albanian Communist party, trained as a guerrilla movement by Tito during World War II, threw off Yugoslav domination after 1948. More than anything else the Albanian communists feared a renewed subjection to the Yugoslavs. When Khrushchev kept wooing Tito, the Albanians turned to China. Albania was an economic liability, but the Chinese rejoiced in having taken a European communist state from the Russian bloc.

In the midst of the 1962 crisis over Soviet missiles in Cuba, China attacked India again. They took the border zones they wanted. The U.S.S.R., like the United States, was pro-Indian.

The Chinese built up their own organizations in Africa and Asia. They called the Russians traitors to the international communist movement for signing the test-ban treaty. Khrushchev tried to get all other Communist parties to denounce China, but failed. Mao called for Khrushchev's removal, accusing the Russians of illegally occupying Eastern European and Japanese territory.

By the time Khrushchev fell in October 1964, the Chinese had won the support of the North Korean and North Vietnamese Communist parties, and had much influence in Indonesia and Algeria. In Africa they took the lead in sponsoring a major rebellion in the former Belgian Congo (later Zaire). In South America they supported Castroites in the hope of starting revolutions. They had exploded an atomic bomb. They were actively supporting, as were the Russians, the communist efforts in South Vietnam.

But in 1965 a congress scheduled for Algiers was canceled, as the Algerians overthrew their pro-Chinese premier Ben Bella. The Congo revolt was put down. An attempted communist coup in Indonesia failed. The Indonesian army revenged itself heavily on the Chinese minority and on the native communists. Perhaps 500,000 were killed.

In 1965 and 1966 the United States and the U.S.S.R. intervened in an Indian-Pakistani war, bringing about peaceful negotiations and keeping the Chinese out.

Between 1966 and 1969 Chairman Mao put China through a "cultural revolution." Important leaders of the government and party were removed. The Red Guard, youngsters in their teens, erupted into the streets of the cities, beating and sometimes killing older people, destroying works of art and other reminders of China's precommunist past, and rioting against foreigners and foreign influences. The Chinese educational system was completely halted, and something like civil war raged in some of the provinces.

By 1969 about a fourth of the top officials had been purged. Economic production had risen only to about the 1965 level. Occasional executions still took place, but the crisis eased for reasons as obscure as the reasons for its inception. Chairman Mao himself—nearing the age of eighty—disappeared from the news for months at a time, and when he showed himself it was as a relaxed and genial leader. Though Soviet-Chinese tension once or twice broke into open fighting on the frontiers, the two countries kept on talking.

Behind the Chinese-Soviet quarrel lay theoretical disagreements about the best way to impose communist control upon the peoples of

Red Guardsmen outside the Soviet Embassy in Peking, 1966.

Africa, Asia, and Latin America. The Chinese favored direct sponsorship of local communist revolutionary movements; the Russians, "peaceful" economic competition with the capitalist world for the loyalty and admiration of the emerging peoples. The Russians said the communists would win the competition without world war, but would help local "wars of national liberation." The Chinese regarded world war as inevitable. "The bourgeoisie," they maintained, "will never step down from the stage of history of its own accord."

The Chinese insisted that communists alone must take charge of all revolutionary movements from the beginning, and claimed that aid to noncommunist countries was a delusion. They particularly objected to Soviet aid to India, their own enemy. They opposed disarmament. They had wanted Khrushchev to freeze Soviet living standards at a low level and to invest the savings in helping the Chinese catch up, but of course Khrushchev preferred to let his own people enjoy some of the fruits of their own labors.

Remembering their own success as a guerrilla operation that first came to control the countryside and then moved in on the cities, Chinese theoreticians extended this lesson to the whole globe. They regarded Asia, Africa, and Latin America—the underdeveloped areas—as the countryside, and Europe and North America as the cities. From the massed peoples of the backward continents the communists would mount an offensive against the peoples of the developed industrial world and conquer them.

One additional factor in the Chinese-Russian quarrel was that of race. The Russians disliked and feared the Chinese, the "yellow peril" on their borders. The huge masses of Chinese—soon to number one billion people—were crowded into territory bordering on the vast, sparsely populated regions of the U.S.S.R. The threat came from yellow men, which increased Russian fears. The Chinese used race openly as a weapon in their efforts among other Asians, Africans, and Latin Americans, lumping the Soviet Union with the United States as symbols of the evil white intention to continue dominating the colored world. Convinced of their own superiority to the rest of humanity, the Chinese were racists too.

Southeast Asia: Vietnam and Laos

A special problem for the Chinese, Russians, and Americans arose in Southeast Asia as the result of the revolt of the Viet Minh communist forces against France that broke out in French Indo-China (Vietnam) after World War II. During the Korean War, the United States, fearing that the Chinese communists would strike across the border into northern Indo-China, gave substantial assistance to the French. In 1954, when the French had been defeated, a conference of powers at Geneva gave independence to the Indochinese provinces of Cambodia and Laos.

Vietnam, the third and largest portion of the former French colony, was divided along the 17th parallel. The northern section, with its capital at Hanoi, was governed by the communist Viet Minh party, under the veteran communist Ho Chi Minh. The southern portion, with its capital at Saigon, was governed by a Catholic nationalist leader, Ngo Dinh Diem. The Geneva agreements guaranteed free elections.

Between 1954 and 1959 Ngo Dinh Diem created the bureaucratic machinery for a new regime, restored order in areas long held by communist guerrillas, provided for almost a million refugees from the communist North, and resettled in the countryside millions of peasants who had fled to the cities. After the departure of the French in 1956, the Americans helped Diem with money and technical advice.

But Diem failed politically. He canceled the scheduled elections. Together with his immediate family, he governed despotically. In 1958 and 1959, communist-led guerrilla activity broke out again. Now known as the Viet Cong, the guerrillas set up a National Liberation Front. In September 1960, Ho Chi Minh endorsed the Viet Cong movement, which he was already supplying with arms and training. By 1961 the guerrillas were moving freely in South Vietnam, overrunning much of the countryside, murdering, looting, and burning.

Neighboring Laos, though strategically important, was no nation but rather a collection of unwarlike Buddhist tribes, where only a small clique of families traditionally indulged in politics. In 1953 a communist-oriented political faction, calling itself the Pathet Lao and supported by Ho Chi Minh, seized the northeastern portion of the country. The United States tried with massive financial and military aid to build a national Laotian army and establish a firm regime, but succeeded largely in creating corruption and factionalism.

The head of the government, Souvanna Phouma, who was the brother-in-law of the head of the Pathet Lao, reached agreement with him in 1957 to set up a coalition government and neutralize the country, absorbing the Pathet Lao into the army. This the United States resisted, ousting Souvanna Phouma and introducing the right-wing Phoumi Nousavan. By 1960, Souvanna Phouma was working with the Russians, and a portion of the army under Kong Le (not a communist) was working with the Pathet Lao. Soviet airlifts of supplies to their side made it likely that Laos would fall to the communists, and that South Vietnam, Thailand and Burma, would be endangered also.

President Kennedy wanted to neutralize Laos and to convince the U.S.S.R. that otherwise American military intervention would follow. The U.S.S.R. agreed to neutralization, but fighting in Laos between Soviet-backed and American-backed forces continued until mid-May 1961, when Khrushchev realized that the United States was preparing to send marines to Laos.

In July 1962 the decision to neutralize Laos was reached—many years too late. But the Pathet Lao, now a strong force armed with Russian weapons and still supported by Ho Chi Minh, maintained control over the portion of Laos bordering on South Vietnam. This included the "Ho Chi Minh trail," a road down which supplies came from Hanoi for the Viet Cong guerrillas.

Incomplete and unsatisfactory as the Laos solution was, it was much better than any arrangement that could be reached for South Vietnam. American efforts to get Ngo Dinh Diem moving politically failed. In May 1963 Diem's troops fired on a crowd of Buddhists in the city of Hué, protesting against Diem's edict that they might not display flags in honor of Buddha's birthday. Riots followed, and several Buddhists soaked themselves in gasoline and set themselves afire. In August, Diem staged a mass arrest of Buddhists, and in November he and his brother were ousted and murdered in a coup led by generals and countenanced by the United States.

Thereafter the South Vietnamese government changed hands several times, each time by military coup. The longest-lived regime, that of General Nguyen Cao Ky, conducted elections in September 1966, Ky emerging as vice-president under President Thieu. But the rebellion grew. North Vietnamese regular troops appeared in South Vietnam in support of the guerrillas. More

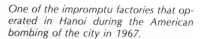

One of the impromptu factories that operated in Hanoi during the American bombing of the city in 1967.

than half a million peasant families were made refugees once more by floods and by terrorism.

Between 1965 and 1967, the United States increased the number of American troops from fewer than a single division to more than 500,000, and began to bomb North Vietnam. This made it impossible for the Viet Cong to conquer the entire country and assured the United States of certain bases along the coast.

President Johnson then tried to bring Ho Chi Minh to the conference table by assuring him that the United States had no long-range intention of remaining in Vietnam and sought no military bases there. In 1966 he suspended the bombing for a time, but Ho Chi Minh insisted that there could be no negotiations until all American troops had left the country. The very act of offering to negotiate with the North aroused uneasiness in the South.

The Vietnam War was the first war in history that could be viewed on television half a world away. The blood and horror of the jungle fighting, the misery of the countless fleeing survivors, the corruption of the Saigon government came home vividly to the American public. The war's mounting costs wrecked President Johnson's domestic programs.

Some voices called for American withdrawal. Others urged that the war be intensified and won. Withdrawal might mean the abandonment of the goals for which the United States had fought the Asian portion of World War II. The communists of the 1970s, like the Japanese militarists of the 1940s, would dominate the Asian continent. But intensification meant fighting a war whose length and severity nobody could predict.

In 1968, as the time for American elections approached, Senator Eugene McCarthy, Democrat of Minnesota, challenged the Johnson administration by announcing his own candidacy for the presidency on an antiwar platform. Another opponent of the war, Senator Robert F. Kennedy, also entered the race. The strength of the antiwar candidates brought about the withdrawal of President Johnson. Ho Chi Minh then consented to open peace talks, which began in Paris but dragged on inconclusively.

The Nixon administration inherited both the war and the negotiations designed to end it. Nixon pledged the eventual withdrawal of all American forces and did indeed begin to reduce them. He planned to "Vietnamize" the fighting by rapidly training and supplying the South Vietnamese forces. The death of Ho Chi Minh in 1969 brought no change to the North Vietnamese government. It continued the war, believing that the Americans had lost stomach for it, and that the communists had everything to gain from more fighting.

In Laos, the Viet Cong grew stronger, endangering the hard-won settlement of the early 1960s. The Viet Cong also overflowed into those portions of Cambodia nearest to South Vietnam, where the Americans and South Vietnamese could not pursue them. Cambodia had as its ruler a French-educated prince, Norodom Sihanouk. He tried to keep Cambodia neutral but believed that China would eventually dominate Southeast Asia and so must be appeased.

He was suspect in Washington and unpopular at home. Many Cambodians, though peaceful, detested the Vietnamese in general, and the intruding Viet Cong and North Vietnamese in particular. In 1970, a coup d'état led by General Lon Nol overthrew Sihanouk. From Peking Sihanouk announced the formation of a government in exile.

Soon afterward American and South Vietnamese troops made an "incursion" into Cambodia. They failed to wipe out the large Viet Cong forces that were their chief target. Public opinion in the United States was deeply opposed to the move into Cambodia. Apparently surprised at this, President Nixon withdrew the forces. As American armies were reduced in Vietnam, bombing and the threat of bombing remained the chief American weapon of war. And by 1970, more and more Americans were revolted by bombing.

Indeed, by 1970, many Americans felt that the Vietnam War would go on forever and could never be won. Our ally, the South Vietnamese government, was both corrupt and cruel. Yet it was also the only possible defense against even crueler communist domination, and thousands of South Vietnamese had believed our promise to support it. The Vietnamese War was creating domestic troubles in the United States perhaps more serious than the importance of all Southeast Asia.

III THE EMERGING NATIONS AND WORLD POLITICS

The Revolt against Imperialism

As in Indochina, so elsewhere World War II speeded the process of liquidating old colonial empires and creating new nations with new economic and political institutions. The Western powers' use of colonial troops increased the self-esteem of the colonial peoples. Wartime propaganda strengthened their wish for independence. Wartime inflation, shortages, conscription of labor, and the enjoyment of war profits by a few added to their sense of grievance.

Moreover, during the war Asians—Japanese—seized Western possessions in the Far East, putting an end to the myth of white supremacy. Though Japan was eventually defeated, Western prestige never recovered. Everybody knew that the French and Dutch had really lost, that British power had been seriously weakened, and that the defeat of Conservatives by the Labour party in 1945 promised new colonial policies. The only real victors in the war were the United States and the Soviet Union, each in its way anticolonial.

The Western tradition itself helped undermine Western colonial power. The West had brought the Bible, the American Declaration of Independence, the French Declaration of the Rights of Man, the Communist Manifesto. You could not insist that "all men are created equal" really meant "white men are created the superiors of colored men." The education provided by the West to a relatively small minority in the colonies taught most of the students that independence could be won only by learning the industrial, technological, and military skills of the West.

These educated black, yellow, and brown men wanted independence. Many were revolutionaries. Some admired the Bolshevik Revolution, and a few received training in Moscow. A great many Westerners wrongly believed that these men were unrepresentative and that the masses still wanted to be ruled by kindly whites. Instead, the city-dwellers and then, more gradually, the peasants, began to demand that the foreigner go. The medical facilities, sanitary engineering, and orderly legal systems introduced by the West lowered death rates dramatically. As the population rose, so did the demand for independence.

Within twenty years after World War II, the British, French, Dutch, and Belgian colonial empires were liquidated. Portugal alone retained its major possessions overseas, largely because the Portuguese government was a conservative dictatorship that would not yield, even to colonial rebellion.

Britain continued to lead the Commonwealth of Nations, which many of its former colonies joined. The Commonwealth remained a major association of trading partners, but its political importance diminished. South Africa left the Commonwealth in 1961, becoming a wholly independent republic. Australia and New Zealand increasingly looked to the United States.

The Far East

During the Second World War, the Japanese had conquered a huge empire, the "Greater East Asia Co-Prosperity Sphere." To rule it they had relied chiefly on exploiting the economic resources of puppet native governments for their own benefit. Although the Japanese were a colored people, they did not emancipate Asians as their propaganda promised. Instead, their armies looted and committed atrocities. They behaved like a master race. They alienated the people they might have won. When the war ended, they were stripped of their overseas possessions.

The occupation of Japan was wholly American. Despite some opposition in American opinion, the emperor was left on his throne, but under the close control of General MacArthur and the forces of occupation. Americans found that the Japanese people did not react to the occupation with hostility. By the time of the peace treaty in 1952, Japan promised to be a democracy of the Western type. The Japanese economy—the only well-developed industrial economy in the non-Western world—overtook France and West Germany, to rank third in the world after the U.S. and the U.S.S.R.

Signs of change and of affluence multiplied. Programs of birth-control education were successful, and the Japanese birth rate became one of the lowest in the world. Peasants migrated to the cities, especially to Tokyo, which surpassed London and New York as the world's largest city. Weekend traffic jams resulted from the rush of Tokyo residents to the beaches in the summer and the ski slopes in winter. Inflation appeared to be the main threat to continued prosperity and to social and economic westernization.

Politically, the democratic parliamentary institutions carefully fostered by the American occupation forces flourished under successive cabinets of the conservative Liberal Democratic party. The left-wing opposition, including both socialists and communists, objected to the mutual security pact binding Japan and the United States. Left-wing demonstrations caused the last-minute cancellation of President Eisenhower's planned visit to Japan in 1960.

Anti-Americanism stemmed from resent-

ment over the continued United States occupation of the island of Okinawa and from the bitter
memory of the atomic blasts. It was fed in the
late 1960s by a particularly violent outbreak of
student extremism. The Japanese university system was halted for months at a time by armed
conflicts between rival groups of students and
between radical students and police.

South Korea also attempted constitutional
government in the Western manner but ran into
serious difficulties. After the Korean War of the
early 1950s, the government of President Syng-
man Rhee came under criticism for corruption
and arbitrary actions. In 1960, massive protests
by students forced the eighty-five-year-old Rhee
out of office. After a period of army rule, a second
constitutional government came to power. The
economy, heavily dependent on American assistance, boomed in the late 1960s. The South Koreans sent troops to fight in Vietnam. In 1970 pressure from communist North Korea remained a
major threat.

Once the Japanese occupation ended in
Southeast Asia, the major Western colonial powers found that they could not restore the prewar
arrangements. The United States gave the Philippines independence in 1946. In 1949, the Dutch
recognized the independence of the Netherlands
East Indies as the Republic of Indonesia, with a
population of a hundred million people. Britain
gave Burma independence outside the Commonwealth (1948) and the Federation of Malaya independence within the Commonwealth (1957). The
port of Singapore at the tip of Malaya, with its
largely Chinese population, secured a special autonomous status (1958). When Malaya joined
with the former British protectorates on the island of Borneo in the Federation of Malaysia
(1963), Singapore at first participated, then withdrew (1965).

The Dutch in Indonesia had not educated
the people for independence. Nevertheless, the
Indonesians at first attempted to run their government along the lines of a parliamentary democracy. Almost everything went wrong. The economy was crippled by inflation and shortages, by
administrative corruption and the black market,
and by the expulsion of experienced Dutch businessmen. The Muslims, who made up the bulk
of the population, proved unable to form responsible political parties.

The outlying islands rebelled against domination by the island of Java, which had the capital
(Djakarta, the former Batavia) and two-thirds of
the population. With Western-style democracy

a failure, President Sukarno, the hero of the Indonesian struggle for independence, installed
"guided democracy."

In 1959 and 1960 he suspended the regime
and vested authority in himself and in the army
and an appointive council. Inflation ran wild, necessities vanished from the market, pretentious
new government buildings were left unfinished
for lack of funds, and all foreign enterprises were
confiscated.

Sukarno fought the new Federation of Malaysia for control of the island of Borneo, where
both states had territory. By intimidation he annexed former Dutch New Guinea (called West
Irian by the Indonesians). When the United Nations recognized Malaysia, Sukarno withdrew Indonesia from membership early in 1965. He also
told the United States "to go to hell with their
aid" and moved closer and closer to Red China.

But a communist coup misfired in the autumn of 1965. There was a wholesale slaughter
of local communists. The anticommunist forces
came to power under military leaders. General
Suharto became president in 1968, reached a settlement with Malaysia, and rejoined the UN. Inflation was brought under control, a five-year
plan was launched, and parliamentary elections
were held.

In Southeast Asia, the communists did not
limit their efforts to Vietnam and Indonesia. In
the Philippine Republic and Malaya too, the communists launched stubborn guerrilla campaigns
that were not checked until the late 1950s. Wherever there were large colonies of "overseas Chinese," some of them became sympathizers of
Mao.

India and Pakistan

The Labour victory in Britain in 1945 made
Indian independence a certainty. But the deep-
seated tension between Muslims and Hindus now
assumed critical importance. When the Hindu
Congress party and the All-India Muslim League
tried to make a working constitution for the new
India, they could not agree. The Muslims had
long been working for a partition into separate
Hindu and Muslim states, and this was in the
end reluctantly accepted by the Hindus. In 1947,
Hindu India and Muslim Pakistan were set up
as self-governing dominions within the British
Commonwealth. India had about eighty percent
of the population.

Pakistan was divided into two parts, widely
separated by intervening Indian territory, West

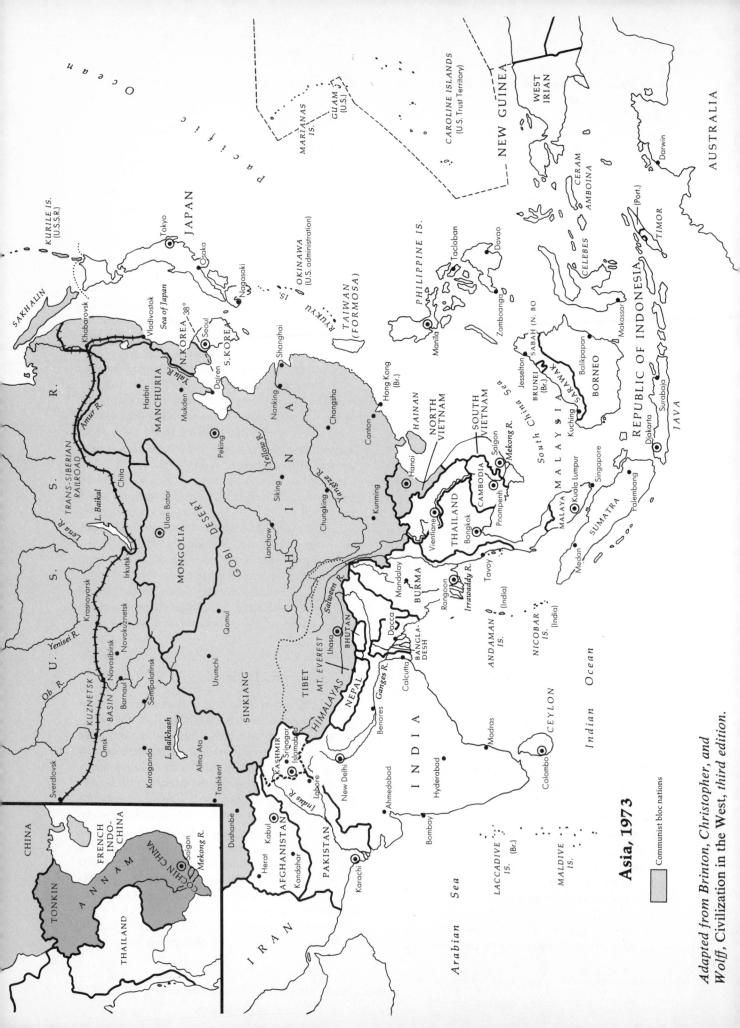

Asia, 1973

Adapted from Brinton, Christopher, and
Wolff, *Civilization in the West, third edition.*

Communist bloc nations

Pacific Ocean

KURILE IS.
(U.S.S.R.)

JAPAN
Tokyo
Osaka
Nagasaki

SAKHALIN

Khabarovsk
Vladivostok
Sea of Japan
N. KOREA
Seoul
38°
S. KOREA
Dairen
Mukden

U. S. S. R.
Amur R.
Lena R.
Chita
L. Baikal
TRANS-SIBERIAN RAILROAD
Irkutsk
Sverdlovsk
Krasnoyarsk
Novosibirsk
Omsk
Barnaul
Semipalatinsk
Novokuznetsk
KUZNETSK BASIN
Ob R.
Yenisei R.

MANCHURIA
Harbin
Yalu R.

MONGOLIA
Ulan Bator
GOBI DESERT

Peking
Nanking
Shanghai
Siking
Yellow R.
Changsha
Canton
Yangtze R.
Chungking
Kunming
Lanchow

C H I N A

Qomul
Urumchi
SINKIANG

L. Balkhash
Alma Ata
Karaganda
Tashkent

HAINAN
Hong Kong
(Br.)
Hanoi
NORTH VIETNAM
SOUTH VIETNAM
Saigon
Mekong R.
CAMBODIA
Pnompenh
THAILAND
Bangkok
Vientiane

South China Sea

TAIWAN
(FORMOSA)

OKINAWA
(U.S. administration)
RYUKYU IS.

MARIANAS IS.
GUAM
(U.S.)

CAROLINE ISLANDS
(U.S. Trust Territory)

NEW GUINEA
WEST IRIAN
AUSTRALIA
Darwin

PHILIPPINE IS.
Manila
Tacloban
Davao
Zamboanga

SABAH (N. BO
BRUNEI
(Br.)
SARAWAK
Jesselton
Kuching
BORNEO
Balikpapan
Makassar
CELEBES
CERAM
AMBOINA
TIMOR
(Port.)

MALAYA
Kuala Lumpur
Singapore
SUMATRA
Medan
Palembang
REPUBLIC OF INDONESIA
Djakarta
JAVA
Surabaja

M A L A Y S I A

BURMA
Mandalay
Rangoon
Irrawaddy R.
Tavoy
Salween R.

TIBET
Lhasa
MT. EVEREST
HIMALAYAS
BHUTAN
NEPAL
Dacca
BANGLA-DESH
Calcutta
Ganges R.
Benares

I N D I A
New Delhi
Ahmedabad
Hyderabad
Madras
Bombay
Karachi

KASHMIR
Srinagar
Islamabad
Lahore
Indus R.
PAKISTAN
AFGHANISTAN
Kabul
Herat
Kandahar
Dushanbe

IRAN

CEYLON
Colombo

Indian Ocean

ANDAMAN IS.
(India)
NICOBAR IS.
(India)

LACCADIVE IS.
(Br.)
MALDIVE IS.

Arabian Sea

CHINA
FRENCH INDO-CHINA
TONKIN
ANNAM
COCHIN CHINA
Saigon
Mekong R.
THAILAND

Pakistan—large and arid—in the northwest, and East Pakistan—smaller, more fertile, and far more densely populated—in East Bengal. The rest of the former British Indian Empire became the Republic of India by the Constitution of 1950. Pakistan, with its smaller population (still well over a hundred million people) and its relatively undeveloped industry, was weaker than India, and at first kept closer political ties with the British Commonwealth.

Violence accompanied partition. It was not possible to draw a boundary that would leave all Hindus in one state and all Muslims in another. Bitter Hindu-Muslim fighting cost hundreds of thousands of lives, as Hindus moved from Pakistani territory into India and Muslims moved from Indian territory into Pakistan. A particular source of trouble was the beautiful mountainous province of Kashmir. Though mainly Muslim in population, it was at the time of partition ruled by a Hindu princely house which turned it over to India. India continued to occupy most of Kashmir, to the great economic disadvantage of Pakistan. The United Nations sought to determine the fate of Kashmir by arranging a plebiscite, but failed to secure the needed approval of both parties.

In domestic politics the two new nations went through contrasting experiences. The chief architect of Pakistani independence, Mohammed Ali Jinnah, died in 1948. Thereafter Pakistan failed to make parliamentary government work or to attack pressing economic difficulties. In 1958 the British-educated army commander, Ayub Khan, took full power. He attacked administrative corruption and the black market. He instituted a program of "basic democracies" to train the population in self-government first at the local level and thence gradually upward through a pyramid of advisory councils. In 1962 a new constitution provided for a national assembly and also for a strengthened presidency, an office that Ayub continued to fill.

But as Ayub grew older, charges of corruption were made against his family and his officials. More and more loudly the teeming and depressed people of East Bengal protested against policies that discriminated in favor of West Pakistan. In 1969 a new military government under General Yahya Khan ousted Ayub. The tension between West Pakistan and the underrepresented and miserably poor Bengalis of East Pakistan in 1970 remained an urgent unsolved problem.

Newly emancipated India suffered a grievous loss when Gandhi was assassinated by an anti-Muslim Hindu fanatic in 1948. But Jawaharlal Nehru at once assumed leadership. India inaugurated a parliamentary democracy of the Western type. Free and hotly fought elections, based on universal suffrage, were conducted among voters who were mostly illiterate and rural. India's worst problem was overpopulation. By 1960 there were over five hundred million people, with approximately fifteen million added annually. The threat of death through starvation was always present.

In 1950, the government launched the first in a series of five-year plans. It permitted the expansion of private industry but stressed government projects: irrigation and flood control, transport and communications, and especially agricultural education. Expert opinion believed that India emphasized industry too much and agriculture too little. The United States helped by furnishing technicians, money, and the surplus grain needed to avert the repeated threat of famine.

In the late 1960s a new strain of high-yielding Mexican wheat was planted experimentally. The initial results were promising. But the very success of the new foods (the "green revolution") threatened a new form of crisis. Farmers displaced from the countryside by new agricultural techniques flooded into the cities of India, where there was no employment for them. Starvation and political unrest always threatened in India. The government-sponsored campaign for birth control was repugnant to many Hindus.

Indeed, Hindu society found it difficult to adopt Western ways. Hinduism taught that each living thing was a soul separated by the very fact of living from the ultimate, universal soul, which is peace, absence of struggle and desire, nonbeing. By turning away entirely from the world, by living without desire, the holiest of men could perhaps attain this nonbeing in the end. But most of humanity—and all animals—were now paying in this world for a sinful life as another personality in the past. The most orthodox of Hindus would harm no living thing. This specifically included the millions of "sacred" cattle that competed with starving people for food. Proposals for curbing the cattle led to widespread riots in 1966.

Hindus believed that a man's sins in past lives were reflected by his status, his *caste*. The poor and humble were poor and humble because their sins had been greater. They could not improve their lot. They could only in subsequent incarnations slowly redeem their wickedness by living as holy a life as possible. Below and outside the caste system were the "untouchables," so called because even their shadow would corrupt a caste Hindu. The Indian Constitution of 1950 abolished the outcast status of the untouchables (Harijans) as undemocratic. But the legal change, however, penetrated Indian custom only very slowly.

In 1964, when Nehru died, and again early in 1966, when his successor, Shastri, fell victim to a heart attack, India chose a new prime minister by due constitutional process. The choice in 1966 was Nehru's daughter, Mrs. Indira Gandhi (her husband was not related to the great Gandhi). The Congress party continued to dominate the Parliament, though torn increasingly by factionalism. Several times Mrs. Gandhi had to offer to resign in order to maneuver in such a way as not to have to do so.

Language made political trouble. Each of a dozen major regions in India had its own tongue. Believing that a common language was essential to a common sense of national identity, the government supported a new national language, Hindi, which became official in 1965. English was an "associate" language. Ardent nationalists deplored this as an "ignoble concession" to colonialism. But English was indispensable: because its modern scientific and technical vocabulary did not exist in Hindi, and because it was the only common language of educated Indians, who could not understand one another's native tongues. The speakers of Tamil in the south were violently hostile to Hindi. The government made some concessions but did not change its aims.

Relations with Pakistan continued strained. Sporadic outbreaks of religious warfare took place, especially near the line dividing Bengal between India and East Pakistan. Neither side would concede anything on the Kashmir question. In 1965 war broke out briefly. The Soviet Union invited leaders of both countries to confer. India and Pakistan agreed to withdraw troops from their common frontier but not to any permanent settlement.

Pakistan judged every country by its attitude toward India. American and Soviet aid to India made Pakistan suspicious of both countries. Pakistan therefore developed a curiously unnatural friendship with China because China was anti-Indian.

The Middle East

The "Middle East" had in Arabia, in the small states along the Persian Gulf, and in Iraq and Iran the greatest oil reserves in the world. Developed by European and American companies, which paid royalties to the local governments, these oil resources directly and indirectly influenced the policies of all the powers. Dissatisfaction over the amounts of royalties led to upheavals in Iran in 1951–1953.

Western European dependence on Middle Eastern oil led to general alarm over the closing of the Suez Canal by Egypt in 1956 and 1967. In 1967 General de Gaulle abandoned Israel, an ally of the French in 1956, and adopted pro-Arab policies, partly because of oil. But except for Iran, no crisis until the 1970s depended upon oil alone. The major issue between 1945 and 1970 was that between the Arabs and Israel.

Since the 1890s Zionism had maintained its goal of creating a new Jewish state on the site of the ancient Jewish homeland. It received a great lift from the Balfour Declaration of 1917, after which the British admitted Jewish immigrants into Palestine. Hitler's slaughter of Jews left those European Jews who survived more Zionist than ever.

But Britain wished to protect its interests in the Middle East by cultivating the friendship of the Arabs, who had long been settled in Palestine and felt that this was their homeland. Finding a compromise impossible, the British turned the problem over to the General Assembly of the United Nations, which proposed to partition the country into an Arab state and a Jewish state. The British withdrew their forces from Palestine in 1948, and the Jews proclaimed the state of Israel and secured its recognition by the UN. The Arab nations declared the proclamation illegal and invaded the new state from all directions. Although outnumbered, the Israelis won the war. A truce, but not a formal peace, was patched up under the auspices of the United Nations (1949).

Israel now obtained more of Palestine than the UN had originally proposed, including the western part of Jerusalem. Jerusalem was the spiritual capital of Judaism, but also of great religious importance to Christians and Muslims. The UN had proposed to neutralize it. The eastern part of "old city" of Jerusalem, however, including the Wailing Wall, the site of Solomon's temple, together with eastern Palestine, remained in the hands of the Arab state of Jordan.

During the 1949 war almost a million Palestinian Arabs fled from Israel to the surrounding Arab states. The United Nations organized a special agency that built camps and gave relief to

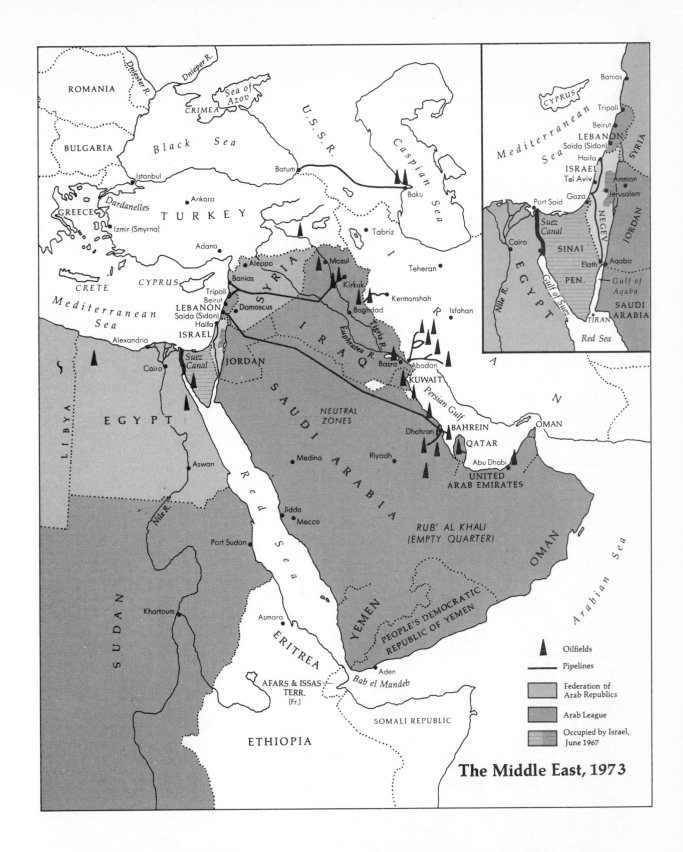

The Middle East, 1973

Oilfields

Pipelines

Federation of Arab Republics

Arab League

Occupied by Israel, June 1967

the refugees, and tried to arrange for their permanent resettlement. The Arab states, however, did not wish to absorb them. Many Palestinians felt that resettlement was defeat. They believed that the Israelis would soon "be pushed into the sea," and that they themselves would return to their old homes. The truce of 1949 was frequently broken in frontier incidents by both sides.

The new state of Israel had an Arab minority of about 200,000. It admitted as many Jewish immigrants as possible, some of them from Europe, but others from North Africa and Yemen, still largely living in the Middle Ages. Welding of these diverse people into a single nationality was a hard job.

Much of Israel was mountainous and some of it was desert. The Israelis used Western talents and training to make the best use of their resources. But they depended on outside aid, especially from the United States. To most Arabs Israel appeared to be a new outpost of Western imperialism, set up in their midst under the influence of Jewish financiers, Jewish journalists, and Jewish voters. It became difficult for the United States and other Western nations to retain cordial relations with the Arabs, who were in any case feeling strong nationalism of their own.

In 1952 revolution against a corrupt monarchy broke out in Egypt. A group of army officers chiefly sparked by Gamal Abdel Nasser established a republic, encouraged the emancipation of women, and cut down the role of the conservative Islamic law courts. Only one party was tolerated, elections were closely supervised, and the press controlled.

Nasser associated the West with colonialism and with support for Israel. He turned for aid to the U.S.S.R. Czechoslovak and Russian arms flowed to Egypt, and Russian technicians followed. Nasser was determined to take the lead in uniting the disunited Arab world to destroy Israel.

Nasser intended a new high dam of the Nile at Aswan as a showpiece of revolutionary planning. He had expected the United States to contribute largely to its construction. But in 1956, John Foster Dulles, Eisenhower's secretary of state, told Nasser that the United States had changed its mind. In retaliation Nasser took over the Suez Canal, hitherto operated by a Franco-British Company. He announced that he would use its revenues to build the dam. The French and British governments, determined to teach Nasser a lesson, allied themselves with Israel. They did not tell the United States of their plans.

In autumn 1956, the Israeli forces invaded Egyptian territory, and French and British troops were also landed at Suez. The Israeli operations were skillful and successful. The British and French blundered badly. The Soviet Union threatened to send "volunteers" to defend Egypt, despite the fact that Soviet troops were busy putting down the Hungarian revolution. The United States refused to support Britain and France.

With the United States and the Soviet Union on the same side of the issue, the United

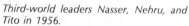

Third-world leaders Nasser, Nehru, and Tito in 1956.

Nations condemned the British-French-Israeli attack. A United Nations force was moved into the Egyptian-Israeli frontier areas. The canal, blocked by the Egyptians, was reopened, and finally bought from the company by Nasser.

In 1958 Nasser experienced some disillusion with Russia. Soviet-sponsored communists who opposed Nasser's aims led a revolution in Iraq. Prompt American intervention in Lebanon and British intervention in Jordan temporarily countered the threat of the spread of Soviet influence. The Russians provided the aid that eventually made possible the high dam at Aswan and much armament for the Egyptian armies. But Nasser made no alliance with either major bloc.

In 1958 Nasser proclaimed the merger of Egypt and Syria into the United Arab Republic. Egypt and Syria were separated by the territories of Israel, Lebanon, and Jordan. Nasser was trying to prevent a coup by Syrian communists. When the Syrians revolted in 1961, Nasser permitted them to regain their independence as the Syrian Arab Republic. The Arab world remained disunited, although Egypt continued to call itself the U.A.R.

After the Suez crisis, Nasser tried one economic and political experiment after another to win grass roots support. With the Egyptian birth rate double that of the U.S., he had to try to feed his fast-growing population. He tried to reclaim land from the desert by exploiting underground water, and to limit the size of individual landholdings so that the surplus might be redistributed to landless peasants. To provide more jobs and to bolster national pride, he also sped up industrialization, often at high cost. Most foreign enterprises were nationalized.

But the temptations of foreign adventure proved irresistible to Nasser. In Yemen, a primitive kingdom in southern Arabia, republican rebels overthrew the monarchy in 1962. Nasser sent Egyptian forces to assist the revolution. Saudi Arabia, most of whose huge revenues came from American oil companies, disliked the Egyptian intervention, which threatened the cause of monarchy and endangered Saudi stability. But Nasser's forces could not win, though they freely used poison gas against their brother Arabs. By 1967 the Egyptian forces had suffered a defeat. The Yemeni republican regime continued to control south Yemen, while monarchists continued active in the north.

In 1967 Nasser demanded the removal of United Nations troops, which had kept Egyptians and Israelis separated since 1956. Secretary General U Thant complied. The Egyptians began a propaganda barrage against Israel. They closed the Strait of Tiran at the northeast corner of the Red Sea, which provided the only water access to the newly developed Israeli port of Eilat.

The Israelis struck the first military blow, knocking out the Egyptian air force on the ground, and hitting also at the air forces of the other Arab states. In six days, they overran the Sinai peninsula, all of Palestine west of the Jordan, including the Jordanian portion of Jerusalem, and the Golan heights on their northern frontier with Syria, from which the Syrians for several years had been launching raids. The third Arab-Israeli war in nineteen years ended in Israeli victory.

This humiliated not only Nasser but the U.S.S.R., which had supplied so much of the equipment he had now lost. The Russians supported the Arab position in the United Nations. They moved token naval forces into the Mediterranean. They denounced Israel and began at once to rearm Egypt.

Israeli armies remained in control of all the territory they had occupied. Had it been possible to begin negotiations soon after the war, much of this could probably have been recovered. As time passed, the Israeli attitude hardened. It became difficult to imagine any Israeli government willing to give up any part of Jerusalem or the Golan heights. Sinai, the Gaza strip, the west bank of the Jordan were different.

Led by Nasser, the Arabs refused to negotiate directly with the Israelis or to take any step that would admit the existence of the state of Israel. The Egyptians kept repeatedly threatening to try again. Blocked again, the Suez Canal was now becoming less crucial because many new oil tankers were too large to pass through the canal in any case and went around the Cape of Good Hope. Although the U.S.S.R.'s ally, Egypt, lost the 1967 war, Russia got naval bases at Alexandria and even in Algeria, which gave the Russians a firmer position in the Mediterranean than ever before.

In 1969 and 1970 Arab Palestinians organized new guerrilla attacks from Jordan, Syria, and Lebanon on Israeli or Israeli-occupied territory. The Lebanese government was balanced between Christians and Muslims, and had always been the most moderating influence among the Arab regimes. Now the Palestinian guerrillas forced it to concede to them the Lebanese territory nearest the Israeli frontier.

European Arab terrorists attacked planes

carrying, or thought to be carrying, Israelis. Israel tried to avenge such acts and prevent their recurrence. At times the Palestinian Arab terrorist movement acted like an independent state, negotiating with the Chinese and compelling Nasser to modify his pronouncements.

In the autumn of 1970, the guerrillas hijacked four large planes in a single day, holding the passengers as hostages in Jordan for the release of certain captives of their own. During the negotiations that followed, full-scale war broke out between the Palestinian guerrillas and the Jordanian government. The Syrians intervened on the side of the Palestinians. Before the U.S.S.R. and the U.S. could get into this dangerous situation, Jordan won. The Syrians withdrew. The Palestinians could no longer use Jordanian territory.

In Egypt, Egyptian raids across the Suez Canal into Israeli-occupied territory in Sinai were countered by Israeli commando raids into Egyptian territory on the west side of the canal, and by air raids into Egypt. During 1970 the installation of Soviet missile sites near the canal forced the suspension of the Israeli attacks. The Soviet involvement in Egyptian defense threatened confrontation between the Soviet Union and the United States.

To avoid this danger, and to enable the Russian military to be withdrawn from Egypt without losing face, the United States, Britain, and France held regular discussions with the U.S.S.R. on the Arab-Israeli conflict. The Israelis insisted that only direct talks between them and the Arabs could lead to a settlement. The Arabs insisted that Israel return all occupied territory before any discussions. In the summer of 1970, however, Egyptians and Israelis agreed to a cease-fire. Then Nasser died suddenly. His successor, Anwar el-Sadat, began by pledging himself to regain all territories lost to Israel.

Among the other Arab states, Iraq, closely aligned with the British after the war, experienced a nationalist uprising in 1958 that ousted the monarchy and proclaimed a republic. Pro- and anti-Nasser factions and pro- and anticommunists thereafter subjected the country to a series of coups and abortive coups. Rebellious Kurdish tribes in the northern mountains contributed to the disorder until they won partial self-government in 1970.

In 1969 and 1970, the Iraqi regime became the most violent and suspicious of all the Arab states. It executed some of its resident Jews and members of earlier Iraqi governments on charges of working for Israel or the American CIA. Nasser himself rebuked the Iraqis.

In Iran, where the Anglo-Iranian Oil Company had the oil concession, the government after the war demanded that the company follow the example set in Saudi Arabia by the Arabian American Oil Company, which paid 50 percent of its profits to King Saud. Supported by a wave of antiforeign nationalism, the politician Mossadeq in 1951 secured the nationalization of the oil company. But the Iranian economy was hurt by an international boycott; and Mossadeq himself was overthrown in 1953 by a coup d'état masterminded by the CIA, which returned to power the young shah, Reza Pahlavi, son of the shah deposed during World War II. The government agreed to pay foreign oil companies to assist in exploiting and marketing the oil.

In Turkey, Atatürk's Republican People's party, the only one allowed in Atatürk's own day, permitted opposition activities after the war. In the election of 1950 it went down to defeat at the hands of the new Democratic party. Western opinion saluted this peaceful shift of power. The new Prime Minister Menderes promoted both state and private industry, built roads and schools, and tried to bring the spirit of modernization to the villages, which contained three-quarters of the population. To propitiate Muslim opinion, he restored religious instruction in the schools.

But Menderes's regime became increasingly arbitrary; it muzzled the press, persecuted the Republican opposition, and restricted the free conduct of elections. In May 1960 student riots touched off a coup by the Turkish army, which overthrew the government, outlawed the Democratic party, and brought Menderes to trial and eventual execution. A new constitution, in 1961, sought to strengthen the legislature and judiciary against the executive.

It was the army, however, that exercised the real power. The new Justice party, with many followers of Menderes, won a majority of the seats in the election of 1965. Tensions persisted between the urban champions of secularization and westernization, represented by army leaders and by Atatürk's old Republican People's party, and the defenders of the conservative Muslim way of life in Turkish towns and villages, who tended to support the Justice party.

Low wages and the lack of employment opportunities at home forced tens of thousands of Turks to take jobs abroad, especially in West Germany and the Netherlands. The marginal quality of much Anatolian farmland, with its thin soil and scanty rainfall, promoted an even greater exodus from the villages to the towns and cities.

Turkey appeared to be suffering a sharp attack of social and economic growing pains.

Turkey's hopes for achieving a quick economic takeoff were thwarted by meager resources, the difficulty in paying for needed imports, especially oil, and the government's inefficient planning. Down to the 1960s, friendship for the United States was warm. It was cemented especially by the brave Turkish fighting in the Korean War. It dwindled because Turkish nationalists disliked NATO and especially because America refused to support Turkey wholly against Greece in the Cyprus question. Anti-American feeling ran high. Some radicals even began to look to the U.S.S.R.—traditionally the bugbear of all Turks.

Africa

The revolution against imperialism reached Africa in the 1950s. But there was clear warning in 1947 when the French massacred the rebels in an uprising on the island of Madagascar off the east coast. After World War II, Ethiopia was taken from Italy and restored to emperor Haile Selassie, who had been ousted in 1935. In 1952 he annexed the former Italian colony of Eritrea. He ruled as an absolute monarch and favored the development of African unity.

Among the northern tier of states bordering the Mediterranean, all Muslim and Arabic-speaking, the former Italian colony of Libya achieved independence in 1951, and French-dominated Morocco and Tunisia in 1956. Morocco became an autocratic monarchy, Tunisia a republic under the moderate president Habib Bourguiba, a veteran nationalist leader.

Algeria, between Morocco and Tunisia, followed, but underwent a grueling war of independence against the French. Its first ruler after independence, Ahmed Ben Bella, favored the Chinese communists. Colonel Houari Boumédienne, who ousted Ben Bella in 1965, was more pro-Soviet. Algeria and Libya strongly supported the Arab cause against Israel, Morocco more feebly, and Tunisia very faintly.

In Libya, a coup d'état in 1969 brought to power a group of army officers. They confiscated Italian- and Jewish-owned property. The United States abandoned its huge airbase in Libya. Colonel Muammar Qaddafi emerged as the Libyan dictator. He was a fanatical Muslim, pro-Soviet,

Kwame Nkrumah of Ghana, left, and Habib Bourguiba of Tunisia in 1958.

anti-Western. His great wealth from oil revenues would soon be at the service of the violent wing of the Palestinian nationalists.

South of the Muslim tier lay the colonies of the French, British, and Belgians, inhabited chiefly by blacks. The West African climate had always discouraged large-scale white settlement except in portions of the Belgian Congo. But in East Africa, especially in the British colonies of Kenya and Uganda, many whites had settled in the fertile highlands. They farmed the land and regarded the country as theirs, as did the large white population of South Africa (a republic after 1961) and Rhodesia.

In West Africa the revolution moved swiftly. The Gold Coast, a British colony, became the nation of Ghana in 1957. Its leader, the American-educated Kwame Nkrumah, began as a democratic leader who understood the need for expert economic planning. But he grew increasingly dictatorial, persecuted his political enemies, and insisted on being worshiped as a virtual god by his subjects. He sponsored unrealistic and grandiose projects that enriched him and his followers. And he became fanatically anti-Western and determined to court Chinese communist favor in an effort to unite Africa into a kind of personal empire. In 1966 Nkrumah was overthrown. His successors tried to revert to sober reality.

The French colonies, huge areas of territory often sparsely populated, all achieved independence simultaneously in 1960, except for Guinea, a small West African state that broke away in 1958 under the leadership of a pro-Russian politician, Sekou Touré. When the French residents left, the country virtually came to a stop. The neighboring states of Mali (formerly French Sudan) and Mauritania also pursued a generally pro-Russian line. In the late 1960s Touré accepted U.S. and World Bank loans to finance a major mining complex.

Some of the newly independent French colonies remained members of the French community with economic ties to Paris. Some—Upper Volta, Niger, Chad, and Gabon—were no more than geographical names without national traditions or tribal cohesion. Others were stable: Senegal, governed by the poet Leopold Senghor; Ivory Coast, under Houphouët-Boigny, who had experience as a deputy in Paris; and the Malagasy Republic (formerly Madagascar), which had a flourishing economy. In Gabon, the French intervened with troops to save the government from a military coup d'état. In others—Togo, Dahomey, Cameroon—coups took place unhindered

and sometimes repeatedly. In 1970, for instance, large numbers of French troops were fighting a war in Chad. The regime in the former French Congo (Brazzaville) was thoroughly procommunist.

In 1960, Nigeria, most important of the British colonies, achieved independence. With sixty million people and large and varied economic resources, it represented a great hope for the future. The British had educated and trained many thousands of Nigerians in England and in excellent Nigerian schools and universities.

Nigeria was divided into four regions, each semiautonomous, to ease tribal tensions. The most severe tensions were those between the Muslim Hausas of the northern region and the Ibos in the east. In the Hausa areas, well-educated, aggressive, and competent Ibos ran the railroads, power stations, and other modern facilities, and formed an important element in the cities. In 1966, when army plotters led by an Ibo officer murdered the Muslim prime minister of Nigeria and seized power, the Hausas rose and massacred the Ibos living in the north.

By 1967, the Ibo east had seceded and called itself the Republic of Biafra. The Nigerian central government embarked on full-scale war to recapture Biafra. The two opposing generals were both graduates of British institutions. Misery and famine accompanied the war. Britain and the Soviet Union helped the Nigerian government. The Biafrans got little help except from the French, who were interested in future oil concessions. In 1969 the Ibos surrendered. Nigeria worked hard on reconciliation and recovery.

In East Africa, the British in Kenya struggled for eight years (1952–1960) against the Mau Mau, a secret terrorist society within the Kikuyu tribe, whose aim was to expel all whites. The Mau Mau murdered white settlers and their families, and Kikuyus who would not join them. The British imprisoned one of its founders, Jomo Kenyatta, and eventually put down the movement. In 1963 they gave Kenya independence. Kenyatta became the first postliberation chief of state.

By 1962 neighboring Uganda attained independence. In 1964 so did Tanganyika, which had been German before World War I. A pro-Chinese communist coup d'état had taken place on the offshore spice island of Zanzibar, which now merged with Tanganyika as the new country of Tanzania. The British-educated Tanzanian leader, Julius Nyerere, thereafter became more notably neutralist. In 1964, Nyasaland became Malawi under Dr. Hastings Banda, formerly a dentist in

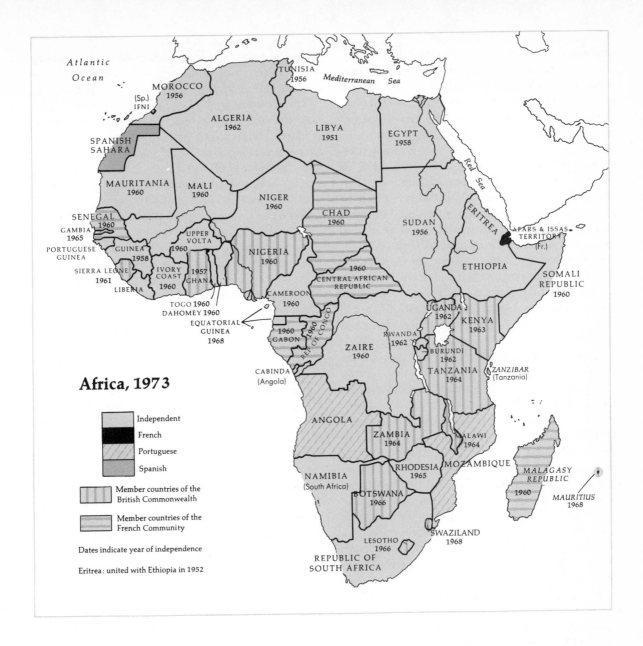

Africa, 1973

Legend:
- Independent
- French
- Portuguese
- Spanish
- Member countries of the British Commonwealth
- Member countries of the French Community

Dates indicate year of independence

Eritrea: united with Ethiopia in 1952

London. Northern Rhodesia became Zambia under Kenneth Kaunda, a Western-educated moderate.

The British had tried to prepare the way for African independence, but the Belgians made no such effort in the huge Central African area of the Congo. When the Belgians suddenly pulled out in 1960, they left a wholly artificial Western-style parliamentary structure. Some tribal and regional rivalries between native leaders led to chaos. A leftist leader, Patrice Lumumba, was assassinated. The province of Katanga, with rich copper mines and many European residents, seceded under its pro-Belgian leader, Moise Tshombe. Other areas revolted. Africans murdered whites or took them prisoner and kept them

as hostages. White mercenaries enlisted in the forces of Tshombe and others.

The United Nations sent troops to restore order and end the Katangese secession. The Chinese supported certain rebel factions, and the South Africans and Belgians others. By 1968 the military regime of General Joseph Mobutu took over. Mobutu renamed the Congo Zaire and changed the Belgian names of the cities.

The Congo troubles overflowed into Portuguese Angola to the south. A local rebellion, at first supplied from the Congo, brought Portuguese military intervention. Angola, which provided Portugal with much of its oil, Mozambique on the east coast, and tiny Portuguese Guinea on the west remained Portuguese despite guerrilla uprisings. The Portuguese regarded these countries as overseas extensions of metropolitan Portugal. Every African who had a certain minimum education obtained the status of an "assimilated" Portuguese. But the guerrilla warfare was expensive and unpopular at home.

Most intransigent of all were the white-dominated Republic of South Africa and its northern neighbor, the state of Rhodesia (formerly Southern Rhodesia). Rhodesia broke its political ties with Britain in 1965 rather than agree to any African participation in political life. In South Africa, the whites included not only descendants of the Dutch settlers, the Afrikaners, but also a minority of English descent. But altogether the whites formed only about twenty percent of the population. The nonwhites included blacks, "coloreds" (those of mixed European and African blood), and Asians, mostly Indians.

The Afrikaners emerged after World War II as a political majority. They held to a narrow and reactionary form of Calvinism, believing that God had ordained the inferiority of the blacks. Their policy was rigid segregation: *apartheid.* Separate black townships to live in, separate facilities of all sorts, no political rights, no opportunity for higher education or advancement beyond manual labor, internment of black leaders—these were the conditions that a series of Afrikaner governments imposed. Emergency laws made it possible to arrest people on suspicion, to isolate them in prison, and to punish them without trial. Severe censorship prevailed, and dissent was silenced.

The South Africans founded two black states on South African territory (1966), Botswana and Lesotho, both previously African reservations. In 1949, defying the UN, South Africa annexed the former German colony and League mandate of South-West Africa (Namibia). Here too the policies of apartheid held sway and aroused black hatred.

The Rhodesians who defied the British in 1965 rather than allow Africans to participate in politics were many of them originally emigrants from South Africa. Boycotted by the British Labour government and later by the UN, they managed to get supplies from South Africa and from Mozambique. But the 1970 victory of the Conservatives in England brought a considerable relaxation of British policy toward Rhodesia.

Latin America

By the end of World War II, most of the Latin American republics had enjoyed political independence for more than a century. But they had much in common economically and socially with the emerging nations of Asia and Africa. They were suppliers of foods and raw materials to the rest of the world. The prices for their bananas, coffee, sugar, beef, oil, nitrates, and copper changed rapidly on world markets. Latin American standards of living were low.

Like the other emerging nations, too, most of Latin America had a racially mixed population: some native-born whites or immigrants from Europe (like the Italians in Argentina), some descendants of the indigenous Indians, and some blacks (chiefly in Brazil and the Caribbean). Although they lived under a so-called democratic system of elected officials and parliaments, in fact their governments were usually military dictatorships, changing whenever a new army officer felt strong enough to challenge the one in power.

Toward the United States, Latin Americans felt a mixture of envy, dislike, and suspicion. The United States was rich and powerful, "the Colossus of the North." Upper-class Latin Americans educated in Europe believed that North Americans lacked true culture. North Americans generally seemed to know little and care less about Latin America. Whenever the United States did pay attention, it intervened in Latin American affairs. Some upper-class Latin Americans knew the majority of the people lived in misery and often had bad consciences. Most of them, however, did not care about the conditions of the poor but only for their own comfort. They hoped that nothing—least of all a social revolution—would disturb the system. So it made them uneasy to find North Americans worrying more about the Bolivian or Peruvian peasant than the Bolivians or Peruvians themselves had ever done.

Craving attention and admiration, yet at the same time longing to be left alone, the Latin Americans made it very difficult for the United States to develop consistent, satisfactory policies toward them. And by and large the Latin complaints about us were true. We were indifferent except when crises arose, and then we tended to intervene. We were tactless, we were crude, we did not understand, our motives were often questionable.

After World War II the Pan-American Union, primarily cultural and going back to 1910 and even before, became the Organization of American States (OAS). The OAS was a means by which all the American nations could consult and reach joint decisions on all important matters of mutual concern. The Alliance for Progress, started by President Kennedy's suggestion, was designed to enable the United States to help the Latin Americans to help themselves. But Latin American suspicions would not go away. And most Latin American countries were run by deeply entrenched oligarchies.

Not every Latin American country, however, was oligarchical or backward. Uruguay, for example, a small country with a population largely European in origin, went further toward creating an advanced welfare state than any other in the world. But the payment of state funds to individual citizens for the many types of benefits available brought the Uruguayan economy near collapse. Venezuela, with rapidly developing oil resources, ousted the last of its military dictators in 1959 and made a transition to moderate democratic rule, though it was still threatened by communists sponsored from outside.

Colombia suffered a lengthy terrorist campaign in the countryside in which many thousands were killed. Even when this drew to an end, the country was still experiencing extremes of wealth and poverty. Brazil, Portuguese-speaking and largest of the Latin American countries, suffered from economic crises and military coups. Its poverty-stricken northeast, where many thousands lived in serfdom on big plantations, contrasted sharply with the luxurious apartment-house and beach life of the big cities. Each of these, too, had its festering slums. Its government was a tight military dictatorship.

Chile, too, plagued by a continual economic crisis and by occasional military intervention, had a democratic government until 1970, when it elected a Marxist, Salvador Allende, as president. Allende won less than 40 percent of votes, but he took office in relative calm. Great storms lay ahead.

Alone in Latin America, Mexico had experienced true social revolution, beginning in 1910, and lasting with interruptions for thirty years. The revolution, however, was marked by violence and insurrection, by revolutionary reformers who became wealthy dictators, and by radical social and economic experimentation. The Catholic Church, which many Mexicans regarded as opposed to reform and indifferent to the welfare of the masses, was a chief target. Foreign oil companies, American and British, were expropriated. At first, labor unions got much power. The government expropriated large estates to free the peasants and began a vigorous program of mass education. A cultural revival was based on native traditions and crafts. Mexican revolutionary painters like Rivera and Orozco won international fame.

The Mexican revolution ran out of radical steam in the 1940s. The new leaders were ready to seek foreign capital and had become less impatient in raising the living standards of the masses. Mexico was dominated by a single political party. Every seventh year its leader was elected president. Each president in turn stepped down peacefully to make way for his successor. The party controlled the unions and showed only an occasional flash of its old revolutionary zeal. Still suspicious of U.S. attempts to influence it, each new Mexican government cemented peaceful and friendly relationships with its neighbor to the north.

By contrast, Argentina had a population almost entirely of European descent, and depended on the export of beef and grain. Its social system rested on a small landlord class. Industrialization and the mushrooming growth of the capital, Buenos Aires, to a city of nearly five million in 1945 enlarged the middle and working classes and deepened popular dissatisfaction.

Elected in 1946, Colonel Juan Perón became a fascist dictator. In 1955 he fell after a military coup d'état. Peron had launched an appeal to the masses, the *descamisados* ("shirtless ones"), and lost much upper-class support. He also quarreled with the Roman Catholic Church. He only worsened Argentina's economic and financial problems by extravagant spending on public works and welfare projects.

After 1955 Peronist sentiment continued strong, and twice (1962 and 1966) a weak elected government was overthrown by a military coup. The army regime installed in 1966 promised to purge Argentina of corruption but aroused much opposition by its repression of academic freedom. The old problems remained unsolved.

They also remained unsolved in Peru, which had a relatively advanced urban life at the time of the military coup of 1968, and in Ecuador and Paraguay, which were still largely rural, as well as in Haiti, which in 1970 still suffered under the brutal dictatorship of Duvalier.

In the postwar years Cuba provided the new revolution. Beginning in the late 1950s under the leadership of Fidel Castro as a guerrilla movement in the hills of the easternmost province (Oriente), it succeeded in ousting the government of Fulgencio Batista in 1959. American attitudes toward Castro had wavered. The Batista regime was corrupt but nobody knew how deeply Castro was committed to communism or to Soviet domination.

After his success, he became more openly pro-Soviet and quarreled bitterly with the United

States, which boycotted Cuban goods. The Cuban economy was dependent upon the export of sugar and tobacco. Castro soon found himself exporting largely to the U.S.S.R. and its satellites, and obtaining most of his imports from them. In 1961, the Kennedy administration backed an expedition of anti-Castro exiles, who landed at the Bay of Pigs and were thoroughly defeated.

In 1962, as we have seen, Castro opened Cuba to the installation of Soviet missiles, leading to the great crisis of October. After the crisis was over, Castro tried to take advantage of the Soviet-Chinese quarrel to extract more from the U.S.S.R. He also tried to export his revolution to Venezuela, to Guatemala, where communists murdered the American ambassador in 1968, and to Bolivia. In Bolivia guerrillas operating under the Argentine revolutionary theorist Ernesto ("Ché") Guevara, formerly a member of Castro's cabinet, were wiped out in 1967. A military coup in 1970, however, brought a leftist government to power.

In 1965, the United States hastily concluded that a revolution in the Dominican Republic was inspired by Castro. Between 1930 and 1961 the Dominican Republic had been ruled by General Trujillo, a corrupt and bloodthirsty dictator. After his assassination Juan Bosch became the freely elected president. But tension between the army

Castro and Khrushchev in New York, 1960.

and the new government led finally to a civil war in 1965. Fearing that communists might take over, President Johnson sent in a division of marines and then tried to internationalize the intervention by appealing to the Organization of American States. Five of the OAS countries, all with conservative military regimes, sent troops to join the Americans. In the elections of 1966, a moderate, Joaquin Balaguer, became president and was reelected in 1970.

No president of the United States in 1965 could possibly have allowed a second Soviet triumph in the Caribbean. But the Dominican episode aroused much opposition in Latin America, where the reappearance of American marines heightened the suspicion that the United States was up to its bad old tricks.

With a population consisting chiefly of East Indians and blacks, deeply at odds with each other, British Guiana also had a strong communist movement, led by an Indian, Cheddi Jagan. When it appeared that independence from Britain would be followed by Jagan's assuming power, the British postponed independence until an effective anticommunist coalition of Jagan's opponents was safely in office. The new state of Guyana was created in 1966.

In 1970 nobody could be optimistic about the future in Latin America. Terrorism spread in Brazil, Argentina, and even Uruguay. Foreign diplomats or local politicians were kidnapped and sometimes murdered. Instability was almost everywhere.

The cold war meant that the U.S. and U.S.S.R. competed for the support of the emerging nations. In their programs of foreign aid, both countries made mistakes. American aid enabled a Ghanaian politician to buy himself a solid gold bed. Soviet aid supplied obsolete and inappropriate agricultural machinery that rusted uselessly on a Guinean dock. It was a mistake for the Americans or Russians to suggest that capitalism or communism would solve the problems of the new nations.

New nations would have to wait for most of the consumer goods they needed until they had educated enough of their own people to do the work of modernizing that would earn the money to buy them. Only then could economic growth and political stability go hand in hand. The American experiment of the Peace Corps, launched by President Kennedy, provided a hopeful step.

READING SUGGESTIONS on Great-Power Foreign Policy and the Emerging Nations: 1945–1970 (Asterisks indicate paperback.)

General Accounts

N. A. Graebner, ed., *The Cold War: Ideological Conflict or Power Struggle?* (*Heath). Divergent interpretations.

D. Donnelly, *Struggle for the World* (1965). A history of the cold war, tracing it back to 1917.

P. Calvocoressi, *International Politics since 1945* (*Praeger). Factual study.

C. E. Black, *Dynamics of Modernization* (*Harper Torchbooks). Illuminating analysis.

S. Kuznets, *Post-War Economic Growth* (1964). Good analysis.

S. P. Huntington, *Political Order in Changing Societies* (1968); L. L. Snyder, *The New Nationalism* (1968). Wide-ranging and provocative surveys.

The Free World

J. Freymond, *Western Europe since the War* (1964). Good brief manual.

T. H. White, *Fire in the Ashes* (*Apollo). Postwar economic recovery and the role of the Marshall Plan.

M. M. Postan, *An Economic History of Western Europe, 1945–1964* (*Barnes & Noble). Comprehensive review.

L. B. Krause, ed., *The Common Market* (*Prentice-Hall). Useful work.

A. Marwick, *Britain in the Century of Total War* (1968). Assessment of the impact of war on society.

F. Boyd, *British Politics in Transition, 1945–1963* (1964). Solid account.

C. Cross, *The Fall of the British Empire, 1918–1968* (1968). Analysis of a central aspect of Britain's altered position.

S. Hoffmann et al., *In Search of France* (*Harper Torchbooks). Essays on economics and politics in twentieth-century France.

D. Pickles, *The Fifth French Republic*, 3rd ed. (*Praeger). Good political handbook.

P. Williams, *Crisis and Compromise* (*Anchor). Analyzing the failures of the Fourth Republic.

H. S. Hughes, *The United States and Italy,* rev. ed. (*Norton). Guide to postwar Italian politics and society.

M. Salvadori, *Italy* (*Prentice-Hall). Handy introduction.

K. P. Tauber, *Beyond Eagle and Swastika,* 2 vols. (1967). Study of German nationalism since World War II.

A. Grosser, *The Federal Republic of Germany* (*Praeger). Concise history.

G. M. Craig, *The United States and Canada* (1968). Guide to Canada's problems.

T. H. White, *The Making of the President, 1960; . . . , 1964; . . . , 1968; . . . , 1972* (*Signet). Highly informative analyses.

Dean Acheson, *Present at the Creation* (1969). Beautifully written memoirs of the 1950s.

A. M. Schlesinger, Jr., *A Thousand Days* (1965); and T. C. Sorenson, *Kennedy* (*Bantam). Memoirs by aides of President Kennedy.

H. Sidey, *A Very Personal Presidency* (*Atheneum). On the Johnson years.

The Communist Bloc

C. E. Black, *The Eastern World since 1945* (*Ginn). Instructive scholarly survey.

L. Schapiro, *The Government and Politics of the Soviet Union,* rev. ed. (*Vintage). Short authoritative treatment.

Z. Brzezinski, *The Soviet Bloc,* rev. ed. (1967). Solid study of unity and conflict.

Adam Ulam, *Expansion and Coexistence: The History of Soviet Foreign Policy, 1917–1967* (1968).

D. Zagoria, *The Sino-Soviet Conflict, 1956–1961* (*Atheneum); W. E. Griffith, *Albania and the Sino-Soviet Rift* and *The Sino-Soviet Rift* (*MIT). Useful studies.

R. L. Wolff, *The Balkans in Our Time* (*Norton). Informed survey.

The Emerging Nations

S. C. Easton, *The Rise and Fall of Modern Colonialism* (1962). Sweeping survey.

B. Ward, *Interplay of East and West* and *Rich Nations and Poor Nations* (*Norton). Studies by an articulate economist.

F. W. Houn, *A Short History of Chinese Communism* (*Prentice-Hall). Useful recent introduction.

J. K. Fairbank, *The United States and China,* rev. ed. (*Compass); E. O. Reischauer, *The United States and Japan,* rev. ed. (*Compass). Authoritative surveys.

D. J. Duncannon. *Government and Revolution in Vietnam* (1968). Authoritative political history.

B. B. Fall, *The Two Viet-Nams,* rev. ed. (1965); and R. Shaplen, *The Lost Revolution: The U.S. in Vietnam, 1946–1966* (*Colophon). Outstanding.

J. D. Legge, *Indonesia* (*Spectrum); W. N. Brown, *The United States and India, Pakistan, Bangladesh* (*Harvard); S. Wolpert, *India* (*Prentice-Hall). Useful introductory studies.

R. H. Davidson, *Turkey* (*Spectrum); L. Fein, *Politics in Israel* (*Little, Brown); W. R. Polk, *The United States and the Arab World,* rev. ed. (1969); H. B. Sharabi, *Nationalism and Revolution in the Arab World* (*Van Nostrand). Introductions to the Middle East.

J. Hatch, *A History of Postwar Africa* (*Praeger). Clear and helpful guide.

L. G. Cowan, *The Dilemmas of African Independence,* rev. ed. (*Walker). A mine of information.

J. F. Gallagher, *The United States and North Africa* (1963); W. Schwarz, *Nigeria* (1968); J. Cope, *South Africa* (1965). Good studies.

G. M. Carter, ed., *Politics in Africa: Seven Cases* (*Harcourt). Informative.

V. Alba, *Nationalists without Nations* (1968). Attack on the ruling oligarchies as barriers to progress in Latin America.

R. J. Alexander, *Today's Latin America,* 2nd ed. (*Anchor); T. Szulc, *Winds of Revolution: Latin America Today and Tomorrow,* rev. ed. (*Praeger). Suggestive introductions.

C. C. Cumberland, *Mexico: The Struggle for Modernity* (*Oxford); A. P. Whitaker, *Argentina* (*Prentice-Hall); A. Marshall, *Brazil* (*Walker); K. Silvert, *Chile Yesterday and Today* (*Holt); J. E. Fagg, *Cuba, Haiti, and the Dominican Republic* (Prentice-Hall); H. Bernstein, *Venezuela and Colombia* (*Prentice-Hall); M. Rodriguez, *Central America* (*Prentice-Hall).

CHAPTER TWENTY

The World Since 1970

So far in this book we have been dealing with history. Even in the last two chapters, which reviewed the developments in the world at large and in the individual nations of the world between 1945 and 1970, we have felt a certain sense of safety as we have discussed events and tried to interpret them. Of course, new discoveries will be made about the period between 1945 and 1970 and new interpretations will be offered and accepted. But this is true also of the history of ancient Egypt or of the medieval papacy or of England in the eighteenth century.

This chapter is different. It deals with the last ten years: with the 1970s. There is much we cannot yet know. What we know we cannot be sure we understand correctly. We have very little perspective. As these lines are written and this book is being prepared for the printer, it is the early spring of 1980. We think we have earned the privilege of discussing the last ten years in a different way from the way in which we have conscientiously discussed all the thousands of years that went before.

We intend to be impressionistic rather than

thorough or exhaustive. It seems to us that it would serve no useful purpose to chronicle for the last ten years each coup d'état in Bolivia, each atrocity of the Ethiopian government, each new evidence that the United Nations could not do its essential job of keeping the peace, or each new manifestation of human wretchedness in any of the three worlds: the "free" world, the "communist" world, and the "third" world. We intend to generalize, to be more personal in our conclusions, and to say what we think about what we have read in the newspapers and seen on television for a decade. No doubt when this book goes into its next edition, we shall have to eat some of our words. We certainly hope so.

THE WORLD AS A WHOLE: MARCH 1980

The United States

As we write, the United States—in March—is already nearly six months along in the 1980 political campaign for the presidency that will not be decided until November. It is still the only nation that takes a full year to crank itself painfully into a position to make up its mind who its two major candidates will be and which of the two it prefers. And that year is full of loud voices saying passionate and unbelievable things, things that are not even intended to be believed, things that vary depending on the audience.

Politicians say one thing to the National Rifle Association, another to audiences who favor the licensing of handguns in the hope that assassinations and murders may become fewer. Politicians favor increased federal medical programs (which will be expensive), and they promise a cut in taxes at the same time (which would be inflationary)—all the while saying that they have the secret of controlling inflation but cannot quite bring themselves to tell us what the secret is. They favor a policy of peace, of course, but if elected, *they* would not let the Soviet Union push the United States around, and they would vastly increase military spending, while cutting taxes at the same time.

For them to say the unbelievable things they say has become very expensive, costing millions of dollars of their own money—which most of them seem somehow to have—and millions of dollars in contributors' money—sent to them by

public-spirited citizens who claim to have no hope of obtaining favors in return—and millions of dollars of taxpayers' money. Instead of stopping to think about their character, their honesty, their actual behavior, politicians worry about their "images." Does the pancake makeup sufficiently conceal the fact that they might look old, tired, ignorant, drunken, incompetent, lecherous, cowardly, and stupid? And do they appear to be as straightforward, intelligent, honorable, protective, fatherly, sober, and efficient as their campaign managers would like? Are they being "sold" to the American public? Are they properly packaged?

Still ahead of an eager people as we write will be the Republican and Democratic conventions, great "spectacles" in which bands will blare, balloons will pop, and for several days all kinds of irrelevant noises will be made until the delegates get around to performing the function they came for. No doubt, this was once a great American institution and may even have served some useful political or social purpose. But coming during an intensive year of politics, in which every issue has been talked about so often that the public is saturated, weary, bored, cynical— are the two conventions still really the best way in which the public's will can be done? After all the barnstorming, caucuses, primaries, five-minute television "spots," revelations, and declarations of intent that turn out not to have been intent after all, might it not be better to work out a way to do the same thing cheaper and better and in shorter time? Might we not also leave our presidents—once elected—a chance to reflect on the problems we ask them to solve for us? It could only help us, because the problems are in fact serious enough. And for the first time, in 1980, it begins to look as if the problems might after all not be solved and as if all our worlds— first, second, and third—might be destroyed.

International Danger

According to the newspapers of the past two days, for example, the government of Iraq has secretly received from the Italians—eager for Iraqi oil—technological information that would enable Iraq to make atomic weapons. It is generally believed that Israel not only already has that capacity but has such weapons available. India, we know, has for some time had the technology, and, many observers believe, the weapons also. Pakistan has, it is assumed, obtained elsewhere the information and materials that the United

States government has been trying to keep away from all countries not already possessed of them. And in the United States the "secrets" of building effective atomic weapons have been conveniently published in a national magazine that has been upheld in the courts.

What does all this mean for the postwar policy of nonproliferation, the effort to keep atomic weaponry confined to those who already had it: the United States, Great Britain, France, Russia, and China? It seemed certain that other nations would before long have atomic arsenals of their own, and that the restraints that have governed the great powers—who, whatever their other follies and aggressions, have at least not used atomic weapons since 1945—would no longer be effective. With the world full of crazy people, some of them in high political office, what should reasonable people and governments do? When some Idi Amin gets his first atomic weapon, how will he be persuaded not to use it?

The Middle East

Afghanistan

Already several weeks old now was the Soviet invasion of Afghanistan. The Russians had certainly been aggressive before, using their own troops against Hungary in 1956 and Czechoslovakia in 1968. But these invasions, tyrannical and disturbing as they were, were directed against members of the Soviet bloc who, the Soviets feared, might get away. The Russians also backed the North Koreans and the North Vietnamese in the wars in which the United States had backed the South Koreans and South Vietnamese. But, although American troops participated with heavy losses in both—the Korean war ending in a stalemate, the Vietnamese War in an American defeat and withdrawal—not a single Russian soldier was involved in either. Afghanistan, then, was different: it was the first time since 1945 that Soviet troops had been sent into battle beyond the frontiers of the Warsaw Pact.

Why did the Russians do it, especially after having misled the United States into thinking that they would not? Partly, of course, because an Afghan puppet regime, established with Soviet backing but without overt Soviet military participation, was threatened by a mounting tide of Afghan nationalism and anti-Marxism within even the members of that regime itself. Instability among the selected Afghan agents of Soviet policy led to the overthrow of two successive communist-minded Afghan leaders on whom the Russians had been counting. It was unlikely that Moscow really believed, as it professed to believe, that American agents were responsible for the anti-Soviet activity in Afghanistan. The fact remained that the Russians seemed on the point of losing a strategic territory they thought they had won without military action. To keep it, they resorted to such action.

Another reason for the Soviet invasion of Afghanistan was their belief that they could get away with it. They held this belief, no doubt, because Afghanistan was an immediate neighbor of their own and many thousands of miles from the United States. Soviet intervention was easy. Soviet troops could be reenforced and supplied from across the Soviet borders themselves. Planes would be needed only to put down Afghan resistance. Even with the will and determination to counter the Soviet invasion by American force, the United States would have faced almost insoluble problems in bringing such force to bear.

But the United States did not have the will to use force. And this was in some part due to the changes in balance between Soviet and American military strength that took place during the seventies. Not only have the Russians continued to pour into military expenditure three times the annual amount spent by the United States, but they have created two new submarine-launched missiles and three new land-based missile systems. The United States has countered only with the Trident submarine-launched missile and the "multiple reentry vehicles" of Minutemen and Poseidon missiles. American resources and technology, superior to those of the Russians, have nonetheless been overcome by the large Soviet missiles that can deliver far heavier warheads.

The balance of terror has apparently been upset, and our reliance on the Soviets sharing equally our fear of a nuclear war is no longer valid, because a nuclear war started by the Russians would give them an enormous advantage over us. What was unthinkable for so long after World War II has now become thinkable again. A Soviet first strike would leave the United States unable to retaliate with equal effectiveness. The United States can no longer deny the U.S.S.R. the opportunity for second and third strikes.

Quite probably it was this that underlay the Soviet willingness to use force in Afghanistan. Of course, to acquire safe control of that territory would give Moscow a greatly improved position in the Middle East: very close to the Persian Gulf and the oil supplies vital to the West and to the routes along which that oil must travel to reach the West. It was suggested that the Russians themselves had an important interest in newly discovered Afghan gas resources. Who knows what other considerations went into Moscow's decision to act?

The United States responded sharply, perhaps more sharply than the Russians had expected. President Carter declared that the invasion of Afghanistan was more dangerous than any event since World War II. Did he really mean more dangerous than the Berlin crisis of 1948, than the Cuban missile crisis of 1962, than the Vietnam War lasting until 1973? Perhaps what he wanted most to achieve by such words was to tell the Russians—who had apparently misled him about their intentions toward Afghanistan—that he took their actions very seriously.

The president asked the Senate to postpone indefinitely its scheduled debate on SALT II, the second round of the Strategic Arms Limitation Treaty, much favored by Moscow. He abruptly halted the export of American technological items to the U.S.S.R., and refused to allow the massive Soviet purchases of American grain, already contracted for, to be delivered. In view of the continued unreliability of the Soviet wheat crop—because of communist agriculture, unreliable weather, and other causes—this would be a serious blow to the Soviet cattle-breeding industry. Even Argentina could not make up the whole deficit.

The president also strongly recommended that the United States refuse to participate in the Olympic Games scheduled to take place in Moscow in summer 1980. The Senate and the House have almost unanimously supported this recommendation. It could be no more than a recommendation because participation in the Olympics was not a question for the American government but for the United States Olympic Committee. Representing the natural eagerness of the highly trained American athletes to compete, the committee was reluctant to declare that it would not do so. But nobody really thought that the wishes of the president and the Congress would in the end be overruled by the Olympic Committee. In March 1980 it seemed most probable, as the Russians showed no sign of withdrawing from Afghanistan and indeed put down anti-Soviet demonstrations there with cruel rigor, that the United States would indeed boycott the Olympics.

Since the U.S.S.R. had intended these Olympic Games as a tremendous international publicity event, celebrating Russian power as well as athletic ability (which, considering the highly professionalized and government-sponsored nature of sport in the U.S.S.R. was hardly a surprise), the absence of the United States would be a severe blow. Canada and Britain might also be absent. Many Islamic nations and Kenya might also stay away out of sympathy for Afghanistan. The appearance in Moscow of teams from other NATO countries, however, seemed quite possible. The French, consulting their own immediate interests only, would perhaps attend. West Germany seemed to be moving gradually toward a decision to stay away. There would be some kind of Olympic show in Moscow, no doubt, but the worldwide impact that the Russians had been intending would certainly be partly spoiled. And this action, led by the United States, at the very least was a serious annoyance to the Soviet leaders.

In 1980, moreover, the Soviet leaders were aging and personally enfeebled. Brezhnev himself, in power since 1964 and now well along in his seventies, was suffering from a variety of illnesses. Kosygin too was old and unwell. Students of Kremlin politics were speculating about which of the more youthful members of the Politburo might be moving up when Brezhnev died or became wholly incapacitated. But even the youngest members were men in their sixties, Soviet bureaucrats stamped from the same mold as Brezhnev himself; they are mostly engineers, "Brezhnev men," quite unlikely to bring a breath of fresh air or a new outlook to Kremlin policies and behavior.

And Brezhnev's illness in itself made it seem probable that already the army generals and other enemies of détente had taken a major role in making important decisions. Quite likely this development also underlay the Soviet invasion of Afghanistan. Truly, if indeed the generals were gaining more power, future Soviet actions were less predictable than ever.

Iran

The dangers posed by the Soviet invasion of Afghanistan and whatever lay behind it were increased by the other major immediate preoccupation of the United States in early 1980. This was, of course, the case of the American "hostages" in Iran. In Iran, during the 1970s, the shah had moved with great rapidity to modernize the country. He was an ally of the United States and bought vast quantities of the latest armaments from us, including a large and modern air force. His alliance with Washington did not prevent him, as supreme authority in one of the most important oil-producing countries in OPEC (the Organization of Petroleum Exporting Countries), from taking a hard line on oil prices and forcing these up to the disadvantage of his American customers.

In the course of modernizing Iran, the shah ran rough-shod over the traditional beliefs of his people. His police behaved with brutality—quite usual for the Middle East but brutality just the same—to those opposing any of his policies. And opposition came to center in the most conservative religious forces of Shiite Islam, led by holy men—*mullahs,* or as they are called in Iran, *Ayatollahs,* of whom the Ayatollah Khomeini, in exile in France, was one of the most vociferous.

The shah himself showed signs of megalomania in his attempt to associate his own recent royal regime—which had been established by his own father, a humble army officer—with the glories of the ancient Persian Empire of Cyrus, Darius, and Xerxes. This culminated in a kind of vast international jet-set party given by the shah in Persepolis to celebrate what he called the 2,500th anniversary of the Iranian Empire. All of this was hollow, and so, to a great extent also, was the modernization itself.

As skyscrapers multiplied in Teheran and Western-trained Iranian engineers and technologists took over important posts in the petroleum industry, the deeply rooted distaste for such alien activity and affection for the traditional Islamic ways of life asserted themselves more and more. Corruption, graft, and self-enrichment among the top ranks of Iranian officialdom, including the shah's family, became a fact of life that perhaps aroused as much opposition as did the ruthless security and police systems. The American government continued to issue strong messages of support for the shah and his regime until within a few days of the moment when he was ousted from power by a popular uprising. He fled into exile in Egypt and then in Mexico. The Ayatollah Khomeini returned from France and assumed the spiritual leadership of the revolution.

The Iranian Revolution turned out to be an extraordinarily complex movement. The Ayatollah himself and many of his most devout followers had a program reminiscent of the seventh century A.D. rather than the twentieth. They scorned the West and all its wicked modern ways and proposed to govern Iran in accordance with the pronouncements of the Koran and Islamic law only. A considerable group of far better-educated Iranians, who repudiated the shah on the grounds of his regime's ruthlessness but who believed that Iran should be governed by more modern principles than those of the Ayatollahs, strove for recognition and a chance to make their contribution to the new state. The shah's armies melted away, and huge stacks of arms and equipment were simply seized by the population at large.

Soon extreme revolutionary groups, some pro-Soviet, others Marxists of other shades or anarchists in outlook, began to execute out of hand (or after "revolutionary" trials) persons whom they declared to be guilty of committing atrocities under the shah. What we would call kangaroo courts in a few weeks shed an enormous amount of blood, how much of it guilty nobody might ever be able to discover. The northwest region around Tabriz, where a rival Ayatollah was prominent and the inhabitants were largely Turkish in origin, virtually split off from the rest of Iran. In the southeast the Baluchis, in the west the Qashgais, strove for autonomy. The Kurds, as always, were rebellious.

In the midst of these fast-moving events, as the Ayatollah Khomeini's influence was proving enormous but his direct power to control events severely limited, the United States admitted the shah for medical treatment in New York. Extremists in Iran were outraged by the United States' giving shelter to the refugee ex-ruler whom they considered to be a tyrant and whom they wanted to recapture and execute. The moderate Iranian prime minister, Bazargan, fell from power after he had been photographed by newspapermen at a conference in Algiers shaking hands with President Carter's National Security Adviser, Zbigniew Brzezinski. A group of "militants," or "students," invaded and captured the American embassy in Teheran, taking captive fifty Americans. Three others, including the American chargé d'affaires, were held in the Iranian Foreign Ministry. These victims became the fifty-three "hostages."

Whatever the alleged provocation, the seizure of the embassy and the hostages was contrary to all international law and contrary also to the Koran. The Carter administration took the gravest view of the crisis thus caused. Had Teheran been quickly accessible or the embassy there itself vulnerable to an American landing from parachutes, or had there been some other military measure to take that would not in and of itself have led to the murder of the very people we were hoping to save, it would have been easier to think of a quick way out of the crisis. But even after the Ayatollah had produced a new

"Islamic" constitution, giving supreme power to a spiritual leader, or "Faghi," and this constitution had been approved by referendum, even after a new and relatively moderate prime minister, Bani-Sadr, had been chosen and installed in office, it proved impossible to obtain the hostages' release.

As the weeks passed, it became more and more obvious that the "militants" who held the hostages captive would not obey Bani-Sadr or the "Revolutionary Council" with whom he shared uneasy day-to-day power. Even Ayatollah Khomeini—now generally called "the Imam" or savior—could not compel their obedience, despite their much-proclaimed religious devotion to him. Who were these militants? Nobody really knew for certain. Probably most of them were pro-communist Iranians—maybe even including some real students or ex-students. Some may have been non-Iranians, perhaps East German or Italian specialists in terrorism. No other Iranian authority could compel them to make concessions. On their own, they allowed a delegation of three American clergymen to visit the hostages at Christmas, 1979.

The United States proceeded through every legal international channel open to it. The World Court condemned the seizure unanimously. The Security Council of the United Nations condemned it without a Soviet veto. The Carter administration was not only careful to act legally but careful to be seen acting legally. The shah—whose reception for medical treatment in this country rested on an ancient precedent that anybody needing medical care could get it here—had his operations and left, not for Mexico, which refused to receive him again, but for Panama, where despite violent communist demonstrations he received asylum.

Long after the shah had left the United States, the militants, the Ayatollah himself, and members of his government continued to insist that only an American apology for assisting the shah's "tyrannical" regime and a promise never again to intervene in Iranian affairs could bring about the release of the hostages. From time to time, they also demanded the return of the shah himself and his money. No government could yield to these demands. Yet not only did the United States not expel the many thousand Iranian visitors in this country, it allowed thousands more to enter.

There were more ramifications to the matter than this condensed and tentative account could consider in detail. There was the involvement of Henry Kissinger, secretary of state under presidents Nixon and Ford, and of David Rockefeller, chairman of the Chase Manhattan Bank and an influential financier, in persuading President Carter to allow the shah into the United States in the first place. However praiseworthy or justified in itself, this act precipitated the attack on the embassy, of which advance warning had been given. Another was the presence in Teheran, during much of the hostage crisis, of hundreds of American reporters and television cameramen who turned the almost daily demonstrations of Iranians yelling in front of our embassy into a grim kind of international carnival.

The invasion of Afghanistan by the U.S.S.R. in the midst of the crisis over the hostages did give the few visible responsible Iranians great pause. It was, after all, Iran that was more directly threatened by the Soviet move than any other country, even Pakistan. The Ayatollah denounced the Russian actions, and for a time there seemed to be hope that, in revulsion against the actual armed intervention of the U.S.S.R. in the midst of the Muslim world, he might be persuaded, in the interests of Iran itself, to soft-pedal for a while the relatively mild earlier intervention of the United States. But the hope soon passed, and the Ayatollah condemned both the U.S. and the U.S.S.R. equally.

The first response of the American public to the firm but moderate reaction of Washington to events in Iran and Afghanistan was favorable. But as the months passed and no visible improvement could be seen in either situation, and the rival candidates for office in November 1980 denounced President Carter for inaction, it was clear by March that American nerves were fraying and time seemed to be running short. Organizing an "American military presence" in the Persian Gulf area, however, to bring pressure on Iran and to warn the U.S.S.R. against extending its conquests, would take much time, much money, and much skill. It was by no means certain that the United States had enough of any of these.

Moreover, the situation was altered by the shah's renewed illness in Panama. The Panamanian authorities seemed unwilling to have an American doctor perform a second operation, if it were necessary. The Iranian government was preparing an elaborate legal effort to extradite the shah; that is to persuade the Panamanians to surrender him on the grounds of his alleged criminal behavior in Iran. Nobody, not even the Iranian government, thought that this would succeed. But some hoped that once the Panamanian government had received the official demand for extradition, it would be possible to persuade the militants in Teheran to give up the American hostages.

The shah did not wait. Instead, late in March 1980 he flew back to Egypt, leaving the American government dismayed, the peril of the hostages increased, and the future of this crisis more obscure than before.

The Islamic Movement

The Islamic movement, that surfaced so violently in Iran with the overthrow of the shah and the events that followed, was part of a larger current in Islam, of which manifestations had been obvious for some time, although very little public attention was paid to them. The Iranian Islamic explosion showed clearly that the Shiite portion of the Muslim world was at least as affected as the Sunnite by the revival. And it became clear for the first time that at least some of the ancient hatred between the two sects, going back to the seventh century, was being at least temporarily sublimated in a common urge for a self-conscious Islamic assertion that united both sects.

The Libyan leader, Colonel Qaddafi, a militant Sunni Muslim, played a substantial role in financing the Ayatollah Khomeini in France and manipulating his return to Iran, despite the differences between their faiths. The Arab Palestinian nationalist movement, too—both the PLO and some of its other sects—was deeply imbued not only with Arab nationalism but also with Islamic revivalism.

In the late 1970s Islamic nationalism also played a role in the virtual destruction of the state of Lebanon. Here there had always been a delicate balance between Christian and Muslim. With the Palestinian Liberation forces concentrated on Lebanese territory after their expulsion by force from Jordan, the Israelis frequently attacked their bases in Lebanon. The Christian population came under attack from the Muslims and formed militant groups to defend itself. The great city of Beirut was virtually destroyed. The Syrians intervened to maintain a precarious truce.

Islamic nationalism also manifested itself in the sensational but quickly forgotten brief uprising in Saudi Arabia in 1979, when a band of militants who could not at first be identified actually seized the great Mosque in Mecca, holy pilgrimage center for all Islam, and held it for some days against Saudi army attack. A surreptitious French mission helped the Saudi authorities, who in the end ousted the invaders from the Mosque and captured the survivors of the battle.

At first rumored to be Shiites from an outlying region of Saudi Arabia, the militants turned out to be ultra-pious Sunnis under the leadership of a self-proclaimed Mahdi. Their real worry was the departure of the Saudi state from Islamic orthodoxy. Strange though this may seem when applied to the strictest Islamic nation of them all, there was much truth in it.

Modernization in Saudi Arabia, supported by the vast riches derived from oil, had brought some westernization with it. Although liquor was still forbidden and women's place in society nominally remained as subordinate as it had been when the land was a primitive Bedouin state, the presence of many Westerners, the building of high-rise hotels and apartments, the founding of universities to teach Western technological and secular subjects could not help but be accompanied by a certain penetration of Western ideas. It was this against which the Saudi militants had been protesting when they seized the Mosque.

The Saudi government was thrown into consternation by the episode, which revealed vulnerabilities previously unsuspected. "Reforms" were undertaken as the captive terrorists were executed, but the changes could amount to very little more than a temporary purge of careless or incompetent officials. The threat of Muslim militancy remained to trouble the most militant of all Muslim states, and, incidentally, the one on which the United States most depended for support and oil.

Among Muslim states, even Turkey, where Kemal's secularism had been at least nominally in force for half a century, showed signs of religious revival and of disorders partly fueled by it. For the moment, Egypt alone of the major Muslim countries was not, at least overtly, undergoing a Muslim revival. This was largely due to the extraordinary character and popularity of Anwar el-Sadat.

War, Truce, OPEC, Inflation

In 1973, the fourth post-World War II war between the Arabs and Israel began with an Egyptian attack across the Suez Canal, followed by an Israeli countercrossing. The Israelis also advanced against the Syrians. By frenzied "shuttle diplomacy," Secretary of State Kissinger brought about a cease-fire on both fronts. Truce lines were established between Israelis and Egyptians and between Israelis and Syrians, with UN forces inserted between the belligerents.

But the truce only stopped the active combat and put an end to the danger of an immediate Soviet-American confrontation. Showing a new unity of purpose, the Arab oil-producing countries, together with the non-Arab oil producers (Iran, Venezuela, and Ecuador), in OPEC agreed in 1974 to raise the price of oil, and (at the start) to boycott the United States as a punishment for being pro-Israeli. This action set off a worldwide economic crisis, from which in 1980 the world was still suffering in an exaggerated form.

When the crisis began, the Western nations were already suffering from what the economists called "stagflation." This meant that production had slowed down *and* that the price levels were rising at the same time. The developed nations suffered from unemployment and recession, the less developed often from sheer misery. In the United States, with its wasteful habits of gasoline consumption (such as large "gas-guzzling" cars driven too fast and occupied by only one person at a time), there were shortages and annoyance as prices rose.

Five years later the basic problem was not only unresolved but far more serious. Despite all the political and financial horse-trading, neither the Ford administration from 1974 through 1976 nor the Carter administration from 1976 to 1980 had come up with any workable solution. New OPEC rounds of price rises lifted the cost of fuel oil and gasoline in the West to levels that would have seemed incredibly high even in 1975. Oil companies made enormous profits but maintained that they were using them for research and development and resisted efforts to tax them. Inflation then drove up other prices, and by March 1980 American interest rates had risen to an unbelievable twenty percent. The stock market was falling rapidly. Public confidence had pretty well evaporated, and controversial government measures to deal with the crisis remained on the drawing-boards.

Although inflation thus reached its serious levels in 1980 largely as the result of the OPEC actions, themselves arising from the fact that most of the oil-exporting nations were located in the Middle East, there were of course other causes also. One was the American method of financing the Vietnam War. The Treasury borrowed and printed money, deferring payment much as the Germans had deferred paying for World War I. The dollar fell as against all foreign currencies, notably the German mark and the Swiss franc. As the only remaining "international" currency, the dollar had to carry additional burdens.

Economists furiously disagreed about the diagnosis of our illnesses and even more furiously about possible cures. It was certain that no cure for inflation had been devised except recession, perhaps depression, and early in 1980 there were signs that that lay around the next corner. Our short-sighted automobile industry, having clung stubbornly to the gas-guzzlers while insisting that efforts to improve fuel consumption were interference with free private enterprise, now begged for government assistance when failure (as in the case of Chrysler) stared them in the face.

Egypt, Israel, the Palestinian Question

In the years after the truce of 1974 in the Middle East, Prime Minister Sadat showed himself a man of courage and originality. Recognizing that the Egyptian public was sick of the repeated costly wars with Israel, Sadat braved the fury of non-Egyptian Arabs and took a bold peace initiative. An incredulous world saw him actually received and cheered in the Israeli Knesset (Parliament) as he began overtures for a genuine peace treaty instead of another truce that would provide only a breathing space between wars. The road to such a peace was long and rocky and we need not trace it in detail.

It was paradoxically made easier by the fact that the Israeli government had passed into the hands of a strongly right-wing nationalist, Menachem Begin, himself a former terrorist. Had a government led by Golda Meir or her successor, Itzak Rabin, both moderates, entered into such negotiations, Begin and his followers would have attacked it from the right for negotiating with Sadat. But there were not enough politicians to the right of Begin to make his work impossible. The United States too played an important part in the negotiations, with President Carter himself devoting much time and energy to bringing the two traditional enemies together on neutral ground in the United States, notably at Camp David, the presidential retreat not far from Washington.

By 1980, an Egyptian-Israeli peace had been signed and ratified. Israeli withdrawal from the occupied Egyptian territories in the Sinai peninsula had proceeded ahead of schedule. Ambassadors had been exchanged and regular Israeli-Egyptian relations established. Tourists could come and go. Sadat and Begin shared the Nobel

Peace prize. But much remained to be done. The Palestinian question and the status of the West Bank of the Jordan remained wholly unsolved. Camp David had provided that this even more difficult matter was to follow. But before this aspect of the question could come up for further negotiation the Israeli government—sometimes without the approval of some of its members—proceeded to found new settlements on the West Bank. It had been generally understood that this would not be done.

The Israeli actions seemed to jeopardize the next stage in the negotiations. The United States Secretary of State, Vance, presumably with presidential approval, instructed our delegate in the UN to go along with a Security Council vote reproving Israel. After the American vote had been cast, it was suddenly reversed by presidential order. This event of March 1980, in itself perhaps not very significant, had both obvious immediate repercussions and not so obvious long-range implications.

The immediate repercussions were political and had to do with the presidential campaign of 1980 already underway. Many American Jews were dismayed, feeling that the President—who must surely, they reasoned, have approved the vote—was now turning against Israel. In view of Carter's record, this was difficult to document and in any case was perhaps more emotional than logical. To be a peacemaker between two warring states, the chief of a third state must not be seen to favor one of the belligerents exclusively. American Jewish leaders sought and received denunciations of Carter's action (which at best was clearly muddle-headed and inept) from rival politicians and punished him for it at the primary polls in New York.

But in the long run—still a matter for speculation—it seemed likely in March 1980 that no future American government could afford to be as singleheartedly pro-Israel as most past governments. By his statesmanlike peacemaking, Sadat had won substantial American gratitude and popularity. He deserved well of American administrations yet to come. And Egypt had no oil; so it would also be necessary for the United States to stay on close terms with the other Arab nations and by that token to come to grips directly with the Palestinian question.

Arafat and his terrorists were anathema to Israel. They had been guilty of many acts of violence against helpless Jews: to name only two, the murder of the Israeli Olympic team in Germany in 1972, and the fantastic episode of the planeload of Jewish hostages held in Uganda in 1976 and rescued at Entebbe by the Israelis in an extraordinary commando feat. Yet sooner or later, Arafat or his successors would have to be dealt with. As the British had dealt with Gandhi, Makarios, Kenyatta—all of whom took British lives on their way to achieving independence for their states—so Begin, himself a former terrorist, or some Israeli successor would eventually have to face the Palestinians directly. Perhaps the Carter administration had been trying awkwardly to say something like that.

If this were true, it implied that American Jewish leaders would sooner or later come to understand that American public opinion was now more even-handed between Israelis and Arabs than in times past. Our American United Nations representative, Andrew Young, who had exceeded his authority and clumsily tried to get into touch with the PLO, had been dismissed for it. This set off a disturbance, as yet not fully healed, between American Jewish leaders and certain black leaders: for Young was the most highly visible black man in the Carter administration, and his departure rankled.

Sensitive as all such speculations were, the stability of Sadat was perhaps even more sensitive. Alone in the Islamic world, he had boldly shown a willingness to come to terms with Israel, to treat the United States as an ally in his confidence, to expel Soviet advisers, and to defy the Islamic revival by receiving the shah. "Let them jeer," he said of Muslims demonstrating against the shah in Cairo, and he referred repeatedly to the Ayatollah Khomeini as a madman. These policies were bold but they were dangerous.

Next door in Libya, Colonel Qadaffi, who had recently failed in another effort to subvert the Tunisian regime to the west of him, was quite prepared to topple Sadat by fair means or foul. Although the Arab nations could agree on very little, they could agree on their opposition to Sadat, amounting in some cases to fanatical hatred. In Egypt itself there were plenty of Muslim fundamentalists who disapproved of their government. And in a Middle East so unstable that even the Saudi regime was being challenged as insufficiently Islamic, Sadat was surely not safe. If anything happened to him, American hopes would indeed lie in ruins. As this is written, Sadat and Begin are scheduled to visit Washington separately. Before this can be read, further steps may have been taken and our story will be in part out of date. But these underlying fundamental realities are likely to remain.

Anybody who had gone to sleep in 1970, and slept for a decade, waking up in 1980, would perhaps not be altogether surprised at the events in the Middle East that we have been discussing. But it is safe to say that he would be thoroughly astounded by the dramatic change in international relations in the Far East that had come about since he had begun his ten-year nap.

China in 1970 had been our sworn enemy for more than twenty years. Chinese troops had shed American blood in Korea. China had supported our enemies in Vietnam and viciously denounced the United States and worked against it in every portion of the globe. Yet in 1980 our awakening sleeper would find that we had reached with the Chinese communists a relationship so close that it amounted to a working alliance. Our former sworn Chinese friends on Taiwan had been, if not abandoned, at least rudely shunted aside.

Nixon, China, and Russia, 1972

As we noted in the case of Israel's new relationship with Egypt, it would have been hard to imagine any politician to the left of the right-wing nationalist Begin getting away with such a dramatic shift. So in the United States, it is doubtful whether any "liberal" or Democratic president could have gotten away with making advances to China. The Republican President Richard Nixon did take the important initiative, which he would probably have denounced had a political opponent tried it.

President Nixon and Premier Chou En lai exchange toasts in Peking, February 21, 1972.

By 1971, huge Soviet armies were in position along the Chinese frontier, and the old working understanding between Moscow and Peking had long since soured into hostility. Although the Chinese had nuclear weapons and a population of at least one billion, China by comparison with either the U.S.S.R. or the United States was not yet an advanced industrial power. The Chinese were alarmed by their own comparative weakness.

So it was to their interest to welcome and give maximum publicity to Nixon's visit in February 1972. Before Nixon ever went to China, the United Nations gave the Chinese communists the Chinese seat on the Security Council and expelled the Taiwan regime. With the Chinese government itself in a state of disrepair owing to the excesses of the cultural revolution of the years before 1969 and the political infighting thereafter, it was a matter of great prestige for Mao Tse-Tung now to receive Nixon as his guest. Each power opened a diplomatic mission in the capital of the other. The United States made it clear that it would interpose no obstacles if at some future time in some way it should prove possible for Taiwan to join the mainland.

To lessen the obvious shock to the Russians, Nixon followed his Chinese visit with one to Moscow a few months later. In the interval between the trips, the United States, its forces in Vietnam reduced now from more than half a million to fewer than 40,000, resumed large-scale bombing of North Vietnam. And while the Russians denounced this, they did receive Nixon.

His visit to Moscow led to a document, often since forgotten, called "The Basic Principles of Relations between the U.S.S.R. and the U.S.A.," in which both powers accepted peaceful coexistence and committed themselves to resolve disputes by negotiations. The Russians regarded the declaration as a highly important success. With it went a relaxation of tensions: The Strategic Arms Limitation Agreement (SALT I) limited antiballistic missile systems to fixed numbers of launchers, missiles, and radar installations. Nixon's visit to China thus made possible the new easing of relations with Russia, shown in a number of concrete ways: Soviet purchases of grain, occasional Soviet relaxation of emigration restrictions on Jews, a variety of new trading arrangements.

The American special relationship with Japan was threatened by Nixon's failure to inform the Japanese of his intended visit to Peking. It was also threatened by his taking important economic steps to free the dollar from gold, allowing it to float, and imposing a new customs surcharge on foreign goods, both of which hurt the booming Japanese economy. But the Japanese soon made their own new diplomatic and commercial arrangements with China, apologizing for past Japanese governments' misdeeds there. In the general shake-up of relationships in East Asia, there were even new discussions and an exchange of delegates between North and South Korea, unthinkable only a short time earlier. And in South Korea, President Park assumed dictatorial powers.

Pakistan, Bangladesh, India

The years 1971–1972 saw major changes in South Asia also. In Pakistan the Bengali nationalist Awami League, led by Sheikh Mujib ur-Rahman of East Bengal, (the easternmost, most populous, and poorest part of Pakistan, separated from western Pakistan by all of India) won a majority of the seats in a new Pakistani parliament. The Pakistani leader, Yahya Khan, thereupon nullified the elections, jailed Mujib, and invaded East Pakistan. Hostilities between the native Bengalis and Bihari immigrants from India into East Bengal (both Muslim) had produced many atrocities before the Pakistani armies arrived. But the West Pakistani atrocities against the Bengalis were now on a vaster scale than anything since the Nazi extermination of the Jews in World War II. Bengali refugees numbering *nine million* poured into India.

Late in 1971 the Indians, manifestly unable to settle so many Muslim refugees, invaded East Pakistan and defeated the Pakistani armies. East Bengal became the new independent state of Bangladesh. In West Pakistan, Yahya Khan's government fell, and a pro-Chinese and anti-American politician named Zulfikar Ali Bhutto took power. Throughout, the United States had supported the Pakistanis, who were committing the atrocities and were also certain to lose the war. Washington mistakenly feared that India would destroy Pakistan altogether. American naval maneuvers in the Indian Ocean did not help the Pakistanis and made us more unpopular than ever with the Indians.

The Russians were able to capitalize on American unpopularity, making a treaty with India, and cementing a friendship that grew still warmer when Nixon's meeting with Mao, India's old enemy, took place. In the aftermath of the victory over Pakistan, Mrs. Gandhi behaved with much restraint. Bhutto managed for some years to cling to office in the new truncated Pakistan. And independent Bangladesh underwent both political upheaval and dreadful famine.

But the late 1970s continued to see rapid reversals of fortune in the subcontinent. Bhutto, whose regime was authoritarian even for Pakistan, fell victim to an army coup. He was tried for conniving at the murder of a political opponent and eventually executed. Disturbed by troubles among its minorities (Pathans, Sindhis) who objected to Punjabi domination of the country, beset by economic woes, facing an India with increased military resources including atomic capability, Pakistan wavered along under the tight new military regime of Zia ul-Huq until the Soviet invasion of Afghanistan posed the greatest threat of all.

The Carter administration now publicly offered Pakistan military aid. Mr. Brzezinski paid an official visit. After peering genially along the barrel of a rifle pointed up the Khyber Pass, Brzezinski returned home, only to have Pakistan scornfully repudiate as "peanuts" the money he was offering.

As for India, Mrs. Gandhi herself ran into serious trouble. Impatient with slow democratic methods, surrounded by corrupt politicians of her own party, faced with charges that her cherished son, Sanjay, had made use of his position as her son to enrich himself and, among other things, to mismanage a new automobile industry, she instituted a dictatorship. Civil liberties were abrogated, opponents silenced and jailed. Some Indian courts held out against pressure, and in a free election in 1977 Mrs. Gandhi was overthrown by a loose coalition of opposition groups, the Janata party.

But Janata's chief point of agreement was their wish to rid themselves of Mrs. Gandhi, and neither Morarji Desai nor Charan Singh, the two successive Janata premiers, was a sufficiently skillful politician to hold the diverse elements of this new regime together. The rise of a leading Harijan ("untouchable") politician, Jagjivan Ram, to a position where he seemed about to become prime minister may have touched those deep chords of caste prejudice still so omnipresent in India. Mrs. Gandhi, who had been acquitted of the charges against her, fought a hard new election campaign and was triumphantly returned to power. In early 1980 her position seemed more impregnable than ever.

And when the Russians invaded Afghanistan, Mrs. Gandhi was not publicly outraged, but preferred to chat privately with Soviet Foreign

Minister Gromyko and to watch complacently the discomfiture of her greatest enemy, Pakistan, and of the Pakistanis' helpless great ally, the United States. It was, Mrs. Gandhi virtuously said, not unnatural for the Russians to have acted as they did in view of the provocation in Afghanistan, by which she obviously meant to endorse the absurd Russian claim that the United States had been responsible for sabotaging earlier pro-Soviet regimes and thus for provoking Russian action. Mrs. Gandhi was enjoying a sweet revenge. It might, of course, be a short one.

China after Mao

The new Chinese-American relationship established in 1972 remained fairly constant through the 1970s and towards the end of the decade warmed still further. Mao, who had been partly senile in his later years and from whose hands the day-to-day management of affairs had slipped, died. In the course of the struggle for succession, Westerners had a chance to learn a good deal more about the internal affairs of China. Mao's wife, the former actress Chang Ching, had been highly influential, everybody knew, and had taken a harsh anti-Western line, while Chou en-Lai, now also dead, had represented a more "moderate" point of view. This did not mean that Chou was in any sense a less dedicated communist or Chinese nationalist: only that it seemed to him more valuable for China to have reasonably good relations with the United States and to profit by Western technology while China was going through the long period before true modernization could be achieved.

These views came to prevail, as Hua Kuo-Feng, previously little known in the West, emerged as Mao's most important heir. Chang Ching and three other anti-Western hard-liners became known as the "Gang of Four." They were vilified and arrested, and disappeared from sight. In this period, as occasionally before, the wall poster became a valuable source of information to Westerners. These posters were plastered on a wall in Peking in full public view, some of them clearly inspired by the group now gaining power, others spontaneously produced by individual Chinese expressing their own views.

It appeared that the Gang of Four had been responsible for all the excesses of the cultural revolution, and indeed for all the ills that plagued China. Gradually the elderly but extremely able and tough Teng Hsiao-Ping, a moderate about the West, reemerged from the obscurity to which the Gang of Four had been able to relegate him. He had been disgraced but not killed, and he now began to rise to the position of Mao's chief heir. The educational system, crippled by the earlier attacks of 1967–1969, was rehabilitated bit by bit. Foreign trade was opened up wider than before. Delegations to and from the West came and went. China received Western tourists in ever-growing numbers.

Wall posters for a time recorded the violent objections of their Chinese authors to the earlier mistakes. Then public comment gradually was suppressed. And in early 1980, Teng's appointments to important government posts seemed to signify a decrease in power for Hua, and more surprising, for Teng himself. In March 1980, it seemed possible that the Chinese were preparing to delegate power to a collective leadership after Teng should die or even sooner. There was something a bit ironic in the Chinese adoption of a device invented by Tito, whom Peking had so long bitterly denounced. Designed for the time after Tito's death, the device had never been tested and nobody could predict how it might work either in Yugoslavia or China, both countries accustomed to one-man rule.

Southeast Asia

By 1973, after long and difficult negotiations, the United States, South Vietnam, North Vietnam, and the Viet Cong reached an agreement for a cease-fire. The last Americans left Vietnam. Tragedy continued to stalk that country, however. As the communists continued their onslaught, the South Vietnamese government of Thieu eventually fell. Vietnamese who had relied on the United States were left unprotected against their Vietnamese enemies. Many thousands were rescued and received in the United States. Others were not and suffered at the hands of the victorious communists. Saigon was renamed Ho Chi Minh City. In the years after 1975, the Hanoi regime continued to be savagely oppressive.

Bad as things were in South Vietnam, they were worse in Cambodia. Here the "Red Khmers" under Pol Pot, after fierce fighting, overcame the government forces of Lon Nol, supported by a few American military advisers. The revenge of Pol Pot's troops and the brutality of their policies almost defied description. They drove the populations of the cities into the countryside, leaving the capital, Phnom Penh, and other towns depopulated. Many Cambodians died on forced marches or were killed at the whim of one of the communist soldiers. All Western-educated people—which meant French-trained—were systematically exterminated. Doctors and nurses were killed with the rest, leaving no trained medical personnel to help the wounded, starving, and diseased. "Reeducation" in the countryside consisted of forced labor in work battalions. Famine spread. Nothing resembling public order remained.

The wild excesses of the Pol Pot regime were apparently not sanctioned by the Chinese, who were its patrons. By the late 1970s, the Hanoi regime had become embroiled with the Chinese, and sponsored a rival Cambodian government of its own headed by Heng Samrin. Moscow backed Hanoi.

Vietnamese forces attacked Pol Pot's forces, whom the Chinese supported. In order not to have to support Moscow and Hanoi by backing Heng Samrin in the United Nations, the United States found itself supporting the unspeakable Pol Pot as legitimate. Probably Heng Samrin was no better. In fact, as the puppet of the Vietnamese, whom the Cambodians hated, he may well have been even more hated than Pol Pot if that were possible.

By 1979 the Pol Pot regime was grudgingly admitting its own past excesses—not that anything could ever palliate them. Partly in order to relieve Vietnamese pressure in Cambodia and so preserve the Pol Pot "government," the Chinese invaded North Vietnam. There were other reasons too. As relations between Hanoi and Peking had cooled and those between Hanoi and Moscow had grown even warmer, Hanoi had begun to persecute systematically the very large Chinese population living in Vietnam. These Chinese were robbed of their possessions and expelled from the country or allowed to flee.

Many thousands crossed into China, making difficulties for the Chinese authorities in the territories nearest the border with North Vietnam. Others became "boat-people," fleeing from Vietnam by whatever vessels they could find and landing on the shores of Thailand or elsewhere. Often they were slaughtered on arrival. The United States managed to rescue some of the boat people, who included many Vietnamese refugees from communism as well as Chinese. Uncounted thousands more were suffering privation somewhere.

The Chinese invasion of North Vietnam was a massive military operation but was apparently limited in its goals, like the earlier Chinese attacks on India. Peking's troops crossed the bor-

der and came close to Hanoi but had no intention of attacking it directly or of remaining in the country for a long time. The Vietnamese, already engaged in Cambodia, fought back and inflicted heavy losses on the Chinese, but took heavy losses themselves. From a military point of view, the war was probably a standoff. It did not succeed in deterring the continued Vietnamese operations in Cambodia.

In that wretched former country, famine raged and was partly alleviated by international efforts in 1979. Journalists were actually able to see and interview the immediate followers of Pol Pot, who was obviously hoping to save his skin and his regime. In the United Nations, the Soviet Union's followers in the Third World, led by Fidel Castro of Cuba, strove for the recognition of Heng Samrin's regime instead of Pol Pot's. The United States successfully averted this Soviet maneuver, and Pol Pot's representatives remained in the UN. It was hardly a triumph to be very proud of.

The "China Card"

In addition to the measures it took against the Russian invasion of Afghanistan, the Carter administration sent the secretary of defense on an official visit to Peking. This was "playing the China card," forcefully reminding the Russians that relations between the United States and China were close, and not very subtly suggesting American willingness to assist China in any confrontation with the U.S.S.R. In March 1980 there was naturally still much discussion as to whether this was a good idea. Distressed by the invasion of Afghanistan, with whom they shared a common frontier, although a short and mountainous one, the Chinese no doubt welcomed such a visible American warning to Moscow. But perhaps it did not frighten the Russians very much: their armies were still in place on the Chinese frontiers, undiminished by the Afghan adventure. And it may have been inept for the United States to rattle so big a sword when the ultimate American intentions were far from agreed upon.

To complete the picture of disarray and troubles in Asia one should note that South Korea—the great economic success of American policy in the 1960s—was also in political turmoil. The repressive policies of the Park regime, nominally our friend and ally, included systematic persecution of Catholics and other Christians. Corruption had grown indeed. Millions of American dollars were used by highly placed Koreans to bribe American congressmen and industrial leaders. Within the Korean governmental structure, the army and the intelligence agency feuded among themselves and against the president.

In 1979 Park was assassinated, but the coup d'état that followed was mismanaged. Trials of the actual assassins seemed to be imminent early in 1980. Across the border, the North Korean communists were biding their time. As in so many other places, so too in Korea, our friends seemed as reprehensible as our enemies, and perhaps the vast American investment in Korean capitalism and democracy would in the end fall into the hands of Korean communist tyrants.

THE WEST

The view of America's problems abroad in 1980 has so far focused on Afghanistan, Iran, the Middle East, East Asia, and Southeast Asia, with the chief outside participants in the action the Russians, the Chinese, and the Americans. Before we ever began, however, we mentioned the forthcoming American election of 1980 and described the atmosphere of unhappiness in which it seemed certain to be conducted. This atmosphere was of course due largely to the persistent and apparently worsening problems in foreign policy that we have just surveyed. But it was also due to a sense of helplessness at home, which derived immediately from America's own political and economic experiences during the 1970s.

The United States: Watergate and Its Aftermath

In 1972, President Nixon was reelected by a massive popular and electoral vote. His opponent, George McGovern, carried only one state, Massachusetts. Presumably McGovern's social and economic programs, which would have been expensive and inflationary, played a substantial part in the voters' decision. The Republicans had from the first perceived McGovern as the easiest candidate to beat. But during the election itself, Nixon's Committee to Reelect the President (known as CREEP) sent a small group of men to break into the offices of the rival Democratic National Committee located in a Washington housing development called "Watergate." A guard arrested the would-be burglars, whose ex-

ploit was at first regarded as a political prank.

But the early investigations gradually exposed a series of ever-worsening scandals, which by 1974 were preoccupying the American government and public so intently that there seemed little chance to think about anything else. The Senate launched an investigation. President Nixon himself named a special prosecutor, Professor Archibald Cox of the Harvard Law School. Several of the Watergate burglars were linked to the Central Intelligence Agency. The chairman of CREEP was John Mitchell, who had been attorney general in Nixon's first administration.

Some of the burglars had also been involved in the burglary of a Los Angeles psychiatrist's office, where they hoped to find personal information about one of his patients: Daniel Ellsberg. Ellsberg, a former CIA employee, had taken for his own use a long, secret history of the Vietnam War, written for the secretary of defense, and soon known as the "Pentagon Papers." Ellsberg gave these to the press for publication. Not only had the Nixon administration tried to procure (no matter how) evidence against Ellsberg, but when Ellsberg's trial opened, the president and his assistant, John Haldeman, secretly and improperly offered the judge the directorship of the Federal Bureau of Investigation. The prosecution's failure to inform the defense of its activities led to the collapse of the government's case against Ellsberg. CREEP funds had been paid to the burglars.

These were a few of what John Mitchell himself later called the "White House horrors." Independently of the growing Watergate scandal, the Nixon administration found itself embarrassed by evidence that Vice-President Agnew, once governor of Maryland, had then and as vice-president taken kickbacks from contractors, and was guilty of income-tax invasion. Agnew was to be tried by a federal judge in Maryland. The judge accepted a recommendation from the Justice Department not to try the vice-president, who in turn signed a memorandum admitting the truth of the charges against him.

Agnew resigned as vice-president and went free. Many felt that the disgrace was punishment enough, but many felt that the rich and powerful could always get a "special deal" and escape the penalties of their actions. Using a new constitutional amendment for the first time in history, President Nixon appointed a vice-president to succeed Agnew. This was Gerald Ford, Republican leader of the House of Representatives. Ford was confirmed by both houses and became the first appointed vice-president in United States history.

The Nixon administration's troubles were only beginning. Nixon himself, it appeared, had at least "avoided" if not "evaded" income taxes. He had taken a large deduction for the gift to the federal government of his papers as vice-president in the Eisenhower administration. But he had given the papers at a time after such deductions were no longer legal, and the deed of gift had been back-dated. He owed the United States government almost half a million dollars. Nor had he paid state income taxes either in California or in New York. Large sums of public money had been spent on his two luxurious private residences, one in Florida and the other in California. There were grave questions about the handling of vast sums contributed to the Nixon campaign by Howard Hughes, the mysterious millionaire, but handled by Nixon's friend Charles Rebozo, a Florida banker.

As the president's own integrity became more and more questioned, his White House special counsel, John Dean, accused Nixon, Mitchell, and Nixon's two assistants, Haldeman and Ehrlichman, of having ordered a cover-up of the original Watergate attempted burglary. For a time it was Dean's word against theirs. But then it emerged almost accidentally from the testimony of a relatively minor official that Nixon had installed a system of tape-recorders in his White House office and that verbatim records existed of his conversations with his aides. Special Prosecutor Cox soon found himself locked in battle with the White House in an effort to obtain these tapes: unprecedented authentic sources of vital evidence. Nixon held out against Cox's requests.

Pleading executive privilege, the President ordered Attorney General Elliot Richardson to dismiss Cox. Richardson refused and resigned. So did his second-in-command, William Ruckelshaus. The third-ranking officer in the Justice Department complied and Cox was fired. This episode was quickly christened the "Saturday night massacre." It aroused a furious outburst (a "firestorm") of public disapproval. To appease it, Nixon consented to turn over certain tapes to the Federal Judge, John Sirica, who had jurisdiction over the Watergate case. Nixon also found that he had to appoint a new special prosecutor, Leon Jaworski, as successor to Cox. And he had to accept the resignations of Haldeman and Ehrlichman. In disbelief, the public watched the president of the United States being driven by his own actions into a tighter and tighter corner.

When the first transcripts of the tapes were made public, the president was heard conversing with Haldeman, Ehrlichman, and others in the language of the locker room if not of the gutter. And this was after many of the "expletives" had been "deleted." In one of the tapes there was an eighteen-minute gap, in which whatever had been recorded had been erased. Who had caused this? And there were hundreds—perhaps thousands—more tapes, which may or may not have recorded incriminating conversations. For months on end, the president hired and fired one expert lawyer after another in an effort to make good his claim that exposure of the tapes would adversely affect national security and infringe upon presidential privilege.

The Judiciary Committee of the House of Representatives began an inquiry on the advisability of impeaching Nixon. They too had been trying in vain to get the tapes. The Supreme Court unanimously found that Nixon would have to surrender the tapes. Nixon was soon forced to admit what he had so long and so often denied: that he had not only known of the Watergate cover-up but had ordered it.

In August 1974, the House Judiciary Committee voted to recommend impeachment. By then the Senate would overwhelmingly have approved the vote. Nixon was faced with the certainty of becoming the first American president in history to be ousted by the elaborate processes established by the Constitution. Nixon resigned and retired to his estate in San Clemente, California. Although he had repeatedly declared that he would repay the taxes he owed the federal government—even those for a year on which the statute of limitations had run out—he did in fact never repay the amounts owing for that year. The threat of prosecution apparently hung over him as he resigned.

Vice-President Gerald Ford succeeded Nixon. Ford's openness and good humor provided a welcome contrast with Nixon's own secretive and vindictive personality, now fully revealed to all the public who had read or listened to the transcripts of the tapes. The ordeal of Watergate had seemed endless, and the public was generally breathing a sigh of relief and congratulating itself on "how well the system had worked." Indeed, Judge Sirica, the members of the House Judiciary Committee, and many others had given memorable examples of personal probity. At this moment, President Ford, contrary to an earlier promise, gave Nixon a full presidential pardon for any acts he might have committed as president, and so freed Nixon from any danger of criminal prosecution. Ford explained that "no purpose" would be served by exposing Nixon to trial and possible punishment. Many accepted the view that Nixon had "suffered enough" by his unprecedented public disgrace.

Yet public cynicism also rose to new heights. First the vice-president of the United States, Agnew, had "copped a plea" and now the president too had been pardoned by a successor he himself had appointed to the vice-presidency. Had there been a "deal" when Ford was appointed, to the effect that, if Nixon were in danger of the law, Ford would pardon him? The question might be turned aside or answered no any number of times, but public doubts would always remain.

The "law-and-order" Nixon administration had been shown up as a crooked sham. Mitchell, Haldeman, and Ehrlichman—less important figures than Nixon—stood their trials and eventually went to jail. Nixon's serious illness aroused sympathy for his plight. His exemplary behavior as a quiet elder statesman, writing a book of memoirs that would earn him millions, did a lot for his "image" if not for his character.

Gerald Ford, the appointed president, in turn appointed *his* vice-president, Nelson Rockefeller, former governor of New York. For two years and more, the United States was governed by a president and vice-president who had not been duly elected. Rockefeller's enormous personal wealth and the immunity it gave him from the problems of mankind generally, worried many who did not doubt his integrity or ability. The "little guys" who had committed the actual break-ins served long sentences. The masterminds, especially those like John Dean who collaborated with the authorities, got off relatively easily. Did we know, would we ever know, all the "White House horrors"? Should we just "put Watergate behind us" and get on with the neglected business of trying to run the most powerful country in the world?

Nagging questions remain to plague historians. *Why* did Nixon ever order his conversations taped? Was it from his own exaggerated wish to look well in the eyes of posterity? But if so, why did he not at least clean up his language? Had he been insane, as certain reminiscences of his advisers indicated, wandering around the White House talking to the pictures on the wall, or even plotting an army coup? Having made the tapes, why did he not destroy them, instead of perhaps erasing only eighteen-minutes worth from one of them?

Had Nixon calmly said, "I ordered tapes made; they were mine; I have ordered them de-

stroyed; they no longer exist," would the House Judiciary Committee ever have had enough evidence to recommend impeachment? Above all, how could such a talented man with so many qualifications for public service have been so mean, small, deceptive, and in the end, criminal? Long after the thousands of pages of memoirs written by all the Watergate figures, Nixon included, had been read and digested, these nagging questions remained.

Ford and Carter

The American political system, then, "worked" but rather badly. The social and economic system was shaken in 1974 as we saw, by new inflation caused in part by OPEC, in part by the Vietnam chickens coming home to roost, in part by the decline in American productivity. Inflation continued intermittently during the two years of Ford's presidency. "Whip Inflation Now" and the distribution of "W.I.N." buttons was an advertising man's empty stunt. The inflation rate tapered off by election time in 1976. But, for example, many large corporations were found to have been using bribery as an instrument of obtaining business overseas. Lockheed, International Telephone and Telegraph, any number of others, were day after day exposed as having committed illegalities. The Ford administration was certainly a healing interlude after Watergate. But certain things would not be the same for a long time, if ever.

With scandals in industry matching those in politics filling the American newspapers every day, the public faced the elections of 1976 in a mood of disillusionment, helped not at all by the serious financial crisis in the city of New York, which was threatened with bankruptcy. It was not very surprising that the prevailing mood was cynical, echoing the excuses of those businessmen who explained that "everybody has to do it," or "it's the only way to get the business," when asked to explain the giving of bribes.

This was surely one of the factors explaining the rise to popularity of Jimmy Carter, former governor of Georgia, a naval officer with special engineering training on nuclear-powered submarines, who wrote a campaign document on his own behalf entitled *Why Not the Best?* Apart from energy, intelligence, and the determination to be president, Carter had certain other great advantages. He was a Democrat coming after the Nixon-Ford era. He was a deeply and publicly devout Christian, who believed in the sanctity of the individual human being. He was a genuine Southerner (not just a Texan like Lyndon Johnson), the first to aspire to the presidency since the Civil War. And despite that, he appealed to many black voters.

He defeated President Ford in the election of 1976. But gradually the hopes faded that his administration would bring major improvements. Some of this was Carter's own fault. He surrounded himself with close political friends from his days in Georgia politics. One of them, Bert Lance, a banker and Carter's director of the Bureau of the Budget, found himself the object of an inquiry that led to his resignation. (The question of Lance's dealings was still unsettled early in 1980.) Other members of the President's immediate entourage at one time or another came under heavy fire from the press. And many problems that Carter had promised to solve proved intractable.

He had told an eager public that he planned to reduce the huge size of the swollen federal bureaucracy and so cut costs. This proved an empty promise, partly no doubt because Carter underestimated the difficulties. Carter showed himself uncertain and wavering in the face of inflation, which became the besetting domestic problem, as OPEC continued to hit its customers with new price rises for oil. The efforts of the Federal Reserve Board under Carter's latest appointee, Paul Volcker, to reduce the money supply and tighten the economy led early in 1980 to an unprecedented rise in interest rates and were producing clear signs of the recession that orthodox economists said was necessary. The president shied away from direct price and wage controls, and perhaps he was right. His repeated calls for voluntary restraint met with some response but not enough.

Above all, from the first, Carter had trouble with a Congress nominally Democratic in majority, which might have been expected to work with him. Instead, Congress balked almost every one of his major efforts. The press sometimes blamed Carter for not establishing closer personal relationships with the powerful leaders of the Senate and House. It was true that at the beginning of Carter's term, as a new boy in Washington, he hardly knew these people and he may have overlooked opportunities to ingratiate himself with them. But it was surely more important that during the collapse of the Nixon regime and in the interim administration of President Ford— an ex-Congressman himself—the Congress had arrogated to itself many powers and privileges of government that normally belonged to a strong executive. Carter never recaptured these.

The president on many occasions appeared both naïve and vindictive, as when he demanded the resignations of his entire cabinet and then summarily fired two members of it. He simultaneously set up a kind of report-card system for the entire federal bureaucracy, so that every employee's punctuality and performance were to be graded by his superiors. The Carter administration often seemed bumbling, inept, and unpredictable in its handling of both domestic and foreign affairs. This emboldened Senator Kennedy of Massachusetts to challenge the president for the 1980 Democratic nomination in a contest still unsettled when this was written.

Kennedy was the only surviving brother of President John F. Kennedy and Senator Robert Kennedy, both the victims of assassins. His family had been dogged by tragedy, and he had served for more than a decade as senator from Massachusetts. He retained much of the Kennedy legacy of political popularity. On the other hand, his programs for 1980 sounded exactly like those of his two brothers for the 1960s.

He favored a new national health service and other increased social services, which would be enormously expensive and would involve either heavily increased taxes or larger unbalanced budgets and more inflation. Kennedy's opponents disapproved of either method of payment for the programs and so, for the present, oppose the programs too. Persistent doubts about Kennedy's character stemmed from an episode at Chappaquidick, Massachusetts. A young woman in a car with the senator at the wheel was drowned, but her death was not reported by the senator to the police for an inexplicably long time. His explanations of his actions left many of the public skeptical or hostile. By March 1980 it was clear that either he or President Carter would be the Democratic candidate in November.

The Republican presidential choice as of March 1980 was apparently moving towards the former governor of California, Ronald Reagan, a one-time film actor, the darling of the conservative wing of the Republican party, with no experience in national politics and very little knowledge of foreign affairs. Still in the contest against Reagan was George Bush, a Connecticut-born Texan with experience as a congressman, director of the Central Intelligence Agency, United States representative in Peking, and chairman of the Republican National Committee. John Anderson, a long-time Republican congressman from Illinois, a fiscal conservative with an open mind towards innovation started from nowhere and attracted a good many disillusioned Democrats as well as more "liberal" Republicans. Neither Bush nor Anderson seemed to have much chance of nomination.

Other Western Nations

Canada and Britain

In Canada the 1970s, save for two brief interludes, belonged to Pierre Trudeau. He did no better with galloping inflation than any other political leader, and the issue of French separatism in Quebec loomed ever larger.

In Britain, the Conservative government of Edward Heath struggled vainly in the early 1970s with several intractable issues. One was the growing power of the unions to disrupt the economy, signalized by damaging strikes. Second was the persistent weakness of the currency, marked by the freeing of the pound to float downward in value and efforts to control inflation. The third was the agony caused by the continued disorders

Pierre Elliott Trudeau, Liberal prime minister of Canada.

in Northern Ireland, where the British would have liked nothing better than to withdraw, but could not abandon the province to the prospect of uncontrolled bloodshed in a full-scale civil war. And the fourth was the impact of the action of the new military dictator of Uganda, Idi Amin, in expelling 50,000 Ugandan Asians—mostly Indians, Hindu and Muslim—who held British passports. The British accepted most of these as immigrants, with a consequent rise in racist feeling at home in Britain.

Expecting to win an election late in 1973, Heath lost. But Harold Wilson, the Labour leader, did not obtain a workable majority, even after a second election in 1974. The electorate seemed to want a Labour government but to restrict its power. The more extreme Labour proposals, including the "wealth tax," not a tax on income but a levy directly on capital, could not be pushed through. Nor, despite Wilson's proclamation that his government rested on a "social contract" between the Labour party and the unions, was he able to control the actions of the communist-dominated unions. Inflation raged, running at rates above 20 percent. Nor did the other political problems that had plagued Heath prove any more tractable for Wilson.

Underlying Britain's economic troubles was the "British disease": overmanning the factories. Sometimes called "featherbedding" in America, this meant clinging to unnecessary positions. There was also the failure to curb union dictatorship and management's neglect of opportunities to modernize. As the 1970s advanced, Britain got a tremendous boost from the growing availability of North Sea oil. Extracted by drilling rigs and piped into such ports as Aberdeen, the oil was rendering Britain largely self-sufficient. It was the chief reason why James Callaghan, the Labour party leader who succeeded Wilson when Wilson rather suddenly resigned, was able to bring inflation under control. Unlike every other Western European nation, Britain was no longer dependent on OPEC and so did not have to face the inflationary impact of every succeeding price increase in oil. Yet with North Sea resources limited, the gain would be limited in duration.

In other respects, Callaghan did no better than Wilson. Communist penetration of the unions grew ever-more threatening. This did not by any means indicate pro-Soviet penetration, but what was more and more called "Trotskyist" penetration. Without much regard to foreign policy, the "Trotskyists" were Marxists who were determined to bring down the social structure of Britain. Their influence, though muted, could be seen in the words and actions of the leaders of the Labour party's left wing, as hostile to Callaghan as they were to the Conservatives.

Certain notable strikes during the later 1970s, notably that against a small photographic equipment plant at Grunwick, in north London, vividly illustrated the point. Employing mostly Indian immigrant labor, the plant was struck because its owner—like his workers—objected to unionization. Not only was extreme violence used against the workers in the plant, but huge demonstrations were organized involving "Trotskyite" members of mining and other unions not directly concerned. At the Post Office, government employees were pulled out on strike to prevent the plant's receiving or filling mail orders. The general public in the area also got no mail as a result.

Callaghan's weakness in his own party and the public dissatisfaction with such spectacles as Grunwick led to a Conservative election victory in 1979. Margaret Thatcher, the first woman ever to lead a political party in Britain, became prime minister. Mrs. Thatcher, whose own specialty had been education and who had saved the British school system from the leveling attempts of Labour party doctrinaires, proved exceedingly tough in her first year in office.

None of the old problems went away. In Ireland, for example, the IRA blew up a small pleasure boat aboard which were Lord Mountbatten—a member of the royal family, a hero of the naval warfare in World War II, and a former First Lord of the Admiralty—and members of his family. Two of the perpetrators of the act were captured and tried by the Irish Republic, in whose territory the crime had been committed. Inflation once again grew out of control, and Mrs. Thatcher prescribed more austerity.

One of the reasons for lagging prosperity lay in the huge payments that Britain had to make annually to the Common Market. Receiving less from the market than other members and with a standard of living markedly lower than that of France and Germany, for example, Britain nontheless had to contribute more cash than any other country. Public opinion backed Mrs. Thatcher in her announced determination to renegotiate these terms. But other members of the market, notably the French, complained that Britain was now trying to change the rules after having agreed to them. In March 1980, the issue remained very much alive and fraught with dangers.

Within the Commonwealth, Mrs. Thatcher scored what seemed to be a notable success in Rhodesia. Here, continued black pressure for majority rule had by the late 1970s taken the form of three chief groupings; one headed by Bishop Abel Muzorewa, leaning to cooperation with the whites, and the other two—under Joshua Nkomo and Robert Mugabe—hostile not only to the whites and to Muzorewa, but to each other. Rival guerrilla groups regularly committed atrocities, and the country seemed threatened with a bloodbath. After elections returning a majority for Bishop Muzorewa had been widely complained of as unfair, Mrs. Thatcher summoned all parties concerned to London and achieved an agreement. She sent out a new British governor with full authority to conduct new elections. In the face of many difficulties, this was actually done in such a way as to win acceptance as wholly fair. Robert Mugabe, most radical of the three rivals, won a notable decisive surprise victory. A Marxist with ties to Mozambique and Tanzania, Mugabe was conciliatory to his defeated rivals. In March 1980 progress towards the independence of the new country—now to be called by its ancient name, Zimbabwe—seemed assured.

France

In France the Fifth Republic of the Gaullists in the early 1970s began to look more like its predecessors, as charges of corruption grew in intensity and were made to stick. President Pompidou had to replace Premier Chaban-Delmas for paying no income taxes, although the premier had only been taking advantage of a loophole in the laws. After Pompidou's death in 1974, a new election narrowly returned as president Valéry Giscard d'Estaing, who defeated Chaban-Delmas, the Gaullist candidate. Not himself a Gaullist but the chief of his own small party, which had always collaborated with the Gaullists, Giscard was a handsome aristocrat who wanted to avoid the dangers he saw both in American unrestrained capitalism and in socialist bureaucracy. He was technocratic and impersonal, yet had at times a genuine popular touch.

The remainder of the 1970s belonged to Giscard, in unmistakable control of an enormously powerful job. He dramatically broadened women's participation in the government, reformed the divorce laws, introduced a liberal abortion law, lowered the voting age to eighteen, raised the minimum wage, put through a generous unemployment insurance law, and increased the income taxes of the rich, some of whom continued not to pay them anyhow. All these achievements were the products of Giscard's first year in office. Thereafter the pace of domestic reform slowed notably. Giscard could not readily decentralize France and decrease the domination of Paris. While he abandoned nuclear testing in the atmosphere and the proposed mass production of the expensive and uneconomic Concorde airplane, he found inflation as insoluble and worrying a problem as any other Western leader.

As the 1970s drew to a close and a new election for the French presidency loomed for 1981, Giscard came under severe sniping from the left-wing opposition. Scandal suggested that he had improperly accepted presents of diamonds from the tyrannical self-styled "Emperor" Bokassa of Central Africa. He was intransigent in his opposition to any modification of the British terms of membership in the Common Market. In his neo-Gaullist anxiety to avoid seeming to agree with the United States on anything, he proclaimed that France would surely participate in the Moscow Olympic Games of 1980. But doubts persist: a way would perhaps be found not to participate after all. France would then, as a French newspaper put it, not be "aligned with the United States, but independent and more hypocritical." French adventures in the Middle East and Africa form a wholly separate chapter in Giscard's history. Many of them in the end might prove to have contributed to international stability.

Germany

In West Germany, the Social Democrats retained continuous control of the government during the entire decade of the 1970s. In the first years, Prime Minister Willy Brandt, with encouragement from the United States, moved steadily towards an understanding with the communist powers to the east. Painfully, the West Germans hammered out treaties with the U.S.S.R. and with Poland. These meant a full acceptance of the frontiers imposed by the victors of World War II. It was a hard dose for some West Germans to swallow, but the opposition Christian Democrats were split on the issue, and therefore it did not become a political question between the two chief parties. In East Germany, Ulbricht, the aged Stalinist boss, was replaced by Erich Honecker, a communist too, of course, but prepared for discussions with West Germany.

The Berlin issue, which had repeatedly threatened world peace since 1945, was defused by an American-British-French-Soviet four-power pact on the subject. And finally, Brandt completed the job by signing late in 1972 a pact directly with the East German state that looked towards the establishment of normal relations. The Berlin Wall still stood, of course, but the deep separation between the Germanies that it symbolized was gradually lessening. Brandt won the Nobel Prize for Peace. Yet much to the surprise chiefly of foreign observers, Brandt resigned in mid-1974. Brandt's staunch anti-Nazi record during World War II had been matched by his record of anti-communism as Mayor of Berlin afterwards. He seemed to many the incarnation of the "good" German.

But domestic issues had always irritated Brandt. He was embroiled with the unions over wages and under fire from the left wing of his own Social Democratic party. He often showed himself indecisive in the face of crisis at home. He did not sense the danger threatening from the presence in his inner circle of an official named Guillaume, who proved to be an East German spy. Guillaume's exposure led to a crisis, in which Brandt resigned. He was succeeded by Helmut Schmidt.

Also a right-wing Social Democrat, Schmidt had served ably in the two most difficult posts in the West German government, the ministry of defense and the ministry of finance. A good debater, he had coined in 1972 a winning political slogan, "Five percent inflation is less of a tragedy than five percent unemployment." If one stops in 1980 to examine the low figures in each case, one shakes one's head in wonder. Which Western country today would not regard five percent inflation *and* five percent unemployment as a golden economic opportunity?

Especially in the years since Carter's election in 1976, the West Germans under Schmidt's leadership turned towards France and partly away from the United States. To the hard-headed practical Schmidt, Carter's seemingly contradictory policies were puzzling and disconcerting. What was the point, Schmidt more and more publicly asked, of trying to pursue détente with the U.S.S.R., while at the same time denouncing the Soviet disregard for human rights? To Schmidt Carter also seemed to be blowing hot and cold on German issues: criticizing Germany's export of nuclear power technology, changing his mind on the neutron bomb, unskilled in reaching firm positions on monetary questions or even in understanding them.

Alert to the change in German-American relationships, and to the opportunities thus opened for France, Giscard moved towards a new understanding with Schmidt. The two had always gotten along, and German industry, hard currency, and strong position in Europe complemented France's booming agriculture, nuclear military capacity, and close ties with Third World countries. The failure of the Carter administration to put through a new energy policy increased German and French doubts. Like Carter in 1980 and Giscard in 1981, Schmidt in 1980 was facing re-election. His chances were better than either Carter's or Giscard's, as the Christian Democratic opposition leader, Franz Josef Strauss, a highly intelligent Bavarian, was also thoroughly reactionary.

Among the problems the German government had faced with only moderate success was that of terrorism. A gang of anarchist-minded young people (the "Baader-Meinhof" gang) assassinated a number of prominent persons. When arrested, tried, and jailed, some managed to escape and continue their careers of violence. Toughness against terrorists, no matter what threat they posed, seemed to be the only workable answer. Even lawyers for the accused often turned into their accomplices.

Other European States

Italy spent the decade of the 1970s moving from crisis to crisis. The once prosperous economy was sickening even before the OPEC price raises began in 1974. Christian Democratic cabinets came and went. Strikes were endemic. Terrorism, at first only a faint reflection of the efficient German or Palestinian brand, grew worse and worse in Italy, with victims chosen apparently at random and sometimes painfully shot in the knees instead of being murdered. However, former premier Aldo Moro, the most prominent of their victims and a man of great personal decency and piety, was kidnapped and killed by them.

Some of Moro's assassins were found and killed by the police early in 1980. The terrorists, in turn, threatened to kill ten policemen for every member they had lost. After repeated government crises, it seemed likely that the Social Democrats would abandon their communist allies and join the Christian Democrats in a coalition government. As in France, so in Italy, nobody in 1980 any longer believed that there really was such a thing as "Euro-Communism," native communist parties opposed or indifferent to Soviet policies and Soviet dictation. Both French and Italian communist leaders were once more as responsive to Moscow as they had ever been.

In Portugal, Spain, and Greece, the 1970s saw the end of long-established dictatorships of the right. Salazar's replacement as dictator since 1968, Caetano, found himself shaken by the drain on Portuguese human and financial resources imposed by the endless wars to hold on to Portugal's African colonies. At first an army coup d'état in 1973 overthrew Caetano. Then the army officers who had engineered it were in turn overthrown. The communists under Cunhal, a Stalinist, had enormous influence. The African colonies—Guinea-Bissau, and much more slowly, Mozambique and Angola—were cut loose in 1974 and 1975. In Angola, as we shall see, Portuguese withdrawal led to serious and continued fighting.

But in Portugal itself, communist influence gradually waned after 1975. The moderate socialist, Soares, formed a government, and the country gradually moved back to the center. Expropriated landowners had lost large estates in the early excesses of the revolutionaries' zeal. But by 1980, Portugal seemed stabilized in a more moderate pattern.

In Spain, the change that had so long been anticipated both with joy and with dread came when Franco died in 1975. Prince Juan Carlos, his designated heir, took over as king. The necessary processes of constitution-making and free elections went through smoothly. All political shades of opinion had a chance to express themselves. The moderate, Suarez, became prime minister, with a strong Social Democratic and communist opposition on the left. There was no civil war, no bloodshed.

But in the late 1970s troubles multiplied. Against diehard Francoite opposition, the government managed to steer through a program for Catalonian autonomy. The parallel program for the Basques, however, encountered the fierce opposition of terrorist groups. Once again, assassinations multiplied: of moderate Basques, of army officers, of policemen. Though the Basque population at large seemed to favor the government's program, the diehards were irreconcilable. Uncertain of its support on the right or left, the government was in trouble on this issue.

Another issue as old as the first Spanish Republic and the Civil War—that of the role of the Church in education—also aroused much heated controversy. By March 1980 the government had gone a long way towards making secular education more available and reducing the Church's monopoly. But severe opposition had made every move difficult. It was the relatively new question of autonomy for Andalucia—a large, populous, barren region of the south—that caused an embarrassing defeat for the government. Andalucia voted for local autonomy, a concept that was plausible and workable for Catalonia and the Basque territories with their old languages and separate traditions. But when applied to Andalucia the idea seemed to threaten a real disintegration of Spanish national territory and a return to the bad old days when Spain was a mere collection of geographical regions with customs barriers rising between them. The government did not obey the Andalucian votes.

Add to these difficulties the ever-increasing ill health of the economy, and one sees that the new Spanish Republic by early 1980 faced genuine troubles. Yet when one remembered that freedom of speech, freedom of the press, freedom of assembly had been safely and successfully introduced into Franco's Spain, that all sorts of Western literature was now widely read and discussed, and that Spain had truly begun to modernize itself, one cheerfully admitted that here was a major achievement indeed. Perhaps Suarez had now lost touch, as his opponents claimed, but before doing so he had accomplished wonders.

Greece and Turkey

On what newspapermen always called "NATO's other flank" in Greece and Turkey, equally dramatic events took place in the 1970s. Cyprus, 80 percent Greek and 20 percent Turkish in population, was an independent nation under the presidency of Archbishop Makarios. A United Nations force was protecting the Turkish minority against Greek mistreatment, and a guerrilla movement (EOKA) was agitating in the countryside in favor of union with Greece. In addition, the Greek government of the colonels had sent a force of a few hundred army officers, ostensibly to train the Cypriot National Guard. But these officers also engaged in EOKA activities. Makarios asked that the officers be recalled. The colonels in Athens refused. EOKA tried a coup d'état and Makarios fled abroad.

Instantly the Turkish government intervened to protect the Turkish minority. Turkish armies landed on the north coast of Cyprus. As they fanned out and a war with Greece threatened, the colonels' government in Athens collapsed. Former Premier Karamanlis, long in exile in Paris, returned to head a new democratic regime in Athens. "At last we owe something good to the Turks" was a remark widely popular at the time among the people of Greece.

But on Cyprus the Turkish occupation eventually extended to the northern portion (about half) of the island. About 200,000 Cypriot Greek refugees fled south into unoccupied Cyprus. There was much suffering among them. Karamanlis was a man of peace who had always sought good relations between Greece and Turkey. But no Greek premier could recognize the conquest by force of so large a part of Cyprus. Difficulties were made even worse by the feeble Turkish caretaker government. Despite the successes of its armies, it did not command enough political support at home to negotiate directly with Karamanlis. Greek Cypriots blamed the United States for not protecting them against the Turkish invasion. The Greeks of Greece proper blamed the United States for not sympathizing more publicly with the fears for the safety of the Turkish minority that had led to the invasion in the first place.

In Greece, Karamanlis won a secure majority in a free election. In a free referendum the Greek people (1974) rejected a monarchy in favor of a republic. Orderly constitutional legal trials were instituted against the leaders of the colonels' dictatorial regime. Greece seemed truly free again. Makarios returned safely to Cyprus and resumed control of the unoccupied portion of the island. After his death, the succession passed in orderly fashion to popular but not extremist leaders of the Greek community.

The Turkish government of the early 1970s became even weaker as the decade drew towards a close. No political party could command a safe majority. While the issue of Cyprus poisoned relations with Greece, a further dispute arose over oil-drilling rights in the sea floor of the Aegean, which several times seemed to threaten an open clash between the countries. Militant right-wing Turkish youths fought their left-wing opponents in the universities and in the streets. Political assassinations became common. There were signs of religious revival and (along the Syrian border) of Shiite-Sunnite hostility. Violence became endemic. The traditional Turkish attitude of suspicion and dislike for Russia was strongly diluted by new suspicion and dislike for the United States. The economy was in ruins, and homeless waifs, abandoned or thrust out by their parents, wandered the streets of Istanbul living by their wits. The loss of the remittances from Turkish workers abroad in Germany or Sweden that bolstered the economy now grew more serious, as those countries cut down on employment of Turkish workers. Inflation was severe. The 1980s threatened to be an extremely precarious period for Turkey.

THE THIRD WORLD

Castro and Tito

In discussing the headline issues of early 1980, we have repeatedly touched on nations of the Third World: Afghanistan, Iran, Vietnam, Cambodia, and others. As such, the Third World had no international leadership on which it could agree as a model. Fidel Castro, however, tried hard to assert himself as such a leader and achieved a measure of success. Cuban troops went abroad and served the purposes of the Soviet Union in Angola, in Ethiopia's destructive wars against the Somalis in the horn of Africa (the Ogaden War), and against the breakaway Ethiopian province of Eritrea.

Cubans were in Afghanistan in 1979 well before the Soviet invasion. The Cuban troops fought, but they also trained Angolans, Ethiopians, Yemenis, and others to fight. Closer to Cuba itself, Cuban intervention was widely expected in Nicaragua and El Salvador, two Central American states with fully developed revolutionary and counterrevolutionary movements. But the Cubans stayed out while an indigenous Nicaraguan movement overthrew the dictatorial regime of General Somoza and while disorder raged in El Salvador.

Possibly the reason for Castro's failure to assume genuine leadership of a Third World grouping was the fact that everybody knew of Cuba's economic dependence upon the Soviet Union. Castro was an effective ruler of Cuba but also recognizably a Soviet agent. For many radicals in the Third World this was a drawback. For example, in 1979, at a Third World Conference in Havana, Castro lost his fight to have the Third World support the Soviet-backed Cambodian regime of Heng Samrin. Castro was faced by Marshal Tito, eighty-seven years of age and already ailing. Tito was able to prevent Castro's getting the votes he needed on the Cambodian issue. Perhaps more important, the impressive and venerable Yugoslav Marshal spoke as a rebel against Soviet domination in the past, the first genuine communist to reject national subservience to Moscow, and his speech commanded both attention and sympathy. By early 1980, Tito was desperately ill, almost certainly on his death bed.

What would happen after he died, particularly in Yugoslavia, itself a Third World leader ever since Tito's rebellion of 1948 and his old friendship with Nehru? The Western press spoke with foreboding about a possible Soviet invasion, something which the Yugoslav government itself certainly feared. But Tito had taken formidable military precautions to make such an effort terribly expensive for the U.S.S.R. Guerrilla fighting on Yugoslav terrain would make a quick conquest impossible. Once bogged down in Yugoslavia, the U.S.S.R. would be exposed as far from invincible. Moreover, traditional Russian foreign policy, tsarist and Soviet alike, did not act aggressively simultaneously in Asia and in Europe. The Russians for the moment in the spring of 1980 were heavily engaged in Afghanistan. It seemed improbable that they would invade Yugoslavia before that operation had been concluded.

More likely than an invasion of Yugoslavia by Soviet troops would be a quick move by the Bulgarian army into the Yugoslav Republic of Macedonia, long claimed by Bulgaria. Such a move would necessarily be sponsored and supported by the U.S.S.R. It too would bring about a Balkan war. Safe prediction was impossible, but it seemed unlikely that the dangers to the communist bloc would be worth the possible gains.

Internal Yugoslav fragmentation remains a possibility. The elaborate scheme of succession devised by Tito would put both the government and the Communist party under collective and rotating leadership. Nothing like it had ever been tried, and it would require superhuman restraint and maturity to make it work for any length of time. Croatian separatists abroad were still sounding the same nationalist slogans that destroyed Yugoslavia before World War II. The degree of sympathy with which their aims were regarded inside Croatia itself, however, was doubtful.

The Albanian minority in Yugoslavia posed the chief additional danger. But a move by the somewhat tired Albanian regime to invade Yugoslavia or sponsor an effort by the Albanians across the Yugoslav border to join the "mother country" would also perhaps involve more danger than profit for the Albanians themselves. In short, Tito's death when it came would probably produce a precarious situation in Yugoslavia but perhaps not so precarious as alarmists feared. Possibly the worst effect in the long run would be the loss of a recognized leader of anti-Soviet national communism. Fidel Castro could not claim that place.

Africa and Latin America

Along the northern tier of Africa among the Muslim states, Morocco was preoccupied with war over the former Spanish territories, where the pro-communist Polisario movement backed by Algeria posed a major threat. Algeria itself survived the death of Houari Boumédienne and experienced a peaceful succession with no notable change in its pro-Soviet alignment. Tunisia, still nominally governed by the aged and unwell national hero, Bourguiba, lay open to threats from Libya, where Colonel Qaddafi had not forgotten his frustrated ambitions to swallow up his neighbor's country one way or another. The Libyan-led raid of 1979 on the Tunisian town of Gafsa, frustrated quietly by French troops, underlined the point.

South of the Sahara, perhaps the most reassuring development in West Africa was the continued healing of the wounds of the past fierce Nigerian civil war. By 1980 a civilian government was in full control and the country's prosperity had returned.

In former French West Africa, the "showcase" example continued to be the Ivory Coast, with its original administration under the French-educated African Houphouët-Boigny still in place. Here perhaps 50,000 French continued to live and to guide a booming economic development. Air-conditioned skyscrapers, plush hotels, and luxury foods flown in from France for the successful were noticed by all visitors. The natural question whether an explosion might be building up below the surface met with reassuring answers from those who knew the country best.

By contrast, one might single out the former French territory of Ubangi-Shari, which became first the Central African Republic and then the Central African Empire. Its emperor, Bokassa, who had a Napoleonic complex, exploited and savagely mistreated his subjects. When overthrown, he found (with French approval) refuge in the Ivory Coast. And in neighboring Chad, warfare between the northern Muslims and the tribesmen of the south involved French troops. When the northerners won, two of their leaders started their own bloody civil war: Muslim against Muslim, which was still in full swing early in 1980.

In East Africa, the most sensational developments in former colonial territory in the 1970s were those supplied by the indescribably cruel tyrant of Uganda, Idi Amin. We have already mentioned his expulsion of Asians and alignment with the Palestinian terrorists and noted his setback by the Israelis at Entebbe. Uganda was economically depressed and politically a shambles, when Kenya and Tanzania jointly agreed to put an end to Idi Amin's regime. Led by the Tanzanian forces of Julius Nyerere, who had a former Ugandan left-wing politician, Milton Obote, as his client, an invasion toppled Idi Amin in 1979, despite Colonel Qaddafi's Libyan troops sent to help Amin. Idi Amin took refuge in Libya and the grim traces of his abominations were gradually uncovered. But even as a liberated country early in 1980, Uganda remained politically unstable and in deep economic trouble.

It was in Zimbabwe-Rhodesia, the scene of the 1980 free elections orchestrated by Mrs. Thatcher, that the largest questions on the continent remained unanswered. With perhaps 200,000 whites and 10,000,000 blacks, and complete one-man, one-vote democracy now in control, what would the future hold? And how would South Africa, next door, where the whites numbered about 17 percent as against the 2 percent in Zimbabwe, react to the new state? Most authorities early in 1980 were predicting further large-scale departures of whites. Prime Minister Mugabe had promised not to give refuge to South African guerrilla forces in Zimbabwe. On the economic side, for a while at least, the "Marxist" Mugabe would surely encourage foreign investment and development capital. As a Mashona tribesman whose territory included the capital, and as a leader previously repudiated by both Britain and South Africa, Mugabe owed neither country any debts. He would probably remain conciliatory with his defeated rival, Nkomo, a Ndebele tribesman. He would surely be looking to Washington for vast foreign aid.

The prime minister of South Africa in 1980, Pieter Botha, came to power by taking advantage of a scandal involving the administration of his predecessor, John Vorster. Botha made various proposals for limiting apartheid and beginning the long-overdue process of redressing old wrongs. But the pressures from the "narrow" wing of his own governing party prevented many of his ideas from getting off the ground. Rooted in their determination to hold on to political and economic power, the dominant Afrikaner South Africans could surely postpone a bitter day of reckoning but might not be able to prevent it.

In fact, signs of weakness—as in the probable setting free of Southwest Africa (Namibia)—would surely set off internal demands in their own country that the dominant politicians would be unwilling or unable to grant. Here, as elsewhere, the future promised to be both gloomy and terrible.

Latin America

The chief Latin American exception to the old Latin American political formula early in 1980 appeared to be Brazil. Here a dictatorship often marked by violence and repression was gradually beginning to liberalize itself. There was far more freedom of speech, far more relaxation of tension than ten years earlier. Argentina, on the other hand, went through a convulsion in the 1970s, when Colonel Perón returned to power from Spain and then died, to be succeeded by his widow. Her inability to govern led to a second coup and the reappearance of a military regime. With inflation raging and terror widely practiced both by the regime and by its enemies, this richly endowed country stumbled along an obviously hopeless neofascist path. Neofascist, that is, except when it came to exporting grain to the U.S.S.R., which the Argentinians gladly did to fill their purses and to cause chagrin to the United States.

The outlook for the 1980s—and for the subsequent decades of the century—was grim indeed. Violence, terror, and dislocation threatened from all directions. For the statesmen of the next ten years even to muddle through would be a masterly achievement. They deserve in advance of their appearance on the scene our understanding and our prayers.

CHAPTER TWENTY-ONE

Science And Culture In The Twentieth Century

In our century both the physical and the social sciences have advanced at a breathtaking pace. The revolution in physics and astronomy triggered by Einstein transformed many fantasies of science fiction into realities. It enabled men to land on the moon but also created the atomic bomb and still deadlier weapons that could wipe out civilization. The revolution in psychology triggered by Freud cast new light on the role of the irrational forces governing much of human behavior. New techniques developed by biologists raised the possibility of altering nature's programming of human beings. The sinister manipulation of people forecast in novels like Huxley's *Brave New World* and Orwell's *1984* became a disconcerting reality. On the whole, the great leaps forward in science, communications, and the arts enhanced the quality of life in many parts of the world. Yet in other areas the majority of people are still immersed in the struggle to survive.

Physics

Remarkable scientific advances have flowed from the revolution in physics identified with Albert Einstein (1879–1955). Einstein emigrated to the United States when the Nazis came to power in his native Germany, but by then he had already made most of his important contributions. Many other experts also played a role in developing the new theories launched by Einstein, which caused radical revisions in the "Newtonian world machine," the model of the universe that had been accepted for more than two centuries.

As Chapter 15 has noted, many nineteenth-century scientists were convinced that light moved in waves and was transmitted through the ether, which supposedly filled outer space. If the ether did exist, it would be set in motion by the movement of the earth; and a beam of light directed *against* its current would travel with a velocity less than that of a beam directed *with* its current. But experiments conducted by the American physicist, Michelson (1852–1931), in the 1880s showed that light traveled at 186,284 miles per second, whether it was moving with or against the hypothetical current. There was no ether.

In 1905 the youthful Einstein published a paper asserting that since the speed of light is a constant unaffected by the earth's motion, it must also be unaffected by all the other bodies in the universe. The unvarying velocity of light, therefore, is a law of nature, and other laws of nature are the same for all uniformly moving systems. This was Einstein's Special Theory of Relativity, which had many disturbing implications. In particular, it undermined the idea that it was possible to regard space and time as absolute. Both space and time are relative to the velocity of the system in which they are moving. If a rod moves at a speed approaching that of light, it will shrink; at 90 percent of the velocity of light, it will contract to half its length. A clock carried aboard the rod will slow down. If men should ever travel through space at such speeds (which are far greater than those reached by the astronauts of the 1960s and 1970s), they would make a disconcerting discovery on their return. While they think they have been away for six months, by

Einstein in 1920.

the earthly calendar they have been absent for a year!

Space and time, therefore, are closely linked, and time may be regarded as the "fourth dimension." For example, an air-traffic controller needs to know the position of an airplane not only in longitude, latitude, and altitude but also in time. The flight path of a plane must therefore be plotted on what Einstein called a "four-dimensional space-time continuum." This term, which described a law of nature, he also applied to the whole universe.

Einstein linked not only space and time but also mass and energy. His celebrated formula—the most famous in the twentieth century—$E = mc^2$ means that the energy in an object is equal to its mass multiplied by the square of the velocity of light. It means also that a very small object may contain tremendous potential energy. Such an object can discharge radiation very slowly for thousands of years or release it all in a single explosion. This was what happened in 1945 when an international team of physicists found a way to unlock the potential energy in uranium. The result was the atomic bombs dropped on two Japanese cities, Hiroshima and Nagasaki, by American planes in August 1945.

The problem of mass also led Einstein to review the Newtonian concept of a universe held together by the force of gravity. Newton believed that the attraction of bodies to other bodies over vast distances depended on their weight. Einstein soon concluded that it was erroneous to suppose that the gravity—that is, the weight—of an object had anything to do with its attraction to other objects.

Einstein proposed to extend the alternative concept of the magnetic field, in which certain bodies behaved in a certain pattern. He therefore referred to a "gravitational field" in which bodies also behaved in a certain pattern. Einstein did not penetrate the mystery of what holds the universe together, but he did suggest a more convincing way of looking at it. This was the essence of his General Theory of Relativity (1916), which stated that the laws of nature are the same for all systems regardless of their state of motion.

One of these laws of nature had been formulated in 1900 by the German physicist, Max Planck (1858–1947), who expressed in mathematical terms the amount of energy discharged in the radiation of heat. He discovered that the amount of energy divided by the frequency of the radiation always yielded the same very tiny number, which scientists call Planck's Constant. His discovery implied that objects discharge energy not in an unbroken flow but in a series of separate little units, each of which Planck called a *quantum,* a tiny parcel of energy. Quantum physics suggested a basic discontinuity in the universe by arguing that a quantum could appear at two different locations without having traversed the intervening space. It seemed almost absurd. As Bertrand Russell remarked, it was as if a person could be twenty years old or twenty-two, but never twenty-one!

Other physicists, however, made discoveries that reinforced the idea of continuity, with all physical phenomena behaving like waves. The old dilemma of whether light consisted of particles or of waves was therefore intensified. Einstein and others suggested that the only sensible procedure was to grasp both horns of the dilemma. A leading British physicist observed that he taught wave theory Mondays, Wednesdays, and Fridays, and particle theory Tuesdays, Thursdays, and Saturdays!

During the 1920s it became evident that human beings might never be able to answer ultimate questions about the universe. They could not fully understand the behavior of the individual electron, the basic component of the atom. The very act of trying to observe the electron altered its behavior. Study of the electron led another German physicist, Werner Heisenberg (1901–1976), to propose the principle of "uncertainty," which concludes that the scientist has to be content with probabilities rather than absolutes. While an individual electron can jump from one orbit to another, the behavior of large numbers of electrons can be predicted. Although the universe is no longer the world machine of Newton, its activity can still be expressed in the mathematical language of probabilities.

Astronomy, Chemistry, and Biology

The development of twentieth-century astronomy has been closely linked to that of physics. It became the most romantic of sciences because of its concept that the universe is at once finite and expanding, its claim that space is curved, and its concern with the breathtaking distances and quantities involved in light-years and galaxies. These distances and quantities are indeed almost inconceivable. A light-year is the distance traversed by light in one year, roughly 5,880,000,000,000 miles. A galaxy is a vast collection of stars, nebulae (immense conglomerations of gases), and other forms of matter. The Milky Way Galaxy, of which our solar system is a part, contains some thirty thousand million stars and nebulae and is shaped like a disk with a diameter of about one hundred thousand light-years. The popularity of astronomy was heightened by the successful landing of American astronauts on the moon (1969) and by the still greater wonders imagined by the stories and movies of science fiction.

Meanwhile, chemistry introduced plastics, synthetic fibers like nylon and polyester, and a host of other new products affecting our food, clothing, utensils, and other facets of daily living. Chemists assisted biologists in making the breakthrough that began in the 1960s with the discovery of the structure of DNA (deoxyribonucleic acid). DNA is the substance composing the genes, which transmit the inherited characteristics that "program" every individual. Subsequent experiments suggest that "genetic engineering" may make cloning possible," that is, the asexual reproduction of genes.

One of the scientists participating in the

discovery of DNA has called it "perhaps the most famous event in biology since Darwin's book," and a detailed history of DNA is entitled "The Eighth Day of Creation." Like Darwin's thesis DNA has sparked a debate, this time about the wisdom of tampering with fundamental biological forces.

DNA may also lead to more effective ways of dealing with viruses and other carriers of disease. Improvements in medicine and public health have already reduced infant mortality and conquered many once fatal diseases. In the more advanced countries of the world the average life expectancy has increased by twenty to thirty years since 1900.

The Quality of Life

These momentous developments have by no means improved the quality of life everywhere. Extended irrigation, chemical fertilizers, and the planting of high-yielding strains of wheat and corn have increased the food supply in some countries. But in others the population has grown faster than the food supply; the result is a constant exodus from impoverished overcrowded rural areas to the still more crowded slums of the big cities. The severity of the problem is dramatized for Americans by the influx into the United States of millions of illegal immigrants.

For nations with high technology the breakthroughs of science have created new concerns. Humanity could be literally wiped out by weapons such as hydrogen bombs, guided missiles, and biological warfare. While nuclear power plants, pesticides, and other products were at first considered beneficial, many of them have posed new threats to human health and to the natural environment. In addition, some medicines and food additives have produced unexpected and undesirable "side effects." Science has indeed improved life for some but has also made it more complicated and more perilous.

II THE REVOLUTIONS IN PSYCHOLOGY AND THE SOCIAL SCIENCES

The twentieth century has produced not only awesome technological developments but also a deeper understanding of the nature of the human beings employing these new inventions. Following leads from biology, especially Darwin's theory of evolution, the nineteenth century had emphasized the dynamics of change in society. The twentieth, taking its cue from psychology, has emphasized the role of the unconscious in human thought and action and the irrational aspects of people's behavior. Foremost among the thinkers responsible for this emphasis was Sigmund Freud (1856–1939).

Freudian Psychology

Freud was a physician trained in Vienna according to the medical tradition of the late nineteenth century. His interest was soon drawn to mental illness, where he found patients who showed symptoms of very real organic disturbances for which no obvious organic cause could be found. Under analysis, as Freud's treatment came to be called, the patient, relaxed on a couch, was urged to pour out what he or she could remember from earliest childhood. After many such sessions the analyst, Freud argued, could make the patient aware of the source of the disturbance.

From this clinical experience Freud worked out a system of psychology that has had a very great influence on our basic view of human relations. Freud started with the concept of a series of drives with which each person is born. These drives, which arise in the unconscious, are expres-

Sigmund Freud photographed with his fiancée, Martha Bernays, in 1885.

sions of the *id* (Latin for "it"), which Freud used as the most neutral possible term. These drives try to express themselves in action, to get satisfaction and pleasure. Infants are uninhibited—that is, their drives well up into action from the id without restraint from their conscious minds. Restraint comes from those in authority—and there's the problem. Infants experience intense frustration because they are made aware that some of the things they want to do are objectionable to those on whom they are dependent. Infants therefore begin to repress these drives from the id.

In becoming more and more aware of the larger world, children develop what Freud at first called the censor and later divided into two phases termed the *ego* (Latin for "I") and the *superego*. The ego is the individual's private censor, an awareness that, in accordance with what Freudians call the *reality principle*, certain drives from the id—for example, the boy's wish to become his mother's lover—cannot be realized. Freud's concept of the ego has been called "the realm of caution and reason;" it is quite different from the self-gratification implied by the popular term, "ego-trip." The superego is rather like the conscience: it is the individual's public censor, his response as a member of a social system in which certain actions are acceptable and others are not.

Freud viewed both the drives of the id and many dictates of the superego as forces of which the individual is not normally aware. They are part of one's unconscious. In a mentally healthy individual, sufficient drives of the id succeed to make for contentment. But even the healthiest of individuals represses a great many drives from the id. This successful repression Freudians term *sublimation*. They argue that the well-adjusted person somehow finds for a repressed drive a new and socially approved outlet or expression. Thus a drive toward unacceptable sexual activity might be sublimated into the writing of poetry, composing of music, or participation in athletics.

Some people, however, force their drives back into the unconscious without a suitable outlet. The drives, so to speak, fester in the id and cause all sorts of *neuroses* and *phobias*—that is, disorders and fears that have no apparent physical cause. What they have in common is a failure to conform to the reality principle. Neurotic individuals are *maladjusted*, and if the failure to meet the reality principle is total, they are *psychotic*—that is, insane, or living in an unreal private world of their own.

Freud's therapy consisted of the long slow process of *psychoanalysis*. Day after day the patient searched his memories of earliest childhood for concrete details. The listening analyst could pick from this *stream of consciousness* the significant information that pointed to the hidden repression, the blocking that explained the patient's neurotic behavior. Freud gave special importance to dreams, which, he believed, allowed the unconscious to express itself with little control by the ego. Once aware of what had been repressed in the unconscious, the patient might then adjust to society and lead a normal existence.

What is pertinent for the student of history is the very great importance Freud assigned to unconscious drives. Much of human thought, according to Freudians, is only *rationalization*. It is thinking dictated not by the reality principle but by desires of the id. One can measure the distance between the rationalism of the eighteenth century and the Freudian psychology of the twentieth by contrasting the "blank slate" of John Locke's newborn infant with the Freudian view of the infant as a bundle of antisocial drives, as a little untamed savage.

Yet it is most important to note that the Freudians, like Locke, do not want to blow out the candle of human reason. Their therapy, which has Christian as well as eighteenth-century roots, is based on the biblical admonition: "Ye shall know the truth, and the truth shall make you free." But, for Freudians, truth cannot be distilled into a few simple rules of conduct which all men and women, being reasonable and good, can use as guides to happiness. Truth can be reached only by a long and difficult struggle. Many individuals will never reach it and will have to endure all sorts of maladjustments and frustrations. Freudians at bottom are pessimists who do not believe in human perfectibility.

Though Freud termed religion an "illusion," he himself became a cult leader. His faithful disciples long constituted an orthodox nucleus of strict Freudian psychoanalysts. Other disciples parted with the master. The Austrian Adler (1870–1937), who rejected Freud's emphasis on the sexual, coined the familiar term, *inferiority complex*, to designate the behavior of timid individuals or of those who overcompensated for their timidity by aggressiveness. The Swiss Jung (1875–1961) attempted to expand the horizons of psychology by studying the evidence of the human past in literature, mythology, and religious faith. His studies convinced him that there was a *collective unconscious*, a reservoir of the entire human experience that we all possess and tap. It is reflected in *archetypes,* patterns established by prophets, seers, and saviors. Archetypes appear and reappear in religion, legend, literature, and art.

Full psychoanalysis has remained an extremely lengthy and expensive treatment that relatively few patients can afford. For less elaborate therapy, many patients consult a psychiatrist rather than a psychoanalyst or participate in such experiments as group therapy or "sensitivity groups." The Freudian influence on imaginative writing has been very great, as evidenced by "stream-of-consciousness" fiction. It has also affected philosophy and the arts in general. Freud reinforced the intellectual reaction against scientific materialism and bourgeois optimism.

The Social Sciences

The social sciences, too, have greatly modified the Enlightenment's faith in human reason. The Italian Pareto (1848–1923) wrote a pioneering study of sociology, *The Mind and Society* (1916). He claimed that in the nineteenth century Western society was transformed by people who stressed the importance of fresh ideas, new inventions, and unlimited competition. But Pareto predicted that their very success was bound to trigger a vigorous reaction by the defenders of tradition. The result would be more security and less competition, more discipline and less freedom, more uniformity and less variety—in short, the emergence of the totalitarian state.

The new studies of human behavior also opened the way for applying the findings of psychology and sociology to modern democracies as well as to totalitarian regimes. The psychology of motivation interested not only Mussolini and Hitler but also many democratic politicians and experts in the field of advertising. In Britain, for example, Graham Wallas published *Human Nature in Politics* (1908). This widely read book was based on his own campaign for election to a seat on the London County Council. Wallas discovered that the voters seemed more pleased by baby-kissing, chitchat and personal flattery than by appeals to reason or self-interest. A rather similar stress on the need for popular psychology in politics appeared in *A Preface to Politics* (1913) by Walter Lippmann, a young American intellectual.

More recently, "psychohistory" has appeared on the scene. While many historians had long been aware of the importance of emotional factors in determining great events, the practitioners of psychohistory have pioneered in apply-

ing the full range of Freudian concepts to participants in historical events. The results have sometimes seemed extreme, but they have helped to explain the strange behavior of maladjusted individuals like Adolf Hitler and Richard Nixon.

Philosophers, too, questioned the degree of reasonableness to be found in human nature. In Freud's Vienna soon after 1900, a philosophy called *logical positivism* (or logical analysis) appeared. Its proponents insisted that even though only a tiny fraction of human behavior could be called rational, that tiny fraction should be protected and explored thoroughly. Pioneers of this logical positivism were Ludwig Wittgenstein (1889–1951) and Rudolf Carnap (1891–1970), who later emigrated to Britain and to the United States, respectively.

One approach of logical positivism has been explained by the American physicist P. W. Bridgman. When a problem can be answered by what scientists call an "operation" and the answer validated by logical and empirical tests or observations, knowledge can be obtained. But there are many problems for which no such "operation" is possible—for example, whether democracy is the best form of government, whether a lie is ever justifiable, whether a poem is good or bad. Thus most of the great problems raised by history, literature, and other aspects of human experience cannot be solved. For the logical analyst,

A caricature of Kierkegaard.

therefore, to attempt to solve them is a waste of time.

Another pessimistic view of the human condition came from the *existentialists,* who held that existence was both mysterious and difficult. Each person had to cope with it individually and could not avoid feelings of anxiety and guilt. The existentialists looked back to the writings of Nietzsche and the Danish theologian, Kirkegaard (1813–1855). Kirkegaard deplored what he considered to be the dehumanizing influence of the materialistic and antireligious society of his day. In the mid-twentieth century, the leading existentialists were the German Christian philosopher, Heidegger (1889–1976), and the French atheist, novelist and playwright, Jean-Paul Sartre (1905–1980).

Sartre seemed to suggest that one's awareness of existence might penetrate to the level that Freudians called the unconscious. Such penetration allows one to make painful adjustments to a world that appears hostile and meaningless. These adjustments will vary widely from one individual to another. Sartre himself was a harsh and relentless critic of the world around him and found even the communists' blueprint for a better world not nearly radical enough. He has been termed "a rebel with a thousand causes, a modern Don Quixote."* Many intellectuals in the West who had been attracted by his early writings concluded that Sartre's existentialism was too personal, too lacking in structure to qualify as a genuine philosophy.

Still another prescription for the modern quandary came from the *semanticists,* who held that the key lies in semantics, the study of meaning. The leader in this rather naïve therapy was the Polish-American scientist, Korzybski (1879–1950), author of *Science and Society* (1933). By a quite different approach, the Canadian Marshall McLuhan (1911–) concluded that if we all really understood communication and the mass media, such as newspapers and television, we should also understand the "images" they present of public figures. His key phrase was "the medium is the message."

A more philosophical approach may be found in various movements loosely grouped under the label of *historicism.* Historicism has tried to find in history the answers to questions about the structure of the universe and the destiny of humanity. It has reflected the application of Darwinian concepts of organic evolution to history

* New York Times (April 16, 1980).

and philosophy. Once historians abandoned the traditional Judeo-Christian concept of a single creation by a God above nature, many of them found in the records of history a substitute for the concepts of God and Providence.

Among the varieties of historicism Marxism is the most important and serves as a substitute for Christianity. The theological parallels have often been noted by non-Marxists. For an absolute God Marxists substitute the absolutely determined course of dialectical materialism; for the Bible they substitute the infallible writings of Marx, Engels, and Lenin; for the Church they substitute the infallible Communist party; and they replace the Last Judgment by the final revolution and the classless society.

A very different kind of historicism was advanced by the German Oswald Spengler (1880–1936) in *The Decline of the West,* published just at the close of World War I. Spengler found in the historical record that civilizations have an average life span of a thousand years. He traced three Western civilizations: the Hellenic from 1000 B.C. to the birth of Christ; the Arabian-Islamic from that time to about A.D. 1000; and Modern Western, which he claimed began about 1000 and was therefore due to end about 2000. Some critics have claimed that because Spengler saw Germany about to be defeated in 1918, he consoled himself by forecasting the end of Western civilization altogether. Many historians contend that, though Spengler had real insights into the growth and decay of civilizations, what he wrote is not so much history as metaphysics or "metahistory." It goes beyond conventional history to a kind of Wagnerian twilight of the Gods.

Somewhat paralleling *The Decline of the West,* but written by a trained historian, was the multivolume *Study of History* published between 1934 and 1954 by Arnold Toynbee (1889–1975), an Englishman with a strong family tradition of social service. World War I aroused in Toynbee a great hatred of war. He was convinced that it resulted from nationalism, which he once declared was the real, though unrecognized, religion of our Western society.

Toynbee's *Study of History,* though indebted to Spengler's work, is an ambitious effort to trace the reasons for the rise and fall of more than two dozen societies. However, Toynbee was a gentle English Christian humanist, not a German Romantic brought up on Nietzsche's doctrines. He concluded that, in terms of the cyclical rise and fall of societies he traced in the past, our own Western one faces a very serious challenge.

But he refused to abandon hope for its future. We may be facing destruction, but we may possibly avoid it under the influence of a revived Christianity of gentleness and love, perhaps aided by the teachings of Buddhism.

Toynbee's approach has not been well received by the majority of professional historians. They have noted that, while he seems convincing in dealing with societies one knows little about, his conclusions often appear to be superficial when he analyzes societies one does know something about. Moreover, historians are generally democratic in values and skeptics in religion, so that they have little sympathy with prophets of doom and preachers of the need for redemption. They agree that Western civilization has many weaknesses but point also to its continuing vitality and inventiveness.

III LITERATURE AND THE ARTS

Literature

Inventiveness and vitality have characterized twentieth-century literature, even though its authors have often passed exceedingly gloomy judgments on mankind. There were still old-fashioned poets with substantial popular appeal, such as the American Robert Frost (1874–1963), who was in the tradition of Longfellow and Tennyson. Much more surprising was the growing acceptance of experimental poets. The American Emily Dickinson (1830–1886), an almost completely unknown recluse in her lifetime, gained a large following for her introspective poems after her death. T. S. Eliot (1888–1965), born in St. Louis but an adopted British subject, created a great stir with his innovations. The beginning of "The Love Song of J. Alfred Prufrock" (1917) once seemed very strange:

> Let us go then, you and I
> When the evening is spread out against the sky
> Like a patient etherised upon a table.

The concluding lines of "The Hollow Men" (1925) have become part of the vocabulary of many people:

> This is the way the world ends
> This is the way the world ends

> This is the way the world ends
> Not with a bang but a whimper. *

The novel, despite repeated fears that it had become a terminal case, continued to be the most important form of imaginative writing. Its vigorous survival was greatly assisted by its incorporation of many insights from Freud, Jung, and other psychologists. It acquired not only new themes but also gradually freed itself from the traditional bans against printing four-letter words and discussing sex. The new permissiveness soon extended to stage plays and somewhat later to movies.

It would be possible to furnish a long catalogue of pioneers—in drama, the Swedish Strindberg, the Americans Eugene O'Neill and Edward Albee, the English Harold Pinter; in the novel, the American William Faulkner, the German Thomas Mann, the Russian Alexander Solzhenitsyn. But if one had to cite a single pioneer, it would be the Irishman James Joyce (1882–1941). Joyce began with *Dubliners* (1914), an outspoken series of sketches of life in the Dublin of his youth, followed by the autobiographical *Portrait of the Artist as a Young Man* (1916). Then, mostly in exile on the Continent, he wrote the classic experimental novel, *Ulysses* (1922). It is an account of twenty-four hours in the life of Leopold Bloom, a Dublin Jew. It is filled with difficult references, parallels with Homer's *Ulysses,* puns, and rapidly shifting scenes and episodes. And it is written without regard for the conventions of plot and orderly development. Above all, it makes full use of the new psychological approach to an individual's stream of consciousness. The last chapter, printed entirely without punctuation, is the account of what went on in the mind of Bloom's Irish wife as she lay in bed waiting for him to come home. Her thoughts were often too shocking for contemporaries, and *Ulysses,* published in Paris, had to be smuggled into English-speaking countries in the 1920s. Later, it became freely available almost everywhere, and, in the 1960s, was faithfully adapted as a movie.

A successful movie also recorded the mindless violence against individuals that was the theme of Anthony Burgess's *Clockwork Orange* (1963). This was one of a series of novels by British authors that forecast a grim future for the life, liberty, and pursuit of happiness championed by Thomas Jefferson. In 1932 Aldous Hux-

---

* T. S. Eliot, *Complete Poems and Plays* (New York: Harcourt Brace, 1952), pp. 3, 59.

ley (1894–1963), a grandson of the Huxley who had been the most articulate champion of Darwin's theory of evolution, published *Brave New World*. It predicted a society that would totally repudiate natural selection. People would be frozen into a series of castes, from the most intellectual to the most menial. Sleeping children would be brainwashed by recorded messages repeated over and over; adults would be urged to ease the pressures of living by taking a drug to produce a sense of euphoria. They would live together casually without commitments like marriage until about the age of sixty when their lives would be terminated in a quick and easy death.

In 1949 George Orwell (1903–1950) forecast a worldwide recourse to the policies of totalitarian dictators in his novel *1984*. Its most chilling feature was "newspeak," a manipulation of language by rulers in which words were used in a sense directly opposite to their conventional meaning. Yesterday's fiction has proved to be a disturbing indicator of tomorrow's fact.

Painting

In the less politicized realm of painting, a few masters of the old representational tradition have found a large and appreciative public; the American Andrew Wyeth is an example. But the mainstream of painting has continued in the radical experimental vein begun by Monet and Cézanne. In 1905 a group of paintings on exhibit in Paris caused the artists to be labeled *Les Fauves* ("the wild beasts"). What was wild about their work was the deliberate use of bizarre colors—lemon yellow skies, bright red trees, a woman with green hair. The Fauves explained that they were in search of an "intellectual" naturalism rather than the merely visual naturalism of the Impressionists.

The "king of the wild beasts" was Henri Matisse (1869–1954). In the early 1900s, when he was too poor to afford a model, he painted astonishing portraits of his wife. In one of them he used brilliant colors for her clothing and the chair in which she sat, but chalky gray with a touch of pink for her face. The face itself was a perfect oval outlined in black and its features were reduced to a minimum. Later he simplified even further the features of his human subjects, from dancers in swift motion to a child at the piano.

Unlike many contemporary painters, Matisse did not attempt to make the two-dimensional space of his canvases appear three-dimensional. Following the precedent set by Islamic tiles and Persian miniatures, he stressed pattern and color in depicting interior scenes. His paintings are often filled with brightly colored tablecloths, wallpaper, draperies, and rugs. Yet he organized them so skillfully that the result is a striking work of art, not the confused mess it might have become in lesser hands. His fascination with color lasted throughout his career. In his 80s, though crippled and bedridden, he was able to design bold *découpages* (cut-outs), huge artful arrangements of bright-colored paper.

An even longer and more varied career was that of Pablo Picasso (1881–1973). Born and trained in Spain but later an adopted Parisian, Picasso experimented with many styles of painting. The first years of the 1900s were his "blue period," when he painted portraits of melancholy and defeated people, perhaps reflecting the young artist's struggle to gain recognition. These pictures were influenced by El Greco, the sixteenth-century Spanish master whose works he had studied in Madrid. Both artists conveyed emotion by exaggerating and elongating the proportions of their subjects.

In 1905–1906 Picasso introduced more daring distortions after he had visited exhibitions of African masks and recently discovered archaic sculpture from the Mediterranean world. The result was one of his most arresting works, "Les Demoiselles d'Avignon" (the "damsels" were prostitutes, and Avignon was a street in the red-light district of Barcelona). The women have the huge eyes and simplified features of archaic sculptures, and two of them have the distorted faces and magnified noses of African masks.

Like Cézanne before him, Picasso transferred the geometry of the real world to the two dimensions of the canvas. Sometimes he used the techniques of *abstractionism*, reducing human figures to a kind of plane geometry, all angles and lines. Sometimes he turned to *cubism*, a kind of solid geometry that converts living bodies into arrangements of cubes, spheres, and cones. And sometimes he turned to *collage* (paste-up) and glued onto a picture real objects, such as bits of newspapers, wall paper, or playing cards.

After World War I, Picasso resumed more representational painting in the neoclassical portraits of his "white period." But he also continued experiments depicting human or animal figures from two or more angles simultaneously. Misplaced eyes and other rearrangements of anatomy were employed with dramatic effect in "Guernica," often judged to be Picasso's finest work

Matisse's "Piano Lesson."

Picasso's "The Old Guitarist."

Picasso's "Les Demoiselles d'Avignon."

(see p. 492). He completed in six weeks this very large canvas for the pavilion of the Spanish Republic at the Paris exposition of 1937. It was a stark and moving requiem for the horrors suffered by the undefended Spanish town of Guernica when it was bombed by fascist planes during Spain's Civil War.

Dada and Surrealism

The most extraordinary defiance of artistic rules and traditions was made during World War I by a group of alienated intellectuals and artists who called their protest *Dada* (baby-talk for hobbyhorse). In a New York exhibition of 1917, the French Dadaist Marcel Duchamp (1887–1968) entered a porcelain urinal with the title "Fontaine" (fountain). He wanted to show his disgust with conventional art and his admiration for ready-made objects. Duchamp had already aroused a storm of disapproval at the New York Armory show of 1913 with his "Nude Descending a Staircase." This cubist experiment converted the human figure into a series of geometric forms so that it seemed to be followed by its own ghosts. Duchamp had carefully studied photographs of athletes in motion as preparation, but critics denounced his "Nude" as "a collection of saddle bags," "an explosion in a shingle yard."

Another Dadaist, the German Max Ernst (1891–1976) later became a pioneer of *surrealism*. This was the expression in art of the forces of the unconscious, particularly the dreams so emphasized by Freud. It had close ties with the rapidly developing art of the film, particularly the German *Cabinet of Dr. Caligari* (1919), which pictured the hallucinations of a deeply disturbed individual. A landmark of surrealism was a film of the late 1920s, *The Andalusian Dog*, made by two young Spaniards, Luis Buñuel and Salvador Dali. It recorded a razor slicing across a human eyeball and a man literally wiping his mouth from his face.

Forty years later, Buñuel continued to pro-

Picasso's "Dancer and Tambourine."

Surrealism: René Magritte's "Portrait."

duce films with surrealistic sequences. Earlier, Dali became celebrated for his fastidious paintings of bizarre subjects—limp watches, a burning giraffe, and a human torso transformed into a dresser with open drawers. Another Spaniard, Miró, painted a fanciful and more cheerful surrealistic universe, with much emphasis on sun, moon, and stars. The Belgian, Magritte (1898–1967), specialized in enigmatic situations—"Portrait" shows a slice of ham on a plate with a human eye in its center, and "The Listening Chamber" a room containing only a huge apple.

Abstract Expressionism and Pop Art

The rise of Hitler and World War II led many European artists to emigrate to the United States. In the 1940s and 1950s New York was the capital of *abstract expressionism,* the effort to communicate ideas and emotions nonrepresentationally—that is, without living forms. A leader of abstract expressionism was the German exile, Hans Hofmann (1880–1966), who applied brilliant colors with long brushstrokes or by simply pouring the paint onto the canvas. The paint was sometimes so thick that it gave the picture a third dimension. The American, Jackson Pollock (1912–1956), dripped or even hurled automobile enamel on huge canvases to create an arresting spattered effect.

In the 1960s the New York spotlight shifted to *pop art,* a Dadaist reaction to the mass-produced commodities of everyday life. Pop artists pictured over and over boxes of Brillo, segments of comic strips, and rather blurred pictures of movie stars from fan magazines and the television screen. Claes Oldenburg, a Scandinavian-American sculptor, began his justification of pop art:

> I am for an art that is political-erotical-mystical, that does something other than sit on its ass in a museum.
> I am for an art that grows up not knowing it is art at all, an art given the chance of having a starting point of zero.
> I am for an art that embroils itself with the everyday crap & still comes out on top.*

Sculpture and Architecture

The "everyday crap" of pop sculpture included plaster casts of real people surrounded by copies of actual furniture, a three-dimensional

* Quoted in J. Russell and S. Gablik, *Pop Art Redefined* (New York: Praeger, 1969), p. 97.

Pop art: Andy Warhol's "Marilyn Monroe."

comic strip of defeated humanity. At the opposite pole, sculpture in the grand manner had been reborn with the monumental works of the Englishman Henry Moore (1898–). Moore studied Pre-Columbian art, produced by the Indians in Central and South America before the Spanish conquest. His huge sculptures, designed for the outdoors, simplified human and animal figures and created an effect rather like that of cubist painting. Examples are his *King and Queen*, at the Hirshhorn Museum of the Smithsonian Institution in Washington, and the *Reclining Figure*

Henry Moore's "Reclining Figure, II."

Barbara Hepworth's Single Form": memorial to Dag Hammarskjold at the United Nations.

Constantin Brancusi's "Bird in Space."

at the Museum of Modern Art in New York City. Moore's compatriot and fellow student, Barbara Hepworth (1903–1975), fashioned standing abstract forms of great serenity. A handsome example stands outside the headquarters of the United Nations in New York as a tribute to her friend Dag Hammarskjold, the UN secretary general.

In sculpture, as in painting, the wide range and vitality of twentieth-century work have been remarkable. Highly polished metal abstractions were created by the Romanian Brancusi (1876–1957). His "Bird in Space" won much publicity after World War I when a United States customs inspector refused to admit it under the category of art objects because it did not look like a bird to him. The playful French Dadaist, Jean Arp (1887–1966), produced "human concretions," curved and billowing sculptures of highly stylized figures. The Swiss Giacometti (1901–1966) created arresting, greatly emaciated human figures. Alexander Calder (1898–1976) became the best-known American sculptor through his whimsical *mobiles* (so named by Marcel Duchamp). They were suspended from the ceiling on wires and so delicately balanced that the slightest breeze would set them in motion. In contrast, Calder's large sculptural constructions of sheet metal (dubbed *stabiles* by Jean Arp) were often somber and menacing, with such titles as "Black Beast" and "Guillotine for Eight."

In architecture the first half of the twentieth century was marked by a gradual retreat from the neoclassical style of Federal office buildings in Washington and the neogothic trimmings of such skyscrapers as the Woolworth building in New York and the Tribune tower in Chicago. A simpler International Style, devoid of fussy details and stressing wide windows and clean geometrical lines, was developed by the German *Bauhaus* ("building house") under the leadership of Walter Gropius (1883–1969). A pioneering American adaptation was the Philadelphia Saving Fund skyscraper completed in 1932 (and financed entirely from unclaimed deposits of deceased customers). It forecast the popularity of the tall cubes of glass and metal that may be found all over the world today.

"Functional" and "organic" became key words in the architectural vocabulary. Functionalism was described by another Bauhaus leader, Mies van der Rohe, as "less is more." An apartment house or business structure should have a clean, simple design and not pretend to be a Venetian palace or a French château. "Organic" design emphasized the harmony between a struc-

Albert Giacometti's "The City Square."

ture and its environment, as in the prairie houses of Frank Lloyd Wright. Wright made a more dramatic organic adaptation in the 1930s when he designed Falling Water, a house built over a waterfall in western Pennsylvania. He used stones from the creek bed in the walls of the house to stress its relationship to the site.

In the 1950s, near the end of a very long career, Wright made a radical functional experiment in his design for the Guggenheim Museum in New York City. Instead of the conventional series of rooms, he created a vast high interior space through which visitors descend along a spiral ramp bordered by shallow recesses for installing exhibits. They may view paintings at close range and also from a distance. But art experts complain that this arrangement makes it almost impossible to hang paintings effectively. Some assert that Wright intended to make his architecture eclipse everything else.

Music and Dance

In contrast to modern architecture, twentieth-century music has never produced a distinctive style like the functional or the organic. Popular music has attracted large and enthusiastic audiences for its jazz, rock, country, disco and other forms. "Serious" music has been less successful in its experiments—substituting a twelve-tone scale for the traditional eight tones, stressing dissonance over harmony, extending orchestral

Arp's "Human Concretion."

Alexander Calder's stabile "Whale."

sounds by electronic amplification. To the untrained ear the results are often harsh and disturbing, almost unmusical.

One experiment that did gain acceptance was made by the Russian composer, Igor Stravinsky (1882–1971). On the eve of World War I he produced scores for two ballets, *Petrouchka* and *The Rite of Spring,* which greatly expanded the conventional narrow limits of classical ballet. The audience at the Paris premieres reacted violently to the unconventional subjects—a clown and an ancient Russian celebration of spring—and the noisy and earthy music provided by Stravinsky. Eventually they found a place in both ballet and the orchestral repertoire.

In the second half of the twentieth century ballet won the mass audience it had never enjoyed before. It was greatly helped by imaginative choreographers and exceptionally talented dancers, including several defectors from the Soviet Union. More remarkable was the growing popularity of "modern dance," which went far beyond the limitations of classical ballet. Two of its pio-

Frank Lloyd Wright's "Falling Water": the Kaufmann house in Bear Run, Pennsylvania.

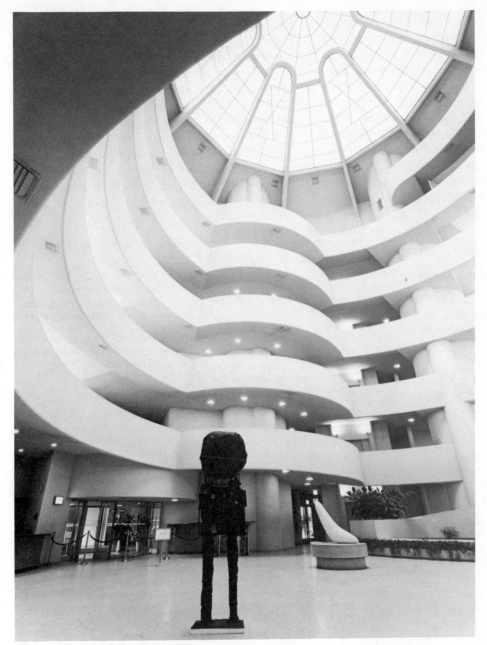

Interior of the Solomon R. Guggenheim Museum, New York: designed by Wright.

neers were the German Mary Wigman and the American Martha Graham. In time a highly skeptical public became enthusiastic supporters of such choreographers as Merce Cunningham, Paul Taylor, Twyla Tharp, Alvin Ailey, and others.

A Final Summary

This review of the cultural achievements of the twentieth century is a sampler, and far from a complete list. It says little about the expan-

sion of popular culture made available by movies, radio, and television and also by swift air travel to distant places. Critics may scoff at their superficiality, yet at their best they have greatly extended the horizons of millions of people, and at their worst exemplify the diversity tolerated by democratic societies.

By contrast, the three great attempts to impose a really totalitarian society in the twentieth century have discouraged intellectual and artistic innovations. Communist China appears to rely on traditional forms of dance, gymnastics, and music to further its political goals. In Nazi Germany science prospered despite the emigration of Einstein and others, but most aspects of intellectual life were suppressed. Artistic and literary experiments, which had flourished in the 1920s and early 1930s, were declared to be "decadent," and leaders of the Bauhaus and other experimental groups left Germany.

In Soviet Russia, too, science has thrived but literary and artistic advances have been at-tacked as examples of "bourgeois decadence." Stalin put an end to such promising cultural beginnings as the films of Eisenstein and the efforts of poets and musicians to find new modes of expression. Like the French revolutionaries of 1789, the Bolsheviks since 1917 have shared the conventional tastes of the old regime they had just overthrown. But, as of 1980, there were few indications that talented individuals in Moscow or Leningrad would be permitted to follow the example of postrevolutionary Paris and promote a revolution in literature and the arts.

READINGS on Science and Culture in the Twentieth Century

The Natural Sciences

R. Taton, ed., *Science in the Twentieth Century* (Basic Books, 1966). Translation of a comprehensive French survey.

H. B. Lemon, *From Galileo to the Nuclear Age* (*Univ. of Chicago). The breathtaking developments in astronomy during the last four centuries.

L. Motz and A. Duveen, *Essentials of Astronomy* (Columbia U., 1977). Another helpful introduction to this exciting science.

D. Kevles, *The Physicists* (*Vintage). A history of this important scientific community through the 1970s.

A. Rosenfeld, *The Second Genesis: The Coming Control of Life* (*Vintage). Evaluates the potential results of recent innovations in chemistry and biology.

H. Judson, *The Eighth Day of Creation* (Simon & Schuster, 1979). Detailed narrative of the discoveries that unlocked the secrets of DNA.

Psychology

J. Rickman, ed., *A General Selection from the Works of Sigmund Freud* (*Anchor). A well chosen anthology.

E. Jones, *The Life and Work of Freud* (*Basic). Abridged edition of a three volume study by a great admirer.

P. Rieff, *Freud: The Mind of the Moralist,* 3rd ed. (*Univ. of Chicago). Up-to-date study stressing the place of Freudian psychiatry in contemporary culture.

R. Appignanesi and O. Zarate, *Freud for Beginners* (*Pantheon). A recent introduction.

E. Bennet, *What Jung Really Said* (*Schoken) and J. Jacobi, *Complex, Symbol, Archetype in the Psychology of C. G. Jung* (*Princeton). Discussions of the theories advanced by a psychologist who disagreed with Freud.

The Social Sciences

H. S. Hughes, *Consciousness and Society* (*Vintage) and *The Sea Change* (*McGraw-Hill). Analyzes the changes in social thought during the generations before and after 1930, respectively.

S. Finer, ed., *Selections from Pareto's Sociological Writings* (Rowman). A good introduction; may be supplemented by Pareto's four-volume *The Mind and Society* (AMS reprint, 1979).

T. Parsons, *The Structure of Social Action,* 2 volumes (*Free Press). A seminal work in American sociological thought.

G. Wallas, *Human Nature in Politics* (Constable, 1908) and W. Lippmann, *A Preface to Politics* (Kennerley, 1913). Pioneering investigations of political psychology.

J. K. Galbraith, *The Affluent Society* (*Houghton) and *The Age of Uncertainty* (*Houghton). Lively assessments by a prominent economist.

Philosophy

M. G. White, ed., *The Age of Analysis* (*Mentor). Well-chosen excerpts from the writings of twentieth-century philosophers.

A. Naess, *Four Modern Philosophers* (*Univ. of Chicago). Discusses Carnap, Wittgenstein, Heidegger, and Sartre.

M. Weitz, *Twentieth-Century Philosophy: The Analytic Tradition* (*Free Press) and A. Ayer, ed., *Logical Positivism* (*Free Press). Introductions to a difficult area of thought.

S. Langer, *Philosophy in a New Key,* 3rd ed. (*Harvard) Widely praised study of the symbolism of reason, rite and art.

W. Kauffman, ed., *Existentialism from Dostoevsky to Sartre* (*Meridian). Selections from existentialist writings with informative commentaries.

R. Harper, *The Existential Experience* (*Johns Hopkins). A sympathetic introduction.

A. Korzybski, *Science and Sanity* (Institute of General Semantics, 1958); M. McLuhan, *Understanding Media: The Extensions of Man* (*Mentor). Two different introductions to semantics.

O. Spengler, *The Decline of the West,* 2 vols. (Knopf, 1945). By the German prophet of gloom.

A. Toynbee, *A Study of History.* The two-volume abridgment by D. Somervell (Oxford 1947, 1957) is the best introduction to this controversial work.

C. Singer, *Toynbee* (*Presbyterian & Reformed). Sympathetic evaluation, which may be contrasted with the more critical studies by I. Berlin, *Historical Inevitability* (Oxford, 1954) and M. Ashley-Montagu, ed., *Toynbee and History* (Porter Sargeant, 1956).

Literature and the Arts

H. Slochower, *No Voice Is Wholly Lost* (Creative Age, 1945). Informative study of the relationship between intellectual and literary history.

F. Hoffman, *Freudianism and the Literary Mind.* (Louisiana, 1957). A useful exploration.

A. Burgess, *Re: Joyce* (*Norton); W. Jones, *James Joyce and the Common Reader* (Oklahoma, 1955). Informative discussions of this important innovator.

H. H. Arnason, *History of Modern Art* (Abrams, 1977). Encyclopaedic introduction to twentieth-century painting, sculpture and architecture.

The Armory Show, 1913 (Arno, 1972). Three volumes reproducing the catalogues and other documents of the historic New York exhibition that introduced the American public to modern art.

J. Russell, *The World of Matisse* (Time-Life 1969); C. Tomkins, *The World of Marcel Duchamp* (Time-Life, 1966); L. Wertenbaker, *The World of Picasso* (Time-Life, 1967); P. O'Brian, *Picasso: A Biography* (Putnam, 1976). Studies of these important pioneers.

H. Richter, *Dada: Art and Anti-Art* (*Oxford); P. Waldberg, *Surrealism* (*Oxford); J. Russell & S. Gablick, *Pop Art Redefined* (Praeger, 1969). Introductions to movements breaking new ground in art.

H.-R. Hitchcock, *Architecture: 19th and 20th Centuries* (*Penguin). Encyclopaedic review.

P. H. Lang, *Stravinsky* (*Norton). Good study of this influential pioneer in the fields of music and ballet.

Index

Hus, John, 268
Huxley, Aldous, 597, 604–5
Huxley, T. H., 605

Iberville, Pierre Lemoyne, Sieur d', 289
Ibsen, Henrik, 437
Id, Freud's theory of the, 601
Illyrian provinces: Napoleon's annexation, 370, 374, 411; Austrian recovery (1814), 375 (*see also* Dalmatia)
Imperialism, 290–91, 456, 513 (*see also* Colonial empires); balance sheet, 462; British, 388, 458–59; and the Industrial Revolution, 382
Impressionism, 439–41, 442
Independent Church (Eng.), 276, 277
Index (Catholic Church), 296, 342
India, 291, 477, 494, 501–2, 519, 557, 559–60; Portuguese settlements, 289; Mogul empire, 289; English colonies, 289, 388; French colonies, 289; and the Seven Years' War, 337, 338, 339; Sepoy Rebellion (1857), 388; British control, 446, 458; Amritsar massacre (1919), 469; and World War I, 501–2; Muslim-Hindu conflict, 502, 557; anti-British movements, 502; agriculture, 559; caste system, 559–60, 582; Chinese invasions (1959, 1961), 551; five-year plans, 559; national language, 560; parliamentary democracy, 559; partition (1947), 557, 559; population, 559; Bengali refugees (1971), 582; elections (1977, 1980), 582–83; nuclear weapons, 573, 582; U.S. relations, 559, 582, 583; U.S.S.R. relations, 553, 582–83
Indian National Congress, 502
Indian-Pakistani Wars: *1965–66*, 552, 560; *1971*, 582
Indians (Native Americans): European exploitation of, 290; and French Catholicism, 289; in Latin America, 568; 19th-century massacres of, 396
Indochina, 394, 459; Japanese invasion, 509; French withdrawal (1954), 529, 553 (*see also* Vietnam; Vietnam War)
Indonesia, 509, 545, 552; independence (1949), 557; communist coup attempt (1965), 552, 557; Sukarno regime, 557
Industrial Revolution, 285–86, 300–1, 379–85, 418; and agriculture, 382; and business cycles, 382, 384; and business legislation, 381; capital and investment, 380; communications, 380; in England, 300–1, 379–85; in France, 381, 382, 394; international repercussions, 381–82; machinery, improvements in, 380; steel and iron smelting, 380; social impact, 382–85; transportation, 380
Inferiority complex (Adler), 601
Ingria province (Sweden), 331
In Memoriam (Tennyson), 437
Inquisition, 371, 401; and Galileo, 295
Instruction (Catherine the Great), 344
Instrument of Government (Eng.), 278
Insurance industry, 266, 295, 297, 298
Intendants (France), 282, 283, 285, 352
International Style, 610
Intolerable Acts (1774), 347
Iran (*see also* Persia), 517, 519, 575–78, 579, 594; oilfields, 502, 560; minorities, 576; Westernization, 503, 575–76; Russian

troops in (1946), 544; coup (1951–53), 560; revolution (1979–80), 576; constitution (1980), 576–77; hostage crisis (1980–81), 575, 576; Islamic movement, 576–77, 578
Iraq, 519; British mandate (1919), 472, 502; oilfields, 502, 560; revolution (1958), 563, 564; execution of Jews (1969, 1970), 564; nuclear capability, 573
Ireland, 379, 529; Catholic revolt (1641), 276, 277; reconquest (1649–50), 277; anti-Catholic laws, 281; incorporated into United Kingdom (1801), 388; famine (1845), 387, 391; emigrato U.S., 387–88; 19th-century reforms, 388, 447; home rule bill (1914), 447; literary revival, 447; Easter rebellion (1916), 495; Irish Free State (1921), 495–96; Republic (1949), 496; and World War II, 496
Irish Land Act (1870), 388
Irish Republican Army (IRA), 529, 590
Iron Curtain, 519
Iron Guard (Romania), 494
Iron Law of Wages (Ricardo), 426–27
Islamic Movement, 578, 580, 593; in Iran, 576–77, 578
Ismail (Egyptian ruler), 458
Israel, 521, 565 (*see also* Arab-Israeli Wars); founded (1948), 560; nationalities in, 562; U.S. support, 562, 579, 580; territory seizures (1967), 563, 579; Palestinian attacks on (1969, 1970), 563–64; Egyptian peace treaty (1980), 579–80, 581; West Bank settlements, 563, 580
Italia Irredenta, 406, 450, 465
Italy, 513, 517, 520, 526, 543; Austrian Hapsburg rule, 327; Napoleonic republics, 365, 368, 370; Austrian possessions restored (1814), 375; revolt (1848–49), 400; liberation movements (1831–49), 402–3; Risorgimento (1849–60), 394, 395, 402, 403–6; French-Austrian War (1859), 394, 403–4; North vs. South, 406, 450; and the Prussian-Austrian War (1866), 409; emigration, 450; war with Turkey (1911–12), 450, 456; colonial empire, 450, 460; and the German-Austrian Alliance (1879), 463; and World War I, 465–66, 486; post-World War I settlement, 469, 472; fascist regime (1921–38), 485, 486–87, 504; syndicates, 487; invades Ethiopia (1935), 504; declares war on France (1940), 507; German front (1944–45), 511; developments (1946–70), 535–36; terrorism, 592
IT & T scandals, 587
Ivanhoe (Scott), 420
Ivory Coast, 566, 595

Jackson, Pres. Andrew, 396
Jacobin clubs (France), 358, 359, 361, 363, 364, 365, 366, 421, 448; Paris commune (1792), 359
Jacobite plots (Eng.), 324
Jacquard loom, 381
Jagan, Cheddi, 570
Jagger, Mick, 529

James I (VI of Scotland; king of England), 272, 282, 310, 321; reign, 273–74; Spanish policy, 274
James II (king of England), 279, 280, 281, 302, 321, 324
James III (pretender), 281
James, William, 436
Jameson, Dr. Leander Starr, 458
Jamestown settlement (1607), 287
Janata party (India), 582
Jansen, Cornelius, 284, 297
Jansenists, Jansenism, 284, 297, 326; and Parlement judges, 326
Japan, 445, 477, 497, 500, 581–82; Dutch in, 290; opened to West (1853), 290, 460; and the Industrial Revolution, 382, 462; political revolution (1868), 460, 462; constitution (1889), 462; imperialism, 462, 556; northern China, occupation of, 462, 469; Pacific island mandates (1919), 472; military dictatorship, 500; Shinto cult, 500; twenty-one demands, 500; invades China (1931, 1937), 501, 503–4; and World War II, 506, 509, 511, 513; U.S. occupation, 513, 517, 518, 556; economic development, 556; political parties, 556; anti-Americanism in, 556–57
Jaworski, Leon, 586
Jefferson, Thomas, 423, 424, 604
Jellachich, Baron Joseph, 412
Jena, battle of (1806), 370, 374
Jenkins, Robert, 336
Jerusalem: partitioning (1948), 560; and the Egyptian war (1967), 563
Jesuits, 290, 326; dissolved (1773), 304; in North America, 289; exiled, 342, 345; in Prussia, 341; and Charles X, 389; reestablished in Spain (1814), 401, 425; expelled from Germany, 450
Jews (*see also* Anti-Semitism): in Austria, 342, 452; in Hungary, 494; in Iraq, 564; in Italy, 487; Nazi persecution of, 491, 511, 512, 541, 560; in Poland, 335; in Prussia, 329, 341; in Russia, 454, 581; in the U.S., 580
Jinnah, Mohammed Ali, 559
Joan of Arc, 419
Johnson, Pres. Lyndon B., 521, 524, 549, 570, 588; meets Kosygin (1967), 550; and Vietnam, 555
Joint-stock companies, 297, 299–300
Joliet, Louis, 289
Jordan, 560, 563, 564; Palestinian guerrilla war (1970), 564, 578
Joseph I (king of Portugal), 345
Joseph II (king of Germany; Holy Roman Emperor), 342–43, 346, 351
Josephine (empress of France), 365, 371
Joyce, James, 604
Juan Carlos (king of Spain), 536, 592
Juárez, Benito Pablo, 394
Julius Caesar, 368, 425
July Revolution (*see* Revolution of 1830)
Jung, Carl, 601–2, 604
Junkers, 329, 330, 335, 341, 374, 408
Justices of the Peace (Eng.), 325
Jutland, battle of (1916), 466–67

Kadar, Janos, 548
Kadets (Constitutional Democrats), 454, 477
Kaganovich, Lazar, 537

Louis XIV (king of France), 266, 279, 280, 282–87, 290, 294, 297, 308, 309, 311, 312, 320, 329, 352, 364, 368, 411, 532; as divine right monarch, 282–83; economic policies, 285–86; reign, 282–85; treaty with Charles II (1670), 279, 286; wars, 286–87, 300

Louis XV (king of France), 298, 302, 336, 338, 352; reign, 326–27, 351

Louis XVI (king of France), 326, 351–52, 357, 391; dismisses Notables, 354; summons Estates General, 354; removed to Tuileries (1789), 356; and the Constitution of 1791, 358; escape attempt (1791), 358; house arrest, 358, 359; trial and death (1793), 360

Louis XVII (son of Louis XVI), 362

Louis XVIII (brother of Louis XVI), 374, 375; reign, 389

Louisberg (Cape Breton Is.), British seizure, 337, 338–39

Louisiana territory, 287, 289, 299; ceded to Spain (1763), 339; returned to France (1800), 369; sold to the U.S. (1803), 369, 396

Louis Philippe (king of the French), 390–91, 396, 431, 439, 448; domestic policies, 390–91; foreign policy, 391; abdication (1848), 391

Louvre Museum, 363

"Love Song of J. Alfred Prufrock, The" (Eliot), 604

Low Counties, painting in, 313 (see also Belgium; Netherlands)

Loyola, St. Ignatius, 304

Lübeck, Treaty of (1629), 269

Lueger, Karl, 452, 488

Lumumba, Patrice, 567

Luneville, Treaty of (1801), 368

Lusitania, sinking (1915), 467

Luther, Martin, 406

Lutheran Church, 329, 492 (see also Thirty Years' War)

Lützen, battle of (1632), 269

Luxembourg, 286, 409, 526

Lvov, Prince Georgi Evgenievich, 477

Lycees (France), 368

Lyrical Ballads (Wordsworth-Coleridge), 419

Lysenko, T. D., 537

Mably, Garbriel Bonnet de, 307

McAdam, Scot, 380

MacArthur, Gen. Douglas, 513, 556

McCarthy, Sen. Eugene, 555

McCarthy, Sen. Joseph, 521

McCormick, Cyrus, 381

Macedonia, 594

McGovern, Sen. George, 585

Machiavelli, Nicolo, 341

Machinery, and the Industrial Revolution, 380

Machine Tractor Stations (MTS), 483, 540

McKinley, Pres. William, 432

MacMahon, Comte Marie de, 448

McLuhan, Marshall, 603

Macmillan, Harold, 527

Madagascar, 290, 459, 566; rebellion (1947), 565

Madame Bovary (Flaubert), 436–37

Madras (India), French seizure, 337

Magdeburg, sack of (1631), 269

Magenta, battle of (1859), 394

Magritte, René, 608

Magyars, 411, 452

"Maids of Honor, The" (Velásquez), 315

Maillol, Aristide, 441

Maine, sinking (1898), 460

Maintenon, Mme. de, 284

Maison Carrée (Nîmes), 424

Makarios, Archbishop, 580, 593

Makepeace Experiment, The (Sinyavsky), 541

Malagasy Republic, 566

Malawi, 566–67

Malaya, 458, 509, 545, 557

Malaysia, Federation of (1963), 557

Malcom X, 524

Malenkov, Georgi, 537, 539

Mali, independence (1960), 566

Malplaquet, battle of (1709), 287

Malta, 369, 375

Malthus, Thomas, 425–26, 434

Manchester (Eng.), 380, 383, 384, 385, 431

Manchuria, 454, 562; Japanese invasion (1931), 501, 503–4; Russian invasion (1945), 513

Mandate system, 472, 500, 502

Manet, Edouard, 439–40

Mann, Thomas, 604

Manson murders (Los Angeles), 524

Mao Tse-tung, 501, 524, 551, 552, 557, 581, 582; Long March, 501; One Hundred Flowers campaign (1957), 551; and the Cultural Revolution (1966–69), 552; death, 583

Marat, Jean Paul, 359, 361; assassinated (1793), 360, 421

March Laws (Hungary), 412

"Maria de' Medici" (Rubens), 315

Maria Theresa (archduchess of Austria; queen of Hungary and Bohemia), 328, 336, 337, 342, 345, 351–52; reign, 342

Marie Antoinette (queen of France), 351–52, 353, 356, 358, 361–62

Marie Leszczýnska (queen of France), 336

Marie Louise (empress of France), 371, 374, 394

Mark, state of (Ger.), 329

Marne, battles of: 1914, 465; 1918, 468

Marquette, Jacques, 289

Marriage of Figaro, The (Beaumarchais), 352

Marriage of Figaro, The (Mozart), 317

"Marseillaise, La," 359

Marshall, George C., 519

Marshall Plan (1947), 519, 521, 532

Marston Moor, battle of (1644), 277

Marvelous Rule of Logarithms (Napier), 294

Marx, Karl, 425–32, 448, 477, 603; First, Second Internationals, 432–33; influences on, 431; writings, 431–32

Marxism, 425, 430–33, 498; basic laws, 430–31; labor theory of value, 432; in prerevolutionary Russia, 454; as a religion, 603; vs. revisionism, 433

Mary II (queen of England), 280–81, 321

Maryland, settlement of, 288

Mary Stuart, Queen of Scots, 265–66, 272, 419

Masaryk, Thomas, 504

Massacre of rue Transnonian (Paris, 1834), 390, 439

"Massacre of Scio, The" (Delacroix), 422, 423–24

Mathematics, 435; 16th- and 17th-century, 294–95

Matisse, Henri, 605, 606

Matsu, 546, 551

Matteotti, Giacomo, 486

Matthias (Holy Roman Emperor), 268

Mau Mau terrorists, 566

Maurice (prince of Orange), 266

Mauritania, independence (1960), 566

Mauritius, Island of, 290

Maximilian (emperor of Mexico), 394, 439–40

Maximilian II (Holy Roman Emperor), 268, 272

Maxims (La Rochefoucauld), 310

Mazarin, Cardinal, 282

Mazzini, Giuseppe, 402, 403

Mecca, uprising (1979), 578

Mechanics institutes (Eng.), 385, 386

Medicine: 19th-century, 433; 20th-century, 600

Mein Kampf (Hitler), 489, 490

Meir, Golda, 579

Mendelssohn, Felix, 421

Menderes, Adnan, 564

Mennonites, 313

Menshikov, Prince Aleksandr Danilovich, 330, 331

Menchevik party, 454, 479, 481

Mercantilism, 297, 298, 458, 462, 495; in Austria, 342; and colonial expansion, 290; in the English colonies, 321; French, 285–86, 297, 298–99; in German states, 298; vs. laissez-faire doctrines, 302, 303; in Latin America, 568; and precious metals, 285, 298, 302; in Prussia, 341; in Spain, 297, 327

Mercenary armies, 269, 272, 321

Messiah (Handel), 317

Metallurgical industry (Eng.), 380

Methodists, 308

Metric system, 363, 371

Metternich, Prince Klemens von, 327, 406, 411; and the Congress of Vienna, 374–75; and the revolutions in Italy, 401, 402; resignation (1848), 412

Mexican-American Wars (1836, 1846–48), 396

Mexico: French occupation (1861–67), 394; revolution (1910–40), 569; elections, 569; shah of Iran in (1980), 576, 577

Michelson, Albert Abraham, 599

Microscope, invention of the, 294

Middle Ages, Romantic revival of, 420

Middle classes (see Bourgeoisie)

Middle East, 477, 516, 519, 560–65, 574–80, 581 (see also individual countries); mandates (1919), 472; Islamic movement in, 578, 580; oilfields, 502, 560, 574–75; nationalism, 502

Mies van der Rohe, Ludwig, 610

Mikhailovich, Gen. Draža, 544

Milan, 535; uprising (1848), 403

Milan Decree (1807), 371

Milky Way Galaxy, 599

Mill, James, 426

Mill, John Stuart, 418, 437; philosophy, 426–27

Millenarian sects, in England, 279

Mind and Society, The (Pareto), 602

Minh, Ho Chi, 553, 554, 555

Minna von Barnhelm (Lessing), 311

Minorca, Island of, 338, 347
Minuteman missile (U.S.), 574
Mirabeau, Comte de, 355
Miró, Joan, 608
Mississippi Bubble (1719–20), 298–99, 300, 326
Mitchell, John, 585, 586, 587
"Mme. Charpentier" (Renoir), 441
Mobutu, Gen. Joseph, 567
Modena, duchy of, 402, 403, 404
Moderados (Spain), 401
Modern dance, 612–13
Moldavia, 331, 402
Molière, 310
Moll Flanders (Defoe), 311
Monarchists, in France, 448
Monarchs: divine right of, 273, 275, 278, 282–83; Enlightenment views on, 305, 306, 307, 320–21; and the Constitution of 1791 (France), 358–59
Monck, Gen. George, 278
Monet, Claude, 440, 605
Monmouth, duke of, 280
Monroe, Pres. James, 396
Monroe Doctrine (1823), 394, 396
"Monte Sainte Victoire" (Cézanne), 440–41, 442
Montesquieu, 301, 305–6, 344, 348, 413
Monteverdi, 316
Montgomery (Ala.), bus boycott, 523
Montreal, fall of (1760), 339
Moon landing (U.S., 1969), 539, 540, 597, 599
Moravia, 472
Moravian Church, 308
Moro, Aldo, 535; assassinated (1980), 592
Morocco, 459, 463; William II's visit, (1905), 463; independence (1956), 529, 565; Spanish Sahara war, 595
Morse, Samuel F. B., 381
Moscow, 330, 333, 335, 484; Dutch colony, 330; Napoleon's occupation (1812), 374; becomes capitol (1918), 479; Olympic Games (1980), 575, 591
Moscow Calling (Daniel), 541
Mossadeq, Mohamed, 564
Mountain (French National Convention), 360–61
Mountbatten, Lord, assassination, 590
Mount Vernon (Va.), 312
Mozambique, 567, 590; independence (1974), 592
Mozart, Wolfgang Amadeus, 317–18
"Mrs. Siddons" (Reynolds), 316
Mrs. Warren's Profession (Shaw), 437
Mugabe, Robert, 590, 595
Muhammad Ali (governor of Egypt), 391, 402
Multilateral (Nuclear) Force (1968), 519
Munich, Olympic Games massacre (1972), 580
Munich Conference (1938), 504
Municipal Corporations Act (1835), 387
Murat, Joachim, 370
Music: 17th- and 18th-century, 308, 316–18; 19th-century Romantic, 420–21, 437–38; 20th-century, 611–12
Mussolini, Benito, 476, 477, 486–87, 492, 493, 495, 496, 497, 504, 507, 602; march on Rome (1922), 486; syndicate system, 487; social policies, 487; foreign policy, 487; Corfu affair (1923), 503; execution (1945), 511

Mutations, 434
Mutualism (Proudhon), 432
Muzorewa, Abel, 590

NAACP (National Association for the Advancement of Colored People), 523
Nagasaki, atomic bombing of, 506, 513, 598
Nagy, Imre, 547, 548
Namibia (South-West Africa), 460, 472, 568, 596
Nantes (France), 326; Vendée drownings (1793), 362; Edict of (1598) revoked (1685), 282, 284, 286, 352, 353
Napier, John, 294
Naples, 327, 336; annexed by Napleon (1805), 370; revolution (1820–21), 400, 401; uprising (1848), 402–3; joins Piedmont (1860), 405
Napoleon I (Napoleon Bonaparte, emperor of the French), 311, 336, 350, 365–66, 393, 394, 425; early career, 365; in the Italian campaign (1796), 365; Egyptian campaign (1798), 365; Brumaire coup (1799), 365–66; as consul (1799–1804), 366; emperor (1804), 366; domestic policies, 366–68; American projects, 369; England, invasion plans (1805), 369; German projects, 368, 370–71; Continental System, 371; invades Russia (1812), 374; exile on Elba (1814), 374; 100 days' reign (1815), 374; Waterloo (1815), 374, 376; exile on St. Helena (1815–21), 374, 376; legacy of, 376, 378; David's painting of, 421
Napoleon II, 394
Napoleon III (emperor of the French; Prince Louis Napoleon Bonaparte), 376, 393–95, 439, 532; campaign (1848), 393; coup (1851), 393; emperor (1852), 394; foreign policy, 394–95, 415; and Italian liberation, 402, 403–4; liberal policies, 395; vs. Bismark (1866), 409–10; capture and exile, 395, 410
Napoleonic Code, 358, 366–67
Narva, battle of (1700), 331
Naseby, battle of (1645), 277
Nasser, Gamal Abdel, 562–63, 564; domestic programs, 563; sends forces to Yemen (1962), 563
Nassau, state of (Ger.), 409
Natal, 458
National Assemblies (France):
—*1789:* 355, 356; Declaration, 357; property confiscations, 357; and the Civil Constitution, 357
—Revolution of 1848, 391–92
—Monarchist victory (1870s), 448
National Convention (France, 1792–93), 359–62, 363, 376; mobilization decree (1793), 362, 376; Right, Left, Plain deputies, 359–60
National debt (Eng.), 300, 324
National Guard: France, 1789, 355; United States, 524, 525
National Health plan (Eng.), 527
National Insurance Act (1911), 447
Nationalism, 306, 388, 395, 400–1, 411, 414–15, 446, 447, 456, 603; in Belgium, 395; colonial peoples, 494, 500, 501; and fascist regimes, 485; in the Middle East, 502, 578

National Liberation Front (Vietnam), 553
Nationalist party (Ger.), 488
National Socialist party (Ger.) (*see* Nazi party)
National workshops (France, 1848), 391, 392, 427
NATO (North Atlantic Treaty Organization), 519, 533, 535, 548, 549, 565
Naturalism, 437
Natural law, 307, 308, 419; and laissez-faire economics, 303
Natural selection (Darwin), 434
Navarino, battle of (1827), 402
Navigation, and maritime trade, 298
Navigation Act (1651), 277
Nazis, Nazi party (National Socialists), 438, 485, 488, 489, 490–93, 541, 598; birth of, 488; intellectual life, 614; Nuremberg trials (1946), 534
Necker, Jacques, 355
Nehru, Jawaharlal, 559, 560, 594
Nelson, Adm. Horatio, 365, 369
Nenni, Pietro, 535
Neoclassic style: architecture, 311, 312, 424, 610; furniture, 363; painting, 421; sculpture, 441
Neo-Gothic style, 424–25, 610
Neo-Guelf movement, 402, 403
Neolithic Revolution, 293
Netherlands, 382, 526 (*see also* Belgium); 16th-century revolt, 265; independence (1609), 266; business activities, 266, 297; United Provinces, 266; and the Thirty Years' War, 266, 269, 272; and the War of Devolution, 286; and the War of the Spanish Succession, 286, 287, 297–98; colonial empire, 287, 289–90; agricultural revolution in, 300; economic leadership, 321; war with revolutionary France, 360, 364, 365; annexed to France (1810), 371
Neurosis, Freud's theory of, 601
New Amsterdam, 287
New Brunswick (Canada), 388
Newcastle, duke of, 325
New Deal programs, 496, 497, 499–500
New Democratic party (Canada), 526
New Economic Policy (NEP), 476, 481
Newfoundland, 287, 289
New France, 289
New Guinea, 460, 472, 557; and World War II, 509
New Harmony (Ind.), 429, 430
New Lanark (Scot.), 429–30
New Mexico, 396
"New Model, The" (Fragonard), 316
New Orleans, 339
New Poor Law (1834), 386, 426
Newton, Sir Isaac, 295, 297, 304, 305, 420, 428, 429, 433, 435, 598; and the calculus, 295; laws of gravity, motion, 599; optics experiments, 295; and rationalism, 302
New York City, 524; as financial center, 460, 497; financial crisis (1976), 587
New Zealand, 389, 458–59, 519, 556
Nibelungenlied, 420
Nicaragua, 594
Nice, 364, 394; annexed to France (1860), 394, 404; Italian claims, 487, 504
Nicholas I (tsar of Russia), 402, 412, 414, 453, 485; becomes tsar, 414; reign, 415–16, 453